NO MAN'S LAND

The Place of the Woman Writer
in the Twentieth Century

Volume 3 • Letters from the Front

SANDRA M. GILBERT AND SUSAN GUBAR

Yale University Press · New Haven and London

Published with assistance from the foundation established in memory of Amasa Stone Mather of the Class of 1907, Yale College.

Set in Baskerville type by The Composing Room of Michigan and printed in the United States of America by Vail-Ballou Press, Binghamton, New York.

Library of Congress Cataloging-in-Publication Data
(Revised for vol. 3)

Gilbert, Sandra M.
   No man's land.
   Includes bibliographies and indexes.
   Contents: v. 1. The war of the words — v. 2. Sexchanges — v. 3. Letters from the front.
   1. English literature—Women authors—History and criticism.   2. English literature—20th century—History and criticism.   3. American literature—Women authors—History and criticism.   4. American literature—20th century—History and criticism.   5. Women and literature—Great Britain—History—20th century.   6. Women and literature—United States—History—20th century.   7. Feminism and literature—Great Britain.   8. Feminism and literature—United States.   I. Gubar, Susan, 1944–   .
   II. Title.
   PR116.G5 1988   820'.9'9287   87-10560
   ISBN 0-300-04587-5 (v. 1 : pbk.: alk. paper)
        0-300-05025-9 (v. 2 : pbk.: alk. paper)
        0-300-05631-1 (v. 3 : cloth: alk. paper)
        0-300-06660-0 (v. 3 : pbk.: alk. paper)

A catalogue record for this book is available from the British Library.

The paper in this book meets the guidelines for permanence and durability of the Committee on Production Guidelines for Book Longevity of the Council on Library Resources.

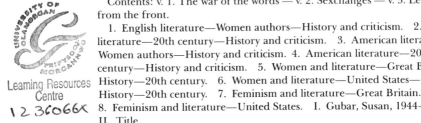

10   9   8   7   6   5   4   3   2

For Ellen Graham and
Carolyn Heilbrun

She carries a book but it is not
the tome of ancient wisdom,

the pages, I imagine, are the blank pages
of the unwritten volume of the new.

—H. D.

. . . O the future shining
In far countries or suddenly at home in a look, in a season
In music freeing a new myth among the male
Steep landscapes. . . .

—Muriel Rukeyser

There are ways of thinking that we don't know about. Nothing
could be more important or precious than that knowledge, however unborn. The sense of urgency, the spiritual restlessness it
engenders, cannot be appeased.

—Susan Sontag

When you have buried us   told your story
ours does not end   we stream
into the unfinished   the unbegun
the possible

—Adrienne Rich

Contents

Preface

How do writers and their readers imagine the future in a turbulent time of
sex war and sexchange? If such a crucially constitutive category as gender
is undergoing radical transformations, what effects do its metamorphoses
have on literary representations of woman, man, the family, and society?
Letters from the Front, this last volume in our three-part *No Man's Land: The
Place of the Woman Writer in the Twentieth Century,* revises the title of Muriel
Rukeyser's war poem "Letter *to* the Front" (1944) in order to argue that, far
from being behind the lines, modern women of letters found themselves
situated on an embattled and often confusing cultural front. As we will
show, all these artists, working in very different genres and adopting a
range of perspectives, dispatched missives recording and exploring some
form of future shock. Embroiled in the sex antagonism that we traced in
The War of the Words and engaged in the sexual experimentations that we
studied in *Sexchanges,* women novelists and poets from the twenties to the
eighties struggled to envision how "the will to change" might inscribe hitherto untold stories on "the blank pages / of the unwritten volume of the
new."[1]

Because we ourselves are enmeshed in the history we examine here,
we too have experienced the continuing repercussions of both a massive
social will to change and a fierce resistance to such change. Within the
academy feminist literary criticism—and gender studies more generally—
has achieved striking success and visibility, as evidenced by the torrent
of books and journals, programs and professorships devoted to these
fields. At the same time, however, an extraordinarily diverse chorus of
voices has lately been raised in protest against either the political or the
epistemological assumptions that shaped feminist theory and practice in
the seventies.

Most notoriously hostile have been such media stars as the late Allan
Bloom and Camille Paglia, both of whom built careers on best-sellers that
sensationalize the threat of feminism or misrepresent the intentions of
the women's movement. According to Bloom, feminism is a major factor
contributing to "the closing of the American mind" because, among other

things, it performs a pivotal role in dismantling "the good old Great Books approach." "The latest enemy of the vitality of classic texts is feminism," Bloom sputters, since the "Muses never sang to the poets about liberated women." In addition, he claims, an age of sexual experimentation has induced in men a deep "nervousness about their sexual performance" while he associates feminist objections to sexual harassment with a "new reign of virtue" similar to "the onset of the Terror" after the French Revolution.[2]

Less nervous than Bloom about masculine aesthetic or erotic performance, Paglia has nevertheless made even more sweeping biologically inflected assertions about gender, insisting throughout *Sexual Personae* (1990) on the intellectual superiority of man (the transcendent culture bearer) and the corollary inferiority of woman (the immanent matter that resists such efforts at transcendence). "Feminism has been simplistic in arguing that female archetypes were politically motivated falsehoods by men," she avers. "The historical repugnance to the grossness of procreative nature has a rational basis: disgust is reason's proper response to the grossness of procreative nature." And, claims Paglia, the nature woman represents to man is part and parcel of the essential sexual nature of the female because of "the albumen in the [menstrual] blood, the uterine shreds, placental jellyfish of the female sea" which is "the chthonian matrix from which we rose," so that "we have an evolutionary revulsion from slime, our site of biologic origin." For this reason, no doubt, Paglia would lump those critics who seek to investigate women's cultural and aesthetic history with all other "feminists [who] have their head up their ass [sic]."[3]

Of course, from the perspective of so-called poststructuralist (or sometimes, tellingly, "postfeminist") gender theorists, the "feminine" is neither aggressively "virtuous" nor ontologically "slimy," neither unmanning nor gross. Yet a disheartening nihilism—perhaps fueled by an odd belief that since nothing unequivocally *is,* nothing can change—often seeps through the rhetoric of even those who would align their projects with the goals of the women's movement. A few examples will suffice here. Questioning the validity for feminism of what one critic has called "truth claims," the Francophile theorist Peggy Kamuf touts the sophistication of an unstable "plurivocality" and "plurilocality" as opposed to the naïveté of a commitment to a contaminated "humanism": "If feminist theory lets itself be guided by questions such as what is women's language, literature, style or experience, from where does it get its faith in the form of these questions to get at truth, if not from the same central store that supplies humanism with its faith in the universal truth of man? And what if notions such as 'getting-at-the-truth-of-the-object' represented a principal means by which the power of power structures are [sic] sustained and even extended?"[4]

Just as disturbingly, Mary Jacobus has celebrated

the French insistence . . . on woman as a writing-effect instead of an
origin [that] asserts not the sexuality of the text but the textuality of
sex. Gender difference, produced, not innate, becomes a matter of the
structuring of a genderless libido in and through patriarchal discourse. . . . The "feminine" in this scheme is to be located in the gaps,
the absences, the unsayable or unrepresentable of discourse and representation. The feminine text becomes the elusive, phantasmal inhabitant of phallocentric discourse.[5]

If, however, the subject disappears into "polyvocality," into an indeterminate
"textuality" in which "every meaning structure attempts to conceal its own
contradictions" and "logical oppositions rest on an aporia, on undecidabil-
ity,"[6] and if *woman* disappears into a writing-effect and her words become
merely phantasmal inhabitants of phallocentric discourse, how can feminist
criticism even begin to discern those systems of representation which have
historically collaborated with oppressive social institutions to limit possibilities for women?

   Equally to the point, how can feminism itself, as a persisting structure of
female desire, express its solidarity with, say, Virginia Woolf's charwomen
Mrs. McNab and Mrs. Bast, or with Gwendolyn Brooks's "Bronzeville
Woman in a Red Hat," a black "cleaning lady" who "hires out to Mrs. Miles"
and—sans aporia—becomes a fated part of the culinary decor: "Child, big
black woman, pretty kitchen towels."[7] At the very least, what Gayatri Spivak
has called "strategic essentialism"—a provisional assumption that there *are*
men, women, and meanings in history—may be politically necessary.[8] Indeed, as Diana Fuss has recently pointed out, "To insist that essentialism is
always and everywhere reactionary is, for the constructionist, to buy into
essentialism in the very act of making the charge; *it is to act as if essentialism has
an essence.*"[9]

   How ironic, then, that some of our own colleagues and coworkers in the
feminist movement should have become complicitous in the reaction formation so incisively described by Susan Faludi in *Backlash: The Undeclared War
against Women* (1991). In this shrewd book, Faludi exposes the ways in which
throughout the eighties television and newspaper journalists, scholars, and
politicians have sought to undermine faith in feminism by convincing
women that its aims have either been met or are hazardous to feminine
health and well-being. Her thesis about a widespread cultural preoccupation
with sex antagonism has been more than borne out not just by the increasingly popular "Wild Man" movement but also by the astonishing media
coverage of the Clarence Thomas-Anita Hill hearings and the William Kennedy Smith rape trial, as well as by the spate of films and recordings in the
early nineties dramatizing violence between the sexes: *Fatal Attraction, The
Silence of the Lambs, Thelma and Louise, 2 Live Crew.*

More generally, Faludi argues that the backlash she analyzes is "a recurring phenomenon: it returns every time women begin to make some headway towards equality, a seemingly inevitable early frost to the culture's brief flowerings of feminism."[10] In other words, the sex war of the eighties is merely the most recent skirmish in the century-long battle we have been exploring throughout *No Man's Land*. Indeed, her notion that backlash needs to be gauged not by losses but by reactions against gains in women's rights and opportunities underscores the dynamics of the literary sex wars we have described. For, as we have argued about modernism in particular, twentieth-century women of letters consistently found themselves in the paradoxical position of benefiting from new economic, educational, political, and sexual freedoms even as they continually encountered images of their embattlement in the signs of their times.

To be sure, since we began our investigation of the place of the woman writer in the twentieth century, modernism itself—its nature and culture—has become an increasingly vexed topic, especially among gender theorists. Specifically, two dramatically opposed views of the relation between women and modernism have emerged among feminist critics. On the one hand, thinkers from Julia Kristeva and Hélène Cixous to Rachel Blau DuPlessis, Alice Jardine, and Marianne DeKoven have celebrated the subversive linguistic *jouissance* that they see as having been facilitated by the "revolution in poetic language," the fragmentation of traditional forms, and the decentering of the "subject" which they associate with modernist experimentation.[11] For these students of the new, the "feminine" is virtually identical with the anarchic impulse that fuels the disruptive innovations of the avant garde, whether that avant garde includes James Joyce or Gertrude Stein, William Carlos Williams or Virginia Woolf. On the other hand, such thinkers as Susan Suleiman, Cheryl Walker, Suzanne Clarke, and Shari Benstock have implicitly endorsed our own view that, first, there is a distinction between the projects of male and female modernists and, second, the feminine should not necessarily be conflated with the so-called avant garde since the rhetoric of innovation—for instance, Ezra Pound's "Make it new"—may, as we have shown, camouflage regressive or nostalgic sexual ideologies even while it inscribes a rebellion against what Walter Jackson Bate has called the "burden of the past."

That we have taken this second position has, of course, been intermittently problematic for us. Because we analyze the sexual anxieties and hostilities which seem to mark the texts of such hegemonic male (and often masculinist) modernists as Eliot, Lawrence, Joyce, Pound, Stevens, and even Williams, we are frequently thought to be attacking or at least disparaging the productions of these artists. And certainly we can understand the reason feelings of aesthetic admiration are accompanied by impulses toward political recuperation among many of our feminist colleagues. Can

Eliot, Lawrence, Joyce, or Stevens be "great" writers, after all, if they are unpleasantly misogynist? (Can Shakespeare be "great," if he is an anti-Semite?) Perhaps these artists can indeed be great precisely because they are "bad"—that is, precisely because their works powerfully reflect (and thus also affect) complex cultural dynamics which less ambitious and accomplished writers elide or ignore. At the same time, perhaps their female counterparts—from Woolf and Edna St. Vincent Millay to Zora Neale Hurston, H. D., Sylvia Plath, and Toni Morrison—are not necessarily "great" to the extent that they are "good" (that is, politically correct) but to the extent that, in their differently engendered ways, they have a rich and fluent access to the shifting currents and contradictions of the cultural unconscious.

In fact, in this final installment of *No Man's Land*, we have elected to examine primarily works by representative women writers who do seem to have such an access to the repository of myths and images, injunctions and contradictions, which registers the psychological effects of social change. To begin with, for the women whose works we study here, such change manifested itself quite dramatically in a problematizing of the traditional middle-class family plot, whose paradigm was described and prescribed by Freud at the turn of the century. That plot—of the nuclear family dominated by a superegoistic father and sustained by a nurturing mother—was supposed to function as a socializing mechanism which reproduced itself in the lives of boys and girls who learned their proper roles in the father's study and the mother's parlor or kitchen. During the course of the century, however, this monolithic plot was gradually put into question by social disruptions whose literary implications we have already studied: the suffrage campaign, the free-love movement, the mass commodification (and marketing) of female sexuality, the emergence of self-defined lesbian communities, the economic and political upheavals associated with World War I, and an increasingly widespread sense of the artifice of gender.

Our emphasis on the ambiguous phrase "family plot," therefore, is intended to reflect not just the fluid combinations and permutations that mark the evolution of the twentieth-century family, not just the changing nature of narrative or "romance" itself but also, in a sense, a burial of what was once, perhaps naively, thought to be a permanent or traditional family structure in the grave or "plot" of the past. In the absence of such a fixed structure, the writers and thinkers whose works we discuss throughout this volume were variously motivated to examine the continuities and discontinuities of history in their attempt to imagine alternative gender organizations for a vexed present and (perhaps even more important) a virtually incomprehensible future, as the "front" of the sex war more and more located itself on the "home front."

At the same time, like the children whose genealogical fantasies Freud

himself analyzed in "The Family Romance of Neurotics" (1909), some of
these writers sought to envision a reconfigured family whose dynamics
would be sufficient to their desires. If, therefore, throughout these pages we
sometimes substitute the phrase "family romance" for the phrase "family
plot," that is because in many cases the writer's yearning to reimagine the
story of gender itself arises from a need to (re)romanticize a (new) family.
Virginia Woolf's *To the Lighthouse* may serve as exemplar here, for through
an allusion to her most famous novel of familial disintegration we might
summarize *the* central theme of our book with this single question: *What does
it mean (for writers and readers in particular) to inhabit a world or text in which Mrs.
Ramsay, once the Great Mother of Victorian culture, no longer appears inevitable or
even visible as a figure for the "feminine"?*

That the feminine as represented by Mrs. Ramsay had begun to lose ontological status by the time Virginia Woolf completed *To the Lighthouse* helps
account for another recurrent motif in the chapters that follow: the concept of
the "female female impersonator," whose masquerade of "femininity" ironically comments on the fictionality of the "feminine" even while implicitly
fetishizing a vanished "womanhood." More generally, however, the disintegration of what had once seemed to be stable gender plots—even stable
identity plots—has led us to explore strategies of impersonation, masking,
and mimicry that also mark writings produced intermittently by both sexes
throughout the century, writings that facilitated meditations not only on the
artifice of the "feminine" but also on the arbitrariness of the "masculine."

In her 1990 *Gender Trouble: Feminism and the Subversion of Identity*, Judith
Butler proclaimed that the "critical task for feminism" should be "to locate
strategies of subversive repetition . . . to affirm the local possibilities of
intervention through participating in precisely those practices of repetition
that constitute identity and, therefore, present the imminent possibility of
contesting them."[12] But as we document here, such tactics of parodic mimicry have long been deployed by modernist and contemporary writers seeking to confront those newly unstable definitions of gender which made
recent feminist theory possible. Sometimes, of course, such masquerades
became almost sickeningly vertiginous, so much so that, on the one hand, a
sense of hollowness or inauthenticity engulfed both the author and her
characters, or, on the other, a sense of revulsion against the absurdity of the
charade of gender led an artist to a theologizing quest for a numinous
"feminine" or "masculine" that would somehow certify the "reality" of personhood. Thus, throughout this book, we also explore how modernist images of a utopian and essentialist Herland (or, for that matter, Hisland)
paradoxically parallel increasingly constructionist views of sexuality.

Letters from the Front is roughly chronological in its organization, with the
first section focusing on writers of the so-called modernist period and the
second devoted to authors who by and large came to prominence during and

after the Second World War, an event which, along with many other critics, we see as a major turning point in the history of literary modernism. While we have not entered the ongoing debate about what has come to be called postmodernism, we do sense a gulf between the sometimes qualified exuberance of an earlier group of writers (Woolf, Millay, Moore, Hurston, H. D.) and the sometimes bleak skepticism of a number of their descendants (Bishop, McCullers, Brooks, Lessing, Spark, Rhys), as well as a further gulf between this World War II generation and the more hopeful artists associated with the second wave of the women's movement (Plath, Rich, Atwood, Wakoski, Carter, Morrison, Kingston). In other words, because in manifold and subtly calibrated ways the themes and dreams of so many of these women are keyed to the rise, fall, and resurrection of a vision of Herland, we continue to believe that women's letters from and about the front are profoundly shaped by the history of feminism.

Although we approached the material in this book together through a series of collaborative discussions and revisions, we divided the responsibilities of drafting most of the chapters. Sandra Gilbert composed the chapters on Woolf, Millay and Moore, and Sylvia Plath; Susan Gubar prepared the chapters on the Harlem Renaissance, H. D., literary reactions to World War II, and the comic fiction of the sixties and seventies. Together, we produced the final chapter, "The Further Adventures of Snow White."

Along the way, we profited from encounters with colleagues and students in a number of pedagogical settings. Sandra Gilbert is grateful to participants in seminars at the School of Criticism and Theory, Princeton University, the Johns Hopkins University, and the University of California, Davis. Susan Gubar is grateful to participants in seminars at Indiana University, and to members of a 1991 NEH summer seminar. In addition, we have much appreciated the help of a number of research assistants: John Beckman, Chris Carr, Lisa Harper, Elizabeth Parr, Kate Remen, Ashley Tidey, Jeanette Treiber, and—especially—Alice Falk, Katharine Ings, Sue Fox, and Dan Wenger, P.M. We were, as always, counseled, guided, and supported by many friends and associates. We would like to thank David Gale, Donald Gray and Robert J. Griffin, along with Joanne Feit Diehl, Edward Gubar, Tricia Moran, Holly Pepe, Garrett Stewart, Susan Van Dyne, Mary Jo Weaver, Marcia Westkott, and Alan Williamson, for valuable advice. Finally, we thank Judith Calvert and Susan Laity for skillful, sensitive editing. And we dedicate this volume to two women whose faith, friendship, and goodwill have sustained us throughout the years of our collaboration: Ellen Graham and Carolyn Heilbrun.

Finally, as always, we want to testify that our mothers—Angela Mortola and Luise David—and our children—Roger, Katherine, and Susanna Gilbert, and Molly and Simone Gubar—have been nurturing presences in our lives, as was, incomparably, the late Elliot L. Gilbert.

I
Engendering the New

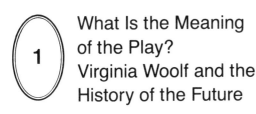

What Is the Meaning of the Play? Virginia Woolf and the History of the Future

With my cheek leant upon the window pane I like to fancy that I am pressing as closely as can be upon the massy wall of time, which is forever lifting and pulling and letting fresh spaces of life in upon us. May it be mine to taste the moment before it has spread itself over the rest of the world! Let me taste the newest and the freshest.
—Virginia Woolf

Now and again Nature creates a new part, an original part. The actors who act that part always defy our attempts to name them. They will not act the stock parts—they forget the words, they improvise others of their own. But when they come on the stage falls like a pack of cards and the limelights are extinguished.
—Virginia Woolf

"Is a play a failure," said Isa, "if we don't know the meaning? And why are we forced to act our parts?" "Is a play a failure," they asked each other, without coming closer, as they watched the first night of a new age take its place irrevocably, with them in the parts of hero and heroine who had given them their parts irrevocably as hero and heroine [sic], "is a play a failure, when we don't know the meaning, but do know that we have to act our parts?"
—Virginia Woolf

Virginia Woolf's posthumously published *Between the Acts* (1941) ends with a primal scene that includes a cryptic meditation on the future, not only the future of gender but also, by implication, the future of the family romance. A representative feminist who had lived through the sexual war of words as well as the startling sexchanges that marked the transition from Victorianism to modernism, this prolific writer concluded her career, fittingly enough, by articulating just the questions about the new that would continue to haunt literary women throughout the twentieth century. As Miss La

Trobe, the indefatigable playwright and pageant-maker, drowses over a drink in a pub, "words without meaning—wonderful words" rise from the "mud" of her unconscious to signal another act in her ongoing dramatization of English history. The protagonists of this episode are to be Giles Oliver, the stockbroker-heir of Pointz Hall, and his wife, Isa; it may appear that their creator plans simply to plunge them into the primordial past, into the "night before roads were made, or houses. . . . the night that dwellers in caves had watched from some high place among rocks," and abandon them there. The narrator insists, however, that in this chaos the pair "must fight" and then "embrace," for "from that embrace another life might be born," not just a new child but (as the ambiguity of "another life" suggests) a new way of being. In the dark night that is the past, Woolf implies, a different future may be engendered.[1]

Her point is further clarified by a draft of the conclusion of *Between the Acts* used here in an epigraph. In this version of the scene, Isa and Giles self-consciously question the nature of the roles to which, in their view, they have been arbitrarily assigned. As they sit "in their shell [the house] looking out at the pageant" and at "the stars [coming] out," it seems "as if another act were beginning; denuded, scaled, stark, and bare," so that the bewildered couple ask each other "'Is a play a failure if we don't know the meaning?' . . . 'Is a play a failure,' they [ask] each other, without coming closer, as they [watch] *the first night of a new age* take its place irrevocably . . . 'is a play a failure when we don't know the meaning, but we do know that we have to act our parts?'" (emphasis ours). Does the backward glance at traveled roads—the long day's journey into history on which Miss La Trobe has taken the Olivers and their guests in the pageant at the center of *Between the Acts*—mandate a forward march into a cryptic future? And is the modern artist's task therefore a double one? Must she look forward as she looks backward, prophesying (or struggling to prophesy) as she preserves? In this draft, even more than in the published text of her final novel, Woolf suggests as much.

In *Between the Acts* Woolf was of course writing about a period and a people themselves precariously situated "between the acts" of two catastrophic wars, between, that is, a painful past and a threatening future.[2] Indeed, she completed her drafts of the novel as the Battle of Britain reached its height, as German planes flew over Rodmell on their way to blitz London, and as bombs fell, too, so near to Monk's House that one, reports Quentin Bell, "burst the river bank[,] and the waters of the Ouse, pouring out over the water-meadows, swept right up to her garden."[3] Quite understandably, then, the novelist might have feared that "the first night of a new age" had begun, an age marked by a regression to the primitive that she associated with war-ravaged London, where "Nature prevails" and "badgers and foxes" might come back because the blackout, the blitz, the paralysis of feeling constitute a "prelude to barbarism."[4]

In brooding on the terrifying assault of the future against the past and the present, moreover, Woolf was no different from many major literary contemporaries striving to make sense of a history whose contours seemed to have determined "the decline of the west."[5] Wrote W. H. Auden in "Spain 1937":

> The stars are dead; the animals will not look:
> We are left alone with our day, and the time is short, and
>   History to the defeated,
> May say Alas but cannot help or pardon.

More hopefully, after confronting the fire-bombing of London, Woolf's friend T. S. Eliot (an air-raid warden) reassured himself in "Little Gidding" (1942) that "history is a pattern / Of timeless moments" and that, as Julian of Norwich had predicted in the fourteenth century, "All manner of thing shall be well / When the tongues of flame are in-folded / Into the crowned knot of fire." But two other long-time associates of Woolf's, E. M. Forster and Edith Sitwell, may well have voiced the misgivings about the first night of a new age that infused all these writers' imaginings of the future. "The pillars of the twenty-thousand-year-old house are crumbling," declared Forster in "Post-Munich" (1939); "the human experiment totters, other forms of life watch." "The Judas-colored sun is gone, / And with the Ape thou art alone," proclaimed Sitwell in "Lullaby" (1942).[6]

But if the urgent, even apocalyptic imperatives bred by the coming of World War II did intensify an inclination in Woolf—as in Auden, Eliot, Forster, and Sitwell—to envision another life born out of the primordial night, the impulse to meditate on a history of the future as well as a future for history was more deeply (and differently) ingrained in her thinking than it was in that of most of her contemporaries. In fact, we shall argue here that throughout Woolf's career a desire to chronicle speculations about the new—particularly new gender roles—was inextricably entangled with speculations about those chronicles of the old that supposedly constituted "history." Woolf was never, of course, frankly prophetic; when she openly fantasized, as she did in *Orlando*, she reinvented and reengendered the past. Nor was she a practical social planner. As Alex Zwerdling has observed, "What eluded her was any understanding of how the present could conceivably lead to the future she imagined. The outline for *Reading at Random*, the cultural history she left unfinished at the time of her death, gives us a sense of this impasse. It is reasonably familiar and straightforward from the Middle Ages through the nineteenth century. But then comes the injunction 'Skip present day. A Chapter on the future.'"[7]

Although the projected "Chapter on the future" remained unwritten, everywhere in her oeuvre Woolf was haunted by often indecipherable or inexplicable images of the future—in her phrase, "orts, scraps and fragments" of the new—chapters of a book or acts of a play that she might never herself transcribe but which continually rose toward her like the "words without meaning" that assail Miss La Trobe.[8] These riddling glimpses of the unknown were fostered by three major projects which consistently engaged her as both a fiction-writer and an essayist. First, they were associated with her frequent attempts to rewrite official "history" so as to provide what the French feminist theorist Hélène Cixous has named "the other history": the history not of "Great Men" but of women and of "the obscure," the history that falls into the interstices between the chronicles of princes and kings so that, when told, it "breaks the sequence" of recorded time.[9]

Second, more specifically, Woolf's proleptic imaginings of the new were inspired by her efforts to excavate *family* history—to investigate the chronicles of the person and the personal, the "family romances" that stand behind both the Carlylean "Lives of Great Men" and the Woolfian "Lives of the Obscure." Third, Woolf's impulse to write a "Chapter on the future" was manifested in her meditations on education, especially in *A Room of One's Own* and *Three Guineas,* texts which simultaneously recounted her rejection of the "old" history, her dream of a "new" history, and her desire for a reengendered education in the new.

As she worked, often at the same time, on all these projects, Woolf recorded what Joyce called "epiphanies"—not epiphanies in which spirit becomes matter, word becomes flesh, but moments in which future becomes present and linear time collapses. As she put it in her late essay "The Moment: Summer's Night," written concurrently with *Between the Acts,* when "you are old, the past lies upon the present, like a thick glass making it waver, distorting it," but when "you are young, the future lies upon the present, like a piece of glass, making it tremble and quiver" (*M* 3). In spite of the despair that ended her life in 1941, the youth that makes the present "tremble and quiver" with intimations of the future lasted throughout her career.

———

The best-known prophetic passage in Woolf's oeuvre is the hortatory last paragraph of *A Room of One's Own,* in which (speaking in her own person and not as "Mary Hamilton"), the author predicts the second coming of Shakespeare's fictive sister Judith (117–18). But in a range of essays, Woolf also ventured into a prophetic mode, although these predictions were less obviously designed to be what speech-act theorists call "performative" utterances than the conclusion of *A Room.* Her manifesto "Mr. Bennett and Mrs. Brown" (1924), for instance, ends with a "surpassingly rash prediction" whose language adumbrates the imagery of the future in "The Moment": "We are *trembling* on the verge of one of the great ages of English literature" (*CD* 119; emphasis ours). Two years later, in "The Cinema," Woolf commented that "sometimes at the cinema . . . the curtain parts and we behold, far off, some unknown and unexpected beauty" (*CD* 185–86). In "On Being Ill" (1930), moreover, she playfully called attention to "the undiscovered countries" (*M* 9) disclosed by, say, influenza, as well as to the "new language" and "new hierarchy of the passions" required for recovery.

The ironic "Royalty" (1939) as well as the more polemical "Why?" (1934) and "The Leaning Tower" (1940), though, formulate predictions as questions explicitly focused on the effects of social changes Woolf had documented in novel after novel. Suppose the metaphorical "Zoo" in which royalty are confined "should be abolished," she speculated in "Royalty," and kings and queens should take up writing careers. "And suppose that among the autumn books of 2034 is *Prometheus Unbound*, by George the Sixth, or *Wuthering Heights*, by Elizabeth the Second, what will be the effect upon their loyal subjects? Will the British Empire survive?" (*M* 240). More earnestly, in "Why?" she asked, "Why not create a new form of society founded on poverty and equality? . . . Why not invent human intercourse?" (*DM* 231), while in "The Leaning Tower," meditating on the preachings of the Auden-Spender generation, she wondered, "How can a writer who has no first-hand experience of a towerless, of a classless society create that society?" (*M* 146).

Virginia Woolf was herself, of course, such a writer, so this last question was as germane to her as it was to her literary juniors. Born into a powerful upper-middle-class family, she was always, as most of her acquaintances observed, a "lady," even when she lectured to the working-class men and women who attended Morley College, and even when she accompanied her husband, Leonard Woolf, to Labour Party meetings.[10] Indeed, by her own admission, she was in many ways "a snob." Yet this lady and snob had lived through, even been an instigator of, many of the radical social changes, and more particularly the sex wars and sexchanges, that we have examined in some detail throughout Volumes 1 and 2 of *No Man's Land*.

The third child of a prototypically Eminent Victorian, Woolf was born when her father, Sir Leslie Stephen, was fifty and had just become the editor of that official history of the lives of great men, *The Dictionary of National Biography*. Even her mother, Julia Stephen, though fourteen years his junior, represented the spirit of a disappearing era because of her association with the Pre-Raphaelite circle grouped around Little Holland House. Perhaps, in fact, because she was not only a quintessential "angel in the house" (as depicted by Coventry Patmore in his verse sequence of that title and limned by Woolf in "Professions for Women") but had also posed for the figure of the Madonna in Edward Burne-Jones's *Annunciation*, Julia early took on the aura of the mythical which intermittently envelops Mrs. Ramsay in *To the Lighthouse*.[11] Certainly, as Woolf herself remarked, "Two different ages confronted each other in the drawing room at Hyde Park Gate: the Victorian age; and the Edwardian age. We were not [Sir Leslie's] children, but his grandchildren" (*MB* 126). As for 22 Hyde Park Gate itself, that tall dark house in which "seventeen or eighteen people lived in small bedrooms with one bathroom . . . between them" (*MB* 161) offered a kind of architectural correlative to the *Mausoleum Book* in which, after Julia Stephen's death, the stricken Sir Leslie set down penitent memories of his familial past, vying with his friend Carlyle, who had included a doleful section on his dead wife, Jane Welsh Carlyle, in his *Reminiscences.*[12]

In the mausoleum of this late Victorian household, however, Virginia Stephen and her sister Vanessa—sloppily dressed, reading Greek, painting, bicycling—incarnated the new, as both were well aware: "We could see the future," recalled Woolf, although "we were completely in the power of the past" (*MB* 126). Thus, even before Bloomsbury had expanded their vocabularies to include such defiantly explicit sexual words as *semen* and *bugger*, the sisters resisted dances, dowagers, and the marriage market onto which their half brother George Duckworth tried to force them. Sir Leslie died in 1904, and Virginia later confessed that had he lived, "His life would have entirely ended mine. What would have happened? No writing, no books:—inconceivable" (*D* 3:208). She rapidly became a journalist, a teacher, and a novelist, besides entering into an egalitarian marriage with Leonard Woolf, whom she described as a "penniless Jew," while Vanessa pursued a career as a "modern" artist and engaged in a radically anti-Victorian sexual life.[13]

"On or about December, 1910, human character changed," Woolf declares in "Mr. Bennett and Mrs. Brown," speaking of the decade from about 1904 to 1914 during which she and her sister first moved definitively toward a future they could only, before Sir Leslie's death, glimpse through the shadows of 22 Hyde Park Gate. The change she goes on to describe is essentially a transformation of socially assigned sex roles: on the one hand, a change in "the lives of the obscure" ("the Victorian cook lived . . . in the lower depths . . . the Georgian cook is a creature of sunshine and fresh air"), and on the other hand, a change in the minds of the powerful ("Read the *Agamemnon*, and see whether, in process of time, your sympathies are not almost entirely with Clytemnestra"). "All human relations have shifted," Woolf concludes her discussion of the "change" manifested in 1910, "those between masters and servants, husbands and wives, parents and children. And when human relations change there is at the same time a change in religion, conduct, politics, and literature" (*CD* 96–97).

What was the significance—playful or serious—of the year 1910? Some critics have argued that this year saw the opening of Roger Fry's controversial show of postimpressionist paintings; others that it marked the date by which, as Quentin Bell has put it, Bloomsbury "was becoming licentious in its conduct, or rather, licence was no longer the privilege of its homosexual component" (*QB* 1:170). In *The Years,* Woolf herself called attention to the death of Edward VII as a defining event (*Y* 191). But in the young writer's personal life, the major event of 1910, as Phyllis Rose has pointed out, was a "massive practical joke," the so-called *Dreadnought* hoax.[14] On this occasion, Woolf, her brother Adrian, and several friends impersonated the Emperor of Abyssinia and his entourage in a mock inspection of the British Navy's "most formidable . . . most modern and . . . most secret man o' war." The twenty-eight-year-old Virginia Stephen blacked her face and dressed in a caftan, a turban, and "a very handsome moustache and beard" (*QB* 1:157), flaunting both a sexchange and a racechange which made headlines when the imposture was discovered and a "very good looking" young lady "with classical features" was found to be "one of the party" (160). And because the whole hilarious experience revealed the gullibility of His Majesty's Navy, the *Dreadnought* hoax itself became, in Rose's words, "a primal event, the acting out on [Woolf's] part of her own rebellion against paternal authority."[15]

Such an acting out of rebellion was doubly significant because it was not isolated. During the decade for which the year of the *Dreadnought* hoax marked a turning point Woolf had not only earned money and married out of her own class, she had begun to work regularly for the suffrage movement, definitively renounced the ideals of decorum espoused by her Duckworth half-brothers, and entered into an advanced living arrangement at 39 Brunswick Square, where she shared a house with her brother Adrian and three other young men—including her husband-to-be, Leonard Woolf.[16] Although Quentin Bell reports Vanessa insouciantly explaining to George Duckworth that "it's quite alright . . . you see it's so near the Foundling Hospital," Virginia's longtime friend Violet Dickinson protested that "Julia would not have liked it" (*QB* 1:175).[17] But Julia was, of course, dead, and so was the age she incarnated.

As for the young men, even they represented a kind of authority that their fellow tenant had begun to mock. In a parodic review of *Euphrosyne*, a volume of verse published privately by Clive Bell, Lytton Strachey, Leonard Woolf, and others in 1905, Woolf began her lifelong attack on the "Oxbridge" system. The smug "melancholy" of the aspiring poets ("a decadence . . . beyond the decadence of Swinburne himself") proved, she ironically declared, that "there is much to be said surely for that respectable custom which allows the daughter to educate herself at home, while the son is educated by others abroad," for the bliss of the university "is one of those parental fictions, like the existence of the Good Santa Claus" (*QB* 1:205–06).

By 1920, then, when Woolf reviewed Leonie Villard's *La Femme anglaise au XIXème siècle et son evolution d'après le roman anglais contemporain*, she spoke out of her own personal rebelliousness about "the story of the Englishwoman's progress from 1860 to 1914" (*BP* 30). For as Rebecca West would later remark, this English novelist, whether dressed in a gown she had tailored (in defiance of George Duckworth) out of drapery material, in an "Abyssinian" caftan, or in one of her own somewhat eccentric frocks, herself constituted "a very new picture" unlike "any portrait that has yet been painted."[18]

Woolf's interrogations of past and future were thus not merely abstract speculations. Rather, they were questionings of her own history and of the history she might make. She knew that, like the role played by the actress Ellen Terry that she depicted in a late essay, hers was a "new part, an original part."[19] But what was the meaning of the play in which, as a woman artist who had moved far beyond Victorian constraints, she had to act this part? "Mlle Villard," she noted in her review of *La Femme anglaise*, "would be the first to agree that not even a woman . . . can say for certain what the words 'emancipation' and 'evolution' amount to. . . . Energy has been liberated, but into what forms is it to flow?" (30).

The dialogue between past and future that Woolf's question implies became a subject of her fiction not long after her father died, and perhaps as part of her "rebellion against paternal authority," she began by couching the issue in mock histories that not-so-subtly satirized the lives of great men that Sir Leslie's friend Carlyle had proclaimed the substance of history itself.[20] From the *Memoirs of James Stephen*—Woolf's eighteenth-century ancestor—"written by himself for the use of his children," to Leslie Stephen's own *Mausoleum Book*, there was a tradition of family biography, and although Woolf's youthful works are comic rather than lugubrious, two of them fall into this Stephen family category: "Friendships Gallery" (1907), a playful life of Violet Dickinson, wittily printed and bound in violet and presented to its subject as a birthday present, and "Reminiscences" (1908), a memoir of Vanessa addressed to Vanessa's children. But "The Journal of Mistress Joan Martyn" (1906), the first and best of her early quasi-historical fictions, departs radically from both the narcissism of Sir Leslie's *Mausoleum Book* and the in-joking of "Friendships Gallery" and "Reminiscences" to examine general questions about time and change.

Woolf wrote the forty-page "Journal of Mistress Joan Martyn" in August 1906, when she and Vanessa were enjoying "a sort of honeymoon" on a month-long vacation at an Elizabethan manor house in Norfolk.[21] Divided into two parts, the piece recounts the researches of one Rosamund Merridew, a successful scholar, into "the system of land tenure in medieval England" (*CSF* 33), including her discovery of a fifteenth-century diary in which, for the second half of the story, twenty-five-year-old Joan Martyn, the daughter of a small landowner, speaks to the present from the distant past. Throughout, in her characterizations of both the woman historian and the historical woman, the novice author skillfully organizes her material so that "the accent falls a little differently" on people, places, and things, as she was eventually to propose that it must do in female writing (*CR* 156). From the start, moreover, Woolf makes it clear that she and her modern protagonist are consciously committed to the production of what we would now call women's history.

To begin with, although Woolf's cousin Katharine Stephen was the vice-principal of Newnham College, Cambridge, and Woolf herself had been educated at home by such scholars as Clara Pater and Janet Case, Rosamund Merridew represents a kind of feminist fantasy on the part of the still fairly sheltered young artist, for Rosamund—far more than most of Woolf's close female associates—is well-known, well-established, and not the least ambivalent about her career.[22] "I have won considerable fame among my profession," she explains with disingenuous frankness, adding that "I am not absolutely unknown in one or two secluded rooms in Oxford and in Cambridge" (*CSF* 33). As determinedly single as Woolf's much later creation Lily Briscoe, Rosamund, unlike Lily, has no doubt that she *can* write, *can* think, and *has* mastered the academic world that so baffles the artist in *To the Lighthouse.*

And Rosamund, again defining an issue that would always concern Woolf, has mastered that world on her own terms. She has, she confides, carried on a "famous argument" with "much zeal in the Historians' Quarterly," defending her digressions on "the life of the time" which seem to some scholars "fitful and minute" but which really illuminate those lives of the obscure that, like her author, she sees as historically crucial. Her illustration of this point is telling: "A sudden light upon the legs of Dame Elizabeth Partridge sends its beams over the whole state of England, to the King upon his throne; She wanted stockings! & no other need impresses you in quite the same way with the reality of medieval legs; & therefore with the reality of medieval bodies, & so, proceeding upward step by step, with the reality of medieval brains; & there you stand at the centre of all ages: middle beginning or end" (34).

Later, when Rosamund visits Martyn's Hall—"one of those humble little old Halls . . . which survive almost untouched, . . . for centuries & centuries" (35)—Woolf aligns herself with this view of history: Jasper Martyn, the heir of the Hall, shows Rosamund a series of family documents, but he is fondest of the family genealogy and "the Stud book of Willoughby" with "the names, the pedigrees, lives, values, descendants" of "dead horses" all "written out like a bible" (42). "Horses or Grandfathers!" he exclaims enthusiastically (43), and Woolf sardonically implies that the official chronicles treasured by traditional scholars are just such absurd genealogical stud books, perpetuated by narcissistic men like Willoughby, perhaps named for the paradigmatic patriarch satirized by George Meredith in *The Egoist* (1879).

Given her choice of Martyn memorabilia to examine, Rosamund picks the diary of "Grandmother Joan," although the heir warns, "I don't think you'll find anything out of the way in her" (45). And she is right to do so, for in her fashion fifteenth-century Joan Martyn is as remarkable as twentieth-century Rosamund. Through Joan's diary, in fact, Woolf touches on issues that were to concern her throughout her career: the overlooked or forgotten power of women in earlier societies (what the historian Mary Beard was later to call "woman as a force in history"); the role of "Anon"—the wandering singer, the prophetic wisewoman—in shaping culture; and the importance of (women's) writing as the locus of a dialogue between past and future.[23]

Significantly, Joan's father and older brothers are away when Joan begins her diary, and her description of the family estate focuses on the authority of her mother: "What a noble woman she is. . . . It is a great thing to be the daughter of such a woman, & to hope that one day the same power may be mine. She rules us all" (46). Joan's mother, moreover, is no anomaly, for the world Joan inhabits is in many ways matriarchal, though not matrilineal. Imagining marriage, the young woman puts herself in her mother's place ("If I marry well, the burden of a great name & of great lands will be on me. . . . In my husband's absence I shall rule his people" [51]), and she conceives of the land itself in female terms ("Norfolk & the parish of Long Winton in Norfolk is to me what my own grandmother is" [52]).

But Joan cannot entirely accept her mother's dream of what the future may bring to England. "She seems to look forward to nothing better than an earth rising solid out of the mists that now enwreathe it" (60), the diarist confides—to, that is, a time of prosperity in which extant social structures would remain essentially unchanged. In a move that foreshadows later intellectual strategies Woolf tempers Joan's admiration for her mother by sketching the young woman's fascination with two other figures: Master Richard, a wandering singer, and the aged Dame Elsbeth Aske, another folk artist, who "would tell you stories . . . till the air seemed to move & murmur. . . . And they thought that she could tell the future too" (55, 62). Because, like the young Virginia Stephen, Joan longs to be this kind of visionary, she struggles, with a yearning that would never desert Woolf herself, to define a newness that might be utterly different, though she cannot ultimately name it: "What it is that I want, I cannot tell, although I crave for it, and in some secret way, expect it. For often and oftener as time goes by, I find myself suddenly halting in my walk, as though I were stopped by a strange new look upon the surface of the land which I know so well. It hints at something; but it is gone before I know what it means. It is as though a new smile crept out of a well known face; it half frightens you, & yet it beckons" (60).

The enigma at the center of the recorded past, Woolf implies here, is an intimation of a future that cannot be deciphered. Yet such an intimation must be articulated: its articulation is, indeed, at the heart of the act (and art) of writing, and specifically of female writing. For Joan is not only *a* reader and writer, she, a woman, is paradoxically enough *the* writer—the scribe, as it were—of her illiterate family. At the conclusion of Woolf's manuscript, as

Joan's father confesses his own anxiety about the future ("We may be washed off the face of the earth, Joan" [61]), he consoles himself by thinking about his daughter's writing: "Our descendants shall have cause to respect one of us." But Joan, like Woolf, wants a great deal more than the "respect" of the future. She wants to imagine it. Each morning, she says, "with my cheek leant upon the window pane I like to fancy that I am pressing as closely as can be upon the massy wall of time, which is for ever lifting and pulling and letting new spaces of life in upon us" (48). To write—to be a (woman) scribe—is not only to record the past which is the matrix (the mother or grandmother) of the present, but to write to and about the future, even when its lineaments are incomprehensible or elusive.

"The Journal of Mistress Joan Martyn" ends abruptly, more or less in medias res, and the surviving manuscript never resolves certain plot problems that a more conventional fiction writer would have thought important. At one point we are told that Joan never married; at another point, that she is about to be married. But Woolf's disregard of such matters hints that what really interested her was the creation of the complementary characters of Rosamund Merridew and Joan Martyn. And that interest was itself prophetic, for as a novelist and essayist, Woolf herself was half Rosamund Merridew, a researcher into a new kind of history, and half Joan Martyn, a searcher for a history of the new.

To be sure, even in her role as Rosamund Merridew, Woolf did not actually produce historical chronicles, for as she explains in her "novel-essay" *The Pargiters* (1933), "It would be far easier to write history [than fiction, but] that method of telling the truth seems to me so elementary, and so clumsy, that I prefer, where truth is important, to write fiction" (9). Nevertheless, from *The Voyage Out* to *Between the Acts* she meditated on the relationship between that official public history constituted by the masculine stud book and the unofficial private history represented by the lives of women. In this respect, her work foreshadows the research that was soon to be undertaken by a range of real women historians, some of whose writings (for instance, Eileen Power's *Medieval People* [1924]) she would later read, some of whose scholarship (like Mary Beard's *Woman as a Force in History* [1946]) she would not live to know.[24]

When Woolf (and Rosamund Merridew) began thinking about history, however, such enterprises were virtually nonexistent in her circle: most investigations of the past that she had studied proceeded on the Carlylean hypothesis that past and present were principally shaped by heroes and hero worship. As for women, with the exception of "worthies" like Elizabeth I and Jeanne d'Arc, female human beings mostly existed on the margins of the historical record. As late as 1921, the American historian Arthur Schlesinger observed that "if the silence of historians is taken to mean anything, it would appear that one half of our population have been negligible factors in our country's history. Before accepting the truth of this assumption, the facts of our history need to be raked over from a new point of view. It should not be forgotten . . . that all of our great historians have been men and were likely therefore to be influenced by a sex interpretation of history all the more potent because unconscious."[25]

Although she very likely never encountered Schlesinger's statement, Woolf echoed it in *A Room of One's Own*, remarking that "it was certainly an odd monster that one made up by reading the historians' [views of women] first, and the poets' afterwards—a worm winged like an eagle; the spirit of life and beauty in a kitchen chopping up suet" (46). To remedy the situation, she suggested that the students of Newnham or Girton "should re-write history," for "it often seems a little queer as it is, unreal, lop-sided" (47). Woolf's self-consciously alienated remarks summarized a criticism, and pointed to a project, central to her work even while they recalled the disaffection of Jane Austen's Catherine Morland, who complains in *Northanger Abbey* that history tells her "nothing that does not either vex or weary [her]. The quarrels of popes and kings, with wars or pestilences, in every page; the men all so good for nothing, and hardly any women at all—it is very tiresome."[26]

Even before she invented Rosamund Merridew, Woolf had embarked on this project. According to Quentin Bell, one of her first serious efforts at composition was *A History of Women*, attempted in 1897 when she was just fifteen, the manuscript of which has evidently been lost (*QB* 1:51). By the time she wrote her first novel, *The Voyage Out* (1915), a task that occupied some six years of vision and revision, she had begun more openly than in "The Journal of Mistress Joan Martyn" to question the histories of men that formed the staple of the early reading prescribed by Sir Leslie Stephen. Bell notes that Woolf's adolescent studies included James Froude's *Carlyle*, Thomas Babington Macaulay's *History of England from the Accession of James II*, Carlyle's *French Revolution*, Thomas Arnold's *History of Rome*, and Edward Gibbon's *Decline and Fall of the Roman Empire*.[27]

The last was to become a virtual leitmotif in her first novel, whose arrogant St. John Hirst—slyly modeled on Lytton Strachey but with a name that recalls *Jane Eyre*'s priggish St. John Rivers—exclaims to the book's ingenuous heroine, Rachel Vinrace, "D'you mean to tell me you've reached the age of twenty-four without reading Gibbon?" (*VO* 154) and promptly lends her volume one. At first Rachel loves the historian's words, which "seemed to drive roads back to the very beginning of the world . . . and by passing down them all knowledge would be hers" (174). But the young woman changes as she is initiated into female sexuality (her initiation is arguably the central theme of the novel), and her alienation from both the masculine way of thinking and the male history represented by Gibbon and Hirst becomes increasingly pronounced. "I don't like it," Rachel finally declares of Gibbon's history, for "read as she would, she could not grasp the meaning with her mind. 'It goes round, round, round, like a roll of oil-cloth'" (201). Her dislike is echoed by Mrs. Thornbury, like Rachel an English visitor to the South American town of Santa Marina where most of the tale's action is set: "'*The Decline and Fall of the Roman Empire?* . . . A very wonderful book, I know. My dear father was always quoting it at us, with the result that we resolved never to read a line'" (200).

But Gibbon and St. John are not the only targets of satire in *The Voyage Out*. Early in the novel, Richard Dalloway (who here displays a very different personality from the one he has in the later *Mrs. Dalloway*) makes a brief appearance in which he admiringly formulates just the "vision of English history" Woolf most disliked: "King following King, Prime Minister Prime Minister, and Law Law," with Britain's imperialism "a lasso that opened and caught things, enormous chunks of the habitable globe" (51). And that Rachel encounters the Dalloways when all are being carried to various British outposts on a ship called the *Euphrosyne*, in a continuing mockery of the unlucky verse anthology published by Strachey and his friends in 1905, suggests that such colonization is an intellectual as well as a political gesture which can capture and captivate some women along with most men. Another, if more sympathetic, object of satire is the kindly but ineffectual Miss Allan, who is "reading the 'Prelude,'" partly because she always read the 'Prelude' abroad, and partly because she was engaged in writing a short *Primer of English Literature*—Beowulf to Swinburne—which would have a paragraph on Wordsworth" (103). She describes her manuscript to Rachel in a series of literary clichés: "'Age of Chaucer; Age of Elizabeth; Age of Dryden,'" and confides, "'I'm glad there aren't many more ages. I'm still in the middle of the eighteenth century" (253).

Against the "oil-cloth" history of "Laws" and "Ages," Woolf sets Rachel's struggle to reimagine the past, and the effort of her fiancé, Terence Hewet, to reinvent the present and the future. For Rachel, the transformations wrought by time are enigmatic yet extraordinary: "If one went back far enough, everything perhaps was intelligible; everything was in common; for the mammoths who pastured in the fields of Richmond High Street had turned into paving stones and boxes full of ribbon, and her aunts" (67). Later, journeying down the Amazon, she and Terence confront what Woolf hints has a deeper historical meaning than Dalloway's vision of English "King following King"—a native village of "strange wooden nests" in which keen-eyed women are "squatting on the ground in triangular shapes" and where the form of a "lean majestic man" causes an "Englishman's body [to] appear ugly and unnatural" (284). This primordial village, concludes Terence, "makes us seem insignificant, doesn't it?" (285).

Finally, although he is unable to save Rachel from the fever of gender that consumes her at the end of the novel, Terence proposes alternatives to Hirst's pomposity and egotism. Terence wants to "write a novel about Silence," about "the things people don't say," and, foreshadowing an argument in *Three Guineas*, he attacks Hirst for his obsession with "his sacred career," a preoccupation that means "no one takes [St. John's sister] seriously, poor dear. She feeds the rabbits" (213): that is, her only purpose in life appears to be domestic nurturance. Thus, after Terence and Rachel become engaged, he seeks "to sketch an outline of an ideal education. . . . Their daughter should be required from infancy to gaze at a large square of cardboard, painted blue, to suggest thoughts of infinity, for women were grown too practical; and their son—he should be taught to laugh at great men, . . . at men who wore ribands and rose to the tops of their trees" (294–95).[28]

The debate between official and unofficial history begun in *The Voyage Out* continued in Woolf's next novel, *Night and Day* (1919), which approaches the issue by literalizing the problem of literary inheritance as Edith Wharton had done in such tales as *The Touchstone* (1897) and "The Angel at the Grave" (1901).[29] Katharine Hilbery, the book's heroine, is the granddaughter of the great Victorian poet Richard Alardyce, to whose memory her family keeps a kind of shrine, containing manuscripts, his "gigantic gold-rimmed spectacles," and his "pair of large, worn slippers" (15). Burdened by the "glorious past" Alardyce symbolizes, Katharine feels dwarfed and depressed. Yet, daunting as the Alardyce history is, Woolf subverts it in several ways. She shows, to begin with, that the job of writing Alardyce's biography has fallen to his daughter, Katharine's mother, who seems congenitally incapable of the linear logic and concern for official events that ought to characterize any account of a great man's life. "She had no difficulty in writing, and covered a page every morning as instinctively as a thrush sings," Woolf explains about Mrs. Hilbery, who is plainly modeled on Sir Leslie's sister-in-law Annie Thackeray Ritchie, "but nevertheless . . . the book still remained unwritten" (40).[30] Indeed, in Mrs. Hilbery's history the accent always falls in the wrong place, so that her book became "a wild dance of will-o'-the-wisps, without form or continuity" (43). Nonetheless, incoherent as Mrs. Hilbery's mind and work appear, she ultimately engineers the denouement of *Night and Day*, giving coherence to Woolf's own narrative. Having decided that "Anne Hathaway had a way, among other things, of writing Shakespeare's sonnets" (305), Mrs. Hilbery returns from a pilgrimage to Shakespeare's tomb to intone a revisionary history in which the names of Katharine and her working-class suitor, Ralph Denham, are definitively linked. As for Ralph, he too plans a subversion of what might be called "old historicism," because, just as Terence Hewet proposes to write a novel about "Silence," Ralph resolves to "write the history of the English village from Saxon days to the present time" (226).[31]

If revisionary history provided a subject for debate in Woolf's first two novels, it became a structural principle in her next work of fiction. In fact, the breakthrough—"some idea of a new form for a new novel"—that the writer decided she had experienced as she began *Jacob's Room* (1922) may be considered a liberation into an art that she saw not only as the future of fiction but also as the future of history.[32] As many critics have observed, *Jacob's Room* is a radically innovative biography, an account of the life of a largely opaque or absent subject in which, although the work is always elegantly coherent, the accent falls differently on people, places, and events.

To be sure, this novel is as thematically haunted by history as its predecessors were. Betty Flanders and her children visit "the raised circle of the Roman camp" on Dods Hill (*JR* 19). Jacob and his friends seek to master history at Cambridge, where Jacob writes an essay on the topic "Does History Consist of the Biographies of Great Men?" (39). The stones of Cornwall and their place in the life of "primeval man" become subjects for a historian's "conjectures" (53). "Plato continues his dialogue in the British Museum" (109). Jacob travels to Italy and Greece, planning to write "something in the style of Gibbon" (136). And Evan Williams has "the political history of England at his fingertips" (143).

But, comments the narrator, "When a child begins to read history one marvels, sorrowfully, to hear him spell out in his new voice the ancient words," and for this reason she inflects "the very moment of history" (98) that constitutes Jacob Flanders's lifetime differently from the way Gibbon—and her own father—would have, so that everything seems slightly skewed. Betty Flanders's domestic life is depicted at length while her decision to send Jacob to Cambridge takes place, as it were, offstage. Jacob's romantic relationships with a series of young women, obliquely rendered, supplant most other external happenings in his life and society. The very events that will lead to his death in World War I and give his surname allegorical force are reported almost parenthetically and juxtaposed with images representing the "lives of the obscure": the Cornish farm wife "Mrs. Pascoe . . . in her cabbage-garden looking out to sea"; Greek women on the steps of the Parthenon, "jolly as sand-martins in the heat" (175).

Two sentences near the end of *Jacob's Room* epitomize this sort of reinflected chronicle-making. Half asleep, Betty Flanders hears the "dull sound" of guns, "as if nocturnal women were beating great carpets," and thinks, "There was Morty lost, and Seabrook dead; her sons fighting for their country. But were the chickens safe?" (175). Such a progression of ideas might seem bathetic or even heartless, but in this context Woolf clearly wishes to make the point Rosamund Merridew would have made. Behind the public march of time that determines Jacob's fate, a private domestic life moves silently forward. Although a voice in Whitehall "decree[s] that the course of history should shape itself this way or that way, being manfully determined . . . to control the course of events" (172), Betty Flanders, who has for some time wanted to keep chickens, has at last got a chicken farm.

If Woolf learned in composing *Jacob's Room* that writing fiction could be a way of writing history, she also intuited that the history she most needed to write was the history of the family and of the individual psyche as those narratives were formed by the social structures of which the family is a microcosm. Both Rosamund Merridew and Joan Martyn had brooded on this history, with Rosamund resolutely renouncing the institution of marriage and Joan ambivalently acquiescing in it while longing for a different, unknowable future. Is Rosamund Merridew Joan Martyn's future? If not, what is Joan Martyn's future to be—and has the structure of the family changed to allow her to "taste the newest and the freshest" for which she yearns? From *Mrs. Dalloway* on, these are major questions to which Woolf's fictive histories address themselves.

The family and its discontents are not, of course, absent from *The Voyage Out, Night and Day,* and *Jacob's Room.* On the contrary, both are intransigently present in all these books, so much so that they have barely been historicized but seem, instead, to represent virtually timeless gender imperatives which determine the fates of both the famous and the obscure. In *The Voyage Out,* for instance, Rachel's struggle is not just a struggle against male-defined history but a conflict with the male-dominated sexuality that seems an inexorable force in history. Thus, although Terence strives to imagine new modes of learning for their hypothetical children, Rachel is ultimately destroyed by her inability to cope with the power of heterosexual desire as it shapes the patriarchal family. When Richard Dalloway furtively embraces her on board the *Euphrosyne,* she finds him "terrifying" and later has dreams of tunnels and "barbarian men" prefiguring the hallucinations induced by the fever that kills her. After her engagement to Terence, moreover, Rachel finds herself being congratulated by her friend and mentor, Helen Ambrose, but feeling obliterated by this paradigmatic wife and mother, who is a first sketch for Mrs. Ramsay, just as Ridley Ambrose is a first study of Mr. Ramsay.

The scene between the two women, set in the heart of the jungle, is the novel's most bizarre, even surrealistic episode:

> A hand dropped abrupt as iron on Rachel's shoulder; it might have been a bolt from heaven. She fell beneath it, and the grass whipped across her eyes and filled her mouth and ears. Through the waving stems she saw a figure, large and shapeless against the sky. Helen was upon her. Rolled this way and that, now seeing only forests of green, and now the high blue heaven, she was speechless and almost without sense. At last she lay still, all the grasses shaken round her and before her by her panting. Over her loomed two great heads, the heads of a man and woman, of Terence and Helen. [283]

Just after this comes the primal scene in which the British party encounters the women squatting in triangular shapes and the lean majestic man who make its own civilization seem insignificant. What Kate Chopin had in *The Awakening* called "the mother-woman"—the woman completely given over to sexuality and maternity—is gigantic, yet at the same time no more than a "triangular shape," while her man, lean and majestic, is upright, phallic, indomitable. Like the Ambroses, the eternal pair of mother-woman and lean majestic man is somehow larger than life: "In comparison with this couple most people looked small" (9). The gender structures they represent therefore appear inescapable except through death.[33]

Certainly the sexual outsiders Woolf depicts in *The Voyage Out*—the pompous homosexual St. John Hirst, the spinster historian Miss Allan, the misandric flirt Evelyn M.—offer Rachel no viable alternatives to the sex roles that sicken her. By contrast, *Night and Day* does introduce the character of the self-sufficient New Woman Mary Datchet. In this novel, nevertheless, the traditional family seems still a changeless structure: Mr. and Mrs. Hilbery function as comic successors to the Ambroses, and the four young people do an Austenian courtship dance throughout the work until they are boxed by Mrs. Hilbery into two neat unions at the end: "'Katharine and Ralph. . . . William and Cassandra'" (497). Indeed, even Mary Datchet has won her independence only by austerely repressing her love for Ralph Denham.

Similarly, throughout *Jacob's Room*, the family is frozen in its traditional bourgeois configuration. Early in the book the widowed Betty Flanders imagines her husband timelessly preserved under the ground on which she dwells: "Seabrook lay six foot beneath, dead these many years. . . . Doubtless his very face lay visible beneath, the face of a young man whiskered, shapely, who had gone out duck-shooting and refused to change his boots." Perpetually young, the lost Seabrook Flanders, "Merchant of this city" (16), has become a kind of Freudian dead father, whose law still governs Betty's works and days. Even her illicit relationship with Captain Barfoot conforms, metaphorically speaking, to this law. It is, after all, Barfoot who recommends that Jacob go to Cambridge, Barfoot who "advises chickens," Barfoot who requires her approval of his political ambitions. And Barfoot's hegemony is further manifested by the helplessness of his invalid wife Ellen, confined to her bath chair, "civilization's prisoner" (25), and silently enduring his extramarital relationship with Betty Flanders.

As for the other characters who appear in *Jacob's Room*, most are as fixed in their positions as Seabrook, Betty, Captain Barfoot, and Ellen. The vicar's wife wanders on the moor, dreaming of a different life, but "she did not lose her faith, did not leave her husband, never read her poem through" (27). Clara Durrant, who longs to escape gentility and reveal her feelings to Jacob, is trapped in a cage of decorum. The "fallen" women Florinda and Fanny

Elmer—along with the adulterous Sandra Wentworth Williams—represent sexual options that are merely scandalous, while Jacob himself, an eldest son and a Cambridge man, is the "destined inheritor" of the society whose double standard condemns such women to marginality and leaves the feminist Julia Hedge in a perpetual, futile rage.

Tellingly, it is the death of Jacob, the heir apparent, that disintegrates this seemingly primordial system. Young women who sicken at the prospect of marriage, or who refuse it, are almost infinitely replaceable, Woolf implies.[34] But precisely because in a patrilineal economy the chosen son must inexorably ascend to power, his death alone can put the whole social enterprise in question. "'What am I to do with these, Mr. Bonamy?'" demands Betty Flanders as she holds the dead Jacob's empty shoes toward his best friend. For no one but the prototypical son can step into the shoes of the heir, and the horse that the hero should have ridden is now riderless, like the runaway steed whose appearance in Hyde Park chillingly prefigures the annihilation of Jacob (167), a representative of what many saw as a whole generation of sons, in Flanders fields.

That until *Jacob's Room* Woolf's novels should have represented the family as a timeless structure is historically reasonable, if not entirely accurate. As her own sense of the generation gap between Leslie Stephen and his children indicated, the institution of the family—and particularly the sex roles it promulgates—had begun to change considerably by, say, the year 1910. But it was the Great War, with its asymmetrical impact on men and women, that dramatized and accelerated social transformations already set in motion by the late nineteenth-century women's movement.[35] Katherine Mansfield's complaint about *Night and Day* that it is "a novel in the tradition of the English novel" whose message is that "the war never has been" (*QB* 2:37) clearly reflected her consciousness of this phenomenon. But Mansfield's remarks also revealed her understanding of a point that soon became crucial in Woolf's artistic development: the disintegration of the Victorian family was accompanied, given Woolf's fascination with "the other history," by a disintegration of the traditionally "plotted" novel.[36]

It is no coincidence, therefore, that Woolf discovered "some idea of a new form for a new novel" as she began work on *Jacob's Room,* because the revisionary history that became her structural principle as well as her thematic focus specifically chronicled the faltering of the family romance that had long shaped the patterns and purposes of fiction.[37] Certainly both *The Voyage Out* and *Night and Day* are structured by that romance and by the marriage-or-death plot that it has almost always necessitated. But in their odd inflections of events (*Jacob's Room*), their curious juxtapositions (*Mrs. Dalloway*), or their rapid expansions and contractions of time (*To the Lighthouse, Orlando, The Waves, The Years, Between the Acts*), Woolf's subsequent novels refuse to accommodate to the imperatives of the family even as they record the demise of traditional sex roles and meditate on the engendering of the new.

Woolf's major rethinking of family history begins with *Mrs. Dalloway*, which simultaneously examines the deadliness of the world Jacob Flanders died to save, traces the public and private histories which shaped that world, and asks who or what might inherit no longer viable structures. As many have noted, heterosexual passion, the force that devastated Rachel in *The Voyage Out* and was celebrated by Ralph and Katharine at the end of *Night and Day*, has almost completely disappeared in this novel.[38] Although at first the book's heroine seems to *be* her sex role—she is "Mrs. Dalloway; not even Clarissa any more; . . . Mrs. Richard Dalloway" (14)—she is fundamentally "virginal," having felt desire only once, in the distant past, for a woman, Sally Seton. During her reunion with her old lover, Peter Walsh, in fact, Clarissa is drawn into a Popeian mock-heroic battle of (male) pocketknife against (female) needle (66), while between herself and her husband there is "a gulf" (181) which emphasizes the nunlike chastity that leads her to sense "an emptiness about the heart of life" and to believe "narrower and narrower would her bed be" (45–46).[39]

The relationship between Septimus Warren Smith and his wife, Lucrezia, has, of course, failed far more theatrically than the one between Clarissa and Peter or between Clarissa and Richard. To begin with, the shell-shocked Septimus had only married Rezia after the death of Evans, the man he really loved, "when the panic was on him—that he could not feel" (131). When we first encounter Rezia she is inwardly lamenting, "I am alone; I am alone!" (35). Grown thin with pain, she has removed her wedding ring, and "their marriage [is] over," Septimus thinks "with agony, with relief" (101). Even the elemental mechanisms of sexuality horrify this traumatized veteran, whose war-induced revulsion against the institutions of government and the family intimate what Jacob Flanders might have felt had he survived. "The secret signal which one generation passes, under disguise, to the next," decides Septimus, "is loathing, hatred, despair" (134), so that when Rezia longs for "a son like Septimus," he insists that "one cannot bring children into a world like this . . . . or increase the breed of these lustful animals" (135).

Most other couples in the book are, if not so catastrophically troubled, at least alienated. Hugh Whitbread's wife, Evelyn, whom Clarissa has visited in a nursing home "times without number," is often "a good deal out of sorts" (7). Lady Bradshaw has "gone under" the subtle tyranny of her husband, the oleaginous physician Sir William Bradshaw (152). Peter Walsh seems inclined to forget Daisy, the faintly disreputable (she is divorced) young fiancée he left in India, because his unrequited love of Clarissa "had sapped something in him permanently" (241). Even the bloomingly healthy young aristo-

crats Lord Gayton and Nancy Blow lack the power "of communicating feelings"; they will "solidify young," and be, when they are alone, "rather dull"
(270).
    Nor are same-sex relationships redemptive in this society of crumbling
couples. To be sure, in strikingly sexualized imagery Clarissa Dalloway imagines the sensation of "yielding to the charm of a woman" as

> a sudden revelation, a tinge like a blush which one tried to check and
> then, as it spread, one yielded to its expansion, and rushed to the
> farthest verge and there quivered and felt the world come closer,
> swollen with some astonishing significance, some pressure of rapture,
> which split its thin skin and gushed and poured with an extraordinary
> alleviation over the cracks and sores! Then, for that moment, she had
> seen an illumination; a match burning in a crocus; an inner meaning
> almost expressed.

But the mystic meaning is only *almost* expressed, and "the close withdrew;
the hard softened" (47). Clarissa's romance with Sally Seton was similarly
evanescent if equally ecstatic, even while, as a bond "between women just
grown up" who "spoke of marriage always as a catastrophe" (50), its remembered urgency reemphasizes the "cracks and sores" of traditional family
structures.
    More problematic than Clarissa's relationships is the metamorphosis of
Septimus's homoerotic *Blutbrüderschaft* with his officer, Evans, into a partnership with death. As Septimus sits in Regents Park, he mistakes Peter
Walsh for the lost Evans and raises his hand in greeting "as the dead man in
the grey suit came nearer" (105). And just as troublesome, Miss Kilman's
lesbian passion for Clarissa's daughter, Elizabeth, has left her in a torment of
frustrated desire. As the two take tea together, Miss Kilman gobbles an
éclair, feeling that she is "about to split asunder. . . . The agony [is] so ter-
rific. If she could grasp [Elizabeth]; if she could clasp her, if she could make
her hers absolutely and forever and then die. . . . But to sit here, unable to
think of anything to say . . . she could not stand it" (199–200).
    Perhaps because of all these failures, then, the most crucial relationship in
Mrs. Dalloway is a bond between two people who do not know each other,
never meet, and appear to have nothing in common: Clarissa Dalloway and
Septimus Warren Smith. Yoked by the violence of Septimus's suicide and
Clarissa's uncanny empathy with his act, this unlikely pair, who unknowingly
shadow each other through a postwar June day in London, dramatize the
arbitrariness of social and sexual destinies which leave the one feeling (in
the role of hostess) like "a stake driven in at the top of her stairs" (259) and
the other feeling (in the role of mad veteran) exposed "very high, on the back
of the world" (103). At the same time, as secret sharers of an invisible tie
more central in the novel than any of the familial bonds in which they and

a range of other characters are fixed, Clarissa and Septimus reveal the artifice of all relationships through the symbolic coupling into which Woolf guides them.

What factors so drastically fragmented and reformed the connections between all these characters? As she had in earlier novels, Woolf explores two histories throughout *Mrs. Dalloway:* the official public history which constitutes the genealogical stud book of "The Journal of Mistress Joan Martyn," and the private history incarnated in Joan Martyn's diary. Most obviously these two ways of recording time are represented by "Big Ben . . . with his majesty laying down the law, so solemn, so just," and by "the other clock, the clock which always struck two minutes after Big Ben" and which "came shuffling in with its lap full of odds and ends . . . all sorts of little things . . . on the wake of that solemn stroke" (193–94). Compared earlier in the novel to "a young man, strong, indifferent, inconsiderate . . . swinging dumb-bells this way and that" (71), Big Ben keeps track of the almost redundantly repetitive public events—war, invention, "King following King, Prime Minister Prime Minister, and Law Law"—which make up the history children are taught in school. Metonymically associated with love (for Clarissa, meditating on "the miracle" incarnated in the old lady next door, has just begun to dwell on love when the other clock comes shuffling in), the alternative history that the "other clock" symbolizes only *seems* to be a chronicle of "little things." In fact, Woolf shows, such trifles may have as much power for changing the world as the *dumb*-bells deployed by Big Ben—and those little things may have more potential for healing wounds in the body politic.

Woolf further dramatizes this contrast between the two histories in the set pieces interpolated into the chronicle of a day in June which patterns the action of *Mrs. Dalloway.* First, the episodes of the motorcar (which carries "the enduring symbol of the state" [23]), of the skywriting airplane (29–30), and of the marching soldiers "drugged into a stiff yet staring corpse by discipline" (77) evoke the official history that led to the war on which this novel broods. But that history has already been put in question here; its outlines are blurry and enigmatic. Even the sex of the figure in the car is "now in dispute," and the true lineaments of its face will be known only when the state itself has been annihilated and "London is a grass-grown path" (23). The airplane "ominously" inscribes what may be intimations of the future on the silent surface of the sky, "but what word was it writing?" (31).[40] And the wreath-carrying "stiff yet staring boys" are a "corpse" appearing out of nowhere for no discernible reason.

The "other history" which Woolf envisions in similar set pieces—the episode of the gray nurse, the description of the tube-station crone, and a brief epic simile comparing the London evening to a woman—is equally enigmatic. And just as the Big Ben history is associated with the public world, masculinity, technology, and the war, this alternative record is embodied in the private, the feminine, the natural. The gray nurse who metamorphoses into a "spectral presence," a "giant figure at the end of the ride," confronts the "solitary traveller" with his own insignificance, but as he advances toward her cryptic shadow, she comes to represent a female enigma at the heart of nature, so that the narrator plaintively asks "to whom does the solitary traveller make reply?" (88). The tube station crone, who has endured through "all ages" (122), sings an untranslatable song: "ee um fah um so / foo swee too eem oo" (124).[41] The London evening, like "a woman who [has] slipped off her print dress and white apron to array herself in blue and pearls," is "constrained . . . to partnership in her [London's] revelry" (245), but to what end these sisters or lovers—the hour and the city—conspire is not clear.

What is clear is that the tension between the forces represented in these contrasting passages—culture and nature, male and female, public and private, what has changed and what might endure—severely questions traditional social and familial hierarchies. The dialectic between these two sets of forces is reiterated in the contrast between two sets of characters in *Mrs. Dalloway:* on the one hand, characters associated with war, empire, Parliament, the *Times,* and Harley Street, and on the other hand, characters associated with the household, the private world of women, and the other clock. Obviously Richard Dalloway, the M.P. who serves on committees set up to deal with "his Armenians, his Albanians" (182), falls into the first category, as do Peter Walsh, the former colonial administrator who believes that "one [has] to respect" the patriotic zeal that drugs marching boys "into a stiff yet staring corpse" (77); Hugh Whitbread, who has a "little job at Court"; and the perniciously public-spirited doctors, Holmes and Bradshaw. But so, too, do several female figures whose identification with public history has overridden or distorted private allegiances.

Such a character is Lady Bruton, who "should have been a general of dragoons herself" (159), although she has been "debarred by her sex and some truancy, too, of the logical faculty" (275) and is united to Clarissa Dalloway by a "feminine comradeship which went beneath masculine lunch parties" (160). Another is Miss Kilman, who has, according to Richard Dalloway, "a really historical mind," and who has "made her way in the world" (200), although her "dismissal from school during the War" (16) because she was not appropriately xenophobic has left her embittered and marginalized. But perhaps the most crucial representatives of Big Ben history are the prime minister, that "thick gold-laced man" (264) who incarnates imperial power, and Septimus Warren Smith, the upwardly mobile working-class veteran whose sanity has been sacrificed to the social order the prime minister represents, in spite of his diligent prewar studies of "Shakespeare, Darwin, *The History of Civilisation,* and Bernard Shaw" (129).

At the same time, Septimus's madness and suicide demonstrate, far more than the death of Jacob Flanders, both the ferocity and the fragility of the patriarchal enterprise, a point which aligns this scapegoat who wants to "tell the Prime Minister" that the "trees are alive" (102) with the other history of nature and nurture. For even while Septimus's most grandiose paranoid fantasies parody, and therefore subvert, the central tenets of heroes and hero worship by which the masculinist stud book organizes itself, his final self-immolation is triggered by a loathing of the history that has shaped and sacrificed him. Parody: at one point, he decides that "he, Septimus, the lord of men [has been] called forth in advance of the mass of men . . . to learn the meaning, which now at last, after all the toils of civilisation—Greeks, Romans, Shakespeare, Darwin, and now himself . . . must be told to the Cabinet" (101–02). Loathing: just after a scene in which Septimus, making hats with Lucrezia, perceives his wife as "a flowering tree" through whose branches he can see "the face of a lawgiver" (224), he defies Dr. Holmes and plunges to his death, as if in allegiance to the nurturing, antipatriarchal law Rezia embodies. And his final cry, "I'll give it you!" (226), further indicates the ambiguity of his affiliation with public history. On the one hand, it emphasizes his acquiescence in a system of destruction: "I'll give *it*"—the death you want—"[to] you." On the other hand, it underscores his threat to an establishment he longs to destroy because it has destroyed him, Evans, and Rezia: "I'll give it [*to*] you!"—I'll show you, I'll shatter you as I shatter myself.

But of course there are many figures less equivocally associated with the other history in *Mrs. Dalloway*. These include the "flowering" Lucrezia, who mounts "the appalling staircase" of time, "laden with Holmes and Bradshaw," and "triumphs" over them because of her allegiance to the law of love rather than of "proportion" (225), and the wild young Sally Seton, whom Clarissa once desired and who accused "Hugh Whitbread, of all people . . . of kissing her in the smoking-room to punish her for saying that women should have votes" (276). Other notable characters in this group are Mrs. Walker, the cook, to whom "one Prime Minister more or less . . . made no difference at this hour of the night [among the] soup tureens, and pudding basins" (251); "old Ellen Barnet," Clarissa's childhood nurse, now a cloakroom attendant and repository of women's history, who "remembered mothers when they were girls" (253); and that Victorian relic Miss Helena Parry, who "had no . . . proud illusions about Viceroys, Generals, Mutinies" (271).

But the queen of this "other history" is Clarissa Dalloway herself. "Mistress of silver, of linen, of china," Clarissa wonders "how she had got through life on [a] few twigs of knowledge" and reflects that she knows "nothing; no language, no history; she scarcely read a book now, except memoirs in bed," the last suggesting her exclusive interest in the personal lives that underlie

public deeds.[42] Yet precisely because of her failure to know the difference
between the Armenians and Albanians who so engage her husband's attention, Clarissa has, as Peter Walsh admiringly realizes, the "gift . . . to be; to
exist; to sum it all up in the moment" (264). Ultimately, therefore, in terms of
the novel's structure, Septimus's death is not primarily a sign of his defeat by
Holmes and Bradshaw or a gesture of defiance toward the system their
sanctimonious sermons sustain. Rather, it is a tribute to Clarissa, a tribute to
the "terror" and "ecstasy" of the personal life over which she rules. And
Clarissa meditates that "there was an embrace in death," because this "mistress" of domesticity understands that through his self-immolation the
young man has drawn close to her, signaling his agreement that authoritative public men like Sir William Bradshaw, "a great doctor yet obscurely
evil," "make life intolerable" (281).

Yet what of Clarissa's puzzling discovery that Septimus's suicide "made
her feel the beauty; made her feel the fun" (284)? In *Sexchanges,* we argued
that this flash of excitement (which may at first seem heartless) at least in part
reflects the society hostess's realization that paradoxically, because of the
nihilism of the war, she and the values she stands for have gained a new
power over a public world, a world of which young men like Jacob and
Septimus are no longer destined inheritors. Certainly, moreover, Woolf's
depiction of the prime minister through Ellie Henderson's eyes ("He looked
so ordinary. You might have stood him behind a counter and bought
biscuits—poor chap, all rigged up in gold lace" [261]) mocks the statesman's
hollowness as well as the decline of the system he symbolizes. In addition,
Woolf's portrayal of the dignitary from Peter Walsh's perspective ("the thick
gold-laced man who was doing his best, and good luck to him, to look important" [264–65]) similarly suggests the debilitation of officialdom, while Peter's enthralled vision of Clarissa as a mermaid "lolloping on the waves and
braiding her tresses" (264) as she says goodbye to the prime minister emphasizes both her enduring magic and her ability to bid farewell to the history of
great men that she never really understood.

Still, although "energy has been liberated" here (albeit in painful ways),
"into what forms is it to flow?" Is Clarissa Dalloway now a destined inheritor,
replacing those lost heirs Jacob and Septimus? Woolf implies that she simultaneously is and is not, establishing a tension between the book's title and its
heroine's first name which replicates the conflict between Big Ben history
and the other clock history. On the one hand, this heroine is presented by the
book's title as merely her sex role, which is the wife of Richard Dalloway,
M.P.—as, that is, a paradigmatic inhabitant of a perpetual family structure.
On the other, she is characterized throughout with increasing intensity as
Clarissa, her Ur-self, until at the end she generates "terror" and "ecstasy" by
appearing in this guise: "It is Clarissa," says Peter Walsh. For there she *is.*

But as the private Clarissa, Woolf's protagonist is not just engaged in a dialectic with the public Mrs. Dalloway; she is also allusively set against literary history's most famous Clarissa, the heroine of Samuel Richardson's novel about masculine predation and feminine martyrdom.[43] As such, she reminds us, first, of the monitory tradition in which Richardson was working, the mode of the conduct book, which advises the female reader of her proper role in society as guardian of chastity even as it awards special significance to the private sphere in which that role is undertaken. At the same time, in tension with Richardson's Clarissa as well as with her identity as Mrs. Dalloway, Woolf's Clarissa also suggests that a revision of the concepts of wife and of martyred virgin is now possible. For just as she persistently remains herself behind the mask of Mrs. Dalloway, this basically virginal Clarissa resists the martyrdom of sexuality. Unlike Richardson's heroine (or Woolf's own Rachel Vinrace), she triumphs through a survival which, when juxtaposed with the death of Septimus ("the lord of men") and the potential deadliness of the label "Mrs. Dalloway," is perhaps the truest source of the terror and ecstasy she instills in onlookers—terror because *they* may not have such a capacity for endurance, ecstasy because she *does*.

Nevertheless, since Clarissa is a contemporary of the men who sent Jacob and Septimus into death and madness, she cannot be an actual inheritor; instead, it is her glory that she is a survivor. What heir, then, will take up the position once occupied by the dead soldiers? Sally Seton, of course, has five sons at Eton, all down with the mumps; beautifully made-up Nancy Blow has appeared at the party with athletic Lord Gayton, who still has "his duties" although he will solidify young; and even the Bradshaws have a son at Eton, also down with the mumps. But in the terms of Woolf's novel (in which none of these figures has a central role), the fated icon of the new is Clarissa's enigmatic daughter, the girl she calls (to Peter Walsh's annoyance) "*my* Elizabeth" (73; emphasis ours).

Named for a distant queen who will recur as an emblem of (female) authority in a number of other books by Woolf, Elizabeth is a boyish girl who likes "being alone in the country with her father and the dogs" and who reacts with distress to stock romantic definitions of the feminine: "People were beginning to compare her to poplar trees, early dawn, hyacinths, fawns . . . and it made her life a burden to her" (204). Physically different from the Dalloways, who are "fair-haired; blue-eyed," she is dark, with "Chinese eyes in a pale face," and seems like "an Oriental mystery" (186). But, Woolf assures us, she is an heiress of a tradition of female "public service" that is too often forgotten, for her Dalloway ancestresses were "abbesses, principals, head mistresses, dignitaries, in the republic of women" (209). Given the gap opened in history by the deaths of Jacob and Septimus, it may be Elizabeth who will step into the breach, becoming, perhaps, a doctor or a farmer (206).[44]

Yet as an icon of the new, what does this Elizabeth, not a queen but an acolyte of the *republic* of women, portend? With her enthrallment to the tormented Miss Kilman, her loyalty to her father, and her refusal of florid romanticism, what can she mean about the future? In a crucial description of this destined inheritor riding up Whitehall into the center of the public city, Woolf depicts the girl as if she were an indecipherable hieroglyph: "To each movement of the omnibus the beautiful body in the fawn-coloured coat responded freely like a rider, like the figure-head of a ship. . . . The heat gave her cheeks the pallor of white painted wood; and her fine eyes, having no eyes to meet, gazed ahead, blank, bright, with the staring incredible innocence of sculpture" (206). Is this new and mysterious Elizabeth—this cryptic figurehead of a ship sailing into the unknown—the form into which liberated energy will now flow? Here the novelist herself appears to be pressing closely upon the massy wall of time in a first attempt to write the "Chapter on the future" that, as she knew, is logically unrecordable.

The process through which a new kind of history of the past might modulate into a history of the future became a major subject in Woolf's next novel, *To the Lighthouse*. Here, however, the wartime death of the male destined inheritor (Andrew Ramsay) is an apparently marginal event, while the death of the wife and mother (Mrs. Ramsay) is central, and the question of who or what might now fill the traditional role of angel in the house is equally important. Yet Woolf suggests in the middle section of the novel, "Time Passes," and to a lesser extent in its concluding section, "The Lighthouse," that there is a metonymic, if not a causal, connection between the public war that slays Andrew, the sex role that debilitates Mrs. Ramsay, and the dialectic between the two histories that threatens to destroy but then actually preserves the Ramsays' house to some unknown end. Most important, though, Woolf here embodies the mystery of the future, with all the questions about new forms that it implies, in an icon of the new analogous to Elizabeth Dalloway but far more closely examined: Lily Briscoe.

Like Elizabeth, Lily is an oddity in her world, a woman whose primary allegiance is, as Woolf believes Elizabeth's will be, to the republic of women. And like Elizabeth's newness, Lily's strangeness is signaled by her "Chinese eyes" (29), which mark her as an outsider in the English society she inhabits, and through which she will gain her own distinctive vision of past, present, and future.[45] But while part of the adolescent Elizabeth's differentness is attributable to her not yet having grown into her destined sex role, Lily is from the start maturely "other" than those around her, for she is already an adult woman of thirty-four when she appears in "The Window," the first section of *To the Lighthouse*. Moreover, by the end of the novel, when she realizes that she has "triumphed" over Mrs. Ramsay's injunction to "'Marry,

marry!'" (260), Lily, now forty-four, has a precise—indeed, a Woolfian—grasp of the history that has liberated her from the bonds of matrimony.[46]

Meditating on the failure of the marriage between Minta Doyle and Paul Rayley that Mrs. Ramsay had so enthusiastically engineered and on how she, Lily, "stood here painting, had never married, not even William Bankes," she imagines herself victoriously explaining to the dead matriarch that "it has all gone against your wishes. They're happy like that; I'm happy like this. *Life has changed completely*" (260; emphasis ours). And indeed, life *has* changed, not just for Lily and the Rayleys, but, with Prue and Andrew dead, for Mrs. Ramsay's other descendants, Nancy, Cam, and James as well, all of whom seem almost as alienated from traditional sex roles as Lily herself. For just as Lily cannot even "imitate from recollection . . . the self-surrender" with which Mrs. Ramsay had responded to her husband's perpetual demands for sympathy (224), Nancy wonders "in a queer, half dazed, half desperate way, 'What does one send to the lighthouse?' as if she were forcing herself to do what she despaired of ever being able to do" (218), while Cam and James, silently swearing to "fight [Mr. Ramsay's] tyranny to the death" (251) (as their mother never had) appear as a "serious, melancholy couple" (230), only reluctantly joining their father on the long-deferred expedition to the lighthouse.

Of course, at the beginning of the novel Lily cannot quite foresee the triumph in store for her, nor is she entirely certain that she wants it. Thus, when Mrs. Ramsay argues that "an unmarried woman has missed the best of life," the younger Lily must gather "a desperate courage" to "urge her own exemption from the universal law. . . . She liked to be herself; she was not made for [marriage]" (77). During Mrs. Ramsay's dinner party, too, Lily several times reveals her ambivalence toward the social system that preaches marriage and assigns some roles to women, others to men. Accurately diagnosing the silent Charles Tansley's misery at table, for instance, she reflects that "on occasions of this sort it behoves the woman, whatever her own occupation may be, to go to the help of the young man opposite . . . as indeed it is their [men's] duty . . . to help us, suppose the Tube were to burst into flames" (137).

Later at the same meal, moreover, Lily finds herself suddenly both enraptured and terrified by "the heat of love" that Paul and Minta radiate: "It is so beautiful, so exciting, this love that I tremble on the verge of it." But then, having decided that "she need not marry, thank Heaven: she need not undergo that degradation," she tells herself that love "also is the stupidest, the most barbaric of human passions" (154). And Woolf shows that such ambivalence is not unique to Lily. The history which will give this unmarried painter her victory has already been set in motion in "The Window," as it had been at a comparable point in the novelist's own life. Lily remembers, for example, that even while Minta was falling in love with Paul and entering into the engagement that would issue in her failed marriage, the bride-to-be had a hole in her stocking that meant to William Bankes "the annihilation of womanhood, and dirt and disorder" (257). When, on the very day of her betrothal, Minta loses her grandmother's brooch, the loss prefigures a symbolic lack: in the future, the unhappily married Minta will no longer have "the sole ornament" (116)—the ceremonial pin, as it were—that fastened her to the roles and rules of the past.

Woolf signals a similar disruption of the social order quite early in the novel, when Mrs. Ramsay's daughters, even the exemplary Prue, "sport with infidel ideas which they had brewed for themselves of a life different from hers," a life "in Paris, perhaps; a wilder life; not always taking care of some man or other; for there was in all their minds a mute questioning of deference and chivalry, of the Bank of England and the Indian Empire, of ringed fingers and lace." In addition, although these rebellious girls do respect the imperatives that have created Mrs. Ramsay, they do so in much the same alienated way in which Lily marvels at "the heat of love": "To them all, there was something in this of the essence of beauty, which called out the *manliness* in their girlish hearts, and made them . . . honour [their mother's] strange severity, her extreme courtesy" (14; emphasis ours).

Precisely because she is not a member of the family, however, Lily definitively incarnates differentness in this novel, and it is therefore quite frequently through her Chinese eyes that Woolf portrays the Ramsays' marriage, as if this "old maid" were really a kind of spy from the future, a "new maid" whose estranged perspective could best illuminate the forms of the past. Strolling in the garden before dinner, Lily catches sight of the Ramsays and observes them with a mixture of elegiac affection and alienated awe: "So that is marriage . . . a man and a woman looking at a girl throwing a ball. . . . And suddenly the meaning which, for no reason at all . . . descends on people . . . came upon them, and made them . . . the symbols of marriage, husband and wife" (110–11).

As symbolic figures, the Ramsays are almost exaggeratedly "feminine" and "masculine." Lacking first names that would individualize them, both *become* their sex roles more fully than does Mrs. Dalloway, whose recurrent "Clarissa" interrogates the official *couverture* imposed by her status as wife and mother. In the seventies and eighties a few scholars sought to demonstrate that Julia Stephen, the original of Mrs. Ramsay, was less conventionally feminine—more worldly and aggressive—than her fictional counterpart, and that Leslie Stephen, upon whom Mr. Ramsay was patterned, was less traditionally masculine than his daughter's portrait of him indicates. But biographical accuracy is not the point here.[47] What engaged the writer's attention throughout *To the Lighthouse*, what she filtered through the lens of

Lily's Chinese eyes, were the historically determined social and sexual meanings that Julia and Leslie Stephen represented. Even before Lily begins to meditate on them, Woolf conveys those meanings through the multiple perspectives generated by the fluidly dissolving and resolving free indirect discourse of "The Window," always linking femininity and masculinity to the two histories she has been exploring since "The Journal of Mistress Joan Martyn." Most theatrically, she depicts the sensual yet agonistic confrontation of symbolic male and female in the almost hallucinatory primal scene witnessed by the six-year-old James, when Mr. Ramsay intrusively demands sympathy from Mrs. Ramsay as she sits reading to her son in the window of the summer house. Because he is a child, James is not only resentful of his father's interruption, he is in his fashion as bemused as Lily by the meaning of marriage. But because he is still entrapped in an oedipal thralldom to his mother, he is not dispassionate about the significance of coupling but shocked by the apparent violence and exploitation such a relationship releases.

As husband and wife face each other and converse, the seated Mrs. Ramsay seems to her son "to pour erect into the air a rain of energy, a column of spray. . . . and into this delicious fecundity . . . the fatal sterility of the male plunged itself, like a beak of brass, barren and bare" so that "standing stiff between her legs, very stiff, James felt all her strength flaring up to be drunk and quenched by the beak of brass, the arid scimitar of the male." And a minute later, James imagines his mother rising "in a rosy-flowered fruit tree laid with leaves and dancing boughs into which the beak of brass, the arid scimitar of his father, the egotistical man, plunged and smote" (58–60).[48]

A classic phallic mother with the magical power to generate a "fountain and spray of life," Mrs. Ramsay is also a flowering tree, like Lucrezia Warren Smith or the ideal woman of Yeats's "A Prayer for My Daughter"—a poem whose definition of the feminine haunts this book. As that figure, Mrs. Ramsay becomes a lawgiver whose allegiance is to (private) love rather than to (public) order. Associated with militarism (a scimitar), predation (a beak), death (fatal sterility), and technology (a beak of *brass*), Mr. Ramsay is also, obviously, a classic phallus, which smites as it invades the fecundity of the female, who bids him to "take his ease" in the house of her body and the body of her house, to "go in and out, enjoy himself" (59). And the desirous James, hating the "egotistical man," himself in his jealousy replicates his father's egotism: standing very stiff between his mother's knees, he becomes not only a phallus for her (as Freud argued all babies are for women) but a phallus himself, as he intuits the secret meanings of "masculine" and "feminine."

Although Woolf presents James as translating these meanings into images of dreamlike intensity, she often depicts the impact of sex roles comically, even parodically. Charles Tansley imagines Mrs. Ramsay as an earth

mother, "stepping through fields of flowers and taking to her breast . . .
lambs that had fallen; with the stars in her eyes and the wind in her hair"
(25), in a passage that echoes the satiric description of Elizabeth Dalloway
("People were beginning to compare her to poplar trees, early dawn, hyacinths"). Similarly, William Bankes, deciding that "the Graces assembling
seemed to have joined hands in meadows of asphodel to compose [Mrs.
Ramsay's] face," pontificates to her, "'Nature has but little clay . . . like that of
which she moulded you'" (46–47). And the alienated Lily, following Andrew's advice to "'think of a kitchen table . . . when you're not there'" in
order to understand Mr. Ramsay's work on "'subject and object and the
nature of reality,'" envisions the "angular essences" of the philosopher's
projects incarnated in "a scrubbed kitchen table . . . lodged now in the fork
of a pear tree" (38).

But Lily's more serious meditations throughout "The Window" prefigure
the atmosphere of loss and skepticism that will permeate "The Lighthouse."
Distanced from straightforward identification with the "femininity" that
marks Mrs. Ramsay's every gesture, Lily wonders blankly, "What was the
spirit in her, the essential thing" (76), and although, when the older woman
talks of marriage "the house seemed full of children sleeping . . . ; shaded
lights and regular breathing" (77), the painter despairs of ever understanding the archaic meaning this maternal figure radiates, despairs of ever pressing into the "secret chambers" of Mrs. Ramsay's "mind and heart" where
stand "tablets bearing sacred inscriptions, which if one could spell them out,
would teach one everything" (79). Desiring "unity" or "intimacy itself, which
is knowledge," Lily realizes that nothing can happen to make her one with
the sexual enigma the traditionally womanly woman represents. Thus the
artist sees this woman who has no first, personal name through "Chinese
eyes"—and portrays her on canvas as a cryptic "triangular purple shape"
(81).[49]

Interestingly, the shape into which Lily simplifies a "mother . . . famous
for her beauty" (81) replicates both the triangular shapes of the primitive
women Rachel Vinrace encounters in *The Voyage Out* and the "wedge-shaped
core of darkness" that Mrs. Ramsay imagines as her own inner essence. What
gives force to the Ramsays as symbols of marriage, this Woolfian reiteration
implies, is precisely the continuity between social definitions of woman and
man and this paradigmatic couple's own self-definitions. At rest in the core
of herself, Mrs. Ramsay looks up toward the beam of the lighthouse—the
maternal lighthouse that James will remember as a "silvery, misty-looking
tower with a yellow eye" (276)—and it seems to her "like her own eyes
meeting her own eyes" (97): subject and object cohere in the reality she
inhabits. Similarly, if more comically, Mr. Ramsay calls upon "qualities that in
a desolate expedition across . . . the Polar region would have made him the

leader" (54) to aid him on his journey through the alphabet of thought from Q to R.

And because neither Ramsay experiences any radical dissonance between self and role, both unproblematically promulgate, as well as represent, the "universal law" of marriage, along with what they see as the equally universal law of sexual difference that necessitates the institution of marriage. Urging all young people to "Marry, marry!" Mrs. Ramsay sees two rooks outside her window as a primordial couple, "Joseph and Mary" (122), while Mr. Ramsay tenderly admires "a hen, straddling her wings out in protection of a covey of little chicks" (34). Mrs. Ramsay maintains sex distinctions in the nursery, softening a boar's skull with a shawl so that it will not frighten her daughter Cam while assuring her son James that its horned masculine reality remains intact (172–73). Revering Mrs. Ramsay's beauty, Mr. Ramsay "exaggerate[s] her ignorance, her simplicity" (182) while worrying about his son Andrew's "chance of a scholarship," although his wife claims that she would be just as proud of the boy if he did not win one. Together, husband and wife continually collude in recreating the sex roles they symbolize: "She liked him to believe in scholarships, and he liked her to be proud of Andrew whatever he did" (103).

Like Big Ben and the other clock, therefore, Mr. and Mrs. Ramsay embody the two different histories with which Woolf was so concerned. On the one hand, Mr. Ramsay is a living avatar of the masculine stud book (other spokesmen for the official record of "King following King and Law Law" are his student Charles Tansley and his disciple William Bankes).[50] On the other hand, Mrs. Ramsay, preserving her grandmother's French recipe for *boeuf en daube*, is a bearer of the alternative history of the private, the domestic, that was also the subject of Joan Martyn's journal. For even while she realizes that lovers "must be danced round with mockery," Mrs. Ramsay also believes that nothing "could be more serious than the love of man for woman," nothing more serious than the births and growth of children, or than the events that mark the lives of the obscure: milk soup for the laundress, sanitary dairies, fifty pounds for the greenhouse roof.

Thus, when Mrs. Ramsay considers "the dahlias in the big bed," and begins wondering about "next year's flowers," Mr. Ramsay merely notices "something red, something brown" (101–02); when Mr. Ramsay begins discussing square roots, Mrs. Ramsay thinks, "A square root? What was that?" (159). *Her* roots belong to the natural realm of flowers, Mr. Ramsay's to the cultural kingdom of mathematics. Nearsighted, she sees only the quotidian details that, like stitches in the stocking she is knitting, make up the fabric of the world she creates and inhabits. Farsighted, her husband sees only the monuments of unaging intellect that define the public past like letters in an alphabet that extends from an originatory A to an apocalyptic Z. As symbols of marriage, then, the couple collaborate to bring the two histories they represent into a harmonious union in which, different as every object is for each of these two subjects, a mutual reality is continually reconstituted. Yet even while husband and wife labor at this project, Woolf shows that both the sex roles they have adopted and the histories behind those roles have already begun to weaken. Not only do Lily Briscoe and William Bankes resist, respectively, marriage and remarriage, not only do Mrs. Ramsay's daughters "mutely" question stereotypically masculine and feminine institutions, but such institutions have a fragility that Woolf documents through ironic allusions and odd juxtapositions of phrases.

Most obviously, Mr. Ramsay's continual booming reiteration of passages from "The Charge of the Light Brigade," especially the line "Some one had blundered," prefigures a more calamitous charge into "the valley of Death" that the destined inheritors of patriarchal society, among them his cherished son Andrew, would be forced to undertake during the Great War. Tennyson's words outline the fate of these doomed heirs: "Theirs not to make reply, / Theirs not to reason why, / Theirs but to do and die."[51] More comically, Mrs. Ramsay, gazing at what might be fresh molehills in the garden and thinking that "a great mind like [her husband's] must be different in every way from ours," produces a significantly muddled meditation: "All the great men she had ever known, she thought, deciding that a rabbit must have got in, were like that, and it was good for young men (though the atmosphere of lecture-rooms was stuffy and depressing to her beyond endurance almost) simply to hear him, simply to look at him. But without shooting rabbits, how was one to keep them down? she wondered" (108).

Has a rabbit, a timid but tenacious herbivore, "gotten in"—not only into Mrs. Ramsay's garden but into the brigade of heroes and intellectuals already poised for a charge into the valley of death? Even Mr. Ramsay seems to be implicitly considering this possibility, for as he prepares to talk what, with Freudian ambiguity, he calls "some nonsense" about history ("Locke, Hume, Berkeley, and the causes of the French Revolution") to the young men of Cardiff, he asks himself skeptically, "Does the progress of civilization depend upon great men?" (67), and irreverently tells himself the story of "how Hume was stuck in a bog" (104).

Similarly, triumphant though Mrs. Ramsay is as she presides toward the end of "The Window" over her sacramental boeuf en daube and a ceremonial cornucopia of ripe fruit, she is deeply, even mysteriously pessimistic. Indeed, unlike Joan Martyn's mother, who dreams of future prosperity for all England, Mrs. Ramsay seems not only to be a wedge of darkness but to look forward into a heart of darkness. Even as she prescribes marriage and preserves a familial past, she thinks enigmatically, "It will end, it will end. . . . It will come, it will come," and then reflects that "she had been trapped into saying something she did not mean" (97). But the indeterminate *it* which will end (her life? the life she represents?) and will come (her death? the death of the order she incarnates?) is precisely what she does, prophetically, mean. This point is reinforced by the grim story of "The Fisherman's Wife" that she reads to James, for the desirous heroine of that tale (like Mrs. Ramsay, defined only by her sex role) cannot finally bend the world to her will and ends up defeated both by the male cultural realm her husband inhabits and by the natural world that the fish rules.[52]

To be sure, Mrs. Ramsay's victory at the dinner table, like the accession of the fisherman's wife to the throne, is a resonant one. Enjoying a sense of profound security as she dishes out boeuf en daube, she produces another ambiguous meditation: such security "partook, she felt, carefully helping Mr. Bankes to a specially tender piece, of eternity" (158). But the confusion works two ways here to emphasize that, archetypal though this quasi–earth mother is, even her moment of eternity is paradoxically transient. For if Mrs. Ramsay is helping William Bankes to a tender piece of eternity, she is also helping him to a piece of beef that will soon be consumed. Both she and Woolf plainly recognize this, for as the matriarch rises to leave the room she hears the voices of her husband and his friend Augustus Carmichael chanting lines about change and journeys and the passage of time—"all the lives we ever lived and all the lives to be" (165–66)—and knows that the scene she is leaving "was vanishing even as she looked," that "it had become . . . already the past" (167–68).

A new order first fully manifests itself in the surface disorder of "Time Passes," the ten-year night that separates "The Window" from "The Lighthouse," subject from object, with a dense "down-pouring of immense darkness," of, that is, apparently unmediated "reality." Beginning with a key line from Mr. Bankes—"Well, we must wait for the future to show" (189)—this extraordinary set piece shows, first, the two histories collaborating in a destruction of the past; then, an engulfment of culture by nature; and, finally, a tentative restoration of a (new) history, a (new) culture, through the intervention of the obscure but obscurely powerful cleaning women Mrs. McNab and Mrs. Bast.

As her own pessimism and her ritual passage from the dining room in "The Window" foretold, Mrs. Ramsay, the maternal angel in the house, is the first avatar of the past to die. The deaths of her daughter Prue (in childbirth) and her son Andrew (in the Great War) follow, as if to suggest that after the loss of the mother all coherence is gone and the center can no longer hold. But these deaths—on the one hand, events in private history (Mrs. Ramsay's, Prue's), and on the other, facts in the public record of masculine politics and military policy (Andrew's)—are all reported parenthetically, as the two histories confound and annihilate each other in a breakdown of traditional distinctions. Now the "little *airs*" of nature (191) become *heirs* of the empty house within whose walls what was once, in Yeats's words, "accustomed, ceremonious" begins to fade and perish; and "stray airs"/heirs indeed become "advance guards of great armies" (194).[53]

At the same time, as the invading airs of nature tear at the maternal shawl with which Mrs. Ramsay had covered the ferocity of the boar's skull, the warring heirs of culture, embattled in France, conspire to further the unveiling of bare reality: "There came later in the summer ominous sounds like the measured blows of hammers dulled on felt, which . . . still further loosened the shawl and cracked the teacups" (200). By the time Mrs. McNab and Mrs. Bast, charwomen who represent the only *ewig weibliche* that might survive the death of the Victorian matriarch, arrive to restore the house, the order Mrs. Ramsay so painstakingly maintained has collapsed into a confusion of categories: "A thistle thrust itself between the tiles in the larder. The swallows nested in the drawing-room. . . . Giant artichokes towered among the roses" (207), and Mrs. Ramsay herself is a "faint and flickering" image seen through a "telescope" focused on a past that seems even more distant than it really is (205).[54]

Finally, therefore, after the two women have brought the house back to a "rusty laborious birth" (210), after the survivors of the ten-year night have returned to an at least superficially restored structure, Lily wonders, "What does it mean. . . . What can it all mean?" (217). Although she thinks dazedly that "here she was again" (214), she knows Mr. Ramsay is right when he melodramatically declaims, "You will find us much changed." Puzzling out a "question . . . of some relation between those masses" to which she had in her painting reduced the Ramsays, she finds herself in "a house full of unrelated passions" (221) and must acknowledge that with the death of Mrs. Ramsay, the matriarch, of Prue, destined heiress of her mother's role, and of Andrew, heir of his father's scholarship, she may have entered a world in which she is not only a representative New Woman but, more unnervingly, a kind of no-woman. Indeed, if the prewar summerhouse in some sense symbolized Beulah, the biblical "married land," the postwar house, with its disjunctions, discordances, and despondencies, may symbolize not simply a no man's land in which nobody knows exactly what to do but, more specifically, a no woman's land in which the private history Mrs. Ramsay preserved has been swallowed up in a new and drastically altered public history.

What will be the thrust of that history? Here, pressing upon the massy wall of time, Woolf comes closer than ever before to confronting the enigma of a future created by "the words 'emancipation' and 'evolution.'" When Lily, thinking of the determinedly modern Rayleys, who have passed from being "in love" to being "excellent friends" (259), exults, "They're happy like that; I'm happy like this. Life has changed completely," she echoes Woolf's comment that "energy has been released"—the energy of the new. But the novelist implicitly asks, "Into what forms is it to flow?" Does the metamorphosis of the Ramsays into the Rayleys, a matter of a few letters yet also of a major historical transformation, bode well for the world? Does Lily's refusal (or inability) to offer Mr. Ramsay the stereotypically feminine sympathy he still demands mean that she is not a New Woman but a no-woman? Certainly she herself fears as much: "Any other woman in the whole world would have done something, said something—all except myself, thought Lily[,] . . . who am not a woman, but a peevish, ill-tempered, dried-up old maid, presumably" (226).

The ancient strategies of "womanhood" also elude Minta, who merely hands her husband his tools in a "business-like, straightforward, friendly" way (259); Nancy, who does not know what to send to the lighthouse; and Cam, who loves her father but refuses to submit to his "crass blindness and tyranny" (253). Only "kind old Mrs. Beckwith" (221), a relic of the past in this revisionary company of the future, has preserved the ways of Mrs. Ramsay's generation. Yet all these New Women (or no-women) would probably share Lily's (and Woolf's) ambivalence toward "the roar and crackle" of heterosexual love, which "repelled her with fear and disgust. . . . But for a sight, for a glory it surpassed everything in her experience" (262). The fire that Mrs. Ramsay lit is irretrievably gone, and so is the cornucopia of custom and ceremony over which she presided. The woman who grew in the shape of Yeats's flourishing hidden tree has been felled. Lily and Nancy and Cam are free not to marry; Minta cannot and need not become an inexhaustible fountain of sympathy for her husband. Lily and Woolf are in one sense glad. Yet what of James's memory that his mother "alone spoke the truth; to her alone could he speak it" (278)? And what of Woolf's parenthetical comment about husband and wife, at the end of "The Window": "Every word they said now would be true" (183)?[55]

Sailing at last to the lighthouse, Mr. Ramsay is, in effect, sailing with his two children into the future, a voyage out on which, tellingly, the patriarchal historian of a changed society rather than the matriarchal preserver of family history must lead the youngest son and daughter. Watching and painting on the shore, Lily is the new historian: her picture will record the changing "relation of the masses" that signify, among other things, the two histories of the past. As she weeps for Mrs. Ramsay and for a world without Mrs. Ramsay, wondering, "Could it be, even for elderly people, that this was life?—Startling, unexpected, unknown?" Macalister's boy takes "one of the fish and cut[s] a square out of its side to bait his hook with. The mutilated body (it was alive still) was thrown back into the sea" (268). Surrounded by brackets and bracketed by Lily's cries of "Mrs. Ramsay," the passage clearly connects Mrs. Ramsay with the creature that must be sacrificed to allow her survivors to fish a new life from the sea of time.[56]

Or rather, the mother and father together deliver the vision, the two histories complementing each other one last time in the riddle of Lily's painting, whose images are not fully revealed to the reader. The ghost of

Mrs. Ramsay knits in the window, subject looking out toward the unattainable object of the lighthouse at which Mr. Ramsay, who is "reading very quickly, as if he were eager to get to the end" (301), has almost arrived. Periodically intoning lines from William Cowper's "The Castaway" ("We perish, each alone") the "great man" who is guardian of the old history journeys toward his death, toward the end of his book, toward a future in which, as he remarks to old Macalister, "Their children would see some strange things" (304).[57] Just before he steps ashore, his children finally come to love and mourn him, realizing that metaphorically as well as literally he too will soon be lost. "They both wanted to say, Ask us anything and we will give it you." And much as Mrs. Ramsay, gazing at the distant lighthouse, had thought, "It will end. . . . It will come," Mr. Ramsay "might be thinking, we perished each alone, or he might be thinking, 'I have reached it. I have found it'" (307–08): the promised end.

Is the rock on which *this* nearby lighthouse rests "stark and straight," ineffably unfamiliar, R, the letter toward which Mr. Ramsay has struggled all his life? R: a reality unsoftened by the shawl of "femininity" that made the earlier lighthouse into "a silvery, misty-looking tower" (276)? As the great man prepares to leap ashore, he appears to his son "for all the world . . . as if he were saying, 'There is no God,'" and to his daughter as if he were "leaping into space." His debarkation, Woolf implies, is the mysterious step into the future that is the leap of faith, so Lily comments, "He has landed. . . . It is finished" (308–09).

But if Mr. Ramsay has landed, if *it* (the past? the voyage out? the work of art?) is finished, what has begun?[58] Is Lily, as her name indicates, a (new) flower in the garden Mrs. Ramsay planted? Does this New Woman/nowoman—one who, in her own view, does not know how to *be* a woman—represent, as an Easter lily would, a resurrection and transformation of the sacrificed Mrs. Ramsay, mother-artist of the domestic, into artist-mother of the new? On what trinity was Woolf brooding here? The Holy Family of Mr. Ramsay and Mrs. Ramsay, father and mother of the past whose private/public histories are united in a mystical daughter, Lily, the icon of the future? Or the trinity of God the Mother (Mrs. Ramsay in "The Window"), God the daughter-artist (Lily), and God the Holy (and wholly) Ghost (Mrs. Ramsay in "The Lighthouse")?[59]

Because she is only *pressing* against the massy wall of time, Woolf presents us here with a text that can be interpreted multiply, even endlessly. Indeed, whether Lily's painting hangs in an attic or becomes, in effect, Woolf's elegy for the past and question to the future, Lily has had her vision, has made her picture and brought a narrative about time and change to an indeterminate conclusion whose only definitive facts, aside from the completion of the painting itself, are the death of Mrs. Ramsay and the arrival of her survivors on the rock of the cryptic lighthouse to which, paradoxically, her whole life had pointed. Woolf would never again depict in any depth such traditional "mother-women" as Helen Ambrose, Mrs. Hilbery, Betty Flanders, Clarissa Dalloway, and Mrs. Ramsay. In fact, her vision of Lily's vision gave birth, within a year, to an "unwilled" fantasy about a human being who transcends sexual categories altogether—the man/woman (hence, no-man/no-woman) who is the protagonist of *Orlando*.

What would Lily's life have been like had she been set free to rove through history and discover that the "universal law" of marriage (and sex roles) was as much an artifice as her clothes or her painting of the relation of masses, as Mrs. Ramsay's boeuf en daube, or as Mr. Ramsay's metaphysical alphabet? How would the engenderings of history appear to such a radically new kind of being? Would the two histories—the masculine chronicle of Big Ben and the feminine record of the other clock—remain divided? These are issues that Woolf addressed in *Orlando*, the book she almost involuntarily began immediately after elegizing the archetypal husband and wife in *To the Lighthouse*. For in this apparent *jeu d'esprit*, even as she transcribed a history of the transformed self which continued her long-standing critique of the standard "lives of great men," she also proposed the possibility of an alternative life while exploring the implications of such a reengendered existence.

The daughter of Leslie Stephen had, of course, long been fascinated by the personal yet often "official" genre of biography and its relation to "official" public historiography. By the time she came to compose *Orlando*, she was ready for what she called "an escapade; the spirit . . . satiric, the structure wild," and further for the creation of what Leon Edel has seen as "a full-fledged theory of biography" formulated in response to both the Carlylean hypotheses of her father and the more radical postulates of such contemporary intellectuals as Lytton Strachey, debunker of *Eminent Victorians*, and Harold Nicolson, author of a treatise on biography published by her own Hogarth Press.[60] Equally to the point, she was ready for an effort to reexamine history as it might have been experienced by an unmothered being utterly free from the gender imperatives fostered by the traditional family romance.

"Truthful but fantastic": this paradoxical phrase from Woolf's *Diary* illuminates *Orlando*, for the lord/lady Orlando is a nobleperson first encountered as a young man in the sixteenth century, followed through the courts of Elizabeth I and Charles II to an ambassadorship in Turkey where *he* becomes a *she*, then seen as a literary lady aristocrat in eighteenth- and nineteenth-century England, and last presented as a prizewinning female author in "the present moment" of airplanes and motorcars. Yet in the free-flying sweep and scope with which it wings over the gravities of history, this fantastic life is, as Woolf insisted, truthful—true to its author's ongoing effort to reimagine history, and true to her developing sense of the increasing range of hermeneutic possibilities through which women's lives might be understood.

Of course, far more fantastically than Lily Briscoe or Elizabeth Dalloway, Orlando is an "outsider," and thus in some sense as mad (*furioso*) as Ariosto's *Orlando Furioso*. Born a nobleman, he has "a liking for low company, especially for that of lettered people" (28), and even when he is taken up by Queen Elizabeth, he has little enthusiasm for court doings. During the Great Frost, when London seems to hang suspended on the ice of an eternal moment, he falls in love with the androgynous Sasha, a Russian princess for whom he "want[s] another landscape and another tongue" (47), a place and a language outside the official history forming all around him. When Sasha sails away in the flood of time that suddenly breaks up the ice, Orlando retreats to his country estate to become a writer, although in the world of letters he is still an outsider. Gulled and galled by the literary impresario Nick Greene, he is haunted but mystified by the enigmatic face of Shakespeare and feels that no battle his ancestors fought was "half so arduous as this which he now undertook to win immortality against the English language" (82).[61]

Again, as the English ambassador to Constantinople and the ex-ambassadress living alfresco among a band of gypsies, he/she never quite fits in. In the first case, *he* alarms the English by making a disreputable marriage to one Rosina Pepita, and in the second, *she* disturbs the gypsies by writing poems, admiring sunsets, and longing for her English manor house. Finally, back in England, the Lady Orlando is always slightly out of step with the march of time around her. In the eighteenth century, she dresses as a man to visit (and hear the tales told by) the communities of fallen women who walk the London streets. In the nineteenth century she marries and produces "lachrymose blot[s]" of sentimental poetry, but her husband is an eccentric explorer, not a Victorian patriarch, and her ladylike verse is "much against her natural temperament" (243). In the twentieth century she wins a prize for her poem "The Oak Tree" but wires her husband a comically encoded comment on the meaning of literary achievement—"'Rattigan Glumphoboo'"— "which summed it up precisely" (282). Always on the margins of history, she nevertheless glimpses Elizabeth, Shakespeare, Charles II, Nell Gwynne, Alexander Pope, the Carlyles, and even, in the book's first draft, one "Volumnia Fox"—a sobriquet for Virginia Woolf herself.[62] But her glance passes over these luminaries with the luminous indifference of, say, a lighthouse beam. Within sight of shore, she is always offshore, at sea in the wilder waters of history.

At the same time, however, as Woolf depicts him/her, Orlando *is* history, if only because the light of his/her mind illumines time for Woolf's readers, and his/her stately mansion, with its symbolic 365 bedrooms and 52 staircases, is the house whose endurance through change is a metaphor for human duration. Whether offshore or on the edge of time, Orlando's supposedly marginal perspective becomes the vantage from which we must view the world as we grapple with the terms of history. In fact, as Woolf ranges over them—obliquely envisioning them, slyly appropriating them, subversively revising them—the terms of history become Orlando's terms: history itself becomes Orlando's story, the tale of a body now male, now female, embodying that thread of alternative truth Woolf was to call in *A Room of One's Own* "the common life which is the real life" as opposed to "the little separate lives . . . we live as individuals" (117).

Thus, the family romance of this parentless creature is a novel narrative indeed—generalized, parodied, and ultimately transcended through Orlando's fantastic intersections with history. As Woolf simultaneously redefines and questions conventional periodization, the so-called Elizabethan period recapitulates her protagonist's childhood and preadolescence, with a timeless preoedipal frost and an oedipal flood exaggerating and mocking the meaning of "growing up." Similarly, the seventeenth century, with its sexchange, offers Orlando a new kind of adolescence, comically marking a moment of sexual transformation and self-realization, while the eighteenth century represents her ostensible (that is, what should be her) "young ladyhood." Finally, the nineteenth century coincides with her bemused confrontation of patriarchally defined female maturity (wedlock, maternity), and the twentieth, with its adumbration of an apocalyptic "new world," reflects her finally mature "moment of being," her liberating encounter with "the Captain self, the Key self, which amalgamates and controls them all" (310), that ontologically authoritative self (free from "universal" sexual laws) for which Lily Briscoe had yearned. In this uncanny conflation of the personal and the political, moreover, both official history's processions of king following king and the permutations of the lives of the obscure that constitute the other history appear, to quote Wallace Stevens, "more truly and more strange."[63] And specifically, the history Woolf had always defined as masculine becomes feminine too. It becomes, indeed, what she had heretofore implicitly defined as a contradiction in terms: a public history of the private woman—just as Orlando, returning at last from Turkey to England, becomes England's figurative land-lady, the Lady Or-land-o, Ur-land-o, Her-land-o.

Orlando began, of course, as a fantasy biography/family history of a woman Woolf loved: Victoria Sackville-West, the wife of the theorist of biography Harold Nicolson, whose commonly used nickname, Vita, means "life." Her friend's *Vita Nuova* thus resonantly suggests the New Life that might become the life of the New Woman. Therefore, just as many of the illustrations in the book are pictures of Vita or her Sackville ancestors, many plot details reflect crucial facts of Vita's biography.[64] And for the most part, Woolf's fantastic transformations of these details empower Vita. As many critics have observed, *Orlando* was a tribute from Virginia to Vita; indeed, it was, in Nigel Nicolson's phrase, "the longest and most charming love letter in history."

Thus Vita's fictional *Vita Nuova* grants her not just the one "life and a lover" she asks for as Orlando but many lives and many lovers. Thus, too, because Vita had grown up feeling like a boy, posing, at the height of her affair with Violet Trefusis, as a wounded soldier named "Julian," and haunted by anxiety about her "dual" sexuality, Woolf assures her that, yes, if she felt like a boy she was a boy.[65] In fact, as if responding to the hope Vita expressed in her (then unpublished) autobiography that "as centuries go on . . . the sexes [will] become more nearly merged on account of their increasing resemblances," Woolf suggests in her metamorphoses of history and sexuality that centuries have gone on and the sexes have merged or were never wholly separated—for "different though the sexes are they intermix" (*O* 189).[66] Thus, finally, where Vita was ultimately barred from inheriting Knole, the family estate, because of her sex, Woolf grants her perpetual possession: the dispossessed man/woman has not 1 but 365 rooms of her own, implying that she has inherited not just a place in time but time itself.

Yet even in this loving fantasy, Woolf was unwilling or unable to imagine the "Chapter on the Future" that Orlando/Vita might initiate. True, Orlando has won a prize for her poetry, and thus has moved a step beyond Lily, who expects *her* picture to be hung in the attics. In addition, although we know she has had a child (tellingly, in the Victorian period), her house is hardly full of the "shaded lights and regular breathing" that characterize Mrs. Ramsay's ménage, for she has not made maternity a career. Furthermore, compared to Mr. Ramsay, her husband is a comic figure, whose interminable, if intrepid, journeys around Cape Horn parody and thereby subvert Ramsay's polar expedition across the wastes of thought from A to Z.

Still, despite *Orlando*'s exuberance, Woolf cannot lean as hard as she might like against the massy wall of time, so that this joyous mock-biography ends in a scene more riddling than the line that completes Lily's painting. As Orlando prepares her house for a visit from a "dead Queen"—Elizabeth I, returning, presumably, as a female savior to revitalize and resurrect history—the destined inheritor of the ages bares her breast, on which pearls shine like great lunar eggs, an airplane hovers overhead carrying her husband, and a mysterious wild goose, a figure for that itinerant man, leaps into the heavens. The tableau suggests the possibility of an annunciation, but an annunciation issuing in *what*? What rough beast, what wild child, is journeying toward Orlando's house of time to be born? The form of the future is hidden, although the force of the new has begun to manifest itself.

In spite of the questions *Orlando* raised and could not answer, the fact that it was a fantasy-biography of a real woman whom Woolf loved empowered the writer herself. "How extraordinarily unwilled by me but potent in its own right . . . *Orlando* was!" she exclaimed in her diary (*D* 3:168). She seems to have felt that *Orlando* was a self-authoring book about a self-authorizing heroine—for, indeed, the unmothered and untutored Orlando does create (and re-create) herself in much the way that her revisionary history asserted its claim on Woolf's consciousness. Perhaps for this reason the very act of transcribing Orlando's transformative history helped Woolf imagine ways that such women as Elizabeth Dalloway and Lily Briscoe might unite the history of the other clock with Big Ben history on their own new terms and, just as important, helped her realize that as a thinker she might appropriate a transformed history to propose new ways of interpreting and teaching the records of past and present, a task she was to undertake in both *A Room of One's Own* and *Three Guineas*.

From the start, as her contemptuous comments on the verse collection *Euphrosyne* indicate, Woolf's attitude toward the elitist, masculinist education of "Oxbridge" was both hostile and ironic. In fact, it is arguable that her two longest and most famous feminist treatises are not so much about the rights of women as about the rites and wrongs of higher education.[67] *A Room*, of course, begins and ends at "Oxbridge," with an intermediate scene in the British Museum, that "huge bald forehead . . . so splendidly encircled by a band of famous [male] names." Presenting itself as a lecture intended for undergraduate women, this founding work of feminist criticism includes many bemused glimpses of the Oxbridge scene not unlike those of Castalia, the protagonist in Woolf's early satire "A Society." (Asked if Oxbridge professors helped "to produce good people and good books," Castalia replies, "It never occurred to me that they could possibly produce anything" [*MT* 21].)[68] Especially significant are Woolf's visions of academic processions, lineups of learned men which express her long-standing sense of dispossession from the masculinist march of time taught as official history.

As early as *Jacob's Room*, a Woolfian narrator had watched with wistful irony as the men of Cambridge enter King's College Chapel: "Look, as they pass into service, how airily the gowns blow out, as though nothing dense and corporeal were within. What sculptured faces, what certainty, authority controlled by piety, although great boots march under the gowns" (*JR* 32). Half a decade later the same procession passes, only this time it seems more ludicrous to a narrator who now, after her reexaminations of history in *Mrs. Dalloway*, *To the Lighthouse* and *Orlando*, defines her attitude toward university education more self-consciously: "Many were in cap and gown; some had tufts of fur on their shoulders; others were wheeled in bath-chairs; others, though not past middle-age, seemed creased and crushed into shapes so singular that one was reminded of those giant crabs and crayfish who heave with difficulty across the sand of an aquarium" (*ROO* 8).

In *Three Guineas*, whose earliest editions were illustrated with Diane Arbusesque photographs of dons and judges, soldiers and solicitors in bizarre official regalia, Woolf addresses the procession of male professors directly. To those who have been denied a place in the solemn patriarchal line, she says, the university

> may well appear a world so remote . . . that any criticism or comment may well seem futile. . . . We watch maces erect themselves and processions form, and note with eyes too dazzled to record the differences, let alone to explain them, the subtle distinctions of hats and hoods. . . . The words of Arthur's song in *Pendennis* rise to our lips. . . .
>
>> I will not enter there,
>> To sully your pure prayer
>> With thoughts unruly.
>
> [23][69]

But while Woolf kept a spiritual distance from academic processions and humanistic professions, while she consistently refused to "enter there," she did eventually formulate a body of "thoughts unruly" linking the question of education with those questions about the new that increasingly haunted her.

To be sure, even in Woolf's early novels, authoritative young men from St. John Hirst to Jacob Flanders assert their privileges, especially in those passages where Woolf is analyzing the processes of masculinist history, still unable to imagine viable feminist educational or cultural alternatives.[70] But precisely because such young men marched like culture's princes through her early fictions, the writer half-consciously identified with the domesticated women, who seemed so thoroughly excluded from history.[71] Indeed, the radical alienation of such women seemed simply an extreme version of the marginalization experienced even by British "ladies"—the group she later called the "daughters of educated men." Chapter four of *A Room* therefore begins with a discussion of the Countess of Winchilsea's lament on the inequities of female education: ▪

> How are we fal'n, fal'n by mistaken rules?
> And Education's, more than Nature's fools,
> Debarr'd from all improve'ments of the mind,
> And to be dull, expected and dessigned?[72]

What pedagogical system might have been redemptive for Anne Finch, Countess of Winchilsea—or for Rachel Vinrace *and* Jacob Flanders? As early as "A Society," Woolf had sought to envision an alternative education that would allow students to view the old through the lens of the new.[73] But just after she wrote *Orlando,* she undertook to outline a series of redefinitions of colleges and curricula, even of campus landscapes, which focus on learning that is in process rather than static and on a humanistic canon that is regenerative rather than regressive.

At a crucial moment in *A Room,* for instance, the "bristly," unblooming cactuses raised by Castalia's aunt in "A Society," which are emblematic of the old patriarchal college, are transformed into the untamed spring blooms of a mythical women's college with the appropriately verdant name of Fernham, where Woolf's narrator is vouchsafed a glimpse of "a bent figure, formidable yet humble"—the brilliant classicist Jane Ellen Harrison, whose studies of ancient Greek culture aided in uncovering the matriarchal origins of what had been seen as a primordially patriarchal society (*ROO* 17).[74] And in "A Woman's College from the Outside," Woolf offered an even more utopian portrait of Newnham/Fernham. Her heroine is a student whose name, Angela, implies that she is no longer an angel in the house but now an Angela in the halls of academe, which the girl exultantly defines as "this good world, this new world, this world at the end of the tunnel" (*BP* 8–9).

At last, in *Three Guineas,* Woolf united her ideal education with a metamorphic vision of a classless, egalitarian culture:

> Let [your college] be built on lines of its own. . . . Let the pictures and books be new and always changing. . . . Next, what should be taught in the new college, the poor college? Not the arts of dominating other people. . . . The poor college must teach only the arts that can be taught cheaply and practiced by poor people. . . . the arts of human intercourse [and] the little arts of talk, of dress, of cookery that are allied with them. The aim of the new college, the cheap college, should be [to] discover what new combinations make good wholes in human life. [33–34][75]

Rejecting the rigid and rigidifying processions of the past without rejecting the past itself, Woolf here integrates official history with the unofficial arts of the other history that had always been marginalized or ignored.[76] Thus, like Ralph Denham in *Night and Day,* who abandons the practice of law to write *A History of the Saxon Village,* or like Miss La Trobe, who in *Between the Acts* would imagine history woven together not by a procession of tufted academics but by "a long line of villagers in sacking," the author of *Three Guineas* finally sought to conceptualize a canon of the humanities which would definitively incorporate a record of, in Carolyn Kizer's words, "the private lives of more than one-half of humanity."[77] In doing so, moreover, this woman who also suggested that the *Dictionary of National Biography* would be improved if the "lives of maids" were included, implicitly proposed that researchers study the history not just of the forgotten "daughters of educated men" (*TG* 166, 466) but also of the arduous "lives of the obscure"—the lives of charwomen like Mrs. McNab and Mrs. Bast in *To the Lighthouse.*[78]

Yet despite Woolf's explicit commitment to "a society of outsiders" founded "on equality and poverty" (113), many of her prescriptions for educational renewal, and for the transformation of sex roles such renewal might bring, have seemed to some readers to be both impossibly utopian and unconsciously elitist.[79] In one way or another, all were responding not just to slippages in Woolf's thought but to the boggling enormity of the task this would-be historian of the future had set herself. Charges of snobbery and lack of realism are the consequences of crucial contradictions: on the one hand, Woolf recommended five hundred pounds a year and a room of one's own, while on the other, she preached poverty and equality (even, in *The Pargiters*, insisting that penniless working-class women had a better chance to become professionals than their upper-class sisters); on the one hand, she sympathetically quoted Arthur Quiller-Couch's remark that "'a poor child in England has little more hope than had the son of an Athenian slave to be emancipated into that intellectual freedom of which great writings are born'" (*ROO* 112) and on the other, she directed *Three Guineas* solely to the daughters of educated men. Plainly Woolf could barely begin to imagine the details of the revolution she desired. In fact, as Zwerdling has commented, "What eluded her was any understanding of how the present could conceivably lead to the future she imagined."[80] What transformations of society and sexuality could make the world habitable for Elizabeth Dalloway, Lily Briscoe, and Orlando? Or indeed, what could change the lives and fates of Septimus and Lucrezia Warren Smith, Mrs. McNab and Mrs. Bast?

That such metamorphoses were unthinkable and would have to be unprecedented is made clearest, first, by the possibilities Woolf could never really articulate and second, by the paradoxes she could explain but not resolve. In *A Room*, for instance, she prescribes the creation of a "woman's sentence" but cannot actually define its characteristics (80).[81] Similarly, later in the essay she tells us that the imaginary novelist Mary Carmichael has "broken" the sentence and "the sequence," but beyond the words "'Chloe liked Olivia. They shared a laboratory together'" (87), she gives us as little of Mary Carmichael's revolutionary novel as she does of Lily Briscoe's revisionary painting. And of course the resurrection of Mary's great foremother, Judith Shakespeare, is scheduled for an indefinite future and dependent on a series of hortatory "ifs" ("if we live another century or so . . . and have five hundred a year each of us. . . . If we have the habit of freedom. . . . If we escape a little from the common sitting room" [117–18], and so forth). Is the new not only what cannot be known but what cannot possibly happen in the real world, cannot possibly be translated into ordinary language?

Certainly the quandary that epitomizes all the complications of *Three Guineas* suggests as much. Situating herself on a bridge over the Thames, Woolf admonishes her readers to fix their eyes "upon the procession . . . of the sons of educated men" who pass through Westminster, the Houses of Parliament, the City, and to reflect that "we too can [now] leave the house, can mount those steps, pass in and out of those doors, wear wigs and gowns, make money, administer justice." But, she asks, "Do we wish to join that procession, or don't we? [For] what is this 'civilization' in which we find ourselves? What are these ceremonies and why should we take part in them?" (60–63) Ultimately, confronting the danger that a New Woman may risk becoming a no-woman, she declares:

> We, daughters of educated men, are between the devil and the deep sea. Behind us lies the patriarchal system; the private house with its nullity, its immorality, its hypocrisy, its servility. Before us lies the public world, the professional system, with its possessiveness, its jealousy, its pugnacity, its greed. The one shuts us up like slaves in a harem; the other forces us to circle, like caterpillars head to tail, round and round the mulberry tree, the sacred tree, of property. It is a choice of evils. Each is bad. Had we not better plunge off the bridge into the river? [74]

And her only solution to the dilemma she describes is what Mary Ellen Chase called an impossible ideal—professional women's adoption of vows of "poverty, chastity, derision, and freedom from unreal loyalties" (80).

The extreme difficulty of these vows is signaled by the fact that, although they can be seriously discussed, they can be defined only through linguistic dislocations. In particular, the key, quasi-religious terms *poverty* and *chastity* signify something quite other than what they ordinarily would: "By poverty is meant enough money to live upon. . . . By chastity is meant that when you have made enough to live on by your profession you must refuse to sell your brain for the sake of money" (*TG* 80). And that Woolf herself understood the paradoxes implicit in such redefinitions of traditional concepts is made plain by her wry comment that "the English language is much in need of new words" (40).

In a world of old words, how can a new life be defined? Woolf seems finally to have decided that only cryptic images, linguistic disruptions, or annunciations and epiphanies could reveal oblique glimpses of that history of the future in which the public world and the private house might join at last to shape a society where Lily Briscoe need become neither Mrs. Ramsay nor Charles Tansley.

After she had completed *Orlando* and *A Room of One's Own,* and during and after the time she spent researching and writing *Three Guineas,* Woolf produced three novels which depend on such visionary obliqueness: *The Waves* (1931), *The Years* (1937), and *Between the Acts.* Although they are very different from each other, each in its own way represents the demise of the old and the birth of the new through images or interludes of enigma, paradox, ambiguity.

The Waves is, of course, both the most overtly experimental and the most apparently ahistorical of Woolf's novels. Fragmenting the psyche into six almost allegorical creatures—Susan, the "mother-woman"; Jinny, the erotic woman; Rhoda, the anxious metaphysician; Louis, the poet; Neville, the homosexual classicist; and Bernard, the novelist—and constellating them around Percival, the "hero," Woolf juxtaposes the human lifetime(s) of this six-pointed star with the natural time of a day marked by the rising and setting of the sun and the breaking of waves on the beach. Thus the structure that patterned *Mrs. Dalloway*—*a day in the life of . . .*—is reversed to become *a life in the day of . . . .* And the introspective soliloquys of the six protagonists, all for the most part set in a highly stylized present tense, similarly mark time by transcending it through a series of infinitely expanded "moments of being."

But even while this novel seems largely freed from the material detritus of past and present in order to focus intensely on issues of time and timelessness that go beyond the questions raised by Big Ben and the other clock, the work addresses the twin problems of history and the new through both form and substance. Formally, for instance, as a hybrid genre that Woolf called a "play-poem" (*D* 3:139), it answers a question she had asked about the New Woman-novelist in *A Room*, the text she completed just before embarking on *The Waves*. Noting there that "we shall find [woman] providing [herself with] some new vehicle, not necessarily in verse, for the poetry in her," she asked "how a woman nowadays would write a poetic tragedy in five acts—would she use verse—would she not use prose rather?" (80) A prose play-poem divided into nine parts (like Barrett Browning's nine-part *Aurora Leigh*, a hybrid verse novel Woolf knew well), *The Waves* implicitly becomes the woman's poetic play of the future.

The action of this poetic play, moreover, elegizes and deconstructs an absent hero, Percival (named for the knight of chivalric romance) over whom "we hang vibrating" as we did over the cryptic Jacob Flanders (*JR* 73). But Percival is from the start presented much more ironically than Jacob was. "Smoothing his hair, not from vanity . . . but to propitiate the god of decency," Percival is a faithful servant of the empire, on his way to India. Remarks Bernard, "He is conventional; he is a hero. The little boys trooped after him across the playing-fields. They blew their noses as he blew his nose, but unsuccessfully, for he is Percival" (260). Later, imagining this quasi-Victorian "hero"'s progress through India in an absurd advance that mocks the solemn processions of *Jacob's Room*, *A Room of One's Own*, and *Three Guineas*, Bernard intones: "Behold, Percival advances; Percival rides a flea-bitten mare, and wears a sun-helmet. By applying the standards of the West, by using the violent language that is natural to him, [a fallen] bullock-cart is righted in less than five minutes. The Oriental problem is solved. He rides on; the multitude cluster round him, regarding him as if he were—what indeed he is—a God" (269). And soon after this, the six friends receive the shocking news that Percival's "horse stumbled; he was thrown" (280).

Unlike his knightly namesake, this Percival does not survive and triumph in duels and jousts. Unlike Jacob Flanders, he does not die on a battlefield. Rather, like the imperial history he incarnates, this Percival rides a flea-bitten mare that stumbles and throws him, so that he dies not with a bang but with a whimper. And his destined inheritor, in the terms Woolf establishes throughout *The Waves*, is his affable opposite, Bernard, who defines himself as "a man without a self": a new man, purified of that "straight dark bar" of the masculine ego, that "shadow shaped something like the letter 'I'" excoriated in *A Room of One's Own* (103).

Yet, as in her educational treatises or indeed in *To the Lighthouse* and *Orlando,* Woolf could go only so far in defining the newness Bernard perceives and represents. His transformed consciousness consists most frequently of unanswerable questions. As he parts with his friends after their last meeting, he wonders, "Was this then, this streaming away mixed with Susan, Jinny, Neville, Rhoda, Louis, a sort of death? A new assembly of elements? Some hint of what was to come?" (370). And after deciding that he is "a man without a self," he asks, "But how describe the world seen without a self? There are no words. Blue, red—even they distract. . . . How describe or say anything in articulate words again?" (376).

The linguistic problem of Bernard's selflessness is compounded by an episode that may have occurred in his childhood. Running away from the schoolroom with Susan, Bernard claimed that the pair had come to "Elvedon," a new and magic country where a "lady sits between the two long windows, writing" and the "gardeners sweep the lawn with great brooms." Announces Bernard, "We are the first to come here. We are the discoverers of an unknown land" (186). But is the writing lady of Elvedon a figment of Bernard's imagination? Or is Bernard the fiction that the lady—Virginia Woolf, say, writing by the window at Rodmell—creates as she gazes toward the indeterminate lighthouse of the future?[82]

Certainly, besides being recorded by a woman writer, Bernard's story, or rather the story of the hexagonal being to which he belongs, is governed by a female figure, at first "couched beneath the horizon" (179), who raises the lamp of the sun that will shape the day which is his life, a girl who "tire[s] her brows with water-globed jewels" (278) and who at the end of the novel restarts the cycle as she once again "lifts the watery fire-hearted jewels to her brow" (379). Is the history of this "man without a self"—not a no-man but a new man—really a cover story for the new history made by woman?[83]

The Years is in many ways just such a history, "a novel of fact," in Woolf's phrase, which she intended, she explained in *The Pargiters,* as a study of the "transformation" from the time of "our great grandmothers" to the "present day" and after (*P* 8–9). In fact, the original plan of the work was "to give a faithful . . . account of a family called Pargiter, from the year 1800 to the year *2032*" (9; emphasis ours), but, as usual, the novelist was unable to imagine that "Chapter on the Future" she was always hoping to compose. Still, even in its final, somewhat less ambitious form—moving from 1880 to the "present day"—*The Years* breaks the sequence of Big Ben time, uniting official records with those traced by the other clock to show how women yet newer than Orlando and Lily Briscoe as well as men at least as new as Bernard have come into being. Significantly, moreover, the major "events" on which at least eight sections of this eleven-section book depend are deaths—deaths which indicate the gradual erosion of the old order and its replacement by an exhilarating yet mystifying future.

Emphasizing Woolf's sense of the fragility as well as the centrality of the acquiescent wife-mother in the traditionally gendered scheme of things, Abel Pargiter's wife, Rose, is the first to die, in 1880; her death, like Mrs. Ramsay's, heralds changes on which the rest of the novel meditates. Unlike Mrs. Ramsay, however, Mrs. Pargiter is neither beautiful nor powerful. Rather, as we first encounter her in her sickroom, she represents the decadence to which Mrs. Ramsay's role might have led, had that "happier Helen of our days" (*TTL* 43) not died quite suddenly in the middle of the night. Indeed, "decayed but everlasting, lying in the cleft of the pillows," the invalid Mrs. Pargiter seems to her rebellious daughter Delia to be "an impediment to all life" (*Y* 22). No longer an angel in the house, she must be whisked away so that time can move forward.

The other literal or literary deaths on which *The Years* broods are less extensively examined: the death of Parnell in 1891; the death of Antigone about which Sara Pargiter reads (in 1907, in an English translation produced by her cousin Edward); the deaths of Eugenie and Digby Pargiter, revealed in 1908; the death of Edward VII in 1910; the death of Abel Pargiter in 1911; the death of the Pargiters' dog Rover in 1913; and, offstage, the deaths of countless young men in the Great War, symbolized by the dates (1914, 1917, 1918) of the next three sections. Although only obliquely rendered or merely implied (as in the demise of soldiers), all these deaths decimate the ranks of the past and emphasize the newness of the "present day."

As she moves her readers toward that final cryptic moment of being—a family reunion of the surviving Pargiter brothers and sisters with their descendants and friends—Woolf frequently alludes to the official history, family history, and classical education that always concerned her.[84] But the novelist—who had thought of calling this book "Here and Now" (*P* xv)—is clearly most fascinated by the questions raised in the text's bravura coda, with its detailed examination of the enigmas of the present. Here we encounter two third-generation Pargiters—Peggy (a doctor) and North (a farmer) who are the New Woman and New Man, largely free of the Victorian knots and nots in which their parents had been enmeshed. To Peggy, indeed, the past is "beautiful in its unreality" (333) and the present is a moment in which, while practicing her profession, she tries to explain the oddities of her family to the "friend at the Hospital" with whom she evidently has a relationship not unlike the utopian friendship of Chloe and Olivia in *A Room*. And to North, the present, especially his role in it, poses a series of key Woolfian questions: "But what do I mean, he wonder[s]—I, to whom ceremonies are suspect, and religion's dead; who don't fit . . . don't fit in anywhere?" (410).[85] As for the older generation, most, in particular the sisters, have changed radically over the years as they formed and were reformed by the social revolutions that have brought them to the edge of the future. The eldest sister, Eleanor, has become a world traveler. The middle one, Delia, worked for Home Rule in Ireland. The youngest, Rose, was a militant suffragist. Now, as North and Peggy realize, their descendants have a chance of inhabiting "another world, a new world" in which people would "live differently" (422–23), for, as the mysterious foreigner Nicholas Pomjarovsky exclaims in a toast, "The human race . . . is now in its infancy," but "may it grow to maturity!" (426) What might that new world of human maturity be? Again, Woolf can only struggle to define it through cryptic epiphanies. When Delia brings the caretaker's children into the party, these new beings of another class entertain the guests with an untranslatable song whose bizarre combination of dignity and "hideous noise" can only evoke from Eleanor the interrogative response "Beautiful?" (429).[86] Then, as she and her siblings stand by the window, watching the sunrise, "the old brothers and sisters" seem to the younger generation "statuesque" (432), like enigmatic icons of a past unrecoverable in a present barely understood. Finally, as the party disperses, Eleanor watches a young man and girl alight from a taxi, unknowable emblems of the new, like the pair who enter just such a taxi at the end of *A Room*. In the future that is arriving along with their taxi, where are this man and woman going and what will they become?

In her last novel, *Between the Acts,* Woolf definitively argues a case for the artifice of history. Here, through the brilliant device of a play within the novel, she questions the "reality" of both histories—that of the public world and that of the private house—while suggesting the arbitrariness, as well as the enigma, of the destiny to which history leads. Of course, Woolf's drama and the pageant mounted by her fictive Miss La Trobe are set in a house that is "historical." Situated in the "very heart of England" (16), Pointz Hall holds in its walls, its grounds, its very placement on the land, a chronicle of past and present. Unlike the centuries-old Orlando, the Olivers have owned this stately home for "only something over a hundred and twenty years" (7), but its Barn (always capitalized) is "as old as the Church" (26) and reminds "some people of a Greek temple, others of the middle ages" (99), while the names of most of the nearby villagers (who will play in Miss La Trobe's pageant) are "in Domesday book," and Mrs. Sands, the cook, who has "never in all her fifty years been over the hill" beyond the town (31), has seen the sands of time pass in her kitchen. And opposite the dining-room window hang two portraits: a male ancestor leading his horse, who evokes the masculine stud book, and a mysterious lady in a forest glade, who is not an ancestor, but who radiates "the still, distilled essence of emptiness, silence" (37), the riddle of the unrecorded past, in the core of the house.

Beneath these pictures, the Olivers—old Bart, of the Indian Civil Service, retired, his widowed sister Lucy Swithin, his son Giles, a stockbroker, and Giles's wife, Isa—assemble for lunch, along with two guests, the oversexed "wild child" Mrs. Manresa and her homosexual protégé William Dodge. Both Bart and Lucy meditate on history, Bart precisely, officially, and Lucy confusedly, wonderingly. "From an aeroplane," Bart remarks, "you could still see, plainly marked, the scars made by the Britons; by the Romans; by the Elizabethan manor house; and by the plough, when they ploughed the hill to grow wheat in the Napoleonic wars" (4). Lucy broods on an "Outline of History": "thinking of rhododendron forests in Piccadilly; when the entire continent [was] populated, she understood, by . . . she supposed, barking monsters . . . from whom presumably, she thought . . . we descend" (8–9). Although both are obsessed with the past, Bart identifies the marks of culture on nature, while Lucy is fascinated by the nature behind culture.[87]

Giles, Isa, Mrs. Manresa, and William Dodge, however, are almost wholly focused on the present. Giles competes for success in the city, crawling "round and round the mulberry tree, the sacred tree, of property" (*TG* 74). Mrs. Manresa, evidently married to a "nouveau riche" Jew, quaffs champagne and makes herself up seductively, unselfconsciously playing the oxymoronic part of benign femme fatale.[88] William Dodge, a clerk, struggles to dodge the onus of "perversion." And Isa, the most introspective of the group, writes not-very-good poems "in a book bound like an account book lest Giles might suspect" (*BA* 50). At thirty-nine, she is "the age of the century," and her preoccupations are, Woolf implies, routine anxieties: a newspaper story about the sexual violence a band of troopers at Whitehall inflicted on a naive girl (20), a recurrent vision of herself as the "last little donkey in the long caravanserai crossing the desert," bearing "the burden that the past laid on me . . . what we must remember: what we would forget" (55).[89]

Like a kind of congregation, all these characters and others gather on the terrace after lunch to be instructed by a pageant "*drawn from our island history*" (76), an eccentrically inflected chronicle produced by the "swarthy, sturdy" lesbian Miss La Trobe, about whom "very little [is] actually known" (58) but who has "the look of a commander pacing his deck" (62) as she embarks on an outline of history which is Woolf's own final attempt to reinvent the march of time.

As a gloss on the chronicle structured by Big Ben, Miss La Trobe's pageant is notable for a number of reasons. To begin with, England is "born" as a girl child, played by the little villager Phyllis Jones, and grows into a queen, Elizabeth, portrayed—amusingly—by Eliza Clark, a shopkeeper "licensed to sell tobacco." Only in the nineteenth century does male power assert itself, in the shape of "Budge the publican" (160), cast as an archetypal Victorian constable who proclaims, in parodic Kiplingesque imperialist rhetoric, that all the world must "Obey the Rule of my Truncheon," although "to direct the traffic orderly, at 'Yde Park Corner, Piccadilly Circus, is a whole-time, white man's job" (163). But because Miss La Trobe's emphasis is more on private history than public life—and on periods defined through queens (Elizabeth, Anne, Victoria)—the "ages" that, say, Miss Allan in *The Voyage Out* had sought to record are virtually reperiodized. There is a Restoration comedy but no Restoration, an Age of Reason but no Romantic period. Gaps and absences point up the playwright's idiosyncratic choices, forcing the audience to ask such questions as one colonel's plaintive "Why leave out the British Army? What's history without the Army, eh?" (157).

At the same time, the pageant's range of genres (Elizabethan drama, Restoration comedy, sentimental Victorian divertissement) allows Miss La Trobe (and Woolf) to reappropriate and re-author English literary history, as if Judith Shakespeare had been all along alive, well, and writing her unwritten works in "the very heart of England" as naturally as the "birds that sang in the hedge" (*ROO* 49). Even more radically, the interventions of cows and rain, proving that "Nature takes her part" (*BA* 197) too, momentarily elide the distinctions between nature and culture that, at least in the nineteenth century, reinforced the "law" of the Victorian constable's truncheon while pointing to the arbitrary way the cultured mind interprets the "part" nature plays.

In addition, the interaction between the persistent procession of villagers *"Digging and delving, ploughing and sowing"* (124) and the featured acts of the pageant juxtaposes the lives of the (supposedly) obscure with the deeds of the (apparently) great to question all definitions of obscurity and greatness. And most crucially, those definitions are further questioned by the pageant's cast itself, a troupe of "ordinary people" who move through time clad in extraordinary costumes—bedspreads, cardboard crowns, sixpenny brooches—to offer comical yet oddly convincing impersonations of heroic figures.

La Trobe: the name of this subversive pageant's author evokes the phrase *la trouve robe*—French for "wardrobe mistress"—and Miss La Trobe is just such a wardrobe mistress of the ages, a purveyor of costumes whose procedures recall Woolf's argument in *Orlando* that "there is much to support the idea that it is clothes that wear us and not we them" (188).[90] For if a villager can represent Elizabeth I, is it not possible that the queen, too, despite her royal inheritance, is in some sense necessarily a representation of herself? As Elizabeth, Eliza Clark, the shopkeeper, "looked the age in person. And when she mounted the soap box in the centre . . . her size made her appear gigantic." Moreover, adds Woolf, who continues ironically to point out similarities in the face of the superficial differences between a shopkeeper and a monarch by noting the shopkeeper's prowess in her own sphere, *this* Eliza "could reach a flitch of bacon or haul a tub of oil with one sweep of her arm in the shop" (83).

"The Victorians," comments Lucy Swithin later. "I don't believe . . . that there ever were such people. Only you and me and William dressed differently" (175). While William demurs that this must mean "'you don't believe in history,'" Woolf implies that history *is* simply people dressed differently— in different garments, different roles, different pieces of cardboard. Thus, when Mr. Streetfield, the clergyman, struggling to make sense of the afternoon's entertainment, opines that "we act different parts; but are the same," for "did I not perceive Mr. Hardcastle here . . . a Viking? And in Lady Harridan . . . a Canterbury pilgrim?" (192), Woolf herself sanctions his interpretation. At the end of the pageant, "reluctant to go," the actors linger and mingle: "Budge the policeman talking to old Queen Bess. And the Age of Reason hobnobb[ing] with the foreparts of [a] donkey. . . . Each still act[ing] *the unacted part conferred on them by their clothes*" (195; emphasis ours). History, says Woolf, is no more than this arbitrary wardrobe supplied by an enigmatic author. And time, tellingly, is marked by "the tick, tick of the gramophone" (154), a contrivance not for calibration but for representation, as if the "ages" were artificial reproductions of impersonations, copies of copies.

Miss La Trobe's strategy for signaling the arrival of the "Present Day" is inspired. "Mopping, mowing, whisking, frisking" (184), a band of impudent children emerges from the bushes holding up mirrors to the audience, so that those who considered themselves observers must realize they are objects as well as subjects in a reality based on roles and clothes. Uneasily, all turn away, embarrassed by the artifice this unexpected denouement has forced them to confront—all "save Mrs. Manresa who, facing herself in the glass use[s] it as a glass" (186). "Wild child" that she is, is this unruly woman the wild card in the decorous deck surrounding her? Does her calm acceptance of cosmetics mean that she is making up not just her face but a new role?

The question is scarcely answerable, for the new in *Between the Acts,* as in all Woolf's late novels, can be known only by its indeterminacy, even its fictionality. With the audience "dispersed" (196), Miss La Trobe stalks away, groaning that her play was "a failure." Then, as if nature were still undertaking to "play her part,". a flock of starlings attacks "the tree behind which she had hidden," creating "a whizz and vibrant rapture . . . life, without measure, without stop devouring the tree" (209). A kind of annunciation, sexual in its ferocity, the preternatural onslaught liberates in the disconsolate playwright an idea for her next work. "'I should group them,' she murmur[s], 'here.' It would be midnight; there would be two figures, half concealed by a rock" (210). And shortly after this, as she drowses over a beer in the local pub, the words of the new world rise toward her, "Words without meaning—wonderful words," so that, again, "Suddenly the tree was pelted with starlings. She set[s] down her glass. She hear[s] the first words" (212).[91]

Those are the first words of the drama in which Giles and Isa, seated in "great hooded chairs" (219), find themselves at the end of *Between the Acts*, a play about "the first night of a new age." Yet again, the issue of that new age is undecidable. Throughout Miss La Trobe's pageant, the recurrent refrain "The King is in his counting house / Counting out his money. / The Queen is in her parlour / Eating bread and honey" (122) had emphasized the obdurate persistence of traditional sex roles despite costume shifts and changes of backdrop. But now, Woolf implies, husband and wife must confront each other: "Alone, enmity was bared; also love. Before they slept, they must fight; after they had fought, they would embrace. From that embrace another life might be born. But first they must fight as the dog fox fights the vixen, in the heart of darkness, in the fields of night. . . . The night that dwellers in caves had watched from some high place among the rocks" (219).

Another life might be born: as when Woolf imagined the starlings' attack on the tree or the moment when Orlando bares the moon eggs on her breast to the wild heaven, she here hints at the possibility of an annunciation, an intersection of primordial forces leading to the birth of the new.[92] The battle of the sexes is not over; in fact, a kind of ultimate battle, Woolf predicts, is about to begin. Yet that battle might bear fruit in what new life, what new creature? An ambivalent woman artist like Lily Briscoe? A wild child like Mrs. Manresa, the happily artificial queen of history's pageant? A New Woman who is, in conventional terms, no woman, like Miss La Trobe, the mother and artificer of that pageant? Or a new being of all sexes and none, like Orlando?

Because both the battle and the embrace must occur—are already occurring, Woolf implies—in a "heart of darkness" like the archaic shadow that enveloped "the dwellers in caves," this historian of the future cannot see to say. But her revisionary use of Conrad's resonant phrase, an echo dating back to *The Voyage Out*, where Rachel journeys down the Amazon into a sexualized "heart of the night" (265), points not to the darkness in the human heart but to that at the heart of gender, the mystery of the relationship between Mr. and Mrs. Ramsay, the king in his counting house and queen in her parlor, Giles and Isa, that must now be reinterpreted.

In *Night and Day*, that "novel in the tradition of the English novel," Katharine and Ralph had sung to each other in the old way out of their own sexual hearts of darkness. In *The Years*, North—the New Man—feels himself to be "in the heart of darkness; cutting his way toward the light" (411) as he struggles to understand his relatives' words at the family reunion.[93] But now the darkness has risen to hold the very future of gender in the enigmatic heart of a drama that has just begun a new act and a new age. Leaning as hard as she can against the massy wall of time, Woolf knows that she herself, as a new being, must play a part and teach others to play their parts in that coming age. Still, she realizes that Miss La Trobe, the wardrobe mistress of history, has not yet designed the costumes or written the lines.

2

Female Female Impersonators:
The Fictive Music
of Edna St. Vincent Millay
and Marianne Moore

It is a dangerous lot, that of the charming, romantic public poet, especially if it falls to a woman.

—Louise Bogan

Family, I discover that I have nothing to give readings in, I *must* have long dresses, trailing ones. The short ones won't do. If Norma hasn't yet done anything to the greenish chiffon & rose scarf then *that* dress ought to be made up very long and drapy—more like a negligée than a dress, really.

—Edna St. Vincent Millay

In the late Forties Marianne Moore walked into a milliner's shop and asked to be fitted as Washington Crossing the Delaware.

—Bonnie Costello

If I were not the recipient of a donated French brocade emerald jacket and purple velvet skirt of papal quality I could be mistaken for a mere citizen of Times Square at the rush hour.

—Marianne Moore

"What is the essential nature of fully developed femininity? What is *das ewig Weibliche?*" asked the psychoanalyst Joan Rivière in an essay on "Womanliness as a Masquerade" (1929), and her answer implied, paradoxically, that the essence of what the nineteenth century had often called "true womanliness" was pure artifice. "The conception of womanliness as a mask," Rivière mused, "throws a little light on the enigma" of "fully developed femininity."[1] Writing in London two years after the publication of *To the Lighthouse* and one year after *Orlando,* this theorist—best known as a translator of Freud—was analyzing the phenomenon Woolf had, in different ways, dramatized in both novels: the interrogation of sex roles necessitated by an age of surprisingly rapid sexchanges. For regardless of whether Rivière's speculations were accurate, they were a product of just the history of social transforma-

57

tion that led to the disappearance of the woman who "naturally" knew how to be Mrs. Ramsay, the history that fostered the uncertainties of Lily Briscoe and Cam, along with the indeterminacy of Orlando.

Even our current phrase "sex *roles*" may itself be seen as a consequence of that history. Although the notion that "all the world's a stage / And all the men and women merely players" elaborates a seemingly timeless metaphor, it is a relatively new idea that the categories "men" and "women" may be as artificial as the parts of "schoolboy" or "lover." In particular, for centuries ministers, physicians, and philosophers had presupposed the essentializing concept of "woman" that Rivière questioned when she suggested that the "ewig Weibliche" might be simply a masquerade.[2] Even Freud, despite brilliant meditations on the difficult *construction* of "femininity," seemed ultimately to believe that there was such a quality as "womanliness." When he asked, "What do women want?" he implied that there were, ontologically, such beings as "women."[3]

As we argued in *Sexchanges,* however, from the turn of the century onward sexologists increasingly called attention to the artifice of gender, and, no doubt as a consequence of this, from Rivière onward the very notion of femininity was put ever more radically in question. By the time *The Second Sex* appeared in 1949, Simone de Beauvoir was frequently defining all women as what we here call "female female impersonators," intimating a necessary disjunction between everywoman's self and the self-presentation Western culture labels "feminine." In particular, de Beauvoir saw femininity as a function of costume and makeup. "Even if each woman dresses in conformity with her status," she declared, "a game is still being played":

> Artifice, like art, belongs to the realm of the imaginary. It is not only that girdle, brassiere, hair-dye, make-up disguise body and face; but that the least sophisticated of women, once she is 'dressed,' does not present *herself* to observation; she is, like the picture or the statue, or the actor on the stage, an agent through whom is suggested someone not there—that is, the character she represents, but is not. It is this identification with something unreal, fixed, perfect . . . that gratifies her; she strives to identify herself with this figure and thus to seem . . . justified in her splendor.[4]

Interestingly, without examining their gender implications Erving Goffman repeatedly cites such passages from *The Second Sex* throughout his study of social "impression-management" and "theatrical performance," *The Presentation of Self in Everyday Life* (1959). The "teams" of "players" who appear on Goffman's cultural stage are usually male, defined through such job categories as "lawyer," "diplomat," "shoe salesman," and so forth. But when a "team" is female, its job category is simply "woman," implying that being a "woman" entails a set of professional performative acts exactly equivalent to the theatrical activities involved in being (that is, in appearing to be) a lawyer or shoe salesman.[5]

In her *Pornography and Silence: Culture's Revenge against Nature* (1981), Susan Griffin presents a view of women's role-playing which addresses the same cultural phenomena, at the same time suggesting parallels between female female impersonation and the long history of black mimicry that we will explore in connection with the Harlem Renaissance. Woman's "false self," Griffin argues, "is the pornographic idea of the female. We have learned to impersonate her. Like the men and women living in the institution of slavery, we have become talented at seeming to be what we are not."[6]

In support of her claim, Griffin offered as paradigmatic examples of female female impersonation several anecdotes about Marilyn Monroe. According to Monroe's friend Simone Signoret, Griffin observed, the star "rarely dressed anything like the self we know as 'Marilyn'" when she was not on camera and referred to "the costume required to create [her] illusory self as her 'Marilyn getup.'"[7] In the same vein, the French theorist Luce Irigaray has written about the "masquerade" of femininity, echoing Rivière's essay and proposing, as Griffin does, that such female female impersonation results from the fact that in patriarchal culture women are inevitably "exiled from themselves."[8] We are speculating here, however, that such self-exile, along with the impersonation it entails, may have been exacerbated by just the historical circumstances—the sexchanges and social changes—that have empowered such feminists as Griffin and Irigaray to study the artifice of "femininity." Certainly, as Woolf portrayed her, Mrs. Ramsay found it "natural" to "be" the person her name delineated. But for Mrs. Ramsay's female descendants, newly aware of the arbitrariness of sex *roles*, there was no comparable continuity between inner feelings and outer mask, between consciousness and costume.

What are the *literary* consequences of such a discontinuity? Since fiction by definition entails feigning, while poets have often tended to imply the confessional "sincerity" of the lyric speaker, we are likely to find more surprising marks of the (female) masquerade inscribed in the lives and works of twentieth-century women poets than in novels or plays written by women. Of course, modernist and postmodernist verse by both sexes has long called attention to the fictionality of every poem's supposed speaker. *Personae* was, after all, the title of Ezra Pound's third book (1909) and of several later editions of his collected poems, while one of the newest words the New Critics introduced to readers was *persona*, meaning "mask" and intended to emphasize the gap between the writer in the world and the poet on the page.[9] But despite pervasive attention to the artifice of poetic identity, a number of twentieth-century male artists reacted not only against what they saw as the "feminization" of the literary marketplace but also against what they feared was the "effeminacy" of some male predecessors by laying claim to a masculinity that was both "authentic" and "ordinary."

Among the most prominent of the male modernists, a number guaranteed their manhood, along with the performative possibilities it offered, by adopting stereotypically male roles which seem to have reflected not just economic but also psychological necessities. T. S. Eliot worked in a bank; William Carlos Williams was a physician; Wallace Stevens was an insurance lawyer.[10] The imperatives that drove them were perhaps most clearly formulated by Stevens, who mused in an early meditation, "Poetry and Manhood": "Those who say poetry is now the peculiar province of women say so because ideas about poetry are effeminate." His answer to this charge consisted of a list of "man-poets" that included Homer, Dante, Shakespeare, and Milton.[11] That, in Stevens's opinion, true "man-poets" in the twentieth century were not—or at least *should* not be—impersonators, that they should be "naturally" masculine, became plain in a letter he wrote to Harvey Breit in 1942. "It was only a few years ago when Joaquin Miller or Walt Whitman were considered to be approximations of a typical image [of the poet]," Stevens commented rather nervously, "But were they? Weren't they recognized by people of any sense at all as, personally, poseurs? They belong in the same category of eccentrics to which *queer-looking actors belong. . . .* The contemporary poet is simply a contemporary man who writes poetry. *He looks like anyone else, acts like anyone else, wears the same kind of clothes,* and certainly is not an incompetent" (emphasis ours).[12]

In contrast to this view, Stevens's female contemporaries seem to have tried not to look "like anyone else," as our epigraphs from Moore and Millay are meant to show. Because in our century the "woman's part" has been culturally redefined as a specialized professional role which in its singularity balances a greater range of specialized male roles, the woman poet may have felt a particular obligation to prepare a distinctively feminine face to "meet the faces that [she] meet[s]." Indeed, where for J. Alfred Prufrock a preoccupation with costume (with, say, a "necktie rich and modest") becomes a sign of failure to achieve the authenticity implicit in a voicing of "the overwhelming question," for the woman poet a literal and figurative concern with clothing and "makeup" was often an enabling strategy which allowed her the *being* in the world that it denied Eliot's unmanned speaker.[13]

Precisely, however, because this woman of letters, newly conscious of the artifice of her gender, "played" a public part that was unavailable to most of her ancestresses, she may at times have found herself far more radically estranged from her aesthetic persona than were her male contemporaries from theirs. On the one hand she was often empowered by her estranged female female impersonation to produce poetry that commented on both the feminine and the masculine from the ironic perspective of the actor who knows that there is a radical gulf between "me" and "her." But on the other, because audiences—both readers and observers—frequently reified the female artist in the feminine role she played, she herself was always in danger of being trapped behind the rigid mask of a self that she secretly despised as inauthentic.

In broadly comic terms, Dorothy Parker's "The Waltz" (1933) wittily fictionalizes the experience of such female female impersonation. Stumbling around a dance floor with a man she dislikes, Parker's protagonist mouths "feminine" platitudes—*"Why, thank you so much. I'd adore to. . . . Oh, they're going to play another encore. Oh, goody. . . . Tired? I should say I'm not tired. I'd like to go on like this forever"*—while, in her mind, she viciously comments on her partner and her "part": "I don't want to dance with him. I don't want to dance with anybody," "I should say I'm not tired. I'm dead, that's all I am."[14] Obviously, the hilarious tension between this unwilling dancer's words and her thoughts allows Parker to analyze social rituals in which both author and heroine are engaged. Yet ultimately Parker can imagine no way out of the ballroom of gender for her speaker. Even while female female impersonation facilitates a critique of culture's central pas de deux, Parker implies, the costume of womanhood may inexorably dictate steps that are no joke.

Parker's "The Satin Dress" (1926) makes this point more explicitly and grimly. The speaker of this ballad begins her stitchery with enthusiasm for what she imagines will be a liberating gown: "Where's the man could ease a heart / Like a satin gown?" But as the speaker sews, she realizes that the task of constructing her "bold" dress may be both interminable and fatal: "They will say who watch at night, / 'What a fine shroud!'"[15] The dress of the female female impersonator may free her into an exhilarating fictionality, yet it may also finally shroud her. For a poet, in particular, the artifice of "the feminine" threatened aesthetic reification even while it fostered creativity. The astute Parker, simultaneously empowered and oppressed by her own comic masquerade, would likely have agreed with Louise Bogan's assertion that the role of "charming, romantic public poet" was, for early twentieth-century women, both a powerful part and "a dangerous lot."

In October 1917 the Neighborhood Playhouse in New York presented a new one-acter by Wallace Stevens. Set in a curiously surrealistic seventeenth century, "Bowl, Cat and Broomstick" is a facetious piece of literary criticism in which the three title characters explore the idea that "there is a special power in the poetry of a beauty" by meditating on the portrait of a French poet named Claire Dupray provided as the frontispiece to a collection of her poems. With comic verve, the characters (and the play) end up excoriating both the image and the imagination of the hapless Claire.[16] In doing so, Stevens's minidrama simultaneously underscores the surprising fetishization of the woman poet in a twentieth century of which the work's seventeenth century is a bizarre reflection, emphasizes the aesthetic dissonance that marked the careers of male and female poets in the period, and indicates the intensity of the irony with which contemporary men of letters confronted these new developments. Perhaps more important, the play's action points to a situation that twentieth-century women poets both exploited and resisted as, deploying the strategy of female female impersonation, they struggled to transform themselves from art objects to artists.

"Bowl, Cat and Broomstick" opens with Bowl, an ascetic aesthete, translating Dupray's verses for his admiring disciple Cat. Broomstick, a "hard-looking" skeptic, arrives, and the three turn their attention to the book's frontispiece, speculating on Dupray's age, as well as on the relations among her age, her sex, her beauty, and her art. "She cannot be more than twenty-two," declares Bowl, adding that that "is an age . . . when a girl like Claire Dupray, becomes a poetess." "Say poet—poet. I hate poetess," remonstrates Cat, but Broomstick dryly observes that "poetess is just the word at twenty-two!" (25). Further analysis of Dupray's work seems to prove the justice of his derogation of "poetesses," for the verse of this beauty sounds as extravagantly sentimental as any produced by the "lady writers with three names" whom many modernists deplored.[17] "This emotional waste," Broomstick notes, "is all thirty years old at the least. . . . I might even put it in the last century" (32). The play proves his judgment correct: the three friends discover, to the mortification of Bowl and Cat, that the poet is really fifty-three years old—and "Damn all portraits of poets and poetesses," cries Cat in chagrin (34).

On the surface, of course, the stylish intellectual farce these characters enact is intended to instruct audiences in the distinction between appearance and reality while it advances the self-consciously "twentieth-century" aesthetic espoused by Pound, Williams, and Stevens himself: poets should "make it new," and even old Broom(stick)s should sweep the world clean of the past's trashy sentimentality.[18] But why does the fastidious *philosophe* of "Sunday Morning" dramatize his allegory of art in terms of male critical gullibility and female poetic pretentiousness? Why does he title his play with an allusion to witchcraft—"bell, book and candle"—that simultaneously demonizes the domestic and deprecates the feminine? A line spoken by the enthusiastic Bowl, as he struggles to balance erotic admiration with aesthetic evaluation, provides a clue: "It is a new thing that the eyes of a poetess should bring us to this" (27). For although Broomstick ironically responds that they "are not living in the seventeenth century for nothing," the creator of this bemused trio of (miss)readers would certainly have noticed that in the year he was composing his playlet "a new thing" was happening on the New York literary scene: Bowls and Cats all over town were talking about "the poetry of a beauty," a poetry that was thought by all to have a very "special power."

Edna St. Vincent Millay—whose last name rhymes with "Dupray"—had actually begun her meteoric career as "poetess" in 1912 at the age of twenty, when her "Renascence" placed fourth in a contest sponsored by *The Lyric Year,* inspiring protest from many readers who thought it ought to have won. The talented ingenue from Maine was immediately taken up by wealthy benefactors, who arranged for her to attend Vassar College and who joined in feting her at parties in New York. Her own excitement at this debut was more than matched by the adulation of her admirers. Some years later, in 1918, when she auditioned for the Provincetown Players in front of the writer Floyd Dell, he wondered if the "slender little girl with red-gold hair . . . could possibly be Edna St. Vincent Millay, the author of that beautiful . . . poem 'Renascence.'"[19]

But by 1918 Millay had even more triumphs to her credit than "Renascence" (triumphs Stevens would likely have known), for throughout her college years she continued publishing poetry and garnered even more attention for her acting.[20] That this youthful poet was as physically lovely as Claire Dupray can only have contributed to her success: in the spring of 1914, the photographer Arnold Genthe posed her against a background of magnolia blossoms for a well-known portrait which might have served as the frontispiece on which Stevens's harried critics brood (figure, next page). But that Millay was apparently as productive as she was attractive may have contributed to the ambivalence she aroused in some male contemporaries. It seems relevant here not only that her first collection, *Renascence and Other Poems,* appeared shortly before "Bowl, Cat and Broomstick" was performed and six years before Stevens published his own first volume of poetry but also that *Renascence and Other Poems* was either praised or blamed for poetic strategies that were all "thirty years old at least."[21]

Millay continued to forge a brilliant public career throughout the twenties and thirties. In 1919, she wrote and directed a play of her own, *Aria da Capo,* for the Provincetown Players, and in 1920 her bravura *A Few Figs from Thistles* was published to such acclaim that she became, in one critic's words, "the unrivaled embodiment of sex appeal, the It-girl of the hour, the Miss America of 1920."[22] In 1922—the *annus mirabilis* which saw the appearance of *The Waste Land* and *Ulysses*—she produced a volume with the highly traditional title poem "Ballad of the Harp-Weaver," for which (in 1923, the year of Stevens's *Harmonium*) she became the first woman to win the Pulitzer Prize in poetry. In 1924, she began a series of lucrative reading tours in which she regularly captivated crowded houses. Throughout these years, too, she was awarded numerous honors (the first a Litt.D. from Tufts, at the age of thirty-three), and in the thirties she began to broadcast her poems over the radio. As early as 1926, Edmund Wilson had observed that "like Mencken, the prophet of a point of view, [Millay] has . . . become a national figure," and by 1936 few readers would have questioned Elizabeth Atkins's

Edna St. Vincent Millay, June 1914; photo by Arnold Genthe (courtesy the Museum of the City of New York, Theater Collection)

assertion that (far from being at least thirty years out of date) "Edna St. Vincent Millay represents our time to itself, much as Tennyson represented the period of Victoria to itself, or Byron the period of Romanticism."[23]

Besides representing what Atkins also called "the incarnation of our *Zeitgeist*," however, Millay stood for another phenomenon: the rise of the publicly active (and well publicized) women poet whose fame was as theatrical as it was literary. Where even the most notable precursors of women like Millay, Amy Lowell, Elinor Wylie, and Edith Sitwell—Elizabeth Barrett Browning, Emily Dickinson, Christina Rossetti—had achieved their reputations in spite (or, indeed, in some cases because) of lives of radical seclusion, these women poets ascended lecture platforms as exuberantly as they gave readings in private salons. Costuming themselves to reflect the self-definitions their poems recorded (Lowell in "high-collared dresses sprinkled with beads" that made her look like "Holbein's Henry VIII," Millay in floating chiffon, Wylie in heavy silver "armor," Sitwell in quasi-Elizabethan robes), they literalized the dream of the "poetess" as dramatic *improvisatrice* that had captivated the nineteenth-century imagination in Madame de Staël's *Corinne* (figure, next page).[24]

On tour in America during the teens, Lowell was "besieged" at "each train depot . . . by hordes of curiosity seekers who surged forward in an effort to catch a glimpse of their new heroine," and when in 1923 Edith Sitwell read her *Façade* to the accompaniment of William Walton's score in London's Aeolian Hall, "the attitude of certain of the audience was so threatening that I was warned to stay on the platform, hidden by the curtain, until they . . . went home."[25] Inevitably the press focused with enthusiasm on such notorious figures. After Millay married, for instance, her kitchen was featured in the *Ladies' Home Journal:* "Polished as a sonnet . . . Light as a lyric . . . Must be the kitchen for EDNA ST. VINCENT MILLAY."[26]

But poetic doings or misdoings that seemed scandalous or melodramatic were, of course, especially compelling to the media. When at the 1915 Harvard Commencement the young e. e. cummings read and discussed one of the gently erotic poems Lowell wrote for her companion Ada Russell, the *Boston Transcript* produced this front-page headline: "Harvard Orator Calls President Lowell's Sister Abnormal." When Millay went to New Mexico in the thirties to recuperate from chronic headaches and poor vision, a local paper proclaimed, "Poet Wins Battle With Death." The Chicago *Journal's* obituary for Elinor Wylie covered both her literary career and her love life ("Elinor Wylie, Poet, Figure in Sensational Elopement, Dies"), and Edith Sitwell's seventy-fifth "birthday party"—in the form of a concert at London's Royal Festival Hall—was attended by a mass of reporters, all, complained the writer, "mad with excitement at the thought of my approaching demise."[27]

Not surprisingly, many men of letters decided that, as F. R. Leavis quipped

Edith Sitwell; photo © Cecil Beaton (courtesy Sotheby's, London)

about Sitwell, such female aesthetic careers belonged "to the history of publicity rather than of poetry," and quite a few longed, with the skeptical
ferocity of Stevens's Broomstick, to sweep away their debased, publicity-
seeking women rivals. Raging against Lowell's transformation of imagism to
"Amygism," Ezra Pound labeled the cigar-smoking New Englander a "hip-
popoetess," while T. S. Eliot defined her as the "demon saleswoman" of
poetry and called Edith Sitwell "EDITH Shitwell." With comparable ferocity, Robert McAlmon delineated Millay as one "Vera St. Vitus" in his roman à
clef *Post-adolescence* (1923), and Thomas Wolfe, in *The Web and the Rock*,
produced a savage portrait of Elinor Wylie as a babyishly narcissistic ice
queen.[28]

More generally, during his early years in London Eliot repeatedly lamented "the monopolisation of literature by women" in both England and America. The *Egoist*, he told his mother in one letter, "is run mostly by old maids" (referring to Harriet Weaver and Dora Marsden) and to his father he explained that, as an assistant editor of that journal, "I struggle to keep the writing as much as possible in Male hands, as I distrust the Feminine in literature, and also, once a woman has had anything printed in your paper, it is very difficult to make her see why you should not print everything she sends in." To his friend Scofield Thayer he wrote even more testily, in the style of Wyndham Lewis's *BLAST:* "Of course, your superior officer is a Lady. They always are. Be PATIENT. . . . Be Sly, INSIDIOUS, even UNSCRUPULOUS. . . . Be to the inhabitants of Greenwich Village a Flail, and to the Intellect of Indianapolis a Scourge. . . . I speak from experience, as asst. (I say ASST.) Editor of the *Egoist.* . . . I am the only male, and three (3) women, incumbents, incunabula, incubae." As late as 1922, after the succès d'estime of *The Waste Land* and the establishment of the *Criterion,* he was pontificating to Pound that "there are only half a dozen men of letters (and no women) worth printing."29

Several decades later, William Carlos Williams brooded on the issue of sexual poetics with equal fervor in *Paterson,* where the most unpleasant representative of female art is the foolish lesbian "poetess" *Corydon,* whose flirtation with a nymphet named *Phyllis* Williams dramatizes in terms of bad metaphors and banal literary history. Tellingly, this episode is a nasty parody of the central *Corydon/Thyrsis* encounter in Millay's *Aria da Capo.* The event that probably triggered *Paterson*'s satire underscores the irritation men like Williams—and Eliot and Stevens—may have often felt as they confronted women's aesthetic success: in November 1918 Alfred Kreymbourg elected not to produce his friend Williams's verse play *The Old Apple Tree* with one of his own plays because he preferred to put his on with *Aria da Capo.* Worse still, Kreymbourg lost the manuscript of *The Old Apple Tree.* The experience must have taught Williams that women writers—banal, publicity-seeking, out-of-date or not—could be troublesome competitors.30 Indeed, he must have felt (like Stevens) that serious readers ought to sweep art clean of the commercially compelling "emotional waste" excreted by such popular artists before men of letters themselves—and their manuscripts—were swept away.

———

Of course, male modernist poets were emphatically *not* swept away by the witches' brooms they may have associated with some of their female contemporaries. On the contrary, although in her own day Millay functioned as a kind of American Poetess Laureate, it was *her* achievement, along with the accomplishments of the women constellated around her, which was rapidly dismissed by the canonizing judgment of time. In 1937 John Crowe Ransom summarized a prolonged critical debate about Millay's "maturity" in a devastating review of Elizabeth Atkins's book-length encomium to her by wryly remarking, "This charming lady found it unusually difficult, poetically speaking, to come of age." Defining Millay as a paradigm of "the poet as woman," he decided that, because of the female writer's "famous attitudes" of sentimentality, her work lacked intellectual interest.[31] In 1958, eight years after Millay's death, John Hall Wheelock made explicit the modernist assumptions on which such comments were based: "The resistance to feeling directly expressed in the first-person-singular lyric, and with a fine Sapphic disregard for 'the objective correlative,' has in our day, been so strong as virtually to eliminate from serious critical consideration the work of such poets as Edna St. Vincent Millay and Sara Teasdale."[32]

That until recently these "poetesses" *have* been eliminated from critical consideration is dramatically revealed by their absence from such major anthologies as Richard Ellmann's *New Oxford Book of American Verse* (1976) and Albert Gelpi's *The Poet in America* (1973), as well as from most "serious" studies of twentieth-century poetry in the last few decades. William Pritchard's *Lives of the Modern Poets* (1980), for instance, contains not one reference to Millay, Wylie, Lowell, or Bogan, nor does Jerome Mazzaro's *Modern American Poetry: Essays in Criticism* (1970). M. L. Rosenthal's influential *Modern Poets: A Critical Introduction* (1960) offers a single allusion to Millay, a reference which illuminates the omissions marking subsequent studies: in a discussion of Elizabeth Bishop, Rosenthal remarks, "In her poems about Negroes and the poor Miss Bishop can be sentimental; these and her love poetry have just the consistency of a typical Millay poem." Ten years after the death of the writer who had once seemed to "represent our time to itself," her name had become a code word for bad art.[33]

To be sure, there were a few women poets whom the tastemaking theorists of modernism did not so rapidly consign to oblivion. H. D., for example, inspired Pound to articulate the aesthetic of imagism, and she retained the friendship of literary men throughout much of a career which eventually lapsed into obscurity. More strikingly, H. D.'s sometime classmate at Bryn Mawr Marianne Moore was frequently treated as an icon of the new, a kind of anti-Poetess Laureate whose work brilliantly avoided other women poets' emotional excesses. In his essay on Millay, Ransom explicitly contrasted the problematic "poet as woman" with Moore, who seemed to fall in a different (and luckier) category, since she did not suffer from the "deficiency in masculinity" that afflicted the author of "Renascence."

Similarly, Wallace Stevens magisterially opined that (unlike the Clare Duprays of this world) Moore was "a poet that matters," and William Carlos Williams continually celebrated her achievements, observing in 1925 that "Miss Moore . . . throw[s] out of fashion the classical conventional poetry to which one is used and puts her own and that about her in its place," in 1948 that "the magic name, Marianne Moore, has been among my most cherished possessions for nearly forty years," and in 1951 that Moore was "a rafter holding up the superstructure of our uncompleted building." Even earlier, Eliot and Pound were among crucial figures who found her work compelling. Although in 1918 Pound worried that "in the verse of Marianne Moore I detect traces of emotion," he praised her poetry, along with that of Mina Loy, for its "arid clarity," while in 1923 Eliot argued that Moore's "aristocratic" verse represented "the *refinement*, not the antithesis, of popular art," contrasting its "satirical" use of language with the "sham ideas, sham emotions, and even sham sensations" of "middle-class art."[34]

Were two canons formed by twentieth-century women who wrote verse—one produced by "poetesses" and another created by anti-"poetesses"? Must contemporary female poets choose between radically opposed literary matrilineages, one poetically "incorrect" from the modernist perspective, and the other aesthetically respectable? If Millay stands for a female tradition that descends from such "bad" (blatantly sentimental) nineteenth-century poetasters as L. E. L., Felicia Hemans, and Lydia Sigourney, does Moore stand for a female poetic tradition that descends from a "good" (intellectually vigorous) nineteenth-century artist like Emily Dickinson? Certainly, as one recent critic has put it, Millay and Moore, as representative women poets, "seem to have little in common even if we wish to say both practice versions of subversion—or compliance." Indeed, according to Charles Molesworth, Millay "was a poet who might instructively serve as Moore's exact opposite."[35] Yet we want to suggest that, notwithstanding the differences between these two, there are surprising similarities, similarities reflecting comparable strategies of female female impersonation that shaped both writers' careers as each sought, in her own way, to translate the "handicap" of "femininity" into an aesthetic advantage.

To begin with femininity: both Millay and Moore (like such contemporaries as Wylie and H. D.) were early reified, even fetishized, as *women* poets. Millay, wrote Joseph Collins in 1924, "is like a beautiful woman who has a varied, attractive wardrobe, and if one may judge from some of her appearances, she knows how to wear her clothes; but she does not always take the trouble to select discriminatingly or to put them on properly, or at least as effectively as she might easily do." And Millay's erstwhile admirer Floyd Dell saw her as, variously, "a New England nun; a chorus girl on a holiday; the Botticelli Venus."[36] In just these years, however, T. S. Eliot was implicitly defining Moore as the "It girl" of the avant garde intelligentsia, pointedly celebrating her not for the absence but for the presence of femininity in her oeuvre: "Miss Moore's poetry is as 'feminine' as Christina Rossetti's, one never forgets that it is written by a woman; but with both one never thinks of this as anything but a positive virtue."[37] And that this appropriately "mod-

ern" artist *looked* as feminine as Genthe's tenderly girlish Millay (or as
Thomas Wolfe's coldly beautiful Wylie or Pound's palely Greek H. D.) was
continually emphasized by Williams and by the many other admiring observers who became as obsessed with her tricorne hat and cape as Millay's
and Wylie's fans had been with the gowns of those "poetesses" (figure).[38]

Interestingly, as Moore's reputation among intellectuals began to decline
during the fifties and sixties, even positive analyses of her work increasingly
emphasized its stereotypically feminine qualities. As early as 1923, Robert
McAlmon matched his portrait of "Vera St. Vitus" in *Post-Adolescence* with an
equally biting caricature of Moore as a librarian-poetess, Martha Wullus—
"a churchgoing, cerebralizing moralist" who "isn't emotionally developed
much" but who looks, at least to one of the men she knows, like "a Dresden
doll thing with those great contemplative Chinese eyes of hers, and that
wisplike body with its thatch of carrot-colored hair. So picturesque too in her
half-boyish clothes."[39]

But such reifications intensified with time. In 1945 Randall Jarrell attacked Moore's war poetry and even his later, celebratory "Her Shield"
(1953) commented somewhat ambivalently on her "restraint," noting that
"in her poems morality usually is simplified into self-abnegation," and adding that "some of the poems have the manners of ladies who learned a little
before birth not to mention money, who neither point nor touch, and who
scrupulously abstain from the mixed, live vulgarity of life."[40] Later still,
M. L. Rosenthal spoke of her "fastidiousness," which risked "precious and
recherché impressions"; Roy Harvey Pearce noted her "propriety," her "po-
lite and lady-like presence," and her "quite feminine realism"; and Henry
Gifford described her poetry as "exact and curious like the domestic skills of
the American woman in ante-bellum days."[41]

Marianne Moore had become exactly the kind of public incarnation of
the zeitgeist that Millay was earlier. In 1955, she was asked to name a new
Ford automobile and suggested, for the model that was ultimately (despite
her best efforts) called the Edsel, such labels as "The Resilient Bullet," "The
Intelligent Whale," "Pastelogram," "Turcotingo," and "Utopian Turtletop."
When she read at the Boston Arts Festival in 1958, "a crowd of something
like five thousand persons" was waiting to applaud her.[42] By the sixties, she
was confiding her breakfast menus to *Glamour* ("half a grapefruit or orange
juice, honey, an egg, hard-boiled or scrambled, a piece of Pepperidge white
toast"), besides discoursing on fashion to *Women's Wear Daily* and the *New York
Times* ("The military cape is the most graceful wrap we have—," "A narrow
sheath or pant . . . does not set a hippomoid figure off to advantage").[43] And
finally, in 1968 she threw out the first baseball of the season at a Brooklyn
Dodgers game. A classically American crowd pleaser, she had also become,
in her tricorne hat and great cape, an icon of eccentric but distinctively
female art. Perhaps it was inevitable then that, like Millay, she was entirely
excluded from Pritchard's *Lives of the Modern Poets*.

Marianne Moore; photo George Platt Lynes (courtesy Rosenbach Museum and Library, Philadelphia, Pennsylvania)

But Millay and Moore had more in common than feminizing publicity, for although both may have thought of the poetic imagination as gender-free at the beginning of their careers, both eventually adopted the mask of "the feminine" as an equivocally empowering stance that allowed them to work from the positions of fetishized femininity in which critics had placed them and to use the newly public roles of twentieth-century Poetess Laureate or anti-Poetess Laureate as "free" (precisely because "female") spaces from which they could question many of the conventions of their culture.[44] In doing this, both were no doubt responding to a classic feminine problem that has recently been theorized by the film critic Laura Mulvey but most succinctly defined by John Berger: "A woman must continually watch herself. She is almost continually accompanied by her own image of herself. . . . And so she comes to consider the *surveyor* and the *surveyed* within her as the two constituent yet always distinct elements of her identity as a woman."[45]

Or, to put the matter as another major twentieth-century woman writer has formulated it, both Millay and Moore were affirming the belief expressed by one of Isak Dinesen's speakers that "the loveliness of woman is created in the eye of man. . . . A goddess would ask her worshipper first of all: 'How am I looking?'"[46] But because, like Dinesen, Millay and Moore were citizens of an age whose women were increasingly conscious of the range of costumes available to them and thus increasingly aware of the radical transformations the very concept "woman" was undergoing, both perceived the dissonance between "surveyor" and "surveyed" far more clearly than their nineteenth-century precursors had. For the freedom with which, say, twentieth-century woman writers like Virginia Woolf and Radclyffe Hall imagined their heroines donning and doffing male as well as female garments implied a newly intense consciousness of the artifice associated with wearing feminine as well as masculine garb, while the cultural disintegration of the supposedly natural womanliness historically attributed to a character like Mrs. Ramsay meant that *being* a woman really meant *seeming* to be a woman.

To be sure, Elizabeth Barrett Browning had been a somewhat theatrical female invalid while Emily Dickinson had melodramatically posed not just as "a woman—white" but also as countless other characters, including a "little girl—old-fashioned, dutiful," a swaggering "Uncle Emily," and an "Empress of Calvary."[47] Yet neither of these poets, caught up in imaginary roles, had lived a life so public that as she ironically distanced herself from the role or roles she adopted she also simultaneously illuminated and interrogated the configurations of female self-fictionalizing. Both Millay and Moore, however, responded to the age-old Western surveyor/surveyed dichotomy that Berger has outlined by employing just the techniques of female "masquerade" described by theorists from Rivière to De Beauvoir and Irigaray, from Goffman to Griffin. More specifically, both appear to have adopted a mode of female female impersonation defined in the 1940s by Karen Horney.

In a study of Horney's "social psychology of women," Marcia Westkott explains that the woman Horney classifies as an "onlooker" simultaneously participates in and detachedly dissects the drama of her own life. "Critically observing herself and others," writes Westkott, "may be the way that a woman is looking at herself being looked at. She becomes the omniscient observer of her own sexualization, the voyeur of the voyeurs of her . . .

body." As such, she complies with male demands for stereotypical femininity even while she rebels against them, "her superiority logged in stinging . . . observation and judgment."[48] Thus, as if sardonically acquiescing in Edmund Wilson's assertion that "merely to be a woman is, as a rule, a career in itself, of which her poetry is bound to be a by-product, but a by-product that may reflect fundamentals," both Millay and Moore quite deliberately wrote "as women." But not in the way, say, Hélène Cixous prescribes, passionately inscribing the milk and blood of the female body. Rather, they wrote as *beings* who impersonated "woman," in order to investigate both "female" costume and the very concept of "the feminine."[49]

Of course, as their reputations suggest, Millay and Moore impersonated and analyzed very different sorts of "feminine" personalities. A comment by the poet-critic Elder Olson implies the degree of consciousness with which both adopted public characters that also infused their verse: "Marianne Moore was very much the spinster schoolteacher. And Edna Millay was the medieval princess, fatigued by too many chivalric romances."[50] Millay generally presented herself as a prototypical femme fatale; Moore depicted herself as a paradigmatic old maid.[51] And the self-consciousness with which each responded to, and reinforced, her own female reification is evident even in their most casual sketches of themselves.

In 1920, for instance, Millay scribbled "a lewd portrait of myself" for Edmund Wilson:

> Hair which she still devoutly trusts is red . . .
> A large mouth,
> Lascivious,
> Asceticized by blasphemies.
> A long throat,
> Which will someday
> Be strangled . . .
> A small body,
> Unexclamatory,
> But which,
> Were it the fashion to wear no clothes,
> Would be as well-dressed
> As any.[52]

Decades later, in the course of an interview, Moore chattily produced a similarly high-spirited self-analysis, though one that suggested a very different female image. For where Millay had wryly depicted herself as seductive, Moore, gazing at a photograph of herself, transformed her physiognomy into a comically spinsterish menagerie:

> I'm good natured but hideous as an old hop toad. I look like a scarecrow. I'm just like a lizard. . . . I look permanently alarmed, like a frog.

I *aspire* to be neat, I try to do my hair with a lot of thought to avoid those explosive sun bursts, but when one hairpin goes in, another seems to come out. . . . A crocodile couldn't look worse. My physiognomy isn't classic at all, it's like a banana-nosed monkey. (She stops for a second thought.) Well, I do seem at least to be awake, don't I?[53]

Dissimilar as these self-portraits are, they suggest what was for early twentieth-century women poets a link between definitions of the feminine associated with artful transfigurations of female anatomy—with, for instance, long trailing dresses or a "purple velvet skirt of papal quality"—and definitions of the literary based on fictions of feminine destiny, a link between the perceived body of the feminine poet and the body of her work. And although such a link was originally forged partly by positive as well as negative male reactions to female aspirations, it ultimately made the achievements of these writers especially vulnerable to attacks by modernist male theorists, for whom good poetry involved what Eliot called an "escape from personality." In fact, as we argued in our analysis of "Tradition and the Female Talent," the critical struggles associated with the emergence of poetic modernism were consistently sexualized: "bad" verse was stereotypically feminine (conservative, effusive, lacking in ambition) while "good" poetry was stereotypically masculine (innovative, cool, ambitious). Or, as William Carlos Williams put it, bad poetry is made "of sugar and spice and everything nice" while good poetry is made "of rats and snails and puppy dog's tails."[54]

As the modernist aesthetic was gradually institutionalized during the first half of the century, therefore, the accomplishments of Millay and Moore came to seem increasingly marginal, so much so that younger women who might have turned to them as heartening examples were often surprisingly ambivalent toward these important precursors. Traditional "poetesses" like Millay had been defined as offensively emotional and anachronistic; ostensible innovators like Moore were seen as precious and recherché. The canon reflected in Pritchard's *Lives*—Hardy, Yeats, Robinson, Frost, Pound, Eliot, Stevens, Crane, Williams—had become for women as well as men *the* canon of the respectably modern.

Sylvia Plath determined not to write "simple lyrics like Millay," and Anne Sexton expressed a "secret fear" of being "a reincarnation" of Millay, while Adrienne Rich censured Moore for being "maidenly, elegant, intellectual, discreet," and even Moore's protégée and sometime disciple Elizabeth Bishop nervously mused on "Marianne's monogram; mother; manners; morals," adding quizzically that "I catch myself murmuring 'Manners and morals; manners *as* morals? or is it morals *as* manners?'"[55] Yet if we reread the apparently disparate but now similarly noncanonical works of Millay and

Moore, bearing in mind these writers' paradoxical deployment of "the feminine" as a response to the feminization-as-trivialization with which contemporary literary culture greeted them, we shall discover that both women were actually part of a poetic tradition whose stylized dramatization of "womanliness" was in a number of significant ways to shape the achievements of such mid-century artists as Sylvia Plath, Anne Sexton, Adrienne Rich, and Elizabeth Bishop.

That Edna St. Vincent Millay was fatigued by chivalric romance even while she acted the part of a femme fatale was plain from the first, notably scornful jingles included in *A Few Figs from Thistles* (1920). These early verses function as wittily feminine manifestos of the New Woman's determination to be free. Celebrating sexual liberation ("My candle burns at both ends; / It will not last the night"), they reveal this self-assertively sexy and consciously feminist young author's determination to revel in modern woman's unprecedented erotic autonomy—

> And if I loved you Wednesday,
>   Well, what is that to you?
> I do not love you Thursday—
>   So much is true.[56]

More, they use what W. H. Auden was later to call "the joke of rhyme" to question (as in "Grown-Up") the bourgeois imperatives of domesticity:

> Was it for this I uttered prayers,
> And sobbed and cursed and kicked the stairs,
> That now, domestic as a plate,
> I should retire at half-past eight?

[138]

Finally, employing transparently "simple" narrative modes, they interrogate the ways women—*other* women—have been put, like plates, on patriarchal shelves. "The Unexplorer," for example, proposes an ironically "ordinary" myth of origins:

> There was a road ran past our house
> Too lovely to explore.
> I asked my mother once—she said
> That if you followed where it led
> It brought you to the milk-man's door.
> (That's why I have not travelled more.)

[138]

Yet this poem's apparently calm and casual conclusion has a Frostian bite: for the speaker, Millay implies, the "road not taken" leads to exactly the same destination as the road taken, since, for most women, all roads lead in the most constraining sense to home.

From a severely modernist perspective such texts might not be considered serious works, yet it can be argued that in their impudent way they begin to make claims about the early twentieth century's battle of the sexes that are directly related to those made by, say, Eliot's "Cousin Nancy" or even by his "Love Song of J. Alfred Prufrock." But if Eliot masked himself as a balding young gentleman poised (as in one of his earliest lyrics) "on the doorstep of the Absolute" in order to question those changes in "unalterable law" which had liberated Miss Nancy Ellicott to dance "all the modern dances" and stride destructively across "the barren new England hills," Millay posed as an apparently conventional femme fatale—at once a cheerful flapper and a weary princess—in order to propose further changes in what had hitherto been "the unalterable law" of romance governing women's lives.[57] Her awareness of the artifice and even duplicity entailed by her pose is dramatized not simply by her public costumes but by the fact that when she wrote much of *A Few Figs from Thistles* she was living a literary double life.

Millay had begun writing magazine sketches under the pseudonym "Nancy Boyd" shortly after she graduated from Vassar and moved to Greenwich Village. According to her sister Norma, she did this work "For a livelihood. . . . But foremost always was her poetry."[58] Yet the insouciant perspective on "femininity" that "Nancy Boyd" expressed in popular pieces published in *Vanity Fair* and other stylish journals reflects on the stance adopted by "Vincent" Millay: in particular, a number of the sketches in "Nancy Boyd"'s *Distressing Dialogues* (1924) and elsewhere focus on the artificial construction of the feminine, on the reification of woman's body, and thus on the alienating disjunction between appearance and reality, mask and self, to which female flesh is subject.

The Arnold Genthe photograph that had been a triumph for "Vincent" Millay, for example, was represented by "Nancy Boyd" as an absurdity. "Why is it that the girls of so many of our best families, the hope of our land, as you might say," inquires Millay's alter ego, "insist upon getting all safety-pinned up into several yards of mosquito-netting and standing about on somebody's golf-links while Arnold Genthe takes their photograph?"[59] At the same time, "Boyd" argues in sketches entitled "Powder, Rouge and Lip-Stick" and "Madame a Tort!" that, given cultural definitions of femininity, a woman who abandoned apparently absurd strategies of self-presentation was as silly as one who did not. When the wife in the first sketch responds to her husband's insistence that she relinquish makeup, she appears in a "magnificent black and silver evening gown, above which rises a rather boyish neck, sun-burned into a V, a . . . sallow face with a pale mouth, a pink and gleaming nose, and no eyebrows whatsoever," explaining that now, "I'm my own sweet, simple, natural, girlish self." At this, however, the man tells her, "You look like the very devil!" (120).

Similarly, in the second piece a sculptor unwillingly subjected to the ministrations of two Parisian beauty experts abandons her work and becomes "a slave to the most exacting of tyrants"—her mirror—when she discovers that it is her fate to be an art object, not an artist. "My skin was smoother and whiter than an infant's," she exults, "My cheeks were a delicate rose, my lips were carmine. . . . My hair was a mass of gentle undulations, and its color—its color was the most wonderful thing I had ever seen" (173). Again, in "Ships and Sealing-Wax," a revisionary dialogue between Alice (of *Wonderland*) and the walrus, the walrus's proposal that people should "stop talking . . . of sex" elicits from Alice a frantic search "in her vanity-bag" for a "powdapuf." For the "subject of sex" requires, according to "Boyd," that this storybook heroine "encrust her countenance with a thin layer of white lead" (273).

Makeup and making up, masking and masquerading: for the comedian that Millay sometimes became, these were crucial elements in the wonderland of femininity. And although the woman who gained her greatest fame as a soulful, presumably sincere (and sometimes apparently sentimental) lyricist seemed to have a very different attitude toward her own sexuality, one of the so-far uncollected "Boyd" pieces makes explicit the poet's sense that "Edna St. Vincent Millay" was just as fictive a construct as any other fainting heroine. In "Diary of an American Art Student in Paris," the supposed journal of a flighty flapper, "Boyd"'s speaker visits a cafe where she is told that "the girl sitting at the next table [is] Edna St. Vincent Millay" and is surprised to find her "eating an enormous plate of sauerkraut and sausages." "Such a shock," she comments. "I have always imagined her so ethereal."[60]

The themes and forms of Millay's verses often suggest that she was hardly less ironic about gender imperatives than "Nancy Boyd" was. Indeed, some of her most "sincerely" impassioned verses implicitly question the conventions of eros, for, as Jane Stanbrough has noted, many of these poems tend to emphasize the ways the female speaker who acquiesces in romance is rendered vulnerable: the ways love (and the male lover) wound, scar, and obliterate woman.[61] And other texts in Millay's *Collected Poems*, including even a number of works in the ostensibly romantic sonnet cycle *Fatal Interview*, radically undercut the aesthetic of heterosexual love, denying or deriding the emotional imperatives that would leave women drowned in desire.

Specifically, from *A Few Figs from Thistles* onward, Millay masquerades as a femme fatale in order to expose the artifice and absurdity of romance while re-creating conventional love scenes as interviews fatal to male rather than female lovers. Seducing her paramours with glittering rhymes and stylishly crafted sonnets, she betrays them in closing stanzas or final couplets that mock and shock. The early "Passer Mortuus Est," for instance, begins with a brisk redaction of a classical theme:

> Death devours all lovely things:
> Lesbia with her sparrow
> Shares the darkness,—presently
> Every bed is narrow.
>
> [75]

But where a dutifully Catullan mistress would have had to be consigned to the mournful earth, a modern woman—a dancing and smoking Cousin Nancy—flirtatiously flips her posturing lover into oblivion:

> After all, my erstwhile dear,
> My no longer cherished,
> Need we say it was not love,
> Just because it perished?[62]

Similarly, some sonnets note the needs of the flesh with amused detachment but redefine romance (and even marriage) as a comic game, so that the female vulnerability occasionally stressed in more "serious" works becomes merely a temporary problem. The speaker of "I shall forget you presently, my dear" admits her wish "that love were longer-lived, / And oaths were not so brittle as they are" but cheerfully reminds her lover that

> . . . so it is, and nature has contrived
> To struggle on without a break thus far,—
> Whether or not we find what we are seeking
> Is idle, biologically speaking.
>
> [571]

The speaker of "I, being born a woman and distressed" concedes that desire may leave her "undone, possessed," but warns her lover, "I find this frenzy insufficient reason / For conversation when we meet again" (601).[63] And although the protagonist of "Oh, oh, you will be sorry for that word!" responds to her husband's insulting "What a big book for such a little head!" by appearing to acquiesce in his patronizing misogyny—"You will not catch me reading any more: / I shall be called a wife to pattern by"—her light-hearted remarks end with a threat:

> And some day when you knock and push the door,
> Some sane day, not too bright and not too stormy,
> I shall be gone, and you may whistle for me.
>
> [591]

To be sure, in *Fatal Interview* the flippancy of these stanzas is translated into a rhetoric of greater hauteur. Yet even here, as she explores the nuances of passion, Millay balances assertions of power against confessions of vulnerability. "Women have loved before as I love now" revises chivalric romance to cast its speaker as a Guinevere or Isolde whose autonomous consciousness is the controlled center, not the hapless calamity, of romantic idyll: "in me alone survive / The unregenerate passions of a day / When treacherous queens, with death upon the tread, / Heedless and wilful, took their knights to bed" (655). "Well, I have lost you; and I lost you fairly" confesses to "some nights of apprehension and hot weeping" but characterizes the speaker as a female Good Soldier, tough and generous: "I might have held you for a summer more, / But at the cost of words I value highly. . . . Should I outlive this anguish . . . I shall have only good to say of you" (676).

Equally to the point, Millay sets into the sequence, at key intervals, sonnets which echo some of her earlier more sardonic poems in their emphasis on both the evanescence of love and the ultimate indifference, or at least the *distance*, of love's artificer, the supposedly impassioned woman poet. At the outset, sonnet II, "This beast that rends me in the sight of all," declares that "this love, this longing, this oblivious thing . . . Will glut, will sicken, will be gone by spring" (631), while sonnet VIII offers a threatening revision of Andrew Marvell's "To His Coy Mistress":

> Yet in an hour to come, disdainful dust,
> You shall be bowed and brought to bed with me.
> While the blood roars, or when the blood is rust
> About a broken engine, this shall be.
> If not today, then later; if not here
> On the green grass, with sighing and delight,
> Then under it, all in good time, my dear,
> We shall be laid together in the night.
>
> [637][64]

Perhaps the most anthologized sonnet in *Fatal Interview*, "Oh, sleep forever in the Latmian cave" (LIII), ties the myth of Endymion and Diana to the poet's bittersweet victories over *her* Endymion. Just as the human hero of the ancient myth is preserved "oblivious" in an eternal slumber by the moon goddess's power, so the nameless man to whom Millay addresses *Fatal Interview* is, as it were, embalmed alive in her poems, while she, like the moon, seems to "wande[r] mad." Yet, as the work's couplet suggests, her apparent madness, like the moon's, is a sign of her divinity: ". . . she wanders mad, being all unfit / For mortal love, *that might not die of it*" (681; emphasis ours). And indeed, sonnet XX ("Think not, nor for a moment let your mind"), the most crucial aesthetic statement in the sequence, hints that this woman as poet-artificer will not just survive love, she will transcend it. Resurrecting the Keatsian trope of the nightingale-artist as a personification of beauty, Millay proclaims her freedom from those pressures of romance which would wound the eroticized heroine:

> Beauty beyond all feathers that have flown
> Is free; you shall not hood her to your wrist,
> Nor sting her eyes, nor have her for your own
> In any fashion; beauty billed and kissed
> Is not your turtle; tread her like a dove—
> She loves you not; she never heard of love.
>
> [649]

"I too beneath your moon, almighty Sex"—a sonnet from the later *Huntsman, What Quarry?*—reappraises a notably modern love life with calm self-scrutiny and summarizes a key assumption that underlies even the most theatrical sufferings in *Fatal Interview.* "Such as I am," the speaker boasts, ". . . I have brought / To what it is, this tower" of art, and "*it is my own*" (688; emphasis ours). Throughout these frequently antiromantic poems about romance, Millay deliberately impersonates not so much a fatally afflicted heroine as a femme fatale whose adventures are energized by, and issue in, proud independence. But unlike the male-created femme fatale who haunted the Victorian imagination—say, Haggard's Ayesha—she is ironic about her triumphs: as we shall see, the masquerade of poetic form, as well as the double consciousness of "Vincent"/"Nancy Boyd," facilitates a distancing of desire. And unlike the femme fatale created by turn-of-the-century women (Olive Schreiner's Lyndall or even Edith Wharton's Lily Bart) Millay as poetic speaker surmounts the plots that would wound her.[65] For her, it is never fatal to be a femme fatale because she can always turn in detachment from entanglement: she can always deploy the vengeful arts of *linguistic* "making up."

A number of Millay's narrative and dramatic poems explore further aspects of the sexual war of the words in which even as romantic sonneteer she was so frequently engaged. The angry mourner who speaks the early "Keen," for instance, celebrates "Death, that took my love / And buried him in the sea, / Where never a lie nor a bitter word / Will out of his mouth at me" (171), while "The Concert" depicts a woman who insists on going to a concert alone because her lover "would put yourself / Between me and song" (186). Later, "Rendezvous" critiques the conventions of a stylized affair between an older woman and a younger man in "Nancy Boyd"'s tone of weary sarcasm: "I wish you had not scrubbed—with pumice, I suppose— / The tobacco stains from your beautiful fingers. And I wish I did not feel like your mother" (341). "Armenonville," describing a similar situation, depicts the woman's alienated consciousness, inexorably "my own," disrupting the ritual dialogue of lovers:

There swam across the lake, as I looked aside, avoiding
Your eyes for a moment, there swam from under the pink and red
   begonias
A small creature; I thought it was a water-rat . . .
. . . .
. . . and when suddenly I turned again to you,
Aware that you were speaking, and perhaps had been speaking for some
   time,
I was aghast at my absence, for truly I did not know
Whether you had been asking or telling.

[476]

More dramatically, a late poem "spoken" by Sappho (a figure often in Millay's mind) repudiates the legend that the poet died for love of the ferryman Phaon, declaring unapologetically that "I die, that the sweet tongue of bound Aeolia never from her throat be torn, that Mitylene may be free / To sing, long after me," and adding, "Phaon, I shall not die for you again. / There are few poets. And my own child tells me there are other men" (452).

   Early and late, Millay's preoccupation with the Bluebeard story illuminates the imperatives that drive many ostensibly romantic lyrics as well as openly antiromantic poems. In 1922, in comic prose signed not by "Nancy Boyd" but by "Edna St. Vincent Millay," she produced "The Key," a revisionary satire in which Bluebeard's seventh wife, an aspiring writer, simply has no interest in unlocking the door to her husband's forbidden room. Instead, forgetting the key that obsesses the arrogant king she married, the wife broods over "a folio of white paper" she longs to fill. The egotistical Bluebeard murders her because, in her self-absorption, her mind has become "a secret thing to him" and because "It May Annoy Blue-Beard More to Neglect the Secret Chamber than to Open It."[66]

   An early sonnet, "Bluebeard," likewise expresses contempt for the fairytale king but from a different angle: the "Secret Chamber" of the man's mind is merely "an empty room, cobwebbed and comfortless," which he pathetically "kept / Unto myself, lest any know me quite" (566). And in a posthumously published verse "Journal" Millay offers yet another perspective on the old plot:

Speaking of Bluebeard, might it be
The story is a pleasantry?—
What lovely fun! There in the vault
The obedient wives,—being those at fault—

While helped to half the kingdom she
Who had the sense to use the key!
[509]

Different as they are, all these versions plainly struggle with the problems
posed by male power and female rebelliousness. Is wifely refusal the solution? Womanly scorn? Or feminine usurpation of masculine authority?

The feminism implicit in Millay's meditations on Bluebeard as well as in
her identification with Sappho comes to the surface just as clearly in her
verses about and for women as it does in her dissections of the ideology of
romance. In fact, she produced a range of poems that implicitly support a
point Simone de Beauvoir made about the "backstage" world of the women
we are defining as female female impersonators:

> Confronting man woman is always play-acting; she lies when she
> makes believe that she accepts her status as the inessential other, she
> lies when she presents to him an imaginary personage through mimi-
> cry, costumery, studied phrases. . . . With other women, a woman is
> behind the scenes; she is polishing her equipment, but not in battle;
> she is getting her costume together, preparing her make-up, laying out
> her tactics; she is lingering in dressing-gown and slippers in the wings
> before making her entrance on the stage; she likes this warm, easy,
> relaxed, atmosphere. . . . For some women, this warm and frivolous
> intimacy is dearer than the serious pomp of relations with men.[67]

The Millay poems that express this intimacy with other women include
her elegies for her friends Dorothy Coleman ("Memorial to D. C.") and
Elinor Wylie, as well as the generalized "To a Young Girl" and the more
specifically personal "The courage that my mother had." "To a Young Girl,"
especially, implies a "backstage" female bonding in "impression-management"
that is intimately loving even while its strategy may seem as cynical as those
de Beauvoir describes. Beginning with a rhetorical question—"Shall I de-
spise you that your colourless tears / Made rainbows in your lashes, and you
forgot to weep?"—the speaker goes on to prescribe the beauty made up, as it
were, by at least an impersonation of feminine feeling:

> I only fear lest, being by nature sunny,
> By and by you will weep no more at all,
> And fall asleep in the light, having lost with the tears
> The colour in the lashes that comes as the tears fall.

> I would not have you darken your lids with weeping,
> Beautiful eyes, but I would have you weep enough
> To wet the fingers of the hand held over the eye-lids,
> And stain a little the light frock's delicate stuff.
>   [238][68]

More openly polemical, Millay's rousing feminist sonnet "To Inez Milhol-land" begins as a paean to the glamorous, Vassar-educated suffragist who was the first wife of Eugen Boissevain, later Millay's own husband. "Read in Washington, November eighteenth, 1923 at the unveiling of a statue of three leaders in the cause of Equal Rights for Women," this piece plays elegantly with rhetorical negations ("Upon this marble bust that is not I / Lay the round, formal wreath that is not fame") to move toward a sisterly affirmation expressed through an ironic prescription of what should *not* be done: "Take up the song; forget the epitaph" (627). At the same time, through the odd tension between the poem's title ("*To* Inez Milholland") and its use of the first person pronoun, this work emphasizes both the political commonality of Milholland/Millay and the public reification they share. For is "this marble bust that is not I" (not) Inez or (not) Edna? And to which of these feminist female impersonators accrues the problematic "round, formal wreath that is not fame"?

"To Inez Milholland" is an interestingly complex polemic, and many of the poet's other feminist verses are equally moving, but Millay's most notable analysis of the courage of women and the authority of female experience is offered in her finest sonnet sequence, "Sonnets from an Ungrafted Tree." This beautifully poised, Frostian narrative, included in the early, prize-winning volume *The Harp Weaver* (1923), is also in a sense shaped through negation, though very differently from "To Inez Milholland." Located in a grim New England that is as reminiscent of the bleak northwest Massa-chusetts of Edith Wharton's *Ethan Frome* (1911) or the forbidding rural landscape of Susan Glaspell's *Trifles* (1916) as it is of Frost's New Hampshire, "An Ungrafted Tree" explores the privations of a failed marriage with the same subtlety and intensity that mark Wharton's and Glaspell's precursor texts.

Unlike them, however, Millay's sequence tells the story of marital disin-tegration entirely from the point of view of a disillusioned childless woman ("an ungrafted tree") who has left her husband but, hearing that he is ill, has come "back into his house again / And watched beside his bed until he died, / Loving him not at all." And where in "To Inez Milholland" Millay's celebration of what in *Fatal Interview* she calls "the wind" of womanly "en-durance" is only implicit, here she documents her argument with domestic details symbolic of both the daily drudgery against which her protagonist's spirit must contend and the determination to survive through which this woman transforms housewifery into heroism.

Sawdust and laundry, jelly jars and kettles—these are the paraphernalia of the world that encloses the New England wife, but in "An Ungrafted Tree" such apparently negligible things become, as William Carlos Williams would have them do, intractable ideas. More, just as the setting of the narra-tive signals the poet's affiliation with Wharton and Glaspell, her theatrical deployment of "trifles" throughout the sequence expresses what may well have been a conscious allegiance to the theme and plot of Glaspell's one-acter, a work that the young writer-actress would have known well through her own participation in the Provincetown Players.[69] Whether she was directly influenced by the playwright, Millay tells the story of "An Ungrafted Tree" as Glaspell does *Trifles:* not through an accumulation of melodramatic public events but through the accretion of "small" domestic incidents, and thus supports Glaspell's argument that the codes male-defined law supposes to be significant may be less crucial than the language of "trivia" which a feminine hermeneutics can decipher.

"I guess they're not very dangerous things the ladies have picked out," opines the county attorney at the end of *Trifles* as the sheriff's wife and the neighboring farm wife secretly gather up the "little things"—a dead bird, a badly stitched quilt—that might convict their neighbor of homicide.[70] Yet although Millay's theme is not murder but mourning, for her, as for Glaspell, such objects illuminate a state of mind close to madness. Lighting a fire for comfort, the protagonist of "An Ungrafted Tree" sees beyond it to further desolation: "A pack of hounds, the flame swept up the flue!— / And the blue night stood flattened against the window, staring through" (609). Hearing "The heavy oilskins of the grocer's man / Slapping against his legs" and fearing human contact, she hides "in the cellar way," where

> She saw the narrow wooden stairway still
> Plunging into the earth, and the thin salt
> Crusting the crocks; until she knew him far,
> So stood, with listening eyes upon the empty doughnut jar.
>   [610]

Later, gazing into the backyard where snow is melting, the trapped woman sees "the brown grass exposed again, / And clothes-pins, and an apron" that had "long ago . . . Blown down . . . To lie till April thawed it back to sight," and thinks, as she confronts Eliot's cruelest month, "That here was spring, and the whole year to be lived through once more" (616). Fearing her husband will "die at night," she paces her house and notices in the morning when she makes tea that "*She had kept that kettle boiling all night long, for company*" (619). And although the verses in which Millay recounts these apparently trifling incidents are comparatively conventional quasi-Shakespearean sonnets (with an *ababcdcdeffegg* rhyme scheme), the poet emphasizes the weariness of such "trivial" detail through her principal swerve from the standard form: all final couplets end with a seven-beat line whose extra length suggests the length of the days and nights through which the protagonist must drag herself.

Besides dramatizing the tedium of this woman's life, Millay examines the origins of wifely bitterness, sardonically revealing that, as a high-spirited young girl, her heroine had struck up a flirtation with the boy who was to become her husband because "he flashed a mirror in her eyes at school / By which he was distinguished" (614) and then recounting how youthful eroticism had forced the young woman into a bad marriage. But as the writer's earlier critiques of female immobilization had already implied, passive yielding to social expectations ultimately leads to total imprisonment: lying in bed, the woman dreams of "the magic World, where cities stood on end . . . Remote from where she lay—and yet—between, / Save for something asleep beside her, only the window screen" (617). No more than a "something asleep," an inert object, the husband nevertheless constitutes a wall between his wife and the vitality of the outside world.

Significantly, only when the husband dies does he become a figure of tragic dignity, even an icon of new life for his widow. The concluding sonnet, one of the finest in the sequence, examines the inscrutability of death in a manner reminiscent of such great modernist meditations as Rainer Maria Rilke's poem "Leichen-Wäsche" ("Corpse-Washing"), D. H. Lawrence's short story "Odour of Chrysanthemums," or Robert Frost's verse narrative "Home Burial": "Gazing upon him now, severe and dead," the New England wife is

> . . . as one who enters, sly, and proud,
> To where her husband speaks before a crowd,
> And sees a man she never saw before—
> The man who eats his victuals at her side,
> Small, and absurd, and hers: for once, not hers, unclassified.
>
> [622]

But Millay's perspective on this scene is notably different from the visions offered by her male contemporaries.

Rilke, for instance, emphasizes the corpse washers' recognition of the dead man's authority: "Und einer ohne Namen / Lag bar und reinlich da und gab Gesetze" ("And one without a name / Lay bare and cleanly there and set down laws"). The widow in Lawrence's story feels "fear and shame" at the otherness of her dead husband: "Life with its smoky burning gone from him, had left him apart and utterly alien to her." And the grieving young mother in Frost's poem stresses the bleakness of every death: "The nearest friends can go / With anyone to death, comes so far short / They might as well not try to go at all. . . . from the time when one is sick to death, / One is alone, and he dies more alone."[71] Millay's protagonist, however, feels joy that this new stranger is "not hers, unclassified," and by implication exults that she is no longer *his* and classified. This once-troublesome lover can now become an empowering figure for the woman who gazes on his body precisely because he is *not*, he is "no man."[72] As in "The Buck in the Snow," the title poem of Millay's next volume, the death of the male of the species seems to leave his mate oddly free and curiously vital: when death "bring[s] to his knees, bring[s] to his antlers / The buck in the snow," the poet suddenly imagines "Life, looking out attentive from the eyes of the doe" (228).

As if to clarify the unnerving implications of these poems, Millay's friend Elinor Wylie gave a prominent place in her last volume, *Angels and Earthly Creatures* (1929), to an ironic "epistle" entitled "The Broken Man," a poem whose ambivalent deconstruction of male glamour summarizes a project to which both these female female impersonators seem to have been intermittently dedicated. At the age of seven and a half, the speaker explains, she fell in love with the tiny, perfect figurine of a man, whose "eyes were gold; his hair a sable silvered." But after her father gave her the figurine, "Poor love, compounded out of clay and sand, / How often were you broken in my hand!" Finally, her father had the figure mended with an iron pin so that, in retrospect, the poet sees that this damaged object was "the image of my lord . . . The broken man, who broke my heart in half."[73] At the least, the thematics of such verse would seem to support Louise Bogan's comment that "modern female verse tends to vilify and belittle the masculine charms, much of it being written just after or just before some disillusion handed to the woman by the man."[74]

But if Wylie belittles her "poor love," she seems to feel guilty, pointedly struggling to make the worst of what she may secretly consider a good bargain. For Millay, however, the recurrent trope of the broken man frequently leads to less equivocal enactments of female triumph because, more consciously than Wylie, this artist links male defeat to the destructiveness of masculinist history and the concealed misogyny of chivalric romance. *Aria da Capo*, the play whose production so vexed William Carlos Williams, is here a central text. Ostensibly a light-hearted comedy of manners in the self-reflexive mode of Pirandello, Millay's most popular drama and the one she regarded as her best counterpoints the romantic frivolity of a stylized Pierrot and Columbine with the pastoral calamity that overtakes two shepherds, Corydon and Thyrsis, when they are forced by Cothurnus, the "Masque of Tragedy," to act out a miniature two-man war and kill each other.[75]

Written at the end of World War I, the play offers a fatigued commentary on male battles, with Columbine complaining, "What a mess / This set is in! . . . / [Cothurnus] might at least have left the scene / The way he found it."[76] At the same time, the merry harlequinade which is rapidly resumed by the commedia dell'arte lovers can be taken as a pacifist critique of the civilian tendency to want to return to the superficiality of "life as usual." But the work's title (Aria *da Capo*), which emphasizes the repetition compulsion that marks cycles of militarism, and Columbine's bemused detachment ("How curious to strangle him like that, / With colored paper ribbons" [43]) suggest that Millay feels something very like the feminist scorn for the problems of

Cothurnus's minions that Virginia Woolf was to express a decade and a half later in *Three Guineas*.

A less successful play, *The Lamp and the Bell* (1926), brings to the surface the specifically female, if not explicitly feminist, imperatives of *Aria da Capo*. Recounting the overtly sisterly but covertly lesbian love of Beatrice ("Rose Red") and Bianca ("Snow White"), this rather hectic historical drama culminates in a romantic triangle in which the two women are separated by their mutual passion for a handsome prince named Mario.[77] But after Bianca— the "good" Snow White—marries the charming ruler, Beatrice, now a queen who carries everywhere a symbolically phallic sword of her own, manages through a series of mischances to kill him. Is it odd that his death brings the two women together again?[78] As schoolgirls, Beatrice and Bianca had expressed their love in terms that, repudiating heterosexual romance and replacing the male-female bond with sisterly love and loyalty, might have predicted Mario's ultimately "broken" manhood:

> BIANCA: You are a burning lamp to me, a flame
> The wind cannot blow out, and I shall hold you
> High in my hand against whatever darkness.
> BEATRICE: You are to me a silver bell in a tower.
> And when it rings I know I am near home.
>
> [95]

But despite celebrations of female survival or intimacy, Millay could not deceive herself about the history in whose context she as impertinent femme fatale, her New England woman as durable widow, and Bianca and Beatrice as sisterly lovers achieved their moments of victory. "The Road to the Past," she wrote in a poem of the thirties, runs "past many towns, past hell seen plainly" (353). For as Millay grew older, the masculine destructiveness that she had light-heartedly satirized in *Aria da Capo* came to seem increasingly oppressive. In the middle twenties she was deeply involved in attempts to save Sacco and Vanzetti from execution; the thirties found her horrified by the Spanish Civil War and the encroaching shadows of fascism in Europe; during the forties she dedicated her talent to propagandizing for the Allies during World War II, lamenting such Nazi atrocities as "the murder of Lidice." Thus the strangely empowering image of the dead man with which "Sonnets from an Ungrafted Tree" concludes was supplanted five years later by a more frightening figure of death as a lover and of a lover as deadly, a figure that the poem "Wine from These Grapes" specifically politicizes.

"Wine from These Grapes" appeared a few pages away from the title poem of *The Buck in the Snow* (1928) and provided Millay with the title for a subsequent collection. The poem is clearly informed by her rage at the case of Sacco and Vanzetti (about which she also wrote "Justice Denied in Massachusetts"), and its central image draws upon Julia Ward Howe's "He is trampling out the vintage where the grapes of wrath are stored."[79] But its conclusion is far more sinister than the apocalyptic optimism that marks "The Battle Hymn of the Republic." Beginning "Wine from these grapes I shall be treading surely / Morning and noon and night until I die," the poem moves to a curiously morbid climax:

> Stained with these grapes I shall lie down to die. . . .
> Death, fumbling to uncover
> My body in his bed,
> Shall know
> There has been one
> Before him.
>
> [234]

Rewriting the last sonnet of "An Ungrafted Tree" so that the gazing woman herself becomes no more than a dead creature, these lines evoke the old trope of death as what Emily Dickinson once called "the supple suitor."[80] But then, disturbingly, the speaker implies that before it is chilled by the embrace of death, her body will already have been contaminated by *another* love—"one / Before him"—whose clasp is even more horrifying. Who is this lover more terrible than death? The poet does not specify, but the context in which she sets "Wine from These Grapes" implies that he is one among "Those without Pity" who denied justice in Massachusetts and who have deformed history by relegating the innocent to "the belly of Death."[81]

From the mid-twenties on, Millay alternated between vengeful imaginings of this deadly lover's death and sometimes sardonic, sometimes savage diatribes against his ubiquitous powers, diatribes which become increasingly fierce as the poet is forced to acknowledge their futility. The bitter sonnet sequence "Epitaph for the Race of Man" in *Wine from These Grapes* predicts a time when "Man and his engines [will] be no longer here. / High on his naked rock the mountain sheep / Will stand alone against the final sky" (701). Grimly tracing the progress of history, Millay records the rise and fall of (male) arrogance:

> Safe in their linen and their spices lie
> The kings of Egypt; even as long ago
> Under these constellations, with long eye
> And scented limbs they slept, and feared no foe.
> Their will was law; their will was not to die:
> And so they had their way; or nearly so.
>
> [706]

And a curse-poem in the same volume, "Apostrophe to Man," subtitled "on reflecting that the world is ready to go to war again," frankly articulates the message implicit in the sonnets: "Detestable race, continue to expunge your-self, die out. . . . Put death on the market; / Breed, crowd, encroach, ex-pand, expunge yourself, die out, / *Homo* called *sapiens*" (302).

That such curses were mere fantasies is conceded in a series of yet more helplessly angry poems. "Huntsman, What Quarry?" (1939) records a dia-logue between an obsessive fox-hunter and a girl who offers herself to him along with "supper and a soft bed" if he will "let the fox run free": although "he smell[s] the sweet smoke" and "look[s] the lady over," the hunter cannot bring himself to renounce the joys of killing (333–34).[82] And "An Ancient Gesture" in Millay's posthumously published *Mine the Harvest* (1954) ques-tions the epic posturings of an archetypal hero, setting them against the gestural primacy of an epic heroine to suggest that the only redemption of a male-dominated culture might come from the suffering—and survival—of women like the protagonist of "An Ungrafted Tree."

> And I thought, as I wiped my eyes on the corner of my apron:
> This is an ancient gesture, authentic, antique,
> In the very best tradition, classic, Greek;
> Ulysses did this too.
> But only as a gesture,—a gesture which implied
> To the assembled throng that he was much too moved to speak.
> He learned it from Penelope . . .
> Penelope, who really cried.
>
> [501; ellipses Millay's]

Yet even as this verse subverts the political glamour of the itinerant Ul-ysses, its ultimate irony is precisely Penelope's stationary helplessness as well as the helplessness of the poem's speaker—the uncontrollable weeping of both women. To be sure, both express their pain with conscious theatricality: Penelope in effect founds a female "tradition" of gestures which Ulysses appropriates and Millay inherits. But the pain itself is inescapable. In fact, the darkening of Millay's vision in this period suggests that the once insou-ciant flapper / femme fatale has had to accept the fatalities of a society in which, just as woman cannot say to man, "expunge yourself, die out," she cannot claim that someday, "I shall be gone and you may whistle for me."

Poignantly, Millay's sense of powerlessness has gradually been associated with an internalization of the guilt earlier projected onto Cothurnus and his shepherds, onto some of her lovers, and onto the "cruel of heart" who dominate history. The speaker of "The Plaid Dress," for instance, re-proaches herself with the "violent plaid / Of purple angers and red shames" that characterize her metaphorical clothing, begging, "Strong sun, that bleach / The curtains of my room, can you not render / Colourless this dress I wear?" (348). By implication, the woman who cannot change the world must be maddened and demoralized by the futility of her own gestures, by angers and shames, by "the yellow stripe / Of thin but valid treacheries . . . The recurring checker of the serious breach of taste."

Even worse, as immobilized as Penelope in her female role, this woman— surely akin to the aging, disillusioned poet—realizes that she is now trapped in the costume she once elected, that like the apparently liberating frock in Parker's "The Satin Dress," her gown has become "a fine shroud." Some fifteen years before she wrote "The Plaid Dress," Millay had depicted the protagonist of "An Ungrafted Tree" confronting a winter clothesline laden with "garments, board-stiff, that galloped on the blast" and then discovering a lost apron, emblem of an inexorably recurring female role (616). More radically, however, the Millay of "The Plaid Dress" recognizes that she has in a sense *become* her dress:

> No more uncoloured than unmade,
> I fear, can be this garment that I may not doff;
> Confession does not strip it off,
> To send me homeward eased and bare;
>
> All through the formal, unoffending evening, under the clean
> Bright hair,
> Lining the subtle gown . . . it is not seen,
> But it is there.

[348; ellipses Millay's]

What exacerbated Millay's sense of reification was, paradoxically, one of her most heartfelt endeavors: her propagandizing for the Allied cause during World War II, specifically with *The Murder of Lidice,* written for the Writers' War Board, and the hortatory collection *Make Bright the Arrows* (1940). Even as Millay struggled with these projects she feared that she was producing "not poems [but] posters" and astutely analyzed the effect her aesthetically problematic publications might have on her already fading public image. That she was not wrong, moreover, is made clear, as Susan Schweik has observed, by the snide reception of these writings in middlebrow as well as highbrow circles.[83] As Schweik also notes, Millay tried to attribute to these reviews her "very handsome . . . all but life-size . . . nervous breakdown" at the war's end, confessing to Edmund Wilson that "there is nothing on this earth which can so much get on the nerves of a good poet, as the writing of bad poetry. . . . Finally I cracked up under it."[84]

But in fact Wilson himself, along with Millay's biographers, reports that this artist had "cracked" repeatedly over the years—and arguably her breakdowns were consequences not just of the tension between public (speaker) and private (poet) fostered by wartime propagandizing but also of the periodic and quite literal breaking down of the machinery that kept public (poet) and private (self) in some sort of precarious equilibrium. Certainly the pain implicit in "The Plaid Dress" suggests as much. At the same time, the notably feminine image of the *dress* through which Millay chooses to represent both her anxious self-analysis and her despairing sense of reification underlines yet again her often theatrical, sometimes exultant, sometimes ironic self-presentation as distinctively "feminine." If Penelope is known by her tear-stained apron and the speaker of "The Plaid Dress" by her garment of guilt, so Millay's earlier women characters are marked by the "long dresses, trailing ones" in which the poet herself gave readings and these characters are marked as well by the domestic objects that surround them: candles and kettles which supplement and complement their wardrobes.

Two late verses, "Thanksgiving Dinner" and "The Fitting," indicate both the advantages and the disadvantages the poet experienced in metaphorizing stereotypical items of femininity. In "Thanksgiving Dinner" she imagines a woman walking smilingly through the "broken garden," because she knows she can live, and feed her "love"—both her lover and her love for him—on "steaming, stolid winter roots" (330). And in "The Fitting," she describes a session with a dressmaker in which the irony made possible through what we have been calling "female female impersonation" is emphasized by the distance between the speaker's thoughts of her lover and the activity of seamstresses who are "turning me, touching my secret body, doing what they were paid to do" (343). If one occupies a "female" position with lucid detachment, these verses hint, one is free to celebrate the real values such as nurturance or endurance that the construction of femininity facilitates, even while, paradoxically, one comes to perceive the artifice of what are now called sex roles.

More darkly, however, "Thanksgiving Dinner" depicts the poet's garden as broken, frozen, static so that she must have recourse to "the woody fibres of the overgrown / Kohl-rabi . . . the spongy radish coarse and hot." And as the garden stiffens, dividing itself into underground roots that only survive in darkness and a rigid wintry facade seen by the world, so the poet is definitively split.

Similarly, while obliquely celebrating "my secret body," "The Fitting" dramatizes—and mourns—this split. The labor of the oppressed dress-maker, a "hard-working woman with a familiar and unknown face," illustrates both the difficulty and the pain associated with the constructed image through which the female female impersonator must speak (she "set her cold shears against me,—snip-snip; / Her knuckles gouged my breast"); and the poet's response documents the self-exile experienced by such an impersonator ("My drooped eyes lifted to my guarded eyes in the glass, and glanced away as from someone they had never met" [342]).

Had this poet ever allowed herself to meet a self other than the woman so laboriously fitted into a public costume? Many of her letters home—littered to the end with "cute" slang—imply that the girlish mask of the flapper

"Nancy Boyd" had inexorably invaded the body of the artist who asked only that her life be her "own." And that the femininity of this mask was itself problematic is suggested by what may well be the etymology of the name "Nancy Boyd": *Nancy boy* was in this period a colloquialism for "an effeminate man" or a "catamite," a derivation which underscores the artifice of an arduous masquerade.[85]

Finally, then, Ransom was not altogether mistaken in assuming that "this charming lady found it difficult . . . to come of age."[86] Artistically, the poet struggled persistently toward a maturity in which she could use the artifice of femininity without being used by it. Nevertheless, a description of Millay's early surroundings offered by Edmund Wilson may have been even more revealing than that astute observer realized. Above Millay's bed, recalled her onetime suitor, "was a modern painting, all fractured geometrical planes that vaguely delineated a female figure, which the Millay girls called *Directions for Using the Empress*. . . . The picture [according to Norma Millay] was 'an abstract portrait of Vincent's mechanical dressform, the Empress,' which gained and lost weight by an intricate system of adjusting nuts and screws."[87] Like her early nom de plume, Millay's youthful preoccupation with her mechanical dress form may have been prophetic. And perhaps Wilson's own comment on the dress form was equally telling: "When we later learned that the inventor of the Empress had killed himself, we understood it perfectly."

———

Millay's posthumous *Mine the Harvest* includes a poem that hints at ways in which what Marianne Moore called "efforts of affection" link McAlmon's Vera St. Vitus, the "It girl" of the antimodernists, with his Martha Wullus, the unlikely contemporary who was the "It girl" of the intellectuals. Millay's "The Strawberry Shrub" offers a close analysis of a plant that is "old-fashioned, quaint as quinces":

> More brown than red the bloom—it is a dense colour;
> Colour of dried blood; colour of the key of F.
> . . . .
> . . . But no, as I said, it is browner than red; it is duller
> Than history, tinnier than algebra . . .

[455]

The poem praises this emblematic bush for just the apparently ladylike virtues of modesty and humility that the self-effacing Moore celebrated throughout her career: the strawberry shrub hides "its fragrance . . . it is not exuberant. / You must bruise it a bit: it does not exude; it yields."

It may be that Millay had been reading Moore when she wrote these lines, but the question of direct influence is not directly relevant. For as the precise observations of, say, "An Ungrafted Tree" suggest, the poet who wrote "The Strawberry Shrub" had long been interested in "that detail outside ourselves that brings us to ourselves," to borrow a phrase of Adrienne Rich's.[88] What she might well have intuited in the work of her apparent aesthetic opposite was a similar sense that such details, humble and "duller / Than history," incarnate the durability and the deliberate differentness of the quality historically labeled "the feminine."

Readers from Randall Jarrell to Bonnie Costello have noted the ways in which, throughout her career, Moore's observations of the natural world tended to emphasize the paradoxical strength of supposed weakness, the power of supposed dullness. The poem "Nevertheless," from the 1944 volume of that title, begins by praising "a strawberry / that's had a struggle" and works toward an ironic maxim: "The weak overcomes its / menace, the strong over- / comes itself."[89] Perhaps more famously, the later "His Shield" meditates on how the legendary Presbyter John, like the mythical salamander whose skin he wears, triumphs by being as willing as Millay's strawberry bush to "yield." Without greed and immune to flattery, this emblematic figure lives in "unpompous gusto" so "he can withstand // fire and won't drown." Beyond the envious will to self-aggrandizement that constructs history, he understands "the power of relinquishing / what one would keep; that is freedom" (144).

It is a freedom, however, that Moore at least subtextually associates with a female alienation from—or, to put the case more strongly, a female refusal to be complicitous in—history. Further, we would argue, it is a freedom this poet learned to imagine through her self-creation as a "spinster" outsider, that is, through a process of female female impersonation which paralleled (although it differed from) Millay's.

Moore's initial construction of herself as what Elder Olson called a "spinster schoolteacher" involved—as many critics have pointed out—her whimsical accumulation of a menagerie of animal masks, many of which recurred in the comic similes she employed when she analyzed a photograph of herself in the interview quoted earlier: "an old hop toad," "a crocodile," "a banana-nosed monkey." Where the young Millay attempted to turn the arbitrariness of sex roles to her own account by seeking long trailing dresses in which to impersonate a femme fatale, the young Moore seems at times to have tried to transcend sex roles altogether by repudiating her humanity itself.

Yet Moore was as conscious as Millay of costume, of artifice—aware that, as she put it in "His Shield," "everything is battle-dressed" (144), including woman. "Those Various Scalpels," which Margaret Holley has called the poet's "Portrait of a Lady," is here a central text, for in this work Moore acknowledges and analyzes her ambivalence toward just the extravagantly feminine strategies of self-presentation that Millay adopted.[90] Like André

Breton's "My Wife," "Those Various Scalpels" updates the Renaissance
mode of the *blazon* to anatomize the sumptuous appearance of a woman who
has armored herself in the weapons of seduction:

> . . . your hair, the tails of two
> fighting-cocks head to head in stone—like sculptured scimitars re-
> peating the curve of your ears in reverse order: your eyes,
> > flowers of ice and snow
>
> sown by tearing winds on the cordage of disabled ships; your
> > raised hand,
> an ambiguous signature: your cheeks, those rosettes
> of blood on the stone floors of French chateaux,
> with regard to which the guides are so affirmative—your other
> > hand,
>
> a bundle of lances all alike, partly hid by emeralds from Persia
> and the fractional magnificence of Florentine
> goldwork. . . .
>
> > . . . your dress, a
> > magnificent square
> cathedral tower of uniform
> and at the same time diverse appearance—a
> species of vertical vineyard rustling in the storm
> of conventional opinion. . . .
>
> > [51][91]

With its courtly rhetoric, this piece enacts its speaker's quasi-erotic enthrallment not merely to the lady it describes but more particularly to the brilliant
artifice of her costume—her dress, for instance, both culturally monumen-
tal ("a / magnificent square / cathedral tower") and defiantly evocative of
nature ("a / species of vertical vineyard rustling in the storm / of conventional opinion").

But by the end of the poem, Moore has fastidiously withdrawn from the
aggressive surface of her female subject's stylized sexuality. Are the items of
appearance she has listed "weapons or scalpels?" she wonders, adding,

> > Whetted to brilliance
>
> by the hard majesty of that sophistication which is superior to
> > opportunity,
> these things are rich instruments with which to experiment.
> But why dissect destiny with instruments
> > more highly specialized than components of destiny itself?

Lurking behind Moore's final question—behind her withdrawal from the conflicted desire evoked by the splendidly attired image of woman—is a protest against the biological essentialism formulated in Freud's notorious claim that "anatomy is destiny." For Moore implies that the destiny dictated by anatomy is inexorable enough without the intensification (of "femininity") produced by the woman's self-dissection into a catalogue of seductive body parts or the poet's dissection of her into a catalogue of stereotypical tropes ("your eyes, / flowers of ice and snow," "your cheeks, those rosettes / of blood"). In this regard, a small revision Moore made between the *Selected Poems* (1935) and the *Complete Poems* (1967) is telling. In *Selected Poems* "Those Various Scalpels" concludes "Why dissect destiny with instruments which / are more highly specialized than the *tissues* of destiny / itself?" (74; emphasis ours). The substitution of the more generalized (and weaker) *components* for the original *tissues*—with its ambiguous reference to biological tissues and tissues as textiles—underscores this woman artist's repudiation of the relation between sexuality and sex role, anatomy and destiny.

Tailored and neat though she was in "real life," then, Moore claims in poems that the garments of her spirit must be in some sense outlandish: "Pig-fur won't do, I'll wrap / myself in salamander-skin like Presbyter John," she declares in "His Shield" (144), but even earlier she had been drawn to the "invisible or visible" plumet basilisk, whose amiable chameleon acrobatics proved that "bird-reptile social life is pleasing" (21); to the elephant with "fog-colored skin" (40); and to giraffes whose "long lemon-yellow bodies" are "sown with trapezoids of blue" (64). A librarian of zoology, she appears, figuratively speaking, to have kept file cards on all the animal traits she could incorporate into the "outfit" with which she met the world, as if she yearned to become an imaginary toad in the real garden of her life.

That Moore was concerned with the fashions required by such self-fashioning, however, is made plain not only by the *blazons* of the early "Those Various Scalpels" and her later pontifications on miniskirts and pantsuits to *Vogue* and the *New York Times* but also by a youthful comment on clothing. In her late twenties, planning a trip to New York where she hoped to meet other young writers, she confided a crucial travel preparation to her brother which suggests she might well have agreed with Millay's assumption (formulated in so many of *her* letters home) that clothes make the woman (poet): "I have an airdale coat and I'm goan to New York on Monday. . . . It's a simple coat, black with blue and green stripes, . . . it has leather buttons about the size of a buckeye. . . . It is finished with catch-stitching inside and the finest quality of black satin."[92]

But where Millay's "professional" clothing choices were usually, like the personae in her poems, both stereotypically and sardonically feminine, Moore refused the conventional attire of romance in life as in art. Her striped airdale coat with "buttons about the size of a buckeye" adumbrates not only the coats, hides, pelts, and skins sported by the protagonists of her poetic bestiary but also the dashing tricorne hat and great cape which were eventually to become the signatures of her spinsterish eccentricity. Yet in its modesty ("a simple coat") and its refusal to flaunt extravagance ("finished with catch-stitching *inside* and the finest quality of black satin"), the young Moore's chosen "professional" costume evokes precisely the humility that she saw as Presbyter John's shield, even the yielding dullness she associated with his freedom. "Become dinosaur- / skulled, quilled, or salamander wooled," she advised in "His Shield," "more ironshod / and javelin-dressed than a hedgehog battalion of steel, but be / dull" (144).

For Moore, such modest "dullness" was as much a weapon as the various scalpels represented by Millay's seductive gowns or "Nancy Boyd"'s "pow-dapuf." "The staff, the bag, the feigned inconsequence of manner, best bespeak / that weapon self-protectiveness," she confessed in the early "In This Age of Hard Trying. . . ." And Marguerite Young's later comment, "She is so unfashionable that she seems extremely fashionable," suggests one way the weapon of spinsterish dullness and nonchalance brought her both social and aesthetic victories.[93] In addition, though, just as the young Moore's airdale coat concealed a lining made from the finest quality of black satin, so the modesty of her poetic persona hid extravagant fantasies, some self-assertive but many hostile toward just the history of (male) self-assertion that had so enraged Millay.

The recurrent figure of the dragon in Moore's work, for instance, is frequently associated with dreams of superhuman power.[94] Speaking with apparent objectivity about the plumet basilisk—an "amphibious falling dragon, [a] living fire-work" (20)—Moore notes that he "meets his / likeness in the stream . . . king with king" and "portrays / mythology's wish / to be interchangeably man and fish" (23). But the desirous subtext of this piece of reportage comes to the surface years later in "O To Be a Dragon," when Moore confesses her personal involvement with "mythology's wish":

> If I, like Solomon, . . .
> could have my wish—
>
> my wish . . . O to be a dragon,
> a symbol of the power of Heaven—of silkworm
> size or immense; at times invisible.
> Felicitous phenomenon!
>   [177; ellipses Moore's]

Yet even Presbyter John, whose "shield / was his humility," was in Moore's view a kind of dragon—an "inextinguishable salamander." Equally, as legendary ruler of a medieval land of heart's desire, he possessed an "unconquerable country of unpompous gusto," where "gold was so common none considered it; greed / and flattery were unknown," and "rubies large as tennis- / balls conjoined in streams" (144). "At times invisible"—shielded by his coat of humility—Moore's Presbyter John nevertheless wielded such moral authority that his was, like the dragon's, "the power of Heaven."[95] Such power is also, of course, implicit in the art of the moralizing fabulist, which many critics have ascribed to Moore. A spiritual descendant of Madame de Genlis—whom Ellen Moers characterized in *Literary Women* as a model "educating heroine"—as well as of La Fontaine and his associate Madame de Sévigné, Moore was as much a didact as she was an autodidact.[96] Thus, while her modesty concealed fantasies of power and luxury the way her "simple coat" hid a black satin lining, her humility overlaid, but did not obliterate, a deep hostility to the "greed and flattery" she associated with male-dominated history. If the "power of Heaven" could be wielded by the fabulous Presbyter John and the fabulist La Fontaine, it could also be commanded by the moralizing spinster schoolteacher who was, on the one hand, neat and trim, on the other, acerbic and censorious.[97] In fact, just as Millay's early impudent *Figs* often seem designed to taunt male suitors, so a number of Moore's early epigrammatic verses frequently seem meant to daunt the male figures (and by implication the male readers) to whom they are addressed by forcing them to attend to lessons taught by a disdainful instructress as apt to scold as to reward little boys for what they regard as their chief achievements.

"Pouters and Fantails," a group of poems which appeared in the May 1915 issue of *Poetry* just a month before T. S. Eliot made his debut in that journal with "The Love Song of J. Alfred Prufrock," introduces Moore in this chastising mood. "That Harp You Play So Well," for instance, begins with modest, feminine praise: "O David, if I had / Your power, I should be glad," and goes on to celebrate the "stout continents of thought" produced by "Blake, Homer, Job, and you."[98] Suddenly, however, daughterly affirmation modulates into teacherly censoriousness:

> But, David, if the heart
> Be brass, what boots the art
> Of exorcising wrong,
> Of harping to a song?
> The sceptre and the ring
> And every royal thing
> Will fail. Grief's lustiness
> Must cure that harp's distress.

What has David done to deserve this unexpected sermon? Plainly his heart has turned to "brass" because of his proclivity for conquest, his hardened manipulation (and ultimate sacrifice) of Uriah the Hittite to his own lust for Uriah's wife, Bathsheba, and because he subsequently begot a self-aggrandizing history that would rebuke him by the death of his son Absalom. Yet Moore's reproach here has further implications, for she links the biblical king's heart of brass with a contamination of the harp, and, by associating David with "Blake, Homer, Job," she implies a shadowy connection between the spoils of (male) history and the despoiling of (male) art, a connection that can be severed only through the yielding to defeat represented by "grief's lustiness" and incarnated in Job, the one nonartist in the group. Thus, the young author of "That Harp You Play So Well" does not, like the speaker of "Prufrock," *mourn* a lost or unattainable authority; rather, she *counsels* the loss of authority, a divestment of power that would function, paradoxically, to enable authorship.

The dismissiveness of "That Harp" predicts a moralizing stance that marks much of Moore's work in this period. "To an Intra-Mural Rat," in the same issue of *Poetry*, is even more censorious toward its interlocutor ("You make me think of many men / Once met, to be forgot again"), while such other 1915 verses as "To Statecraft Embalmed," "To Military Progress," and "To a Steam Roller" are more scornful still in their chastisings of masculinist swagger.[99] "To Statecraft Embalmed," for instance, apostrophizing a mummified ibis that symbolizes the dead and deadening authority of the pharaohs, begins with pure contempt—"There is nothing to be said for you"— and includes a moving protest against the "hard plumage" of politics and policies that would deny life: "As if a death mask ever could replace / life's faulty excellence!" (35) Still more fiercely, "To Military Progress" excoriates the implicitly masculinist "mind / like a millstone" whose grindings inspire "black minute-men / to revive again, / war / at little cost" (82), while "To a Steam Roller" compares such a mind to a machine which crushes "all the particles down / into close conformity, and then walk[s] back and forth on them," adding, with freezing irony, "As for butterflies, I can hardly conceive / of one's attending upon you" (84).

Such overt misandry was associated with a commitment to the feminist movement that was at least as intense as Millay's. In 1915 Moore and her mother were members of the Woman Suffrage Party of Pennsylvania, on whose behalf the poet attended meetings, distributed leaflets, and hung banners. Remembering Moore's reports of her activism, Elizabeth Bishop became heatedly defensive of her friend and mentor. Citing "several references critical of her poetry by feminist writers," Bishop specifically referred to the woman who was Millay's great heroine, asking, "Do they know that Marianne Moore . . . paraded with the suffragettes, led by Inez Milholland on her white horse, down Fifth Avenue?"[100]

Equally to the point, in the same fine memoir, Bishop noted that Moore's "Marriage" is "a poem that says everything . . . Virginia Woolf has said. . . . It is a poem which transforms a justified sense of injury into a work of art."[101] Bishop's insight was acute, but besides elaborating the feminism embodied in Moore's early epigrammatic verses, "Marriage" (composed in 1923) also helps us understand this poet's continuing construction of a female mask which both complemented and contradicted Millay's. For, feminist though it is, this complex meditation on a central patriarchal institution, a work Moore called "an anthology" of quotations, is a crucial statement of bemused alienation spoken by an exuberant outsider. Indeed, it is more through its noncommittal alienation than through its committed feminism that this extraordinary text reveals the direction in which Moore's pose as spinster schoolteacher would take her.[102]

To be specific, "Marriage" is clearly spoken by someone quite aloof from what Adrienne Rich has called "compulsory heterosexuality."[103] Not that it is what Rich might call a "lesbian" poem; it is simply a soliloquy that stands entirely outside romance to look at the conventions of that institution from, as it were, an extraplanetary perspective—or perhaps more accurately, from the point of view of an entirely self-sufficient, apparently asexual creature, a genius of an amoeba, say. With scrupulously objective phrasing, the first lines of the poem establish this perspective while, through reiteration of the neutral pronoun *one*, they promise to take no sides:

> This institution,
> perhaps one should say enterprise
> out of respect for which
> one says one need not change one's mind
> about a thing one has believed in,
> requiring public promises
> of one's intention
> to fulfil a private obligation:
> I wonder what Adam and Eve
> think of it by this time.

[62]

Some of the changes Moore made in the poem as she worked through various drafts emphasize her own intention to remain at least superficially nonpartisan. Laurence Stapleton notes that the passage which begins, "Eve: beautiful woman— / I have seen her / when she was so handsome / she gave me a start," and which then goes on to offer a comic picture of Adam and Eve resolving yet reiterating differences (says Eve, "'*I* should like to be alone'; / to which the visitor replies, / 'I should like to be alone; / why not be alone together?'" [62–63]), was originally overtly feminist:

> Adam
> I have seen him when he was so handsome that he gave me a start
> then he went off
> appearing in his true colours

the transition fr. Apollo to Apollyon
being swift like Jack before and after the beanstalk.[104]

But Stapleton goes on to observe, "As the thinking about Adam's possessiveness and desire for power continues, a conclusion is made: 'this division into masculine and feminine compartments of achievement will not do . . . one feels oneself to be an integer / but one is not one is a particle / in an existence to which Adam and Eve / are incidental to the plot.'" In fact, what the writer evidently comes to understand is the degree of her own puzzlement at "this institution," a puzzlement both facilitated by, and issuing in, profound indifference. For although marriage may require "all one's criminal ingenuity / to avoid," it is nevertheless an "amalgamation which can never be more / than an interesting impossibility," and if Eve is "the central flaw / in that first crystal-fine experiment" of the creation, the "shed snake skin . . . not to be returned to again" is an "invaluable accident / exonerating Adam," who is himself no more than "a crouching mythological monster" (63).

As Bishop claimed, Moore, writing five years before the publication of *A Room of One's Own* and thirteen years before *Three Guineas*, makes a number of proto-Woolfian points: Adam treads "'chasms / on the uncertain footing of a spear,' / forgetting that there is in woman / a quality of mind / which as an instinctive manifestation / is unsafe" (64), forgetting, that is, the irony frequently deployed by those who are subordinated. And although, like some of Woolf's patriarchs, Adam deludes himself into believing that he has achieved "the ease of the philosopher" paradoxically "unfathered by a woman," he "stumbles over marriage," the bizarre contrivance of "unhelpful Hymen!" More to the point, when five o'clock comes and "'the ladies in their imperious humility / are ready to receive you,'" Moore, like Woolf, interjects her opinion of such gatherings: "Experience attests / that men have power / and sometimes one is made to feel it," adding further, in a quotation from M. Carey Thomas that anticipates the photographs of bizarrely garbed male leaders in *Three Guineas*,

> She says, "Men are monopolists
> of 'stars, garters, buttons
> and other shining baubles'—
> unfit to be the guardians
> of another person's happiness."

[67]

Ultimately, however, Moore dispassionately withdraws from both parties to unhelpful Hymen's pact, noting that while "he loves himself so much, / he can permit himself / no rival in that love," she "loves herself so much, / she cannot see herself enough," and wondering, "What can one do for them— / these savages / condemned to disaffect / all those who are not visionaries /

alert to undertake the silly task / of making people noble?" (68). Her declared intention to assemble the poem out of "statements that took my fancy which I tried to arrange plausibly" (271) is therefore revealing, for the collage of quotations that Moore has constructed persistently supports her own pose as a bemused researcher. Indeed, where the verbal shreds of history accumulated by the speaker of *The Waste Land* all become parts of *his* sensibility, so that, as Hugh Kenner once suggested, his "Voice" represents all voices—"the European mind" articulating itself—the shards of language brought together by the author of "Marriage" seem like three-by-five cards, notes for a dissertation on a subject the writer is trying (with difficulty) to understand.[105] Thus, where Eliot's art of allusion entails assimilation, Moore's involves alienation.

By the end of "Marriage," then, the very notion of marriage has been reduced to a rhetorical gesture whose hollowness fails to reconcile the rhetorical debate that "he" and "she" have carried on throughout the poem: "the statesmanship / of an archaic Daniel Webster," observes the poet, "persists to their [the couple's] simplicity of temper / as the essence of the matter," yet that statesmanship turns out to be mere oxymoronic sloganeering ("'Liberty and union / now and forever'") objectified in empty symbols and theatrical gestures: "'the Book on the writing table; / the hand in the breast pocket'" (69–70). Well might such an institution require "all one's criminal ingenuity / to avoid" (62), not for political reasons but because, from this disaffected perspective, it is so absurd.

"One is a particle / in an existence to which Adam and Eve / are incidental to the plot": this is the position to which Marianne Moore came, as she realized that her ingenuity had empowered her to avoid the minuets not only of marriage but of sexual flirtation. Even before she began "Marriage," she had hinted at her disdain for the hierarchical relationships associated with romance in a culture where "men have power / and sometimes one is made to feel it." In 1916 she published in *The Chimaera* a mysterious diatribe later omitted from the *Complete Poems*. Entitled "To Be Liked By You Would Be a Calamity," the piece implicitly defines liking and loathing as catastrophic equivalents in what appears to be sexual combat:

> "Attack is more piquant than concord," but when
> You tell me frankly that you would like to feel
> My flesh beneath your feet,
> I'm all abroad—I can but put my weapon up and
>   Bow you out.
>
> Gesticulation—it is half the language.
> Let unsheathed gesticulation be the steel
> Your courtesy must meet,

Since in your hearing words are mute, which to my senses
Are a shout.[106]

"Battle-dressed," the spinster-poet here has silent recourse to "un-
sheathed gesticulation," coolly bowing her threatening interlocutor out of
the room of her life and herself out of the "plot" of erotic liking. If "Marriage," published two years later, was franker in its contempt for couples as
"savages," "The Arctic Ox," produced some three and a half decades later
still, demonstrates the unswerving constancy of Moore's belief that to be
liked (by a man) might be a calamity. Speaking admiringly of the Arctic ox
"(or goat)," she notes of such creatures that

> While not incapable
> of courtship, they may find its
>   servitude and flutter, too much
> like Procrustes' bed;
> so some decide to stay unwed.

[194]

As more biographical material about Moore's family becomes available,
psychoanalytically inclined readers will no doubt begin to draw conventional
conclusions: her father's early disappearance from the household as well as
the resulting closeness Mary Warner Moore established with her son,
Warner, and her daughter, Marianne, might be seen as having stifled their
adult sexuality. After the publication of *The Wind in the Willows* in 1908, Mary
Moore was regularly "Mole," Marianne was "Rat," and Warner "Badger":
this series of playful animal names would seem to have perpetuated an
asexual childishness.[107] At the same time, though, participation in an ingenuous alternative life must also have reinforced Moore's feminist inclination
to deconstruct patriarchal history from the perspective of a nonparticipant
in crucial sexual institutions even while it allowed her to reconstruct a history
of her own: a *natural* history in which she and her familiar familial animals
played a central part. Thus, coming at the questions which concerned
Millay—the relations between the sexes, the course of events that constituted "Western culture"—from a radically different position, the author of
"Marriage" was eventually to express a notably similar point of view.

A brief early poem hints at the sophistication with which this censorious
"spinster" would embark on her project of historical analysis. "He Wrote the
History Book" is addressed with benevolent sarcasm to the child of one Dr.
C. M. Andrews, a boy who said, at the age of five or six, "My name is John
Andrews; my father wrote the history book" (276). Here the poet uses little
John's naïveté implicitly to interrogate the monolithic idea of "history":

> There! you shed a ray
>   of whimsicality on a mask of profundity so

> terrific, that I have been dumbfounded by
> it oftener than I care to say.
> *The* book? Titles are chaff.
>
> [89]

Moore's culture may childishly tell her that there is *a* book of human history, that "titles"—representing different visions, different "stories"—are "chaff," but such a notion dumbfounds her. Yet she is ironically pleased with the boy for having brought to the surface his father's assumptions, concluding her verse with "Thank you for showing me / your father's autograph." And it is the father's autograph, that signature of propagandistic interpretation, on which she trains her sights in one of her most brilliant meditations on history: "Virginia Britannia."

"Virginia Britannia" begins quietly, mellifluously, with an evocation of the natural landscape in which America's earliest drama of colonization was played out: "Pale sand edges England's Old / Dominion. The air is soft, warm, hot / above the cedar-dotted emerald shore" (107). But Moore's theme here is neither the charm of the South nor the triumph of America. Rather, as in the later "Enough"—another work meditating on the Jamestown colony, which bitterly observes, "Marriage, tobacco, and slavery / initiated liberty" (186)—she wants to question the platitudes of patriotism. Thus her first stanza moves gravely toward a key image of the grave of one of the English interlopers who, as the poet will later tell us in a sly understatement, were at least as "odd" as the Indians whose land they usurped:

> The now tremendous vine-encompassed hackberry
> starred with the ivy flower,
> shades the church tower;
> And a great sinner lyeth here under the sycamore.
>
> [107]

Although Moore's note reports that the inscription on the gravestone of one Robert Sherwood piously describes him as "a great sinner who waits for a joyful resurrection" (279), her text emphasizes the imperialistic sinfulness, rather than the Christian piety, that he represents. For, reviewing the history of England's Old Dominion, she records simultaneously the oddity and the evil of colonial voracity, emblematized by Captain John Smith's coat of arms: an "ostrich with a horseshoe in its beak—i.e., invincible digestion" (279), bearing the motto *Vincere est vivere* (To conquer is to live).

The people of that "Rare Indian" Powhatan have, after all, long since died out, and "an almost English green" has been established where, "among un-English insect sounds, / the white wall-rose" climbs; and "care has formed walls of yew / since Indians knew / the Fort Old Field and narrow tongue of land that Jamestown was." Yet "the terse Virginian"—the one remaining

true native—is the mockingbird, "the mettlesome gray one," whose cry
dominates the pseudo-English landscape over which it presides, while
"the work-mule and / show-mule and witch-cross door and 'strong sweet
prison' / are a part of what has come about—in the Black / idiom—from
'advancin' back- / wards in a circle'" (107–09).

Nor have the women who inhabit or inhabited this countryside escaped
the deformations of history. If Pocahontas became a "feminine / odd Indian
young lady!" and her British counterpart was an "odd thin- / gauze-and-
taffeta-dressed English one!" the contemporary plantation mistress is
equally peculiar, "feeding" from a "crested spoon" in her "French plum-
and-turquoise-piped chaise-longue." Similarly, because "priorities were cradled in this region not / noted for humility," even the "one-brick- / thick
serpentine wall built by / Jefferson" to enclose the University of Virginia is
associated, through its snakiness, with corruption. For, declares Moore in
one of her most forceful political statements,

> . . . Like strangler figs choking
> a banyan, not an explorer, no imperialist,
> not one of us, in taking what we
> pleased—in colonizing as the
> saying is—has been a synonym for mercy.
>
> [110]

Finally, therefore, along with the mockingbird, only the "mere brown
hedge sparrow"—incarnating a natural history that coexists with human
history in blessed ignorance—is a redeemer, fluting "his ecstatic burst of
joy." Beyond his song, little consolation can be discerned except that offered
by what Wallace Stevens called "the isolation of the sky at evening," a distance
from "civilization" in which

> . . . clouds, expanding above
> the town's assertiveness, dwarf it, dwarf arrogance
> that can misunderstand
> importance; and
> are to the child an intimation of what glory is.
>
> [111]

Unlike Stevens, however, whose line comes toward the end of a poem ("Sunday Morning") celebrating the humanizing progress of theological history,
Moore would *de*humanize the human, teach man to conquer the male will to
conquer and to acquiesce, instead, in the inhuman humility of the natural
world. And unlike Wordsworth, to whose "Intimations Ode" her last line
plainly alludes, she would undo the humanizing experience which brings
"thoughts . . . too deep for tears" and return to her readers the innocence of
the child who does not just perceive "clouds of glory" but sees, also, glory in

simple clouds. Last, like some severe prophetess, she would warn the "arrogance / that can misunderstand / importance" about the "cloud no bigger
than a man's hand": the cloud of an abiding natural history whose laws
inexorably lead the "strong [to] overcome / itself" and which will eventually,
therefore, "dwarf arrogance."[108]

That the arrogance of patriarchal history must ultimately be dwarfed is a
point Moore also makes in numerous other poems. "No Swan So Fine," for
instance, with its well-known description of a Louis XV "chintz china" swan
"with fawn- / brown eyes and toothed gold / collar on to show whose bird it
was," begins with a quote from the *New York Times Magazine*—"No water so
still as the / dead fountains of Versailles"—and ends with a kind of gently
gloating satisfaction: "The king is dead" (19). And although the china swan
still "perches" among ironically named "everlastings," it is clearly *not* "so
fine" as the real swan, whose "swart blind look *askance*" (emphasis ours)
underscores the arrogance of the gold-collared bird's maker and owner. In
"No Swan So Fine" Moore revises "Ozymandias" to point as succinctly as
Shelley did to the futility of a history emblematized by material possessions;
in "The Jerboa" she explores such presumptuousness through an accumulation of details that in itself enacts, even as it examines, the nausea of surfeit.

"*Too Much*," the first section of "The Jerboa," turns to the Roman and
Egyptian origins of Western civilization to consider, with detached contempt, the lives of "those with, everywhere, // power over the poor" (12). The
more complex a culture, Moore suggests, the more it deforms nature, first
by attempting to possess what should be free, and second by perverting
natural purposes. The Egyptians, who "understood / making colossi and /
how to use slaves"

> . . . had their men tie
> hippopotami
>   and bring out dappled dog-
>   cats to course antelope, dikdik, and ibex;
>   or used small eagles. They looked on as theirs,
>   impalas and onigers. . . .
>
>   [10]

Diverted by "dwarfs here and there," Egypt's "Princes / clad in queens'
dresses" and "queens in a / king's underskirt" were served by depersonalized attendants who "were like the king's cane in the / form of a hand." Nor
were these people who "liked small things" a historical anomaly, for the
opening stanzas of "*Too Much*" tell how "a Roman had an / artist, a *freedman*"
(emphasis ours) devise a grotesquely huge "pine cone / or fir cone—with
holes for a fountain," which, significantly, was to be placed on Rome's notorious Prison of St. Angelo and which is "known // now as the Popes'." Moore's
sardonic remark that this bizarre object "passed / for art" expresses her

disdain for the way in which the Roman master who ordered it both distorted the creative energies of the "freedman"-artist and misrepresented nature. At the same time, her emphasis on the endurance of the absurd cone—"known // *now* as the Popes'"—indicates her sense that much of history, perhaps of culture, has been shaped by such deformations of nature.

After an afternoon spent with Marianne Moore, the journalist Marguerite Young wrote in 1946: "She has a box of wild bird feathers of all kinds wrapped in tissues and a blue-jay claw. She offered me some eagle down, which she says is getting scarcer. She offered me a blue-jay claw."[109] Against the extravagant nature of the art produced by hierarchical culture, Moore set, in her life as in her work, the economical art of antihierarchical nature. The second section of "The Jerboa," "*Abundance*," continues the celebration, begun late in the first section, of the jerboa, "a small desert rat, / and not famous, that / lives without water" but "has happiness," explaining that "one would not be he / who has nothing but plenty." And lest readers mistake the poet herself for a zoological connoisseur not unlike the lords and ladies of ancient Egypt, she makes her moral explicit:

> Africanus meant
> the conqueror sent
>   from Rome. It should mean the
>   untouched: the sand-brown jumping-rat—free-born; and
>   the blacks, that choice race with an elegance
>   ignored by one's ignorance.
>
> [13]

Possession and enslavement, arrogance and ignorance—these are the fruits of "civilized" history, and only those outside history (the creatures who have a timeless natural history of their own) or marginalized by history (the "choice race" of the blacks, or the forgotten race of Powhatan and Pocahontas) are free of cultural pollution. Moreover, it is the endurance of the freest of these creatures—the nonhuman ones—which dwarfs human arrogance. The jerboa still has "a shining silver house // of sand," but the Pharaohs, as Millay put it, only "nearly had" their way: the king (of Egypt as of France) is dead.

In one of the few negative passages Moore's admirer Randall Jarrell ever wrote about her, the usually astute Jarrell complained that in idealizing certain animals the author of "The Jerboa" was falsifying the nature of a nature which is after all red in tooth and claw: "The way of the little jerboa on the sands—at once True, Beautiful, and Good—[Miss Moore] understands; but the little shrew or weazel, that kills, if it can, two or three dozen animals in a night? the little larvae feeding on the still-living caterpillar their mother has paralyzed for them? We are surprised to find Nature, in Miss Moore's poll of it, so strongly in favor of Morality; but all the results are implicit in the sampling—like the *Literary Digest,* she sent postcards to only the nicer animals."[110] Jarrell's observation is in a sense correct: but his point is precisely one that Moore herself, a college biology major, might have made. Seeking to imagine alternatives to the voracity of history, the jerboa's celebrant strives to depict the alternative history that might be constructed by what Jarrell contemptuously calls "the nicer animals." Jarrell goes on to wish "Miss Moore had read a history of the European 'colonization' of our planet (instead of natural histories full of the quaint animals of those colonies)," which reveals the surprising depth of his misunderstanding. Moore had carefully studied *both* histories and wanted to substitute one for the other.

Because the author of "The Jerboa" *was* a feminist, she particularly associated the "European 'colonization' of our planet" with a colonization of the feminine. Even more clearly than the representations of subordinated "Feminine / odd" young ladies in "Virginia Britannia" or the dilemma confronted by "Marriage's" "ladies / in their imperious humility," the image of Ireland explored in the comparatively early "Sojourn in the Whale" makes this point. Oppressed and impoverished, conquered Ireland endures "her" tribulations in the belly of voracious England as Jonah struggled for his survival in the indifferent gut of the whale, while Britain's imperialists rationalize away her rebellious impulses and predict her ultimate resignation: "'There is a feminine temperament in direct contrast to ours, / which makes her do these things. . . . Compelled by experience, she will turn back; // water seeks its own level'" (90). Tellingly, however, Moore responds to this smug braggadoccio with a sly smile: "'Water in motion is far / from level.' You have seen it, when obstacles happened to bar / the path, rise automatically." Perhaps, she implies here, the alternative narrative possibility signified by colonized peoples/women/animals will endure and be "yielded" forth from the confining chronicle of imperialist culture in the same way that the biblical prophet was liberated from his imprisonment within the great fish.[111]

Although the natural history that Moore valued so much more highly than the tale of the European colonization of our planet was not always specifically figured as female the way colonized Ireland is, that history was frequently a record of animals who were tropes for special forms of female desire, especially the desire for self-protection in male-dominated society and the desire to escape from such a society. Indeed, if one reads Moore's natural history with care, it becomes plain that her "nicer animals" often are either female, similar to females, or associated with females. In "He 'Digesteth Harde Iron,'" for instance, the ostrich "watches his chicks with / a maternal concentration—and he's / been mothering the eggs / at night six weeks." In the face of such quasi-feminine commitment to nurturance, human excess becomes particularly vicious.

Six hundred ostrich brains served
at one banquet, the ostrich-plume-tipped tent
and desert spear, jewel-
gorgeous ugly egg-shell
  goblets, eight pairs of ostriches
in harness, dramatize a meaning
always missed by the externalist.

[100]

What is dramatized is the meaning of the history of the colonization of
our planet, and particularly the colonization of the female principle. Moore
again celebrates the virtues of that principle in the extraordinary watchfulness of the paper nautilus, in the poem of that name, who does not "con-
struc[t] her thin glass shell" for "authorities whose hopes / are shaped by
mercenaries" but to shelter her eggs because "love / is the only fortress /
strong enough to trust to" (121, 122). Unlike the harnessed ostriches—or,
indeed, Oliver Wendell Holmes's cosmically adventuring "Chambered
Nautilus"—Moore's patient mollusk represents the durability of the female
as surely as does the resilience of Ireland or the abiding watchfulness of the
woman portrayed in Millay's "Sonnets from an Ungrafted Tree."[112] And it
was very likely Moore's female female impersonation that made it possible
for her to appraise stereotypes of the feminine in such a way that she could
articulate such a fundamentally feminist possibility.

Like Millay's, however, Moore's originally artful and often ironic female
female impersonation ultimately threatened to entrap her in precisely the
role she had at first examined with distancing irony. Specifically, she seems to
have internalized guilt and anxiety about her conspicuously public position
even while she understood herself to have been reified (by others as well as by
herself) in the part she had chosen to play. The wartime "In Distrust of
Merits," simultaneously one of Moore's most frequently anthologized and
controversial productions, illustrates both these points. As Susan Schweik
reminds us, this widely read polemic was frequently cited by contemporaries
as "a model of transparent earnestness," a prototypically "good" war poem,
in comparison to the propagandistic trash produced by Millay, "the 'bad'
woman war poet who is excoriated in these discussions as often as Moore is
extolled."[113] But the quasi-official rhetorical posturings of the poem resemble the fervent hortatory stance adopted in, say, The Murder of Lidice. In fact,
it was Jarrell's understandable irritation at the "blindingly moral" terms of
the text which caused him so seriously (and surprisingly) to misread Moore's
grasp of the colonization of our planet. More recently, Helen Vendler,
among others, has dismissed the work because of its "unwise explicitness"
and "banality of outcry."[114] But to the extent that such problems are real
ones in the poem, they would seem to have been fostered by an almost

parodic enactment of precisely the role of spinster schoolteacher that elsewhere served this writer so well.

The line "We / vow, we make this promise / to the fighting—it's a
promise—'We'll / never hate black, white, red, yellow, Jew, / Gentile, Untouchable'" sounds like nothing so much as a lesson delivered to fifth
graders after the pledge of allegiance and before the air raid drill. And
unlike the acerbic pedagogy of "To Statecraft Embalmed" or "To a Steam-
roller," this is a lesson delivered on *behalf* of an official establishment to those
whom it would control. Even the skepticism with which Moore here and
there undercuts her sermonizing (for instance, "We are / not competent to /
make our vows") is ultimately turned against herself, as she identifies completely with the forces of militarism that she had elsewhere ironically chastised. "There never was a war that was / not inward; I must / fight till I have
conquered in myself what / causes war," the poet confesses with what is
intended as exemplary humility but slides into naive grandiosity.

Oddly, then, as public spokeswoman *and* scapegoat for Allied morality,
Moore became a representative of just the history she had deplored in "The
Jerboa" and "Virginia Britannia." Considering this strange development,
the most perspicacious remark in Jarrell's troublesome 1945 essay is his quip
that because "Miss Moore is reviewed not as a poet but as an institution,"
perhaps she really ought to "be placed in Fort Knox for the duration."[115]
"Emotion overpowered me," Moore was later to apologize, defining "In
Distrust" as "a protest—disjointed, exclamatory" rather than a poem, just as
Millay had called her wartime writings posters.[116] But what appears really to
have overpowered the poet here was the public feeling that, as "an institution," she was expected to have, rather than the private vehemence she
expressed in "To Military Progress" when she rebuked "black minute-men"
who would "revive again, war // at little cost" (82).

By the time Moore had become such an institution that she was confiding
her breakfast menus to *Glamour* and her fashion tips to *Women's Wear Daily,*
the identification with officialdom "disjointedly" expressed in "In Distrust of
Merits" had begun more explicitly to permeate her writings. A number of
critics have remarked on the jingliness that marked much of her late verse,
especially the occasional poems in the *New Yorker,* while Marie Borroff has
noted the poet's surprising (and longstanding) stylistic indebtedness to the
"promotional prose of feature articles and advertisements." Significantly,
some of Borroff's most striking examples are drawn from advertisements
for women's fashions and home furnishings:

> Accounts in Moore's poems of the 'white pin-dots on black horizontal
> spaced- / out bands' on the back of the newt (p.6), the 'pink and black-
> striped, sashed or dotted silks' of racehorses (p.162), and the decora-
> tions on the uniforms of the palace guards of the Sultan Tipu, 'little

woven stripes incurved like buttonholes' (p.241) have their truest counterparts in 'cool grey-and-white stripes, white piqué touches' (advertisement for women's suit-dresses, *Times*, 6/7/44, p.13), 'bare-midriff
swim suit accented with bands of navy or red' (*Times*, 6/4/44, p.7), and
'skinny streaks of beige, turquoise or licorice sharply drawn on the
chalkiest white cotton knit' (advertisement for women's dresses, *Times*,
1/1/56, p.46).[117]

Borroff argues persuasively that Moore usually made brilliantly revisionary use of such formulas. Yet as the critic also admits, the second stanza of
"Saint Nicholas" (like a number of other passages from Moore's late work) is
"unmistakably inspired in content and idiom by Madison Avenue itself."[118]
In fact, in the context not only of Moore's whimsical yet apparently unironic
struggle to name the ill-fated car that became the Edsel but also of her
earnest replies to *Glamour* and *Women's Wear Daily*, these lines seem remark-
ably sincere:

> If you can find no striped chameleon,
> might I have a dress or suit—
> I guess you have heard of it—of *qiviut?*
> and to wear with it, a taslon shirt, the drip-dry fruit
> of research second to none;
>   sewn, I hope, by Excello;
>   as for buttons to keep down the collar-points, no.
> The shirt could be white—
>   and be "worn before six,"
> either in daylight or at night.
>
>   [196]

Such sincerity would be amusing, indeed charming, if it were not associated
with Moore's gradual reification into the figure she had earlier more wittily
impersonated. As a *qiviut*-loving eccentric, she might, after all, have been a
delightful minor poet. But as the major poet who produced, among many
other subversive texts, "Those Various Scalpels," "Marriage," "Virginia Britannia," and "The Jerboa," she could afford no more than a pretense of
lovable idiosyncrasy. Shirts "sewn by Excello" might facilitate her masquerade, but they could hardly have been (as toward the end of her life they
threatened to become) its reward.

Certainly the costume of the younger Moore's mind had been grander.
Refusing to comply with the exigencies of "annoying romance" (in "A Car-
riage from Sweden"), coolly distanced from the ill-fitting fashions of "Marriage," this poet had been liberated to imagine civilizing alternatives to
"civilization," options that she feared those trapped by the acquisitive imperatives of culture could not see. Thus, playfully dressed as Washington cross-

ing the Delaware—wearing a skirt *and* a cloak *and* a tricorne—and thereby signaling her "old maid"'s freedom from heterosexualized femininity, she was, consciously or not, casting herself as the leader of a new kind of war for independence. As president of the apparently whimsical but really fantastically serious state of ostriches and nautiluses, unicorns and virgins, she would lead her creatures across the Delaware into a different history. Cleansed of the excess—the *"Too Much"*—signified by Edsel and Excello, her New World would be the old order of birds, beasts and flowers, of marginalized women and enslaved peoples, resanctified.

———

What are the implications of the female female impersonation that Millay and Moore, albeit with varying degrees of success, deployed as a defense against trivialization, an offense against masculinism? What caused these two very different figures to attempt such an artistic strategy? In other words, how were these two women empowered to move from what was in the nineteenth century an aesthetic of renunciation underlying women's poetry to a twentieth-century aesthetic of self-dramatization?[119] The suffrage movement in which both were involved surely played a part here, along with the fact that both must have understood themselves to have a fuller lineage of literary ancestresses than the apparently scanty maternal heritage to which, say, Elizabeth Barrett Browning, Christina Rossetti, and Emily Dickinson were able to turn.

Millay wrote sonnet sequences as indebted to Louise Labé's Renaissance verses, Rossetti's "Monna Innominata," and Barrett Browning's *Sonnets from the Portuguese* as they were to the sequences of Shakespeare and Meredith or the sonnets of Keats and Wordsworth. Similarly, in a 1931 review of Emily Dickinson's letters, Moore described the Amherst poet in terms that would be equally applicable to herself: as a writer, Moore declared, Dickinson "flash[es] like an animal," has a "Japanesely fantastic reverence for tree, insect, and toadstool," and has a "conciseness . . . as extreme as her largess." In 1962, moreover, Moore published what Donald Hall calls "a curiosity": a dramatization in four acts of Maria Edgeworth's novel *The Absentee*, in which "in general the female characters have the best lines."[120]

Among their contemporaries, too, both singled out women poets for special praise. The only review of a verse collection that Millay ever published was an encomium to Elinor Wylie, whom she regarded as "one of the most distinguished writers of our time" and for whom she produced a far more elaborate elegy than even her impassioned public panegyric to Inez Milholland. And just a year or two after she discovered her affinity with Wylie, Millay confided in a letter to Edmund Wilson that she was "quite thrilled by some of" Louise Bogan's poems, adding, "Isn't it wonderful how the lady poets are coming along? 'Votes for Women' is what I sez!"[121] As for

Moore, long before she became a mentor to the young Elizabeth Bishop, she had written several glowing reviews of H. D.'s poetry, praising her "immortalizing of minutiae" along with her "fastidious prodigality," and concluding, tellingly, that "in H. D.'s work . . . we have heroics which do not confuse transcendence with domination.[122]

Nevertheless, as if to acknowledge the literary battle in which they were implicitly engaged, both these artists consciously measured their own achievements against those of male contemporaries, and they frequently aligned themselves with those contemporaries. Millay's letters to such literary men as Arthur Ficke, Witter Bynner, Edmund Wilson, and George Dillon far outnumber her letters to literary women, while a series of parodic verses in which, she boasted, she had mounted a "murderous" attack on T. S. Eliot is probably her most venomous literary production.[123] Moore's reviews of works by major male writers—particularly Eliot, Stevens, Pound, and Williams—far outnumber her reviews of works by female writers, and a "modest disclaimer" she once made to the British poet Kathleen Raine explains the ratio, as if to bring to the surface the complexities of this poet's affiliation complex: "'Yes, I know they did say I was the best woman poet in this country; but you see, Miss Raine, that means nothing, just nothing at all; because here in America not more than two, or perhaps three, women have ever even *tried* to write poetry.'"[124] Perhaps, then, the best way to understand both the meaning of and the motive for the accomplishment of these poets is to set their oeuvres, if only briefly, against the male modernist accomplishment canonized in Pritchard's *Lives of the Modern Poets*.

"The centuries have a way of being male," wrote Wallace Stevens in a central critical essay, "The Figure of the Youth as Virile Poet" (1943), and he went on to outline key aspects of what became Harold Bloom's theory of influence:

> When we look back at the face of the seventeenth century, it is at . . . the Miltonic image of a poet, severe and determined. . . . from which a younger figure is emerging, stepping forward in the company of a muse of its own, still half-beast and somehow more than human, a kind of sister of the Minotaur. This younger figure is the intelligence that endures. It is the imagination of the son still bearing the antique imagination of the father. It is the clear intelligence of the young man still bearing the burden of the obscurities of the intelligence of the old. . . . For this Aeneas, it is the past that is Anchises.[125]

Clearly, for both Millay and Moore the literary past was no Anchises. To be sure, both thought that the history of "the European 'colonization' of our planet" had to be revised and resisted, but "the burden of the obscurities of the intelligence of the old"—that burden to which much of Eliot's criticism was directed, which Pound confronted in the *ABC of Reading*, which Williams sought to cast off in *In the American Grain* and *Paterson*, and which is in some sense the burthen of Pritchard's *Lives*—was alien to these women.[126]

Unlike most of their nineteenth-century female precursors, neither was daunted by cultural injunctions telling aspiring women not to write, not to read: both were extraordinarily successful public figures, and Moore was, in fact, a powerful editor during her years on *The Dial*. But neither, seeking to delineate "with accurate speech the complications of which [they were] composed,"[127] would have felt that such speech had to repudiate the linguistic achievements of immediate precursors, if only because neither seems to have felt a need to defile or deconstruct the "monuments of unageing intellect" created by male forebears. Millay wrote sonnets at a time when every serious critic *did* "scorn . . . the sonnet," and she was no doubt able to do so because (like her friend Elinor Wylie) she felt affinity rather than antipathy for her Romantic precursors, sensing that their egalitarian ideals and valorization of nature were empowering for women. Moore elevated Hazlitt's (and Keats's) Romantic concept of "gusto" into a critical principle that she stubbornly advocated in the face of her friend Eliot's rejection of Romanticism and rehabilitation of the (supposedly anti-Romantic) metaphysical poets.[128] In addition, as Robert Lowell noted, Moore consistently drew on the particularizing strengths of the great tradition of the nineteenth-century novel that was shaped by women: she was "an inventor of a new kind of English poem, one . . . able to fix the splendor and variety of prose in very compressed spaces. . . . One thinks of Jane Austen and George Eliot."[129]

Indeed, it is arguable that for both Moore and Millay the artifice—even eccentricity—of the verse forms in which they chose to write functioned metaphorically in the same way their costumes functioned literally: to dramatize the artifice and arbitrariness of female poetic identity. Millay's love sonnets, for example, allowed her to enact an erotic role reversal comparable to the one Christina Rossetti defined in her prefatory note to "Monna Innominata," letting her show what might have happened "had such a lady [as Beatrice or Laura] spoken for herself."[130] But because, unlike Rossetti, Millay was working in the sonnet form at a time when, to most male modernist contemporaries, it seemed "thirty years old at the least," the sonnet itself became a kind of archaic costume in which the rebellious poet sometimes seriously, sometimes parodically attired herself to call attention to the antiquated garb of femininity. Whether the corset of form in which Millay encased her ideas was Shakespearean or Petrarchan, the very process of rhyming and measuring that the composition of any sonnet entails would in effect let her become what Horney called "the voyeur of the voyeurs" of the "body" of her work.

At the same time, however, the mastery with which Millay deployed the sonnet form (even Alan Tate conceded that her "best sonnets would adorn any of the great English sequences") made it just as crucially a garment in which, as we noted earlier, she could in the octave seduce (male) readers and then in the sestet or concluding couplet betray them.[131] Her posthumously published "I will put Chaos into fourteen lines" is in fact a manifesto for this essentially vengeful project:

> I will put Chaos into fourteen lines
> And keep him there; and let him thence escape
> If he be lucky; let him twist, and ape
> Flood, fire, and demon—his adroit designs
> Will strain to nothing in the strict confines
> Of this sweet Order, where, in pious rape,
> I hold his essence and amorphous shape,
> Till he with Order mingles and combines.
> Past are the hours, the years, of our duress,
> His arrogance, our awful servitude:
> I have him. He is nothing more or less
> Than something simple not yet understood;
> I shall not even force him to confess;
> Or answer. I will only make him good.
>
> [728]

As Debra Fried has pointed out in a fine essay on "Gender and Genre in Millay's Sonnets," "Millay's 'I will put Chaos' ends in such a way as to suggest that the controlling process it describes has been enacted in the sonnet as we read it. . . . In Millay's figure, the woman poet binds 'Chaos'—a kind of male anti-muse . . . with the 'strict confines' of her ordering art." And at least in part she did so because, as Fried adds, "For a woman writing poetry in the years between the wars, the . . . shaky fiction of new sexual freedom for women made the sonnet an apt form in which to scrutinize the inherited stances of men toward women and poets toward their muses."[132]

As late as 1976, Elizabeth Bishop was employing the same strategy, intermittently attiring the body of her thought in forms whose artifice allowed her both to test the limits of the aesthetic and to triumph over the limitations of the emotional. The famous villanelle "One Art," for instance, inexorably rhymes *master* and *disaster* to lead proleptically to the apparently calamitous final quatrain:

> —Even losing you (the joking voice, a gesture
> I love) I shan't have lied. It's evident
> the art of losing's not too hard to master
> though it may look like (*Write* it) like disaster.[133]

Here the "one art" of "losing" is conspicuously controlled by the one art of language with which the poet tames loss by setting the poem up so that she literally "writes it" before the reader's eyes and thus turns the nakedness of pain into a costume of victory. Even more explicitly, in the late "Pink Dog" Bishop employs the metaphorical garb of strict form, in this case rhyming triplets, both to commend and ironically to comment on the camouflage of costume:

> Carnival is always wonderful!
> A depilated dog would not look well.
> Dress up! Dress up and dance at Carnival![134]

Although Moore's innovative and, for an English poet, almost unprecedented use of prosaic-sounding syllabics would seem to place her at the other end of the aesthetic spectrum from both the more conventional Bishop (with whom she was frequently aligned) and the sonnet-writing Millay, her prosodic choice, too, let her call attention to the artifice of female poetic identity, as well as to the artifice of poetry itself. Consistently insisting that she was not really "a poet," Moore documented that claim in the first version of "Poetry," where she declared, "I too dislike it," and where she responded to Tolstoi's assertion that "poetry is verse; prose is not verse. Or else poetry is everything with the exception of business documents and schoolbooks" by impudently remarking that it is not "valid / to discriminate against 'business documents and // schoolbooks'; all these phenomena are important" (267).[135]

To be sure, this self-presentation can be, and has been, attributed to Moore's often-avowed "humility." As Bonnie Costello puts it, in this writer's work "the prosaic, conversational tone, the long, meandering, run-on lines and shifts of figurative level, give the impression of nonchalance. She is not, she seems to suggest, writing anything so grand as a poem."[136] At the same time, however, by transforming "prose" into "poetry," Moore challenges the historically privileged status of "poetry" while, with a kind of quiet arrogance, she proves that *she* can make poetry out of anything, including a business document or a schoolbook. In addition, just as the process of formal mastery allows Millay the sonneteer, or Bishop the villanelle writer, to become a voyeur of the aesthetic victory at which readers will also gaze, so Moore's use of syllabics lets her watch herself being watched as her meticulous counting converts "prose" into an innovative "poetry"—a poetry, like the many-armed glacier that is the subject of "An Octopus," characterized on the one hand by "relentless accuracy" in its "capacity for fact" and on the other by "neatness of finish!" (76).

More usefully than the long and complex "An Octopus," "An Egyptian Pulled Glass Bottle in the Shape of a Fish" serves as a paradigm comparable to Millay's "I will put Chaos":

> Here we have thirst
>   and patience, from the first,
>   and art, as in a wave held up for us to see
>   in its essential perpendicularity;

    not brittle but
    intense—the spectrum, that
      spectacular and nimble animal the fish,
      whose scales turn aside the sun's sword by their polish.
                                                                            [83]

Although counting reveals that the two stanzas of this piece are measured
into units of four, six, twelve, and twelve syllables, the apparently casual
enjambments, understated rhyme, and counter-stressed rhythms ("the
fish/polish") do give what Costello calls an "impression of nonchalance." Yet
the poem's very appearance on the page calls attention to the artifice by
which it is organized, while its argument that in the artifact which is its
subject "art" is "as in a wave held up for us to see" self-reflexively emphasizes
the skillful generic costume of the poet, whose own nimble "scales" brilliantly
attract, reflect, and refract the swordlike gaze of the reader just as the fish's
"scales turn aside the sun's sword by their polish."[137] To return to Berger's
formulation, surveying the "surveyed" in her self, Moore controls the reactions of a voyeuristic audience by flaunting her skill at what, despite its
apparent aesthetic neutrality, paradoxically becomes a mode of female female impersonation.

    Significantly, in their various ways these women poets chose obviously
rigorous prosodic strategies far more often than did their most notable male
contemporaries. When Millay and Moore were counting lines and syllables,
Eliot, Pound, Williams, and even Stevens were frequently seeking to disrupt
closed forms and traditional stanza patterns.[138] Acknowledging their newly
public role as *women* poets, Millay and Moore had to find stylistic as well as
stylish ways of (re)presenting themselves to the world. They made use of
what were for their time eccentric aesthetic strategies, although neither felt
that "the Miltonic image of a poet, severe and determined," obliged her to
fortify her work through *structural* allusions to such traditionally "high"
poetic forms as the ode, the pastoral elegy, the epic—all modes to which
their male contemporaries, even at their most innovative, consistently (if
implicitly) returned. Historically, as we have argued elsewhere, the emerging male poet has constructed his poetic self through an identification with
the specifically male tradition represented by such forms, just as the growing
boy has constructed his personal self through what the theorist Nancy
Chodorow has called a "positional" identification with the official insignia of
masculinity, an identification, that is, with abstractions representing the role
and rank of the father.[139] Thus, even the modernist poets who struggled
against the burden of the past by seeking to "make it new" at least covertly
referred to the conventions that marked the tradition into which they hoped
their individual talents would be assimilated, and they did so precisely in
order to assert their own sovereignty in the company of their precursors.[140]

But women appear to have had, historically, no such need to create poetic identity through a positional identification with paternal genre; rather, from Anne Bradstreet in the seventeenth century and Anne Finch in the eighteenth century to Elizabeth Barrett Browning and Emily Dickinson in the nineteenth, female poets have more often associated themselves with the personal: they have worked in narrative or occasional modes (including the "verse novel" and the sonnet sequence) whose explorations of, and relations to, specific places, persons, and events might be said to represent the culturally privatized and particularized realm that is literally or figuratively maternal. Thus, although they led unprecedentedly public lives and had been empowered by historical change, both Millay and Moore, along with H. D., Sitwell, and Bishop, appear to have seen it as the job of the poet to create *her*self through costumes and forms directed—like novels, letters, and journals—to the special moment in which the female Aeneas, unhampered by Anchises, finds herself.

"Where there is personal liking we go," wrote Moore in her early "The Hero," proposing a paradigm of nobility who looks "upon a fellow creature's error with the / feelings of a mother—a / woman or a cat" (8–9). At their best, neither she nor Millay considered it necessary (or perhaps even possible) to speak in the ostensibly universal voice of the poet—the voice that cries and whispers in *The Waste Land*, the voice that meditates on aesthetics in "Notes toward a Supreme Fiction," the voice that explores America in *Paterson*, the voice that utters cultural disillusionment in *The Cantos*.[141] Each, on the contrary, spoke as the highly particularized, private self she had constructed for, as it were, public consumption, and for each her formal choice became a kind of story in which, consciously or not, she impersonated herself.

But what of Stevens's "muse . . . still half-beast and somehow more than human, a kind of sister of the Minotaur?" It is perhaps through this anomalously powerful figure, rather than through the struggling "virile poet," that Millay and Moore would have located themselves both *in* Stevens's text and *out* of it. Certainly, confronting a history in which one's ancestresses have often been mythologized as "half-beast" (whore) or "more than human" (virgin), one might well decide to become, through brilliant metamorphosis, a femme fatale or a "spinster," a "romantic" sonneteer or a "prosaic" moralist. Thus the female female impersonation practiced by these two poets in both life and art reminds us that, as Marcia Westkott remarks in her commentary on Horney, woman's "alienation is informed not only by her visualized presence . . . her being taken as a fetish by others and therefore by herself" but also "by her marginality" so that "she is detached even when she is engaged, because she is the other, the outsider, the intruder." Yet to put the case more positively, such alienation means that the woman—here, the woman poet—is, to quote Westkott again, "the outsider who . . . can see

through the pretensions" of the powerful and construct aesthetic modes
which seek, at least implicitly, to deflate those pretensions.[142]

Most crucially such aesthetic modes seek to address the main issue that, if
we return from the seventeenth century of Stevens's mythical "sister of the
Minotaur" to the one inhabited by his more "realistic" Claire Dupray, we will
find couched in Broomstick's defensive irony, Bowl's determined naïveté.
Staring at the vexed portrait of the poetess, Broomstick asks: "Does the voice
of tragedy dwell in this mouth?" And Bowl answers: "I was not thinking of
that. I was thinking merely of the expression it gives to the portrait. That
expression is vitally biographical" (27). Stevens is plainly being ironic here
but the observations of his characters are accurate about Millay and Moore.
Whether frankly scrutinizing lovers and animals or more "objectively" meditating on Penelope and Pocahontas, each worked out of a secret feminine
assumption that "the personal is the poetical." To be sure, Moore declared in
"To a Giraffe" that it is "in fact fatal / to be personal" (215)—but by this, she
explained, she meant that it is "undesirable // to be literal," so that both she
and Millay, as avatars of that new being "Claire Dupray," attempted a mode
of female female impersonation that was "vitally biographical" even as it
subverted standard biography by suggesting its artifice.

Elizabeth Bishop's "In the Waiting Room," one of her finest works, suggests the cultural arbitrariness to which these poets were addressing themselves. In this poem the seven-year-old Bishop—or, rather, the persona
"Elizabeth"—accompanies her Aunt Consuelo to a dental appointment,
where the child reads a *National Geographic* that contains bizarre pictures of a
volcano, a set of married explorers, a dead man labeled "Long Pig," and
naked African women with "horrifying" breasts. But when "suddenly, from
inside, / came an *oh!* of pain / —Aunt Consuelo's voice—," the little girl has
a remarkable insight into the artifice of identity which reflects a number of
the points we have been making here:

> . . . I felt: you are an *I*,
> you are an *Elizabeth*,
> you are one of *them*.
> *Why* should you be one, too?
> I scarcely dared to look
> to see what it was I was.
> I gave a sidelong glance
> —I couldn't look any higher—
> at shadowy gray knees,
> trousers and skirts and boots
> and different pairs of hands
> lying under the lamps.
> I knew that nothing stranger

had ever happened, that nothing
stranger could ever happen.[143]

There is, says Bishop, "nothing stranger" than being a human being, than
being, specifically, a *female* human being (with "those awful hanging
breasts").

Such a sense of virtually metaphysical strangeness was of course intensified for Bishop, as it had been for her modernist precursors, by what we
have seen was an increasingly widespread cultural feeling that received social roles were no longer unproblematically natural. What roles or clothes,
however, could replace the odd "trousers and skirts and boots" of the past?
Neither Moore nor Millay—nor, for that matter, Bishop—was ever able
fully to imagine an answer to that question. Indeed, none of the three
appears to have formulated the question itself with the clarity that marked
Woolf's dream of a "chapter on the future." When Moore, for instance,
confronted the issue, she lapsed into teacherly tartness: "*So far as the future is
concerned, / 'Shall not one say, with the Russian philosopher, / "How is one to know
what one doesn't know?"'*" she inquired snappishly in an early (1915) version of
"The Past is the Present" (88). As for Millay, the despair that characterized
such late works as "Epitaph for the Race of Man" and "The Plaid Dress" was
reiterated in the posthumously published "Few come this way," another
examination of the Frostian "road not taken" in which a revision of "The
Unexplorer" hypothesizes not just that the past is the present but that the
past is the future:

> Few come this way; not that the darkness
> Deters them, but they come
> Reluctant here who fear to find,
> Thickening the darkness, what they left behind
> Sucking its cheeks before the fire at home,
> The palsied Indecision from whose dancing head
> Precipitately they fled, only to come again
> Upon him here,
> Clutching at the wrist of Venture with a cold
> Hand, aiming to fall in with him, companion
> Of the new as of the old.
>
> [454]

Given that a painful past seemed to these artists to be leading toward
either a vertiginous or a repetitious future, feelings of estrangement were
no doubt inevitable. A generation younger than Moore and Millay, Bishop
was to develop her own strategies for dealing with such alienation; like the
earlier group of women expatriates whose exploits we discussed in *Sexchanges*, she became preoccupied with "questions of travel," with a search for

a geography that would be enabling rather than unnerving. But her bemused memoir of Moore suggests that she understood why, for her modernist precursors, the dilemma of "the feminine," intensified by the gaze of a
voyeuristic public, had to be confronted through the deliberate "strangeness" of literal or figurative costume: "long dresses, trailing ones," a tricorne
hat and a "great cape," heavy silver "armor against the world."[144] Indeed,
whether intentionally or not, she summarized a central imperative of the
modernist woman poet's career in the advice she offered to a naked and
hairless female dog in faraway Brazil: "Dress up! Dress up and dance at
Carnival!" If the new is unknowable or terrible, one can at least *play* with the
disguise of the old. Thus, throughout their careers, some of Bishop's most
powerful female precursors had for better or worse attired themselves in the
artifice of the feminine so that they could produce ironic but vitally biographical portraits of the artist as that supreme fiction, woman.

Ain't I a New Woman? Feminism and the Harlem Renaissance

3

A disingenuous and unmanly *Position* had been formed . . . which is this,
That the Negro's though in their figure they carry some resemblances of
manhood, yet are indeed *no* men.

—Morgan Godwyn

My sons, deftly sapped, of the brawn-hood of man, self-rejected and
impotent stand,
My daughters, unhaloed, unhonored, undone, feed the lust of a dominant
land.

—Georgia Douglas Johnson

Why do they see a colored woman only as a gross collection of desires,
all uncontrolled, reaching out for their Apollos and the Quasimodos with
avid indiscrimination?
    Why unless you talk in staccato squawks—brittle as seashells—unless
you "champ" gum—unless you cover two yards square when you laugh—
unless your taste runs to violent colors—impossible perfumes and more
impossible clothes—are you a feminine Caliban craving to pass for Ariel?
    An empty imitation of an empty invitation. A mime; a sham; a copy-cat.
A hollow re-echo.

—Marita O. Bonner

At the climax of Jessie Redmon Fauset's novel *There Is Confusion* (1924), the white-masked heroine, Joanna Marshall, dances the regal, symbolic role of "America" to the delight of an audience that begins clapping and chanting, "Let's see your face, America!"[1] A moment of tension follows the removal of her mask, after which the dark-skinned Joanna proudly proclaims, "There is no one in the audience more American than I am. My great-grandfather fought in the Revolution, my uncle fought in the Civil War and my brother is 'over there' now," and renewed applause signals her stardom. But, even at this moment of New Womanly triumph, Fauset's narrator speculates that

121

perhaps Joanna's performance "would not have succeeded anywhere else but in New York, and perhaps not even there but in Greenwich Village" (232), an admission that qualifies her triumph. And although Joanna's ambitious dreams have come true on this Greenwich Village stage, the success of her career is further qualified by her future husband's belief that, for black men and women, such performances before white audiences are degrading: "I'm still a slave," he thinks about his own role-playing in a racist culture and by extension about hers, still "an entertainer" (196).

Joanna's wish to pull off the white mask to reveal her black skin and her fiancé's conviction that even were Joanna unmasked she would be dissembling arise from the disgust they feel at being forced to play a part, at being reduced—in Marita Bonner's words—to "an empty imitation. . . . A mime; a sham; a copy-cat." Both Bonner and Fauset are amplifying critical and creative meditations on the centrality of the mask in African-American culture and the problem of inauthenticity it bequeaths, studies highly influential during the Harlem Renaissance but still ongoing today. W. E. B. Du Bois, considering the "double-consciousness" of "the Negro," who "is born with a veil," examined "a peculiar sensation, . . . this sense of always looking at one's self through the eyes of others." And Paul Laurence Dunbar protested against "the mask that grins and lies, / It hides our cheeks and shades our eyes."[2] Along with Du Bois's and Dunbar's insights, Fauset's speculation that the "minstrel" or "funny man" portrait of the black man was "painted in order to camouflage the real feeling and knowledge of his white compatriots" laid the groundwork for such contemporary theorists as Henry Louis Gates, Jr., and Houston Baker, Jr., who trace the evasions, lies, and circumlocutions inflicted by a mimicry that the successful black artist transforms into aesthetic form through a process Gates terms *signifying*.[3]

For all these thinkers, black impersonation begins as an enforced necessity, a punishment imposed by racist representations of African-Americans, a mode of survival in a hostile environment. A curiously acerbic and condescending passage by Nietzsche in *The Gay Science* explains why. The "instinct" of acting "developed most easily in families of the lower classes who had to survive under changing pressures and coercions, in deep dependency, . . . [among people] who always had to change their mien and posture" until they became "masters of the incorporated and inveterate art of eternally playing hide-and-seek, which in the case of animals is called mimicry." Snobbishly equating the "mimicry" of "the lower classes" with the camouflaging or protective coloring of animals, Nietzsche went on to consider the playacting of women. "Reflect on the whole history of women: do they not *have* to be first of all and above all else actresses? Listen to physicians who have hypnotized women; finally, love them—let yourself be 'hypnotized by them'! What is always the end result? They can 'put on something' even when they take off everything. Woman is so artistic."[4]

In spite of Nietzsche's condescension, his analysis underlines the causal connection between dependency and mimicry that made acting a particularly resonant trope for black women in the 1920s and 1930s. Perhaps because, as Zora Neale Hurston put it, "only three generations separate[d] the Negro from the muteness of slavery" and the "deep dependency" bred of a system that equated blacks with animals; perhaps because she and her contemporaries lived in an age of unprecedented female female impersonation, the literary women of the Harlem Renaissance frequently used their art to focus on the mimicry deployed by black female characters.[5] To these writers, exquisitely conscious of the degradation of a survival purchased at the price of integrity, the flamboyant performances of African-American entertainers must have seemed a startlingly new phenomenon during the modernist period.

The most famous of these performers—Josephine Baker—has been described by Phyllis Rose as "a female impersonator who happened to be a woman."[6] Appearing in *Shuffle Along* (1922) and *The Chocolate Dandies* (1924), shows that featured blacks on Broadway for the first time, and later in the Paris *Revue Nègre* (1925), Baker's most astonishing success came when she established herself as the personification of negritude in so-called cannibal or savage dances. Two images in particular capture the entertainer's consciousness of being a spectacle of black womanhood for a white audience. In one photograph, wearing blackface, crossing her eyes, and using her distorted grin and splayed feet to make herself grotesque, Baker mocks the mockers of black women, whose parts in nineteenth-century minstrel shows were actually played by white men. There she parodies a white man representing a "Funny Old Gal." What Marjorie Garber calls "the anomaly of the black face in blackface" is matched in another image by the oddity of Baker's trademark, seductive "banana skirt," which Rose describes as looking "like perky, good-natured phalluses" in "jiggling motion" and which was redesigned for the Ziegfeld Follies with dangerous weapons resembling tusks or bayonets.[7]

Baker exemplified the magnetism of a host of black personalities who constructed their public images on and off the stage throughout the first two decades of the twentieth century: the show girl Valaida Snow posing as a can-can girl; the actress Ethel Waters as a boyish tramp; the singer Ida Forsune as a wealthy gent; the arts patron A'Lelia Walker as a middle-eastern adventurer; the entertainer Florence Mills as a star-spangled Dixie; and especially the film star Louise Beavers as Aunt Delilah. Yet despite the comic intent evident in some of these performances, the photograph of Louise Beavers suggests that self-presentation could shade into self-parody, contaminated by a fundamentally racist culture (figure, next page).

Perhaps for this reason, the female female impersonations of modernist women of color did not resemble Millay's and Moore's efforts to dramatize

"Aunt Delilah's Pancakes": Louise Beavers in *Imitation of Life*, 1934 (courtesy
Photographs and Prints Division, Schomburg Center for Research in Black
Culture, the New York Public Library, Astor, Lenox, and Tilden Foundations,
658-5)

the inauthenticity of the feminine. Instead, the women of the Harlem Renaissance and the characters of their fictions, encountering a series of
racially inflected stereotypes, often longed to discover or recover the authentic (black) feminine. A similar dynamic to that implicit in the image of Louise
Beavers—where mirroring the stereotype traps the actress in the image—
worked itself out in one of Zora Neale Hurston's more exotic charades.
When she was touring Vermont with the novelist Fanny Hurst, who was
distressed that her companion would be assigned to servants' quarters or
refused entrance altogether, Hurst managed to get Hurston served at a hotel
by introducing her chauffeur-friend—wearing a red headscarf and a colorful frock—as "Princess Zora": "Who would think," Hurston soliloquized
afterward, "that a good meal could be so bitter."[8] The author's conflicted
dramatization of "Princess Zora" adumbrates the debilitating stereotypes
with which many literary women of the Harlem Renaissance struggled, roles

that were partially responsible for the obscurity that attended the ends of their lives as well as (until quite recently) the marginality of their place in literary history. Significantly, the photographs usually used to represent the three major female novelists of the Harlem Renaissance—Fauset, Nella Larsen, and Hurston—dovetail with feminine stereotypes that have been erected by a number of literary-critical appraisals of their works.

The most widely distributed photograph of Jessie Fauset presents her decorously garbed in black, decorated with a string of cultured pearls and her Phi Beta Kappa key (figure, below). This portrait of a lady suits the written descriptions of her composed by Claude McKay, who claimed that "Miss Fauset is prim and dainty as a primrose, and her novels are quite as fastidious and precious."[9] Similarly, the drama critic Theophilus Lewis believed that

Jessie Redmon Fauset, from *The Crisis Magazine*, February 1924, 163 (courtesy Moorland-Spingarn Research Center, Howard University)

the world of her fiction certified respectability as the highest virtue and an old Philadelphia ancestry as the most precious possession:

> A comfortable income, derived from pill mongering, embalming cadavers, the catering business or some other traffic, is taken for granted. A finishing school o.k. is desired but not required of young ladies. Young men must present a college degree and no back talk. With those preliminary qualifications clutched tightly in their fists, the boys and girls are ready for action in a realm where love is the sweetest thing—and the greatest thing. They are, in short, readying to live, move and have their being in a world God would take pleasure in having created if God were a top-crust colored woman—which perhaps He is.[10]

According to Robert Bone, Richard Wright was thinking of Fauset, who was the literary editor of *The Crisis*, when he objected to "the prim and decorous ambassadors [of the Harlem Renaissance] who went a-begging to white America, dressed in the knee-pants of servility, curtsying to show that the Negro was not inferior."[11]

If Fauset's fiction has been dismissed as the ameliorative product of a proper lady, Larsen's prize-winning novels were quickly pigeonholed as the self-indulgent therapy of a tragic mulatto. A photograph by Carl Van Vechten captures this pose by featuring dizzying patterns of black and white, not only in the polka-dot dress and the geometrically lined background but also in the contrast between the light face and the dark hat Larsen is wearing (figure, opposite). The brooding eyes, gazing beyond the space enclosed by the photograph, almost seem to forecast the characterizations of Larsen and her heroines as "mixed-up," "illegitimate," "neurotic," and "morbid," judgments that caused many critics to ignore the social dimension of her fiction and argue with Hiroko Sako that "Nella Larsen is not concerned with race problems in the ordinary sense."[12] Often, too, the writer's supposed neuroses were visited on her heroines. Typically, discussions of *Quicksand* dismiss the novel's heroine, who "is finally engulfed by a quagmire of her own making," as well as the author, whose "prudish attitude toward sex, and . . . simple equation of 'nice things' with the pursuit of beauty" are thought to condemn her central character to banality.[13] Critics who follow this tack see Larsen and her novels as fatally flawed by the author's divided sexual, racial, and class allegiances.

Hurston shared with Fauset and Larsen a fascination with costumes of the mind, which found expression at the beginning of her *Mules and Men* (1935). There she explains that her own "negroism" had fit her "like a tight chemise. I couldn't see it for wearing it"; only after college in New York and "the spyglass" furnished by anthropology could she see herself "like somebody else and stand off and look at my garment."[14] The author's conflicted dramatiza-

Nella Larsen (courtesy the Beinecke Rare
Book and Manuscript Library, Yale
University)

tion of "Princess Zora" and her need to gain the distance of scholarship in order to watch herself: both testify to her extraordinary self-consciousness about impersonation, an awareness that explains her delight in collecting "lies" (or tall tales) and adopting different personae. Few of the many photographs of Hurston illustrate the mobility of her literal and literary impersonations better than the two portraits taken by Carl Van Vechten and used by Alice Walker for the front and back covers of her anthology *I Love Myself When I Am Laughing . . . And Then Again When I Am Looking Mean and Impressive*. Wearing a feather in her hat and a fur-collared coat, Hurston is presented as looking (rather than being) mirthful or meditative, jauntily funny or vaguely dangerous. And in her life, as Fanny Hurst has explained, Hurston lived "laughingly," "raffishly," and "with blazing zest for life," but she remained "a woman half in shadow."[15]

Exactly that sense of humor and mystery infiltrates the description of Hurston provided by her contemporary Louise Thompson. According to Nathan Huggins, Thompson "remembered her talking on the phone: 'Here's your little darky' and telling 'darky' stories, only to wink when she was through so as to show that she had tricked them again."[16] Wallace Thurman and Langston Hughes were less kind in their depictions, sarcastically intimating that Hurston profited from and fortified racist stereotypes. Thurman's portrait of Sweetie May in *Infants of the Spring* (1932) attacks Hurston as a token, a sellout who was willing to gain what she could by pandering to the racist notions of whites: "She was a great favorite among those whites who went in for Negro prodigies. Mainly because she lived up to their conception of what a typical Negro should be." Her repertoire of "earthy, vulgar and funny" tales, as well as "her darkies always smil[ing] through their tears," proved to Thurman that she "knew her white folks." Similarly, claiming that Hurston need never have written books "because she is a perfect book of entertainment in herself," Langston Hughes concluded that "to many of her white friends, no doubt, she was a perfect 'darkie,' in the nice meaning they give the term—that is a naive, childlike, sweet, humorous and highly colored Negro."[17]

The prim, proper Victorian lady; the tragic mulatto as femme fatale; the entertaining darky or royal princess: precisely the roles within which Fauset, Larsen, and Hurston were encased constitute the most powerful subjects of their respective fictions. Populated by characters repeatedly drawn to anachronistic, doomed, or self-subverting stereotypes, the narratives composed by women novelists of the Harlem Renaissance recurrently return to the question posed in the nineteenth century by one of these authors' most important black precursors, Sojourner Truth. That Truth's query—"Ain't I a woman?"—remained pertinent during the Jazz Age can be demonstrated most economically by quoting Virginia Woolf's touchstone feminist text. In *A Room of One's Own* Woolf declares, "It is one of the great advantages of being a woman that one can pass even a very fine negress without wishing to make an Englishwoman of her" (52).[18] Overtly protesting imperialism and racism, the quotation nevertheless raises Truth's question: Isn't "a very fine negress" also "a woman"? and does the adjectival "fine"—meant (undoubtedly) to certify physical attractiveness—hint at precisely the fetishization of the (looked at) "negress" that distinguishes her from the "woman" (who does the looking)?

In spite of what later accounts of the Harlem Renaissance that consistently erase or discount female achievements claim, black women played a crucial role in the transformation of African-American culture at the beginning of the twentieth century, and they did so to criticize the feminism defined by their white counterparts. For, as Barbara Christian has observed, the central "problem" of their art "was not whether black women were heroic, but whether they were women at all."[19] Yet because the New Negro of the Harlem Renaissance was implicitly male, they also questioned the emancipatory movements that shaped black modernism. Novelists like Fauset, Larsen, and Hurston therefore found themselves in the situation of the contributors to a recently published anthology evocatively entitled *All the Women Are White, All the Blacks Are Men, But Some of Us Are Brave*.[20]

Rosemary Bray has analyzed the "conflicting agendas" faced by women who are not white, blacks who are not male: "The parallel pursuits of equality for African-Americans and for women have trapped black women between often conflicting agendas for more than a century. We are asked in a thousand ways . . . to take sides against ourselves, postponing a confrontation in one arena to address an equally urgent task in another." Bray's insight that the movement for racial equality has been understood as a pursuit by and for African-American men and that feminism has been read as a pursuit by and for white women informs the contributions of the women of the Harlem Renaissance. In diverse ways, the novelists of the period elaborate upon Bray's point that "black men and white women have often made claims to our loyalty and our solidarity in the service of their respective struggles for recognition and autonomy, understanding only dimly that what may seem like liberty to each is for us only a kind of parole."[21] For many of the women artists in the Harlem Renaissance, the New Negro and the New Woman were just two more fictive roles furnishing opportunities for charades that were only a "parole." "Ain't I a [New] Woman?" Fauset, Larsen, and Hurston asked repeatedly about themselves and about heroines trapped in a succession of masks. Yet the power of their portraits of anachronistic ladies, tragic femmes fatales, Topsylike pickaninnies, and African queens emanates at least in part from an answer in the negative.

Two representations of family, and specifically of the dilemma of daughterhood, composed by Zora Neale Hurston at the start of her literary career clarify why Fauset's protagonists question the vision of the New Woman, why Larsen's heroines rebel against the values of the New Negro, and why all three authors remain highly skeptical about female impersonation. Michele Wallace has decried the "desperate masquerade" of black women who seek to adopt, adapt, or abrogate stereotypes of femininity, and for Fauset the New Woman constitutes just such an impersonation, as does the New Negro for Larsen.[22] In the play *Color Struck* (1926) and the autobiographical short story "Isis" (1924), Hurston foregrounds the dynamics of female psychosocial development through an elegy on the dead daughter whose tragic destiny (in the play) can be countered only by the desperate masquerades undertaken by Fauset's and Larsen's characters and by the desirous masquerade enacted by the protagonist in Hurston's own portrait of the artist as a young girl (in the story). Taken together, then, *Color Struck* and "Isis" can be understood as a myth of origin not only for Hurston but for many of the literary women of her generation.

To the extent that Hurston exploits vernacular to foreground the darker-skinned and economically impoverished figures who are either absent or marginalized in the works of Fauset and Larsen, her texts sustain the dichotomy usually drawn between her own commitment to Southern agrarian "folk" as opposed to Fauset's and Larsen's interest in urban, bourgeois black life.[23] Yet *Color Struck* resembles the work of Fauset and Larsen in establishing the deadly effect of societally induced self-hatred on women of color. Through it Hurston shows how the black mother's obsession with white-defined standards of beauty transforms her and her daughter into fatal or fated females, for it dislocates the black man from paternity and turns the family into a killing field. Indeed, this play presents the internalization of racism as a danger to the future of people of color, a virulent strain handed down from mother to daughter, a poisoned gift that will result in the devolution of the black family and imminent race suicide.

The four-scene play—set first inside a "Jim Crow" railway coach taking couples from Jacksonville to a cakewalk contest, then at the dance hall in "the onliest colored town in de state," Eatonville, and finally twenty years later in the heroine's one-room shack—documents the insecurity of dark-skinned Emma Beazeley, who refuses to accept her dancing partner's protestations of love.[24] In spite of John Turner's efforts to explain that "de darker de berry, de sweeter de taste!" (94), Emma convinces herself that he wants a "light colored" rival and so refuses to dance with him at the cakewalk contest. The last scene of the play repeats this encounter, but with more catastrophic results. An older, wiser John has returned to propose marriage, only to come up against Emma's continued belief that he desires "some high-yaller dickty-doo" (99). She has since borne a sickly child out of wedlock to a white man. John tries to convince Emma to get a doctor for the child, but she hesitates to leave him alone with her daughter, for she jumps to the conclusion that he will molest her. Emma forces him to leave. By the time the doctor arrives, it is too late. Drawing a sheet over the dead girl's face, the doctor rebukes Emma for waiting an hour before sending for him. In response to his query, "Why didn't you come?" Emma speaks the last line of the drama, "Couldn't see" (102).

John recites the moral of the play—"She so despises her own skin that she can't believe any one else could love it!" (102)—but he is powerless against Emma's conviction about his desire for lighter-skinned women, a belief that reflects her own self-hatred. Observing her daughter, John taunts Emma for "talkin' 'bout *me* liking high-yallers—" (100), a view borne out by her response to his injunction to get "some good colored" doctor: she "wouldn't let one of 'em tend my cat if I had one!" (101). *Color Struck* suggests that Emma is

so blinded by a sense of inferiority about her own color that she literally
strikes down her own child, who dies because of Emma's suspicions about
her own unattractiveness. As at the end of Larsen's novel *Quicksand* (1928),
the dead offspring signifies the death of the central character's sense of self-
worth, the end of the line that should be her lineage.

Just as *Quicksand*'s Helga Crane does not want to give "life to creatures
doomed to endure such wounds to the flesh, such wounds to the spirit, as
Negroes have to endure,"[25] Hurston's deluded Emma, who dreads the sexual vulnerability of her sick daughter, uncovers a motif in black women's
literature that sets itself in opposition to the stereotypical image of the adoring mammy of white children in order to meditate on the painful dilemma of
black mothers, a tradition derived at least in part from Elizabeth Barrett
Browning's "Runaway Slave at Pilgrim's Point" (1850). The speaker of Barrett Browning's dramatic monologue, having been raped by her white master, is driven to infanticide because her baby has "the *master's* look." At the
contemporary end of this tradition, Toni Morrison's brilliant novel *Beloved*
(1987) analyzes the anguish of a mother who loves the children she attempts
to kill, drawing on a major trope developed by earlier African-American
literary women.[26]

A historical depiction of a black community on a southern plantation in
1862, Shirley Graham's play "It's Morning" (1940), for example, counterpoints the bright future of emancipation with the figure of a mother holding
in her arms the daughter who has to be killed to be saved from sexual slavery.
Not slavery but lynching and rape constitute the dangers facing mothers and
children in a number of texts by modernist women of color. In a poem
entitled "Black Woman" (1922) by Georgia Douglas Johnson, the speaker
confronts the "cruelty and sin" awaiting black children by concluding, "I
must not give you birth!" Three of Johnson's short plays—"Plumes" (1927),
"Blue-Eyed Black Boy" (193?), and "A Sunday Morning in the South"
(1925)—depend for their suspense on the life of a child hanging in the
balance between a powerfully felt but powerless maternal protectiveness and
a murderous society which threatens the survival of the black child.[27]

Staged in 1916 and published in 1920, *Rachel*—the best-known work of
Hurston's contemporary Angelina Weld Grimké—focuses on its heroine's
tragic decision to relinquish her foster child and give up a maternity made
too painful by a racist society that abuses black children. Similarly, in the
short story "The Closing Door" (1919) Grimké's central character, horrified
at becoming "an instrument" that produces "men children—for the sport—
the lust—of . . . mobs," smothers her baby and shuts the door on her own
future.[28] Although Chandler Owen, one of the editors of the *Messenger*,
called for "a *New Negro mother*, no longer a '*white man's woman*,' no longer the
sex-enslaved '*black mammy*' of Dixie—but the apotheosis of triumphant Negro womanhood,"[29] a number of black literary women analyzed Helga

Crane's conviction that "giving birth" is a "sin, an unforgivable outrage. More black folk to suffer indignities. More dark bodies for mobs to lynch" (75).

Yet Hurston's Emma destroys her daughter not to wrest control from a white owner or mob but because of unjustified suspicions about her black suitor. Indeed, despite John's reiterated desire to marry Emma and adopt her child, Emma persists in imagining a rivalry between herself and the girl, much as she had earlier fabricated a competition between herself and a lighter-skinned dancer. The fatal insecurity of the color-struck woman makes the black family a virtual impossibility here. When Jessie Fauset and Nella Larsen imagine the resurrection of the light-skinned girl-child and chart her evolution into maturity, they dramatize the ways in which she continues to struggle within Emma's script, for their heroines subscribe to a depreciation of black femininity and encounter the secondariness of the black man cut off from the paternal authority that should be his.[30]

The protagonists of Fauset and Larsen respond quite differently to the ways in which the mastery of black men is attenuated by a racist culture; like Emma, however, they oscillate between competing allegiances to white and black men, white and black societies. Regardless of whether they decide to pass as white, Fauset's and Larsen's protagonists become trapped in suicidal modes of impersonation that drain them of authenticity. For Fauset and Larsen, black women who overvalue whiteness or white men are destined to suffer a kind of antinarcissism that condemns them to mimic bankrupt roles which, in turn, further encase black men in no-manhood even as they ensure the devolution of the race. In other words, Fauset and Larsen frequently center their novels on color-struck characters who are granted the light skin Emma so cherishes and who, like Emma's daughter, suffer its poisonous effects in the lies of their lives, the shame of the shams they perpetuate.

If Hurston studies the destruction of the light-skinned daughter in *Color Struck*, her story "Isis" presents the dark girl who exploits tactics of impersonation unrelated to "passing," stratagems that enable the heroine to live and create; the story therefore shows Hurston's aesthetic project in contrast with those of Fauset and Larsen. In this tale, eleven-year-old Isis Watts, who loves to perch on the gatepost in order to glimpse the road that leads to Orlando, repeatedly defies her grandmother's admonition to act like "a lady."[31] Inventive and rebellious, Isis goes off to dance at a neighborhood barbecue, where three white figures mirthfully view her as "our little gypsy" (16). Looking for a means to evade her grandmother, Isis drives off in their "heavenly chariot," explaining to the white lady "that she was really a princess": "She told them about her trips to the horizon, about the trailing gowns, the gold shoes with blue bottoms—she insisted on the blue bottoms— the white charger, the time when she was Hercules and had slain numerous dragons and sundry giants" (17). When Isis is returned home, the white woman saves her from a whipping by giving the grandmother five dollars and inviting Isis to come "to the hotel and dance for me. I could stand a little light today" (18). Because Hurston's young heroine loves adventure and believes that the white woman "could understand" her, she does go off, offering to sing a song. The "feeling that Grandma had been somewhat squelched did not detract from Isis' spirit at all" (18).

As a self-portrait, "Isis" introduces several tropes to which Hurston would return in later works. In the essay "How It Feels to Be Colored Me" (1928), Hurston describes her "favorite place" as a child in Eatonville as "atop the gate-post." Wandering off on horses or in automobiles, Hurston saw the gate-post as a "Proscenium box" in which she could "enjoy the show" or join it, if her family did not interfere. As in "Isis," it is the "white people" who "liked to hear me 'speak pieces'" and "gave me generously of their small silver for doing these things," while "the colored people . . . deplored any joyful tendencies in me, but I was their Zora nevertheless." Similarly, in *Dust Tracks on a Road* (1942), Hurston's autobiography, she again describes herself taking "a seat on top of the gate-post" from which she would hail white travelers for whom she furnished "a great deal of amusement," even though her grandmother, who "had known slavery" and who found her "brazenness . . . unthinkable," warned her, "They's gowine to lynch you, yet." Like Isis, a youthful Hurston had sworn an "oath of Hercules," the figure whose dedication meant "follow[ing] . . . the steep way to the blue hills of fame and glory." In all of these works, as in *Their Eyes Were Watching God* (1937), where Janie Crawford looks down the road from the front gate, the imagination is linked to a vision of what Janie calls the "change and chance" of the "far horizon."[32]

Drawing on formative autobiographical material, "Isis" repudiates traditional, middle-class norms of femininity, choosing instead the indeterminacy of mimicry. Rebelling against her grandmother's admonition—"youse too 'oomanish jumpin' up in everybody's face dat pass" (9)—Isis whistles, sits with her knees separated, plays with boys, pictures herself as a dragon-slaying Hercules, and determines to shave her grandmother's whiskers, all activities that "Grandma Potts felt no one of this female persuasion should do" (11). At the same time, she also imagines herself as a princess, a Spanish dancer, and a Madame Tragedy. Known as "Isis the Joyful," then, she functions not only as a wild child who embodies Hurston's vision of creativity as impersonation but also as a divine child who exemplifies the author's life-long quest to reconstruct ancient images of black female spirituality.

The sheet used as a shroud for Emma's dead daughter in *Color Struck* recalls Du Bois's effacing veil, but in "Isis"—which was originally entitled "Drenched in Light"—the tablecloth that Hurston's character wears as a costume to turn herself into a dancer evokes the veil of her namesake, the goddess Isis. "My veil no one has lifted," the Egyptian goddess proclaims in rituals celebrating her mysterious relationship to the principles of generation and regeneration. In fact, the goddess Isis—addressed by Egyptians as the "Mother in the *horizon* of heaven" (emphasis ours)—seems a fitting prototype for Isis Watts, a child drenched not in the white light of Judeo-Christianity but in the celestial light of Hurston's reconstructed emblems of African creativity.[33] According to Du Bois, "the spell of the African mother pervades her land. Isis, the mother, is still titular goddess, in thought if not in name, of the dark continent."[34] Hurston's early fascination with the figure of African Isis, which Du Bois connected to "the mother-idea," may be related to a later image, that of the veiled black woman who appears in her description of a voodoo priestess in *Tell My Horse* (1938):

> "What is the truth?" Dr. Holly asked me, and knowing that I could not answer him he answered himself through a Voodoo ceremony in which the Mambo, that is the priestess, richly dressed[,] is asked this question ritualistically. She replies by *throwing back her veil and revealing her sex organs.* The ceremony means that *this is the infinite, the ultimate truth.* There is no mystery beyond the mysterious source of life. The ceremony continues on another phase after this. It is a dance analogous to the nuptial flight of the queen bee. The Mambo discards six veils in this dance and falls at last naked, and spiritually intoxicated[,] to the ground. It is considered the *highest honor for all males participating to kiss her organ of creation,* for Damballa, the god of gods has permitted them to come face to face with truth (emphasis ours).[35]

To the extent that the child Isis and the priestess Mambo embody Hurston's vision of gifts of spiritual power, we shall see that their depiction dovetails with her more aesthetically ambitious consecration of black female sexuality in *Their Eyes Were Watching God.*

Certainly in her mature work Hurston seems to vouchsafe her heroines not the self-destructive masquerade of passing we will examine in Fauset's *Plum Bun* (1928) and Larsen's *Passing* (1929) but a shape-changing multiplicity of masks, names, roles, and personae. Yet the end of "Isis" functions to qualify the triumphant mutability of its heroine's identities and to link her to the seemingly more decorous or doomed heroines of Fauset and Larsen. For Isis turns her back on her own community, lets herself be bought by the white people's money, relishes the defeat of her censorious but nonetheless nurturing grandmother, and faces a future in which she functions as a spectacle in an alien and inevitably alienating world.

That Isis's lies, charades, and dancing are discouraged by her grandmother while encouraged by the white woman reflects Hurston's tangled relationship to white and black readers.[36] At the end of the story, moreover, a white man describes Isis's cleaving to his female companion with a phrase— "you've been adopted" (18)—that invokes the often stifling effect of Hurston's patron or "adopted godmother," Mrs. Osgood Mason. As in

Hurston's autobiography, *Dust Tracks on the Road*, in "Isis" white people furnish aesthetic impetus and support, but they also threaten to control black speech. The singing, dancing child, who is supposed to perform in order to bring "mirth" and "a little of her sunshine" into the white woman's soul (18), recalls not only the pickaninny Topsy in Stowe's *Uncle Tom's Cabin* but also the figure Hurston calls "the pet Negro."[37] "Isis" therefore charts Hurston's ambivalent attitude toward her artistry, specifically her acknowl-edgement that an art formed within the black community must inevitably be played out for a white audience that exiles the artist from her own origins.

Thus, Hurston crafts a tale equivocal enough to encompass the sense of inauthenticity that haunts the seemingly quite dissimilar characters created by her female contemporaries. Like the tellers of the "lies" she recalls in her anthropological study *Mules and Men*, she finds some comfort by trusting to the naïveté of the white reader or spectator: "He can read my writing but he sho' can't read my mind"(5). Yet, Hurston's Isis, performing for and before whites, ultimately resembles the heroines of *There Is Confusion, Plum Bun, Quicksand,* and *Passing,* all of whom turn themselves into surveyed spectacles, the object of the gaze of a community whose racism continually shapes and threatens their survival. Significantly, too, the source of Hurston's own re-siliency, as well as that of her heroine, resides neither in New Womanly assertion nor in New Negro programs of uplift but in old tactics of dissimu-lation furnished from African-American folk culture, and we shall see that authors as different in sensibility as Fauset and Larsen share her skepticism. For whether their characters pass as New Women or New Negroes, whether their masquerades are desperate or desirous, together they diagnose the plight of the black woman who feels herself to be a mime, a sham, and a copy-cat.

Although these same characters often seek the freedom and autonomy we associate with early twentieth-century sexual and racial movements of emancipation, their authors undercut the ideology of the new to which so many of their contemporaries subscribed. Exploiting the novel of manners to critique American racism, Fauset viewed the New Woman as a white woman, whose feminism the black woman must repudiate in order to rein-vent the masculinity of black men. Revising the psychological novel to inves-tigate the bankruptcy not only of European but also of African-American culture, Larsen presented the New Negro movement as life-threatening to the autonomous black woman. Hurston pioneered a different kind of recon-struction: using anthropological methods to excavate a folk legacy beyond racism and sexism, she resurrected not the black New Woman but an older, wily or wild conjure woman from African Ur-cultures.

According to the literary women of the Harlem Renaissance, who sought to negotiate between the competing claims of white New Women and male New Negroes, feminist and black liberation agendas only generated spurious roles for black women. Even their adherence to relatively conventional narrative forms signals a shared suspicion about the relevance of ideologies of the new to the social and psychological situations of black women. If Fauset's repudiation of feminism led her to embrace an anachronistic model of ladyhood, if Larsen's rejection of racial uplift caused her to promulgate an image of the femme fatale, if Hurston's anthropological excavations encouraged her to mystify or essentialize the power of the feminine, all three novelists nevertheless dramatized desperate and desirous charades in which the "woman" who is a "negress" takes center stage to act out the liabilities and the liminality conferred on black women by the social revolutions associated with feminism and the Harlem Renaissance.

At a crux in Jessie Redmon Fauset's *Plum Bun* (1928), two sisters meet inside New York's Penn Station and one pretends not to know the other. Light-skinned Angela Murray, the heroine who left her home in Philadelphia after her parents' death, has passed as white in New York by transforming herself into Angèle Mory: "She was seeing the world, she was getting acquainted with life in her own way without restrictions or restraint; she was young, she was temporarily independent, she was intelligent, she was white."[38] Although she had planned to welcome her darker sister, Virginia, to New York, the unexpected arrival of a white suitor causes color-struck Angèle to disclaim any kinship with (or even recognition of) Virginia. This "sacrifice of a sister" (159) demonstrates that sisterhood is not powerful when it involves those whom Mary Church Terrell called "sisters of the dominant race" or, in this case, a sister posing as a member of the dominant race.[39] When Angela turns herself into the young, independent, white Angèle, she becomes a paradigmatic New Woman. But, as Fauset repeatedly shows, for the woman with roots in the black community, the New Woman can only be an impersonation, a charade that divides her from that community without providing her with alternative sources of empowerment. Although *Plum Bun* is usually dismissed as retrograde melodrama, it can be read as an indictment of the racism and sex antagonisms that afflict white society in general and feminists in particular.

That "white" Angèle Mory rather than "coloured" Angela Murray represents feminism becomes clear through Fauset's depiction of the young woman's evolution in New York. To Angela color stands in the way of "the good things of life which could come to you in America" (46): it is "nothing short of a curse" (53) that "narrow[s] her confines" (64). Passing as white, on the other hand, means "launch[ing] out 'into a freer, fuller life'" (80). She has therefore left Philadelphia and found an apartment in Greenwich Village. In New York she enrolls in the art institute at Cooper Union, befriends a number of independent white women, and becomes involved with a wealthy white man. Although "no boyish stowaway on a ship had a greater exuberance in going forth to meet the unknown than had Angela as she entered her class that first afternoon" (93), and although the other students greet her as "Miss New One" (94), Angèle discovers that passing as (or even being) a New Woman is not as liberating as she had expected. Fauset questions through her representation of feminist activities feminism's ostensible goals—specifically its emphasis on economic and professional individualism, its ideal of sisterhood, and its advocacy of free love—and their accessibility to black women.

The "strong," "pronounced" New Women (112) Angèle meets in New York advocate audaciously unconventional ideas about female independence; all, however, are shown to be implicated in highly conventional and subtly tainted situations. Paulette Lister, who seems "mistress of herself and of her fate" (105) and who argues that "any woman is better than the best of men" (128), nonetheless lives with a man; she defines her philosophy as getting what she wants: "I use my wiles as a woman to get it, and I employ the qualities of men, tenacity and ruthlessness, to keep it. And when I'm through with it, I throw it away just as they do" (105). The salon hostess Martha Burden, who "doesn't believe in marriage" (195) but is nevertheless married, explains to Angèle that "God doesn't like women" who are condemned "to play a game" to entrap men; the older woman then goes on to instruct Angèle in the rules of that game: "You must always like or appear to like him a little less than he does you. And you must make him want you. But you mustn't give" (145–46). Similarly, despite European travels, a profession as a librarian, and ambitions to become an actress, Rachel Salting ends up preaching to Angèle the "gospel of marriage," which is "an old, old story" (213), and a story, as told by this Jewish girl in love with a Catholic man, no less complicated by ethnic prohibitions against interfaith relationships than the "old story" that forbids interracial marriage.

For all their advocacy of freedom, then, these women are trapped in manipulative, hypocritical, or traditional relationships with men. Together they reinforce a point that at this stage in the novel Angela has accepted but that will be revised by the novel's ending, namely that "men had a better time of it than women, coloured men than coloured women, white men than white women" (88). When she enters into a flirtation with the white, wealthy Roger Fielding, moreover, Angèle finds herself engaged in a sexual battle that is a lost cause. Playing "Angel" (140) to this "blond, glorious god" (129), she refuses to be a "sentimentalist," acknowledging to herself that "she wanted Roger and what he could give her" (143), namely the gifts of courtship that she hopes will solidify into "golden keys which could open the doors to beauty and ease and—decency!" (142). Knowing that "men paid a big price for their desires," she determines that "her price would be marriage," dues she wishes to exact through the "dangerous game" taught to her by Martha

(183). But she is unprepared for the "duelling" (190), the "trial of strength" (191), and the "conflict" over what he calls "free love" (192). Characterizing the relationship between white men and women as warfare and defining the rhetoric of free love as the white man's ploy to gain sexual possession of the female, Fauset exploits the language of battle to indicate that Angèle's "weapons were those furnished by conventions" but her fight is against yearnings for intimacy which sabotage her from within. In spite of her tactical efforts to resist sexual compliance—"because viewed in the light of the great battle which she was waging for pleasure, protection and power, it was inexpedient" (199–200)—Angèle eventually capitulates, but on her own terms. Refusing to be kept, she attributes her "surrender" to the "generosity of her heart": "If this were free love the freedom was the quality to be stressed rather than the emotion." Although Angèle convinces herself that, poised on "a threshold," she is entering "on a new, undreamed of phase of being" (204), the plot of *Plum Bun* demonstrates that female "kindness" breeds male "indifference." All of her efforts to please Roger lead to his "increased sullenness, remoteness, wariness" (226) until he insults her, ending the relationship not only by flirting with a woman more acceptable to his class-conscious father but also by insisting, "You knew perfectly well what you were letting yourself in for. Any woman would know it" (231).

To the extent that Fauset emphasizes the contradiction between Angèle's faith "that she alone of all people in the world was exempt from ordinary law" (232) and her inexorable confinement within that law, she alludes to the literary stance of her major white contemporary, Edith Wharton. As Elizabeth Ammons has argued, "the whole issue of marriage for profit in *Plum Bun* evokes several Wharton novels—*The House of Mirth, Summer, The Custom of the Country*"—and, as Carolyn Wedin Sylvander has pointed out, early advertisements and reviews of Fauset's first novel praise her for crafting "an art as impersonal as that of Mrs. Wharton."[40] Like Lily Bart rejected by her suitors at the end of *The House of Mirth* and like Charity Royall abandoned by Lucius Harney in *Summer*, Angèle is scorned by Roger Fielding and therefore loses her value as an ornament, becoming "like any one of a thousand other pitiful, frightened girls thronging New York" (234).

The nursery rhyme to which the title of *Plum Bun*, as well as its section titles, alludes—

> To market, to market
> To buy a Plum Bun
> Home again, home again
> Market is done

—indicates that Angela, who had moved into the market to buy her freedom, must realize that she is herself an object of exchange, a delicacy which will be consumed in spite of her own consuming ambitions because in white society "everything was for men" (229). Significantly, then, at the climactic scene when she arrives in Penn Station to greet her sister, Angèle wears a veil, a costume which recalls Du Bois's metaphor of black entrapment and which symbolizes her efforts to pass as white as well as her confinement in white-defined standards of femininity.

Just as important, when she rejects her sister, Angèle uses a formula from a childhood game that consisted of impersonating ladies—"Really you have the advantage of me. No I'm not Mrs. Jones" (159)—a sentence that marks Angèle's effort to keep up with the (white) Joneses as well as Fauset's relationship to Edith (Jones) Wharton. Predictably, too, the ironies which perplex so many of Wharton's heroines seem destined to entrap Angela even after Roger Fielding's rejection has led her to leave the "market" of whites and go "home again" to her roots. Angela discovers that Anthony Cross, the art student to whom she has been attracted, is actually passing as white (and therefore is a perfect match for her) at the same time that she learns that he has become engaged to her sister, even though Virginia loves a childhood friend, Matthew Henson, and Anthony really wishes to marry Angela. Like Wharton's heroines Angela becomes afflicted with a passivity born of the consciousness that "whatever move I make is always wrong" (314).

Yet, as if to elaborate on the sentence "No I'm not Mrs. Jones," Fauset swerves from her white precursor to the extent that she sets her critique of feminization in an explicitly racial context. While "white" Angèle confronts the listlessness of her "double life" (252) in a room of her own in downtown New York without Roger, "coloured" Virginia, "leading an utterly open life, no secrets, no subterfuges, no goals to be reached by devious ways," feels at home uptown in Harlem (243). For this reason, after Roger's desertion Angèle determines to reclaim her relationship not only with Virginia and Anthony but also with the black community. In search of companionship, security, and "home," she decides at the beginning of the process of disclosure that will culminate in her full acceptance of her racial identity: "When it seemed best to be coloured she would be coloured; when it was best to be white she would be that." At this moment, a "great sense of peace, of exaltation descended upon her" and the narrator explains that Angela "could have said: 'I will arise and *go unto my father'*" (253; emphasis ours).

The phrase is an important one, for just as the New Woman's feminism in *Plum Bun* entails a battle of the sexes with sexual exploitation disguised as an ethic of free love, so racial consciousness means bonding with black men. In *Summer*, Wharton depicted the capitulation of her heroine to paternal Lawyer Royall as at least implicitly a female tragedy emblematizing the inexorable Law of the Father;[41] Fauset, however, represents her heroine's turn to the father as a return to origins which have been repressed by the laws of the land. At the moment Angèle considers transforming herself back into Angela, then, she begins thinking of the safety of marriage, of giving instead of taking, and of relinquishing her quest for autonomy: "Perhaps this selfish-ness [of her past life of New Womanly independence] was what the posses-sion of white blood meant; the ultimate definition of Nordic Supremacy" (275). When she determines to disclose her racial roots to Anthony, there-fore, she feels that "she wanted to be a beloved woman, dependent, fragile, sought for, feminine; after this last ordeal she would be 'womanly' to the point of ineptitude" (296–97).

In spite of her bemused identification of womanliness with ineptitude, Angèle's resumption of the appellation "Angela" further enables Fauset to criticize the racist underpinnings of (white) feminism. As Angela begins to test her white friends against her new racial consciousness, she learns that Rachel Salting, for example, "wouldn't marry a nigger in any circumstances" (313) and that even the progressive Martha Burden wonders whether "col-oured people aren't natural born quitters" (338). As at the start of her heroine's art education—when a white girl looked at a painting of "an old coloured woman" and exclaimed, "I never think of darkies as Americans" (70)—Fauset illuminates the view of Angelina Grimké that "the white women of this country are about the worst enemies with which the colored race has to contend."[42]

Race, not gender, functions as a true bond, or so *Plum Bun* goes on to imply. While passing, Angèle had kept her distance from the other black art student at Cooper Union, Miss Powell. But after both win scholarships to study abroad and Miss Powell's is rescinded because of her color, Angela realizes that "they were more than 'sisters under the skin,'" for they are "connected in blood, in racial condition, in common suffering" (340–41), and she rejects her own scholarship, publicly avowing her racial origins to journalists, who publish a story under the headline "Socially Ambitious Negress Confesses to Long Hoax" (352). Fauset's plot hints at the same point Elise Johnson McDougald made when she claimed that "the Negro woman's feminist efforts are directed chiefly toward the realization of the equality of the races, the sex struggle assuming the subordinate place,"[43] for the "So-cially Ambitious Negress" in *Plum Bun* is viewed as a "Hoax" because of racist, not sexist, discrimination.

Yet an even more important aspect of Angela's decision to "go unto my father" is effected through Fauset's invocation of her major black precursor, Frances E. W. Harper. Harper's *Iola Leroy, or Shadows Uplifted* (1892) focuses on a light-skinned woman who rejects the marriage proposal of an attractive white doctor, thereby refusing to pass or to "cast her lot with the favored race" and instead dedicating herself to "serv[ing] the race which needs me most." After working as a teacher in the South, Iola moves to the North where she marries a light-skinned man who has also rejected opportunities to pass and who embodies her ideal of "high, heroic manhood."[44] Fauset directly invokes Harper's plot when, late in the novel, Angela also receives and rejects a proposal from a white man, choosing instead a man like herself. In opposition to Roger, who had followed his father's wishes by choosing a socially acceptable mate and seems "like a cross baby," Anthony Cross appears to be "a man, a real one, someone not afraid" (321). By making this distinction, though, Fauset strives to redefine masculinity in such a way as to defuse the economic and social power of Roger Fielding and infuse the passive, tormented Anthony with potency.

Alluding to *Iola Leroy* in order to certify the masculinity of black men, *Plum Bun* examines the figure of the no-man that Wharton had also delineated but does so to analyze the ways in which a racist society degrades black men. Paradoxically, the very extremity of that problem produces a female literary tradition that seeks to reinvent masculinity. All of the black male characters in Fauset's novel, beginning with Angela's father, are shown to be resourceful combatants in a racial struggle that inflicts humiliations which the black woman can ease only by reestablishing at least a semblance of masculine authority. At the start, the fate of Angela and Virginia's parents illustrates the deadly effects of emasculation on both sexes.

Light-skinned Mrs. Murray, who occasionally passes for a "joke" (19)—that is, for a brief adventure or on a whim—becomes ill during one of her holidays from blackness and is taken to "a hospital to which no coloured woman would ever have been admitted except to char" (58–59). When her husband, arriving to take her home, is greeted by a hostile clerk, he is forced to pretend to be his wife's chauffeur. Immediately after this episode, he becomes ill and dies, and his loving wife mysteriously passes away soon after. These sorts of coincidences, which most critics consider faults in Fauset's novel, function symbolically, for the deaths of the parents in effect document the fatality of a charade that places Mrs. Murray in the position of the wealthy, racist "Madame" for whom she had earlier worked as a maid even as it plummets Mr. Murray back to the role of coachman he had performed for the same white woman. In spite of his "patriarchal aspect almost biblical" (22) inside the family and despite his trickster ruse, the father's vulnerability in the world outside the home may be said to kill him and his wife.

Two social scenes—one at the movies and one in a restaurant—further show how the humiliations to which black men are subjected afflict black women with the burden of bolstering shattered male pride. While still living in Philadelphia, Angela purchases film tickets for her date, Matthew Henson, but the attendant in the lobby tells him, "she can go in, but you can't" (75). Immediately, we are told, "Angela could feel [Matthew's] very manhood sickening under the silly humiliation of the moment" (75). Although Angela had been peeved in the past by his attentions, in this instance she leaves the theater, becoming "very kind to him in the car," because she is "suddenly conscious of the pain which must be his at being stripped before the girl he loved of his masculine right to protect, to appear the hero" (76). This incident, which causes her to quit her life in Philadelphia, returns to her memory when, as Angèle, she is dining in New York with Roger Fielding. During the second episode, surrounded by "the glitter and perfection of crystal and silver, of marvellous napery and of obsequious service" (132), Angèle watches Roger turn three "'coons,'" a young couple accompanied by a fatherly man, out of an elegant café. His racism, which horrifies her, causes him to pervert the ideas promulgated by the separatist Marcus Garvey: Roger "had black-balled Negroes in Harvard, aspirants for small literary or honour societies. 'I'd send 'em all back to Africa if I could. There's been a darkey up in Harlem's got the right idea, I understand; though he must be a low brute to cave in on his race that way; of course it's merely a matter of money with him. He'd betray them all for a few thousands. Gosh, if he could really pull it through I don't know but what I'd be willing to finance it'" (133). Even before this tirade, Angèle had noted the self-consciousness of the young couple. While she sympathizes with the boy's distress at being turned out of the café, Angèle is particularly sensitive to the girl, who had "affected at first a gay hardihood," but then her "courage had had to be translated anew into a comforting assurance" to her companion: she "could not relieve her feelings, for she must comfort her baffled and goaded escort" (136).

As Roger's reference to Garvey demonstrates, even the most charismatic Harlem leaders can become grist for the racist mill that is American society in Fauset's novel. W. E. B. Du Bois, fictionalized as Van Meier, appears in a scene which celebrates the powerful societal forces at work in the Harlem Renaissance but which also proves that these forces are not sufficiently potent to rid whites of their prejudice. Angèle, attending a lecture with her white friends, hears Van Meier speak poetically about the personal sacrifices racial "chauvinism" should inspire. Yet although the black members of his audience are "transformed by racial pride as princes in a strange land in temporary serfdom, princes whose children would know freedom" (219), Angèle's white companions respond by flirting with Van Meier or by wondering about the "portion of white blood" in his veins (220).[45]

But it is by means of the character of Anthony Cross that Fauset most forcefully documents a point made by a contributor to a 1923 issue of the *Messenger* that the "New Negro Woman" must help teach her male peer "to spurn and overcome the fatal, insidious inferiority complex of the present, which . . . bobs up ever and anon to arrest the progress of the New Negro Manhood Movement."[46] Introduced as a Spaniard characterized by "curious sadness" as well as a "half-proud, half-sensitive tendency to withdrawal" (102), Anthony is nevertheless associated in Angèle's mind with her father, for when she deflects his marriage proposal early in the novel she thinks with distaste of wash days in the shabby house inhabited by her parents. But after she has decided to go unto her father, she listens sympathetically while Anthony reveals his heritage.

Anthony's black father and light-skinned Brazilian mother had suffered in Georgia from the white community's jealousy of the father's wealth and the mother's beauty: their farm was burned; the father was shot and his fingers, toes, and ears cut off by "souvenir hunters"; and the mother had become "a madwoman, . . . haunted by a terrible fear" not of whites but of blacks, whom she believed to be "cursed": "otherwise why should we be so abused, so hounded" (289–90). That, unlike Anthony's mother, Angela responds to the cross of his history by repudiating her white mask becomes only one sign of her renunciation of New Womanly ambition. The plot of this novel emphasizes the opposition between such ambition and race pride by portraying the climactic moment of racial revelation through Angela's refusal to accept the art scholarship she has won.

But although Angela insists on validating the masculinity of her beloved, *Plum Bun*'s plot emphasizes his impotence. Anthony's declaration that he was going to tell Angèle about his blood elicits admiration from her: "Here was honour, here was a man!" Yet the contradiction between his vow "always to hate [whites] with a perfect hatred" (291) and his earlier marriage proposal to her when he believed her to be white escapes her entirely. In addition, his entrapment in an engagement to Virginia, toward whom he feels only a protective sort of affection which matches Virginia's passionless sense of gratitude, proves his resignation to "the ceaseless warfare which most coloured people wage," a battle that means, he explains, "they have to stop their fight for the trimmings of life in order to hang on to the essentials which they've got to have, and for which they must contend too every day just as hard as they did the first day" (338). Fauset repeatedly certifies Anthony's superior authority *because* of his vulnerability; while the narrator and heroine affirm his masculinity, the narrative presents the necessity of Angela taking upon herself the responsibility of making a man of him.

In direct contrast to the fiction of many of such white contemporaries as Wharton and Woolf, then, the conclusion of Fauset's *Plum Bun* demonstrates the compatibility of men's and women's quests for liberation from debilitating social scripts. On the one hand, Angela's move to Paris and her dedication to her art hint that she is more than capable of New Womanly autonomy, but on the other, her homesickness there forces her to judge her New Womanly ambitions against the values of domesticity and find her adventurous life wanting. The final scene of the book shows that, unlike the white New Women, black women *can* revise traditional roles for both sexes. Having witnessed the destruction caused by color-struck or passing women—her own mother, Anthony's mother, herself—Angela will construct a sufficient black family to create a future for her race.

Because Virginia has finally been united with her childhood sweetheart, Matthew Henson, she sends Anthony as a "present" (377) to her sister. That he appears on Christmas implies that Anthony Cross will be reborn through his reunion with Angela, as will she through him. In a tale that begins with Angela and Virginia singing "Am I a Soldier of the Cross" and "Dying Christian" (21, 25), it is fitting that in a sense the conclusion dramatizes the biblical injunction "No man comes unto the Father except through me" (John 14:6). Although the female is an object of exchange between white men, Angela's bearing of the burden of Cross hints that if black women sacrifice their ambitions for independence they can resurrect their wounded male doubles and themselves, thus entering into newly egalitarian sexual relationships. "There ought to be a tag on me somewhere," Anthony remarks at the conclusion of *Plum Bun*, as Angela receives her sister's "package" (378) and he becomes the gift outright. Here, then, Fauset subscribes to a view expressed in a 1923 issue of the *Messenger*, namely that upon the shoulders of the "New Negro Woman" rests "the big task to create and keep alive in the breast of black men, a holy and consuming passion to break with the slave traditions of the past."[47]

Nella Larsen's fiction, which reads like a direct indictment of Fauset's project, satirizes not only programs of racial uplift but also the supportive feminine role they prescribe. For Larsen, as for Fauset, black liberation entails a recuperation of the no-man, but *Quicksand* and *Passing* examine the ways in which that recuperation embeds the black woman in a series of desperate pretenses and thereby destroys her because there is no place for female desire in the economy of the New Negro movement. Like Jean Toomer, whose work she knew, Larsen suggests that "man dominates because of limitation" and the limitations placed on black men by a racist society cause them to straitjacket women of color into a role designed to counter myths of hypersexuality—the anachronistic role of the desexualized lady.[48] When Larsen's heroines go unto their fathers, they encounter black men whose mimicries of white patriarchs are as destructive to women as the model upon which they are founded. Indeed, whether confronted by segregated white or black cultures, *Quicksand*'s Helga Crane feels herself to be fraudulently passing herself off, even though she never attempts to pass for white. According to Larsen, then, the New Woman of color who subscribes to the values promulgated by the Harlem Renaissance will be turned into a mime, a sham, a copy-cat.

At least in part, Helga's reaction against African-American schools, salons, and saloons can be attributed to her biracial background. Born of a Danish mother whose black husband abandoned her, Helga Crane has been viewed as a typical tragic mulatto, a self-divided character fated to suffer the consequences of liminality. But what Larsen emphasizes through Helga's alienation from black as well as white societies is not only a psychological ambivalence that might seem neurotic but also a segregated social network of lies that traps her heroine behind a succession of masks. At a circus performance which highlights Helga's dilemma, she confronts a humiliating image on a stage. Watching two black entertainers dancing and singing a ragtime song, Helga sits motionless while the rest of the audience applauds in delight. Filled "with a fierce hatred for the cavorting Negroes on the stage" (83), she realizes that she has been decked out too: as in the nursery rhyme she recalls—"Hark! Hark! The dogs do bark"—African-Americans seem like "beggars" to Helga, whether dressed in rags or in velvet gowns. During her frequent, solitary returns to the circus, she gazes at gesticulating ragtime figures who reflect her own tawdry impersonations, charades complete with costumes, masks, and lying lines that are provided not only by white spectators but by black actors as well.

As such critics as Hazel V. Carby and Deborah McDowell have noted, *Quicksand* begins by launching a scathing satire against the doctrine of racial improvement promulgated by Booker T. Washington in the South and the racial revolution advocated by Du Bois in the North.[49] In the first chapter of the novel, Helga determines to leave "the finest school for Negroes anywhere in the country" (3), and Larsen uses her heroine's alienation to ridicule the hypocrisies of racial "uplift" movements (5). As Helga's progress takes her from the South to Chicago, New York, Copenhagen, and finally back, moreover, Larsen implies that the Harlem Renaissance and even the most enlightened white cultures, as well as those agrarian regions associated with a return to African-American roots, furnish no place for the independent black woman.

Educators at Naxos, an anagram of (Anglo-) Saxon but also a reference to the island on which the mythical Ariadne was abandoned, conform to what is "expected of them" (3) by racist authorities; to ensure conformity the school, which has "grown into a machine" exemplifying "the white man's magnanimity," acts like "a big knife with cruelly sharp edges ruthlessly cutting all to a pattern, the white man's pattern" (4). In particular the girls at Naxos are cut into pattern young ladies. Directing her charges to "act like ladies and not like savages from the backwoods," the appropriately named Miss Mac-Gooden forgets that they "had actually come from the backwoods." Helga, considering the older teacher's spinsterhood, sardonically muses that prim Miss MacGooden's "ladyness" means that "things in the matrimonial state . . . were of necessity entirely too repulsive for a lady of delicate and sensitive nature to submit to" (12).

Like Miss MacGooden, the dean of women also derives from one of the "first families." When she preaches against dark-complexioned people wearing bright colors, Helga defends her own colorful clothing by reasoning, "These people yapped loudly of race, of race consciousness, of race pride, and yet suppressed its most delightful manifestations, love of color, joy of rhythmic motion, naive, spontaneous laughter" (18). In fact, although Helga

experiences a moment of doubt about leaving Naxos, it is the school's snobbish, repressive model of the lady that seals her resolve. In a final interview
with the principal, Dr. Anderson, Helga decides to quit her position as a
college instructor when he expresses his appreciation of her through "that
trite phrase, 'You are a lady'" (21).

But if black centers of education in the South seem dedicated to "the
suppression of individuality and beauty" (20), two female characters, one in
Chicago, the other in New York, demonstrate to Helga that the Northern
liberal circles Fauset celebrates are no less constricting. After traveling to
Chicago, Helga lands a job as companion to Mrs. Hayes-Rore, a specialist on
"race problems" (35) whose lectures to the Negro Women's League of Clubs
in New York combine "patchworks of others' speeches and opinions" with
"ideas, phrases, and even whole sentences and paragraphs . . . lifted bodily
from . . . [the] published works of Wendell Phillips, Frederick Douglass,
Booker T. Washington, and other doctors of the race's ills." Even when for
variety she sprinkles these set pieces with "a peppery dash of Du Bois" or "a
few vinegary statements of her own," this "prominent 'race' woman" seems
to Helga to be reiterating "the same old thing" (38). In addition, Helga's
skepticism about the platitudes of Mrs. Hayes-Rore, whose name sounds like
"haze-roar," deepens into a critique of urban black culture when she lives in
Harlem with Mrs. Hayes-Rore's niece, Anne Grey.

To be sure, at first Anne Grey and her connections in New York fill Helga
with a "magic sense of having come home" to a black community composed
of sophisticated people who share her "contempt and scorn of Naxos and all
its works" (43). Quickly, though, the newcomer feels a discontent that reflects
Larsen's dissatisfaction with what she saw as contradictions in the ideology of
the Harlem Renaissance. For the seemingly sophisticated Anne Grey "hated
white people with a deep and burning hatred," but she "aped their clothes,
their manners, and their gracious ways of living." Anne asserts that "the
most wretched Negro prostitute that walks One Hundred and Thirty-fifth
Street is more than any president of these United States"; however, she
"turn[s] up her finely carved nose at [blacks'] lusty churches, their picturesque parades, their naive clowning on the streets" (48).

While conversations in Harlem circle around racial discrimination, a
bored Helga wonders, "Why must the race problem always creep in?" (52).
Larsen depicts the insularity of the place she presents as the most enlightened black intellectual center. The only alternative to such stultifying conventionality appears equally stupefying to Helga. At first, a trip to a cabaret
filled with the "reek of flesh, smoke, and alcohol" as well as "extraordinary
music" drugs Helga into the ecstatic oblivion of dance. But even amid the
vertiginous "sooty, black, shiny black, taupe, mahogany, bronze, copper,
gold, orange, yellow, peach ivory, pinky white, pastry white" shades of skin
color, she rebels and refuses to participate because of "a shameful certainty

that not only had she been in the jungle, but that she had enjoyed it" (59). At least in part because of the influence of her mother's monitory story, at this point in the narrative Helga's dread of the "jungle" signifies her unintentional internalization of Miss MacGooden's strictures against savagery and her anxiety about her own eroticism. If, like her mother, Helga experiences desire for a black man, will she find herself alienated from her origins and ultimately abandoned? Yet both Mrs. Hayes-Rore and Anne Grey have made it clear to Helga that a white partner must also be unthinkable because "race intermingling" is "disgusting" (39, 62).

Helga flees Harlem because she refuses to become either a lady in Anne Grey's circles or a savage in the bar. Increasingly encased inside "a smoldering hatred" at being "shut up, boxed up, with hundreds of her race" (54), Helga responds with relief to her white uncle's gift—a payoff to get rid of her—and she accepts his advice to visit her white relatives in Copenhagen: "Why, she demanded in fierce rebellion, should she be yoked to these despised black folk?" (55). Helga determines that her new life will be lived "where she belonged" (67), in a city "where there were no Negroes, no problems, no prejudice" (55). But ironically, when she goes into white society she is turned into a savage queen, a figure reminiscent of "Princess Zora." The welcoming admiration of Aunt Katrina and her husband, Herr Dahl, is tainted by their fetishization of Helga, who is transformed into "some new and strange species of pet dog being proudly exhibited" (70). Elaborating on precisely the "pet Negro system" which Hurston later attacked, Larsen suggests that the black woman within even the most outwardly tolerant white society will be turned into "a curiosity, a stunt" (71).

Throughout *Quicksand* Larsen exploits the vocabulary of clothing to analyze the grammar of selfhood, but nowhere as methodically as in the section of the novel devoted to Copenhagen. Decked out in earrings, glittering shoe buckles, barbaric bracelets, and flashy colors, Helga is made to feel "like a veritable savage": "'As if I had horns, or three legs,' she thought" (69–70). Because of the language barrier, she smiles silently in response to the admiration she elicits, but her face soon becomes "a fixed aching mask" (71). At this point in the novel Helga, put before a staring populace as "a decoration. A curio. A peacock" (73), represents Larsen's views on African-American performers who gained celebrity in Europe throughout the Jazz Age. Excited by the leopard-skin coats, the dangerously high-heeled shoes, the batik dresses which are purchased for her, Helga is "incited to make an impression, a voluptuous impression," so that "after a little while she gave herself up wholly to the fascinating business of being seen, gaped at, desired" (74).

The allure of attention wears thin, however, when it becomes clear that the Dahls are using her to gain social standing. Indeed, to the extent that her aunt counters Helga's anxieties about miscegenation and pushes her into the arms of the socialite portrait painter Axel Olsen, Katrina Dahl plays pimp to

Helga the whore, or paid entertainer. As a character of her aunt's devising, Helga is supposed to "secure the link between the merely fashionable set to which [her aunt and uncle] belonged and the artistic one after which they hankered" (90), a role described most explicitly by the suitor, who is painting her portrait. When she rebuffs his sexual advances and he decides to propose, he argues (illogically but fiercely) that by holding out for marriage, she has exhibited her intrinsic corruption: "'You have the warm impulsive nature of the women of Africa, but, my lovely, you have, I fear, the soul of a prostitute. You sell yourself to the highest buyer. I should of course be happy that it is I. And I am'" (87).

Olsen's degrading view of Helga also surfaces in his picture of "some disgusting sensual creature with her features," a portrait that he judges to be "the true Helga Crane" but which she insists is not herself at all (89). Repelled by his certainty of her acceptance, she rebels against her own commodification on the marriage market: "I'm not for sale. Not to you. Not to any white man." The repetition compulsions of this scene—"You refuse me?"; "Yes . . . I refuse you"—as well as Axel's look of "a puzzled baby" (87) recall episodes in Fauset's and Harper's novels. Just as important, Axel's vision of Helga as a whore represents the flip side of Miss MacGooden's and Anne Grey's fastidious, ladylike modesty or even its historical underpinnings: as our epigraph from Marita Bonner indicates, the purported promiscuity of the black woman, her "gross collection of desires," instigated the mimicry that was black female passionlessness in the first place.[50]

Helga's quick fall in society's perception from decorous lady to savage reiterates Elise Johnson McDougald's point in "The Task of Negro Womanhood" that the "Negro woman" knows "that what is left of chivalry is not directed toward her" and evokes the shocking initial scenes of Pauline Hopkins's novel *Contending Forces* (1900).[51] There, Grace Montfort is initially presented "as a dream of beauty" whose "willowy" form and "creamy" complexion compose "a most lovely type of Southern beauty" (40). When the Southern community in which this model lady lives suspects that her husband may free his slaves, however, rumors spread that there is "negro blood in [her] veins" (45). Soon after her husband is murdered she is bound to a whipping post and lashed by men determined to possess her sexually. The fast fall of "Grace" from the pedestal to the whipping post, from the prototypical Southern belle to the prey of predatory white men, underlines the fragility of black female sex roles, given their racist underpinnings. Similarly, *Quicksand* meditates on the fictionality of the roles of lady and savage for a heroine forced to repress desire in the black community in part because she is viewed as the epitome of sexuality by whites. Like Hopkins, Larsen analyzes not only how middle-class feminine roles furnish no protection against the quicksand effect of racism but also how both white and black models of femininity—dependent, as they are, on each other—make the "Socially Ambitious Negress" feel, as Fauset's Angèle does, like a "hoax."

In her rejection of Axel Olsen, Helga claims that she could never marry a white man because he "might come to be ashamed of me, to hate me, to hate all dark people," as her mother had done (88). As if to confirm her dread, her aunt and uncle, disappointed in her, see her as "insufficiently civilized" (91), an attitude that generates a nostalgic ache in her for America. Listening to Dvorak's "New World Symphony," with its undertones of "Swing Low, Sweet Chariot," instills a greater homesickness that propels her back to Harlem. Her experience in Copenhagen gives her a new, important sense of sympathy for her father, whose yearnings for "his own kind" may have precipitated his repudiation of her mother and the "formal calm" of her "Nordic" culture. Determining, as Angela had, to go unto her father, a man whom Helga now feels "able to forgive" (92–93), she returns to America, where she will clarify the nature of the relationships black men seek to have with her. But Helga's pursuit of eroticism, previously inhibited because of her mother's abandonment, enables Larsen to diagnose the problem black men pose for black women. Specifically, the concluding chapters of *Quicksand* imply that the middle-class New Negro—a man who is shown to suppress his own eroticism—represses women of color as effectively as do traditional black men.

Although Harper's and Fauset's heroines reject white lovers to embrace darker ones who are dedicated to racial uplift, Larsen's confront the inadequacies of the New Negro. Both James Vayle, Helga's fiancé and assistant principal at Naxos, and Dr. Anderson, the principal, who later moves to Harlem and marries Anne Grey, suffer from the hypocrisy—even the frigidity—exacted by programs of racial uplift designed to counter old stereotypes of hypersexual black men. Just as the ladies at Naxos horrify Helga because of their denial of sexuality James, at the beginning of the novel, seems alarmed at the "ancient appeal by which she held him" (8) and helpless against a sensuality he can neither deny nor accept. When Helga later returns from Europe and meets a blushing, awkward James at a gathering in Harlem, he still appears "embarrassed and uncertain" (100) about his continued attraction to her. James Vayle, whose last name evokes Du Bois's influential metaphor,[52] emblematizes Larsen's disillusionment with an upward mobility framed in terms that alienate black men from their own eroticism and encase them in a masquerade of respectability.

This "snobbish, smug, servile" man (129), who accepts the petty proprieties of Naxos and is ambitious to become the principal of the school, seems quite different at the Harlem party from Dr. Anderson, the "new man" (16) who quits that post. Helga, who feels "very sorry" for James, nonetheless turns away from him and falls into the arms of Anderson, whose kiss causes "a long-hidden, half-understood desire" to well up in her "with the suddenness of a dream" (103–04). But when Anderson retreats from "the ecstasy which had flooded her" (105), it becomes clear that he experiences the same ambivalence about eroticism that torments James. The "irrepressible longing" awakened in Helga leads Anderson to an apology that leaves Helga feeling "belittled and ridiculed" (106–07). Because he has certified his earlier admiration of "the lady" by marrying Anne Grey, a woman dedicated to passionlessness and white mimicry, he cannot even acknowledge the "desire [which] had burned in [Helga's] flesh with uncontrollable violence" (109).

Paradoxically, the only place in which desire does find an outlet in *Quicksand* is the church into which Helga retreats from a storm, but this sanctuary turns out to be ruled by an ersatz, uxorious patriarch. There, surrounded by the "wild, ecstatic fury," the "almost Bacchic vehemence" (112–13), of a predominantly female congregation, the proprieties of Naxos, Harlem, and Denmark drop away. If, at the beginning of the novel, Helga is an Ariadne deserted amid the manners and morals of Naxos, she only finds Bacchic release through what is characterized as a patriarchal religion. Praying, "Forgive them, Father" (111), the women in the church welcome Helga as "a scarlet 'oman" or a "los' Jezebel" (112) and she, feeling "an echo of the weird orgy resound in her own heart," falls "forward against the crude railing." The narrator ambiguously explains: "In that moment she was lost—or saved" (113); however, the women who "dragged themselves upon their knees or crawled over the floor like reptiles" in the church recall the jungle creature in the nightclub and the pet in Copenhagen. Although the congregation seems to bring her "back into the mysterious grandeur and holiness of far-off simpler centuries" (114), this will remain a specious recovery of origins, one which will deny her humanity and cage her in a less complicated but equally fictive and far more brutal world.

The "fattish yellow" (115) Reverend Mr. Pleasant Green becomes the instrument of Helga's revenge against Anderson as well as an outlet for her passion. Dedicating herself to God and man, Helga determines to marry this man of God and go to his tiny Alabama hometown, where the community serves "the worth and greatness" of her husband (119). Indeed, his avuncular pomposity stimulates the adulation of "the female portion of the flock": "The greater his own sense of superiority became, the more flattered they were by his notice and small attentions, the more they cast at him killing glances, the more they hung enraptured on his words" (120). Initially, Helga gratefully worships the pastor in order to be "filled with the glory and the marvel of God," and she therefore ignores "the atmosphere of self-satisfaction which poured from him like gas from a leaking pipe" (121–22). Yet, to go unto the father in *Quicksand* clearly means returning to agrarian poverty and familial submission to a vulgar patriarch. As the narrator's satiric descriptions indicate, a nostalgic return to the Pleasant Greens eulogized in local-color or regionalist literature only solves the problem of the New Negro's renunciation of desire through a regression to repressive patriarchal structures.

Eventually the burdens of housekeeping and childbearing inculcate in

Helga a "sick disgust" (124) that results in anorexia and feelings of suffoca-
tion. To the extent that she tries to use her religion as "a kind of protective
coloring, shielding her from the cruel light of an unbearable reality" (126),
she is only passing as a Christian. To the extent that she tricks herself into
believing in a man she knows to be a pompous sham of a patriarch, she is also
only passing as a wife. The bearing of a fourth child (which is too weak to
live) plunges her into pain and unconsciousness, from which she awakens
filled with hatred not only of her husband but also of the "white man's God"
(130) in whom blacks place a "childlike trust in full compensation for all woes
and privations in 'kingdom come.'" Sinking in a "quagmire" (133) but determined "to get herself out of this bog into which she had strayed" (134), she
awakens into conscious anger and the determination to leave, but she discovers she cannot desert her children. In "snatches of sleeping and waking,"
time runs out at the end of the narrative when she begins to have her fifth
child (135).

Awakening into desire and drowsing into sensuous fantasies about Anderson, horrified by the pains of the domestic confinement and biological
labor inflicted by her husband, unable to escape because of her tie to her
children, and drowning in despair, Helga Crane at first suggests that Larsen
is revising Kate Chopin's *The Awakening*. But from the beginning of the novel
it is clear that the major white female precursor for Larsen, as for Chopin, is
Charlotte Brontë.[53] With its emphasis on clanging bells demanding obe-
dience, poorly prepared food, and the mindless conformity of its staff,
Naxos resembles Lowood in *Jane Eyre* as well as Madame Beck's school in
Villette. Helga, characterized by a "lack of acquiescence" (7) which frightens
her so much that she almost faints when she decides to leave, recapitulates
Jane Eyre's breakdown in the red room after her revolt against John Reed.
But Helga's refusal to conform to the school's standards and her sense of
being unfitted for teaching also echo Lucy Snowe's profound alienation in
Brussels. That Helga experiences the "rebellious state of her feelings" as a
"formidable antagonist, nameless and ununderstood" (100) within her further links her anger to that experienced by Brontë's protagonists.[54] Like
Brontë's orphans, and especially like Lucy Snowe, who remains at school
during "the long vacation," Helga envies the other students who "went home
for the vacations" (24).

Both Brontë and Larsen consistently present female confinement in
male-dominated society through metaphors of entrapment. No wonder,
then, that Mrs. Hayes-Rore, a mentor who resembles Miss Marchmont in
Villette, sends Helga to a niece whose name, Anne Grey, invokes Anne
Brontë, the author of *Agnes Grey*. In addition, Jane Eyre's efforts to renounce
her attraction to Rochester and Lucy Snowe's attempts to bury her desire for
Graham Bretton serve as a background for Helga's repression of her passion
for Anderson. Jane's isolation on the moor ends in her collapse before St.

John Rivers's vicarage and Lucy's loneliness drives her out into a storm
where she finds asylum in a Catholic church; Helga is driven by her restlessness out into a storm and ends up collapsing inside a church. At the conclusion of *Quicksand* Larsen seems to ask what would have happened to Jane
Eyre if she had married the missionary St. John. And what would have
become of Lucy Snowe, if she had capitulated to the sublimation of desire
represented by the "nun" who haunts the school in which she is employed?
    Even more important, though, Larsen draws on Brontë's analysis of fe-
male disease—agoraphobia, claustrophobia, anorexia, schizophrenia—to
diagnose the wounding dis-ease of sex roles cast in racial modes, for Helga's
biracial roots signify the self-division bred by the inadequacies of two segregated cultures which work together to drain Helga—the product of both—
of any sense of her own reality. "Why couldn't she have two lives, or why
couldn't she be satisfied in one place?" (93). Whereas *Jane Eyre* and *Villette*
imply that women in patriarchal culture are split between docility and rebelliousness, *Quicksand* revises this tension so that Helga quite consciously confronts the imitative and hence fictive roles of the lady and the savage from
the beginning to the end of her pilgrimage.
    From Miss MacGooden, trying to turn "savages from the backwoods" into
"ladies," to Mrs. Hayes-Rore, whose speeches are examples of bricolage (or
plagiarism), and Anne Grey, who apes the tastes of middle-class white
women, Larsen's characters substantiate Helga's speculation at the circus:
thinking about African-Americans' "slavish imitation of traits not their
own," she asks, "Why their constant begging to be considered as exact copies
of other people?" (83). Even the traditional hymn "Showers of Blessings,"
sung by the wailing women in the church, cries out to a white father god for
"less of self and more of Thee" (112), as if to expand upon Larsen's critique
of Christianity as another kind of "slavish imitation." Besides lamenting the
impact on black women of a psychological sense that they are doomed to
enact what Fanny Hurst called "an imitation of life," Larsen raises crucial
issues about representation for the black woman artist. The interrelation
between the black female character's anxiety that she is a mime and the black
literary woman's dread that her fictions are merely "a hollow re-echo" is
clarified by Larsen's next and last novel, *Passing*, as is her pessimistic assessment of the social revolutions associated with the New Negro and the New
Woman.
    This narrative grants Helga Crane her wish of "two lives" by splitting the
protagonist into two women: the ladylike matron Irene Redfield and the
exotic, passionate Clare Kendry. Sufficiently light-skinned to pass, decorous
Irene rejects this option, choosing instead to dedicate herself to her husband, their two sons, and the social activities of Harlem: she is the prototypical New Negro. But impetuous Clare, who has masqueraded as white, married a racist, and decided to reconnect with her abandoned black roots,

accepts "no allegiance beyond her own immediate desire" (144): she is the quintessential New Woman. A number of critics have examined the ways in which these two seemingly antithetical characters are doubles within the ironic framework of Larsen's title. For Irene, who values respectability, security, and racial uplift above all else, passes by conforming to middle-class standards of propriety, whereas the passer Clare rebels against her own "pale life" by pursuing "Negroes, to be with them again, and to talk with them, to hear them laugh" (200).[55] Just as important, however, the novel's emphasis on writing and specifically on letter-writing extends Larsen's psychological study of inauthenticity to examine an aesthetic issue, for the book opens with Irene reading one letter and led to remember an earlier one, both composed by Clare.

With its "long envelope of thin Italian paper" and "its almost illegible scrawl," Clare's "alien" and "mysterious" communication in Irene's morning mail looks like a "thin sly thing" (143) purloined from the unconscious. This letter and the other that it recalls enable Larsen to examine the relation between Irene as reader and Clare as writer. Clare's missive is a letter from the front, sent by a woman who has crossed the color line but who now "ache[s] to see more" of her friend and her friend's home in Harlem. It does not conciliate Irene, however, who was subjected to the racism of Clare's white husband.[56] Irene had torn the first letter "into tiny ragged squares," thrown them from a train, and watched the pieces "scatter, on tracks, on cinders, on forlorn grass" (178). This memory returns to her as she reads the second letter, which gives her a "dim sense of fear, of panic" (181). Because its style seems "too lavish in its wordiness, a shade too unreserved in the manner of its expression," it arouses "again that old suspicion that Clare was acting, not consciously, perhaps—that is, not too consciously—but, none the less, acting" (182). Irene tears it up as well, this time flinging the pieces into the wastepaper basket.

If we interpret Clare as Larsen's portrait of the artist, she illuminates a connection between writing and passing. For Larsen, the black female writer inhabits a white world, but longs through her artistry to regain contact with her origins. According to *Passing*, when the black woman who has been integrated into and then estranged from white society takes up writing, her communication is condemned as a form of "acting": the reader (Irene) rejects the author's quest for contact with "negroes" as inauthentic.[57] Clare's two letters, torn up and thrown away, dramatize the inefficacy of writing as an effort to pass or negotiate between black and white milieus. In response to Clare's pleas—"I am so lonely, so lonely" (145)—Irene determines on "the basket for all letters, silence for their answers" (192). Through the epistolary framing device Larsen dramatizes her own dilemma as a novelist: the black woman writer, camouflaged inside white culture, is encased inside a spurious role that can only inculcate self-loathing and cut her off from the black community she seeks to regain; however, that community condemns her efforts to reconnect as disloyalty to the race. Through the image of the furtive, sly letter, with its "extravagantly phrased" wishes (145), Larsen also hints that she identifies writing with the liberation of female libidinal energies that are "unsafe" (144).

The New Womanly Clare, passionately committed to sexual experimentation and later to an effort to escape the confinement of marriage and motherhood, is as destined for destruction as is Helga in *Quicksand*. Indeed, Helga Crane's devolution from Naxos to her fall inside the church forecasts Clare's fall to her death, for both, garbed in red dresses, dramatize Larsen's view that the black New Woman will be castigated as—and literally transformed into—a fallen woman. In *Passing*, though, this fate appears to be inflicted by a female friend whose entire life is predicated on the fact that she "did not look the future in the face" (224). Terrified that the discovery of Clare's black origins will cause her husband to divorce and thereby liberate her, Irene fears the breakup of her own marriage: "If Clare was freed, anything might happen" (236). Although Irene realizes "she couldn't now be sure that she had ever truly known love," she nevertheless decides "to keep" her husband because "security was the most important and desired thing in life" (235). Through the figures of mean-spirited, destructive Irene in *Passing* and those of Miss MacGooden, Mrs. Hayes-Rore, and Anne Grey in *Quicksand*, Larsen rejects the rejection of feminism by her contemporary, Fauset.

The New Negro Irene, who is endowed with smug, middle-class pieties and proprieties, imagines the New Womanly Clare as a prototypical femme fatale: seductive, conflicted, destructive, and infused with transgressive knowledge. Indeed, she uses this iconography to justify her murderous assault on Clare. According to Larsen, the woman committed to racial uplift destroys not only the autonomy of other women but her own ambitions as well. *Passing* hints that, because only a few middle-class black women in the first decades of the twentieth century had managed to gain the security of middle-class matrimony which many white women had attained in the nineteenth century, they rejected New Womanly efforts to liberate themselves from traditional roles, although those roles diminished their lives and their loves. Taken together, Larsen's novels suggest that the black New Woman will be destroyed by racial liberation movements, while the New Womanly black writer will succumb to self-defeating forms of mimicry or compose works that fall on deaf ears. That Larsen's writing career after *Quicksand* and *Passing* was terminated by her shock at a charge of plagiarism (which was quickly rescinded) seems bitterly appropriate because her fiction analyzes the problem not only of personal inauthenticity but also of aesthetic imitation for women of color.[58]

Just as Sojourner Truth's "Ain't I a woman?" invites both a yes and a no answer, the query "Ain't I a New Woman?" is answered both positively and negatively in the fiction of Fauset and Larsen: "Yes" in terms of aspiration (desire for economic independence, physical liberty, sexual autonomy); "No" in terms of ideology (white-specific standards of beauty, access to professional success, stereotypes of a transgressive but attractive or at least tolerated femininity).[59] Only impersonation enables the characters of Fauset and Larsen to shuttle between yes and no, to play at being the New Women a racist culture never lets them be. Perhaps for this reason Zora Neale Hurston, an author exquisitely aware of the links between racial consciousness and mimicry, ultimately turned away from the sense of inauthenticity such social masquerades bred and toward a spiritual definition of black female power.

The subject of representation and the discontents of the African-American woman writer finds its fullest expression in *Dust Tracks on a Road*, Hurston's evasive autobiography, in which the author claims about "My People" that, "We would rather do a good imitation than any amount of something original." In spite of her ironic acknowledgment here of the belatedness of copies in relation to "something original," Hurston goes on to boast, "We love audiences when we get to specifying. . . . We just love to dramatize" (*D* 300–304). Earlier, in one of her contributions to Nancy Cunard's *Negro Anthology* (1934), Hurston had argued that "the Negro . . . [who] is famous as a mimic" is "in no way damage[d]," because "mimicry is an art in itself" and "self-despisement" only occurs in "a middle class [that] scorns to do or be anything Negro."[60] This idea of the representational flair of African-Americans led Hurston to speculate that her race—or, indeed, race as a category—is a fiction: "Maybe, after all[,] the Negro doesn't really exist. What we think is a race is detached moods and phases of other people walking around. . . . Could be the shade patterns of something else thrown on the ground—other folks, seen in shadow" (*D* 304).

At various times in her life and works, Hurston's advocacy of impersonation as a mode of self-presentation helped her resolve the problem of the anachronistic ladies and femmes fatales depicted in Fauset's and Larsen's fiction, causing such critics as Robert Hemenway, Barbara Johnson, and Mae Henderson to emphasize her chameleonlike changes of moods and phases, voice and political stance.[61] But even the most savvy and spirited shape changing did not necessarily lay to rest anxieties about women's entrapment within spurious roles, as Fauset and Larsen had demonstrated, as Hurston's "Isis" had intimated, and as a number of the poets of their generation knew. Representative in this regard was Gwendolyn Bennett, who journeyed toward a vision of black female divinity that would also help Hurston heal the pain of ontological insecurity and psychic fragmentation.

In "Fantasy" (1927), for example, Bennett "sail[s] in my dreams to the Land of Night / Where you were the dusk-eyed queen"; and in "To a Dark Girl" (1923) the "brownness," "darkness," and "sadness" of her heroine lead the poet to advocate the excavation of a powerful female identity that may have existed before slavery and that in any case serves as an antidote to the suffering inflicted by slavery:

> Something of old forgotten queens
> Lurks in the lithe abandon of your walk
> And something of the shackled slave
> Sobs in the rhythm of your talk.
>
> Oh, little brown girl, born for sorrow's mate,
> Keep all you have of queenliness,
> Forgetting that you once were slave,
> And let your full lips laugh at Fate![62]

Here Bennett hints that her brown girl can save herself from the fate to which she would otherwise be consigned—becoming sorrow's mate—by forgetting her slavery and remembering her queenliness.

Forgetting slavery was an imperative for Hurston, a writer who sought to transcend the tragic and formulaic productions of the thinkers she derided as "Race Champions." The "terrible struggle" that made Africans "Americans," according to Hurston, was not of their creating, but it placed them at "the center of the national stage, with the spectators not knowing whether to laugh or to weep." If the Civil War said, "On the line!"; if Reconstruction said, "Get set!"; and if the generation before hers said, "Go!" she determined to be "off to a flying start": one "must not halt in the stretch to look behind and weep."[63] Amy Jacques Garvey captured the implications for black men of such a race into the future when she warned, "Mr. Black Man watch your step! Ethiopia's queens will reign again, and her Amazons protect her shores and people. Strengthen your shaking knees and move forward, or we will displace you and lead on to victory and glory."[64]

For Hurston, too, the strategy of excavating the queenliness of African-American women—founded in part on repression of the immediate past, in part on imaginative leaps of faith forward into an ancient past—involves a recovery of powers daunting to "Mr. Black Man." At the same time, it transforms mimicry into mythology, establishing in women a spiritual primacy that liberates the black heroine and her creator from the submission Fauset prescribed as a racial duty and Larsen mourned as a sexual inheritance. Indeed, the enigmatic opening of Hurston's now-classic *Their Eyes Were Watching God* may refer to the necessity of "forgetting" the immediate past in order to move forward into the ancient past. The "Watcher" who, we are told at the beginning of the book, is man "turns his eyes away [from the horizon] in resignation, his dreams mocked to death by Time"; however, "women forget all those things they don't want to remember, and remember everything they don't want to forget. The dream is the truth" (1). Although all the male characters in the novel capitulate to time and death, its heroine passes through a series of social roles—farmer's wife, mayor's lady, and migrant worker's mate—by keeping her eyes on the horizon (associated with Isis) and on its dream until she emerges as the embodiment of truth.

A god-haunted work, *Their Eyes Were Watching God* demonstrates how the writer who called herself the "Queen of Niggerati" solved the problem of the New Negro intellectuals she caricatured as "Negrotarians."[65] The solution, a spiritual one, is encapsulated in her autobiography:

> I have had the corroding insight at times, of recognizing that I am a bundle of sham and tinsel, honest metal and sincerity that cannot be untangled. My dross has given my other parts great sorrow.
>
> But, on the other hand, I have given myself the pleasure of sunrises blooming out of oceans, and sunsets drenching heaped-up clouds. I have walked in storms with a crown of clouds about my head and the zigzag lightning playing through my fingers. The gods of the upper air have uncovered their faces to my eyes. I have found out that my real home is in the water, that the earth is only my stepmother. My old man, the sun, sired me out of the sea. [*D* 347]

Also "a bundle of sham and tinsel, honest metal and sincerity," the heroine of *Their Eyes Were Watching God* gives herself up to the pleasure of blooming sunrises; walks in storms amid the zigzag lightning; finds her real home in the waters of the sea; and sees the uncovered faces of the gods. The title of Hurston's novel can thus be understood as a "lie": while the eyes of most of the characters are watching a variety of gods, our eyes are watching the apotheosis of a goddess.

Of course, as a number of critics have noted, *Their Eyes Were Watching God* is primarily a bildungsroman that recounts the development of Janie Crawford from the sensual awakening she experiences under a pear tree when her grandmother marries her off to Logan Killicks, to her elopement with Joe (Jody) Starks, the "big voice" (27) who becomes mayor of an all-black town similar to Hurston's hometown, Eatonville, and finally to her union with Tea Cake Woods, the younger man who teaches her "de maiden language all over" (109).[66] And her progress represents not only the fruition of her eroticism—Logan "desecrat[es] the pear tree" (13) and Jody cannot become "a bee for her bloom" (31) while Tea Cake *Woods* can and does—but also an evolution from agrarian poverty and its inheritance of slavery, through a form of white mimicry among the black bourgeoisie to the emergence of a black separatist community.

As Janie Killicks, the heroine of this novel is forced by her grandmother, Nanny, into a marriage of security because Nanny has herself been traumatized by a white master who impregnated her and by his jealous wife who beat her, as well as by the fate of a daughter who was raped and became mad. Then as Janie Starks, Hurston's central character is silenced by her entrepreneurial husband's desire to make her "de mayor's wife" and a "lady" (56, 28). But finally as Janie Woods, she lives in an egalitarian, migrant community that provides her with both work and play. Framed by her return to Eatonville from burying Tea Cake after a storm, the narrative of Janie Crawford Killicks Starks Woods charts its heroine's ascendancy in wisdom. Janie loses her dream of the truth of the horizon in her first relationship, recovers but contains it in a secret compartment of her psyche closed to her second partner, and reaches it through the death and resurrection of her beloved third consort.

Janie's first two partnerships generate an alienation from men that causes her to divide herself into a facade of acquiescence and a buried self of resistance, a rebelliousness that surfaces and engages her in a battle of the sexes. After Nanny decides to marry Janie off because she will not have "menfolks white or black . . . makin' a spit cup outa you" (19), Logan objects that Janie is "powerful independent around here" and suffers a "terrible ache in [his] body" because she has "put [into] words" his "held-in fears" that she might desert him; and so he threatens to "take holt uh dat ax and come in dere and kill yuh" (29, 30) when she scorns his hardworking but drab life. Jody builds a post office, a general store, and a big white house that makes all the other houses in town look like servants' quarters and thus appears far more ambitious than Logan. But in a mimicry of a white patriarch, Jody stops Janie from "speech-makin'" (40), forces her to tie her hair up in a head rag "lak some ole 'oman" (47), keeps her shut inside his store as "Mrs. Mayor Starks" (50), proclaims that "somebody got to think for women and chillun and chickens and cows," and slaps her face, causing Janie to cease being "petal-open anymore with him" (67).

Just as Janie hurts Logan when she speaks the words of his held-in fears, she retaliates against Jody's abuse with a verbally humiliating retort: "When you pull down yo' britches, you look lak de change uh life." By "playin' de dozens," as one character puts it, Janie effectively robs Jody of the "illusion of irresistible maleness that all men cherish, which was terrible" (75). That Janie's mouth functions as a weapon appears likely not only to Jody but also to the community. Janie's friend Phoebe explains that "it's been singin' round here ever since de big fuss in de store dat Joe was 'fixed' and you wuz de one dat did it" (78). Predictably, then, Jody looks "baggy" (77), as if Janie's curse has turned him into the money- and windbag that he has shown himself to be. While Janie's disillusionment with her first marriage means her "first dream was dead, so she became a woman" (24), her second induces a kind of schizophrenia, for she looks like a "shadow of herself going about tending store and prostrating itself before Jody," while she salvages a vision of herself sitting "under a shady tree with the wind blowing through her hair and her clothes" (73). If only through such self-division, she is refusing to become the "nigger woman" defined by Nanny as "de mule uh de world" (14).

Nanny's belief that the "nigger woman" is "de mule uh de world" illuminates Hurston's decision to write not about the New Womanly independent life she was herself living but instead about the seemingly more conventional lives of agrarian folk. As if meditating on Du Bois's insight that "our women in black had freedom thrust contemptuously upon them,"[67] Hurston eschews the model of the New Woman. Older than the New Woman, the female characters in her novel are also wiser, for they have always confronted the problems posed by female employment, sexuality, and autonomy as well as the crisis of masculine virility which, we have claimed, characterized white society during the first half of the twentieth century. At the same time, Janie's refusal to become de mule uh de world informs not only her subsequent anger at Nanny but also the demise of her first two relationships: she will not work a mule on Logan's farm, and she rebels against Jody's decision to exclude her from the funeral service for Matt Bonner's yellow mule.

Janie's struggles with Logan and Jody recall what Hurston calls the "no-man's land" on which the sexes battle in her short stories "Spunk" (1925), "Sweat" (1926), and "The Gilded Six Bits" (1933). All of these tales examine the effects on both sexes of a culture that denies black men the money, confidence, or jobs that confer authority on white men. The resultant black male insecurity turns into either hostility against or exploitation of black women.[68] Whether cuckolding Logan or hexing Jody or eventually shooting Tea Cake, the heroine of *Their Eyes Were Watching God* is patterned not only on early female fictional antagonists in the battle of the sexes but also on the wild women and conjurers of *Mules and Men*. About wild women in the area in rural Florida where her storytellers reside, Hurston-the-anthropologist claims in a deadpan tone that "Negro women *are* punished in these parts for killing men, but only if they exceed the quota" (*M* 65). Her joke surfaces as a maxim spouted by the black men at the end of *Their Eyes Were Watching God*, who fear that "de nigger women kin kill up all de mens dey wants tuh" (280). Although Hurston clearly has her doubts about the basis for this belief, Big Sweet, a character who shows up in a number of works, typifies the racy, wild woman, for "if God send her a pistol she'll send him a man" (*D* 187). With her switch blades and razors, she is "uh whole woman and half uh man," who boasts, "Ah got de law in mah mouf" (*M* 162, 190). When humiliating Logan, fixing Jody with the law in her mouth, and warning Tea Cake not to leave her or "Ah specks tuh kill yuh dead" (119), Janie also acts like a conjure woman.

According to Hurston's anthropological work, inexorable laws issue from the mouths of priestesses in the suppressed religion of Hoodoo or Voodoo. *Mules and Men*'s Marie Leveau in New Orleans is imagined accompanied by a rattlesnake, turning white policemen into barking dogs, rising out of the waters of a lake, and walking upon its waters to the shore. Since her death Leveau has been mythologized as part Circe, part Christ: the embodiment of black magic. A devotee explains to Hurston that, either as a destroyer or a preserver, "Marie Leveau is not a woman when she answer the one who ask. No. She is a god, yes" (204). Significantly, the story of Leveau precedes the ceremony in which Hurston herself was initiated into the secret rites of the hoodoo priestess. Naked, stretched face down on an altar with her navel on a snakeskin during three days of fasting, Hurston emerged for a ritual in which a white veil was placed over her head: when the veil was lifted, she was crowned with power that resembles the life-giving potency of Hurston's Isis or her Mambo. Learning "all of the Leveau routines," Hurston nevertheless explains that "in this book all of the works of any doctor cannot be given" (212).[69] Yet it is possible to argue that in *Their Eyes Were Watching God* Hurston encoded the magical transformation of woman into god that Leveau typifies and Hurston herself sought.

When Janie progresses toward the horizon and truth in the last section of the novel, she no longer works or rests like a mule but instead plays with Tea Cake Woods, who holds out the promise that Janie, the daughter of the lost Leafie, will at last bloom. Checkers, cards, piano playing, fishing, hunting, dancing, gardening, and even an imaginary guitar constitute the "love game" that serves as an alternative to Nanny's vision of "sittin' on porches lak de white madam" (109). The idyllic lives of Janie and Tea Cake on the "muck" (122) of the Everglades—with its jooks, its blues, its feasts, and its tale-telling—partake in an egalitarian, working-class culture, for while Janie shoots, hunts, works in the fields, and "tell[s] big stories herself" (128), Tea Cake helps fix supper with her at the end of the day. Wearing overalls and thick boots, Janie finds her freedom through neither ladylike conventionality nor New Womanly independence but in communal interdependence with the blacks whom her new acquaintance, "color-struck" Mrs. Turner (142), disdains for "singin' ol' nigger songs!" and "cuttin' de monkey" (135).

But behind the lovers' union and informing it are several episodes that create distrust between them, factors that pick up on the image of currency so crucial in, for instance, "The Gilded Six Bits." Janie's autonomy, symbolized by the fact that she is older than Tea Cake and by the inheritance from Jody Starks which gives her economic independence, causes her to fear that, like the wealthy widow Annie Tyler who went off with the younger Who Flung, she may be exploited, broken, and humiliated by Tea Cake. Annie Tyler "had waited all her life for something, and it had killed her when it found her" (114). When, without Janie's knowledge or consent, Tea Cake steals two hundred dollars from Janie so he can experience "how it [feels] to be a millionaire," he sets up a big chicken dinner and pays "all the ugly women two dollars *not* to come in" (117), appearing suspiciously like his predecessor, Jody. Although Tea Cake wins the money back, he convinces Janie to put all her savings in the bank because "Ah no need no assistance tuh help me feed mah woman. From now on, you gointuh eat whutever mah money can buy yuh and wear de same" (122). What Hurston claimed about the masculinity of the lover who inspired her to compose *Their Eyes Were Watching God*—his "manliness, sweet as it was, made us both suffer" (*D* 253)—applies to Tea Cake too.

Even on the muck, Janie fights Tea Cake when she becomes jealous of another woman, and Tea Cake whips Janie to prove that "Janie is wherever *Ah* wants tuh be." Horrified by Mrs. Turner's homage to Janie's Caucasian traits and this color-struck woman's disdain for his dark skin, Tea Cake "didn't whup Janie 'cause *she* done nothin'. Ah beat her tuh show dem Turners who is boss. Ah set in de kitchen one day and heard dat woman tell mah wife Ah'm too black fuh her" (141). Not only does "being able to whip her reassur[e] him in possession" (140); it also leads his male companions to fantasize about hitting a woman who never raises her hand in retaliation: "Wouldn't Ah love tuh whip uh tender woman lak Janie! Ah bet she don't even holler. She jus' cries, eh Tea Cake?" (141). Given these scenes, it may be that Hurston's heroine, like Annie Tyler, has also found a love capable of killing her.

As described in *Dust Tracks on a Road*, Hurston's most important love affair (and the impetus for her greatest novel) was a relationship rife with competition. Indeed, the similarities between this affair and the marriages in the fiction imply that the New Womanly author in Harlem found herself just as enmeshed in problems of masculinity as do poor, southern women. Hurston's lover, A. W. P., "flew hot" when Hurston offered to loan him a quarter for carfare back from her apartment on 116th Street to his own place on 61st Street: "He was a *man!* No woman on earth could either lend him or give him a cent. If a man could not do for a woman, what good was he on earth? His great desire was to do for me. *Please* let him be a *man!*" The incident indicates why "he wanted to do all the doing, and keep [Hurston] on the receiving end," but "my career balked the completeness of his ideal" (253).

Because of A. W. P.'s lack of confidence in himself and his inability "to whip his woman mentally," a "war" over Hurston's autonomy ensued. Even his physical violence did not stop her from feeling herself "his slave"; however, "the telephone or the doorbell would ring, and there would be my career again." When Hurston finally left A. W. P. and sailed to Jamaica, "everywhere I set my feet down, there were tracks of blood. Blood from the very middle of my heart": "So I pitched in to work hard on my research to smother my feelings. But the thing would not down. The plot was far from the circumstances, but I tried to embalm all the tenderness of my passion for him in 'Their Eyes Were Watching God'" (256–60). As Kathleen Davies has pointed out, the "choice of the word 'embalm' is highly significant," suggesting Hurston's power to kill and preserve the beloved in order to protect herself, which is precisely what the conclusion of her novel accomplishes.[70] Killing and preserving, embalming and balming: the plot of *Their Eyes Were Watching God* works in mysteriously providential ways to consecrate the wild conjure woman Janie.

The ending of *Their Eyes Were Watching God* solves the tension between the heroine's adoration of Tea Cake and the female thralldom and abuse that such adoration can lead to through the intervention of unleashed powers of nature that exact a revenge against even the marginalized, playful, and relatively free culture on the muck. As in George Eliot's *Mill on the Floss*, in which a flood annihilates a world inhospitable to Maggie Tulliver's desires, in *Their Eyes Were Watching God* a hurricane wreaks havoc, creating a topsy-turvy world of misrule: "Wind and water had given life to lots of things that folks think of as dead and given death to so much that had been living things" (151–52). As in other visions of apocalypse—"The Dead shall live, the Living die / And Music shall untune the Sky"—the storm heralds a new world order, a baptism, in this case, to purify a culture at odds with fully realized female potential.[71]

Corpses surrounded by wild animals, rattlesnakes in trees, tar-paper roofing sailing through the air, fish in yards: "the monster" (150) or "monstropolous beast" (153) or "tired mammoth" (154) that was Lake Okechobee first rolls in its bed and then effects a virtually apocalyptic destruction. That, given a racist society, the promised end of female fulfillment must be spiritual is signaled by the burial of the dead chapter in which Tea Cake is forced to clear the wreckage and separate the white bodies destined for coffins from the black to be thrown in pits: "They's mighty particular how dese dead folks goes tuh judgment," Tea Cake observes (163). The climactic scene of *Their Eyes Were Watching God*—which portrays Janie swimming against the current, holding on to the tail of a cow upon which a dog squats and growls, and Tea Cake fighting the dog who bites him—could hardly be more surrealistic. It leads to the equally eerie logic of the novel's denouement: Tea Cake's pride at saving Janie—"Ah want yuh tuh know it's uh man heah" (159); the hydrophobia that turns him into a maddened dog; his growing suspicion and hostility toward Janie, whom he blames for his illness, much as Jody Starks had; and Janie's realization that she will have to shoot him because he has aimed a rifle directly at her breast."The pistol and the rifle rang out almost together. . . . Janie struggled to a sitting position and pried the dead Tea Cake's teeth from her arm" (175).

"Ah loves him fit tuh kill" (168), Janie declares about Tea Cake and she kills her lover to save herself and their love. Although during the storm "the eyes" of Janie, Tea Cake, and their companion, Motor Boat, "were watching God" (151), the topsy-turvy world of the storm turns her *god* Tea Cake into a *dog*, as if to indicate how Mrs. Turner's color-struck values have infected him with a rabid need to assuage his insecurity by dominating women. At the same time, as in "The Burial of the Dead" section of *The Waste Land*, the dog Tea Cake becomes at the end of *Their Eyes Were Watching God* may be Anubis, the Egyptian dog-god of the Isis-Osiris myth. For Tea Cake's devolution from god to dog and his death result in Janie's rebirth and his own transformation into a divine consort.[72]

To Jody Starks, who had made himself out to be "God Almighty" and who had classified women with cows, Janie (later to be saved by a cow) had argued, "Sometimes God gits familiar wid us womenfolks too and talks His inside business" (70). And, given the folkloric material in *Mules and Men*, the storm itself could be said to signify female access to the divine. A storyteller in *Mules and Men* recounts a tale about the wind and the water, which are both women: Mrs. Wind and Mrs. Water become tired of hearing each other boast about their respective children, so when Mrs. Wind's children arrive for a drink of water, "Mrs. Water grabbed 'em all and drowned 'em." Thus, "When you see a storm on de water, it's de wind and de water fightin' over dem chillun" (138–39). The hurricane in *Their Eyes Were Watching God* is further linked to female power through the figure of Marie Leveau, for she brings thunder, lightning, wind, and waves, as well as through Hurston's new name as a priestess of voodoo: she is called "the Rain-Bringer" (*M* 209), and a lightning symbol is drawn down her back from her right shoulder to her left hip because "this was to be my sign forever. The Great One was to speak to me in storms" (210).

Just as Hurston imagined herself in her autobiography as walking "in storms with a crown of clouds about my head and the zigzag lightning playing through my fingers," the author of *Their Eyes Were Watching God* uses the storm that Tea Cake identifies as the "mother of malice" (161) to elaborate subversively upon a comment that one male character makes about wild Big Sweet's potency: "Well, you know what they say—a man can cackerlate [calculate] his life till he git mixed up wid a woman or git straddle of a cow" (*M* 134). Although Janie had been forced to marry Logan so as not to be used as a "spit-cup" for men, even though she had soaked up "urine and perfume with the same indifference" in her marriage with Jody, she discovers with her hydrophobic lover that all along "she was the world and the heavens boiled down to a drop" (19, 73, 72).

The courtroom scene at the end of the novel positions Janie between a hostile black audience whose tongues were "cocked and loaded, the only real weapon left to weak folks," and sympathetic whites, "who didn't know a thing about people like Tea Cake and her" (176). Determined to fight "lying thoughts" by speaking the truth, Janie tries to explain that "Tea Cake couldn't come back to himself until he had got rid of that mad dog that was in him and he couldn't get rid of the dog and live. He had to die to get rid of the dog" (178). And through a death that is described as a sacrifice, he is transfigured: "Tea Cake, the son of Evening Sun, had to die for loving her" (169). Elsewhere in the novel the narrator explains, "All gods who receive homage are cruel. All gods dispense suffering without reason. Otherwise they would not be worshipped" (138). In opposition to Joe Starks, whose favorite expletive was "I god," and Mrs. Turner, who had "built an altar to the unattainable—Caucasian characteristics for all," Janie's divinity is her black womanhood, and at the end of the novel it is born through suffering, for "Half gods are worshipped in wine and flowers. Real gods require blood" (139). As a divinity propitiated by Tea Cake's blood, Janie manages to have her cake and eat it too.

The "great sermon about colored women sittin' on high" (15) that Nanny had wanted to preach is finally provided by Hurston's novel, which consecrates a woman whose "dream is the truth" (1). The pear tree, the "change and chance" of the "far horizon," and Tea Cake, who looked in life "like the love thoughts of women" (101), join together in Janie Crawford Killicks Starks Woods's final vision of the Herland she emblematizes: "Tea Cake, with the sun for a shawl. Of course he wasn't dead. He could never be dead until she herself had finished feeling and thinking. The kiss of his memory made pictures of love and light against the wall. Here was peace. She pulled in her horizon like a great fish-net. Pulled it from around the waist of the world and draped it over her shoulder. So much of life in its meshes! She called in her soul to come and see" (183–84). As a consort, Tea Cake brings Janie the shawl of the sun's radiance as well as the fishnet of the horizon, drapery not like the shroud of Emma's dead child in "Color Struck" but resembling the veil used as a crown of wisdom by the Mambo and by the initiates of Marie Leveau. As a muse, Tea Cake inspires "pictures of love and light," a prophetic writing on the wall.

A fisher of men who is kissed by the memory of a man who bit her in life, Janie has tasted the seeds of her Tea Cake, who functions eucharistically to bring her beatification. Childless not because she is sterile like a mule but because she is a complex multitude in her own singular being, Janie is sufficient in herself for dialogues of self and soul: "She called in her soul to come and see." No wonder, then, that Phoebe becomes an ephebe, a convert growing "ten feet higher from jus' listenin'" to Janie and deciding "tuh make Sam take me fishin' wid him after this." Having "done been tuh de horizon and back" (182), Janie of the many names wears it as a garment suitable for the woman who has matured from the inventive child Isis.

Taken together, the women artists of the Harlem Renaissance accomplished what the grandmother in Hurston's *Their Eyes Were Watching God* sought to achieve against great odds: "Ah wanted to preach a great sermon about colored women sittin' on high, but they wasn't no pulpit for me. Freedom found me wid a baby daughter in mah arms, so Ah said Ah'd take a broom and a cook-pot and throw up a highway through de wilderness for her. She would expound what Ah felt. But somehow she got lost offa de highway and next thing Ah knowed here you was in de world. So whilst Ah was tendin' you of nights Ah said Ah'd save de text for you" (15–16). As Nanny intimates, the "highway [which] shall be called the Holy Way" through the wilderness exists so "the ransomed of the Lord shall return, / and come to Zion with singing; / everlasting joy shall be upon their heads; / they shall obtain joy and gladness, / and sorrow and sighing shall flee away" (Isa. 36:8–10). Made "straight in the desert," this highway reveals "the glory of the Lord" (40:3–5) to Hurston's inheritors: in *Mama Day* (1988), for example, Gloria Naylor uses the apocalyptic power of a hurricane, the divinations of a conjure women, and the sacrifice of a beloved man "who looked just like love" to pay homage to Hurston's text.[73] But even the far more pessimistic works of Fauset and Larsen, dedicated to those who strayed from the highway, prepare the way so that the sorrow and sighing of the ransomed shall flee away.

Saving the texts of their precursors and providing highways through the wilderness of the contending forces set in motion by feminism and the Harlem Renaissance, Fauset, Larsen, and Hurston expounded a great sermon on the tribulations and triumphs of the woman who was also a negress, one that established fertile traditions enabling their black successors to ask, in the words of Audre Lorde, "which me will survive / all these liberations?"[74] It was a sermon from "no pulpit" that repeatedly returns to the Bible to define freedom for its authors. As for Hurston in particular, to the extent that she created a vision of divinity to heal the anxieties she shared with a generation grappling with the artifice of gender, she threw a highway through the wilderness of sexual antagonisms and impersonations that confounded her contemporary H. D., whose eyes were also watching "the Lord become woman."[75]

H. D.'s Self-Fulfilling Prophecies: Theologies of the Family Romance

4

> For too many centuries women have been busy being muses to the artists. . . . I wanted to be a muse, and I wanted to be the wife of the artist, but I was really trying to avoid the final issue.
>
> —Anaïs Nin

> What was my character anyway? My real *me* was a creature I dared not look upon—it was terrorized by loneliness, frozen by a sense of futility, obsessed by a longing to *stop*. No one had ever heard of that Me. If they had, they would have thought it was an interesting pose. The mask was tightly adjusted.
>
> —Ruth Benedict

> If you want to know more about femininity, enquire from your own experiences of life, or, turn to the poets.
>
> —Sigmund Freud

> Mother? Mamma. But my mother was dead. I was dead; that is, the child in me that had called her mamma was dead.
>
> —H. D.

The women writers of the Harlem Renaissance, as well as the white female female impersonators we have discussed, prove how varied were the uses to which feminine mimicry could be put, especially when it was employed deliberately, even vengefully, either to submerge the individual woman within her background—what Jacques Lacan calls a "camouflage" effect, one similar to the technique "practised in human warfare"[1]—or to outline more clearly her foregrounded fictive lineaments. Although, as Mary Russo has noted, "to put on femininity with a vengeance suggests the power of taking it off," at the midpoint of her career the American expatriate H. D. literally took off her clothing to put on her femininity, as if glossing Nietzsche's "they can 'put on something' even when they take off everything."[2] Eventually, however, she stripped herself of a plethora of feminine personae that enabled her, first, to meditate on the aesthetic and sexual frigidity her masquerades exacted and then to envision, much as did Zora Neale Hurston, a numinous female spirituality—a lost center or essence—that could counter the dissembling artifices of femininity.

Few poets in the twentieth century were more frequently fictionalized than the poet H. D., whose initials functioned as a signet suggesting sovereignty to replace her name, Hilda Doolittle. Dating back to her early days in Pennsylvania were the impressions of her sometime fiancé, Ezra Pound, who called her "Dryad." From her husband Richard Aldington's characterization of her as "Astraea" to Edith Sitwell's description of her as "Atalanta," H. D. was imagined as a chaste, beautiful nymph, the figure her companion Bryher identified with Artemis. Whether likened to a witch, as in D. H. Lawrence's portrait of her in *Aaron's Rod* (1922), or celebrated as an American Aphrodite, as she was by Horace Gregory, feminizing publicity linked H. D. to a pagan spirituality, contributing to the problem of fetishization that *"Personne,"* or "Nobody," as she sometimes called herself, confronted. For, to the dismay of her friend Norman Holmes Pearson, she frequently found herself praised as "a kind of Greek publicity girl" by her admirers.[3]

Oddly, according to Louis L. Martz, imagism—an effort to make the *im*personal poetical—sustained the reification of this poet by setting in place what he calls H. D.'s "Greek mask."[4] In addition, she constructed images of herself through strategies of self-presentation related to those deployed by other female female impersonators, although the most striking of her poses can be found neither in publicity photos nor on the lecture circuit but in a private scrapbook consisting of pictures taken by Bryher in 1920 and arranged by Kenneth Macpherson during the early thirties. These photographs, in which H. D. appears nude in a remote, sylvan scene, perpetuate an image of the poet as an antique, virginal divinity. Poised on the rocks at the edge of the sea or lying recumbent on the earth (see figures, next two pages), she disdains the clothing of culture, placing herself in a natural setting that evokes the archaic stance of the isolated, erotic, and sacred Greek nymph, a creature "At Home—in Paradise," to quote one of Emily Dickinson's meditations on female nudity.[5]

In the words of Diana Collecott, these portraits therefore "endorse earlier readings of H. D. as 'Oread,'" but they also seem to elaborate upon Isak Dinesen's point quoted earlier that "the loveliness of woman is created in the eye of man. . . . A goddess would ask her worshipper first of all: 'How am I looking?'"[6] And the album in which they appear includes equally resonant collages composed of statues of the gods on which H. D.'s head has been superimposed (see figure, page 170). Yet the fact that these photos were taken by a woman—who rescued H. D. from a life-threatening illness during pregnancy, supported her artistically and financially, lived and traveled with her

H. D. (courtesy the Yale Collection of
American Literature, Beinecke Rare Book
and Manuscript Library, Yale University)

intermittently throughout her life, and eventually adopted her daughter—
frames their significance, as does their appearance in a scrapbook put together by a man who both married Bryher and directed H. D. (whom he
loved as a "god or goddess") in the film *Borderline* (1930).[7] For throughout
her life H. D. enacted her charades with women as well as with men.

Given their resemblance to popular turn-of-the-century paintings and
photographs of naked nymphs lying prone on the earth or perched in trees,
such as Gabriel Guay's "Poem of the Woods" (1889), Albert-Joseph Penot's
"Autumn" (1903), or Anne Brigman's "The Dryad" (1906), these images of
H. D. indicate that she watched herself being watched by those who shared
her understanding of the aesthetic history of the female nude.[8] A voyeur of
the voyeurs of her body, to reiterate John Berger's terms, H. D. accepted

H. D. (courtesy the Yale Collection of American Literature, Beinecke Rare Book and Manuscript Library, Yale University)

demands for stereotypical femininity even as she rebelled against them. But her verse frequently documents her distress at the toll taken by such a balancing act, a distress at least partly apparent in the photograph that juxtaposes the poet's severed head with the stony immobility of a Greek statue. As if meditating on Joan Rivière's view of the feminine masquerade as (in the words of Tania Modleski) a "*compensation* on the part of the woman for having usurped what she perceives to be a 'masculine' authority" which might have "'unsexed'" her, throughout her poetic progress H. D. examined the liabilities, the problematics, of female female impersonation.[9]

H. D.'s sense of the spiritual source of her authority takes on added resonance when one considers the argument with Sigmund Freud in which she engaged during the two periods in 1933 and 1934 when she undertook analysis at Berggasse 19. During her sessions with Freud, begun because of her breakdown during the Great War and her dread of another war and another breakdown, the poet asked herself a disarmingly direct question: "Do I wish myself, in the deepest unconscious layers of my being, to be the founder of a new religion?" (*TF* 37). She was responding to the suggestion that she was suffering from what Freud termed *megalomania*, a "suppressed desire to be a Prophetess" (51). As Susan Stanford Friedman has shown, the question of religious belief in general and H. D.'s identification with divinity in particular comprised the substance of the poet's quarrel with "the Professor."[10] H. D. was convinced that Freud was blind to spiritual realities,

4.Bronze charioteer profile bust.Delphi.

H. D. (courtesy the Yale Collection of American Literature, Beinecke Rare
Book and Manuscript Library, Yale University)

specifically to the idea of immortality, and she considered the trancelike
states that he labeled her "only actually dangerous 'symptom' " to be part of a
mystical "inspiration" (41, 47).

If we place H. D.'s impersonations of nymph, dryad, priestess, or goddess
in the context of her later speculation that she might be the founder of a new
religion, it becomes clear that in her finest work she solved the problem of
the narcissism and frigidity evident in some of her aesthetic mimicries by

transforming herself into a spiritual poet, indeed into a deeply revisionary theologian. We will argue, moreover, that she managed to move from the dramatic verse of the teens and twenties to the long poems of the forties only when, like other women of letters, she self-consciously manipulated the images through which she continued to define herself. For H. D., such distance was attained through an examination of her situation as a woman poet in the twentieth century, specifically of the literary implications of the family romance that, following Freud, we used in *The War of the Words* to map the three lines of development available to the modern woman of letters.

Thus, H. D. evolved beyond submission to a paternal literary lineage, which Freud defined as the normative father-daughter paradigm; she suffered the renunciation of (aesthetic) desire that Freud saw as the source of female "frigidity"; and she eventually recuperated what Freud called "the original mother-attachment" through the recovery of a female muse of her own. H. D.'s efforts to achieve literary potency therefore can serve to summarize the various stages of development that we have used to define the twentieth-century woman writer's affiliation complex.[11] At the same time, her poetic progress implies a critique of Freud's theory of female maturation, for it demonstrates how the so-called normal attachment to the father figure can plunge a woman into a self-abnegating, frozen numbness that will thaw only if contact is made with the maternal attachment Freud labeled regressive. Paradoxically, then, throughout the twenties and thirties H. D. passionately wrote about the "sense of futility" that, in one of our epigraphs to this chapter, Ruth Benedict describes as a lonely obsession with "a longing to *stop*" and that H. D. associated with the longing to stop loving, writing, and living.

Through her evolution from paternal to maternal models of creativity, H. D. developed a visionary feminist aesthetic that addressed her scribbling sibling rivalry with her male peers as well as the tensions between the surveyor and the surveyed, the poet and the woman, the lover of women and the lover of men. Drawing upon a hubris suitable to the mythic characters she had exploited as poetic masks—Demeter, Calypso, Circe, Cassandra—but relinquishing these masks entirely, the "Greek publicity girl" eventually transformed the iconography of Christianity into a heretical, hermetic female genealogy. In her quasi-epic *Trilogy* (1944–46), H. D. used her role as "Prophetess" to formulate a theology of the family that consecrates the matriarchal divinity invoked in her autobiography: "This is Gaia, this is the beginning. This is the end. Under every shrine to Zeus, to Jupiter, to Zeupater or Theus-pater or God the Father . . . there is an earlier altar . . . beneath the carved super-structure of every temple to God-the-father, the dark cave or grot or inner hall or cellar to Mary, mère, Mut, mutter, pray for us."[12]

Why did H. D., the winner in 1915 of the Guarantor's Prize offered by
Poetry magazine and in 1917 of the Vers Libre contest sponsored by the *Little
Review*, a poet widely reviewed and anthologized as the perfect imagist after
the publication of *Sea Garden* (1916), produce her *Collected Poems* in 1925, as
if to signal the end of her career? And why, too, did she refrain for more than
a decade from publishing any volume of poetry after *Red Roses for Bronze*
(1931)? Why did H. D. arrange the verse she had composed but not published between 1931 and 1941 in a collection entitled *A Dead Priestess Speaks*?
And why, finally, did she destroy many of her prose manuscripts dating from
the 1920s and 1930s, dismissing others as "too self-centered or 'narcissistic'"?[13] Until the 1980s, critics discussed either her "crystalline" imagistic
verse or her book-length late poems, neglecting the ways H. D. used dramatic monologues—conversations of a conflicted "I" with an agonistic, godlike "you"—to depict her engagement in an unbalanced literary battle which
threatened to issue in a sense of futility: an obsession with a longing to stop.[14]

Early examples of these one-sided poetic dialogues illuminate Rachel
Blau DuPlessis's view that H. D. struggled "not to be reduced, to be neither
muse nor poetess,"[15] an endeavor that highlights her debt and her resistance
to her male peers. That two of the most prominent mythologists of H. D.'s
time—Ezra Pound and D. H. Lawrence—were also "initiators" in her poetic
development suggests that the myth of origins she eventually dedicated to
"Mary, mère, Mut, mutter" was the result of their visionary company. While
H. D. began her mythological impersonations under their influence, the
roles they allotted her threatened to undermine her own aesthetic independence. After her engagement to Pound was broken in 1912, H. D. associated
his image of her with the "Pounding" sentence pronounced both in her novel
HERmione (composed 1927) and her memoir *End of Torment* (composed
1958), namely, his assertion, "You are a poem, though your poem's
naught."[16] Similarly, after the death of Lawrence, H. D. believed she was
the model for Isis in his *The Man Who Died* (1929), although in the brief time
during World War I that she had befriended him she had resented his
criticism of her poetry ("Your frozen altars") as well as his admonition to her
to limit her perspective to "the woman speaking" ("How can you know what
Orpheus feels?")—or so she intimates in *Bid Me to Live* (composed 1939),
her roman à clef about their relationship (136, 62).[17] Two poems, "Toward
the Piraeus" (1924) and "Eurydice" (1917), analyze the connection between
H. D.'s Greek impersonations and the sense of vulnerability that characterized her relationships with her male contemporaries.

Specifically, both poems identify the protection furnished by the "Greek
mask" with an elite classicism that marks the poet as a true bard, the female
double of a masterful man of letters, even as they dramatize the sinister
competition that the mask provokes, prolongs, and protects against. At the

same time, "Toward the Piraeus" and "Eurydice" explain why H. D.—who received substantial acclaim with her first publications—suffered so many doubts about her work, for in the early stages of her development the poet felt herself to be trapped inside a literary and sexual romance that propelled her from the father-daughter affiliative relationship to a virtual renunciation of poetic desire. Reified within the images of herself that she constructed in dialogues with both Pound and Lawrence, the youthful H. D. adopted a series of feminine masks that energized but nevertheless threatened to mute her voice.

Although "Toward the Piraeus" begins with a scathing denunciation of the no-men most modern men have become (*"puny, passionless, weak"*) and with a request for a masterful man (*"one / to fright (as your eyes) with a sword, / men, craven and weak"*), it proceeds to express not only the female poet's need for a strong mentor but also her dread that he will obliterate her (*CP* 175–76). The male poet, partially modeled on Pound, is both an initiator of the female poet's artistry and a danger to it.[18] "You would have broken my wings," the female speaker admits: "You would have snared me"; however, "the very fact that you knew / I had wings," as well as "the very fact that you saw," means that she is "set . . . apart" and endowed with the gift of song. A typical example of what DuPlessis calls H. D.'s "romantic thralldom,"[19] the poet's initial request—*"Grant us your mantle, Greek!"*—quickly evolves into an acknowledgement that the master who inspires her verse also might isolate her and usurp her voice:

> . . . the very fact that you saw,
> sheltered me, claimed me,
> set me apart from the rest
>
> Of men—of *men*, made you a god,
> and me, claimed me, set me apart
> and the song in my breast,
> yours, yours forever—
> if I escape your evil heart.

[176]

Explaining to this godlike man with an evil heart that "I loved you," the ensnared speaker likens herself to "the Pythoness stand[ing] by the altar," for she waits and watches, unable to "break from my trance to speak" the word of love. H. D. proceeds sarcastically to meditate on an alternative, fulfilling relationship with the male poet, "had you been true," or "were I not wise," or (most scathingly) "if you were great" (177). Finally, "if I had been a boy," she speculates, the male bard might have left the bed of his mistress and "summoned" her (178, 179). Instead, however, he endangers her so that she retreats from him. In the final stanzas of the poem, even their common disdain for "the puny race" is not enough to bind them together, because H. D. sees the woman poet locked into a fatal battle with her paternal competitor:

> It was not chastity that made me wild, but fear
> that my weapon, tempered in different heat,
> was over-matched by yours, and your hand
> skilled to yield death-blows, might break

> With the slightest turn—no ill will meant—
> my own lesser, yet still somewhat fine-wrought,
> fiery-tempered, delicate, over-passionate steel.

[179]

At least in part, "Toward the Piraeus" articulates H. D.'s dedication to a kind of poetry which exacts an abnegation of love from the woman who must remain "cold, cold, cold" so as not to be reduced to a silent beloved; the male poet's fleeting erotic encounter—with "the flame / of the woman, tall like the cypress tree"—represents the "lethargy of love and its heat" as opposed to the "fiery-tempered" and "over-passionate" desire of aesthetic ambition. Not poetic dedication, however, but fear motivates her coldness, a coldness at odds with her belief that she would have "watched / and burned" at seeing his "great head, set on the throat, / thick, dark with its sinews." "Toward the Piraeus" thus also serves as an apology on the part of the woman writer who finds it necessary to withdraw from a relationship that has the potential to destroy her. The masculine poet's frightening eyes like a sword, as well as the weapon of his art, could break the delicate steel of the feminine writer's "lesser" artistry. Entrance into Piraeus, the gateway to Athens, appears to be barred by a possibly murderous mentor whose evil heart has been filled by "curious lies."

The hauteur of the male poet in "Toward the Piraeus" and his erotic encounter with "the woman, tall like the cypress tree" recall Ezra Pound's revolt against late nineteenth-century Romanticism and his mythologizing of H. D.: rejecting the "slow-moving pageantry of hours that languidly / Drop as o'er-ripened fruit from sallow trees," the poet who frequently memorialized H. D. as a "tree-born spirit of the wood" decides in his "Revolt: Against the Crepuscular Spirit in Modern Poetry" (1909) to "dream great deeds, strong men, / Hearts hot, thoughts mighty."[20] If as a writer H. D. could become an icon of the new, she would have to distance herself from a female tradition that, according to Pound, reeked of soggy sentimentality. In Pound's early poems about women writers, the male poet seeks to "make it new," while the female poet is accused of precisely the literary anachronism with which Wallace Stevens charges his fictional poetess Claire Dupray, namely that she "imitates the point of view and the feelings of a generation ago."[21]

Throughout Pound's poetry, moreover, while the beloved lady in general and H. D. in particular inspire the erotic longing that energizes the bard, "marriage means art death" because of "the semi-stupor of satisfied passion."[22] This view, which explained his attraction to the courtly love traditions of Provençal poetry, caused Pound to imagine his beloved in terms that stress her embodiment of a natural world outside of culture: she is not only the moss-grown tree in "Hilda's Book" and *A Lume Spento* (1908) but also, by the publication of *Personae* (1908–10) and *Ripostes* (1912), the doomed yet radiant Persephone, symbol of springtime flowering.[23] Yet this identification of the female with the object of the male gaze ("A woman well to look upon"), with nature ("She swayeth as a poplar tree"), and with silence ("Her lips part, tho no words come" ["Hilda's Book"]) shaped a view that would have been especially perplexing for H. D., namely that the female of the poetic species functions as the object or the muse and not the author of verse. Therefore the aspiring woman poet must learn, as the Pound character explains in *HERmione*, "Love doesn't make good art" (*HER* 149).

On the one hand, in the naming scene at the tearoom of the British Museum, Pound the facilitator looks at H. D.'s verse and informs his Dryad, "this is poetry"; on the other, Pound the censor and editor "slash[es] with a pencil" (*ET* 18). A similar dynamic plays itself out in his "Ortus" (1913), which Cyrena Pondrom views as a poem about H. D., where Pound claims to have "laboured" to "give her a name and her being," for he entreats her to "enter [her] life" and to "learn to say 'I'"; however, she "has no name, and no place" of her own making.[24] Within a setting that evokes the tearoom near the British Museum in which Pound signed "H. D., Imagiste," below her verse, the woman poet of Pound's "Tea Shop" (1926) no longer functions as the male poet's muse and she is therefore demoted from the mythological to the temporal realm where, "not so beautiful as she was," she "will turn middle-aged."[25]

Similarly, in "Tempora" (1926) Pound comically, affectionately, but definitively labels H. D.'s literary ambition sacrilegious:

> The Dryad stands in my court-yard
> With plaintive, querulous crying.
> (Tamuz. Io! Tamuz!)
> Oh, no, she is not crying: "Tamuz!"
> She says, "May my poems be printed this week?"
> The god Pan is afraid to ask you, may my poems be
> printed this week?[26]

Before and after the composition of "Toward the Piraeus," H. D.'s poetic entanglement with Pound apparently demonstrated to both of them that— whether he flattered her with a "tribute such as some courtier might pay to a queen who played at classicism" or "tampered with [her as with] an oracle, . . . bang[ing] on a temple door, . . . dragg[ing] out small curious, sacred ornaments"—he "did not proffer her the bare branch that was the strip of wild naked olive" (*HER* 172).[27]

Pound's subsequent charge in the *Cantos* (1930) that "the female / Is an element, the female / Is a chaos / An octopus / A biological process" must have contributed to H. D.'s later suspicion that, despite his hymns to the Eleusinian Demeter, to Circe, and to the Dionysian Lynx (all figures she imagined as portraits of herself), Pound could accept neither her spiritual nor her poetic authority. Given these images of the feminine, it seems fitting that Pound apparently asked the sculptor Gaudier-Brzeska to fashion his head of the poet in the shape of a phallus.[28] For by 1931 Pound was conceptualizing originality as "the phallus or spermatozoid charging, head-on, the female chaos," just as he was linking the innovations of modernity with "man," to whom is "given what we have of history, the 'inventions,' the new gestures, the extravagance, the wild shots, the new bathing of the cerebral tissues."[29]

As he evolved a mythology of male aesthetic potency in the *Cantos*, Pound increasingly denied women any attribute other than biological fecundity. While he celebrates Odysseus, Confucius, John Adams, and Mussolini, admonishing himself to "think of thy plowing," he is assured of woman's intellectual incapacity:

> Two span, two span to a woman,
> Beyond that she believes not. Nothing is of any importance.
> . . . .
> The stars are not in her counting,
> To her they are but wandering holes.[30]

Even the Confucian ideogram is used as a kind of *patrius sermo* and imagined by Pound in emphatically phallic terms as "pictorially the sun's lance coming to rest on the precise spot verbally." Because "man's phallic heart is from heaven / a clear spring of rightness," Pound's Wang declares in the *Cantos*, "the heart shd / be straight, / The phallos perceive its aim." In the grotesque logic of anti-Semitism, then, Pound's portrait of the "procurer" Levine labels the Jew "the brains behind the female suffrage movement in England," while the poet's critique of a bankrupt Anglo-American culture dubs it a "gynocracy." In addition, Pound's effort to glorify masculinity led him to claim that the phallus "inspire[s] primitive religions": "the phallus is not the cock= / it is the COCK ERECT= / obj. of worship—."[31]

Like her struggle with Pound, H. D.'s contest with D. H. Lawrence was fought over the spiritual forces their classical allusions invoked. Lawrence wrote in 1917 to Cecil Gray about "my 'women'" (among whom he listed "Hilda Aldington"), moving from an insistence that they embody "an impure and unproud, subservient, cringing, bad fashion" to the admission that they nevertheless represent "the threshold of a new world, or underworld, of knowledge and being," resembling that of "the Greeks—Orphicism." H. D., horrified like Lawrence by the senseless suffering she associated with the Great War, would have agreed with him that "the old world must burst, the underworld must be open and whole, new world."[32] Yet H. D. also knew that Lawrence, "shout[ing] his man-is-man, his woman-is-woman at her," was mistaken about artistic consciousness which was, to her mind, "sexless, or all sex" (*BML* 136, 62), a point she makes in "Eurydice," where she nevertheless dramatizes the rivalry between the male and female poet by conforming to Lawrence's advice and "stick[ing] to the woman-consciousness" (*BML* 62).

Not abandoning the male, as she does in "Toward the Piraeus," but here abandoned by him, H. D.'s Eurydice broods upon the "arrogance" and "ruthlessness" of an Orpheus who has left her in the hell she is now destined to inhabit eternally. If in "Toward the Piraeus" the female speaker prays for *"one / to fright (as your eyes) with a sword,"* only to find herself "claimed" and "set . . . apart" because "you saw," in "Eurydice" it is the male poet's gaze that dooms the woman—"broken at last"—to a solitary, tormented life-in-death:

> why did you turn?
> why did you glance back?
> why did you hesitate for that moment?
> why did you bend your face
> caught with the flame of the upper earth,
> above my face?
>
> [*CP* 52]

In Hades, where "everything is crossed with black" and "worse than black, / this colourless light," the female poet is divorced from the colorful world of birds, beasts, and flowers her male peer inhabits.

Resorting, as she had in "Toward the Piraeus," to the subjunctive, the poet explains that if she "could have caught up from the earth, / the whole of the flowers of the earth," she "could have dared the loss" (53) of the earth. But instead she has been consigned to a buried life by "you who have your own light, / who are to yourself a presence, / who need no presence" (54). And, far from bestowing upon her a true picture of herself, Orpheus's ruthless glance only entangles Eurydice in his own self-projections: "What was it you saw in my face? / the light of your own face, / the fire of your own presence?" (52). Again, although the stationary female poet loses "the earth / and the flowers of the earth, / and the live souls above the earth" (53), the male poet has an autonomy that makes him seem not only impervious but also indifferent.

In spite of "all your arrogance / and your glance" (54), however, at the end of the poem H. D.'s Persephonelike Eurydice defies Orpheus by turning her rage into a satanic light that fuels a curse poem. In hell Eurydice becomes a daunting rival of the god of song, proclaiming that her "hell is no worse than your earth," arguing "nor [is] your presence, / a loss," and exulting, "I have the fervour of myself for a presence / and my own spirit for light" (55). Lost to Orpheus, she has found herself, for she has been tempered by a heat that turns his absence into her own presence. Amid the blackness, the poet's intensity illuminates landscapes which, if described, would tempt Orpheus back to hell, to another glance back, and to her own plunge "into a place / even more terrible than this." The mysteriously defiant final lines of "Eurydice"—"Before I am lost, / hell must open like a red rose / for the dead to pass"—warn that she is so determined to keep "the flowers of myself" that, rather than lose herself, she will let hell bloom on earth, as she and her legions, not Orpheus, trespass between the worlds of the living and the dead.

The source of H. D.'s attraction to Lawrence and of her intimation of his ambivalence about her poetic aspirations can be found in both writers' work. Besides their common efforts to infuse a bankrupt modern society with energy derived from pagan mythology, H. D. and Lawrence identified that energy with the woman in the underworld who embodies a sensual wisdom that serves as a spiritual alternative to the skepticism of contemporary life. Enamored of Eurydice's realm, Lawrence celebrates in "Medlars and Sorb-Apples" (1921) the "wonderful . . . hellish experiences, / Orphic" that lead him "down the strange lanes of hell"; and his "Bavarian Gentians" (1923), revising many of the images in H. D.'s "Eurydice," praises the "torch-like" flowers, resembling "black lamps from the halls of Dis," that might guide the poet down to the "sightless" realm "where Persephone goes."[33]

A number of the poems in *Look! We Have Come Through!* (1917), Lawrence's paean to his wife, explain why H. D. repeatedly associated Lawrence's artistry as well with a linguistic intensity she admired. In his "Gloire de Dijon" (1912), a poem she often invoked in her later narratives about Lawrence, he "linger[s]" to "watch" a golden woman swaying in the sunbeams that transform her into a self-sufficient presence, a "full-blown yellow / Gloire de Dijon [rose]" (*LCP* 217).[34] Yet Lawrence's exultant songs of "a Man Who Has Come Through" contrast sharply with Eurydice's stasis, for his personae typically visit the daemonic underworld of the female in order to revitalize their lonely but triumphant autonomy. "Hymn to Priapus" (1917), a poem about the death of Lawrence's mother, repeats a stanza—

> My love lies underground
> With her face upturned to mine,
> And her mouth unclosed in the last long kiss
> That ended her life and mine—

to explain that, while the speaker "will not forget, / The stream of my life in the darkness / Deathward set," he also departs from the buried woman, knowing he "has forgotten, / Has ceased to care. / Desire comes up, and contentment / Is debonair" (*LCP* 198–99).

Even in "Medlars and Sorb-Apples," Lawrence's "Orphic" hero travels "down the strange lanes of hell, more and more intensely alone," relishing "the exquisite odour" of Orpheus's "leave-taking." And in the later "Bavarian Gentians," instead of being relegated to the hell of abandonment by another's glance, the male poet himself dares the loss and actively seeks the "darkness invisible" in which Persephone is "enfolded in the deeper dark / of the arms Plutonic." Lawrence's development would only have confirmed H. D.'s realization of their differences, for the "female" fruits he prefers in *Birds, Beasts and Flowers* (1923) turn from the "orgasm of rupture" he tastes in the rotten "Medlars and Sorb-Apples" to the even more exposed "fissure" of "over-ripe" figs whose "moist, scarlet lips" affirm female sexuality, disgusting the poet who likens the fissure of the ripe fig to "a wound" or "a prostitute . . . making a show of her secret" (*LCP* 280–81, 282–84).

As several critics have demonstrated, Lawrence's fear that "there is no getting of a vision . . . before we get our souls fertilised by the *female*" may have spawned the humiliating sense of dependency that explains his growing insistence that "the only gods on earth are men." Indeed, the "phallic knowledge" Lawrence celebrated in the "leadership" novels of the twenties led to his belief that "woman as the goddess in the machine of the human psyche is a heroine who will drive us, like a female chauffeur, through all the avenues of hell, till she pitches us eventually down the bottomless pit." Birkin's curse of "Cybele, the accursed Syria Dea," in *Women in Love* (1920) prefigures not only Lawrence's conviction that "a race falls when men begin to worship the Great Mother" but also his belief that "all the germs in the list of bacteriology are not so dangerous for a child as mother-love."[35] But perhaps the "[Third Song of Huitzilopochtli]" (1926) best illuminates Lawrence's commonality with Pound, their identification of masculinity with the source of spiritual potency:

> Man that is man is more than a man.
> No man is man till he is more than a man.
> Till the power is in him
> Which is not his own.

> [*LCP* 806]

By 1917, H. D. has already cast Lawrence as arrogant in "Eurydice" because—in H. D.'s words—"you would say I was trespassing, couldn't see both sides, as you said of my Orpheus. I could be Eurydice in character, you said, but woman-is-woman and I couldn't be both. The *gloire* is both" (*BML* 176). Warding off his disdainful critique of her "frozen altars," the heroine of H. D.'s *Bid Me to Live* first explains that Lawrence's "vaunted business of experience, of sex-emotion and understanding . . . might be all right for

men, but for women, any woman, there was a biological catch" (135–36).
Then, although H. D.'s fictional surrogate sees Lawrence as Orpheus (51)
and "Dis of the under-world, the husband of Persephone" (141), she believes
that their relationship fails because of *his* sexual squeamishness or puritanism. An erotic charade in *Bid Me to Live* presents Rico (Lawrence) flaming
out with desire that is shattered when Julia (H. D.) responds. In other words,
after the overture of his gaze—which awakens her and causes her to reach
out to him—he is portrayed withdrawing, as Orpheus does in "Eurydice."
     H. D.'s Eurydice therefore resembles the speaker of "Toward the Pi-
raeus": both struggle with roles to which they have been consigned because
of the male poet's "glance." To be sure, the masks of Pythoness and Eurydice
presumptuously mark the woman poet as an aristocratic equal of her lordly
competitor. Indeed, the mask functions as a kind of armor that guards the
woman poet from male assaults against the aesthetic presumption it signifies.[36] Deploying what we have called female female impersonations, H. D.
questions as rigorously as do Millay and Moore those conventions of eroticism and of verse writing which appear to be traditionally grounded in
female immobilization, for both "Toward the Piraeus" and "Eurydice" exploit mythic personae to protest against the male lover-artist who threatens
to control the female lover-artist. Yet the origin of the feminine mask, constructed in part by the gaze of the male spectator, as well as the vulnerability
associated with the mythic script to which it refers, suggests that it threatens
to blind or muffle the woman poet by turning her into the object surveyed.
While H. D. brooded upon Pound's and Lawrence's mastery in the first two
decades of her long career, she confronted the empowering glamour and
the painful frigidity brought about by her absorption with her male peers
and by her dread that artistry itself somehow required ruthless strategies of
objectification.

———————

     Although allegations of sexual frigidity may have been leveled against
women in modern times as often as the Victorians raised the specter of
female impurity, few extended literary studies of the temper and toll of
frigidity were produced. In mid-career H. D. provided just such an analysis,
one which emphasizes the immobility and self-absorption of the woman who
suffers the cold because she fears the fires of art or love will consume her.
Many early critics faulted the poet's Hellenism as itself frigid; however,
throughout the twenties and thirties her prose and poetry passionately
counterpoint the red roses, fiery darts, and honeyed lips of love with the cold
hands, wind-driven snows, and white stones of a withdrawal that she analyzed with exceptional clarity.[37] Punishment, refuge, defiance, neurosis:
H. D. diagnosed frigidity as an aesthetic and a psychosexual condition that
leads the woman poet to a life-in-death. Thus, one persona explains about

her relationship to the male or the male muse, "I was dead / and you woke me, / now you are gone, / I am dead" (*CP* 222).

At two crucial moments H. D. invoked *The Winter's Tale*. She named her fictional surrogate Hermione to mourn her own sense of inanimate life-in-death: in Shakespeare's play, the jealous king Leontes sentences his wife Hermione to death, although a sculptor re-creates her image in a statue. And H. D. called her daughter Frances Perdita: in the play, Hermione's child, Perdita, is saved from a death sentence and transformed into a pastoral shepherdess who eventually brings her mother miraculously back to life. The mother as a stone statue, the exiled lost daughter: in H. D.'s poetic and novelistic winter tales, she adumbrates the insights of recent feminist theorists of female psychology. Kim Chernin describes women whose social selves are splintered from their buried identities as "frozen. Turned to stone. Made inert," and goes on: "Few guess that this wasteland is inevitable for those who have unclothed the paper doll who pretends to be a woman."[38]

A number of poems in *Hymen* (1921) and *Heliodora and Other Poems* (1924) yoke H. D.'s sense of immobilization with reified, mythic female figures killed into art or consigned to marginality by the same sort of glances that torture the central characters of "Toward the Piraeus" and "Eurydice." Of course, as divine creators of life, magical consorts of heroes, legendary beauties, or visionaries, such mythological characters as Demeter, Circe, Helen, Cassandra, and Telesila function as avatars of power as well as ancient prototypes who enabled H. D. to study women's history. Yet just as H. D.'s novel about Pound is written from the perspective of Hermione, who "froze into a statue" (*HER* 66) and whose nickname, "Her," exemplifies her objectified case, many of H. D.'s lyrics and monologues demonstrate her attraction toward and rebellion against the transformation of the female artist into a work of art. "Demeter," who creates life itself, sits "wide of shoulder, great of thigh, / heavy in gold," on "a mighty plinth," and laments, "They have wrought me heavy / and great of limb." And "Circe," who has the art to turn each of the men on her island into "his own self," is effectively imprisoned in her palace, for after Odysseus's departure she would renounce all of her "power and magic / for your glance" (*CP* 111, 119, 120).

When seen by men or gods, the poet's personae find it almost impossible to be see-ers or seers themselves. Indeed, many of the characters with whom H. D. identifies are literally or figuratively petrified. Helen, whom "all Greece hates," "reviles," and "sees unmoved," is a wan, white figure who could only be loved "if she were laid, / white ash amid funereal cypresses" (*CP* 154–55). The ambiguity of the lines "Greece sees unmoved, / God's daughter" functions to present both a voyeuristic Greek populace, unmoved or unsympathetic, and a fetishized maid, to be loved only in rigor mortis. Even the more prophetic "Cassandra" suffers from "fire / searing my eyeballs and my eyes with flame," for she is trapped in a trance of daemonic possession which neither fully possesses her nor fully withdraws from her: "when will you leave me quite? / when will you break my wings / or leave them utterly free / to scale heaven endlessly?" (169–70). Like Helen, Cassandra knows that she "frightens" men, in her case because Hymen's "look" has burnt her face with its light (170).

Just as paralyzed, "Telesila," a poet-warrior sculpted in Argos with a scroll of poetry at her feet and a helmet in her hand, is wooed by two antithetical gods, stymied by the eroticism of "Love" and that of the equally fevered "War" (186). Personae not fixed in stone suffer internal conflicts similar to Telesila's. H. D.'s Penelope in the poem "At Ithaca," for instance, appears to be torn between her devotion to her warrior-husband, which requires her to undo her "web of pictures," and her wish for closure, which makes her see "my work so beautifully / inwoven" that she wants to "keep / the picture and the whole" (164). Indeed, Penelope meditates on precisely the stasis to which H. D.'s "Fragment Thirty-six" alludes: "*I know not what to do: / my mind is divided*" (165).

In the Sapphic reinvention, moreover, H. D.'s competing loyalties to love and to art result in a kind of deadlock:

> My mind is quite divided,
> my minds hesitate,
> so perfect matched,
> I know not what to do:
> each strives with each
> as two white wrestlers
> standing for a match,
> ready to turn and clutch
> yet never shake muscle nor nerve nor tendon;
> so my mind waits
> to grapple with my mind.
>
> [167]

The poet of these lines about self-division introduced the book in which they appear with an epigraph about a glacial landscape of "chill, snow-ribbed sand" and "frozen lily-leaf" that leads her to want to "mould a clear / and frigid statue" of marble (*CP* 147–48). Meant "to grace / your inaccessible shrine," this "frigid statue" recalls many of H. D.'s earlier poems about the virgin-huntress Artemis and Pallas Athene, armored devotee of her father, Zeus. One poem in *Heliodora*, "Lethe," links the lure of chastity with the suicidal wish not for "word nor touch nor sight / Of lover," but for "the roll of the full tide to cover you / Without question, / Without kiss" (190).

The prose H. D. wrote in the twenties extends her examination of immobility, linking it to her characters' disappointment in love relationships, their blocked artistic aspirations, and their feelings of personal unreality. To the extent that Hipparchia, the protagonist of the first part of the novel *Palimpsest* (1926), decides "betrayal was her safeguard. She must wear it, tempered armour wrapped about her spirit" (74), she is a typical H. D. heroine. Her frigidity with her lovers as well as her inability to write signify her debilitating sense of paralysis. Looking at her own hand, Hipparchia thinks, "It was as if a heavy marble hand had been broken from the draped body of some exiled Muse or early unfashionable Aphrodite" (42). *Palimpsest* goes on to analyze the enervating effect on women of the sense of objectification Hipparchia suffers, for her successor in the second section, Raymonde Ransome, feels that she is left with a choice "between Limbo where we are or that salt pillar, Lot's wife" (122), while the central character of the third part, Helen Fairwood, lives on a tightrope and "in danger . . . of losing, in the very torment of this balance, the whole clue, of standing frozen, nullified" (192).

Whether petrified or fractured into body parts, H. D.'s vulnerable heroines feel themselves to be coldly inanimate. As if glossing the image of the stone statues photographed with H. D.'s head superimposed on them, Hermione feels that "her wrists were doll wrists" (*HER* 166); her head a "marble weight" (73); "her heart was frozen" (226).[39] Both *Palimpsest* and *HERmione* depict the fatal attractions of frigidity for women who are survivors of failed heterosexual relationships, most of which are patterned on the subordination of a daughterly woman to a distant or untrustworthy patriarch. The thralldom women experience in erotic relationships with men, H. D.'s work implies, inevitably leads to the problem Freud identified with an alternative line of development when the woman, "turning her back on sexuality altogether," relinquishes "her phallic activity and therewith her sexuality in general and a considerable part of her masculine proclivities in other fields" ("FS" 198). H. D. swerves from Freud, however, by interpreting such renunciation not as a stage distinct from the "ultimate normal feminine attitude in which [the young girl] takes her father as love-object" but as a damaging repercussion of the female fetishization inflicted by a heterosexuality based on the father-daughter paradigm ("FS" 198).

As if illustrating Karen Horney's and John Berger's point cited in Chapter 2 that a woman must continually watch herself being watched, H. D.'s characters relinquish aesthetic and sexual activity and instead obsessively look at themselves. Wondering over her jewels and dresses in order to keep "proving, to myself my own reality,"[40] the heroine of her novel *Hedylus* (1928) is fixed in a narcissism that also distinguishes the protagonists of *Palimpsest*: Hipparchia, who dwells on her own mirror image ("Hipparchia loved the silver cold Hipparchia" [55]); Raymonde Ransome, who sees other characters as projections of herself ("in avid clarity, Ermy gave her Raymonde" [118]); and Helen Fairwood, who imagines the impact of her image on others ("he should step across the threshold of the door . . . when the blue, blue slim creature with the heavy blue collar of blue stones should rise, 'you'" [197]).

At the moment H. D.'s fictional surrogate in *HERmione* breaks off her engagement by explaining to the Pound figure, "I love Her, only Her, Her, Her," Hermione's erstwhile suitor calls her "Narcissa" (170). And Hermione's love of the vaguely sinister, Swinburnean young woman named Fayne seems at least in part to substantiate his view—and Freud's belief as early as "On Narcissism" (1914)—that homosexual desire constitutes a regression to a self-love that guards against mature individuation.[41] Although a number of critics have recently praised H. D.'s prose narratives of the twenties and thirties, moreover, the repetitive self-absorption of plots that consistently turn all the characters into mirrors of the heroine and her author causes these texts to come perilously close to modernist Harlequin romances. A sign of their passivity, the narcissistic gaze of H. D.'s personae, like their frigidity, nevertheless protects them from men, even as it functions as a covert form of resistance to men.

In *Red Roses for Bronze*, the last book of poetry H. D. published before her thirteen-year poetic silence, she examined the dialectic between the feminine model's sculpted form and the female author's vengeful visions of herself as a sculptor. The title poem, in particular, is wistful in its wish for an aesthetic victory that might defend the woman artist against erotic desire, even as it uncovers the anger implicit in literary as well as literal frigidity. But the poem begins with an "if" that expresses the poet's hopeless sense that she is destined to be defeated. "If I might take a weight of bronze," she explains, "and hammer in / the line beneath your underlip," or "if I might ease my fingers and my brain / with stroke, / stroke, / stroke, / stroke, / stroke at— something (stone, marble, intent, stable, materialized)," then "peace, / even magic sleep / might come again" (*CP* 211). Thus, violently retaliatory strokes replace erotically desirous strokes as the poet-sculptor disdains the "you" who would only deign to give her a "casual sort of homage" (212). But the anxious repetitions of this verse ("stroke, / stroke, / stroke, / stroke, / stroke") hint that she is unable to wrest aesthetic victory from her male antagonist, a man who is also her love object.[42]

Although the speaker of "Red Roses for Bronze" counts "most men ignoble by your height" (212), she wants to "turn and tear and rip" this man, to "force you to grasp my soul's sincerity" (213). Specifically, what she would do is lure him to her studio, fashion a sculpture of him as "Mars / or maybe Actaeon / the Huntress / bids her hounds / to leap upon," and "make a thing" at which "all, seeing it, would stare, / so that all men (seeing it) / would forsake all women" (214). Self-consciously motivated by jealousy of another woman, the speaker nevertheless directs her rage against the "tall god" she would murder through her "mastery," for she "would set your bronze head in its place," like a modern-day Judith severing the head of Holofernes. Dedicated—despite her book's title—to substituting bronze roses for red, the poet would sculpt roses that "would endure" (215), unlike the red roses of her rival.

Yet the desire for such mastery is tempered by the poet's own hopeless sense of enchantment and entrapment. In "Trance," for example, the speaker stares "till my eyes are a statue's eyes, / set in, / my eye-balls are glass, / my limbs marble, / my face fixed / in its marble mask" (*CP* 244). Just as the voice of the "Sea-Choros" translated from *Hecuba* calls out, "I am lost, / I am dead" (*CP* 240), the poet writes her own "Epitaph," appearing to resign herself to a living death: "'I died of living, / having lived one hour'" ("Epitaph," 299). The verse H. D. composed but did not publish between 1931 and 1944, later arranged in *A Dead Priestess Speaks*, contains a number of portraits of the woman artist as dead or dying. "I, being dead" is a Dickinsonian phrase articulated by Delia of Miletus, the dead priestess who imagines her own funeral (*CP* 371). Endowed with a "secret song" (373), Delia had "found / a new brew of bay" as well as "honour," and her followers "carved upon the stone / that I was good" (374, 375, 377). Wanderer, herbalist, spinner of fine threads, singer, and witch, she has not died, it seems, because of a hostile or indifferent community. "Priest," another poem in this collection, helps explain Delia's elegy on her own death in terms of the poetic death H. D. seems to have suffered in mid-career and implies that the poet's renunciation of aesthetic ambition for more than a decade was the inevitable result of her sense that she might be losing the literary battle of the sexes.

"Priest" is infused with an almost incomprehensible acerbity about a paternal literary potency that the speaker views as a kind of necrophilia, a sign that thralldom has less to do with real men and more with haunting presences within the female psyche. The ironic poet here begins with two seemingly unrelated but actually causal facts: "Now you are a priest, / and she is dead."[43] The priest himself, according to the female speaker, realizes his power comes from the dead woman: "You say, / 'she alone gave me prescience'" (*CP* 419). What troubles H. D. is the priest's plentiful praise for a woman who is dead because (unlike the buried woman) the speaker "will not die, / and you will not praise me that I live" (422). In fact, she comes to realize that

> you prefer a woman under the earth,
> you heap roses above a grave;
> a woman under the earth
> is safe,
> a woman dead
> is beloved.
>
> [423]

As elsewhere, the abandoned poet survives through coldness. Indeed, her heart and love are "cold" so as "to withstand / even your fire" (427).

As if refuting Poe's belief that the death of a beautiful woman "is unquestionably the most poetical topic in the world,"[44] H. D. goes on to discount the priest's verbal potency: "your words, / spoken like a king . . . don't count, //

your words don't mean anything" (430). By the end of the poem, the speaker taunts the priest with his promise that his departure from her will result in their meeting at the ends of their solitary journeys. Clinging to his beloved, he has lost not only H. D. but also her visionary gleam: "*O, my friend, / where is your wisdom? / the end is the beginning; / O, my priest, / where is your robe?*" (431). In spite of her scornful judgment, however, she admits that her own life is "measureless," that is, it is both ongoing and without poetic measures. She herself "can not tell"; she "can not take tablet and wax / and make words" (429).

As the "dead priestess," then, H. D. speaks about the fearful burden of female (poetic) autonomy. Just as the poet Hedylus burns all his manuscripts in the novel named after him, H. D. suffered a crisis of confidence in her own creative survival at mid-career. Thus, the fiction of the thirties reiterates Delia of Miletus's self-definition, "I, being dead." Not only is the narrator of *Kora and Ka* (1934) a Ka, which "lives after the body is dead"; his companion, Kora, is described as "heavy stone" reassembled from "various bits of marble, foot, hand, and severed torso."[45] And the numb heroine of *Nights* (1935), who seeks in sex the feeling of being sexless, ends up committing suicide by walking out onto an icy lake, leaving behind "fervid stream-of-consciousness" prose that resembles H. D.'s own associative novels.[46] Whether H. D.'s surrogates die, boast, apologize, assuage, denounce, or imagine a retaliation, they struggle with their dread of imminent (aesthetic) obliteration. Although, like Dickinson, H. D. turns the master who poses this threat into a muse who inspires these works, the cost is great, for she increasingly defines language as a weapon that not only could but would be turned against her.

"Chance Meeting," a poem H. D. left unpublished and uncollected, dramatizes a disillusionment with linguistic mastery that would make the writing of poetry ethically troubling. Acknowledging her initial worship of the male poet—"I thought your thought / was rare, / made maps for men, / the words you write / are chart and rudder in a storm"—"Chance Meeting" documents H. D.'s dread that her own artistry would somehow harm that of her male peer: "I thought my thought / might spoil your thought" or "I thought my thought / would slay" (*CP* 233). But the male author, who "dip[s] stylus in the beauty of the translatable / things you know," is contrasted with the female creator, whose insights are "untranslatable" (231–32). "You thought as poets think," H. D. charges her antagonist, an odd accusation coming from a poet. Declaring that "the things I have / are nameless," the speaker believes that her male rival's ability to turn the world into words means "the spell / had passed you" (232, 236). Her original hope that they might share each other's inspiration has been undermined by her realization that he has "wrecked" numerous others by praising their "worthless" songs and by using them as "oracle" or "seer": "you bled them of their genius," leaving them "without love / and without power" (234–35).

If the poetic imagination is vampiric, how could H. D. continue her career? With what words could she find a spell to resurrect the priestess? Once again, the disappointed female "I" concludes by denouncing the inadequate male "you": "The spell / had passed you" because "you did not sense the wings beyond the gate" and "you could not see, / you could not touch and feel" either "the sea-sand" or "the sea-shell." Again, too, the subjective mood forecasts an impossible future: "If you had caught my hand," the speaker thinks, "we would have . . . sipped / a nectar" that would have destroyed her male companion's familial and erotic attachments, demanding "headier loves / than your heart knew" (236). A lyricist of unrequited love, H. D. suffered from feelings of anger, loneliness, and betrayal that nevertheless forecast her subsequent efforts to find a nameless vocabulary to speak the spell of wings beyond the gate, of the sea-sand and the sea-shell, and of the headier love she envisioned in *Trilogy.*

But intimations of that headier love appear in *A Dead Priestess Speaks* when the sense of insufficiency suffered by H. D.'s personae and their anger at men are countered by an extraordinary act of voyeurism. "The Master," composed in 1933, shortly after Freud published his essays on "Female Sexuality" (1931) and "Femininity" (1932), is spoken by a quarrelsome acolyte of the father of psychoanalysis ("I flung his words in his teeth" because "his tyranny was absolute" [*CP* 452]). However, the poet's rage against a mentor "who set [her] free / to prophesy" (458) dissipates after she watches a hieratic female dancer: "She is a woman, . . . her arms are the waving of the young / male" (455); "she needs no man, / herself / is that dart and pulse of the male" (456).[47] A mysterious sign of the instability of conventional gender markers, the dancer holds out the promise of negotiating between fire and ice, the lures of passion and asceticism: "For a woman / breathes fire / and is cold, / a woman sheds snow from ankles / and is warm" (454). That H. D.'s vision of a "white heat / melt[ing] into snow-flake" and her redefinition of the relationship between the feminine and the masculine appear during her therapy with Freud in a poem about surveying a female figure explain how important she found his admission "that the girl did not invariably transfer her emotions to her father" (*TF* 175), an insight she would fully examine in *Trilogy.*

"I will rise / from my troth / with the dead," H. D. vowed in "Wine Bowl" (*CP* 241). "So having died, / raise me again," she prayed in "Myrtle Bough" (262). As Gary Burnett has explained about the "verbal treadmill" of H. D.'s repetitions and silences in the middle of her career, the "chosen 'death' of a poet is nothing if not fruitful."[48] Dwelling with the dead through a linguistically strained withdrawal from desire, the author of *A Dead Priestess Speaks* began to discover a truth beneath gender:

> there is no "he and me,"
> there is no "you and she,"

there is no "it must be."

["Sigil," *CP* 411]

Although the sentence "'I love you'" leaves H. D. "cold" (418), the death of love opened the door to a different eros and a poetry about its raptures. The woman robed in "white, / as fitting the high-priestess" (372), rose from the dead by finding a clue to the mystery behind he and me, you and she, it must be.

Even taking into account H. D.'s movement from the Greek masks of, say, "Eurydice" to the more personal voice of "Chance Meeting," *Trilogy* comes as a revelation, for here the poet uses neither the mask nor the personal voice of one speaking to an antagonistic poetic peer. The resurrection H. D.'s *Trilogy* celebrates is her own rebirth as a poet, a regeneration made possible by a number of related prose experiments that furnished the strategies she employed to distance herself from her earlier impersonations. Indeed, besides its ambitious scope as a book-length poem, what is perhaps most striking about *Trilogy* is the prophetic strength of the poet's voice, no longer articulated through a Greek mask, no longer quarreling with a troublesome helpmate. H. D.'s affirmation of survival in this quasi-epic poem may be a response less to the Great War or the Second World War (its ostensible origins) than to the literary war between the sexes and to her own emergence as a poet who had survived the death sentence "I, being dead."

To the extent that it charts a shift from the death of the male and his symbols of power to images of female spiritual primacy, *Trilogy* meditates on H. D.'s survival in a world that must have quite literally seemed a no man's land. After the deaths of her brother and father during the Great War, the poet suffered the dissolution of her marriage with Aldington as well as the losses of Pound, Lawrence, and Macpherson, and then, just before writing *Trilogy*, the death of Freud. The sliced walls and fallen roofs in the opening poem describe her experience of the London blitz, but ruin "here and there" presents World War II as a palimpsest for the Great War and for all wars. Although "the bone-frame was made for / no such shock," the poet explains, "the frame held," and she poses the question that this work repeatedly seeks to answer: "What saved us? what for?" (*CP* 1:511).[49] Various responses to this question emerge in *The Walls Do Not Fall, Tribute to the Angels,* and *The Flowering of the Rod,* the three sections of *Trilogy,* as the poet-priestess moves through three stages of spiritual growth: election and calling, justification and adoption, and sanctification and glorification, a process that leads not to a Pauline recognition of the depravity of Adam purified by the grace of God's son but instead to a mystical vision of the poet's psychic pain purged by divine maternal and paternal compassion.[50]

Amid "ruin everywhere" H. D. immediately establishes her spiritual election, for "inspiration stalks" her:

> unaware, Spirit announces the Presence;
> shivering overtakes us,
> as of old, Samuel:
>
> trembling at a known street-corner,
> we know not nor are known;
> the Pythian pronounces—we pass on.
>
> [1:510]

Is the Pythian the Spirit announcing itself to the poet or the poet pronouncing herself? Oracle and priestess, "the Pythian" is also an appellation of the Delphic Apollo. H. D. had seen a vision, the "writing on the wall" which Freud viewed as "symptom" and which she termed "inspiration," and one of its central images was the "tripod, . . . symbol of prophecy, prophetic utterance or occult or hidden knowledge; the Priestess or Pythoness of Delphi sat on the tripod while she pronounced her verse couplets, the famous Delphic utterances which it was said could be read two ways" (*TF* 49, 51).

Endowed with the power of divination, the poet as Pythian meditates on the endurance of the "skeleton" as opposed to "the flesh" which "melted away, / the heart burnt out, dead ember" (*WDNF* 1:510). That "the heart burnt out" suggests why the answer to the question "what saved us? what for?" will not involve H. D. in erotic relationships, which had so disappointed her earlier. That she speaks as a "we" in contact or synonymous with the Pythian signals the poet's will to evade disappointment through redirecting her desire to a spiritual realm which might infuse her with ecstasy, enabling her to transcend gender and attain in her own verse couplets the oracle's wisdom.

The "we" of *The Walls Do Not Fall* are "bearers of the secret wisdom" (8:517), who "know each other / by secret symbols" (13:521). Even when the poet speaks as "I," she represents these others because, as in the earlier poem "The Dancer," she is both priestess and priest. H. D.'s "we" signifies her refusal to "stick to the woman-consciousness," a marked divergence from her earlier dramatic monologues. Still feeling outcast, though, the poet knows she has been rejected by a secular society: representatives of a fallen world have "shout[ed] out, / your beauty, Isis, Aset or Astarte, // is a harlot." Prophetic like Samuel, Delphic like Apollo, ancient and divine like Isis, Aset, or Astarte, H. D. refuses any gendered definition in her quest for the *gloire*, which is "sexless or all sex." Dedicated not to the flesh or the heart but to the skeletal frame, the prophetic speaker of *Trilogy* functions as an interpreter and sign of the divine. Thus, she hungers not for human relationship but "for the nourishment, God" to which her "true-rune[s]" will turn (2:511).

A sibyl or oracle, the priestess speaks for and to humanity, and what she says is not her own. Uttering words not of her own making, under the stimulus of a divinely inspired ecstasy, the Pythian is possessed by an otherness which authors and authorizes the delivery of the word. The poet's need to counter literary arrogance by claiming a selfless, receptive aesthetic potency, as well as her Moravian heritage (which H. D. had defined as the source of her own spiritual and aesthetic "gift"), make prophecy a suitable mode, one that draws, moreover, on the feminizing publicity of nymph or dryad which had earlier characterized her. Strengthened by the realization that the visionary describes herself "as a vessel of divine inspiration, not as a creative genius," and by the "scriptural injunction that God often elects the weak to confound the strong," H. D. could use the stance of prophet to make sense of many of her personal experiences: her frigidity becomes a chastity dedicated to an elected life; her abandonment by men is a sign that her desire should shift toward spiritual union with the divine; her experience of being dead foreshadows a miraculous resurrection; her visions—hallucinations, trances, dreams—liberate her from conventional female roles by attesting to her spiritual vocation even as their content eventually presents the female as the first principle in the universe.[51] To begin with, though, the poet's certainty of spiritual election is followed in *The Walls Do Not Fall* by a series of calling poems: the poet cries out, summoning a vision of redemption and rebirth, but she also constructs images of her internal conviction of a divine call.

Book 1 of *Trilogy* prepares for the attainment of spiritual consummation by repeating a number of the motifs we have traced in H. D.'s earlier poetry. First, in the most famous poem of *The Walls Do Not Fall*—"There is a spell" (4:513)—she uses the images of pearl and shell to speculate that what saved her and what constitutes a secret, safe sign of grace is the imperviousness associated with her youthful "crystalline" artistry and frigidity. Second, in a series of related poems she engages in a conversation with a cynical "you" who questions the values of her "scribblings" (10:518), although here her survival emboldens her to view herself as the inheritor of an aesthetic lineage now endangered by warmongers and crass utilitarians, stimulating from her a passionate defense of poetry. Finally, *The Walls Do Not Fall* links supplications, prayers, catechisms, and entreaties to the good father H. D. had sought first in her earlier initiators and later in Freud. Demonstrating an aesthetic control lacking in many of her earlier works, these calls for a paternal protector—Amen, Ra, the All-father, the Holy Ghost—breed a confusion bordering on "madness" (30:533), as well as self-doubt about "imagery // done to death" (32:534–35).[52]

Both the new aesthetic control and the futility of the paternal quest shape H. D.'s evolution in the next two books of *Trilogy*, where the poet finds a voice that eschews the arrogance of her male rivals and that licenses her finally to articulate the prophetic utterance to which all her surrogate characters had laid claim. Indeed, the secret signs she discerns in *The Walls Do Not Fall* become visible wonders in the second and third books of *Trilogy* where, as Pythian or priestess, H. D. distances herself by looking *at* the feminine, rather than being looked at *as* the feminine. Both *Tribute to the Angels* and *The Flowering of the Rod* develop the paradox that spiritual love can be experienced only when the feminine is reached through the masculine, when the father or brother provides access to the mother or sister. The structure of *Tribute to the Angels* depends on a series of prayers to the masculine powers Azrael, Uriel, and Raphael, invocations that are interrupted by the appearance of a "Lady," to whom the poet acts as "Bridegroom" (39:571), but that resume after that vision has been fully apprehended. In addition, *The Flowering of the Rod* describes the potency of two Marys through the eyes of a male character, Kaspar, whose brilliant but nevertheless disturbing interpretive skills stand for those of H. D.'s "Professor," Freud.

Yet, unlike Freud, who examined the "masculinity complex" (in which the growing girl persists in a fantasy of being a man) as an abnormal line of development of the young woman "cling[ing] in obstinate self-assertion to her threatened masculinity," H. D. uses the masculine presences in *Trilogy* to analyze the complications Freud "refrained from touching on," namely those "which arise when a child, disappointed in her relation with her father, returns to the abandoned mother-attachment, or in the course of her life repeatedly shifts over from the one attitude to the other" ("FS" 198, 209). Although, as Susan Stanford Friedman and Rachel Blau DuPlessis have demonstrated, H. D. repeatedly wrote about lesbianism as "sister love" in her prose, only after her analysis with Freud and the composition of her tributes to him did she poetically approach her "two loves separate" ("The Master," *CP* 453); in books 2 and 3 of *Trilogy*, H. D. examines Freud's view that she represents "that all-but extinct phenomena, the perfect bi—."[53] What concerns her here in *Tribute to the Angels*, however, are less the sexual dynamics of bisexuality than the linguistic, creative, and spiritual resonance of shifting from disappointing father attachments to the originatory but abandoned female figure.

Tribute to the Angels addresses this paradox or tension most directly:

> what is this mother-father
> to tear at our entrails?

> what is this unsatisfied duality
> which you can not satisfy?
>
> [9:552–53]

H. D.'s sense of unsatisfied duality expresses her positions as a child attached to both parents; as an expatriate allied with two continents; as a palimpsestic writer obsessed with, for example, the correlation between the Bethlehem (Pennsylvania) where she was born and the Bethlehem of Christ's birth; as a translator shuttling between two languages; and by extension as a woman attracted to both men and women, to the roles of muse and artist, to femininity and poetry. In *Tribute to Freud* an especially useful passage that begins with a series of puns on "pairs" and "matches" explains, "There were two's and two's and two's in my life. . . . There were two of everybody (except myself)" (31–32).

What the verse form of *Trilogy* represents is this sense of unsatisfied duality, for its unrhymed or off-rhymed couplets serve as a stanzaic form that confronts the problem of two's and two's and two's. A marked divergence from the style of H. D.'s earlier verse, the couplet in *Trilogy* combines its two lines in a variety of ways, which recall the verse couplets of the Pythoness of Delphi (*TF* 51). Although a number are open grammatically, the space between the couplets separates them visually. In addition, many of H. D.'s couplets are self-contained statements that reinforce each other: "This is no rune nor riddle, / it is happening everywhere" (*TA* 21:559). Some are enjambed syntactic units: "I am sure you see / what I mean" (22:560). Others are end-stopped to represent a modulation, equation, or translation of two terms: "this is the flowering of the rood, / this is the flowering of the reed" (7:551). Emphatically unheroic, H. D.'s couplets function less like Augustan couplets than like the conclusions to Shakespearean sonnets, for they set off lines as "special and perhaps a trifle fragile." Paul Fussell's description of the couplet as "a vigorous enclosure . . . into a compact and momentarily self-sufficient little world" highlights the similarity of this form to the seashell within whose enclosure the poet originally seeks shelter.[54]

Like Millay and Moore, then, H. D. persisted in a rigidly formal strategy, in opposition to the willed disruption of traditional stanza patterns that was characteristic of many of her male contemporaries. The couplet form also provided her with an opportunity to meditate on one of the principal points she wished to make about the mysteriously transformative nature of belief: "the same—different—the same attributes, / different yet the same as before" (39:571). Emphasizing the interchangeability of terms, the couplet enabled H. D. to become a medium of the indeterminate, a role she may have learned through the autobiographical, psychoanalytic, and translation work of the thirties and early forties, genres that assume meaning to be ambiguous and multiple. Besides shaping the couplet form, repetition ("the same") with a change ("different") helps explain two crucial sequences of poems in the second book of *Trilogy*, specifically the alchemical redefinition of language and the appearance of the Lady. While *The Walls Do Not Fall* testified to the poet's sense of election and calling, *Tribute to the Angels* in these two sequences moves through the next stages of prophecy, elaborating on the justification and adoption of the poet-prophet, whose fantasy of a mother tongue and whose vision of a female muse of her own will empower her to repair the defaced image of divinity in the soul.[55]

The poem in which H. D. articulates her unsatisfied duality begins with a gem inside an alchemical bowl, another variation on the pearl in its shell or the worm inside its cocoon but also a reference to the Delphic tripod:

> Bitter, bitter jewel
> in the heart of the bowl,
>
> what is your colour?
> what do you offer
>
> to us who rebel?
>
> [9:552]

As we noted in our discussion of sexual linguistics in *The War of the Words*, alchemical art, which has traditionally been defined as a fiery purification that transforms decomposing dross into precious stone, is identified throughout *Tribute to the Angels* with the poem-bowl in which language will be transmuted into a mother tongue.[56] H. D.'s efforts to liberate the multiple potential of words through neologisms, anagrams, puns, and alternative spellings cause her to emphasize the look and sound of the signifier. The play between *word* and *sword*, *Osiris* and *O Sire is*, *ruin* and *rune*, and *haven* and *heaven* means that words function in precisely the way the poet had claimed in *The Walls Do Not Fall*—like "anagrams, cryptograms, / little boxes, conditioned // to hatch butterflies . . ." (39:540). To those who decry female art as sorcery or black magic, the recipe by which H. D. now turns "a word most bitter, *marah*" into "mer, mere, mère, mater, Maia, Mary," and finally into "Mother" (*TA* 8:552) or *venery* into *venerator* in poems 11 and 12 may be said to produce "poison," but such poison is "food for the witches' den" (11:554).

Seeking a new language that will consecrate what has been desecrated by her culture, H. D. is propelled by the unsatisfied duality between mother and father to reestablish the primacy of words linked to "candle and script and bell," the female witchcraft that "the new-church spat upon" (1:547). Besides valorizing the sorcery of such earlier avatars as Calypso and Delia of Miletus, H. D. also seeks a new relationship to her redefined, refined words, for she wishes to find a way of evading names that label the word-jewel in the bowl. Resisting her "patron," who says "'name it'" (13:555), she explains,

> I do not want to name it,
> I want to watch its faint
>
> heart-beat, pulse-beat
> as it quivers, I do not want

to talk about it,
I want to minimize thought,

concentrate on it
till I shrink,

dematerialize
and am drawn into it.
[14:555]

The color of the jewel in the bowl has "no name" (poems 13 and 14), although it gives off a rhythm (a "heart-beat, pulse beat") and a "fragrance" that seem to promise the possibility of an otherness invisibly permeating the self. What the poet seeks through the minimalization of thought is a shrinking or incubation within the box or bowl of the poem, a dematerialization into the word's beat or fragrance: "I can not name it"; "I do not want to name it" (13, 14:555).

The urgency of not-naming is a direct reaction against the arrogance H. D. had earlier attributed to initiators who "dip stylus in the beauty of the translatable things you know," while "the things I have / are nameless, / old and true" (CP 232). But it is also a retort to the traditional conclusion of the prophetic books in the Bible: "You shall not add to the word I command you, nor take from it" (Deut. 4:2, Rev. 22:18). In Tribute to the Angels, John's admonition—"if any man shall add // God shall add unto him the plagues" (3:548–49)—stands for the closed revelations of Judeo-Christianity that must be controverted by the hermetic priestess dedicated to new apprehensions of the ancient not-named. Let "the word of Christ dwell in you richly," Colossians advises (3:16); H. D. would dwell in the word, for this indwelling empowers her to add her not-named words in an ongoing process of revelation.

The fantasies of a mystical awareness different from rational, adult perception and of shrinking into language appear in both H. D.'s fiction and her visionary writing, where they presage a return of consciousness to "some strange exact and precious period of pre-birth" (P 220). To enter this period of prebirth means becoming like a child and shedding gender: "While I live in the unborn story," Julia of Bid Me to Live explains, "I am in the gloire," that state which is both the child and all sex (177). This "heaven" is defined in Notes on Thought and Vision (written 1919) as "womb vision," a phrase that consolidates maternity and creativity: although the brain and the womb are "both centres of consciousness, equally important," H. D. comes to believe that "the majority of dream and of ordinary vision is vision of the womb."[57] In direct contrast to the terrifying obliteration of the self in The Walls Do Not Fall, womb vision is attained in a submerged but protected state called "jellyfish consciousness," a phrase H. D. would have associated with the scientific as well as the mythic term *medusa:* encapsulated in transparent fluid, the visionary is "like a closed sea-plant, jelly-fish or anemone."[58] A "balloon or diving-bell . . . seemed to hover over me," H. D. explained about another such moment of being, and "a second globe or bell-jar [arose] as if it were from my feet. I was enclosed. I felt I was safe but seeing things as through water" (*TF* 130).

H. D.'s desire for incorporation into the word, like her womb vision, seems at first unrelated to her subsequent invocation of the seven angels and her apprehension of the Lady, who first manifests herself in the flowering of a burnt-out tree, then displays herself in a dream, and finally presents herself in her own person. But the angels—whose candles the poet lights in tribute—converge back into the prism of the Lady, who is defined as "all-colour; / where the flames mingle // and the wings meet, when we gain / the arc of perfection" (*TA* 43:573). Just as the poet sought dematerialization in the word-jewel-fragrance, she finds fulfillment in being adopted by the Lady—"we are satisfied, we are happy"—and the "jewel / melts in the crucible," turning into "a cluster of garden-pinks / or a face like a Christmas-rose" (574). Clearly the melting of the not-named words in the crucible, as well as the poet's happiness, serves as an antidote to the rigor mortis H. D. had earlier suffered as a stony image of herself.

Although H. D. "had thought" to address the angels, it is the Lady who appears to the poet, whose refrain in one poem—"We have seen her" (29:564)—modulates into the repeated phrase of another—"We see her" (30:565)—to culminate in the assertion "But none of these, none of these / suggest her as I saw her" (31:566). Negatives abound in the subsequent portrait of this Lady because she must be distinguished from fetishized forms of the feminine found "in cathedral, museum, cloister" (29:565). The poet is careful to remind us through her liturgy of negative attributes that this Lady, whom "you" name "Holy Wisdom, / *Santa Sophia*, the SS of the *Sanctus Spiritus*" (36:568), is "no symbolic figure" (39:570); this Lady "wasn't hieratic, *she wasn't frozen*" and "she must have been pleased with us, / for *she looked so kindly at us*" (38:569, 35:568; emphasis ours). H. D., who had previously been objectified by the "glances" of male contemporaries, here distances herself by looking at the feminine Lady whose "attention" focuses solely on the woman poet. Remembering herself watching the Lady who, in turn, had gazed back at her, H. D. experiences neither the fragility nor the frigidity she had previously lamented. Instead, encapsulated as in womb vision, she is "satisfied, . . . happy" (43:573), giving "thanks that we rise again from death and live" (23:561).

Dedicated to a strategy of not-naming, H. D. admits that even her negative language cannot fully explain what she sees. Conversationally, deferentially, however, the poet does elaborate on the figure who is "the same" as,

say, John's portrait of the virgin mother of God or the troubadours' lady
praised by Pound, but "different," too:

> I grant you the dove's symbolic purity,
> I grant you her face was innocent
>
> and immaculate and her veils
> like the Lamb's Bride,
>
> but the Lamb was not with her,
> either as Bridegroom or Child;
>
> her attention is undivided,
> we are her bridegroom and lamb;
>
> her book is our book; written
> or unwritten, its pages will reveal
>
> a tale of a Fisherman,
> a tale of a jar or jars,
>
> the same—different—the same attributes,
> different yet the same as before.
>
> [39:571]

The poet, as "Bridegroom or Child," is the Lady's divine consort (even—
oddly enough—Her son), so that together they represent the muse/poet or
mother/child dyad. But H. D. is also the Lady's literary descendant, for the
Lady carries a book of "blank pages / of the unwritten volume of the new"
(38:570): on the one hand, this tabula rasa ratifies H. D.'s own poem, for it
means that the Lady "was satisfied / with our purpose, a tribute to the
Angels" (41:572); on the other, the blank book, which could be inscribed
with not-named words, may be the next book of *Trilogy*, the story of a Fisherman and of jars at the center of *The Flowering of the Rod*.

As Deborah Kelly Kloepfer has argued, *Tribute*'s "Lady, unlike the biographical mother, validates [H. D.'s] writing: stripped of her maternity, she is
better able, paradoxically, to 'mother'" the daughter-poet.[59] At least three
factors explain why the Lady as not-mother imbues the poet with a "new
sensation" (22:559). Traditionally, the maternal Lady carries a male child,
the divine son or word, but here, because there is no son, the poet can stand
in that position; personally, too, H. D. felt her mother favored her brother
and devalued her own "gift"; and as a grown woman, H. D. probably associated biological maternity with physical vulnerability and psychological pain
because of the stillbirth she suffered in 1915, the life-threatening illness that

accompanied the birth of Perdita in 1919, and the abortion she underwent in 1927.[60]

Through the Lady's sign, the flowering of a burnt-out tree, H. D. recovers "the Sceptre, / the rod of power . . . crowned with the lily-head" that is a healing caduceus in *The Walls Do Not Fall* (3:512). The flowering rood/reed is also, of course, the cross, no longer a symbol of crucifixion but now an image of the Christmas rose as well as the biblical rod of Aaron. Implicitly, then, H. D. criticizes *Aaron's Rod,* a novel in which D. H. Lawrence's surrogate, Lilly, asserts that "the woman must submit" to "the male godliness, the male godhead," which Lawrence defines in terms of the flowers sprouting from the rod of Moses's brother.[61] She also transforms Pound's "tree spirit" dryad into a "new Eve" who will retrieve what the old Eve lost in the garden; the Lady in *Trilogy* holds "the Book of Life" (*TA* 36:569), which will be inscribed not with Adam's names but with the poet's own not-naming. Because the poet-priestess has excavated what Freud called "the original mother-attachment" in a way that authenticates her spiritual and literary quest, the burnt wood of the blossoming tree imbues her with "a new sensation" (22:559), just as the Lady heralds "a new phase, a new distinction of colour" (40:571). For H. D. this newness consists of a female aesthetic presence that can counter the earlier burden of her poetic patrilineage.

What characterizes all the poet's images of the Lady is the potency of the nurturing feminine figure, which confounds Freud's idea of female castration. While Freud had based his view of H. D.'s penis envy on the equation "book means *penis,*" she associates the Lady's book with her own words, with herself as word.[62] In a dialogue between Freud and H. D. to which Norman Holland first called attention, the Professor showed her his favorite bronze statue: his figurine of Pallas Athene was "perfect," according to Freud, "*only she has lost her spear*" (*TF* 69).[63] At the end of *Tribute to Freud,* H. D. brandishes the flowering rod of an orange branch that Freud has given her, turning it into the golden bough that might empower her to transport the Professor from the waste land of his skepticism to the promised land where her own beliefs blossom. When she celebrates her own adoption by the feminine muse who resurrects the tree of life in *Trilogy,* H. D. substantiates the claim in "The Master" that in and of herself *"woman is perfect"* (*CP* 455). In the next book of *Trilogy,* moreover, H. D. did—at least imaginatively—transport her "blameless physician" to the Herland she sought to consecrate.

———

Having been adopted by the Lady, H. D. progresses in the final section of *Trilogy* toward the last two stages of her spiritual growth: sanctification and glorification, which restore the image of God in the prophetess and assure her eternal blessedness. This is achieved in *The Flowering of the Rod* by leaving the place of crucifixion so as to arrive at the regeneration of Christmas, a move forward into the past made possible by the poet's storytelling. Both the prose and the verse translations H. D. undertook before writing *Trilogy* had immersed the poet in a quest for narrative: the novels' persistent script of abandonment by men and survival with women, the promise in autobiography and psychoanalysis of the reconstruction of a coherent life story, and the plays' classical myths. In comparison to Eliot's *Waste Land* (1922) or his *Four Quartets* (1943), Pound's *Cantos* (1934–59), and Williams's *Paterson* (1946–58), *Trilogy* is structurally eccentric because it narrates a parable of gender not invented by the poet's imagination (or so she intimates) but instead simply discerned. H. D., exploiting the strategies she had acquired through her prose and her translations, confronts the one line of development Freud himself had considered as mysterious as the "Minoan-Mycenaean civilization behind that of Greece" ("FS" 195), namely the (literary) daughter's continued attachment to her maternal origins.

In *The Flowering of the Rod* H. D. retells the story of the days before Christ's death from the unexpected perspective oι two figures in the gospel—the wise man Kaspar and the whore-convert Mary Magdalene, here called Mary Magdala—before the sequence concludes with a vision of Mary, the mother, in the ox stall. Thus, the final book of *Trilogy* embodies the emergence of the poet's narrative voice in a story if not of her own making, of her own fashioning. Claiming to discern "what men say is-not" (6:582), H. D. establishes her tale as a gospel, a good *spell* ("story") that "everyone knows," although "it is not on record" (12:587). Modestly, the poet merely transcribes what "some say": "some say it never happened, / some say it happens over and over" (20:593).

Like *Trilogy* itself, *The Flowering of the Rod* reverses chronology, moving retrogressively from Kaspar's confrontation with Mary Magdala, who wishes to obtain one of his jars of myrrh, to his appearance in the ox stall with the christening gift of another. Kaspar's two jars of myrrh make an imagistically logical conclusion to the poem, for they represent the poet's success in finding a form that can contain without confining. No longer fearful that the jar of "water-about-to-be-changed-to-wine" is "too circumscribed" (*WDNF* 31:534), H. D. makes her jars a symbol of aesthetic shape: beautiful, sealed, intact, unbroken objects of exchange that will become gifts and that are "a-jar somehow," as Robert Duncan explains, because of the fragrance they emit, a scent that recalls the fragrant jewel-word inside the alchemical bowl.[64] The gum resin of a tree or that tree itself, myrrh is a perfume, an incense, an embalming ointment, and a healing salve, but it is also an aphrodisiac.[65] Shell, cocoon, box, and bowl are now ready to reveal their previously secret hoard, as the poet makes a "bee-line" to the remuneration of "food, shelter, fragrance" (*FR* 7:583) where myrrh will become "mère, Mut, mutter, pray for us."

Just as Christ was "an outcast and a vagabond" (11:586), both Kaspar and
Mary are aliens in their society. The inheritor of an ancient alchemical tradition, Kaspar owns the jars that hold "priceless, unobtainable-elsewhere
myrrh" (13:587), a "distillation" which some said "lasted literally forever."
As a heathen, he represents a prebiblical lore that acknowledges the power
of daemons, termed *devils* by the Christian world. But his education is a
patrimony in an exclusively male tradition that assumes "no secret was safe
with a woman" (14:589). The Arab Kaspar is shown to be a bit of a prig so it is
highly incongruous that Mary Magdala should come to him in his "little
booth of a house" (13:587). Unmaidenly and unpredictable, she is as much
of an outcast as he, if only because of her ability "to detach herself," a
strength responsible for her persistence in spite of Kaspar's insistence that
the myrrh is not for sale. Before the jar actually changes hands, however,
H. D. dramatizes the discomfort of Simon the leper, host of the Last Supper,
who views Mary as a destructive siren. This "woman from the city" who
seems "devil-ridden" to the Christian is recognized by Kaspar as a living embodiment of the indwelling daemons of "Isis, Astarte, Cyprus / and the other
four; // he might re-name them, / Ge-meter, De-meter, earth-mother // or
Venus / in a star" (25:596).

H. D.'s reinvention of the biblical portrait of the prostitute Mary Magdalene implicitly criticizes traditional interpretations of the gospel. "By replacing Mary Magdalene with Mary, the mother," Rosemary Radford
Ruether explains about Christian history, "the Church replaced a dangerously unconventional role model with a conventional" one.[66] Like Lawrence
in *The Man Who Died*, H. D. reverses this substitution by emphasizing that
Jesus's first disciple was an "unbalanced, neurotic woman, // who was naturally reviled for having left home / and not caring for housework" (12:586–
87). But Lawrence, who had associated H. D.'s "Orphicism" with "Magdalene at her feet-washing," rejected Mary Magdalene as ghoulish in *The
Man Who Died;* his Christ turns instead to Isis.[67] H. D.'s unconventional
woman reminds us that Mary Magdalene plays a crucial role in the gospel;
remaining faithful to Jesus at the tomb, Mary is rewarded by being the first
to witness the resurrection. *Trilogy* excavates the whore as a representative of
Isis: only after this does H. D. (who knew that Lawrence's story "was not my
story" [*TF* 142]) return to the scene in the booth to describe the vision
granted to Kaspar through the intervention of this insubordinate Mary.

At the climax of *Trilogy*, Kaspar reenacts the poet's experience with the
Lady when he reads in the light on Mary's hair "the whole secret of the
mystery" (*FR* 30:601). After seeing earth before Adam and Paradise before
Eve, he hears an "echo in a shell," which seems to come down "translated"
from prehistorical times. That "the *echoed syllables of this spell* / conformed to
the sound // of *no word he had ever heard spoken*" (33:602–03; emphasis ours)

suggests that the spell of the seashell presented in *The Walls Do Not Fall* has been comprehended and that Kaspar is understanding precisely the language of not naming H. D. had striven to imagine in *Tribute to the Angels.* What he believes himself to have heard is so resonant that it appears italicized in a stanzaic form radically different from the couplets in which the rest of the text is composed:

> *Lilith born before Eve*
> *and one born before Lilith,*
> *and Eve; we three are forgiven,*
> *we are three of the seven*
> *daemons cast out of her.*

[33:603]

This enigmatic message implies that a matriarchal genealogy was erased from recorded history when an archaic female trinity, exorcised as evil, was cast out of human consciousness. Or is Mary now freed of her daemons because Eve, Lilith, and the shadowy one before Lilith have been forgiven, their desires no longer entwined with death, labor, pain, shame, and expulsion from paradise? Lilith dared to pronounce the Ineffable Name and articulated her sexual preferences, and so her presence promises a prelapsarian vision quite different from that of Genesis: created not out of Adam, but out of dust, Lilith predates the Bible and evokes a submerged but now recoverable time of female strength, female speech, and female sexuality, all of which have mysteriously managed to endure in Mary Magdala. Imbued with the mystery of the not-named "*one born before Lilith*," Kaspar has in a sense recaptured Mary Magdala's lost ancestors, establishing the family tree that sanctifies her.

But who is the one born before Lilith? The not-named last figure in Kaspar's spell may be the oldest female principle in Biblical tradition, Sophia, who was present at the creation: "When God established the heavens, I was there . . . I was beside him, like a master workman" (Prov. 8:27, 30). A "breath of the power of God," Wisdom "can do all things, and while remaining in herself, *she renews all things*" (Wisd. of Sol. 7:25, 27; emphasis ours). As a number of theologians have noted, John's description of Jesus as the originatory Word of God is a palimpsest of earlier depictions of Sophia, although only Matthew explicitly identifies Sophia with Jesus.[68] Pictured "at the crossways" or "beside the gates of the city," Sophia is a teacher whose "wisdom is more precious than pearls" (Prov. 8:11).

Having unsuccessfully sought a dwelling place among humanity, Sophia "has taken her seat among the angels" (1 Enoch 42:1–2). In Roman Catholicism, she prefigures Mary the mother while in Gnostic tradition she is linked to Eve and Isis. Significantly, too, Sophia speaks of herself in terms of the flowering rod and the fragrance of myrrh:

> I grew tall like a cedar in Lebanon,
>   and like a cypress on the heights of Hermon . . .
> Like cassia and camel's thorn I gave forth the aroma
>   of spices,
> and like choice myrrh I spread a pleasant odor . . .
> Like a vine I caused loveliness to bud,
>   and my blossoms became glorious and abundant fruit.
>
> [Sirach 24:13–17]

To be sure, any effort to turn H. D.'s not-naming into a fixed theology is bound to transform the reader into the "you" of *Tribute to the Angels,* a figure who advances the figure of Sophia in the glib logic that defines what the poet hopes to keep unnamed. But just as Western theology teaches that all the names for God are analogies, H. D.'s one born before Lilith shatters the male monopoly on God language.

The sight of Mary Magdala's hair becomes the site of the revelatory spell so that, as Susan Schweik has explained, perhaps for the first time in Mary Magdalene's textual history she is given "something else to do with her hair than wipe feet."[69] Why then is knowledge of the echo in the shell vouchsafed Kaspar and not Mary? Perhaps, as Deborah Kelly Kloepfer has argued, Kaspar serves as intermediary to the sexual Mary Magdala whom H. D. "does not dare entreat without a symbol of difference (the magus) to mark the boundaries she fears crossing over."[70] Writing in *Tribute to Freud* about the brother who was her mother's favorite, H. D. recalled her attempts as a child to "stay with my brother, become part almost of my brother" so that "perhaps I can get nearer to *her*" (33). If the poet of *Trilogy* gets nearer to the masterful Kaspar, she can through this male impersonation approach the feminine. Just as H. D. imagines herself as the bridegroom of the Lady in *Tribute to the Angels,* just as she sought to get nearer Pound and Lawrence so as to gain access to "the mother [who] is [their] Muse, the Creator" (*ET* 41), so in *The Flowering of the Rod* does she gain access through Kaspar to the female as an object of desire, enabling her to express and camouflage her desire for women.

Certainly, the vision Kaspar attains while watching Mary Magdala is not only erotic in its invocation of Lilith but also in its imagery of "the flower, thus contained / in the infinitely tiny grain or seed," which "opened petal by petal, a circle" around a "dynamic centre" that "would go on opening . . . to infinity" (31:601). But Kloepfer may exaggerate when she claims that H. D. "casts herself as the male . . . to explore a forbidden access to [the female]" because the voice of the poet who describes Kaspar's vision is quite distinct from his voice, which is not recorded.[71] Although the poet "stay[s] with, become[s] part almost" of Kaspar to "get nearer" to both Mary figures, H. D. also separates herself from him in order to explore the psychology of her male initiators. By watching the male gazing at the female, the narrator of *Trilogy* extends her analysis of sexual poetics to understand the dynamics of female objectification in psychoanalysis. In particular, as a wise man who "knew the scene was unavoidable" (24:595), Kaspar is what many critics have taken him to be, a fictionalization of Freud, the sage who discerned primal scenes, and so H. D. completes her own analysis with the Professor by examining his analysis of her and of the feminine.

Just as H. D. traveled with some trepidation to Berggasse 19, H. D. describes Mary Magdala going to Kaspar's little booth of a house to get the jar of myrrh. In the notebook which H. D. kept, against Freud's wishes, during analysis, she explained that "perhaps I will be treated with a psychic drug, will take away a nameless precious phial from his cavern. Perhaps I will learn the secret, be priestess with power over life and death" (*TF* 117). Like Freud, Kaspar is suspicious of women, yet he is a "master" (*FR* 18:591) who some take to be "Abraham" or "God" himself (20:593). His "unobtainable-elsewhere myrrh" is as priceless as the discoveries Freud makes when he is described in the *Tribute* as striking oil—a business symbol apt for both Kaspar and Freud, self-defined merchants. Both Freud and Kaspar are wise men and healers, recipients of Semitic, patriarchal educations that have taught them how to decipher medical and poetic symbols.

H. D. distinguishes herself from Kaspar by indicating that, in spite of his remarkable sensitivity to Mary Magdala, his apprehension of her divinity contradicts his suspicions of her "disordered, dishevelled" appearance, for the "hedges and fences and fortresses" of his mind deny the mystery he has himself perceived (34:603). With "her hair—un-maidenly—" Mary exasperates Kaspar's sense of propriety, his intimation that "it was hardly decent of her to stand there, / unveiled, in the house of a stranger" (15:590). Although the female provides Kaspar access to prelapsarian "promised lands, lost" (31:601), which he himself identifies with matriarchal majesty and sexuality, "What he thought was the direct contradiction / of what he apprehended" (35:604), for the defenses of masculine consciousness can neither discount nor recount this insight. After "a slender girl / holding a jar" appears to him, he struggles to retain a sense of his own identity: "He said *I am Kaspar*, / for he had to hold on to something" (39:606–07). Indeed, we are informed by the poet that "no one would know exactly" how the jar of myrrh was transferred from Kaspar to Mary, "*least of all Kaspar*" (40:608; emphasis ours).

In this reading, H. D. is more closely aligned with Mary Magdala than with Kaspar, an alliance that allows her to bring to the surface the critique of psychoanalysis that Susan Stanford Friedman has traced in *Tribute to Freud*. On the one hand, Freud had described the oceanic bliss of the child in the preoedipal stage before separation from the mother; on the other, he had defended himself against this intuition of the mother's primacy through theories of female secondariness. *Tribute to Freud* tactfully recounts H. D.'s efforts to seek her mother through her therapist and examines her sense that "the Professor was not always right" (98, 101) by dramatizing Freud's anxiety that at seventy-seven he was too old to engage the affections of his forty-four-year-old analysand (" *you do not think it worth your while to love me* '" [16, 62]); by documenting his dislike of being put in the female role ("'I do *not* like to be the mother in transference—it always surprises and shocks me'" [146–47]); by recording his discomfort at her erotic attachments to women ("'No—biologically, no'" [152]); and by confronting his disbelief in female artistry: "He said (as I remember) that women did not creatively amount to anything or amount to much, unless they had a male counterpart or a male companion from whom they drew their inspiration" (149). Somewhat disingenuously, H. D. adds, "For some reason, though I had been so happy with the Professor (Freud-*Freude*), my head hurt and I felt unnerved" (152).

Because of Kaspar-Freud's defenses, then, the transaction whereby he hands the alabaster jar of myrrh to Mary Magdala is not depicted in the poem, although it may be that the myrrh is not given by Kaspar because Mary Magdala already possesses it through her own transformative powers:

> I am Mary, she said, of Magdala,
> I am Mary, a great tower;
>
> through my will and my power,
> Mary shall be myrrh;
>
> I am Mary—O, there are Marys a-plenty,
> (though I am Mara, bitter) I shall be Mary-myrrh.
>
> [16:590]

Like the poet of *Tribute to the Angels,* this Mary has the capacity to translate bitterness, *marah,* into mère, mater, Maia, Mary and Mother. As a statement about psychoanalysis, *Trilogy* reverses the hierarchical relationship of the (male) doctor to the (female) patient, implying that Kaspar-Freud is reduced to a silent decoder, an interpreter, even a voyeur of the patient who supplies the dream. The analysand is the creator of visions that the analyst witnesses and his discomfort at this secondary role causes him to discount the feminine principle he encounters in those hieroglyphs of the unconscious.

In the last poem of *Trilogy,* a nativity scene, H. D. takes to one logical conclusion Freud's efforts from "The Moses of Michelangelo" (1914) to *Moses and Monotheism* (1939) to rescind the law of oppression instituted by the monotheism of Mosaic law.[72] Disrespectfully, indeed almost comically, she transforms the Jewish skeptic into the wise man and transports him to the adoration. At the end of *The Flowering of the Rod*, Kaspar brings a gift, a jar of myrrh, to the mother in the manger who holds in her arms a branch of myrrh. As with the other Mary, he can only give what she already possesses:

> But she spoke so he looked at her,
> she was shy and simple and young;
>
> she said, Sir, it is a most beautiful fragrance,
> as of all flowering things together;
>
> but Kaspar knew the seal of the jar was unbroken.
> he did not know whether she knew
>
> the fragrance came from the bundle of myrrh
> she held in her arms.
>
> [43:612]

Myrrh, a scent of love and death, has also been linked to incest, for Mary Magdala identified herself (the "Mary [who] shall be myrrh" [16:590]) with Myrrha, the mother of Adonis, who was changed into a myrrh tree because she seduced her father. Weeping at her suffering, swelling with sap, Myrrha produces tears of myrrh as well as the baby Adonis. "To be *Myrrha*," as Susan Schweik has explained, is to experience "a violent feminine desire for the patriarchal law (represented by that ultimate form of *père*-version, father-daughter incest)."[73] Thus, the myrrh tree represents the (f)rigidity H. D. suffered when she took father-figures for the objects of her desires. Here, though, the bundle of incense as incest taboo protects Mary from the law of the father. In addition, myrrh becomes not only the flowering wood of book 2's Lady, but also, in its fragrance and its position within the arms of Mary, the child and the word.

The last poem of *Trilogy* remains radically indeterminate, dedicated to the not-naming of the poet-priestess. One could claim about this Mary with myrrh in her arms, as with the Lady, that "the Child was not with her" (*TA* 32:567). Linked to Mary Magdala through the gift of myrrh and therefore no longer alone of all her sex, Mary surrounded by the fragrance previously associated with the jewel-word in the poem-bowl reminds us that "*In the beginning / was the Word*" (*WDNF* 10:519), and the word here is cradled by a woman before whom the wise men bow down speechlessly. But when Balthasar, Melchior, and Kaspar kneel before the "shy and simple and young" Mary, H. D. knew that her readers would supply the divine child—the word made flesh—at the center of a story that culminates in the crucifixion and deification of the son. In addition, the significance of that story here, as in the Bible, may be clearer to the wise man who has heard the echoing spell than to the two women who embody it. Not-naming the child, H. D. tells a tale that could lead to a "different" future or that might result in the "same" recycling of the past. In either case, though, by representing Mary Magdala, "*the incense-flower of the incense-tree*" (*FR* 19:592), and the Virgin Mary holding the bundle of myrrh in her arms, H. D. reinstates Wisdom, Sophia, as Jesus.

Finally, then, the poet who had suffered a renunciation of poetic desire here sanctifies her own creativity. For the first line of the last poem—"But she spoke so he looked at her"—reverses the paradigmatic relationship between the male glance and female utterance in H. D.'s earlier dramatic monologues, where the poet's persona speaks *because* of the male gaze. Mary with her flowering rod at the end of *Trilogy* also modifies the revision of Freud's theory of female castration begun in *Tribute to the Angels*. The phallus is only a translation of the scepter of Caduceus, the tree of life, the book, the bundle of myrrh, the baby, the word, with each substitution opening the way for the next in a series of displacements. Read, like the priestess of Delphi's couplets, two ways—backward and forward—no one term in H. D.'s chain of associated images emerges as privileged in the series scepter-tree-book-bundle-baby-word. To term Mary with her myrrh the phallic mother, as some Freudians might,[74] is to avoid H. D.'s hints that the phallus is merely a fictively privileged sign for what the mother possesses—her self-possession —and therefore an evasion of her inescapable autonomy.

The two jars of myrrh, about which "no one can tell which is which" (41:610), represent the commonality of the prostitute and the madonna, the whore and the mother. Like the four Marys of Virginia Woolf's *A Room of One's Own*, H. D.'s "Marys a-plenty" heal the divisions between sexuality and maternity, creativity and procreativity, nurturance and knowledge.[75] Mary, sister of Martha, Mary of Bethany, Mary, mother of James, and Mary, wife of Clopas coalesce into a community, countering the paternal figures of H. D.'s earlier verse. Kaspar's crucial role in conferring a gift to the gifted constitutes H. D.'s poetic tribute to Freud's healing belief that "in mental life nothing which has once been formed can perish— . . . everything is somehow preserved and . . . in suitable circumstances (when, for instance, regression goes back far enough) it can once more be brought to light."[76] Thus, *Trilogy* moves back to a scene that illuminates what Kim Chernin has called "the no-man's-land that stretches between first bonding to the mother and the later relationship to the father."[77]

Trilogy's concluding vision is set after a series of poems celebrate a magical landscape, one in which "the snow fell" and "the desert blossomed" (36, 37:605) as a maternal Kaspar cherishes the foal of a newly born camel "under his cloak" (38:606). This "bearing [which] was difficult," like the unnamed child to come, centers the work on birth. When in the ox stall "he did not know whether she knew," Kaspar exhibits the modesty that has characterized the speaker of *Trilogy* throughout its three books. Together, then, they pay tribute to the birth of "the *gloire*" which is "all sex," when "there is no 'he and me,' / there is no 'you and she.'" As Kaspar, Mary in the ox stall, and the not-named child residing in the womb vision of the "unborn story," H. D. has turned the "two's and two's" in her life into three.

"I go where I love and where I am loved" (2:578): the scene of "food, shelter, fragrance" (7:583) to which *Trilogy* goes is one in which H. D. can imagine the complications that arise when the child "returns to the abandoned mother-attachment" or "repeatedly shifts over" from mother to father and back again ("FS" 209). Through this trinity, too, *Trilogy* meditates on a spiritual adoration. Not only is the Incarnation—a biological, linguistic, and spiritual event—female as well as male, but divinity itself resides in the self-sufficiency of "all flowering things together" rather than in the separateness of a father god. While H. D. composed her *Tribute to Freud* to acknowledge the authority of her master, in *Trilogy* Kaspar stands aside "like an unimportant altar-servant" (*FR* 42:611) when he places his tribute on the floor of the ox stall. The prophecy in H. D.'s "The Master" is fulfilled:

> no man will be present in those mysteries,
> yet all men will kneel,
> no man will be potent,
> important,
> yet all men will feel
> what it is to be a woman.
>
> [*CP* 460]

Retelling the story of her encounter with all the wise men who were her initiators, *Trilogy* presents them finally acknowledging the vision of female divinity they read but can neither comprehend nor accept. The claim H. D. made about Kenneth Macpherson's experimental films could be used to characterize her most pacific war work: "Pro patria indeed, if that pro patria is a no-man's land . . . of plausible perfection."[78] No man's land has been transformed into Herland through the spelling of *Trilogy*, as in "The Master," where the woman dancer with a "purple flower / between her marble, her birch-tree white / thighs . . . needs no man, / herself / is that dart and pulse of the male," a fact that leads the poet to name her "that Lord become woman" (456, 461). H. D.'s Kaspar and her Marys a-plenty, as well as the not-named baby in the ox stall, are aspects of a self-ordination that *Trilogy* performs for its glorified priestess. *Content* for her masters, through the creation of *Trilogy* H. D. finally became con*tent* with her own physical and poetic survival, born of an intimation of that Lord become woman. Working in an ambitious genre—the long poem—that presented unique problems in female literary history even while participating in a revisionary spiritual tradition mined by many female precursors, H. D. healed herself of the frigidity she had earlier suffered by confirming her sense that women could extricate her from a debilitating thralldom to men and by constructing a theological alternative to the religious system that perpetuates such thralldom. In her later poems H. D. would continue to delineate the "family romance, this trinity which follows the recognized religious pattern: *Father*, aloof, distant"; "*Mother*, a virgin, the Virgin . . . an untouched child, adoring, . . . building a dream, and the dream is symbolized by the third member of the trinity, the *Child*, the doll in her arms" (*TF* 38). Freud's "Delphic" injunction—"*Know thyself*" (72)—taught H. D. to sanctify herself through a trinity to which her mythologies returned because of her stubborn belief that bliss was it in that romance to abide. When, at times, her chain of associative substitutions turns father into mother, mother into virgin, virgin into child, child into doll, doll into sister, sister into brother, brother into god, god back into father, she seems entangled in an infinitely recyclable repetition compulsion of translation-work. But, as with her redefinitions of the phallus in *Trilogy*, the refusal of stasis defamiliarizes the family romance so that it becomes a surrealistic system of mutability. The poet who creates father, mother, and child pays homage to the holy family as a paradise perpetually lost and regained.

"*Kennst du das Land, wo die Zitronen blühn?*" (*TF* 109): Goethe's poem at the end of *Tribute to Freud* brings H. D. to "the promised lands, lost" (*FR* 31:601) which Kaspar reaches in *Trilogy*. The "lyrical interrogation and the implication that the answer is given with it" capture H. D.'s imagination, as does the landscape which boasts "the myrtle of Aphrodite and the laurel of Apollo": "It is: do you know the Land—but you do know it, don't you?" This undiscovered country is "strange," "foreign," a place "of classic associations," traversed by "the soul"—"Miriam or Mignon, we may call her" (*TF* 110, 109)—in a pilgrim's progress through garden, house, and hall, to the narrow bridge her Professor knows can take them over terrifying chasms and gulfs to the Olympian mountain crowned with clouds. While the statues in Freud's study "stare and stare and seem to say, what has happened to you?" the poet likens herself to a "child, poor shivering and unprotected," seeking her guardian's help. But as soul speaks to self, Mignon to Goethe, Miriam to Moses, and H. D. to Freud, pleading questions turn into words of endearment—"o mein Geliebter," "o mein Beschützer"—to issue in "simple affirmation" (111) as she leads the way to that "mental" paradise Freud had intuited, where nothing can perish, where everything is somehow preserved.

II
The Burden of the Future

Illustration on preceding page: Remedios Varo, *Woman Leaving the Psychoanalyst,* 1961, oil on canvas (copyright © 1993 ARS, New York/VEGAP, Madrid; by permission of Walter Gruen, Mexico City)

5

Charred Skirts and Deathmask: World War II and the Blitz on Women

There is too much fathering going on just now and there is no doubt about it fathers are depressing. Everybody nowadays is a father, there is father Mussolini and father Hitler and father Roosevelt and father Stalin and father Lewis and father Blum and father Franco is just commencing now and there are ever so many more ready to be one.

—Gertrude Stein

The War she endured was different.

—H. D.

The place I am getting to, why are there these obstacles—
The body of this woman,
Charred skirts and deathmask
Mourned by religious figures, by garlanded children.
And now detonations—
Thunder and guns.

—Sylvia Plath

After H. D. had followed the swastikas chalked on the Vienna pavement directly to Freud's door, she realized that in analysis she would have to conceal her dread of war because of her Jewish Professor's vulnerability, but her fear of militarism was let loose during the London blitz. Enduring "the full apocryphal terror of fire and brimstone," she learned to "switch" her mind into the "dimension out of time" that she presents as a *"haven / heaven"* in *Trilogy* (*CP* 543). Yet she remained "sick to death of tensions and tiredness and distress and distorted values and the high pitched level and the fortitude" demanded by nearly a hundred days of bombing.[1] And her later texts about the Second World War grew increasingly pessimistic about the war's impact on the relationship between the sexes. From *Helen in Egypt* (begun 1952) to *Thorn Thicket* (composed 1960), H. D.'s poems and prose examined

211

the claim Helen makes about her sister that "the War she endured was different"—different from the First World War and from the war experienced by men—because, as this memoirist put it about herself, "the War was my husband."[2] As if generalizing about what it might mean to live in an erotic partnership with destruction, H. D.'s companion, Bryher, declared, "The First War had opened a few doors but . . . the Second slammed many of them shut."[3]

Although, as Bryher's comment suggests and as we argued in *Sexchanges*, the Great War became a crux that elicited gloom about masculine paralysis from many literary men while exciting glee about female mobility in many literary women, World War II functioned differently in the literary imagination of both sexes. Writing in occupied France, Gertrude Stein contrasted the freedom she had attained in the First World War with her subsequent sense of disaster: "You begin a thing in one war and you lose it in the next war. From war to war."[4] Stein's 1937 protest against too much fathering, which we have used as our first epigraph here, represents the reactions of many of her female contemporaries who also experienced in World War II a resurgence of patriarchal politics. Her sentiments were echoed by the heroine of Doris Lessing's *Martha Quest* (1952) who fears about the Second World War that "this new war was in some way necessary to punish her."[5] Although many literary women enlisted in intelligence, propaganda, and refugee work, they often intimated that what had been gained in the earlier conflict was lost in the later.

Elizabeth Bowen's short story "The Demon Lover" (1945), read as a ghost story exploring the impact of the two wars on the relationship between the sexes, dramatizes the ways in which World War II destroyed women's traditional sphere—the domestic world of the home—and unleashed male hostility against women. When Mrs. Drover, the central character, returns to her bombed townhouse, she finds a mysterious letter from a fiancé who had been reported missing in the Great War. This letter from the dead is a reversal of the usual trope in which the envelope encloses news of death. She stealthily escapes from her damaged house to avoid the man, for he had "never been kind" to her. But when she enters a waiting taxi, she discovers that he is its driver, and he sweeps her screaming "into the hinterland of deserted streets."[6] Although Mrs. Drover had been effectively freed from an unsatisfying relationship by the Great War, her suffering during World War II seems to represent a return of the repressed. Haunted by guilt, Bowen's central character appears to suffer a punishment related to her survival after the disappearance of her fiancé in World War I.

From the forties on—that is, from the wartime writing of Virginia Woolf, Elizabeth Bishop, Edith Sitwell, Kay Boyle, Gwendolyn Brooks, and Carson McCullers to the postwar work of H. D., Harriet Arnow, Muriel Spark, and Doris Lessing—a surprising number of poems, stories, and novels by women focused on the vulnerability of female characters alienated from or threatened by their so-called defenders. More striking than, say, Stein's attacks on fathers Hitler and Mussolini were such women's critiques of the forces fighting for father Roosevelt and father Churchill. During the same period in which Pearl S. Buck argued that "psychologically and emotionally, war sets women back both in man's mind and in their own,"[7] a number of literary women presented not only fascist but also Allied militarism as a logical extension of misogyny. Why did the contemporaries of women from Bryher and Stein to Lessing perceive the Second World War as a threat to the second sex?

According to Stein, World War I was "a nice war, a real war, a regular war," while "certainly nobody no not anybody thinks this war is a war to end war."[8] Her remark points to one of the major differences between the two world wars, for World War *II* was only one of a sequence of wars. As a repetition, the Second World War was perceived by both sexes with much less idealism than had accompanied the beginning of the Great War, which haunted their memories. For men, and in particular for literary men, the earlier war marked a historical and imaginative watershed: "Never such innocence again," Philip Larkin explained in his poem "MCMXIV" (1960). Directly addressing "a conscript of 1940," Herbert Read recalled about the last group of soldiers, "We went where you are going, into the rain and the mud," and warned the next generation of combatants, "We think we gave in vain. The world was not renewed." Keith Douglas, demoralized by a repetition of warfare that proved the futility of the brilliant protest poetry of the Great War, hopelessly concluded about Isaac Rosenberg's earlier "Break of Day in the Trenches," "Rosenberg I only repeat what you were saying." In addition, even those literary men who, in C. Day Lewis's words, wrote war poetry to "defend the bad against the worse," suffered from the feeling of belatedness explained by Stephen Spender's remark that the poetry against "fascism had already been written . . . during the Spanish war."[9]

For women, and in particular for feminists like Ray Strachey and Vera Brittain, women's economic decline during the interwar years generated skepticism about government propaganda which encouraged female mobilization. Of course women were urged to join the war effort as, say, WACS (Women's Auxiliary Corps) or Wrens (Women's Royal Naval Service) or as Rosie the Riveters in the factories. By the early forties, the female labor force in Britain and the United States had expanded by over 40 percent, approximately three-quarters of it consisting of married women. Mrs. Laughton Matthews, the director of the Wrens, almost echoed triumphant female responses to the earlier war in her claim, "This war has exploded so many of the old theories about women."[10] Yet a number of recruitment posters had to be taken out of circulation when protests were lodged against the glamour they cast over dangerous, difficult jobs, while other come-ons presented war work as a necessary but only temporary departure from women's more important homemaking and childrearing responsibilities: "Some jubilant day mother *will* stay home again, doing the job she likes best—making a home for you and daddy," the Adel Precision Products ad promises about its pencil-factory workers.[11]

As auxiliary units, ruled by the military but not legally within it, many English and American women's corps received no insurance, no benefits, and no ranks equivalent to those of men. Not surprisingly, too, soon after the war women's military organizations were characterized as an "expression of free-flowing penis-envy"; they represented, it was thought, "the masculinity complex institutionalized, pure and simple."[12] Mrs. Matthews was prescient, if powerless, when she added to her assertion that "facts have shown that women can do anything" the proviso that "we must see that [female recruits] are not disappointed as they were in many ways after the last war." In spite of the economic freedom gained by, say, the subjects of the film *Rosie the Riveter*, women might have interpreted War Department brochures explaining that "a woman worker . . . is a substitute—like plastics instead of metal" to mean that, as a substitute, the female war worker was to be exchanged as soon as possible for the real thing. Even the most celebratory books about the female war effort concluded with the conciliatory proclamation, "The majority of girls are looking forward to running homes of their own, not to running a man's job." Understandably, then, Margaret Mead complained about the "continuous harping on the theme: 'Will the women be willing to return to the home?'" a question "repeated over and over again . . . by those to whose interest it will be to discharge women workers, regardless of whether they are wives, widows, or spinsters, as soon as the war is over." And one year after the war, three million American women, as well as over a million British women, were laid off or left their wartime jobs.[13]

But if the women who entered the labor force and the services paradoxically faced a heightened rhetoric about women's proper place in the home, both men and women knew that, as an adumbration of a third World War or even a fourth, the Second World War could never be considered a "Great" war. Indeed, if World War II had any singularity, it was as the first *total war*, waged by all against all. The whole female population, not just the women serving in the air and armed forces, was no longer insulated from the brutality of the battlefield. As Paul Fussell has observed, "The Second World War, total and global as it was, killed worldwide more civilian men, women, and children than soldiers, sailors, and airmen."[14]

Although during the 1914–18 conflict many women were protected by the sharp demarcation between the safety of the home front and the fighting in no man's land, during World War II civilians throughout Europe were affected by bombings, air raids, blackouts, evacuation, rationing, geographical dislocation, housing and food shortages, or enemy occupation. For this reason, literary men and women shared a common abhorrence of assaults that seemed virtually apocalyptic: while Dylan Thomas's "A Refusal to Mourn the Death, by Fire, of a Child in London" (1945) lamented, "Deep with the first dead lies London's daughter," Edith Sitwell envisioned humanity crucified and "blind as the nineteen hundred and forty nails / Upon the Cross."[15] Concentration camps, trajectory guns, long range rockets, "strategic" raids, military mistakes, firebombings, and atomic bombs closed the gap between home and war front, displaying the vulnerability of women and the domestic sphere.

Even as technology rendered civilians more vulnerable, it made possible a kind of depersonalization that insulated crews in large bombers and transport aircraft from the reality of destruction: "When those on earth / Die, there is not even a sound," a flyer admits in James Dickey's poem "The Firebombing" (1964), which recalls Dickey's own experiences, and he therefore becomes "enthralled" by "aesthetic contemplation" of the destruction he has created. "You only see the first plume and first fall," John Ciardi's pilot observes in "Take-Off over Kansas" (1947), so "you think, 'It was not human after all.'"[16] The irrationality as well as the deprivation of military life combined with the increased destructive capabilities of the machinery of war to fill many men with dread, although Robert Graves has pointed out that a larger proportion of the military was occupied with civilian-oriented duties than ever before and John Press has argued that some soldiers "enjoying, albeit with a twinge of guilt, the green pastures of Kenya, the pleasures of Egypt, or the imperial grandeur of India might reflect that they were a great deal safer and more comfortable than people in the cities and towns of Britain."[17]

But of course the airplane and zeppelin that Yeats envisioned pitching "like King Billy bomb-balls in / Until the town lies beaten flat" destroyed countless men trapped inside fox holes, submarines, and bombers.[18] One of the most moving American war poems—Randall Jarrell's "The Death of the Ball Turret Gunner" (1945)—dramatizes the terrible vulnerability of the man operating machine guns set into the plexiglass belly of a B-17 or B-24 bomber; speaking from death's kingdom, Jarrell's airman first finds himself awakened by flak, then, "When I died they washed me out of the turret with a hose."[19] Many servicemen suffered not only from the guilt and anesthetization Dickey and Ciardi describe but also from the miseries of combat, imprisonment, and dislocation depicted in Jarrell's verse.

No longer encased in the static but symbolically resonant trenches of no man's land, soldiers participated in a mobile war that was broadcast on radios and filmed in movies. For, as Paul Fussell has observed, "Compared to all previous wars, the Second was uniquely the Publicity War."[20] From the perspective of both men and women, media coverage brought the war home, as if to illustrate the expansion of the "theater" of war from the battlefield to the home front, and espionage played a much more prominent role in the Second World War than it had in the First: the enemy was potentially anyone anywhere. World War II therefore ended the possibility of a separate sphere for women; it seemed less a generational conflict between fathers and sons than a road to universal apocalypse, or so the firebombing of Dresden and the atomic bombing of Hiroshima and Nagasaki demonstrated. In fact, the only separate sphere created was in the ghettos and camps where Jews were segregated into male and female barracks as part of a process that led to total depersonalization and death. That the enemy had also defined itself in explicitly masculinist terms meant that women were inexorably involved in the ideological debates that distinguished World War II from the nationalist struggles of the Great War. Because fascism in Germany and Italy evolved as a reaction against the emasculation associated with World War I and the Depression, the fascist "father" regarded his leadership as a sexual mastery over the feminized masses.

The potentially infinite sequentiality of world wars, the technological advances in destructive capability, the obliteration of a safe home front, the extensive media coverage, the genocide, and the ideological threat of fascism: all these horrified men and women both. Yet many literary women also felt victimized by men who were presumably on their own side. Certainly feminist polemicists, as well as women novelists and poets, mourned the suffering of their male contemporaries. But in spite of (or perhaps because of) the sense of grief and alienation literary men recorded, literary women also feared that male vulnerability in wartime would result in hostility toward or violence against women. While total warfare called into question any stark dichotomizing of home and combat fronts, the two most persistent images of women in literature written by men—the whore and "the girl he left behind"—tended to place women in a realm of their own even as these character types were often judged by highly conventional norms of compliancy or loyalty on the one hand and indifference or betrayal on the other. Not only did the whore and "the girl he left behind" tend to blur into each other; they both also modulated between masculine desire (for a refuge from battle) and masculine dismay (at the insufficiency of that refuge). As we shall see, then, even those men who were distressed by the hypertrophied masculinity spawned by the crisis of war often attempted to cope with their fear of emasculation by reconstructing a sexual mythology of separate spheres.

Literary women's responses to World War II, frequently an articulation of dread, have long gone unheard because we have failed to realize that they were grappling with ideologies that reified gender arrangements as rigidly as they had been demarcated in the Victorian period but in a newly sexualized way. Far more explicit about the connection between heterosexuality and masculine bonding than the literature produced during the Great War, the works of literary women and men record mutual hopelessness about the confusion of sex with death that was turning men into demon lovers and women into their willing victims. Indeed, for those literary women who reacted to the "thunder and guns" as Sylvia Plath did in the sixties, World War II marked the demise of a dream of Herland that had shaped earlier feminist fantasies and the rise of a recognition that within the no man's land of history all that subsisted behind the fictionalized mythologies of femininity were the "charred skirts and deathmask" of the dead woman, a no-woman.

Elizabeth Bishop's "Roosters" (1946) is scathing in its denunciation of war as a battle cry of virility, and it reads like a brilliant gloss on two questions posed in a letter by Virgina Woolf: "Musn't our next task be the emancipation of man?" and "How can we alter the crest and the spur of the fighting cock?"[21] Bishop's answers, like those of many of her aesthetic compatriots, remain gloomily equivocal about the possibility that women will be able to disentangle definitions of manhood from warfare. "Roosters" uses the image of the fighting cock to link masculinity with militarism in a trope exploited by feminist polemicists and women artists; it also uncovers the association of guns and virility in the texts of literary men who were equally concerned that a battle of the sexes threatened to turn the war into a virtual blitz on women.

"Roosters" begins by satirizing militarism as a masculinism that awakens the sleeping speaker "in the gun-metal blue dark."[22] With their "protruding chests / in green-gold medals, dressed," Bishop's cocks arise "with horrible insistence," screaming their "uncontrolled, traditional cries." Gloating and floating over "our beds" and "our churches," they screech a refrain—"This is where I live!" or "Get up! Stop dreaming!"—that wakes "us here" to "unwanted love, conceit and war" (36). Bishop's fowls are endowed with an "excrescence" which "makes a most virile presence," and they therefore seem physically programmed for violence: "The crown of red / set on your little head / is charged with all your fighting blood" (37). Given Bishop's pun on the word *cock*, her roosters imply that militarism must be understood as stupid, biological cruelty motivating a senseless but inexorable masculine territorial imperative. The cockpit of a plane is here represented as the site of ceaseless cockfights and the cocked firearm is simply an "excrescence." Yet the whole world is terrorized, for "making sallies / from all the muddy alleys," the roosters mark out "maps like Rand McNally's" (36).

To be sure, after crowing as "poor Peter" weeps at his betrayal of Christ, one of Bishop's roosters reappears during what appears to be a turn in the poem as a chanticleer whose spurs are composed of Peter's tears, suggesting that "'deny, deny, deny' / is not all the roosters cry" (38). Yet Bishop's poem does not solve the problem of escalating hatred through a simple affirmation of Christian love. Although Peter's forgiveness, like the sun that rises at the end of "Roosters," has caused a number of critics to view its development as a redemptive "mov[e] from a country morning to the morning of Christianity," there is a disturbing similarity in the language used to describe the kamikaze cocks falling from midair ("Down comes a first flame-feather") and that used to delineate Peter's treacherous "falling, beneath the flares."[23] Equally sardonic are the rhymes of the poem ("sallies," "alleys," "McNally's" or "guess," "bless," "forgiveness") as well as the speaker's judgment that "St. Peter's sin / was worse than that of Magdalen / whose sin was of the flesh alone" (37).

In addition, the poet's question "How could the night have come to grief?" is ambiguous. For while it might suggest self-criticism on the part of the speaker (how could I have thought that the night would come to grief?), it also can be read as sad acknowledgement (how terrible that the night did come to grief). Finally, the dawn in the last verse stanza—

> The sun climbs in,
> following "to see the end,"
> faithful as enemy, or friend—

is equivocal (was Peter an "enemy, or friend"? the "end" of the night's destruction or the "end" of life as the speaker had known it?), and the rising sun (during the war associated with Japan) succeeds only in making the cocks "*almost* inaudible" (39; emphasis ours). The poet therefore implies that the songs they have sung, which have "flung" them in "dung," subsist even in "those cock-a-doodles" said to "bless."

An attack not only on male aggression but also on male mythologies of heroism, "Roosters" further deflates the rhetoric of unwanted love, conceit, and war by demonstrating how the fighting cocks, who turn the world into a barnyard, transform wives into hens who lead lives "of being courted and despised":

> Cries galore
> come from the water-closet door,
> from the dropping-plastered henhouse floor,
>
> where in the blue blur
> their rustling wives admire,
> the roosters brace their cruel feet and glare
>
> with stupid eyes
> while from their beaks there rise
> the uncontrolled, traditional cries.

[35]

Either the rustling wives admire the cruel feet and stupid eyes of the crowing cocks or the hens lie dead "with open, bloody eyes" while the cocks' "metallic feathers oxidize." To the extent that the poem articulates Bishop's sense that in wartime women can only watch and wait or die, it poses a question— "Roosters, what are you projecting?" (36)—that informed the responses of a number of Bishop's contemporaries who depicted women "courted and despised" as whores, wives, and mothers. But a critique of the trope of militarism as masculinism that the roosters were projecting emerged even before the outbreak of the war in feminist polemics that assumed women were in a privileged situation from which to oppose fascism as the extreme but logical conclusion of masculine domination.

According to Mary Beard, the Nazis, who were trained "in isolation from women," consisted of "battalions of bachelors" and, borrowing a title from Hemingway, she argued that these "'men without women'" constituted "a menace to the liberties of women."[24] For Winifred Holtby, fascist ideology, which evolved as a reaction against the Continental women's movement and which curtailed women's new-won freedoms in Germany and Italy, effectively removed women from the work force and denied them any right but the right to produce and sacrifice the next generation of sons. Identifying D. H. Lawrence's doctrine in *Aaron's Rod* (that "men must submit to the greater soul in a man for their guidance; and women must submit to the positive power-soul in man for their being") with Goering's glamorization of leadership in *Germany Reborn* ("From the first moment that I met and heard [Hitler] I belonged to him body and soul"), Holtby protested in 1935, "But a world of hero-worshippers is a world in which women are doomed to subordination."[25] Similarly, in *Three Guineas* (1938), Woolf declared that dictators always insist it is the "essence of manhood to fight," and she therefore speculated that the fascist states might be able to reveal "to the younger generation at least the need for emancipation from the old conception of virility" (186, 187).

Katherine Burdekin's 1937 dystopia, *Swastika Night* (which Daphne Patai views as a major influence on George Orwell's *1984*), analyzes fascism as male domination: her novel presents Europe after seven centuries of Nazi hegemony as a feudal state in which a "Reduction of Women" program has arrogated women to the submissive, physical function of breeding and re-stricted them to ghettos while Nazi rulers bond in homosexual attachments and legalize their rights to rape women and remove all male children over one year of age from their mothers.[26] The inauguration of Hitler's new society occurs in a scene that connects the triumph of fascism with the fateful emergence of a misogyny so lethal it does not merely "reduce" women; it mutilates and destroys them. A lonely, last holdout encounters the body of a naked young woman on a roadside, a mangled body which convinces him of the impossibility of public dissent: "The hair had all been pulled out, leaving nothing but a ghastly red skull-cap of blood. The body was covered with innumerable stabs and cuts that looked as if they had been made with a pen-knife. The nipples had been cut off" (84).

Although this victim was murdered because she had scorned the idea that women should be "animals and ugly and completely submissive" (82), those who survive acknowledge that "it was beneath the dignity of a German man to have to risk rejection by a mere woman": "*all* women [are] at [men's] will like the women of a conquered nation" (81). Therefore, under the masculinism that is fascism in Burdekin's work, women, living "according to an imposed pattern" that legislates sexual exploitation and inculcates self-hatred, are "not women at all": "The human values of this world are masculine. There are no feminine values because there are no women" (107–08).[27]

Of course, Allied propaganda, like Archibald Macleish's *Fall of the City* (1938) and Edna St. Vincent Millay's *Murder of Lidice* (1942), often relied on the idea that fascism directly threatened women: both texts use grief-stricken or dead women to measure the effects of German aggression. During the war, a series of posters graphically presented the enemy as the man who would rape and murder "our" women. Whether the woman was portrayed as an Aryan-looking mom about to be caught in the clutches of hands resembling claws, or a ravaged corpse lying amid the ruins of a landscape obliterated by the huge face of Adolf Hitler, or a naked prey draped over the shoulder of a predatory Japanese soldier, the female functions as bounty: both the bountiful fertility that must be saved and the booty that constitutes the spoils of war (see figures). Not only could the madonna and child of "Keep These Hands Off!" be torn apart from each other by the grasping fingers, but the woman could be penetrated, as she is in both "This Is the Enemy" posters, by stake, gun, or (given the disheveled and nude figures) the magnified, bestialized masculinity of the German and Japanese enemy.

Identification of fascism with masculinism, as well as women's past non-combatant status, initially led women writers to assume that, as Muriel Rukeyser put it, while "all the strong agonized men" who "wear the hard clothes of war" found it difficult "to remember" why they are fighting, "women and poets see the truth arrive," and they "believe and resist forever."[28] Rukeyser's "Letter to the Front" (1944) goes on to explain that the woman poet speaks for "labor, women, Jews, / Reds, Negroes," a claim comparable to Marianne Moore's vow in "In Distrust of Merits" (1943) that "'we'll / never hate black, white, red, yellow, Jew, / Gentile, Untouchable'" (*CP* 137). Yet the passion for U.S. involvement in a "good" war and the patriotism of "Letter to the Front" are shadowed by Rukeyser's alienation from the forces fighting fascism, her intimation that female lives were being threatened by Allied, as well as Axis, forces.

Although Rukeyser was emphatic in her belief that the war must be won "in love and fighting," in the "Home thoughts from home" included in

KEEP THESE HANDS OFF!

BUY *the New* VICTORY BONDS

G. K. Odell, National Archives of Canada,
C-090883

"Letter to the Front" she admits that "a man fights to win a war, / To hang on to what is his," be it "his own birth" or "his own whore," and she documents the sense of unreality experienced by women who become a symbol of peace:

> We hold belief. You fight and are maimed and mad.
> We believe, though all you want be bed with one
> Whose mouth is bread and wine, whose flesh is home.

[239]

The poet admits, "We are that home you dream across a war"; yet when she hears "the singing of the lives of women" at the end of the poem, she confronts not a mouth of "bread and wine," a flesh that "is home," but instead "the sorrow of the loin," the "sad dreams of the belly, of the lip, / Of the deep warm breast," for "all sorrows have their place in flesh, / All flesh will with its sorrow die." Although she believes "it is time for the true grace of women" to emerge and free "a new myth among the male / Steep landscapes," she can

only imagine resistance and regeneration in negative terms, and specifically in terms of a new form of humanity evolving "not as traditional man" (243).

Rukeyser's conviction that returning soldiers at the war's end would desire a sacramental consummation with women but would encounter a home battle waged against "labor, women, Jews, / Reds, Negroes" helps explain why many women, in spite of their loathing of fascism, felt suspicious of the forces fighting fascism. Indeed, a 1941 essay by Lillian E. Smith and Paula Snelling speculated, "If man dared to thrust into the open his unending secret enmity against woman, there might be less of nation warring with nation; less need for him to merge his longing for superiority into a great mass-lust for power, less need for him to find outlet for his hate." In addition, because, as Smith and Snelling pointed out, "home has no wall around it that will protect it from aerial bombs" and because women were moving toward what Rukeyser called "a wider giving" (217), they confronted the possibility of losing the security and the privileges, as well as the privations, of their traditional domestic sphere.[29]

As Vera Brittain observed, "Modern war struck more fiercely than ever before at those things which meant life to the majority of women—children, homes, education, healing."[30] At the same time, the historical exclusion of women from the military was dramatically challenged by the first draft of unmarried women into the British Armed Forces; according to Winifred Holtby, the technological nature of warfare meant that there was "no reason why, if wars are to be fought at all, women should not be subject to conscription, service and death on the same terms as men."[31] No wonder, then, that the future of feminism itself seemed vexed to some of its most ardent advocates. Woolf's metaphorical ignition in *Three Guineas* of the "vicious and corrupt word" *feminism*, a parodic enactment of Nazi book burning, is the most ironic sign of her frustration at the alternatives available to women, for she cannot burn the words *Tyrant* and *Dictator*, which "are not yet obsolete" (101–02).

While Woolf implies that she looks forward to a time when the word *feminism* will no longer be needed, Gertrude Stein dramatizes her even more intense hopelessness about women's cultural situation. In *The Mother of Us All* (1946), Stein portrays first a disgusted and later an exhausted Susan B. Anthony, who laments the fact that men will not give women the vote and attributes male recalcitrance to male anxiety: "They fear women, they fear each other, they fear their neighbor, they fear other countries and then they hearten themselves in their fear by crowding together and following each other, . . . they are brutes, like animals who stampede, and so they have written the name male into the United States constitution, because they are afraid of black men because they are afraid of women, because they are afraid afraid. Men are afraid." Significantly, however, Stein's suffragist does not look forward to the time when women will win the vote, "because having the vote they will become like men, they will be afraid, having the vote will make them afraid."[32] That the vote is finally won after Anthony is dead and reified into a statue turns the play into an elegy for the spirit of feminism.

"*Dispersed are we,*" Miss La Trobe's gramophone scratches out at the end of *Between the Acts* (196), the play-within-the-novel Woolf wrote just before the war and, as Louise Bernikow has noted, the female modernist community was dispersed by World War II.[33] By the end of the forties the generation of feminist-modernists associated with Stein and Woolf had died or, as in the case of the Paris expatriates, scattered. The bombing of England meant, moreover, that British women of letters lived through substantially different experiences of war than did North American, Australian, and South African literary women. Paradoxically, however, precisely the sense of vulnerability which resulted from the disintegration of women's interwar communities and which is anticipated in Stein's portrait of Anthony's long life of strife produced a brilliant literary tradition that amplifies the battle cries of both sexes. Less concerned with military maneuvers than are the texts of their male contemporaries, many wartime works by women reiterate Burdekin's dread that the war constituted a specifically sexual warfare directed against women.

In Woolf's view, women who attempt to "compensate the man for the loss of his gun" must free not only Nazi but also English airmen "from the machine" ("Thoughts on Peace in an Air Raid" [1940], *DM* 156). Yet in her last work, *Between the Acts* (1941), she is hardly confident about this project. For while the novel includes a play by Miss LaTrobe that pointedly leaves the British army out of English history, militarism is obliquely represented as a threat to women when Woolf's heroine Isa broods on a *Times* article about the gang rape of a nameless, naive girl by troopers. As if to dramatize the narrative consequences of Bishop's insights into unwanted love, conceit, and war and Woolf's point that English and Nazi militarists must be liberated from their ethos of aggression, in *The Heat of the Day* (1948) Elizabeth Bowen's heroine Stella Rodney, who works during the blitz in "an organisation better called Y.X.D., in secret, exacting, not unimportant work," is horrified to realize that she cannot disentangle the identities of her lover, an Axis spy, and his antagonist, his Allied pursuer.[34] Just as her lover, Robert Kelvey, has kept Stella ignorant of his Nazi connections, so his antagonist, Robert Harrison, has proposed to collude in Kelvey's treason in exchange for Stella's sexual compliance. Besides using these male doubles to analyze the commonality of Axis and Allied "intelligence," Bowen further explores World War II as a menacing backlash against the sexual repercussions of the Great War.

Kelvey turned to Nazism after he was first raised in a "man-eating house" (288) dominated by women and then sent to Dunkirk where he received a wound he associates with his emasculated father. Seeking "to be a man in secret" (314), Kelvey illustrates Bowen's thesis that the attraction to fascism is inextricably related to what she calls a "fiction of dominance" (289). As in "The Demon Lover," in *The Heat of the Day* Bowen's central character becomes convinced that "the fateful course of her fatalistic century seemed more and more her own" (147). Like the heroine of Stevie Smith's *Over the Frontier* (1938) who comes to believe that "all holders of privilege" are "ruthless and cruel in their tenure," Stella attains a Woolfian consciousness into her own vulnerable status as an outsider.[35]

In a further elaboration of the war's brutal effect on women, Edith Sitwell's "Lullaby" (1942) presents a nightmarish reversal of Darwinian evolution in which a baboon replaces a dead mother to sing a song of devolution: "And down on all fours shouldst thou crawl," the ape cautions the child who inhabits a world of dry sockets and steel birds, "For thus from no height canst thou fall."[36] The only maternal message of perseverance possible in Sitwell's sterile environment consists of "the discordant cry" of the poem's refrain, "Do, do, do, do," which emphasizes that the endearing "du, du" of traditional lullabies is now a stuttered warning that there is nothing to "do" but return to the dust of the ape's sunless world. Similarly, although in "Letter to the Front" Rukeyser sought an image of innocence to imagine the promise of a future after the war—"You little children, come down out of your mothers" (241)—she believed that "the sad-faced / Inexorable armies and the falling plane" transformed the prophetic woman poet she sought to be into "a childless goddess of fertility" (227).

But Sitwell's tellingly titled "Serenade: Any Man to Any Woman" (1942) is more explicit in attributing linguistic casualties to the brutality Woolf's Isa reads about in the newspaper. For what "any" man says to "any" woman is comparable to the deadly invitation issued by Bowen's demon lover. The cannoneer-speaker of "Serenade" identifies his beloved with a cannon ("Dark angel who are clear and straight / As cannon shining in the air") and woos the woman (who "can never see what dead men know!") by asking her to "die with me and be my love."[37] The ironic reversal of Marlowe's "Come live with me, and be my love" implies that the "universal Flood" of wartime destruction is composed of female, as well as male, "blood." Intoxicated less by love than by death, any man in battle, Sitwell suggests, will sing a demonic serenade of annihilation. Her dramatic monologue thus functions as a meditation on the commingling of eroticism and warfare—of weapon, phallus, and girl—that caused H. D. to view the war as her husband, that shaped Bishop's satiric portrait of fighting "cocks," and that, we will see, became quite common in literature written by men. A shared consternation about what Bishop called the "excrescence" of "virile presence" transformed American and British women's letters *to* the front into letters *from* the front. And, as Rukeyser knew, "When the cemeteries are military objectives / and love's a downward drawing at the heart, . . . every letter bears the stamp of death" (250).

The confusion of love and death, sex and murder, girl and cannon evident in Sitwell's "Serenade" finds a parallel in the chant used to teach marines how to name their instruments correctly: "This is my rifle, / This is my gun, / This is for fighting, / This is for fun." Oddly, though, the metaphorical association of gun with penis sometimes modulated into an identification of gun with female; in *Battle Cry* (1953) Leon Uris's squat sergeant patiently explains this lesson, as he hands out rifles: "'You've got yourselves a new girl now. Forget that broad back home! This girl is the most faithful, truest woman in the world if you give her a fair shake. She won't sleep with no swab jockies the minute your back is turned. Keep her clean and she'll save your life.'" Similarly, a poem entitled "Cannoneer's Lady" (1943), by Lieutenant Morris Earle, contrasts a man's love of woman with his passion for "a howitzer [which] goes to the heart of a man": "In the retch and recoil," he explains, "The cannoneer, loving her, cared for her more / The moment this turbulent outburst began."[38]

With retrospective clarity, a number of male poets—John Ciardi and Lincoln Kirstein, for example—protested the ways military life ritualized masculinity so that, in the words of the historian John Costello, "Soldiers . . . came to regard their weapons as extensions of their virility."[39] While manuals given to U.S. army infantrymen proffered the advice "your rifle, like your girlfriend, has habits for which you must allow," Ciardi satirized "the sex of war":

> The health of captains is the sex of war:
> the pump of sperm built in their polished thighs
> powers all their blood; the dead, like paid-off whores,
> sleep through the mornings where the captains rise.

For Kirstein, the soldier who "feels his courage stir" in a whorehouse "can manage five-minutes' stiff routine / as skillfully as grease a jeep or service other mild machine. // Slips off his brakes; gives her the gas." Kirstein's title—"Snatch" (1964)—ironically conflates his soldiers' efforts to "snatch" pleasure on a furlough with the female "snatch" which is as depersonalized as a jeep or any other "mild machine."[40]

Many photographs of "our boys over there" reinforced the fused images of sex and death that so disturbed men and women of letters. Pinups, barely clothed or naked, adorned bunks and tanks named after women, and posters and drawings of movie stars and models jokingly represented what the men were fighting for (figure, below). With more frontal nudity than in any earlier war, the female figures painted on planes add resonance to the eerily incoherent "US Army Flyer's Lament" which included the refrain "I wish all girls were like B-24's / And I were a pilot, I'd make them all whores."[41] Indeed, when pinups were used to teach camouflage techniques and map reading to new recruits, the targets of desire and destruction became identical. Glossing this phenomenon, Ivor Roberts-Jones, a poet who served as an artillery lieutenant, viewed the bombardment pattern produced by "the

Jane Russell (courtesy the Bettmann Archive, New York)

guns shout[ing] in the narrow valleys" as "little . . . shifts, like a girl arranging her dress, / At the start of the party waiting for the young men."[42]

Perhaps in consequence of all this, World War II marked an increase in the use of the word *fuck* to mean not only intercourse but also assault or exploitation. As Fussell has pointed out, numerous memoirs of veterans record their mechanized sexual experiences of "wall jobs" and "knee tremblers," but one Canadian soldier's reticence captures both the violence and the surrealism of swarms of whores "servicing" the forces: "I won't describe the scenes or the sounds of Hyde Park or Green Park at dusk and after dark . . . . You can just imagine, a vast *battlefield* of sex" (emphasis ours).[43] As Elaine Tyler May explains in her history of the cold-war era, "female sexuality continued to represent a destructive and disruptive force" after the war, perhaps most dramatically when a photograph of Rita Hayworth was attached to the hydrogen bomb dropped on the Bikini Islands and when the name "bikini" was chosen by its designer to establish the swimsuit's explosive effect.[44]

As the texts of Ciardi and Kirstein demonstrate, however, many war works produced by literary men protest, as do those by Bishop, Woolf, and Sitwell, against the excrescence of a hypertrophied virility, thereby agreeing with Cyril Connolly, the editor of *Horizon*, that the "lack [of] patriotic poetry" was a "healthy sign" of "the decline of the aggressive instinct."[45] Ciardi's captains engage in "the sex of war" only to awake among "the dead, like paid-off whores"; Kirstein's soldiers, who "service" whores, are themselves depersonalized in the "stiff routine" of giving "gas." The confusion between gun and penis led literary psychologists of warfare to examine the war as an assault on or a perversion of male sexuality: Lincoln Kirstein's terrified soldier turns to masturbation only to discover that the "big load" of the Jerries' "steel-turned tubes . . . splashes my small load"; John Hersey's *War Lover* (1959) becomes a sadist "when he gets in bed," a female character explains, because "he makes hate—attacks, rapes, milks his gland; and thinks that makes him a man."[46]

According to one critic, men of letters set out to prove "how war stripped man of his manhood, reflected his absurdity and capacity for evil."[47] The mutilated and tormented heroes of novelists from Norman Mailer and George Orwell to those later writers like Joseph Heller and Thomas Pynchon, who resemble the no-men of, say, Wilfred Owen and D. H. Lawrence, enabled some of these authors to engage in a critique of traditional masculinity, at least in part in response to an Axis ideology which associated the male with aggression. Conscious of the impersonality of technologically advanced warfare, literary men extended the point made by their precursors during the Great War, namely that combat could no longer be used as a test of individual heroism or as a masculine initiation ritual. Their most telling lesson of war, after their unmasking of what W. H. Auden called the "lie of Authority," was therefore not far removed from Auden's injunction, "We must love one another or die."

But, just as Auden rewrote this line to read "We must love one another and die,"[48] many men of letters mourned the insufficiency of women and bemoaned the inefficacy of love, responding to the related problems of emasculation (the no-man) and ritualized hypermasculinization (the he-man) by emphasizing the different spheres inhabited by the two sexes. The prostitute became an index of new sexual explicitness, playing a crucial role in commodifying female eroticism. Viewed sardonically, as in Kirstein's serviced "mild machines," or metaphorically, as in Ciardi's "dead, like paid-off whores," the whore functions as an emblem sometimes of temporary relief from warfare, sometimes of warfare itself. As the only available erotic object, the whore can offer sanctuary to the soldier because, in Richard Wilbur's words, her "much touched flesh" furnishes the opportunity to "gently seize" with hands that otherwise "kill all things." Just as frequently, however, exotic Eurasian, Italian, French, and African prostitutes are the proverbial solution to the problem of a "rusty load" that is described in the war song "Lydia of Libya" (1943): "Why are the armies of the world / Fighting for that desert land?" They fight for "Lydia of Libya, / The lady with the lacy lingerie," who has "passed all her courses" in "harem school" and therefore "devastates our forces." Often, too, as in Keith Douglas's "Cairo Jag" (1943), the soldier has to decide between getting drunk or "cut[ting] myself a piece of cake, / a pasty Syrian with a few words of English / or the Turk who says she is a princess."[49]

But of course the rest and recreation furnished by the whore is only a temporary reprieve from the horror of battle: although "Odysseus saw the sirens" as charming, "with snub breasts and little neat posteriors," John Manifold's pilot-Odysseus forgets them when faced with the more portentous reality of "alarming / Weather report, his mutineers in irons, / The radio failing." A poem entitled simply "War" (1943) exploits Homeric allusion to contrast men's vulnerability in war with women's safety: "Innocence, hired to kill, / Lies pitilessly dead. / Stone and bone lie still. / Helen turns in bed." So many of the younger generation of novelists equated "a man of war" with "a man of whore" that, like Vance Bourjaily's heroes, they often considered penicillin a far more important scientific achievement than radar, rocketry, or the atom bomb, an understandable judgment considering that the most traumatic war zone depicted in Bourjaily's *Confessions of a Spent Youth* (1960) is the bathroom of a hospital in which men infected with gonorrhea and syphilis stand, "each with a tortured penis in his hand." The hostility implicit in these scenes erupts in Melvin Tolson's "The Furlough" (1944), a poem that describes how a soldier gazes upon the "silken loveliness" of "a passion-flower of joy and pain / On the golden bed I came back to possess": "I choked her just a little, and she is dead. / A furlough is an escalator to delight / Her beauty gathers rot on the golden bed."[50]

"On the golden bed I came *back* to possess": Tolson's poem implies that the war, by rupturing relationships between the sexes, fostered insecurity and anger in men. Similarly, in "A Woman's a Two-Face" (1943), the "Dear John" letter composed by a female correspondent who claims to be busy causes the soldier-reader to think, "You must be busy, and / I wonder who's the guy."[51] Axis propaganda sought to aggravate such jealousy by producing leaflets to divide Allied fighting men over the ownership of women. Japanese posters, obscene in their racism, informed Australians away "philandering" in Africa that the English were cuckolding them back home and German posters instructed French fighting men that British servicemen were enjoying security and sex behind the lines. But Allied propaganda also spoke directly about and to servicemen's fear of their women's betrayal. Posters enjoining silence as a protection against spies implied that women's talk would kill fighting men. The female spy, a femme fatale or vamp whose charms endanger national security, was sinister in her silence, for her allure could penetrate the security needed to keep the fighting forces safe (figure, opposite).

In the verse and the posters of the period, the most intense hatred of women surfaces in those poems that identify the "boys" as victims of a war that is the whore personified. George Barker's "To Any Member of My Generation" (1944) identifies the war as a dance "in what we hoped was life"; yet, "Who was it in our arms but the whores of death / Whom we have found in our beds today, today?" In "Careless Love" (1944) Stanley Kunitz returns to the gun/girl analogy to analyze the erotic relationship between young soldiers and the "dark beauty" of the guns that comfort them, "for what / This nymphomaniac enjoys / Inexhaustibly is boys." Similarly, just as Karl Shapiro identifies boot camp with "Virginia," a female state that is sickened "with a dry disease," whose sun rises "like a very tired whore" beckoning soldiers to death, Charles Causley exclaims,

> O war is a casual mistress
> And the world is her double bed.
> She has few charms in her mechanised arms
> But you wake up and find yourself dead.[52]

As in World War I, women were presented as posing the threat of contamination, for they could infect fighting men with syphilis. "She may look clean—but . . ." warned captions on posters featuring disarmingly healthy looking girls.[53] The danger of female pollution is used in a 1938 Pulitzer-prize winning cartoon against U.S. involvement in the war that personifies the war itself as a syphilitic whore. And in a famous British poster, feminine accoutrements (both the veiled hat and its vaginal flower) grace a skull that would lure soldiers to dissolution and death (figures, pages 232 and 233). Thus, when Thomas Pynchon's novel *V.* (1961) redefines the "V for Victory"

Fougasse, Trustees of the Imperial War
Museum, London

in terms of the vulgarity, the void, and the vagina of a sinister, syphilitic
Lady V, he may be sardonically referring to the phrase "Victory-girl," which
was used throughout the war years as a euphemism for "whore."[54] In fact,
victory was pictured as a triumphant undressing of the female in the most
popular cartoon strip in England: the nubile cartoon character Jane, who
was dubbed "Britain's Secret Weapon" and relished by the troops reading
the *Daily Mirror,* finally lost all her clothes on V-E day.[55]

Interpreted from this perspective, it seems resonant that the figures
shown under the caption "This Is the Enemy" are females linked pictorially,
almost pornographically, to the villainous, foreign masters of war. As Fussell
has explained about the perspective of combatants, "Civilians were different, more like 'foreigners,' indeed rather like the enemy."[56] At the conclusion of *The Naked and the Dead* (1948), Norman Mailer meditates on the
female civilian as enemy when, in an effort to foster camaraderie, one major

C. D. BATCHELOR.   New York *Daily News.*

"Come on in, I'll treat you right. I used to know your Daddy."

Cartoon by C. D. Batchelor, 1937 (courtesy the *Chicago Tribune*, New York *News* Syndicate)

"jazz[es] up the map-reading class by having a full-size color photograph of Betty Grable in a bathing suit, with a co-ordinate grid system laid over it." Thomas Pynchon echoes this scene at the beginning of *Gravity's Rainbow* (1973), a novel set during World War II, with Slothrop's map of London, which is sprinkled with stars, a firmament of "Carolines, Marias, Annes, Susans, Elizabeths," each marking the place where he has had an affair and each becoming visible a few days before bomb sites of V-2 rockets mysteriously appear.[57]

If the pinup was a "bomb shell," if the gun was a "girl," then the disturbing conflation of sex and death that some men described as a perversion of masculinity, some as its triumph, was often experienced by women as an attack. Perhaps the pinned-up bomb shells who became the targets of men's

Reginald Mount, Trustees of the Imperial
War Museum, London

desire explain why military women continually confronted sexual assaults at
the camps they called "Wolf Swamps" from men who jokingly translated
WAAF (Women's Auxiliary Air Force) as "Women All Fuck." Even female
soldiers and workers, publicly encouraged to keep up their "FQ" (feminine
quotient), were displayed in quasi-pornographic nudity in magazines. And
in 1940 a chorus line in London's Garrison Theatre wore and then stripped
WAAF uniforms.[58] Besides slander campaigns that pictured female combatants as sexually promiscuous or contaminated with venereal disease, WASP
(Women's Air Service Pilots Association) pilots were physically endangered
by hostile male colleagues: when women pilots tested planes to be sent to the
front, their safety was threatened by mechanical failures which were the
result of sabotage—or so they suspected when traces of sugar (sure to stop
an engine in seconds) were found in the gas tank of one WASP plane.[59]

That the images and stereotypes of popular culture affected women poets is apparent from the critical reaction to war poems by Edna St. Vincent Millay, Muriel Rukeyser, H. D., and Marianne Moore. After publishing her polemical volume *Make Bright the Arrows* (1940), Millay endorsed the view of her critics that she had committed "prostitution"; in the wake of the appearance of her pro-war *Wake Island* (1942), Rukeyser was condemned for "promiscuity" and labeled a "Poster Girl"; H. D. was attacked for patching together "religious scraps" in *Tribute to the Angels* (1945), a "quilt" she was said to use "to warm" herself; and Moore's "In Distrust of Merits"—although frequently praised and anthologized—was attacked by her admirer Randall Jarrell, who wished that in this case she had taken "her individuals with their scrupulous virtues and shown them smashed willy-nilly, tortured, prostituted, driven crazy—and not for a while but forever."[60]

H. D.'s old-fashioned quilt and Moore's scrupulous virtues suggest that women were thought to be out of touch with the harsh realities of battle: these caricatured descriptions emanated from an image just as prevalent as (but purportedly the antithesis of) that of the whore. Although endowed with a fidelity that presumably differentiated her from the prostitute, the girl he left behind could, of course, shade into the prostitute. For notwithstanding her faithfulness, the girlfriend, wife, or mother—who symbolizes why men fight, the desirable peace they sought to secure—may also represent a refuge not forthcoming. In addition this character, like the whore, reinforced the notion that women—and thus women writers—remained behind or outside the actual war effort and therefore deprived of the inside experience necessary to express the realities of worldwide combat. Like Bishop's hens in "Roosters," women not "courted and despised" as whores were "courted and despised" as witnesses of male suffering.

The spectatorship shared by literary women living outside Europe was shaped by their alienation from the sons, brothers, lovers, and husbands away at the fronts. In Bishop's language, the separation between the battling cocks and the wives in the henhouse precludes communication, for the women left behind feel hopelessly divided from the men they seek to address. Precisely this estrangement is expressed in Babette Deutsch's "For a Young Soldier" (1944), in which the poet can penetrate neither the subjectivity of the soldier ("Do you dream of what lies behind you / Or ahead?") nor the meaning of the war itself ("How can a woman scale this wall, this war?"). In "To My Son" (1944), therefore, Deutsch admits that the war inducts the soldier into a different language ("How shall we talk / To you who must learn the language / Spelled on the fields in famine, in blood on the sidewalk?"), an idiom that ensures the impotence of the mother: "I cannot hide you now, / Or shelter you ever, / Or give you a guide through hell."[61]

As Susan Schweik has explained, the predominance of the letter form in World War II literature signals the distance between the sexes, a distance that produced the image of the girl he left behind and that is brilliantly captured by a gruesome *Life* magazine photograph in which a woman writes a thank-you note to her boyfriend for the autographed Japanese skull he has sent her (figure, next page).[62] The comfort, security, and normalcy of the female writer "left behind" contrast sharply with the skull, a gruesome memento signaling the impossibility of her comprehending the horror "over there." The shocking juxtaposition between the female figure's complacencies—her elegant hairdo, her jewelry, her expensive suit, her fingernail polish—and the gift of the (autographed) skull symbolizes the resentment many departing servicemen felt about the girl he left behind. One soldier-poet, indefinitely separated from his wife, exclaims, "Your peace is bought with mine, and I am paid in full, and well, / If but the echo of your laughter reaches me in hell." Feelings of estrangement were also inscribed on war memorials: "For your tomorrow / We gave our today."[63]

In spite of the critique of masculine dominance articulated by many male writers, then, a curious unreality permeates positive images of women, who are often viewed as solacing outsiders or resented beneficiaries of male suffering. Whether she is the silent recipient of "V letters" or a photographed face peeping out of the pockets of dead men, the good wife, mother, or mistress in the literature of the Second World War is marked by her absence from the scene of battle which is the scene of the writing. Even in Karl Shapiro's loving poem "V-Letter" (1944), for example, the speaker cherishes the fair face of his beloved "because you wait" and because "you are my home and in your spacious love / I dream to march as under flaring flags."[64] While Shapiro believes his "love is whole / Whether I live or fail," the dead German soldier in Keith Douglas's poem "*Vergissmeinnicht*" (1943) is not saved by his talisman, an autographed picture which is "dishonoured" now that the combatant sprawls in the sun, decaying next to what Douglas sardonically calls "hard and good" equipment. As the only witness who might weep to see "the lover and killer . . . mingled" and mangled, the photographed female is a repository of precisely the humane values which the soldier must repress in wartime.[65]

Although a number of writers express the soldier's guilty sense that his innocent beloved would never accept the person he has had to become under the brutal and brutalizing circumstances of combat, many writers express the soldier's anger at the safety or the infidelity of the girl back home.[66] Besides being potentially unfaithful and fatefully ignorant, the girl he left behind could endanger the lives of fighting men as effectively as the vamp-spy. A host of posters suggest that even well-meaning female civilians pose a security threat: a Finnish poster, for example, presents women's lips locked up, while English cartoons and posters picture gossips as irresponsible and naive in their garrulity (figure, page 237).

Under the pressure of such emotions, many men felt, in the words of the

Arizona war worker writes her Navy boyfriend a thank-you note for the Jap skull he sent her

"A Thank-you Note," *Life*, 22 May 1944 (courtesy Owen/Black Star Publishing)

Fougasse, Trustees of the Imperial War
Museum, London

narrator of Leon Uris's *Battle Cry,* that there were just two kinds of women,
"The ones who waited and the ones who didn't."[67] "Brotherhood of Men"
(1949), Richard Eberhart's poem about the defense of Corregidor, expresses
male nostalgia for the "ones who waited" and specifically for a lost female
world of fertility or faithfulness: Eberhart's embattled recruits, vampires
"drinking the blood of victims" in a hellish fight, are only prevented from
surrendering by a vision of "mother in the midst of terror: / 'Persevere.
Persevere. Persevere. Persevere.'" The epitome of what Eberhart calls "faith
beyond reason," the mother represents humanistic values at odds with the
dehumanizing technology of death, much as she does to James Jones's Robert E. Lee Prewitt, who is torn between a vow to his dying mother—that he
"wont never hurt nobody unless its absolute a must"—and "the jism cord"
that connects him to the army.[68]

George Orwell's *1984* (1949), a novel that contrasts the brutality of "Big
Brother" with the hero's remembrances of the altruism of his mother, is
imbued with nostalgia for a fantasy prewar world, specifically a world in

which his mother tried to protect him even at the cost of her own and his sister's life. What Winston Smith must learn in Room 101, however, is that he can neither have the mother nor kill the father: indeed, when he is brainwashed to "see" five fingers where there are four, he submits to the power of his persecutor and specifically to the state's phallus, the invisible but potent symbol of authority that no single man possesses. Physically and psychologically beaten, Winston—"the last man"—relinquishes the oceanic unity he had with his mother for the perpetual warring of an Oceania ruled by Big Brother. Even though Winston's mother is elegized as a victim of the war, she is also a mother not good enough to protect her son from the vengeance of his big brothers.[69]

Orwell's dystopia reflects the anger with which many male writers, encased in what they call "the womb of war" or "the steel cocoon," articulated eerie parallels between the biological mother and the military to suggest, as John Ciardi later put it, that "the womb of woman is the kit of war." In Jarrell's "The Death of the Ball Turret Gunner," the mother has sent her son to war: "From my mother's sleep I fell into the State," declares the airman "hunched" upside down in the "belly" of the ball turret from which he is virtually aborted: "When I died they washed me out of the turret with a hose."[70] The bomber carrier as grotesque uterus reached its culmination at the end of the war when the plane over Hiroshima, the "Enola Gay," was named for the pilot's mother, and the plutonium and uranium bombs were referred to as "Fat Man" and "Little Boy." The mother who has given her son over to the state has exchanged her birth-giving function for a death-dealing one.

As guilty as Jarrell's mother is the wife of his "Gunner" (1945), for here the soldier sent away from his wife and his cat confronts his death wondering bitterly, "Has my wife a pension of so many mice? / Did the medals go home to my cat?"[71] As survivors, wives and pets—presumably interchangeable—are the beneficiaries of men's suffering and their security therefore appears sinister. Similarly, in "On Embarkation" (1945), by Alun Lewis, sobbing women on railroad platforms are "thinking of children, pensions, looks that fade, / The slow forgetfulness that strips the mind"; and in Lewis's "Christmas Holiday" (1942), when the war begins, "The fat wife comfortably sleeping / Sighs and licks her lips and smiles."[72]

No less quick than Orwell to perceive totalitarianism as a Big Brother controlling the military complex of any and all sides of the war, literary women did not react with Orwell's nostalgia for a prewar world of feminine renunciation and constancy. On the contrary, whether they examine female vulnerability in wartime, as do British and expatriate survivors of the blitz, or analyze their estrangement from the war, as do Americans geographically removed from warfare, they elaborate Bishop's belief that militarism reduces women "courted and despised" to death or spectatorship. In the face of a newly eroticized but highly traditional sexual division of labor, women writers wondered over the survival possibilities of the women in the "left behind" who could neither join forces with nor do battle against the men on their own side.

———

Analyzing the contradictions between the ideology of separate spheres embedded in so much war literature and women's increased participation in public history, many women of letters resemble Muriel Rukeyser in her effort to get "beyond the men of letters, / Of business and of death" (217–18). The new explicitness apparent in depictions of the whore and the girl he left behind, as well as the slippage between these two types, helps explain the sense of dread that pervades women's texts. Certainly the (mythologized) dichotomy between battle and home front, upon which such stereotypes depend, fostered feelings of loneliness, guilt, and anxiety about the ways the war divided the sexes, heightening sex antagonism.

Both in prose and poetry Kay Boyle examined the dangers confronted by the girl he left behind and in particular the sexual onslaughts that threatened to turn her into a whore. The physically free women in Kay Boyle's stories face the violence of sex-starved men as well as the images such men construct as a retaliation against the women they are presumably fighting to preserve but that they are really preserving themselves to fight. The American soldiers on a train carrying war brides in "Army of Occupation" (1947), for example, assault a female journalist with rowdy advances and drunken marriage proposals. In such stories as "Men" (1941) and "Defeat" (1941), moreover, Boyle's female characters either become symbols of home (for prisoners of war whose fantasies threaten to erupt into rape) or images of defeat (for French soldiers who would rather blame the Nazi occupation of their village on women dancing with the enemy than face their own army's failures).[73]

Boyle's long poem *American Citizen Naturalized in Leadville, Colorado* (1944), which focuses on the same linguistic casualties suffered by the characters left behind in Sitwell's and Deutsch's works, describes the inadequacy of both the absurd "G.I. talk" that war brides appropriate and the "alphabet of sorcery" that women in bereavement use. While the war brides jabber in a tongue foreign to them ("'Sweating out three weeks of maneuvers, or sweating the week-end pass, / Or sweating him out night after night,' they'll say, sweet-tongued as thrushes"), the "women in bereavement" look for solace to a seer who resembles no one so much as T. S. Eliot's Madame Sosostris and end up sounding like Eliot's neurasthenic Belladonna as they nervously ask, "What do you see now? . . . Do you see?" *American Citizen* describes the "polka of war brides"—the "mazurka" of women left to collect checks and await furloughs—as a ghastly "*pas seul*":

This is the waltz
Of the wives whose men are in khaki. Their faces are painted
As flawless as children's, their hearts each the flame of a candle
That his breath can extinguish at will.[74]

While many women wrote about the rhythm of military leaves, partings, and letters to express their loneliness, others found distant lovers and husbands drained of reality. According to Margaret Mead, "Just as the man in the cartoon is pictured as looking at his rifle and saying, 'I've given you the best years of my life,' so the young women of the 1940s look at the pictures on their dressing tables, the service pins on their lapels, realizing the years which have been dedicated to absence, to breathless hope and to gnawing fear, and to a break in experience."[75] If the man who went away seemed as insubstantial to literary women as the girl he left behind did to literary men, women of letters often articulated feelings of guilt not unrelated to the resentment at female survival expressed by men of letters. That such anxieties about survival were inevitable is made clear by a poem Eleanor Roosevelt was said to have carried with her at all times for spiritual guidance, a prayer composed by Sir William Stephenson, the Canadian in charge of British intelligence operations in the United States: "As long as there be war / I then must / Ask and answer / Am I worth dying for?"[76]

Popular verse written by and about English ambulance drivers, farmers, nurses, and civil defense workers insisted that women were not left behind, but it lacks the note of exhilaration frequently resounding in comparable texts written by women during the Great War. "I'm only a wartime working girl" begins one song chanted by factory workers trying to confound the monotony of long hours of production:

The machine shop makes me deaf,
I have no prospects after the war
And my young man is in the RAF.[77]

Instead of exulting in the formation of a Herland when men at the front are replaced by women in factories, post offices, and statehouses, not a few female writers moaned that England had become a "Monstrous Regiment" of women: "What host of women everywhere I see!" Alice Coats exclaims, adding "I'm sick to death of them—and they of me." Sexual deprivation, boredom, and self-revulsion, not emancipation, characterize what she experiences:

The newsboy and the boy who drives the plough:
Postman and milkman—all are ladies now.
Doctors and engineers—yes, even these—
Poets and politicians, all are shes.
(The very beasts that in the meadows browse

Are ewes and mares, heifers and hens and cows. . . .)
All, doubtless, worthy to a great degree;
But oh, how boring! Yes, including me.[78]

Besides suffering a "blankness" associated with the dehumanization of military service, war workers become war victims in Stevie Smith's "Who Shot Eugenie?" (1950). As Karen Schneider has pointed out, this poem "expresses Smith's concern that the sanctioned violence of war all too insidiously infects one's consciousness and fatally poisons relations with others, even those whom we do not consider enemies." For, at the conclusion of an account of two female "campaigners," the speaker discovers her dead friend "shot, with a bullet through her head. / Yet every chamber in her revolver was full to plenty / And only in my own is there one that is empty." What Smith depicts as the surrealistic contagion of violence escalates into a sense of unreality in literature about and pictures of the bombing of England.[79]

In magazines and newspapers, photographs depicted women and children as the predominant civilian casualties of enemy blitzes, while pictures of Allied planes dropping bombs over both the Asian and the European fronts tended to represent transcendent Allied power without regard to the dismemberment or death of victims. Although a number of World War II photos of nurses, machinists, ammunition workers, and fire fighters testify to the same exhilarating sense of female camaraderie evident in World War I pictures, what is different are the images of women nearly buried alive by bombs, almost as if they were in fox holes, framed by landscapes of crumbled houses (figure, next page). Within urban settings in which gas, electricity, telephone, transportation, food, water, and even houses were drastically reduced or disappeared altogether, the drudgery and danger of making do were accompanied by a bizarre sense of unreality.

After the months of the "phony war," in which enemy bombers failed to appear in the skies over England, scarcity measures—widely publicized by the government—encouraged women to retain a pretense of normal life through inventive substitutions. Defamiliarization of the home was thereby accompanied by a widespread impersonation of femininity: not only were women encouraged to produce fatless pastries and mock stews and to draw the seams of make-believe stockings on their legs; a Lewis Carrollesque Board of Trade announcement urged civilians to effect a series of metamorphoses which may have implied that, far from being "left behind," they were engaged in battles against the enemy on the home front:

Golf Balls become Gas Masks;
Mattresses become Life Jackets;
Saucepans become Steel Helmets;
Combs become Eyeshields.[80]

(Trustees of the Imperial War Museum, London)

Those children who were not labeled like packages for deportation from the bombed cities to the safer countryside were photographed clutching symbols of a childhood made virtually impossible by the war. Those who were evacuated to foster homes often suffered intense homesickness, or so a poignant story by Sylvia Townsend Warner suggests. "Noah's Ark" (1943) describes the estrangement of two young evacuees who find the lambs and flowers of the countryside tame in comparison with their recollections of the monkeys, serpents, jaguars, crocodiles, and wolves in the city zoo. Indeed, the children take refuge from memories of "corpses . . . heaped up where the old coffee-stall used to be" by lovingly recounting stories about the zoo, "as though wild beasts were meat and drink, home and mother" to them. Even that recourse is taken away at the end of the tale when they are given a newspaper notice: "*Owing to the continuance of blitz bombing the authorities of the Plymouth Zoo have caused all the dangerous animals to be destroyed.*"[81]

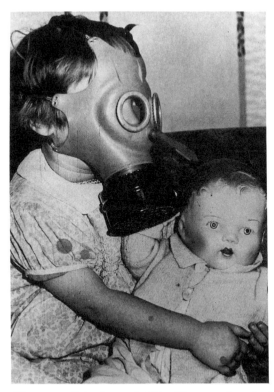

(Trustees of the Imperial War Museum, London)

While Warner's children grieve that there is no Noah's Ark to save the animals in the zoo from the falling rain of bombs, in H. D.'s elegy on the death of a fire-girl (female fire fighter), "May 1943" (1950), the vitality of newly arrived American soldiers contrasts sharply with the fatigue of beleaguered citizens on the home front who have themselves been reduced to an animal state:

> We've slithered so long in the rain, prowled like cats in the dark,
> like owls in the black-out,
> look at us—anaemic, good-natured,
> for a rat in the gutter's a rat in the gutter,
> consider our fellowship,
> look at each one of us,
> we've grown alike, slithering,
> slipping along with fish-baskets,
> grey faces, fish-faces, frog gait,
> we slop, we hop.
>
> [*CP* 496]

H. D.'s denizens of the home front resemble the no-men in the trenches of World War I: slithering in the blackout, anemic but aware of fellowship in suffering, encased in a gutter of mud like rats, as wet as frogs or fish.

Because of their greater proximity to (or engagement in) warfare, the literature composed by British and expatriate American women caused them to emphasize the deaths of women, which Bishop viewed as the alternative to spectatorship. But for a number of American women writers, the widening gulf between men and the women they left behind also led to a loss of communication between the sexes and to female suffering, as Gwendolyn Brooks's verse in *A Street in Bronzeville* (1945) and *Annie Allen* (1949) most tellingly records. The voices of her "Gay Chaps at the Bar" express their hostility toward the girls left behind—sweethearts, unfaithful correspondents—not only at a literal bar but also at the color bar which is sustained by the forces presumably representing democracy.

Brooks's elliptical sonnet sequence about the disillusionment experienced by black veterans uses male speakers whose traumatic experiences of a violent enemy and a racist army have effectively alienated them from the women to whom they return. According to the soldier-speaker of "looking," the women left behind "have no word" with which to leave the soldier: "'Good- by!' is brutal, and 'come back!' the raw / Insistence of an idle desperation." For the veteran-speaker of "mentors," the girl to whom he returns—even if she is "fragrant as the flower she wears"—must be abandoned at the "remotest whisper" of the "reproving ghosts" who haunt him, for his "best allegiances are to the dead."[82] A number of the other "soldier sonnets" in "Gay Chaps at the Bar" display the hostility of returning veterans estranged by their war experiences from the women to whom they return and effectively mentored by the dead men they have had to leave behind.

The speaker of "piano after war," for example, knows that although he may watch and listen to a female pianist whose "fingers, / Cleverly ringed, declining to clever pink, / Beg glory from the willing keys," his pleasure will be interrupted by "a multiplying cry" issuing from "bitter dead men who will never / Attend a gentle maker of musical joy." In the final couplet, his bond to his buried comrades separates him from the woman and her artistry, even as it condemns him to a frigid life-in-death: "Then my thawed eye will go again to ice. / And stone will shove the softness from my face" (52). The male personae of two other poems—"love note I: surely" and "love note II: flags"—send hate mail to women. Doubting the fidelity of the girl he left behind, the first speaker mocks her language of empty promises ("Surely your word would pop as insolent / As always: 'Why, of course I love you, dear'"), concluding that the "wounds and death" of war pale in comparison to the wound she has inflicted, for "I doubt all. You. Or a violet" (57). The second speaker, conflating the flag and the female, contrasts his own "power crumpled and wan" with the "pretty glory," "merry / Softness," and "pert exuberance" of the national emblem and the woman who symbolize what he fights for and whose vitality seems sinister in light of his suffering (58).

Thus the poems of "Gay Chaps at the Bar" evoke "the color bar, justice, and the 'bar' between life and death," as noted by D. H. Melhem; they also, however, speak about the bar that the impotent, hostile veteran sets between himself and the girl he left behind.[83] Traumatized by the color bar, Brooks's gay chaps are horrified by a military establishment so racist that black combatants wonder about the government's white leaders, "Am I clean enough to kill for them?" and respond to that humiliating question by retaliating against women. As Harry B. Shaw has shown, the predicament Brooks's soldiers confront is the irony that "they are fighting the white man more than he was fighting the enemy."[84] What did it mean to the black soldier that he faced the contradiction of fighting for and within a system that denied him full humanity? According to Brooks, this tension would catapult him into rage against women, or so her poem "Negro Hero" implies. The speaker here, based on a mess attendant who won the Navy Cross at Pearl Harbor, confronts the irony that he guards what the white man loves and projects his rage by imagining the United States as a murderous white woman: "Their white-gowned democracy was my fair lady. / With her knife lying cold, straight, in the softness of her sweet-flowing sleeve" (33). While the embittered "Negro Hero" sneers at his own allegiance to this "fair lady," Brooks's mock heroic "Anniad" suggests that black male resentment instilled by racism and war effectively destroys black women.

The heroine of Brooks's stylistically dense verse epic is left by a lover she idolizes, the "man of tan" (84), not only when he goes off to war but also when he returns: "Soldier bare and chilly then / Wants his power back again" (87). Hunting for an antidote to his "impotence" with a succession of whores, and specifically with "a maple banshee" who is more exotic and less dark than Annie, he discovers how "woman fits for recompense" (88). "Wench, whiskey and tail-end / Of your overseas disease / Rot and rout" him (91), sending him back to Annie to be nursed. Brooks's first description of Annie—"Think of sweet and chocolate / Left to folly or to fate" (83)—contrasts sharply with her last portrait: "Think of almost thoroughly / Derelict and dim and done" (93). Indeed, because the actors in "The Anniad"'s plot are presented without voices of their own, the reader is left with an unmediated series of images of sexual disease which contrast sharply with the heroic ideals implicitly evoked through allusions to *The Iliad* and *The Aeneid*.

In the same years that Brooks wrote about the ways the war united soldiers, living and dead, while dividing them from women, such dissimilar artists as Wallace Stevens and Carson McCullers brooded on the same subject. Taken together, their meditations suggest that, even under the duress of suffering, the war functioned to consecrate bonds between men in a manner which isolated women. Stevens returned in one section of *Esthetique du Mal* (1944) to his earlier vision of brotherhood in "Sunday Morning" (1915)—"Supple and turbulent, a ring of men"—to compose a hymn to the fallen "soldier of time" that envisions a redemptive brotherhood set against the survival and separateness of a mysterious, even malevolent, female:

> The shadows of his fellows ring him round
> In the high night, the summer breathes for them
> Its fragrance, a heavy somnolence, and for him,
> For the soldier of time, it breathes a summer sleep.
>
> In which his wound is good because life was.
> No part of him was ever part of death.
> A woman smoothes her forehead with her hand
> And the soldier of time lies calm beneath that stroke.

Stevens—who asked in "Examination of the Hero in a Time of War" (1942), "Unless we believe in the hero, what is there / To believe?"—came to see the poet in wartime as a hero whose masculinity is mysteriously doubled, for "the poetry of war . . . constitutes a participating in the heroic" and the hero "arrives at the man-man as he wanted."[85]

But the shadows of fellows ringed round, the man-man in the military, constitute precisely the problem of McCullers's *Member of the Wedding* (1946), a text that analyzes mysteriously doubled masculinity by examining its heroine's inability to participate in the heroic and, by extension, its author's inability to write a work about war. McCullers's youthful heroine, Frankie Addams, who "wanted to be a boy and go to the war as a Marine," envies her older brother, who has joined the army to see the world, for "soldiers in the army can say we."[86] Within the claustrophobic heat of the kitchen she shares with the black housekeeper Berenice and her six-year-old cousin, John Henry, the war seems like just one more club that excludes Frankie, who "was not afraid of Germans or bombs or Japanese. She was afraid because in the war they would not include her and because the world seemed somehow separate from herself" (21).

Equally afraid that her only true community is composed of freaks, the tomboy Frankie gives herself a new name—F. Jasmine Addams—and believes that she can become a member of the war by becoming a member of her brother's wedding. But after Berenice tells a story about a black boy who "changed his nature and his sex," and John Henry asks, "How did that boy change into a girl?" Frankie, who is fond of exclaiming "Boyoman! Manoboy!" finds out what it means to change from a boy into a girl. She meets a soldier near the sign that reads "Prophylactic Military" and discovers that their conversation "would not join": the soldier talked "a kind of double-talk that, try as she would, she could not follow" (67).

Without a member of her own, Frankie learns that she cannot become a member of the war/wedding but must instead defend herself against the warriors. When the soldier finally takes her upstairs to his room at the Blue Moon Hotel and tries to get her to "quit this stalling" (130), she bites his tongue and brings a glass pitcher down on his head. But even Frankie's rebelliousness is relinquished after her brother and his wife reject her. First she admits that "she must find somebody, anybody that she could join with"—"she might as well ask the soldier to marry with her" (146)—and then she is accosted by "the Law," labeled "Royal Addams's daughter," and reclaimed by her father.[87] That Frankie's last act is watching the painful death of John Henry foreshadows the terrible induction into femininity McCullers would later explore in "The Ballad of the Sad Café," for John Henry has sworn not to tell anyone that Frankie "brained" a "crazy man": "If I tell I hope God will sew up my mouth and sew down my eyes and cut off my ears with the scissors" (132). The meningitis from which he suffers does sew up his mouth, eyes, and ears, just as his death signifies the demise of Frankie's childhood boy-self.

Significantly, McCullers's newly feminized heroine is fair game for a nameless draftee who is as vulnerable and isolated as she is. But *The Member of the Wedding* further analyzes the dynamics of dominance when Frankie's first act upon discovering that she cannot become a member of her brother's wedding is to call Berenice a "nigger" (135), for through Berenice's utopian vision of a peaceful world where there would be "no killed Jews and no hurt

colored people" (92), *The Member of the Wedding* makes an implicit claim that
Zora Neale Hurston articulates in *Dust Tracks on a Road* (1942)—namely
that Hitler's criminal actions in Europe subjected Europeans to the injustices
that had been inflicted on American blacks for centuries (339–42). Admit-
tedly controversial, this point is also established by Ann Petry in *The Street*
(1946), when Lutie Johnson's black employer and ultimate assailant, Boots
Smith, declares that "the people in the government hate Germans, but they
hate me worse," adding, "They're only doing the same thing in Europe that's
been done in this country since the time it started."[88]

     The prostitution of Brooks's Annie as well as the attempted rapes of
McCullers's Frankie and Petry's Lutie represent women's anxiety about even
the most embattled of men, an anxiety attributed by McCullers to the war
effectively wedding men to men. In a poem about a lover away fighting in the
Spanish Civil War, Rukeyser identifies his presence on the battlefield with
her own abandonment:

> I know how you recognized our war, and ran
> To it as a runner to his eager wedding
> Or our immediate love.

>   [230]

"Wedding" himself to the war, Rukeyser's beloved has effectively widowed
her. Whereas civilians were barraged with the injunction to buy "bonds,"
men in the forces and those who wrote about them found little if anything in
which to believe except the unity or camaraderie men achieved by virtue of
the holy bonds they established within the military.

     To begin with, whether male characters are turned into guilty voyeurs of
their own maneuvers or corpses decaying during enemy onslaughts, their
authors record a hopeless sense of emasculation. From Orwell's broken "last
man" to Jarrell's aborted airman, male characters are made to realize that the
gun always wins in its competition with the penis. Many enlisted men recorded their alienation from the aggression of warfare as a rejection of their
commanders: Howard Nemerov, for example, begins his remembrance
about the air war "Hate Hitler? No, I spared him hardly a thought. / But
Corporal Irmin, first, and later on / The O.C. (Flying), Wing Commander
Briggs, / And the station C.O. Group Captain Ormery— / Now there were
men were objects fit to hate."[89] And just as many soldiers, alienated from
their superior officers, turned toward their comrades, finding in what Richard Eberhart praised as the brotherhood of man men fit to love as well as a
fitting way to love men.

     Perhaps the finest novel written about the war, Norman Mailer's *The
Naked and the Dead*, illustrates how even those writers engaged in criticizing
the identification of the gun and the penis paradoxically reify the female to
rectify the relationships between men. General Cummings, a Faustian fas-

cist with repressed homosexual tendencies, derives joy solely from power and specifically from the "phallus-shell that rides through a shining vagina of steel," a fantasy Mailer is presumably ridiculing. Significantly, however, Cummings's obsession with coming is the result of the overprotectiveness of his mother and the bitchiness of his wife. In a telling parallel his working-class double, Croft, is sexually aroused by a machine gun because his wife has been unfaithful to him. Although Mailer's fictional surrogate, Captain Hearn, seeks an alternative to Cummings and Croft's dream of a "League of Omnipotent Men," he eventually discovers that what he needs most is "control and not mating." Finally, then, Mailer's novel confirms Cummings's creed, namely that "the average man always sees himself in relation to other men as either inferior or superior. Women play no part in it. They're an index, a yardstick among other gauges, by which to measure superiority."[90]

The female characters, whether dead, disloyal, or frigid wives; randy girlfriends; or raunchy whores, play no part in the action except as "gauges" located in the "Time Machine" sections that return us to civilian life before the war. Even love, which saves men from the "lie of Authority" and serves as an alternative to Cummings's philosophy of the will to power, is a love between men: when Ridges and Goldstein bear the burden of Wilson's syphilitic body back to the beach at the end of the novel, Wilson becomes their "heart." The brotherhood of Ridges, Goldstein, and Wilson resembles the camaraderie between men described in Joseph Heller's novel about World War II *Catch-22* (1962), where Yossarian is mystically linked to his dying comrade, Snowden. Peter Aichinger's claim that "the appeal to the team spirit is perhaps the only positive motivation mentioned in the novels of World War II" is similarly borne out in *From Here to Eternity* (1951), where James Jones presents two characters (Prewitt and Warden) moving from the here and now of poker, drinking, whoring, and brawling to a fraternity that causes both men to reject their mistresses in order to wed themselves to the military.[91]

Trying to capture the apocalyptic dynamic of war in a poem included in his 1943 essay "Looking Back on the Spanish War," Orwell fixes on its eroticism when he describes the ecstasy of shaking an Italian soldier's hand: "To meet within the sound of guns, / But oh! what peace I knew then / In gazing on his battered face / Purer than any woman's!"[92] Similarly, after describing a prison camp in which "those [who] survived best were feminine," Eberhart claims that "we were at our peak when in the depths," sustained by "visions of brotherhood when we were broken."[93] Although a homoerotic love for "pals" enabled the characters of World War I authors to achieve a union "passing the love of women," as Ford Maddox Ford put it, their descriptions of comradeship are usually more overtly sensual than those of their successors. For the medicalizing of homosexuality in the intervening years had made such homoerotic expressiveness either a crime or a symptom of sickness.[94]

Oddly enough, the morbidification of homosexuality by the medical establishment also contributed to the eroticization of women. In the one arena, the popular "soldier shows"—which enabled men who were gay to subvert antihomosexual policies by wearing dresses, makeup, and wigs and using double entendre to express themselves covertly—the scripts and characters remained blatantly heterosexual, even heterosexist. Soldiers in *This Is the Army* and *Stars and Gripes* performed in chorus lines decked out in WAC uniforms, singing "With a Gun on His Shoulder or a Girl on His Arm, You Can Tell He's a Yankee Doodle Dandy," while male illusionists and caricaturists played the roles of pinups and strippers, bombshells and broads: Marlene Dietrich, Carmen Miranda, Mae West, and Gypsy Rose Lee. Allan Bérubé's account of such shows stresses the encoded freedom homosexuals achieved through government sponsored drag performances that enabled them to "display their camp sensibilities"; fear of exposure, humiliation, and discharge, however, led gay men to camouflage themselves in aggressively heterosexual roles. Similarly, while the buddy system, which encouraged comrades to pair up together and which issued in popular songs like "My Buddy," may have enabled gay lovers to live and work together, as Bérubé claims, it also spawned a fear in men who were sleeping and suffering together that, unless they demonstrated desire for women, they would be forced to confess to a "sick addiction" and be confined to a "psych" ward.[95]

The bonding of what Stevens called the man-man, depicted in war novels as an index of the enlisted man's alienation from his commander, is presumed to be redemptive only when its eroticism does not become explicitly sexual, and it is therefore almost always set against male homosexuality, which is usually diagnosed as a psychotic response to the violence of battle. Worse than being labeled a whore is being called a queer or a fairy, for homosexuals are typically presented in World War II literature as guilt-ridden, pathologically violent, or suicidal. In the effort to differentiate what, in another context, Eve Kosofsky Sedgwick has called "homosocial desire" from homosexuality, both the girl he left behind and the whore play crucial roles, for—as the imagined object of male desire and as the body that links men to men—they ratify men as heterosexual.[96]

Confronting the boredom of "weary hours of waiting," rather than the "dramatic thunder" of military engagement, the soldiers in Timothy Corsellis's poem "What I Never Saw" (1940) sit "together as we sat at peace / Bound by no ideal of service / But by a common interest in pornography and a desire to outdrink one another."[97] While sailors in Bentz Plagemann's *The Steel Cocoon* (1958) object to "the whole mess that made [them] need women" and while they lament that "you never know until the last minute whether you're going to get in or not," often admitting "I just want to get my gun," such sentiments prove that the "satisfying relationship" between men and boys on the ship is "merely a normal expression of the capacity, or even the need, of all men for the love of one another."[98] When pilots, infantry soldiers, sailors, hospital inmates, and prisoners of war become "buddies" or "mates" in World War II fiction, they are united by their love for each other and defended from the charge of deviancy, which such love could provoke, by their scorn for homosexuals and by the credo that "men like to get their guns off."[99]

Understandably, then, many heroines in women's fiction about the war experienced it as a big brotherhood from which they were excluded. Cut off from communication with men, the wife in Dorothy Parker's "The Lovely Leave" (1944) realizes that her husband has found in the service "companionships no—no—wife can ever give [him]," and his leave proves to her that her husband has taken leave of her and virtually married his companions in the military.[100] Far from bequeathing security, women's status as outsiders left behind helped create the suspicion that male bonding in the military would effectively replace domestic bonds and make "left behind" women even more vulnerable. Therefore, in *The Children of Violence* series (1952–69), Doris Lessing analyzes the pregnant Martha Quest's realization that her husband's enlistment satisfies a lifelong hunger for fraternity that excludes her: "It seemed that his whole life had led without his knowing it to the climax of being with those men, his fellows, his friends, parts of himself, in real fighting, real living, real experience at last." Like Parker's heroine, Martha understands not only that "she was married to one of the boys; he would always, all his life, be one of the boys" but also that "the condition of being a woman in wartime . . . was that one should love not a man, but a man in relation to other men."[101] Thus, Lessing examines the dynamics bequeathed by what Stevens called the heroic arrival at "the man-man" and what McCullers considered the "wedding" of the "members" of the war.

———————

After Lessing's Martha Quest learns to "love not a man, but a man in relation to other men," why does she experience the "dangerous and attractive . . . intoxication of war"? And why does Lessing's later *The Golden Notebook* (1962) include a novel written by a woman horrified that her work records the "feverish illicit excitement of wartime"?[102] While literary women from Woolf to Brooks and McCullers protested against militarism as masculinism —worried about a new sexual explicitness that fused the figures of the girl left behind with the whore—and analyzed the homosocial bonding of soldiers or veterans, some of their postwar successors recorded a more intense sense of devastation, for their characters masochistically embrace a constellation of oppressive forces about which they feel helpless. Because, as Keith Douglas explained in "*Vergissmeinnicht*," during the war "the lover and the killer are mingled / who had one body and one heart," some female characters end up fatally in love with the killer. Like Elizabeth Bowen's Stella in *The*

Heat of the Day, they may decide that "from the point of view of nothing more than the heart any action was enemy action now" (142). Enemy action, in light of the feeling expressed by H. D. that the war was her husband, has less to do with militarism as a masculine problem and more with the sadomasochism instilled in male-female relationships shaped by what Lessing later called "the feverish illicit excitement of wartime." As if to elaborate upon that "intoxication" and sexual abuse, H. D.'s *Helen in Egypt* (1961) revises Homer's *Iliad* to focus on a character reared in an atmosphere contaminated by sexual violence: Helen, the daughter of Leda, who was raped by Zeus, has been abducted both by Theseus, who stole her away when she was a young maiden, and by Paris, who took her away from her husband. While *Helen in Egypt*, like *Trilogy*, suggests to some readers that the crisis of global war might enable both men and women to liberate themselves from a destructive sex antagonism that reflects and affects warfare, we will argue that it is significantly more pessimistic than the earlier epic.

Meditating on a question comparable to the one that Simone Weil had raised in her essay "The *Iliad*, Poem of Might" (1940–41)—"What does Helen matter to Ulysses?"—H. D.'s epic recalls Weil's answer: "Troy and Helen matter to the Greeks only as the causes of their shedding so much blood and tears; it is in making oneself master that one finds one is the master of horrible memories."[103] Like the Helen of Stevie Smith's "I had a dream . . ." (1962), who does not know "which of the Helen legends I was,"[104] H. D.'s heroine, the so-called cause of the Trojan War, attempts to extricate herself from the guilt which she has internalized, to disentangle Helen on the Egyptian beach from Helen on the ramparts at Troy. Implicitly revising not only Euripides' play *Helen in Egypt* and Stesichorus of Sicily's *Pallinode* but also Marlowe's, Goethe's, and Yeats's Helens, as well as Pound's Odysseus, H. D.'s verse passages are each prefaced by a prose narrative, one of which explains that "the Greeks and the Trojans alike fought for an illusion" created out of their need to "blame someone" (15).

What does Helen matter to Pound or to other mythologists of warfare, H. D. seems to ask. First, according to *Helen in Egypt*, the Greeks and the Trojans appear indistinguishable to the woman whose face launched a thousand ships: "so they fought, forgetting women, / hero to hero, sworn brother and lover, / and cursing Helen through eternity" (4). Second, the female is denounced as the cause of war. When Helen meets the wounded Achilles on the Egyptian beach, he attacks her ("for you were the ships burnt"), calls her a "witch" (16), and tries to strangle her. In addition, militarism is directly associated with male bonding: "the Command," which links past to present, becomes Achilles' "father, my brother, / my lover, my God"; it is an "iron-ring, unbreakable," "the hierarchy," that promises men, "You shall control the world" (61, 51–52). And finally, the role women play in war is a sacrificial one: not only is Helen punished for the fighting, but she is haunted by

Iphigenia, who was told she was going to wed Achilles, when in reality she was to be sacrificed to the gods in return for fair winds; by Cassandra, who was captured as a slave and raped by the foreign lord Agamemnon; by Clytemnestra, who could only strike back at her husband, Agamemnon, with "the Will-to-Power" (97) and therefore was herself doomed; and by Polyxena, Paris's sister, who was "slain to propitiate a ghost," Achilles (218).

What Helen thinks concerning her sister Clytemnestra—that "the War she endured was different" (99)—is true of herself as well. This difference is at first portrayed through Helen's status as a "phantom" in a "timeless time" (39, 40) that is constantly shifting in a phantasmagoric way. Although in her letters H. D. claimed that the time of the blitz was "very exciting" and that her mind "had switched, as it were, into another dimension," the "dimension out of time" (137) that Helen inhabits seems to turn her into a troubled shadow of herself.[105] What Vera Brittain suggests in her novel *Account Rendered* (1945)—namely that "after this [Second World] War many civilians, both men and women, would develop symptoms of a type hitherto mainly confined to men in the Forces"—is true of Helen, who exhibits the amnesia and anesthetization associated with battle fatigue.[106] Also, like *Account Rendered*, which portrays the recurrence of shell shock in a veteran of World War I who almost hypnotically murders his wife at the onset of the blitz, *Helen in Egypt* analyzes the femicidal impulses of its veteran, Achilles.

In *Account Rendered*, the repentant suffering of the hero and his expiation lead to rebirth: "Redeemed from egoism and fear he was indeed a new man, mentally and spiritually born again" (290). A number of critics have argued that H. D.'s Achilles evolves in a similar pattern, moving from his anger at the mother who forgot to give him immortality to his murderous assault on Helen to a redemptive process that turns him into "the New Mortal." According to this reading, to which most interpreters of the poem subscribe, H. D. agrees with Virginia Woolf that the war, by revealing "the need for emancipation from the old conception of virility" (*TG* 187), could liberate the male sex from aggression.[107] More troubling, however, is H. D.'s insistence throughout *Helen in Egypt* that women are destined to desire men whose repudiation of the mother and hatred of women are strongest. During the primal scene on the beach, when Achilles assaults her, Helen's response is notably erotic:

> O Thetis, O sea-mother,
> I prayed,
> as he clutched my throat
>
> with his fingers' remorseless steel,
> *let me go out, let me forget,*
> *let me be lost . . . . . .*

O Thetis, O sea-mother,
I prayed under his cloak,
let me remember, let me remember,
forever, this Star in the night.

[17; ellipses H. D.'s]

Later, dissenting from the advice of Theseus, the Freud figure, Helen answers affirmatively the question posed by the entire poem: "Does Zeus decree that, forever, / Love should be born of War?" (32). Fully convinced of the identity of "La Mort, L'Amour," she remembers "the hands that ringed my throat // and no moment's doubt, / this is Love, this is Death, / this is my last Lover" (268).

That Helen's desire for Achilles is a courtship with annihilation is confirmed by the identification of Achilles with "Dis, Hades" (199) and of Helen with "Kore, Persephone" (195). *La Mort,* entangled with *L'Amour,* turns the "wheel" or "circle" that weds the woman to the warrior. As one prose gloss explains, Helen remains "almost ready for this sacrifice—at least, for the immolation of herself before this greatest love of Achilles" (245). Indeed, she remains intoxicated by recollections of the attack on the beach, associating Achilles' desire with his rage and her fate with that of Iphigenia sacrificed at Aulis: "We stare and stare / over the smouldering embers," she recalls, "till I felt the touch / of his fingers' remorseless steel . . . / *for I have promised another / white throat to a goddess, / but not to our lady of Aulis*" (269–70; ellipses H. D.'s). Mesmerized by the idea that "what she invoked" may "destroy her," Helen as Circe or witch feels herself encircled by a snarling, prowling Achilles and brought back to the painful but desirous memory of "the touch / of his fingers' remorseless steel." Whereas Woolf called on women to "compensate the man for the loss of his gun," H. D.'s heroine seems to offer herself as a sacrificial compensation to the wounded veteran, Achilles.

H. D.'s flirtation with masochism is apparent not only in her depiction of Helen's adoration of Achilles but also in the later sequence *Vale Ave* (1957), which expresses the poet's own reverence for "the Master of the Air, the Air Marshal," Sir Hugh Dowding, who was commander of the Royal Air Force fighter pilots during the Battle of Britain and one of the possible models for Achilles.[108] In a scene in *Vale Ave* almost verging on the pornographic, H. D. describes how she responds with "agony" to "his hands grasp[ing] my bare thighs . . . that would tear open, tear apart" and "his commanding knees keep[ing] my knees locked": "my own hands clutch and tear, // and my lips part, as he releases me, and my famished mouth opens // and knows his hunger and his power" (47). Finally admitting her own subjugation not only to his "virility" but also to his spiritual primacy in deciphering the mysteries of transcendent truths—"Hugh was right, 'no woman / should explore these devious rites'"—the poet seems to relinquish the authority of the word and its mystical rituals to "the Air Lord and his pride" (57). Her last vision of their union—"he turned to attack her, crowned" (68)—captures not only the violence of his desire but her desire for violent violation.

Similarly, in *Helen in Egypt*, Helen illustrates H. D.'s belief that women are bound to be enthralled not by Paris, the lover, but by Achilles, the warrior, whose impassioned grief over his loss of omniscience—his rage against his mother—will perpetually threaten to obliterate Helen, a script that illuminates H. D.'s feeling that she was married to the war. Like Simone Weil, then, H. D. implies that when women experience a capacity to love in the midst of the brutality of warfare, "this love could only be for the master. Every other way is barred to the gift of loving."[109] The "remorseless steel" of Achilles' fingers ringing Helen's throat resembles nothing so much as the unbreakable "iron-ring" of the military "Command," an echo that enables H. D. to meditate on the enmeshed terms *eros* and *eris*, *L'Amour* and *La Mort*, even as it forecasts Sylvia Plath's "Every woman adores a Fascist / the boot in the face, the brute / Brute heart of a brute like you" ("Daddy," *PCP* 223).

The sadomasochistic love battle H. D. presents through Helen and Achilles surfaces in the relationships between the passengers who are journeying toward war on Katherine Anne Porter's *Ship of Fools* (1962). One of her female characters is haunted by a vision of a murderous struggle in which a man and woman "swayed and staggered together in a strange embrace, as if they supported each other; but in the man's raised hand was a long knife, and the woman's breast and stomach were pierced. The blood ran down her body and over her thighs, her skirts were sticking to her legs with her own blood. She was beating him on the head with a jagged stone, and his features were veiled in rivulets of blood." This anonymous woman, clinging to her mate in "rage and hatred," serves as a prototype for a number of the women on board the *Vera:* the two whores who enjoy being beaten by their pimps, for example, or the imprisoned Condesa who asks to be injected and sent into a drugged sleep by a physician-admirer.[110] Just as disturbingly, in the section of *The Golden Notebook* devoted to World War II, Doris Lessing describes a series of sadomasochistic relationships that prove to her protagonist Anna Wulf "how many women like to be bullied," while in Lessing's *Four-Gated City* (1969) Martha Quest's lover Jack, who had been wounded as a minesweeper during the war, eventually salves his haunting sense of mortality by becoming a sadistic pimp who initiates young girls into what he teaches them to consider degrading sexual acts. For H. D.'s, Porter's, and Lessing's characters, all half in love with death, "the secret ugly frightening pulse of war itself" is, in the words of Anna Wulf, the "delicious intoxication" in "the death that we all wanted, for each other and for ourselves."[111]

Although many critics have read *Helen in Egypt* as a joyous excavation of the maternal principle, Helen's isolation in a ring of supple and turbulent men like Achilles, Paris, and Theseus can be said to symbolize the breakdown of the female community. Without her daughter, her mother, and her sister, Helen is a phantom, a shadow, reduced by the war to a no-woman. Significantly, then, the only mother-goddess in the poem is a mother-in-law, who welcomes an epithalamion in "timeless time" which resembles nothing so much as the *liebestod* of Edith Sitwell's "Serenade." In this respect, H. D.'s late works typify the ways women writers of the fifties and sixties use the occasion of World War II to deliberate not only on the vulnerability of its survivors but also on the disintegration of the dream of Herland.

From Stein's worry about women becoming as afraid as men to Boyle's image of the mazurka of women as a pas seul and Brooks's isolated Annie, the writings of literary women brooded on the breakdown of a feminist dream of women's commonality.[112] From the fifties on, however, literary women as different as Harriet Arnow, Djuna Barnes, Paule Marshall, Muriel Spark, and Jean Rhys developed one of the insights found in *Helen in Egypt*, namely the ways in which the war divided women from one another and instilled various forms of self-division. Survival guilt, shell shock, the fragility of the home, postwar economic declines, sexual violence: all undermined or discredited the dream of Herland celebrated by earlier feminist writers. Three otherwise quite dissimilar works—Arnow's *The Dollmaker* (1954), Barnes's *The Antiphon* (1958), and Marshall's *Brown Girl, Brownstone* (1959)—suggest that the war inducted mothers into a public world that was hostile to their children. Assimilation or adjustment becomes a major theme in these books, one that dramatizes the tragic consequences for mothers complicitous in systems dangerous to their daughters' survival.

Fierce conflicts between mothers and daughters, the inadequacy of the family as a survival mechanism for children, and the threats posed to female artistry are examined in sociological and religious terms by *The Dollmaker*. "How shall we sing the Lord's song in a strange land?" Arnow's heroine wonders after she has been dislocated by the war, and Arnow implies that, exiled from Herland and repatriated inside a dollhouse, the female artist can only become a dollmaker.[113] To the extent that *The Dollmaker* describes the divisions between women and the impossibility of female artistry through a critique of the theory that the Second World War liberated women by catapulting them in unprecedented numbers into the labor market, it prefigures the use of the war as a metaphor in Barnes's and Marshall's works.

In *The Dollmaker* Gertie Nevels saves the money she gains from a brother, Henley, who was killed in the war, to buy "a place of her own," adjoining her father's property. While her husband, Clovis, is away, working in the Detroit war industry, she muses: "Almost every day she would see her father. His land touched her land—her land, *her* land" (134). At first, therefore, Gertie believes that "the war and Henley's death had been a plan to help set her and her children free so that she might live and be beholden to no man, not even to Clovis" (139). Yet, although she plans to stay in Kentucky, planting crops and tracing the war routes of absent husbands for women left behind, Gertie is converted by her mother's Pauline doctrine that wives should "be in subjection unto your husbands" (141) and goes to join Clovis in Detroit. Effectively expelled from the Edenic fields of Kentucky, she lands in the dark satanic mills of Detroit, where natural rhythms are supplanted by the work shifts at the steel factories. Instead of homemade food, furniture, and books, an "Icy Heart" refrigerator dominates her tiny kitchen, while radios, movies, and educators spout a fallen language that is almost incomprehensible to Gertie, who must learn to understand what words like *hillbilly, kike, spic, commie,* and—most important—*adjustment* mean.

That Gertie has lost not only her own land but a dream of Herland is made clear through the fates of her neighbors, her children, and her art. Living among women who work in the war industry, Gertie watches her neighbors juggling paid (industrial) and unpaid (childcare) work and driven to drugs or drink to ease their sense of fragmentation. Although she herself stays at home, thereby escaping the fate of a woman who is "squashed to death in her press" (317), Gertie also feels oppressed, especially by her new dependency on her wage-earning husband: "Here everything, even to the kindling wood, came from Clovis" (338). In addition, she observes her children variously respond to the adjustment that is required of them at school. Given her own ambivalence, she hardly knows whether it is better for them to rebel openly and return home, as her oldest son does, or to conform aggressively, as her oldest daughter does. Worse still, Gertie witnesses the destruction of her most gifted child, Cassy, who is literally split in two by a railroad train that amputates her legs.

Early in the novel Cassy, who has created an imaginary friend named Callie Lou, identifies her with a huge piece of cherry wood that Gertie is in the process of whittling. Gertie is at first unsure whether the figure in the wood is "the laughing Christ with hair long and black like Callie Lou's" or "the Judas she had pitied giving back the silver" (127), but she relinquishes her artistry after her daughter's death. Striking with an ax until "the wood cried out," she splits the image to provide herself with the material she needs to produce the machine-made crosses and painted dolls that sell in Detroit. Gertie discovers that her Christlike self-sacrifice of her land was satanically self-subverting, for her renunciation of her own land has effectively turned her into a dollmaker who consigns her children to a culture perpetually at war. By the end of the novel the war has ended, but violent battles against unionization have begun. While her racist neighbors are celebrating the dropping of the atomic bomb ("Now, I figger them Japs around u atom bomb is kinda like them bugs"), a woman with a wounded husband articulates the general realization of the wives: "I don't guess a woman can ever find a job, now" (494, 495).

More oblique but just as bleak in its depiction of the war as a defeat of women, Barnes's autobiographical closet drama *The Antiphon* takes place in 1939, inside a bomb-damaged ancestral mansion. In a setting littered with battered statues (including a dummy in a British soldier's uniform), an actress-writer attends a family reunion that evokes T. S. Eliot's play of that name. This gathering mourns a primal rape scene, for Barnes's heroine, Miranda, remembers how her father persuaded her to submit sexually to an old Cockney traveler. Looking into a dollhouse, Miranda is haunted not only by her father, a "Devil" with "a raping-hook," but also by her mother, "a *madam* by submission"; both parents had "made / Of that doll's *abattoir* a babe's *bordel*."[114] To the horror of the victim of incest, the collusion of parents has prostituted the child. The ruin of the war becomes the site for the ruin of her life, first, when her brothers attempt to murder her along with her mother and then at the end of the play, when the mother and daughter who had been divided in life exchange costumes and embrace each other in a suicidal union that leaves two entrepreneurial brothers in charge of a world at war. Only the convoluted conceits of Jacobean drama can express the despair Barnes's Miranda experiences not in a brave new world but in the old world of the dollhouse, which is associated with the sexual exploitation of the father and the complicity of the mother.

Like *The Dollmaker* and *The Antiphon*, *Brown Girl, Brownstone* deals with the war as a symbolic assimilation of the mother into a system injurious to her daughter. In Marshall's Brooklyn community of West Indian immigrants, the mother who works in the war industry appears alien and destructive to her children. As if enlarging upon Adrienne Rich's dictum that "the price of external assimilation is internal division,"[115] Marshall implies that the mother who functions as a socializing agent for a hostile society is a war victim who perpetuates war. *Brown Girl, Brownstone*'s Silla Boyce becomes a drudge as she works in the war factories during the night shift and in her kitchen during the days, while her husband, Deighton, idly dreams about the piece of land he has inherited in Barbados. Not only does the "formidable force" of "the mother," as Silla is usually called, "match that of the machines" producing shells, but she also exerts her will by usurping her husband's authority.[116] Specifically, behind his back she writes in his name to Barbados and sells his land in order to gain the money she needs to buy a house in Brooklyn. The forgeries are a fitting symbol of Silla's inability to find security except by conforming to a ruthless ethic of competition and by denying both her love for her husband and her own identity.

As indebted to the images of Eliot's poetry as is Barnes's play, this novel presents Deighton—"a hollow man" (116)—seeking his own obliteration by joining a religious cult in which he relinquishes adult responsibility to a "Father Peace," who teaches that "the word *mother* is a filthy word" (168). Then, after "the mother" has him deported as an illegal alien, he takes a suicidal leap from the boat returning him to Barbados and thereby attains a

virtually mythic "death by water." The earlier section of the novel entitled
"The War" describes the war between this couple, a series of battles which
Deighton loses, to the horror of their daughter Selina, who is revolted by the
way in which her father is "unmanned" and who fights "the mother," whom
she calls "Hitler." Like Brooks, Hurston, and Petry, Marshall explicitly views
World War II as, in Silla's words, "another white-man war" (65). But by the
end of the novel Silla herself has destroyed the female community in her own
home: not only has her daughter left, but the white and black roomers who
befriended Selina in her growing up have been expelled by the force of "the
mother's" will.

Muriel Spark and Jean Rhys, writing later, identify the war with morally
impoverished communities composed not of women but of aging girls, girls
as catty as the bitchy characters in Clare Boothe's satiric *The Women* (1936).
Framed by V-E and V-J day celebrations, Spark's *Girls of Slender Means*
(1963) is set in one of the cheap hostels "which had flourished since the
emancipation of women had called for them"; however, its inhabitants—
who worship "Poise" and produce fake fan letters to literary men so as to sell
handwritten responses—are characterized as superficial and solipsistic.[117]
When an undetonated bomb explodes in the garden and destroys the hostel,
the girls who survive are those who are the most metaphysically and physically slender. Similarly, Jean Rhys's short story "The Insect World" (1976)
describes the competition between "old girls" worn down by fly bombs,
shortages, rationing, and overwork. Rhys's heroine, who "hated most
women," suffers from a nightmare that she has been infected by a noxious,
infected insect world that symbolizes her sense of the home front.[118]

But although both Rhys and Spark analyze the inadequacies of women's
values and relationships, they also dramatize female vulnerability. Rhys's
heroine finds herself shocked by marginalia penciled in a book by its earlier
owner, markings as sinister as the tropical insects described within the volume: on one page, "He had written 'Women are an unspeakable abomina-
tion' with such force that the pencil had driven through the paper," a sentence that fills her with terror at "the hidden horror . . . that was responsible
for all the other horrors" (352). Even more malevolent, amid the joyous
crowds commemorating V-J day in the London rally that concludes Spark's
Girls of Slender Means, a young sailor quietly slips a knife between the ribs of
the girl at his side. For both Rhys and Spark, the war marks the fall of
Herland, the rise of a misogynist Hisland, into which women are assimilated
at the cost of their lives. Toni Morrison's *Sula* (1973), if read as a historical
novel, also identifies the war years with the destruction of women and their
relationships. *Sula* begins with a portrait of Shadrack, a shell-shocked veteran of World War I, and dates the rift in the friendship between Sula and
Nell in 1939 and the death of Sula—whose last name is "Peace"—in 1940,
one year before a large proportion of the people in their town go down to

death on the annual holiday Shadrack has set aside as "National Suicide Day."

That the no man's land of World War I was followed by the no woman's land of World War II made total war an apt image of contemporary women writers' anxiety about their authority and authorship. Meditating on her personal poetic development, Jane Cooper explained that "by 1951 the war had begun to seem like a mask, something to write through in order to express a desolation that had become personal," and she went on to quote one of her poems from that period:

> Guilt, war, disease—pillars of violence
> To keep a roof of symbols over my head.
> Still the rain soaks my bed
> Whenever the wind blows, riddling innocence.[119]

While Cooper echoes Edith Sitwell's "Still Falls the Rain" to record her sense of the hopeless inadequacy of her linguistic shelters, Wanda Coleman, in a poem entitled "No Woman's Land" (1979), presents herself as occupied enemy territory:

> they trample on my sensitivity
> goose-step thru streets of my affection
> line me up before the firing squad of insecurity, shoot me down
>
> when the smoke clears
> my corpse interred
> they sing my praises in a hymn.

Although she concludes the poem with a defiant exclamation—"no white flag of truce / no surrender"—Coleman uses the death mask of the Second World War to protest against a blitz on herself and on "Woman's Land."[120]

Less metaphorically and more historically grounded in the war, the fates of the representative female characters in Marge Piercy's novel *Gone to Soldiers* (1987) delineate the damage done to women forced to imitate feminine or masculine roles after the war to escape the horror of no-womanhood. A female war correspondent, traumatized by the atrocities she has witnessed on the European front, returns to a career of romance writing for women's magazines and to an ex-husband she had previously hated because "he had not valued their marriage enough to preserve it."[121] Another woman, a wasp/flyer put out of commission by the cessation of war, can only continue to pilot planes by wearing men's clothes and passing as a man, a ploy that also enables her to withstand homosexual baiting. A laid-off factory worker, whose Marine lover has been subjected to the murderous brutality of Japanese island combat, finds herself nursing "a man who killed and killed and who weeps about it" (743). Because the dislocation and destruction of the war demonstrated the vulnerability of the family, Piercy implies, perhaps only a reconstruction of strikingly traditional gender roles could salve anxieties about national and personal security, or so the historian Elaine Tyler May has also speculated.[122]

But of course atomic bombs and concentration camps put into question the future of the whole human race, rendering all sex roles strikingly fictive. For two newly married intelligence officers in *Gone to Soldiers*, the "something new" that occurred at Hiroshima resembles nothing so much as a "void. A force that turns people from breathing flesh into an image on stone, like a photograph," that presages the "future . . . [as] a plain of ashes, of sand turned to glass, flesh vaporized, time itself burned up" (755–56). Piercy's Jewish heroine is more personally threatened: she is starved and overworked, undressed and beaten, shaved and numbered in Birkenau, and eventually becomes disabused of her fantasy that she can survive by "imagin[ing] that her body was hidden inside an imitation body. The men could only see the imitation rubber body, but she was the bones hidden inside that they could not see or touch" (626).

Encased in her "charred skirts and deathmask," the speaker of Plath's "Getting There" (1962) reacts to a boxcar of "legs, arms piled outside / The tent of unending cries— / A hospital of dolls" with the vision of a reborn but inarticulate self arising "pure as a baby" out of the "black car of Lethe" (*PCP* 249). Both Plath's sense of herself as a displaced person and her belief that the only utterance available to her is a language of lamentation reflect the elegiac tone that accompanies the crowing of Bishop's cocks, the brooding of Brooks's veterans, the "G.I. talk" of Boyle's war brides, Sitwell's "discordant" lullabies and serenades, the incomprehensible "double-talk" of McCullers's soldier, H. D.'s liebestod, Gertie Nevel's crying wood, and Marshall's and Spark's female forgeries, all signs not only of women's psychological but also of their linguistic sense of loss. As Burdekin's *Swastika Night* had predicted, that loss was related to the "Reduction of Women" to no-women: hens, whores, battered corpses, ghosts, dolls, dollmakers, and aging girls.

Perhaps so many literary women mourned their aesthetic impotence and questioned the viability of female community because of pressures exerted by the war which issued in divisions between, say, black and white, Asian and Caucasian, or Jewish and gentile women, a number of whom found ample cause to blame each other for failures of moral and material support. As we have seen, McCullers, Brooks, and Petry criticized Allied propaganda not only by uncovering the "we" of the war as white and male but also by suggesting that it posed different problems for women of different colors even as it set them at odds. But in writings about the Holocaust and about Japanese-American internment camps, women seemed intent on explaining why women should beware women.

After the revelation of the atrocities in the concentration camps, Jewish writers like Muriel Rukeyser as well as gentiles from Katherine Anne Porter to Sylvia Plath felt that, to quote Plath, "I think I may well be a Jew" ("Daddy," *PCP* 153).[123] Because so many literary women viewed fascist ideology as a form of masculinism, because they suffered militarism as an assault, because they were imbued with the guilt of victimization, and because they saw themselves caught in a threatening assimilation process, not a few of them identified the vulnerability of women with the extermination of the Jews; but even as they examined the metaphorical relationship between womanhood and Jewishness, they confronted the immorality of the analogy.

Such an imaginative equation, of course, has a long history, going back to Margaret Fuller and Olive Schreiner, who observed that prejudice against Jews was a consequence of the same self-certifying mythology that enslaved blacks and women.[124] At the same time, femininity and Jewishness had been conflated in anti-Semitic texts like Otto Weininger's *Sex and Character* (1903), which claimed that "Judaism is saturated with femininity. . . . The most manly Jew is more feminine than the least manly Aryan." Similarly, Hitler, in his efforts to limit German women to traditionally nurturing roles (*Kinder, Kirche, Küche*), promulgated the idea that "the emancipation of women" was the product of the "Jewish mind."[125] An early literary protest against genocide written by a Christian woman, Ada Jackson's *Behold the Jew* (1943) eschews silence in the face of outrage—"If I keep silence all these things / are done of me and in my name, / and mine the guilt of bludgeonings / and massacres"—even as it indicts its readers: "While you read they die."[126] Adumbrating subsequent literary meditations on the Holocaust, Jackson addresses the unnegotiable gulf between Jewish sufferers ("they die") and female as well as male observers ("you read").

For the Jewish observer, of course, the Holocaust demands a witness. Like Rukeyser's "To Be a Jew in the Twentieth Century," a sonnet in "Letter to the Front," later works by writers as different as Adrienne Rich, Irena Klepfisz, Susan Fromberg Schaeffer, Norma Rosen, Cynthia Ozick, and Lore Segal describe Jewishness as a tragic double bind, a gift it is fatal to refuse or accept:

> If you refuse,
> Wishing to be invisible, you choose
> Death of the spirit, the stone insanity.
> Accepting, take full life. Full agonies:
> Your evening deep in labyrinthine blood
> Of those who resist, fail, and resist; and God
> Reduced to a hostage among hostages.
>
> [139]

Besides producing a body of literature dedicated to exploring what it means to be a Jew in the twentieth century and to remembering what Rukeyser described as "Full agonies," identification with Jewish suffering may help explain why the first important works produced by the so-called second wave of feminism relied on a comparison between women and Jews. In *The Second Sex* (1949), Simone de Beauvoir introduced her analysis of the construction of the feminine by deflating stereotypes of "the Jewish character" and "the eternal feminine," reminding her readers that the "Jewish problem" and "the woman problem" are not made by Jews or women. Betty Friedan, considering the housewife in the home and the prisoner in a concentration camp, alluded to Bruno Bettelheim's work on the "zombies" who inhabited Nazi camps. Friedan's *Feminine Mystique* (1963) argued that "the comfortable concentration camp that American women have walked into, or have been talked into by others, is . . . a frame of reference that denies woman's adult human identity."[127]

Significant as the comparison of the concentration camp to the housewife's space was for Friedan, however, for obvious reasons she found it necessary to conclude her discussion by explaining, "The suburban house is not a German concentration camp, nor are American housewives on their way to the gas chamber" (309). Her reservations about the analogy hint at the discomfort it could also produce in non-Jewish women. When Elizabeth Bishop wrote a poem which locates a "Jew in a newspaper hat" and the anti-Semite Ezra Pound in a madhouse, her adjectives for the poet demote him from "tragic" and "honored" to "cranky" and "wretched" not because, as one critic claims, "his simple nobility is smothered by the weakness, fragility, and insipidity of the other inmates" but because his delusions are no less pathetic than theirs. Bishop's title—"Visits to St. Elizabeths" (1950)—alludes to the hospital that housed Pound and she regulates her verse through the nonsensical, indeed cannibalistic, rhythms of "The House that Jack Built" to imply that the suffering of both poet and Jew is contained within an insane structure that even she, an Elizabeth herself, may not be able to escape.[128] From Marianne Moore to Stevie Smith, literary women explored their hatred of anti-Semitism but also their consciousness that, like Moore, they were "not competent" to promise never to hate black, white, red, yellow, Jew or their awareness of what Stevie Smith called the "final treachery of the smug goy."[129] At the same time, a number of women writers responded to the Holocaust by demonstrating that women were as guilty as men of evading their responsibilities for a previously unimaginable evil. Both Kay Boyle's "Winter Night" (1946) and Flannery O'Connor's "The Displaced Person" (1955), for example, use the ethical issues raised by the Holocaust to criticize the naïveté and jingoism of American women.

In "Winter Night," a survivor is driven to relive with the American child for whom she is babysitting a maternal role she played for a motherless girl in the camps. Besides alluding to the impossibility of communicating the terror of the European camps to Americans, the story hints at the survivor's continued entrapment in an experience that breeds grief and rage, for the

Jewish babysitter has cause to resent gentile mothers not only ignorant but somehow luckier than she.[130] "The Displaced Person," which represents Catholic rather than Jewish victims of the Holocaust, more scathingly condemns American women as responsible for the destruction of displaced people. Locating her story on the farm of Mrs. McIntyre, O'Connor shows why Mrs. McIntyre and her hired workers, Mr. and Mrs. Shortley, effectively collude in the murder of a Catholic immigrant who has fled "the ovens and the boxcars" of his native Poland. Ironically, what horrifies them about Mr. Guizac is his effort to rescue his niece from rooms "piled high with bodies of dead people all in a heap, their arms and legs tangled together," by marrying her to a black worker on the farm. Because Mrs. McIntyre and Mrs. Shortley are motivated by precisely the idea of "wise blood" that led to the laws against miscegenation in Europe, they deserve the punishment they receive when they are themselves turned into displaced people.[131]

As distrustful of female merits as O'Connor, Doris Lessing's heroine in *Four-Gated City* confronts what she calls "the self-hater" by coming to terms with the fact that "*I am 'The Germans are the mirror and catalyst of Europe' and also: 'Dirty Hun, Filthy Nazi.'*"[132] In the context of the Holocaust, literary women necessarily confronted the guilt they shared with the rest of the world. Paradoxically, however, the very failure of the metaphorical equation of woman and Jew as well as guilt about its use foregrounded the difficulty of articulating female experiences in anything but borrowed terms. Such an aesthetic problem propels not only the grotesque stories of Boyle and O'Connor but also the very different ironies of, say, Sylvia Plath, for whom the Holocaust became a key metaphor.

Just as the Holocaust clearly called into question the savage nature of Western (and Western women's) culture, the internment of Japanese Americans was experienced as such a catastrophe that its literature only began appearing several decades after the fact. A retrospective poem entitled "To the Lady" (1976) by the Nisei writer Mitsuye Yamada best exemplifies the distrust and rage that resulted from divisions between women set in place by the prison camps. The lady of the title had asked, "Why did the Japanese Americans let / the government put them in those camps without protest?" and the speaker of the poem answers in two bitter stanzas. First, she ironically enumerates the extravagant lengths to which she herself should have gone—"should've bombed a bank / should've tried self-immolation / should've holed myself up in a / woodframe house / and let you watch me / burn up on the six o'clock news"—and then she sarcastically predicts, "YOU would've / come to my aid in shining armor / laid yourself across the railroad track / marched on Washington." The poem concludes with both women's failure— "we didn't draw the line"—a failure that has effectively put them on two different sides: "YOU let'm / I let'm / All are punished."[133]

The "we" which the war turns into an antagonistic "YOU" and "I" in

Yamada's poem has been split as definitively as it is in Ada Jackson's warning "While you read they die." Like their male contemporaries, many literary women believed that World War II marked the end of an age of innocence. Meditating on childhood's end, Muriel Spark's story "The First Year of My Life" (1975) uses the uncanny intelligence of a baby born at the end of World War I to express the author's disillusionment with modernity. Only after hearing former Prime Minister Asquith's claim that since the Great War "'All things have become new'" does this infant smile the knowing grimace of the damned.[134] Preternaturally old before her time, Spark's cynical child foresees that the promised "new" of the post-World War I generation might lead to a recycling of the past in what Lessing called the nightmare repetition of history she herself portrayed in her aptly named *Children of Violence* novels. After the Second World War, women of letters joined many of their male contemporaries in expressing despair at the nightmare repetitions of bankrupt sexual scenarios. Significantly, however, just as the assault on masculinity during World War I produced many of the strongest works associated with male modernism, so the blitz on women during World War II contributed to the formation of a female literary tradition which mourns the demise of the dream of Herland even as it documents female artistic survival behind a mask, a survival achieved only with the rictus of a grin set in place.

In Yeats's House:
The Death and Resurrection
of Sylvia Plath

6

I have a violence in me that is hot as death-blood. I can kill myself or—I
know it now—even kill another. I could kill a woman, or wound a man. I
think I could.

—Sylvia Plath

How did she prepare?

What salt was her shield?
What lime was her spur?
What phosphorus her visor?

—Ted Hughes

Climb to your chamber full of books and wait,
No books upon the knee. . . .
                    What climbs the stair?
Nothing that common women ponder on
If you are worth my hope! Neither Content
Nor satisfied Conscience, but that great family
Some ancient famous authors misrepresent,
The Proud Furies each with her torch on high.

—W. B. Yeats

Well, here I am! Safely in Yeats' house! . . . I feel Yeats' spirit blessing me.

—Sylvia Plath

In 1955 Sylvia Plath published a somewhat conventional little story about the
sort of childhood trauma that has been stock material for many twentieth-
century writers. Entitled "Superman and Paula Brown's New Snowsuit," the
first-person tale, set at the beginning of World War II, recounts an incident
in which the eight- or nine-year-old narrator is unjustly accused of pushing a
neighbor's child into a puddle of oil and ruining the girl's new snowsuit.

Significantly, however, the apparently trivial episode is consistently juxtaposed with references to the war. The narrator wins a prize for drawing the
best Civil Defense signs; watches a classmate parody a Nazi goose step; has
bad dreams about a movie she sees that is set in a Japanese prison camp;
identifies her uncle (who is living with her and her mother "while waiting to
be drafted") with Superman; and listens, "feeling a queer foreboding," as
her mother and uncle "talk . . . of planes and German bombs. Uncle Frank
[said] something about Germans in America being put in prison for the
duration and Mother kept saying over and over again about Daddy: 'I'm
only glad Otto didn't live to see this.'"[1] Moreover, when she remembers
realizing that nobody believed her innocence in the matter of the snowsuit,
the narrator summarizes her experience with what seems an inappropri-
ately large generalization, in which the war becomes both metaphor and
subject: "That was the year the war began, and the real world, and the
difference" (*JP* 275).

That for Plath "the real world" continued to be the world of "the war" is
suggested by both the widely noted and controversial references to the Holocaust and Hiroshima in her *Ariel* poems and her use of a war-haunted quotation from Louis MacNeice's "Aubade" as one of three epigraphs for her
journals: "What have we . . . to look forward to? // Not the twilight of the
gods but a precise dawn / of sallow and grey bricks, and newsboys crying
war."[2] And her obsession with World War II is further demonstrated by her
new version of the story, "The Shadow," written four years later.

Again the piece is set during "the winter the war began" and again the
narrator recounts a childhood incident in which she was unfairly chastised,
this time for biting a neighbor's little boy on the leg during a slapstick fight.
Again, too, the children in the tale design Civil Defense badges, have nightmares about war movies, and admire popular heroes (now the Green Hornet
and the Shadow). But here the connection between the war and the "crime"
for which the protagonist has been punished becomes quite explicit: explains the boy's sister, "My mother says it's not your fault for biting
Leroy. . . . It's because your father's German," and another child taunts,
"How do you know he's not a spy?" (*JP* 149). Worse still, as the tale draws to a
close, the narrator learns that her father, although willing to fight for the
Allies, has been sent to one of the "places out West for German citizens to live
in during the war so people will feel safer about them" (150). When the child
protests that "God won't let it happen," her mother responds, "It's government orders. . . . God will let it happen." "I don't think there is any God
then," the girl concludes, and her mother quietly agrees: "Some people
think that" (151). The good Shadow who teaches children that "Crime does
not pay" (148) and "who knows what evil lurks in the hearts of men" has
definitively modulated into a "shadow in my mind . . . blotting out our half
of the world, and beyond it" (151), a shadow of the battle that has arisen from
the evil lurking in the hearts of men.

The conflation in these two stories of human guilt and divine indifference, of the fall from innocence to experience and the rise of warfare, of struggles between children and battles between and within nations foreshadows a complex set of references to warfare that was increasingly to mark Plath's writing as, in the spring of 1962, she began to break through into the vivid style of the *Ariel* poems. To be sure, the theme of battle, often dramatized as battle between the sexes, though repressed, disguised or evaded in her more decorous early verse, does appear in other youthful prose works. In "Sunday at the Mintons'" (1952), for example, an oppressed elderly spinster fantasizes that her older brother drowns while she flies away, witchlike, uttering a "high-pitched, triumphant, feminine giggle" (*JP* 305). In "Stone Boy, with Dolphin" (1957–58) the protagonist, Dody Ventura, bites the poet Leonard, in a scene that parallels the narrator's biting in "The Shadow" (and that reenacts an incident in Plath's own meeting with her husband-to-be, Ted Hughes).[3] In "The Fifty-Ninth Bear" (1959) the heroine, Sadie (who has the same name as the narrator of "The Shadow"), triumphantly prophesies the appearance of a bear that kills her husband on a camping trip.[4] But as Plath evolved what was to become her mature style, metaphors drawn from World War II frequently replaced delineations of combat between individuals, not only to enact conflicts within the poet herself, torn between guilt over her German ancestry and grief for her German father, but also to explore sexual battles, literary campaigns, the horrifying ruptures of all human history, and the ghastly torpor of a god who, as Plath writes in "Lyonesse," has "had so many wars" that "the white gape of his mind [is] the real Tabula Rasa."[5]

In "Daddy," of course, Plath defines herself as "a bit of a Jew," her father as a "Panzer-man," and her husband as "a man in black with a Meinkampf look" (*PCP* 223–24), while in "Lady Lazarus" she calls her skin "bright as a Nazi lampshade" and her antagonist first "Herr Doktor . . . Herr Enemy" and then "Herr God, Herr Lucifer" (244, 246).[6] In "Fever 103°" the "yellow sullen smokes" of moral as well as mortal illness grease "the bodies of adulterers / Like Hiroshima ash" (231); in "Nick and the Candlestick" the speaker tries to ignore "the mercuric / Atoms that cripple" (242); and in "Cut" she defines her wounded thumb as a "Saboteur" or "Kamikaze man" (235). Even in some of these World War II-haunted poems, however, the metaphors of warfare widen to refer not just to the specific blitzes of that conflict but to all the blitzes on innocence evoked by World War II's initiation of children into the war of life that constitutes "the real world" and "the difference".

In "Cut," for instance, the "many wars" that "the big God" had "lazily" ignored (according to "Lyonesse," written three days earlier) merge with the war in which "Saboteur" and "Kamikaze man" participated, to become the one unending conflict of history which the speaker internalizes as she compares her thumb to a "little pilgrim" whose scalp has been "axed" by an

Indian, her bandage to a "gauze Ku Klux Klan / Babushka," and her flowing blood to "a million soldiers . . . Redcoats, every one" and wonders, tellingly, "Whose side are they on?" (235). Similarly, in "Getting There," the train through whose boxcars the poet imagines dragging herself blurs into "the black car of Lethe," while World War II becomes simply "some war or other," and the earth at the train stop where nurses tend the wounded modulates into "Adam's side, / This earth I rise from, and I in agony" (247–49). Later, in "Mary's Song," as the "Sunday lamb" of God "cracks in its fat," the ovens of "burnt-out / Germany" that "glowed like heavens, incandescent," merge into a horrific pagan/Christian myth of sanctified violence that Plath sees as the true "heart" of her culture:

> It is a heart,
> This holocaust I walk in,
> O golden child the world will kill and eat.
>
> [257]

Even in "Daddy," the Polish town where the frightening Nazi father originated is not just a metonym for World War II: it is an archaic place "scraped flat by the roller / Of wars, wars, wars," and its name "is common" (222). Again, in some of the bee poems the raging insects evoke a range of historical horrors implicit in the "real world" of warfare: in "The Arrival of the Bee Box," for instance, they recall "African hands / Minute and shrunk for export" as well as the "furious Latin" of "a Roman mob" (213), and in "The Swarm" they remind the poet of "the Grand Army" of Napoleon (216). Tellingly, then, when in "Berck-Plage" Plath chose to confront the mysteries of death and dying, she set her brilliant meditation on a beach in Normandy where, according to Ted Hughes, "there was a large hospital for mutilated war veterans and accident victims—who took their exercise along the sands" (293), although in fact her neighbor Percy Key, whose death was the subject of the piece, died in Devon a year after her visit to Berck-Plage. Feeling herself like the "trepanned veteran, / Dirty girl" she calls her "thumb stump" (236), she had come to see history—with its "wall of old corpses" (253)—as built almost entirely out of the disruptions fostered by constant combat.

How did tropes of battle become so pervasive in Plath's work, especially in the late poetry where, as Robert Lowell put it, she became "something imaginary, newly, wildly and subtly created . . . one of those super-real, hypnotic, great classical heroines"?[7] To begin with, the death of Otto Plath in 1940, associated as it was with the onset of World War II, obviously charged the early years of the war and all the war's effects with special resonance for his daughter, allowing the bereaved child to project her own private feelings of rage and guilt into a series of dramatic public events. Obviously, too, as many commentators have observed and as she indicates in "Daddy" that she perfectly well understood, Plath's abandonment by Ted Hughes in 1962 revived her feelings of anger toward her dead father, complicating and intensifying her fury at Hughes's infidelity and bringing back with them the wartime context in which she had first had to confront her grief. Nevertheless, imagery of battle had haunted her writing—her journals as well as her fiction— long before the calamitous but brilliantly productive fall of 1962.

Torn between her acquiescence in the decorum of the fifties and her ambition to become a boldly great artist, between modest pride in her poet-husband's power and immodest competitiveness toward him, between scholarly admiration of an often misogynistic male modernist tradition and secret anxiety about that tradition, Plath seems always to have been doomed to suffer in her own person the sexual battle that marked the century in which she was born. In fact, in her life and art personal associations with public events were shadowed by literary confrontations that could be defined as forms of warfare. Thus, her late poetry, more than the work of most of her female contemporaries, was marked by a dialectical ferocity that summarized a number of the personal, political, and aesthetic struggles in which postwar women of letters were enmeshed. In the end, her engagement with the "war" of sexual history and "the real world" and "the difference" made her into a veteran of combat who, to revise Adrienne Rich's poem on Marie Curie, died not "denying" but *knowing* that "her wounds came from the same source as her power."[8] Ultimately, in the late poems that constitute her most radical letters from the front of sexual combat, Plath was forced, if only obliquely, to meditate on a question that would preoccupy many of her contemporaries and descendants: what would be the nature of a future in which the real world did *not* equal the war and the difference?

"I am afraid of getting older," wrote Plath in 1949, when she was just seventeen. "I am afraid of getting married. Spare me from cooking three meals a day—spare me from the relentless cage of routine and rote. I want to be free. . . . I want, I think, to be omniscient. . . . I think I would like to call myself 'The girl who wanted to be God.' Yet if I were not in this body, where *would* I be—perhaps I am *destined* to be classified and qualified. But, oh, I cry out against it. I am I—I am powerful—but to what extent? I am I" (*LH* 40). "I am I": curiously, that somewhat theatrical adolescent phrase echoes a poet whose works even a precocious teenager might not yet have read—William Butler Yeats, who was to become Sylvia Plath's "beloved Yeats" and in whose house, thirteen and a half years later, she was to die in a suicide that might have been a cry for help or a crying out against being "classified and qualified." For in a late verse called "He and She" (1935) Yeats had used just the phrase the young Plath used in her journal explicitly to examine what she was herself exploring: the relations between male authority and female identity, male creation and female creativity:

> As the moon sidles up
> Must she sidle up,
> As trips the sacred moon
> Away must she trip:
> 'His light had struck me blind
> Dared I stop.'
>
> She sings as the moon sings;
> 'I am I, am I;
> The greater grows my light
> The further that I fly.'
> All creation shivers
> With that sweet cry.[9]

At least as much as they were affected by the wars of history and the history of warfare, the life, death, and poetic resurrection of "the girl who wanted to be God" were affected by her increasingly keen consciousness that the scene of writing had become the arena of a dialogue between a literary "He and She" and by her ambivalent awareness that she was born at a moment when her "I am I, am I" might "shiver" all creation.

Criticism of Plath's poetry has proliferated in recent years, with even those who dislike her work finding it absorbing, as if this young woman who died in 1963 had in some troubling sense led what Keats once called a life of allegory. Most writers, however, treat two separate issues, one moral (commentary on the life), the other aesthetic (analysis of the art).[10] Few consider the connection between the poetic influences that shaped Plath's style and the personal dilemma that became her subject. More specifically, few speculate on what it meant to be a woman, born in America in 1932, reading and trying to write major poetry in the years from 1953 to 1963—what it meant to be a girl who wanted to be God setting out, like a female Stephen Dedalus, to forge an identity, an "I am I," in Wellesley, Massachusetts; at Smith College; at *Mademoiselle;* at Cambridge University; in Spain; in Boston; in London; in Devonshire; and finally in Yeats's house.

But almost by itself such a varied list of places, all equally and (so it seemed) unproblematically accessible to a young woman, suggests how new Plath's historical situation was. Even such modernist foremothers as Edna St. Vincent Millay, Marianne Moore, and H. D.—whom we have defined as the first generation of *publicly* successful women poets—had had to adopt strategies of ironic self-impersonation, costumes of "femininity," in response to the gestures of male readers and rivals who fetishized their sexuality. But because of their achievements and those of other "career" women, the world in which Plath found herself seemed to lie all before her, where to choose. Yet despite its promising openness, that world was notably complex, with its literary tradition(s) fully incarnating that complexity. Plath was born at a time when Yeats, Joyce, Pound, Eliot, and other major male modernists were still writing and publishing, as were Stein, H. D., Millay, Moore, and other major female modernists. Among them, these representatives of both sexes created a dialectic that became an inheritance which may well have been disquieting to an ambitious young woman poet.

Because the young Plath is often depicted as either a sort of neurasthenic sorceress of syntax or a diligent and decorous ephebe of fifties elegance, she is not generally recognized for what she really was: an extraordinarily conscientious student of the peculiarly new literary tradition she inherited. Yet from the first she was a voracious reader who surely understood the implications not just of that tradition but also of the long literary history that she had imbibed, she once confessed, almost as if it were her mother's milk. "I recall my mother . . . reading to me . . . from Matthew Arnold's 'Forsaken Merman,'" she noted, adding, "A spark flew off Arnold and shook me like a chill. . . . I had fallen into a new way of being happy" (*JP* 21). Quite early, too, she must have understood the implications of her gender for the principal genre—lyric poetry—to which she had committed herself virtually from childhood.

During her Fulbright year at Cambridge, for instance, Plath played the part of Phoebe Clinket, the parodic portrait of Anne Finch, the Countess of Winchilsea, as (in Plath's own words) a "mad poetess" (*LH* 190), a "verbose niece who has high flown and very funny ambitions to write plays and poetry," that John Gay, Alexander Pope, and John Arbuthnot created in *Three Hours after Marriage*.[11] Mouthing the absurdities of a savagely satirized woman artist, she gave what her director told her was an "excruciatingly funny" performance, but a performance whose deeper meaning might have been merely excruciating because of the message it conveyed about literary men's attitudes toward literary women's aspirations. By the time she was established at Cambridge, moreover, Plath was exactly what many of her critics are: a sophisticated student of a twentieth-century literary tradition in part constituted out of an implicit battle between highly cultured intellectual men and their female counterparts, writers who seemed either an uncultivated "mob of scribbling women," as Nathaniel Hawthorne called them, or a cultured but presumptuous mass of scrivening women.[12] That Plath saw herself as oscillating among these three groups—as if adopting most of the positions possible in the female affiliation complex—becomes clear in the letters home she wrote from Smith and Cambridge. Articulating her loyalty to male tradition, she expressed her worship of her "beloved Yeats," her admiration for D. H. Lawrence, her reverence for James Joyce, her respect for Dylan Thomas (see, for example,*J* 189, 207, 196), while she hinted at her feelings of rivalry toward these men and, by implication, her sense of her own power in comparison to theirs: "I am learning and mastering new words each day, and drunker than Dylan, harder than Hopkins, younger than Yeats in my saying" (*LH* 243). Simultaneously, though, she indicated her anxiety about being a "scribbling" woman: her poems, she said, are "not quailing and whining like Teasdale or simple lyrics like Millay" (*LH* 277), and she claimed to loathe "the sensationalist trash which is [Djuna Barnes's] *Nightwood*—all perverts, all ranting, melodramatic: 'The sex God forgot.'—self-pity" (*J* 205). Her early sonnet "Female Author" dramatically predicts these feelings: the subject of this female-authored poem "lies on cushions curled/And nibbles an occasional bonbon of sin"; "Prim, pink-breasted, feminine, she nurses / Chocolate fancies in rose-papered rooms. . . . And lost in subtle metaphor, retreats / From gray child faces crying in the streets" (*PCP* 301).

But while she feared becoming a scribbling woman like that female author, Plath expressed her admiration for what she regarded as serious female precursors, noting when she sent her mother some poems from college that "any resemblance to Emily Dickinson is purely intentional" (*LH* 110), praising the brilliance of Dorothy Krook ("a woman on the Cambridge faculty for whom I would sweat my brains out" [255]), enthusing about Marianne Moore ("lovely at her home in Brooklyn" [340]), and "reading Elizabeth Bishop with great admiration" (*J* 321). Even more, she continually dwelt on the example of Virginia Woolf, observing, "I get courage by reading Virginia Woolf's *Diary*," and that she felt "very akin to" Woolf. She found Woolf's novels "excellent stimulation for my own writing" (*LH* 305, 324) and, she added, believed that "her novels make mine possible" (*J* 168).

At the same time, Plath competitively compared herself to these women, at one point noting: "Arrogant, I think I have written lines which qualify me to be The Poetess of America. . . . Who rivals? Well, in history Sappho, Elizabeth Barrett Browning, Christina Rossetti, Amy Lowell, Emily Dickinson, Edna St. Vincent Millay—all dead. Now Edith Sitwell and Marianne Moore, the aging giantesses"(*J* 212). Thus, while repudiating the bitterness, sentimentality, or oversimplification of one part of the female literary tradition and excoriating most women dons at Cambridge as "bluestocking grotesques," she deliberately defined herself as "a woman poet . . . the world will gape at. . . . One of the few women poets in the world who is a rejoicing woman . . . a woman singer" (*LH* 248, 256, and insisted that she wanted to be "a woman famous among women" (*J* 260).

But what were the implications of such a self-definition, arising out of divided loyalties, ambivalences, ambiguities? A casual but crucial sentence Plath tossed off in another letter suggests that one central implication was an extraordinary sense of guilt and consequent terror: guilt over her own power; terror that she might be, should be, punished for her power. Complaining about the burden of domesticity in England, a country that then had not yet discovered "the Cookiesheet, Central Heating, and Frozen Orange Juice," she commented that "if I want to keep on being a triple-threat woman: wife, writer and teacher . . . I can't be a drudge."[13] "Triple threat": the competitive metaphor is telling, for it both explains Plath's early fascination with Arnold's "The Forsaken Merman" and foreshadows her later fascination with images of herself as (or associated with) an arrow, an acetylene virgin, a runaway, a queen bee, a crackling moon, a murderess, a deadly interloper, a ferocious transgressor. Arnold's poem, after all, recounts how a pathetic merman is seduced and abandoned by a "'cruel'" earth-woman who, claiming her own place in the sun, leaves "'lonely forever / The kings of the sea.'"[14] And Plath's later images of her own threatening self record similar—if far more exaggerated—cruelties, from "the upflight of the murderess into a heaven that loves her" described in "The Bee Meeting" to the violently "dancing and stamping" villagers let loose in "Daddy," the man-eating heroine resurrected in "Lady Lazarus," and "the lioness," who elicits "the shriek in the bath" imagined by the Clytemnestralike speaker of "Purdah" (*PCP* 212, 224, 247, 244).

In the spring of 1958, while teaching at Smith, Plath confessed her violence in a journal entry (used here as an epigraph) that fuses impulses toward self-destructiveness with murderous rage toward others: "I have a violence in me that is hot as death-blood. I can kill myself or—I know it now—even kill another. I could kill a woman, or wound a man" (*J* 237–38). But although this passage emphasizes same-sex rivalry ("I could *kill* a woman") and mutes rage at male otherness ("or *wound* a man"), a comparable confession two years earlier at Cambridge had more specifically focused on hostility toward men, suggesting that Plath's use of *wound* in 1958 was a sign of repression or evasion. Even while most women "fight for the father, for the son," she wrote in her notebook, most also have the power to "believe in [men] and make them invincible," along with the complementary power of the vampire, who expresses "*the old primal hate*. That desire to go around castrating the arrogant ones who become such children at the moment of passion" (*J* 100; emphasis ours). And a moment after she wrote these words she alluded to Yeats—"How the circling steps in the spiral tower bring us back to where we were!" (*J* 101)—as if she knew how he might refer to her: as a Helen for whom there was "no second Troy" to burn, as an adept of "the Proud Furies," or as one of Herodias's desirous and demented daughters, blasting through "the labyrinth of the wind."[15]

If Gay, Pope, and Arbuthnot had reacted with irascibility against Anne Finch's poetic presumption by satirizing her as Phoebe Clinkett, Plath's more recent masters—among them, Eliot, Joyce, and Lawrence—had, as we have seen throughout these volumes, responded even more censoriously to what they perceived as the old primal hate of vampire women who seemed to want to usurp not only the literary marketplace but even high cultural authority. The messages conveyed by the life and work of Plath's "beloved Yeats" were particularly complicated, however, for even as Maude Gonne's erstwhile lover praised the powers of Lady Gregory, Dorothy Wellesley, and Maude herself, he deplored the way Con Markiewicz's mind had become "a bitter, an abstract thing," denounced the "vague Utopia" of feminism dreamed by Eva Gore-Booth, celebrated "woman / That gives up all her mind," and prayed that his daughter might "become a flourishing hidden tree."[16] When we read Plath's anxious insistence that she is not a "frustrated or warped man-imitator" (*LH* 256), therefore, we can see that while she did intermittently allow herself to express corrosive rage at men, she had intuited and internalized the male reaction-formation embodied in so many masculinist modernist statements.

Internalizing misogyny, however, she did not immediately respond as women poets from Anne Bradstreet and Anne Finch to Edna St. Vincent Millay and Marianne Moore did, by trying (like the first two figures) to renounce her own power or (like the second two) to disguise or distance it. Rather, her first response was to affirm her strength: "I am making a self, in great pain, often, as for a birth, but it is right that it should be so" (*LH* 223); "by re-forging my soul, I am a woman now the like of which I could never have dreamed" (241). Between this poet and her foremothers a new age of literary equality had intervened, an age that seemed to have made possible sharing her "husband's dearest career" (276), an age that let her live figuratively as well as literally in Yeats's house.

That Plath from the first suspected she *had* been born into such an age is clear even in her early papers. As a teenager she had underlined a passage from one of her mother's college textbooks, John Langdon-Davies' *Short History of Women* (1927), which claimed: "Once both sexes use their reason equally . . . women cannot fail to dominate. Theirs is the stronger sex once nature and art cease their cruel combination against them, because it possesses a greater singleness of purpose and a greater fund of imagination." That there was something problematic about this apparently brave new world, however, is plain even in Langdon-Davies' quasi-feminist prose. After all, his prediction that "women cannot fail to dominate" because theirs "is the stronger sex" elaborates a submerged metaphor of sexual warfare, and it is followed by another, even bleaker passage that Plath also underlined: "Men and women are purely relative terms, and long before the tendencies of our times work to their logical conclusions, men and women, as we know them, will have ceased to exist; and human nature will have forgotten the 'he' and 'she.' According to our own personal feelings we may regret that we shall not live to see that time, or congratulate ourselves on living at a time which antedates it."[17]

Such a comment must have been disturbing indeed to a girl who wanted to be a "rejoicing woman . . . . famous among women," a girl who started out praying to be spared marriage's relentless cage of routine and rote but who then was persuaded that she wanted "to become anchored to life by laundry and lilacs . . . and a man, the dark-eyed stranger, who eats my food and my body and my love and goes around the world all day and comes back to find solace with me at night" (*J* 102).

Perhaps, Plath felt at times, she ought to strive to become a flourishing hidden tree herself or find some other way to give up "all her mind"—her assertively intellectual "I am I." In the spring of 1956, a few months after she expressed her longing for a dark-eyed stranger, this veteran of *Mademoiselle*'s stylish corridors certified her own femininity in a manner that strikingly recalls the strategies of female female impersonation deployed by Millay, Wylie, Sitwell, and Moore. In an article for the Cambridge *Varsity*, she commented on and modeled the latest spring fashions. Entitled "Sylvia Plath Tours the Stores and Forecasts May Week Fashions," the piece features the poet—identified as "Sylvia Plath, American Fulbright Scholar at Newnham"—glamorously attired in a ball gown and a white cocktail dress but gives most space to two cheesecake poses (one on the front page of the paper) where she is wearing a white bathing suit "with black polka dots, bow tied over each hip." Plath enthusiastically sent clippings to her mother, happily autographing one "With love, from Betty Grable" (*LH* 236–37; figure, opposite).

More seriously, in the same year Plath produced a poem which openly confronts the problem posed by a female "I am I." In "Two Sisters of Persephone" the female doubles represent, on the one hand, the poet's ambitious intellectual self and on the other, her dutifully sexualized self. The first, in a "dark wainscoted room," works at a "barren enterprise" and, "wry virgin to the last, / Goes graveward with flesh laid waste, / Worm-husbanded, yet no woman." The second willingly sacrifices herself on the altar of femininity, burning "open to sun's *blade*" (emphasis ours) so that "grass-couched in her labor's pride, / She bears a king" (*PCP* 31–32). On the brink of an age in which "human nature will have forgotten 'he' and 'she,'" one part of Plath seems to have acquiesced in a central male modernist imperative: if a woman is not to become unbearable, she must reconstitute an increasingly imperiled patrilineage not just by impersonating Betty Grable but by bearing—and bearing with—a king.

———————

The connection in Plath's career between the literary history her letters ambitiously review, the power her poems ambivalently renew or repress, and the wound her death ambiguously reveals emerges interestingly in a brief

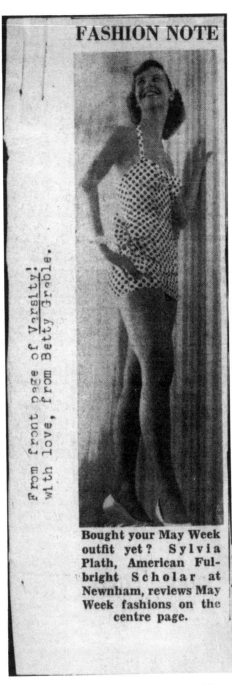

FASHION NOTE

From front page of _Varsity_!
with love, from Betty Grable.

Bought your May Week outfit yet? Sylvia Plath, American Fulbright Scholar at Newnham, reviews May Week fashions on the centre page.

Sylvia Plath models for the Cambridge
Varsity (courtesy the Manuscripts
Department, Lilly Library, Indiana
University)

verse play entitled "Dialogue over a Ouija Board" (1957–58), which, as
Katherine Stern has pointed out, offers an encoded depiction of this artist's
intellectual struggle with her poet-husband Ted Hughes. As Stern notes and
Judith Kroll has documented, the couple had from the first been attracted to
the occult, and there seem to have been literary and (at least in Plath's case)
personal reasons for this interest.[18] In October 1956, shortly after their
marriage, Plath wrote her mother that "Ted and I . . . shall become a team
better than Mr. and Mrs. Yeats—he being a competent astrologist, reading
horoscopes, and me being a tarot-pack reader, and, when we have enough
money, a crystal-gazer" (*LH* 280). A memoir by Hughes reveals that Plath's
"occasional dealings with the Ouija board, during the late Fifties" were
associated not just with Yeats but with her lost father: "Her father's name was
Otto, and 'spirits' would regularly arrive with instructions for her from one
Prince Otto, who was said to be a great power in the underworld. When she
pressed for a more personal communication, she would be told that Prince
Otto could not speak to her directly, because he was under orders from The
Colossus. And when she pressed for an audience with The Colossus, they
would say he was inaccessible." Obviously, the father's role in Plath's Ouija
conversations was problematic—but then so was the Yeats connection: if
Plath and Hughes were to become "Mr. and Mrs. Yeats," would Plath have to
be *Mrs.* Yeats, the entranced transmitter of "metaphors for poetry" to her
genius husband?[19]

Her awareness of such competitive tensions is first dramatized in "Dialogue over a Ouija Board" by the names of her play's two characters: Sibyl
(for Sylvia) and Leroy (for Ted). On the surface Leroy is meant to signify
what Plath sees as Hughes's kingly qualities: he is Le Roi—an avatar of the
king her heroine "bears" in "Two Sisters of Persephone"—and, indeed,
throughout the verse drama he maintains a regal authority. Yet Leroy is also
the name that Plath would in a year use for the male playmate whom Sadie
bites in "The Shadow." And although the "seeress" Sibyl and her antagonist,
Leroy, do not actually come to blows in the play, they are forced to confront
their mutual hostility as they rivalrously strive to interpret the messages
delivered by their attendant spirit, Pan. For when Sibyl asks Pan "*Do you know
how my father is?*" he replies first, "IN PLUMAGE" (which she decodes as in
"wings"), and then "IN PLUMAGE OF RAW WORMS" (at which Leroy observes,
with sardonic triumph, "Worms, not wings" [*PCP* 278–79]).

Finally, after Sibyl expresses her disaffection with the whole Ouija enterprise, complaining that "you've pampered / Pan as if he were our first-
breached brat" (280), both members of this occult wedding openly meditate
on their competitiveness:

> LEROY: Do we have to battle
> Like rival parents over a precocious

Child to see which one of us can call
Pan's prowess our own creation, and not the other's
Work at all?
SIBYL: How can we help but battle
If our nerves are the sole nourishers
Of Pan's pronouncements, and our nerves are strung
To such cross-purposes?
LEROY: At last you glimpse
Some light.
SIBYL: I glimpse no light at all as long
As we two glower from our separate camps,
This board our battlefield.

[284]

And that the battlefield represented by this board was more than a personal one is suggested by the poem "Ouija," contemporary with "Dialogue." There the spirit of the board, "a chilly god, a god of shades," is associated with the "old god" who "writes aureate poetry / In tarnished modes, maundering among the wastes," and who is "godly, doddering" (77–78). Evidently for Plath at this point, both literary history and the contemporary literary man to whom she was married were either threateningly wounding or disturbingly wasted.[20]

The distressing dialogue with twentieth-century male literary tradition in which this woman poet felt herself to be engaged becomes central in Plath's early poem "The Shrike" (1956) and in two short stories, "The Wishing Box" (1956) and "Johnny Panic and the Bible of Dreams" (1958), three texts ostensibly about dreams but really about reading and writing. In these works, however, male tradition is represented not by Yeats or by the old god of "Ouija" but first by Ted Hughes and then by his precursor from the north of England, D. H. Lawrence. "The Shrike" offers a surprisingly frank portrait of the artist as a vengeful bride. "The Wishing Box" counters that depiction with a punitive portrait of the wife as suicide. Longer and more complex, "Johnny Panic and the Bible of Dreams" offers an unnerving narrative of what we might call femicide. But despite differences in tone and genre, the three pieces serve as a single narrative examining simultaneous feelings of rivalry and transgression (or usurpation) that haunted Plath when she contemplated her own creative power.

Although it has the formal polish of what Plath herself defined as her early "Thesaurus poems," "The Shrike" is almost shocking in its self-loathing depiction of wifely competitiveness. As if to evoke "Le Roi" of "Dialogue over a Ouija Board," the work begins by focusing on a husband's kingly imaginative privilege as compared to his less fortunate wife's frustration:

When night comes black
Such royal dreams beckon this man
As lift him apart
From his earth-wife's side . . .
While she, envious bride,
Cannot follow after, but lies
With her blank brown eyes starved wide,
Twisting curses in the tangled sheet
With taloned fingers.

But as might be expected of a triple-threat woman, the envious bride achieves a startling revenge at "bird-racketing dawn,"

When her shrike-face
Leans to peck open those locked lids, to eat
Crowns, palace, all
That nightlong stole her male,
And with red beak
Spike and suck out
Last blood-drop of that truant heart.

[*PCP* 42]

Predatory bird and vampire in one, the deprived (non)dreamer enacts the fury of the blocked writer who was soon to confess to her journal that she was "unable to speak human speech, lost as I am in my inner wordless Sargasso" (*J* 246). At the same time, the denouement of "The Shrike" points toward its author's admission two years later that "I have a violence in me . . . hot as death-blood"—a violence here specifically associated with conjugal (literary) competition.

That such rivalrous rage seemed to Plath deserving not only of self-disgust but also of severe punishment is revealed in the two witty yet disturbing stories, which also meditate on dreaming and its discontents. To be sure, "The Wishing Box" is at least on the surface an ironic tale of female powerlessness. Harold and Agnes, a young married couple, meet at breakfast and discuss his dreams, which are always visions of aesthetic triumph, as if to bring to the surface the literary script that underlies "The Shrike." In one dream, Harold talks about manuscripts with William Blake; in another (as a kind of Le Roi?), he plays the *Emperor* Concerto; in a third, he is introduced to a gathering of American poets in the Library of Congress; and in two others (the ones that most comically relate him to Hughes), he encounters, respectively, a red fox (who presents him with a bottle of permanent black "Quink") and a giant pike.[21] Listening to his accounts of these nighttime events, Agnes, who has few dreams herself—and those are nightmares—is soon "wrestling with the strange jealousy . . . growing on her like some dark malignant cancer ever since their wedding night": "It was as if Harold were spending one third of his life . . . in an exhilarating world from which [she] found herself perpetually exiled" (*JP* 204–05).

Unlike the shrike-wife, though, she attempts no violence against her mate. Rather, at first she plans to study Freud on the sly and fortify herself "with a vicarious dream tale by which to hold Harold's interest each morning" (207), a strategy that recalls both the literary seductions of Scheherezade and the occult wiles of Georgie Yeats. But finally she confesses her inadequacy to her husband, who sets her a series of dream exercises not unlike the poetic exercises Hughes sometimes set Plath. Yet even these do not work, and although she then tries to restore her "shaping imaginative powers" by reading novels, cookbooks, "home appliance circulars . . . anything to keep from facing the gaping void in her own head of which Harold had made her so painfully conscious," the very letters she looks at writhe "like malevolent little black snakes across the page in a kind of hissing, untranslatable jargon" (209), so that finally, insomniac as the heroine of "The Shrike" or Esther Greenwood in *The Bell Jar,* she consumes a "wishing box" full of sleeping pills and dies into the only country of dreams accessible to her.

Like "The Shrike," this tale predates "Dialogue over a Ouija Board," but the tensions enacted in the play and outlined in the poem are examined in the story's obsession with the dream competition between husband and wife and, more specifically, in its emphasis on both the sense of creative inadequacy and the "malignant" jealousy Agnes feels when facing the fertility of Harold's imagination. It is ironic that Plath wrote the story at just the time when she confided to her journal that she had been able to marry her husband because "he was a better poet than I and . . . I would never have to restrain my little gift, but could push it . . . and still feel him ahead" (*J* 172)— and at the time, too, when she was boasting to her mother that she and Hughes "romp through words together," that he was her best critic as she was his, and that she was "glad his book [was] taken first" and proud that he was "always just that many steps ahead of me . . . so that I feel very feminine and admiring" (*LH* 270). For unlike the openly vengeful "Shrike," "The Wishing Box" dramatizes a profound battle within the young poet-wife's psyche, revealing both a traditional female anxiety that she *could* not compete with the élan of the male imagination, and a deep, *Ladies Home Journal* conviction that she *should* not. Better death than the expression of (female) desire, the story seems to say. Or more accurately, death is the most appropriate expression of female desire, the best or only dream a woman can have.

But of course Plath also believed that she could and did compete with Hughes's and other men's imaginative élan, and from the first, in passages from her journals, she acknowledged the violence of her feelings toward her husband. After they met at the party described in "Stone Boy, with Dolphin," she noted that she would like "to give myself crashing, fighting, to" Hughes and that she "would like to try just this once, my force against his" (*J* 112); a few weeks later she was planning a novel about the "position of intelligent woman in [the] world . . . fight, triumph: toleration of conflict, etc." (129). Thus "Johnny Panic and the Bible of Dreams" offers another piece of the painful puzzle that these three dream-obsessed texts together articulate. For in "Johnny Panic," which Hughes saw as "moving straight toward *The Bell Jar* and the more direct poems of *Ariel*" (*JP* 6), the female narrator—"Assistant Secretary in [an] Adult Psychiatric Clinic"—becomes "a dream connoisseur" (*JP* 153), a dedicated transcriber of the nightmares inspired by the god "Johnny Panic," and "this," she says with the bitter pride of a Lady Lazarus, "is my real calling." By comparison with the comically ambitious dreams recounted in "The Wishing Box," however, the nightmares of "Johnny Panic" are intricate, metaphysical poems; more, they are exactly the Plathian nightmares—"dark glowing landscapes peopled with ominous unrecognizable figures" (205)—that Agnes had rejected as inadequate in the earlier story.

Clearly, then, the narrator of "Johnny Panic" is a prophetically visionary version of the poet herself, an impassioned imaginative woman who aspires to record all the dreams contained in the old books begun when "the clinic started thirty-three years ago—the year of my birth, oddly enough." But when finally, after much scheming, she does undertake that task, contriving to spend all night in the hospital copying the "dream book [that] was spanking new the day I was born" (*JP* 164), she quickly learns that her inspired transcription is an awful transgression. Finding her among the files at dawn (Plath's own regular writing time), the clinic director marches her off to a place of punishment where a terrible nurse and "five false priests in white surgical gowns and masks" ritually strip her, anoint her, robe her in "sheets virginal as the first snow," extend her full length on a white cot, and place a "crown of wire" on her head and a "wafer of forgetfulness" on her tongue. The sacrificial shock treatment she then undergoes elicits a vision that, as Hughes implied, energizes and, in a searing blue light, illuminates both *The Bell Jar* and *Ariel*, in particular the poem "The Hanging Man": "At the moment when I think I am most lost the face of Johnny Panic appears in a nimbus of arc lights on the ceiling overhead. I am shaken like a leaf in the teeth of glory. His beard is lightning. Lightning is in his eye. His Word charges and illumines the universe. The air crackles with his blue-tongued lightning-haloed angels" (166).

Quite literally, Plath's association of "Johnny Panic" with divine lightning describes her own experiences with shock treatment, but it seems apropos here that two years earlier she had described her kingly husband-to-be in similar terms—as a "hulking, healthy Adam . . . with a voice *like the thunder of God*" (*LH* 233; emphasis ours). Coupled with "The Wishing Box," therefore, this story explores the problem that Suzanne Juhasz has called "the double bind" of the woman poet: if she empties her head of her own dreams, she dies into what in *Howards End* E. M. Forster termed "panic and emptiness"; but if she ambitiously studies what are, symbolically speaking, her own dreams, she is shocked by a panic that also produces emptiness.[22] Worse still, her panic is triggered not only by a Pandoralike curiosity about the secret facts of her own history recorded in the clinic's musty dream books, but also by her consciousness that her identification of her history with these sacred tomes constitutes a fearful usurpation of literary history itself. Plath is aware, in other words, that when the clinic director shocks her transgressive dream connoisseur out of her mind, he does so because this scribbling woman's appropriation of the dream books challenges his authority over them, his mastery of their mystery.

Plath's awareness of this last point is suggested in particular by the fact that "Johnny Panic" is a strong revision of one of D. H. Lawrence's fiercest sexual allegories, a revision produced just after she had observed in her journal that "Lawrence bodies the world in his words" (*J* 261). Lawrence's "The Woman Who Rode Away"(1928) recounts the misadventure of a "nerve-worn" white woman who at the Christological age of thirty-three escapes from her bourgeois marriage only to be seized by a band of male Indians, ritually anointed, stripped, splayed out on a flat rock by five priests, and offered as a sacrifice to their sun god so that they can recapture "the mastery that man must hold, and that passes from race to race." For, says Lawrence, "Her kind of womanhood, intensely personal and individual, was to be obliterated again, and the great primeval symbols were to tower once more over the fallen individual independence of woman. . . . Strangely, as if clairvoyant, she saw the immense sacrifice prepared." And why must such a sacrifice be prepared? Because the white woman's power has debilitated not only the white men but the Indian men and their traditionally dutiful woman. The moon, says one of Lawrence's noble savages, must be told that "*the wicked white woman can't harm you any more.*"[23]

Like the narrator of "Johnny Panic" and the speaker of many *Ariel* poems, Esther Greenwood in *The Bell Jar* defines herself as a wickedly ambitious woman who wants to "shoot off in all directions" herself instead of being the passive "place the arrows shoot off from."[24] And like the crises to which "The Wishing Box" and "Johnny Panic" allude, Esther's breakdown is precipitated by a confrontation with male modernism, and through it with male literary history. Home for the summer and shut out of a creative writing course she had hoped to take, this fashion-magazine prize winner plans to write her undergraduate honors thesis on *Finnegans Wake*. But when she opens Joyce's magnum opus—a "thick book [which] made an unpleasant dent in my stomach"—she is overwhelmed by the horror of interpretation and, implicitly, by the horror of what she must interpret. When she tries to read, the alphabet itself, as it did in "The Wishing Box," becomes alien and alarming: "The letters grew barbs and ram's horns [and] associated themselves in fantastic, untranslatable shapes."[25] So she decides to "junk" her thesis, the honors program, and even—because it would require her to take a course in the eighteenth century—her college English major. For, says this surrogate self of the Cambridge student who claimed to have so much fun playing Phoebe Clinket, "I hated the very idea of the eighteenth century, with all those smug men writing tight little couplets, and being so dead keen on reason" (*BJ* 102).

———————

Given the ferocious alphabet in which Plath evidently felt ensnared, what literary influences might have liberated her to seize the authority she achieved in *Ariel*? To begin with, paradigms of poetic (if not personal) survival came to her from a woman novelist—Virginia Woolf. As early as 1956 Plath was telling her mother proudly that "all the scholarly boys [at Cambridge] think of me as a second Virginia Woolf," and not much later she confided, "I get courage by reading [Woolf's *Diary*]" because "I feel very akin to her" (*LH* 230, 305). By the time she wrote her radio play, "Three Women: A Poem for Three Voices," in 1962—another text Hughes sees as a crucial transition work from the style of *The Colossus* to the mode of *Ariel*—the kinship was manifesting itself in the very texture and tempo of Plath's verse as well as in its increasingly brilliant illumination of the complex "I am I" that constitutes human consciousness.

In particular, the distinctive cadences of the three introspective women in Plath's verse play appear to have evolved out of the voices of the three introspective women speakers whose lives Woolf explored in her "play-poem" *The Waves*.[26] In addition, the prototypical female personalities Plath's three women represent are consistently analogous to the female types represented by Woolf's Susan, Rhoda, and Jinny, for the first voice is that of a nurturing mother, the second of a woman who feels herself "lacking" in appropriate femaleness, and the third of a woman who wills herself to live seductively but without attachments. Plath's copy of *The Waves* (now in the Smith College Rare Book Room) is the most heavily underlined of all her books, with the exception of a few texts in which she took notes as a student. Even without such evidence of influence, however, a few sample passages from *The Waves* juxtaposed with some representative lines from "Three Women" indicate how the reveries of Plath's women are not only substantively but stylistically shaped by the meditations of Woolf's heroines, for both Woolf's and Plath's "dramatic soliloquies"—Woolf's phrase applies equally well to Plath's verses—generally characterize their speakers through self-defining metaphors, incantatory incremental repetition, and interpolated rhetorical questions.

Comparing school (where she is) to home (where she wants to be), for example, Woolf's earth-motherly Susan thinks that "something has grown in me . . . [at home] gradually I shall turn over the hard thing that has grown here in my side." Similarly, Plath's "first voice," a woman entering labor, thinks, "A power is growing in me, an old tenacity" (*PCP* 180). Later, Woolf's Susan declares, "I am the field, I am the barn" (*W* 242) and still later, having become a mother, she defines herself as "spun to a fine thread round the cradle, wrapping in a cocoon made of my own blood the delicate limbs of my baby" (294). Similarly, Plath's first voice resolves to be "a wall and a roof protecting . . . . a sky and a hill of good" (*PCP* 180) and, having become a mother, she imagines herself as "a river of milk . . . a warm hill" (183).

Just as strikingly, where Woolf's Susan and Plath's first voice are single-minded in their commitment to maternity, Woolf's Rhoda and Plath's "second voice" are faint with the failure of identity, aching with emptiness. Rhoda imagines her defiance of life as "a thin dream . . . a papery tree" (*W* 213), while the second voice, a secretary who has miscarried, fears that "the streets may turn to paper suddenly" (*PCP* 187). Rhoda approaches a puddle and confesses, "I could not cross it. Identity failed me. We are nothing, I said, and fell" (*W* 219), while the second voice insists that "I am found wanting" (*PCP* 177). After the mythic Percival's demise in India, Rhoda broods on death, elaborating upon the assertion of her male double, Louis, that "Death is woven in with the violets . . . Death and again death" (*W* 273), while the second voice, bleeding away her embryonic child, declares, "This is a disease I carry home, this is a death. / Again, this is a death" (*PCP* 177).

Woolf's Jinny, a femme fatale who lives the purely sensual "life of the body," is perhaps less akin to Plath's "third voice," but even between these last two figures there are meaningful resemblances. Jinny claims, for instance, that "I do not settle long anywhere; I do not attach myself to one person in particular" (*W* 296), while the third voice, a student who has given her illegitimate child up for adoption, insists, "It is so beautiful to have no attachments! / I am solitary as grass" (*PCP* 186). Again, Jinny sees "every blade of grass very clear" and gives herself to "a tree . . . the river . . . [the] afternoon" (*W* 206, 351), while the third voice is haunted by "hot noon in the meadows [where] the buttercups / Swelter and melt" (*PCP* 186).

The options for women, say Woolf's novel and Plath's play in a kind of antiphonal chorus, are threefold: the qualified power of maternity, the absolute powerlessness of metaphysical consciousness, and the pseudo-power of seductive indifference. But when exploring those apparently limited options, women can speak in a style marked by unlimited metaphorical energy, a style of liberated self-analysis that persistently explores the crucial "I am I" of female identity. The woman writer, or so Woolf taught Plath, may be destined to be "classified and qualified," but she still has the imaginative strength to articulate the tension between the self that wants to be God and the classifications which would constrain that self.

The explosion of *Ariel* is, then, a breakthrough into further, more lyrically incisive Woolfian self-analyses, accomplished when the poet remembers that "I have a self to recover, a queen." Thus many of the *Ariel* poems continue to echo key passages from *The Waves*, some spoken by Woolf's male characters. Plath's confession in "Tulips" that "I have no face, I have wanted to efface myself" (*PCP* 161), for instance, recalls Rhoda's twice-repeated claim, "I have no face" (*W* 203). Plath's "I think I am going up, / I think I may rise" in "Fever 103°" (*PCP* 232) echoes Rhoda's "I am above the earth now . . . I mount; I escape" (*W* 193). Plath's "Now I break up in pieces that fly about like clubs" (*PCP* 192) in "Elm" parallels Rhoda's "I am broken into separate pieces; I am no longer one" (*W* 248). Plath's "I / Am a pure acetylene / Virgin" (*PCP* 232) echoes Rhoda's "I am unsealed, I am incandescent" (*W* 214). Plath's continual visions of smiling or sinister "hooks" recall Rhoda's "I feel myself grappled to one spot by these hooks [people] cast" (337). And Plath's galloping words with their "indefatigable hoof-taps" (*PCP* 270) echo Neville's "words and words and words, how they gallop" (*W* 232).

Even the difficult processes of composition through which these women artists achieved such images and cadences are similar. Woolf, who suspected she had "not yet mastered the speaking voice," rewrote *The Waves* by "reading much of it aloud, like poetry" while, as Hughes reminds us, Plath began around the time she wrote "Three Women" to "compose her poems more to be read aloud," and indeed to compose them, often, by speaking aloud. The female voice, such a process of composition suggests, must and will be heard—even, in Plath's case, broadcast. The woman writer, neither "Roget's strumpet" (*J* 112) nor the furtive transgressor of "Johnny Panic," can now speak out and up for herself.

Yet when Plath was speaking her last potent self-analyses in what Elizabeth Hardwick, with bewildering censoriousness, once called "plump, diction-perfect, Englishy, mesmerizing cadences," she was in effect speaking from Yeats's house.[27] Given the problematic nature of the tradition Yeats represented for her, how did she achieve such acts of linguistic audacity, even with Woolf's monitory example? We want here to suggest that in the end Plath felt "Yeats's spirit blessing [her]" because she sensed that, despite his ambivalences, Yeats, among male modernists, was the most fascinated by women's creative as well as procreative power. Indeed, in such verse plays as "Cathleen ni Houlihan" and "The Only Jealousy of Emer" as well as in sequences of dramatic soliloquies like the "Crazy Jane" poems, he himself had tried to capture the unique inflections of women's voices, with their pride in sexuality ("'Fair and foul are near of kin, / And fair needs foul,' I cried"), their ambivalence toward patriarchal authority ("The Bishop has a skin, God knows, / Wrinkled like the foot of a goose"), their impassioned assertion of identity ("My body makes no moan / But sings on"), and their amused contempt for male pretensions ("Nine books or nine hats / Would not make [the Bishop] a man").[28]

From the first, Plath's letters to her mother about the flat she eventually rented in Yeats's house reveal her almost mystical sense that dwelling in this symbolic edifice might allay the anxieties she had long felt about her transgressive desire to enter a literary tradition that was not hers but "his." "By an absolute *fluke*," she wrote in November 1962, "I walked by *the* street and *the* house . . . where I've always wanted to live. . . . And guess what, it is W. B. *Yeats' house*—with a blue plaque over the door, saying he lived there!" (*LH* 477–78) If she could inhabit this house, Plath would be not "Mrs. Yeats"— the silent half of an occult team—but, as we would put it today, "Ms. Yeats," the great poet's self-possessed heiress, with a male muse who, unlike the inaccessible "Prince Otto" or enigmatic "Colossus," might obligingly instruct her from the spirit world.

On 19 November 1962, waiting to hear whether she would get the flat, Plath wrote her mother, "I had the uncanny feeling I had got in touch with Yeats' spirit . . . when I went to his tower in Ireland," then added, "I opened a book of his plays in front of Susan [O'Neill Roe, her household helper] as a joke for a 'message' and read, 'Get wine and food to give you strength and courage, and I will get the house ready'" (*LH* 480). And on that day she entered into a daring dialogue with this poetic ancestor. In the horrified conclusion of her own "Mary's Song"—"It is a heart / This holocaust I walk in, / O golden child the world will kill and eat"—she revised and reinterpreted a key passage in his "Two Songs from a Play": "I saw a staring virgin stand / Where holy Dionysus died, / And tear the heart out of his side, / And lay the heart upon her hand / And bear that beating heart away. . . . Whatever flames upon the night / Man's own resinous heart has fed."[29] Acknowledging the stylized barbarism with which the Irish poet invested the Christian myth through reiterated metaphors of hearts and eating, Plath signaled her debt to Yeats's imaginative mythology. Yet in divesting Yeats's sacred heart of its healing resin by evoking the purposeless bleakness of the Holocaust he did not live to see, she indicated her determination to swerve from the earlier writer's visionary teleology.

In the two poems that follow "Mary's Song" Plath also implicitly revised crucial Yeatsian texts. The third stanza of "Winter Trees," written on 26 November, obliquely addresses itself to "Leda and the Swan," describing the trees outside the poet's dawn window as "full of wings, otherworldliness" and noting that "in this, they are Ledas"—but then protesting, "O mother of leaves and sweetness / Who are these pietàs? / The shadows of ringdoves, chanting, but easing nothing" (*PCP* 258). Where the great wings of Yeats's father-god brutalize the "staggering girl" who is *his* Leda, Plath's stately trees are *all* Ledas, governed by a "*mother* of leaves and sweetness" and perhaps even controlling the wings of (male) otherworldliness. At the same time, where Yeats's Leda is "mastered" by the god's engendering of a patriarchal causality that will lead to Agamemnon's death and thence to all of Western history, Plath's Ledas skeptically evoke female "pietas . . . chanting but easing nothing," so that again her poem is both an homage to Yeats and an assertion of independence from the famous "system" that he outlined in *A Vision* (1937).

Even more frankly, "Brasilia," written on 1 December as Plath was preparing for her move to London, reverses the parental wishes Yeats had outlined in both "A Prayer for My Son" and "A Prayer for My Daughter." In the former, Yeats had anticipated "some most haughty deed or thought" waiting upon his infant's "future days" and subtly compared the boy to the Christ child; in the latter he had of course wished his daughter to become a flourishing hidden tree.[30] But in "Brasilia" Plath prays that her son will escape godhood and that *he* will in effect become a flourishing hidden tree:

> O You who eat
>
> People like light rays, leave
> This one
> Mirror safe, *unredeemed*
>
> By the dove's annihilation,
> The glory
> The power, the glory.
>
> > [*PCP* 259; emphasis ours]

Here she appears to have freed herself from the terrors expressed in "The Wishing Box," "Johnny Panic," and even "Dialogue over a Ouija Board" to experience the spirit presence of a male precursor as inspiring but undaunting.

Indeed, Plath may have felt that, by dwelling on Yeats's writings while preparing to dwell in his house, she could learn to resurrect rather than reject the subversive strength he predicted for the woman poet when he told his protégée Dorothy Wellesley (in the poem we quoted as an epigraph) to expect a visit from "that great family / Some ancient famous authors misrepresent, / The Proud Furies, each with her torch on high." Like Wellesley— no "common" woman—Plath took on the revisionary role of a Fury, rising like "God's lioness" from the earth in which those great and greatly misunderstood figures had been shut up at the close of the *Oresteia*.[31] In doing so at, as it were, Yeats's behest, she found a poetic father, a liberating male muse rather than an inhibiting master, to match the poetic mother she had discovered in Virginia Woolf.

With what must have felt like the tacit encouragement of Yeats and Woolf, then, Plath gave herself up to herself and freed her own ambition to be a woman famous among women. Inevitably, her engagement with such enthralling precursors did at times involve her in a kind of Bloomian struggle for authority.[32] Nevertheless, together these literary parents became not primarily antagonists but sacred facilitators: Plath felt Yeats's spirit blessing her as she traced "the spiraling stair of [her] ascent adultward" (*J* 196), and she spoke with awe of Woolf's "blessed diary" (152). Thus through the sacramental benedictions of Yeats and Woolf, the young poet became the person she most feared and desired to be—most terribly, the lion-red queen with her wings of glass, the voracious Lady Lazarus, the glamorously guilty murderess boasting that "If I've killed one man, I've killed two"; and most triumphantly, the fierce virgin whose fallen selves peel away as she ascends to a heaven of her own invention, shivering all creation with her purified "I am I, am I."

The verse in which Plath voiced the claims of her revisionary self reflects her new acquiescence in her own aesthetic strength, for throughout *Ariel* her prosody reveals not what Hugh Kenner dismisses as "the gleeful craft of a mad child" but the mature skill of an artist who has finally entered into an open dialogue with literary history.[33] As many critics have observed, Plath began her literary career with a number of technical experiments. Influenced by Stevens, Thomas, Moore, and Hughes, she counted syllables; consciously drew on strategies of alliteration, assonance, and consonance; wrote, in her own words, "page after page of villanelles and sonnets"; and even, as John Frederick Nims has observed, produced in "Black Rook in Rainy Weather" a poem that "follows the Provençal system of *rimas dissolutas*." Yet as she confessed in "Stillborn," many of her early experiments "do not live" (*PCP* 142) because the decorum with which they are crafted makes them into "stilted artificial stuff" (*J* 164). The breakthrough of *Ariel*, however, is marked, as Nims has argued, by what might seem to be "a severe regression" to "the most basic of English rhythms . . . strict iambic and loose iambic."[34]

In his analysis of Plath's late style, Nims points to a number of lines that can be read as, or recast in, iambic pentameter. Similarly, in an essay on "the line," Sandra McPherson juxtaposes Plath's "Sheep in Fog" with a reworking of the poem "in a sort of blank verse," commenting that "the effect of the transposing . . . is a loss of suspense." But why such a loss of suspense? We would argue that the problem is a consequence of the revision's surfacing what the poem seeks simultaneously to deploy and reject: the traditional strength of "a sort of blank verse." For if *Ariel* is haunted by iambic pentameter—whose ghost presents itself in such diverse poems as "Tulips,"

"The Hanging Man," and "The Bee Meeting"—this is not because the collection is a "severe regression" but because it is a sophisticated dialogue with the prosodic history of English poetry, a battle of words in which this artist is at last ready to hold her own.[35]

While both "Daddy" and "Lady Lazarus," arguably Plath's most mythically vital poems, draw their prosodic strength from the rhythms of "dancing and stamping" villagers whose folkloric energies, claims Donald Hall, make "Mother Goose . . . all mouth and muscle . . . a better poet than W. H. Auden,"[36] these works are newly skillful and willful texts. The girl who rebels against "daddy" speaks in nursery rhymes with sardonic control. The "pure gold baby" who revolts against "Herr God, Herr Lucifer" similarly dances and stamps in anti-Dantesque tercets to truncate not only her contemporary master but a historical master, Dante, by revising, and rising out of, the inferno of her seduced and abandoned consciousness:

> Herr God, Herr Lucifer,
> Beware
> Beware.
>
> Out of the ash
> I rise with my red hair
> And I eat men like air.
>
> [*PCP* 245–46]

Moreover, as both her language and its rhythms indicate, the author of "Lady Lazarus," whether consciously or not, wants to confound the shamanistic image of masculine bardic authority perhaps most powerfully presented by Coleridge in the conclusion of "Kubla Khan":

> And all should cry, Beware! Beware!
> His flashing eyes, his floating hair!
> Weave a circle round him thrice,
> And close your eyes with holy dread.[37]

At the same time, while Plath's line breaks here swerve from Coleridge to transform traditional caesuras into threatening modernist gasps ("Beware" —pause—"Beware"), the basic beat of her poem is fortified by, even as it defies, the classical beat of iambic pentameter. Whole sections can, in fact, be recast not in "a sort of blank verse" but in superbly skilled blank verse, or even, as below, in highly regular heroic couplets:

> Herr God, Herr Lucifer, beware, beware.
> Out of the ash I rise with my red hair.

Our experience as readers of this poem, then, recapitulates what may have been Plath's own conscious or unconscious prosodic doubleness. Behind the apparently ragged, defiantly irregular lines of the "real" text, we sense the rhythm of a kind of ghost text, so that Plath's poem is at many crucial points written simultaneously in blank verse and in "free verse."[38]

A similar point could be made about well-known passages in many other *Ariel* poems, all secretly strengthened by the very prosody whose regularities they refuse or revise. The conclusion of "Ariel," for example, has obviously been shaped to emphasize intellectual meaning through the punning re-iteration of *I, I, Eye* at crucial points in important lines, and Plath's use of what is one of her (and Dante's) hallmarks—a last line isolated from the carefully counted-out stanzas (here, as in "Lady Lazarus," rapid tercets)—equally stresses meaning: the mystery of an apocalyptic denouement that cannot be forced into patterned regularity.

> And now I
> Foam to wheat, a glitter of seas.
> The child's cry
>
> Melts in the wall.
> And I
> Am the arrow,
>
> The dew that flies
> Suicidal, at one with the drive
> Into the red
>
> Eye, the cauldron of morning.
>
> [*PCP* 239–40]

In addition, the line breaks here, with their willed caesuras ("I"—pause— "Foam"), allow us (and the poet) to discover full or half rhymes that would otherwise have been internal: *I/cry, seas/flies,* even *cry/I/flies/drive.*

But again, the strength of this pattern depends on the power of the ghost text which the lines both incorporate and evade:

> And now I foam to wheat, a glitter of seas.
> The child's cry melts in the wall, and I
> Am the arrow, the dew that flies, suicidal,
> Into the red eye, the cauldron of morning.

Significantly, one phrase—"at one with the drive"—does not "fit" into this ghost text, although the fairly regular quatrain above makes perfect sense without it. Perhaps, given the prosodic norm Plath is working against, her brilliant addition of the uncontainable phrase "at one with the drive" is a sign of *excess:* excess meaning that has to insist upon its primacy in the poem, excess rebellion against historical conventions of lineation.

A comparable rebellion marks the last two stanzas of "Stings," arguably Plath's most defiantly self-defining poem. Here there is no excess phrase; the lines of these two stanzas—

> They thought death was worth it, but I
> Have a self to recover, a queen.
> Is she dead, is she sleeping?
> Where has she been,
> With her lion-red body, her wings of glass?
>
> Now she is flying
> More terrible than she ever was, red
> Scar in the sky, red comet
> Over the engine that killed her—
> The mausoleum, the wax house.

[*PCP* 215]

—easily reform themselves into sometimes iambic, sometimes dactylic or anapestic pentameter:

> They thought death was worth it, but I have a self
> To recover, a queen. Is she dead, is she sleeping? Where
> Has she been, with her lion-red body, her wings of glass?
>
> Now she is flying, more terrible than she ever was,
> Red scar in the sky, red comet, over the engine
> That killed her—the mausoleum, the wax house.

But the meanings forced into the poem through the allusion to and disruption of standard patterning are at least as intense as Ariel's determinedly egotistical reiterations of *I* and *Eye*.

In blank verse, these two stanzas appear controlled and meditative, almost the musings of some turn-of-the-century soliloquist. Fragmented and recast as *shreds* of traditional lineation, the stanzas demonstrate their author's mastery of conventional norms even while they arrogantly propose her autonomous power—the braggodocio of her ability to end a line with the stark "but I," the daring of the linguistic split embodied in the defiantly spondaic "red / Scar." The craft here may be gleeful, but it is neither mad nor childish, for the forward movement of the printed text, as it unobtrusively counterpoints itself against the shadowy movement of the ghost text, arises from a confident appropriation of the complex poetic mastery Yeats himself implicitly prescribed when he wrote in "Adam's Curse" that "'a line will take us hours maybe; / Yet if it does not seem a moment's thought, / Our stitching and unstitching has been naught.'"[39]

Plath's consciousness that she had at last entered into a strong dialogue with literary history is clear from her claim to her mother in October 1962 that "I am a genius of a writer; I have it in me. I am writing the best poems of my life; they will make my name" (*LH* 468). She herself understood the powerful skills and, as Ted Hughes has pointed out, the deep well of private inspiration on which she was drawing. And interestingly, Hughes—who, after all, knew Plath the *artist* better than anyone—has represented her "inner gestation and eventual birth of a new self-conquering self" as a battle. After "the *Ariel* voice emerged in full," he has observed, "it never really faltered again. . . . The subject matter [of her poems] didn't alarm her. Why should it, when Ariel was doing the very thing it had been created and liberated to do? In each poem, the terror is encountered head on, and the angel is mastered and brought to terms. . . . In October, when she and her husband began to live apart, every detail of the antagonist seemed to come into focus, and she started writing at top speed."[40]

To be sure, in the same essay Hughes somewhat mystically identified his poet-wife's antagonist with the forces in her that drew her toward death and stasis: on the one hand, the mourned-for "ghost of her father"; on the other hand, "The Other" in herself, "the deathly woman at the heart of everything."[41] And indeed the struggle between death and life, other and self, father and mother, permeates most of her late poems. In "Three Women," the dark earth goddess who is "the vampire of us all . . . Old winter-face, old barren one," is set against the newborn souls of children who are "pure, small images. . . . walkers of air" (*PCP* 181, 183). In "The Other," a female figure with "a womb of marble" inserts herself like "cold glass . . . Between myself and myself" (202). And the paired poems "Daddy" and "Medusa" together play out a ghastly psychodrama whose protagonist is torn between a diabolical father, with his "barb wire" language, and a monstrous mother, whose "wishes / Hiss at my sins" (223, 226).

At the same time, however, the emergence of "the *Ariel* voice" was not just associated with a struggle toward the "birth of a new self-conquering self"; it was marked, like some of Plath's best early poems—for instance, "The Disquieting Muses," "Electra on Azalea Path" and "The Colossus"—by a mythologizing of that self which continually gave public significance to private experience. In "The Disquieting Muses," the blank-faced ladies of the De Chirico painting on which the poet was meditating are unnerving representatives of a guilt-ridden female art, and they can neither be escaped nor openly acknowledged. Facing her "traveling companions," the speaker helplessly swears that "no frown of mine / Will betray the company I keep" (*PCP* 76).[42] Similarly, in "Electra on Azalea Path" the guilt-stricken daughter who dreams "image by image" the *Oresteia* that is her dead father's epic, can only knock "for pardon" (116–17) at the gate of a history that will never forgive her and that is both public (the chronicle of the house of Atreus) and private (the tomb, on "Azalea Path" in a Boston cemetery, of Otto Plath). Finally, in "The Colossus" the speaker, struggling to piece together the incoherent language ("Mule-bray, pig-grunt and bawdy cackles"), as well as the "immense skull-plates" of the dead father who is simultaneously her own lost father and the father-god of a patriarchal tradition, crouches "in the cornucopia" of his gigantic "left ear," hopelessly stranded, her hours "married to shadow" (129–30).

But in the *Ariel* poems the uses of mythology were far more liberating. In "Daddy" and "Medusa," mythologizing personal experience does not imply the repetition compulsion of stories whose fatality is inescapable. As the drafts of "Daddy" reveal, for instance, the last stanza of the poem, with its violently declamatory "Daddy, daddy, you bastard, I'm through," was added as part of a careful revision obviously intended to elaborate on the poem's vampire imagery and, more specifically, to clarify the victory implicit in the ritual exorcism that the speaker has just performed.[43] The Agamemnonlike figure of "The Colossus" had functioned as a cultural superego exactly like that dead father who, Freud wrote in *Totem and Taboo* (1913), constitutes the law in patriarchal society. But in "Daddy" he has been transformed into a more vulnerable Dracula. The simultaneously personal and public monument the poet inhabited in the earlier work has metamorphosed into a demon who inhabits and inhibits *her*—but who can therefore be cast out.

Similarly, in "Medusa" the poet mythologizes a frightening mother figure —originating not just in her own mother but also in "The Disquieting Muses," "The Other," and "The Rival"—as a gorgon/jellyfish whom the speaker, a sort of female Perseus, can at least seek to escape, ambiguously crying "Off, off, eely tentacle! // There is nothing between us" (*PCP* 226). As several critics have noted, the origin of this text, first entitled "Mum," "begins to come clear when one discovers that *medusa*, a stage in the life cycle of the jellyfish, is synonymous with *aurelia*"—the name of Plath's own mother.[44] Where in Plath's earlier work such a coincidence would have implied an inexorable doom, however, a sting that turns the daughter-poet as stony as the gowns of her bald-headed muses, here it leads to a redefinition of myth, mother, and sea creature that may promise the speaker's liberation from her antagonist's "eely tentacle."

Finally, such revisions of private and public myth facilitated more radical redefinitions of linguistic and cultural concepts. For while the emergence of Plath's *Ariel* voice was associated with newly powerful technical strategies and the birth of a newly empowered self-conquering self, it was also evidence of a struggle toward accurate analyses of "the war" and "the real world" and "the difference" through newly confident uses of language. The processes and possibilities of definition, indeed, are at the heart of the *Ariel* poems, whose dazzling chains of metaphors and similes repossess all the terrible territories of experience by renaming them.

Such renamings had always, of course, interested Plath. From the bemused zoology of the opening of "Blue Moles" ("They're out of the dark's ragbag" [*PCP* 126]) to the pregnant wit of the analogies that constitute "You're" ("Mute as a turnip . . . Vague as fog and looked for like mail. . . . Right, like a well-done-sum" [141]), she had sought, perhaps more persistently than most poets, to explain physical and mental phenomena through figuration. But some of the modesty of her early, thesaurus-obsessed poems may be attributed to an insecurity about her own definitional abilities, which was matched by the nervousness about her talents as a dreamer expressed in "The Shrike," "The Wishing Box," and "Johnny Panic." "The word, defining, muzzles," she complained in "Poems, Potatoes" (1958): "word and line . . . shortchange me continually" because when she struggles to deploy them to represent and contest the primacy of a dauntingly *given* world of objects, language "still dissatisf[ies] . . . the potato / Bunches its knobby browns on a vastly / Superior page; the blunt stone also" (*PCP* 106).[45]

From the spring of 1961 onward, however, Plath began to look both at words and at the world they represent from a radically alienated and therefore liberated perspective, refusing the black shoe of received definitions and generating, instead, her own meanings. The middle-period poem "Widow" (1961) frankly meditates on this process, proposing a series of alternative significations for a single word: "Widow. The word consumes itself— . . . Widow. The dead syllable, with its shadow / Of an echo. . . . Widow: that great, vacant estate! . . . Widow, the compassionate trees bend in" (*PCP* 164).

By the time Plath wrote "The Moon and the Yew Tree," on 22 October 1962 (which Hughes sees as also a crucial transition work), poem after poem had enacted the process of redefinition, as if the poet were a shaman simultaneously renaming and reinterpreting everything she encountered. "This is the light of the mind, cold and planetary," the poem begins, focusing on consciousness, but then it moves outward into efforts to define the external landscape:

> The moon is no door. It is a face in its own right,
> White as a knuckle and terribly upset.
> It drags the sea after it like a dark crime. . . .
>
> The yew tree points up. It has a Gothic shape. . . .
>
> And the message of the yew tree is blackness—blackness and silence.
>   [*PCP* 173]

In the same way "Mirror," written the next day, forces the mirror to define both itself and its purpose: "I am silver and exact. I have no preconceptions. . . . Now I am a lake. A woman bends over me. . . . In me she has drowned a young girl, and in me an old woman / Rises toward her day after day, like a terrible fish" (173–74).

In 1962 these redefinitions became increasingly ambitious. The unfinished "New Year on Dartmoor" addresses a young child (her infant son, Nicholas) and uses his estranged perspective to confront both time and snow:

> This is newness: every little tawdry
> Obstacle glass-wrapped and peculiar.
> . . . Only you
> Don't know what to make of the sudden slippiness,
> The blind, white, awful, inaccessible slant.
> There's no getting up it by the words you know.
>
> [*PCP* 176]

With comparable severity, "Berck-Plage" organizes the poet's encounter with death and dying around the distanced observations of an onlooker who refuses to acquiesce in conventional definitions. Beginning flatly with "This is the sea, then, this great abeyance," the poem insistently rejects received physical and grammatical categories. "Electrifyingly-colored sherbets . . . travel the air in scorched hands"; a "black boot . . . is the hearse of a dead foot"; "a green pool opens its eye, / Sick with what it has swallowed"; the speaker herself is "not a nurse . . . not a smile"; the surgeon is "one mirrory eye"; a "curtain . . . flickering from the open window" is both "a pitiful candle" and "the tongue of the dead man" which says, "Remember, remember"; and finally the children watching the funeral from the schoolyard see "a wonderful thing— // Six round black hats in the grass and a lozenge of wood, / And a naked mouth, red and awkward"—the figures of ceremony (attendants, coffin, grave) transformed and reinvented (196–201).

After this, throughout *Ariel* poem after poem dramatizes Plath's victory over the "aureate poetry" of the "old god" either by questioning and repudiating normative definitions or by proposing new kinds of meanings. "A Birthday Present" begins, "What is this, behind this veil, is it ugly, is it beautiful?" (*PCP* 206), while "The Bee Meeting" opens by asking, "Who are these people at the bridge to meet me?" (211) Similarly, "Stopped Dead" opens with "a squeal of brakes. / Or is it a birth cry?" (230) and "Fever 103°" wonders, "Pure? What does it mean?" (231) In a more bleakly comic mode, the speaker of "Getting There," who defines herself as "a letter in this slot" and the earth as "Adam's side," muses, "What do wheels eat?" (248).

Such testings of language and experience, cast in alienated Woolfian cadences versified, if not in Yeatsian stanzas, then with Yeatsian skill, replicate the disaffected perspective on history that informs "Cut," "Getting There," "Mary's Song," "The Swarm," and other poems. Just as important, such explorations prepare for newly assertive claims about the self and the world, many almost obsessively cast in definitional phrases—"I am" or "have," "This is," "You are." The speaker of "Stings," for instance, declares that "*I / Have* a self to recover, a queen" (*PCP* 215). The heroine of "Fever 103°" exults that "*I / Am* a pure acetylene / Virgin . . . Attended . . . By whatever these pink things *mean*" (232). The speaker of "Ariel" boasts that "*I / Am* the arrow / The dew that flies / Suicidal, at one with the drive / Into the red // Eye, the cauldron of morning" (240), simultaneously redefining self, sun, and morning/mourning. And the maternal poet of "Nick and the Candlestick" moves from a sardonic self-renaming ("*I am* a miner") to a loving renaming of her child ("*You are* the baby in the barn) (240, 242; all emphases ours).[46]

These linguistic testings of identity and environment frequently lead to redefinitions of both which virtually constitute prophetic propositions about the *new*, the heretofore unimaginable, substituting for the thesaurus, with its fixed synonyms and antonyms, a lexicon of fresh possibilities. Thus, throughout the *Ariel* poems Plath intermittently (and sometimes hesitantly or painfully) confronts the crucial question implicit in much of her work: what would be the nature of a future in which the real world did *not* equal the war and the difference?

To be sure, in "Superman and Paula Brown's New Snowsuit," the story whose narrator laments her wartime fall into reality and differentness, *difference* refers primarily to the distinction between the young protagonist's prewar political innocence (when her ethnicity seemed to entail no special consequences) and her wartime political experience (when she was blamed in the real world for ruining her playmate's snowsuit, just as German-Americans were unjustly interned). Yet the concept of gender difference is implicit in the contrast between innocence and experience. Indeed, as the parallel between international and sexual battles in such poems as "Lady Lazarus" and "Daddy" demonstrates, for Plath the savage war between men and women was very like a war between sovereign states. Thus the female child's fall into the real world and the difference at the very least prefigures a fall into a sex role bound to vex an ambitious girl who wanted to be God.

In what sort of future might a girl with such extravagant desires escape the constrictions of gender? Although Plath claimed in a late radio interview to be deeply concerned with world politics, she did not have an explicitly political imagination.[47] Moreover, although she had early read Langdon-Davies' prophecies about the future of sex roles with keen attention, she rarely tried to shape her dissatisfactions with gender imperatives into a theory. Nowhere, for instance, do her comments on Virginia Woolf encompass that writer's feminist treatises, nor does she ever address the visions of sex-role transformation implicit in, say, *Orlando* and *Between the Acts*. In spite of her awareness that she herself was living at the front in an age of sexual combat, Plath rarely meditated on the future of gender in her society.

In fact in the late poem "Brasilia," the one work that comes close to futuristic speculation, the speaker ironically withdraws from thoughts of radical change. The piece begins:

> Will they occur,
> These people with torsos of steel
> Winged elbows and eyeholes
>
> Awaiting masses
> Of cloud to give them expression,
> These super-people!—

But then Plath renounces the possibility of such a new occurrence, proclaiming the biological inexorability that would prevent it ("my baby a nail / Driven, driven in") and even praying that he may continue in his ordinariness ("leave / This one . . . unredeemed // By the dove's annihilation" [*PCP* 258–59]).

Nevertheless, in many of her most compelling texts Plath fantasized escapes from sexual difference which parallel some of the strategies for imagining the "sexchanges" of the *new* that were deployed by such artists as Woolf and H. D. Most obviously, perhaps, in *The Bell Jar* as well as in "Getting There," she imagined her own rebirth. Esther Greenwood, plummeting downhill on skis whose motion she has not mastered, strives to unite with "the white sweet baby cradled in its mother's belly" (79).[48] The speaker of "Getting There" rides a train that "is dragging itself, it is screaming . . . Insane for the destination" and ultimately decides:

> The carriages rock, they are cradles.
> And I, stepping from this skin
> Of old bandages, boredoms, old faces
>
> Step to you from the black car of Lethe,
> Pure as a baby.
>
> [*PCP* 249]

And, by implication at least, the "baby" self to be reborn here is a preoedipal creature whose innocence signals an ontological freedom from the contaminations of gender and whose unmarred newness recalls both the ambiguous hopefulness of the new life (that might be) generated at the end of *Between the Acts* and the restorative powers of the myrrh-drenched bundle who appears at the conclusion of H. D.'s *Trilogy*.

That the rebirth of such a purified fantasy self is achieved only at great risk—the screaming train is full of dangers, the ski ride breaks Esther's leg—proves just how radical as well as how crucial the poet's struggle toward the new has become and suggests that from Plath's conflicted perspective the new can only come into being through an annihilation of the old. The poem "A *Birth*day Present" makes this point explicitly by defining the "knife" of change that will "not carve, but enter" to slice the universe from the speaker's "side" as "pure and clean as the cry of a baby" (*PCP* 208; emphasis ours). But some of the assertive self-definitions that we discussed above formulate the violence associated with gender transformation even more directly.

"Ariel" 's self-as-"arrow" flying toward rebirth in the "red . . . cauldron of morning" (*PCP* 240), for instance, incorporates the definition of masculinity proposed by Buddy Willard's mother in *The Bell Jar* ("A man should be an arrow into the future; a woman should be the place the arrow shoots off from") into a prophetic figure of ferocious androgyny. Similarly, the "pure acetylene / Virgin" of "Fever 103°," shedding her sexuality like "old whore petticoats" as she rises into a future whose mysterious objects ("whatever these pink things mean") she can hardly define, regresses to a virginity that, like the innocence of the baby, predates difference but is also as searingly dangerous to the ordinary reality of the past as an acetylene torch. And that, as several commentators have noted, this speaker's obliquely confessed eroticism is feverishly masturbatory ("All by myself I am a huge camellia / Glowing and *coming* and going") reemphasizes her metaphorically androgynous self-sufficiency (232; emphasis ours).[49]

But if both Plath's fantasized arrow-self and her virgin-self are dangerous in their quasi-androgynous transcendence of traditional gender categories, some of her most vengeful yet stereotypically *"female"* selves are equally deadly in their construction of a kind of *super* femininity that also, paradoxically enough, strives toward the new in its elision or evasion of traditional sex roles. In her sardonic revision of biblical parable, the heroine of "*Lady* Lazarus" achieves, in the seductively (albeit parodically) eroticized body of a woman, the resurrection that Jesus had bestowed on a man whose powerless sisters, Mary and Martha, had watched in wonderment. As she rises miraculously from the "grave cave," moreover, this literally and literarily marvelous speaker wryly prophesies a future of further rebirths ("like the cat I have nine times to die") while boasting the terrifying Romantic authority of the bard of "Kubla Khan."[50]

At the same time, as she narrates her story of turning, burning, and rising "out of the ash," the speaker of "Lady Lazarus" unmistakably asserts the legendary regenerative power of the phoenix claimed by D. H. Lawrence, the modernist to whom Plath had ambivalently alluded in "Johnny Panic." Like Lawrence's totemic phoenix who "renews her youth / only when she is burnt," Plath's speaker is, in Lawrence's words, "renewing her youth like the eagle, / immortal bird" ("Phoenix," *LCP* 728). More radically, though,

Plath's flaming, red-haired revenant threatens a resurrection of the feminine that will explode the old order by destroying the power of the patriarchal enemies ("Herr God, Herr Lucifer") who had mistakenly identified
her as their "opus" in the first place. Thus, as she brags "Out of the ash / I
rise with my red hair / And I eat men like air," she preenacts the impassioned warning on which Hélène Cixous was to elaborate later in *The Newly
Born Woman:* "When '*The*' repressed of their culture [sic] . . . come back, it is
an explosive return, which is *absolutely* shattering."[51]

Similarly, in "Stings" the self reincarnated as a queen bee, a "red / Scar in
the sky, red comet," is neither (like the baby and the virgin) presexual nor
(like the male/female arrow) androgynous, but rather *super* sexual in her
generative and regenerative femaleness. Yet she too rises out of a tired
gender order that forced her into "a column // Of winged, unmiraculous
women, / Honey-drudgers," and thence out of the "mausoleum" of sexual
domestication that had previously "killed her" (*PCP* 215, 214). And she, too,
is murderous, both in her rage against the bee-keeping father figure—that
"great scapegoat" whom her sister bees died to kill when they molded onto
his lips, "complicating his features"—and in her achievement of a sexuality
that must destroy every male who mates with her.[52]

Whether they withdraw from the feminine into a preoedipal "purity,"
appropriate a form of androgyny, or fantasize a powerful super femaleness,
Plath's dreams of escape from gender and its discontents are usually as
"blood-hot and personal" as are most of the poems in *Ariel.* In only one piece,
"Wintering," does she even attempt a vision of *communal* female redemption.
Here, instead of contemptuously rejecting the honey-drudgers who winter
"in a dark without window," Plath rejoins in her imagination the population
of the hive, from which the oppressions of masculinity—and thus the *re*pres-
sions of gender—have been eliminated.

> The bees are all women,
> Maids and the long royal lady.
> They have got rid of the men,
>
> The blunt, clumsy stumblers, the boors.
>
> [218–19]

True, the poet's notation at this point that "Winter is for women— / The
woman, still at her knitting. . . . Her body a bulb in the cold and too dumb to
think" hints at a risk to her own sex almost as grave as the danger to the
"men" the female bees have got rid of. Nor does her initial question about
the fate of this female community—"Will the hive survive?"—imply a positive answer. Yet as her drafts for the poem reveal, Plath struggled, achingly,
toward affirmation here. In an incisive analysis of the composition of the bee
sequence, Susan Van Dyne has discussed the ambivalence with which Plath

strove "to assert a compelling prophecy" in the last stanza of this poem, and certainly her first draft of the stanza is more desperate than it is optimistic:

> What will they taste [like] of the Christmas roses?
> Snow water? Corpses? [Thin, sweet Spring.]
> [A sweet Spring?] Spring?
> [Impossible Spring?]
> [Some sort of Spring?]
> [O God, let them taste of spring.]

Finally, though, the compelling prophecy emerged:

> Will the hive survive, will the gladiolas
> Succeed in banking their fires
> To enter another year?
> What will they taste of, the Christmas roses?
> The bees are flying. They taste the spring.
>
> [219][53]

Overcoming the winter of women through an indirect allusion to the "trumpet of a prophecy" with which another of Plath's Romantic precursors —Percy Bysshe Shelley—had predicted the coming of a new order ("O wind, if winter comes, can spring be far behind?") these determinedly regenerative lines imply an affiliation with other women that allows the speaker to move, at least momentarily, away from the solipsism of "Lady Lazarus," the acetylene virgin, and her other reborn avatars. And significantly, "Wintering" is the poem with which Plath had planned to close *Ariel* when in December 1962 she assembled what she considered the final manuscript of the collection, suggesting that if the poet had survived the winter that assaulted the "hive" of her mind, she might well have gone on to propose calmer and more generous fantasies of a future in which the real world did not entail the war and the difference.[54]

How conscious was Plath that she was seeking to confront dilemmas so obdurate that a victory over them might be impossible? That despite the self-annihilation which silenced her claims of regeneration, she understood the extremity of the lexical (and cultural) project she had undertaken in all these poems of redefinition becomes evident in her most open analysis of language, the late "Words," which characterizes words as "Axes / After whose stroke the wood rings, / And the echoes!" Dangerous enough to cause sap to well "like tears," these linguistic implements may be weapons, battle axes, but they are also instruments of *poesis*-as-making which indefatigably carve out "newness" by generating echoes which travel autonomously "off from the center like horses" (*PCP* 270).

Yet in this ambiguous and ambivalent poem—written three days before the ominous "Contusion," four days before the sinister "Edge," eight days before the poet's suicide—the poet also indicates her awareness that such tools of transformation and remediation may not ward off the doom induced by words themselves. The wounded sap modulates into "Water striving / To re-establish its mirror / Over the rock // That drops and turns," and the fallen rock then blurs into one of the fearsome "fixed stars" which "From the bottom of the pool . . . Govern a life." Ted Hughes, himself one of Plath's figures for the literary/historical as well as the private/personal antagonist over whom she triumphed in her composition of the *Ariel* poems, has commented about her final suicidal acquiescence in the fatality of fixed stars, "That her new self, who could do so much, could not ultimately save her, is perhaps only to say what has often been learned on this particular field of conflict—that the moment of turning one's back on an enemy who seems safely defeated, and is defeated, is the most dangerous moment of all. And that there can be no guarantees."[55]

But of course there are some guarantees: they are the poems of the redefined self and world whose newly fashioned words, like indefatigable hooftaps, echo the victory that this poet finally achieved—in her art if not in her life—over the war and the real world, and the difference. For if Plath's body could not sustain her struggle against "the mausoleum" of a history that she feared might want to kill her, her spirit could and did. She is, after all, resurrected every day as a crucial member of the visionary company who inhabit that twentieth-century poetic tradition we might call "Yeats's house."

Because Plath does inhabit Yeats's house, her unquiet ghost continues to haunt readers of both sexes. Indeed, some of the most hostile criticism she has received indicates that her spirit lingers to infuriate the apparently indifferent male authorities against whom she directed many of her most ferocious diatribes. But she is equally haunting to those more neutral male readers who look at her work with mingled admiration and anxiety, reactions which also summarize and perpetuate the sexual battle in which she was one of the mid-century's key combatants. In 1969, for instance, John Berryman with mingled pity and censoriousness wrote of Plath's self-annihilation that "she her credentials / has handed in," while in 1973 Robert Lowell, who had earlier paid tribute to Plath's transformation of herself into "something dangerously wildly new," redefined her as the wielder of a "*miniature mad talent.*"[56] As the most peculiarly privileged of this latter group of readers, however, Ted Hughes best articulates the ambivalence many evidently feel. Speaking in notably Plathian definitional cadences in "Cadenza," he laments that

> . . . I am the cargo
> Of a coffin attended by swallows.

And I am the water
Bearing the coffin that will not be silent.

The clouds are full of surgery and collisions,
But the coffin escapes—as a black diamond,

A ruby brimming blood,
An emerald bearing its shores.[57]

Even when she is dead, says Hughes's poem, this woman poet is irrevocably
alive: her coffin will not be silent; her words endure not just as hooftaps but
as jewels which transform the landscape.

A number of Hughes's critics have observed that following Plath's death
her husband, after writing only a few works, himself fell silent for three
years. But Ekbert Faas, who interviewed the writer on the contours of his
oeuvre in 1970, claims that although "Hughes merely alluded to Sylvia
Plath's suicide in February 1963 . . . the main focus of our discussion—the
story of a quester's descent to save his desecrated bride from the underworld
through his self-sacrifice—bore the obvious imprint of this event."[58] In
Gaudete, Faas argues, Hughes, reflecting his desire for such regeneration,
imagines his hero giving (re)birth to a lost woman, now a sort of earth
goddess and muse. And certainly, whatever the merits of this interpretation,
the poems written by the book's protagonist, printed as an epilogue to the
main narrative, appear to be shadowed by memories of the "event" on which
"Cadenza" also meditates. In one, it is described thus: "You knocked the
world off, like a flower-vase. / It was the third time. And it smashed."[59] In
another, which muses, like "Cadenza," on a coffin that "took a wrong turning": "All I have // For an axle // Is your needle / Through my brains." And
in another, perhaps the most telling in its evocation of that primal scene of
erotic combat on which Plath herself had often brooded, "The sun, like a
cold kiss in the street" is

A mere disc token of you.

Moon—a smear
Of your salivas, cold, cooling.
Bite. Again, bite.[60]

"Bite. Again, bite": Is there no way out of the sexual battle recorded in
Plath's "Stone Boy, with Dolphin" and in Hughes's "Lovesong," with its characterization of "his words" as "occupying armies" and "her laughs" as "assas-
sin's attempts"?[61] Did the blitz on women of which Plath was an unwilling
heiress doom her survivors to repetitions of the same conflict? Or had this

failed Lady Lazarus finally achieved a few glimpses of the new that were inspiring to her *female* contemporaries and descendants? Among women readers and writers Plath has long, of course, been both a charismatic and a controversial figure. Adrienne Rich speaks for what is now several generations when she notes with nervous respect that Plath's "sense of *herself*" as "embattled, possessed" gives her poetry "its dynamic charge."[62] At the same time, Rich is representative in her worry about "the effect on so many young women poets of Sylvia Plath's suicide (an imaginative obsession unfair to Plath herself and her own struggle for survival)" ("Anne Sexton: 1928–1974," *L* 121). Certainly for such women as Anne Sexton, Erica Jong, and Joyce Carol Oates, the poet's self-destruction, signaling defeat in the battle for aesthetic fulfillment, seems at least on the surface to have been of primary concern, just as it was for men like Berryman and Lowell.

As if to confirm Rich's point about the effect Plath's fate might have on other women poets, Sexton—who had worked closely with her in a Boston writing group and who would herself commit suicide eleven years later— commented enviously a week after Plath's death, "I know at the news of your death / a terrible taste for it, like salt."[63] Ten years later, in "Alcestis on the Poetry Circuit (IN MEMORIAM Marina Tsvetayeva, Anna Wickham, Sylvia Plath, Shakespeare's sister, etc. etc.)," Erica Jong bitterly extrapolated a general destiny for the masochistic woman artist from the suicides of Plath and others like her:

> If she's an artist
> and comes close to genius,
> the very fact of her gift
> should cause her such pain
> that she will take her own life
> rather than best us.[64]

And in "The Death Throes of Romanticism: The Poetry of Sylvia Plath," Joyce Carol Oates decided, with comparable disapproval, that the "moral assumptions behind Plath's poetry condemned her to death, just as she, in creating this body of poems, condemned it to death."[65]

Problematic as Plath's fate was for her peers, however, many of her fears and resentments foreshadowed the ways in which the female affiliation complex functioned for her era. Just as a youthful Plath had scorned the "chocolate fancies" of the "prim, pink-breasted" solipsistic "Female Author" who "lies on cushions curled," for instance, Rich quite early in her career protested a culture in which woman is defined as "Time's precious chronic invalid," so that "our mediocrities [are] over-praised . . . slattern thought styled intuition." Similarly, just as Plath had complained that she did not want to be "quailing and whining like Teasdale," Carolyn Kizer attacked "the sad sonneteers, toast-and-teasdales we loved at thirteen . . . When poetry wasn't a craft but a sickly effluvium." As recently as 1991, indeed, the formalist poet Mary Jo Salter was defining the "female 'tradition'" as "wobbly and uneven," and declaring, "The time is overdue to admit that there is something of a vacuum in women's poetry, and that we abhor it."[66]

And finally, just as Plath had rebelled against the fatigue induced by the aureate poetry of the old god who incarnated a male-dominated Western literary tradition, Rich lamented "the great tradition / of human waste": in a dystopic vision of the "Artificial Intelligence" represented by a poetry-writing computer "force-fed / on all those variorum / editions of our primitive endeavors," she claimed for herself at least the "luxury of nausea" ("Artificial Intelligence," *F* 47), while Kizer wrote scorchingly of "man's uniform drabness, his impersonal envelope [and] formal, hard-fibered assurance." Indeed, even the more conciliatory Salter wondered, in her skeptical reappraisal of the "female 'tradition,'" whether "some men poets have been overrated."[67]

As both an icon and an articulator of the new, however, Plath had more positive meanings for her contemporaries and descendants. For one thing, although many saw her motherhood as (to understate the case) vexed by the self-annihilating impulses that led her to abandon her children in favor of her tryst with "Death & Co.," her determination to "write until I begin to speak my deep self, and then have children, and speak still deeper" (*J* 164) was not only pioneering but prophetic. In fact, as we shall argue, by choosing to *celebrate* maternity in such works as "You're," "Three Voices," and "Nick and the Candlestick," Plath virtually initiated what has become a significant genre for the mid- and late twentieth-century women whom we call "mother-poets." Equally resonant was her struggle to imagine modes of being (or bee-ing) that would resolve the problems posed by the war and the real world, and the difference. In some cases, the tropes through which she sought to transcend gender conflict may have directly influenced women writers who survived and studied her; in others, her images and metaphors may have merely paralleled linguistic fantasies through which subsequent poets, too, confronted the major cultural dilemmas associated with femininity. But whether consciously or coincidentally inscribed by others, her visions and revisions of (female) selfhood were almost uncannily representative of the new definitions of womanhood—and, more generally, the gender-inflected definitions of the new—that marked the work of her aesthetic sisters and daughters in the sixties and seventies.

Like Plath's, such innovative imaginings of the possible took many forms. Anne Sexton, for example—the woman poet most frequently aligned with Plath as a member of the so-called confessional school, despite many notable differences between their styles and themes—explored a range of transformative figures for a self freed from constraining sex roles, sometimes plainly echoing Plath's imagery, sometimes anticipating or paralleling solutions arrived at in *Ariel* and elsewhere.[68] In the late "O Ye Tongues," a sequence in *The Death Notebooks* (1974) whose presiding influence is the eighteenth-century mystic Christopher Smart, Sexton fortifies herself first by doubling herself into the quasi-androgynous pair/self "Anne and Christopher . . . my imaginary brother, my twin holding his baby cock like a minnow" and then by elaborating the Plathian motif of the preoedipal baby into an equally Plathian promise of *re*birth: "For birth was a disease and Christopher and I invented the cure. // For we swallow magic and we deliver Anne" (*SCP* 403).[69]

Earlier, in "Somewhere in Africa" (1962) Sexton had anticipated Plath's visions of a resistant super femininity, reimagining what Plath saw as the old god of aureate poetry, and what she herself defined as a patriarchal god of "prayers and psalms" spoken by the "dull" and "windy preacher," as a chthonic woman:

> Let God be some tribal female who is known but forbidden.
>
> Let there be this God who is a woman who will place you
> upon her shallow boat, who is a woman naked to the waist,
> moist with palm oil and sweat, a woman of some virtue
> and wild breasts, her limbs excellent, unbruised and chaste.
>
> [*SCP* 106–07]

A year or so later, in a move that parallels the central trope of Plath's "Fever 103°," Sexton addressed her grandmother in "Walking in Paris" (1963) and invited her, in an effort to "clean off / the mad woman you became," to return to a potent virginity:

> Come, old woman,
> we will be sisters! . . .
> Come, my sister,
> we are two virgins,
> our lives once more perfected
> and unused.
>
> [135–36]

Perhaps because Sexton's verse writing had its origins not (like Plath's) in a meticulous study of aureate poetry but as reconstructive therapy for mental illness, she was inclined at times to strive for even more radical solutions to the riddle of gender confinement.[70] *To Bedlam and Part Way Back* (1960), her first collection, includes both the apocalyptic "Venus and the Ark" and the gothic "Her Kind." In the first, "Two male Ph.D.'s" journey with a missile full of insects, snakes, fish, and rats to the allegorically resonant planet Venus, where the creatures they have transported evolve into different beings.[71] In the second, which is roughly contemporary with Plath's "Witch-Burning," the speaker draws on a traditional metaphor for deviant (female) identity, claiming to be "a possessed witch . . . [a] lonely thing, twelve-fingered, out of mind," but qualifies her self-definition with the remark, "A woman like that is *not a woman,* quite" (*SCP* 15; emphasis ours).[72]

Most radical of all in this respect, however, is "Consorting with Angels" (1962), included in Sexton's *Live or Die* (1966), which glosses an era of widespread preoccupation with sexchanges. Beginning "I was tired of being a woman . . . tired of the gender of things," Sexton here joins the ancient dispute on the nature of angels by metamorphizing the preoedipal baby, the revisionary goddess, the magical virgin, the unwomanly witch, and the apocalyptically mutant fish of Venus into an indeterminate being who transcends definition:

> I was not a woman anymore,
> not one thing or the other. . . .
>
> I've been opened and undressed.
> I have no arms or legs.
> I'm all one skin like a fish.
> I'm no more a woman
> than Christ was a man.
>
> [*SCP* 111–12]

Although she never attained the prosodic skill or the mastery of nuance and metaphor that characterize Plath's poems from 1961 onward, Sexton's search for visions of the new would lead her, eventually, into redefinitions of the erotic (*Love Poems* [1969]), revisions of fairy tales (*Transformations* [1971]) and reinventions of religion ("The Jesus Papers" [1972], *The Death Notebooks* [1974], *The Awful Rowing toward God* [1975]). Philosophically if not stylistically, Sexton took up where Plath left off, delineating a range of issues to which women writers influenced by the second wave of feminism would address their poetic letters from the front of the twentieth century's ongoing sex war.

In their separate ways, Denise Levertov and Diane Wakoski also confronted the problem of the new that Plath and Sexton had sought to solve. Just a year after Plath died, Levertov—always a poet with strong political commitments although never an avowed feminist—published a self-definition that in effect *de*genders her in her aesthetic role even while it draws on the same mythological super femininity to which Plath and Sexton had turned. "Song for Ishtar," alluding to the Babylonian goddess of love and fertility, begins by emphasizing the paradoxical attributes of this muse figure, who is both transcendent/celestial and immanent/material:

> The moon is a sow
> and grunts in my throat

> Her great shining shines through me
> so the mud of my hollow gleams
> and breaks in silver bubbles.[73]

At first, indeed, as lunar animal and silver mud work their wonders, the speaker's identity is indeterminate (although "the mud of my hollow" suggests biological femininity).

But then the poet leaps into a self-definition that evades human sex roles altogether while describing an erotic interaction with the goddess that both mocks and transfigures heterosexual intercourse:

> She is a sow
> and I a pig and a poet
>
> When she opens her white
> lips to devour me I bite back
> and laughter rocks the moon
>
> In the black of desire
> we rock and grunt, grunt and
> shine.

To paraphrase Sexton, Levertov might be saying here "I'm no more a woman / Than Ishtar was a man" even as she hints that a poet who is also a (sacred) pig has moved entirely out of what Plath implicitly defined in "Stings" as the "mausoleum, the wax house" of a gender system that obliges ordinary women to dry dishes with their "dense hair" (*PCP* 214–25).[74]

Elsewhere in this period, however, Levertov is less certain and less daring in constructing tropes for transformation. She is, of course, a mystical poet, perpetually seeking an "archetype / of the world always a step / beyond the world" ("The Garden Wall," *LP* 132), but often frank in her admission that the new and the ineffable are one. In "The Disclosure," a new "creature" is "slowly . . . pushing out" from "the shrivelling gray / silk of its cocoon," but it is virtually indescribable: "*not* a butterfly . . . *not* a furred / moth of the night" but simply "*some* primal-shaped, plain-winged, day-flying *thing*" (133; emphasis ours). Similarly, in "The Unknown," dedicated to Muriel Rukeyser, "one is / lured on" by "supererogatory divinations" so that the very sound of a kettle changing its note, "*the steam sublimed,*" seems to say "*Begin over.*" But although "the awakening is / to transformation, / word after word" (177)—giving language a function not unlike that in Plath's "Words"—the particulars of change remain unspoken, evidently unimaginable.

In Diane Wakoski's major collections from the sixties, too, the new is often the ineffable even while clearly a major object of the poet's desire. Adrienne

Rich, in her influential "When We Dead Awaken: Writing as Re-Vision" (1971), rightly grouped Wakoski with Plath as a pioneering woman poet in whose work "Man appears as, if not a dream, a fascination and a terror" (*L* 36). And in the very titles of some of her later books—*The Motorcycle Betrayal Poems* (1971), *Dancing on the Grave of a Son of a Bitch* (1973)—as well as in many of the *George Washington Poems* (1967) Wakoski re-creates the Plathian rage that she herself formulated in, for instance, the early "Poem to the Man on My Fire Escape":

> Voyeur,
> how limited your investigations become. . . .
> You want to know what's inside a woman—
> underneath her clothing. . . .
> how she bleeds,
> how she creeps in your past?
>
> You are looking in the wrong window; and I hope
> you were frightened by what you saw.[75]

In the introduction to the 1974 reissue of her three earliest books as *Trilogy*, Wakoski offered an incisive self-analysis, explaining that many poems "intend to present a vision of reality as absurd and foolish, often taking the dignity out of [male-dominated] history in order to rewrite it"—in much the way that Plath did in "Daddy" or "Cut." Several other points in this miniature poetic manifesto sound significantly Plathian as well: "In all my collections . . . I created a Diane whose real experiences were dramatized and exaggerated, were presented as surrealist experiences or metaphysical ones [perhaps because] the poems were a way of inventing myself into a *new life*" (xv; emphasis ours). Thus Wakoski continually reimagines herself as an "Empress," a priestess, "the first president's wife" inaugurating a new cycle of history, a moon goddess, an avatar of Isis, a sword with a "starry hilt."

Yet as the wistfulness of her tone often reveals, and as the phrase "motor-cycle *betrayal*" indicates, Wakoski is even more skeptical than Plath about the redemptive possibilities of either *the* or *a* new life. The "first president's *wife*" recycles the gender configurations of the past, while the enthralled lover of the treacherous motorcyclist laments her abandonment by a similarly gendered past. And when, as in the early "To the Lion," Wakoski constructs a speaker who assumes the prophetic powers of a Lady Lazarus—

> I am the girl who visits the sun,
> east of destiny and west of destruction,
> who comes in the rain to remind you of tomorrow
> and the silken trees.

[21]

—she echoes the fatality of Plath's "Words" in her conclusion:

> . . . I am the girl
> who would not know what to do
> if the words came true,
> if stones tumbled in her hands.
> I am the girl who is speaking with words
> and knows words will never break stone. . . .
> and I am the girl who has broken the silence of stone
> to speak
> and in so doing
> has sealed her voice behind fallen rocks
> forever.

Finally then, Wakoski's keenest intimations of the new, like Levertov's remain "supererogatory divinations" rather than fully realized fantasies of transformation—moments of intuition whose meanings remain indeterminate or indecipherable. "Looking for the Sign on Fulham Road (The Star)" (1968) parallels Levertov's "The Unknown" in its simultaneous yearning for a portent of the new and its refusal to determine the nature of what is to be revealed:

> What is the sign
> I was to have received on this road
> today? . . .
> The sign must come like dawn. You cannot see its
> arrival but know when it is there.
> . . . I dip my fingers into a basin of water,
> and see the moon reflected,
> or is it a stone, or a fish,
> flashing away to a darker pool?[76]

Although she has created one of our richest bodies of self-mythologizing verse, and has been consistently concerned with the problems generated by the war and the real world, and the difference, Wakoski has paradoxically been as wary as Levertov about asserting the claims of a seer.

Ultimately, it was to Adrienne Rich that the mantle of feminist prophecy descended, as the phrase "When We Dead Awaken" indicates. Indeed, in this essay Rich outlined her view that, like Plath, women poets of the mid-century must struggle beyond "victimization and . . . anger" into the imagining of unprecedented possibilities: "A new generation of women poets is already working out of the psychic energy released when women begin to move out towards what the feminist philosopher Mary Daly has described as the 'new space' on the boundaries of patriarchy" (*L* 49). While Rich's own efforts to define that new space have been too complex to review in a few pages, we should certainly note that in their inception and intensity they paralleled Plath's as closely as Rich's career did.

Like Plath's, Rich's poetic oeuvre began with both a youthful poetic decorum and a striking allegiance to modernist aesthetic fathers. W. H. Auden pronounced in his introduction to her first book—the prize-winning *A Change of World* (1951)—that her early poems "speak quietly but do not mumble, respect their elders but are not cowed by them."[77] Although his tone is patronizing, his comment is largely accurate. As Rich has herself remarked, her style "was formed first by male poets . . . Frost, Dylan Thomas, Donne, Auden, MacNeice, Stevens, Yeats" (most of them writers equally important to Plath), while in "those years formalism" (as a kind of "decorum") "was part of the strategy" (*L* 40).[78]

Perhaps because she is a more conscious cultural theorist than the author of *Ariel*, Rich critiqued the gender order associated with the tradition represented by her male precursors a bit earlier than Plath did. Between 1958 and 1960, while Plath was still for the most part enthralled by the aureate poetry of the old god, Rich produced the lucidly angry and visionary "Snapshots of a Daughter-in-Law," a ten-part sequence which became the title poem of the volume she published in 1963, the year Plath died. And although she later called this poem "too literary, too dependent on allusion," she conceded that it "was an extraordinary relief to write" it (*L* 45).

Beginning with a series of images of female repression *and* rebellion that have become staples of feminist criticism—the domesticated mother-in-law whose mind "molder[s] like wedding-cake," the "nervy, glowering" daughter who lets "the tapstream scald her arm" out of self-destructive rage, the "thinking woman" who "sleeps with monsters," the sex object who "shaves her legs until they gleam / like petrified mammoth-tusk"—Rich formulated in "Snapshots" a dramatic analysis of the perils surrounding female aesthetic or intellectual transgression, deploying imagery of sexual warfare that summarized the conflicts of several generations. For "the crime" of "cast[ing] too bold a shadow" or "smash[ing] the mold straight off," she observed, the punishment was "solitary confinement, / tear gas, attrition shelling," so that there are "few applicants for that honor" (*F* 38).

But the prophetic conclusion of "Snapshots" resonates as strongly as the poem's earlier depiction of the consequences of the feminine mystique. Here, in a telling revision of a key passage from Simone de Beauvoir's *Second Sex*, the poet transcribes an epiphany of a redemptive woman who will deliver a new life to the female community:

> Well,
> she's long about her coming, who must be
> more merciless to herself than history.
> Her mind full to the wind, I see her plunge

breasted and glancing through the currents,
taking the light upon her
at least as beautiful as any boy
or helicopter,
          poised, still coming,
her fine blades making the air wince
but her cargo
no promise then:
delivered
palpable
ours.

[*F* 38–39]

Significantly, the sentence from de Beauvoir scornfully redacts the god-
dess/muse myths that, in the view of the French feminist, have historically
functioned to *oppress* women: "She comes down from the remoteness of
ages, from Thebes, from Crete, from Chichen-Itza; and she is also the totem
set deep in the African jungle; she is a helicopter and she is a bird; and there
is this, the greatest wonder of all: under her tinted hair the forest murmur
becomes a thought, and words issue from her breasts."[79] But where the
existentialist de Beauvoir sees the reifying sacralization ("she is a helicopter
and . . . a bird") and magical materiality ("words issue from her breasts") of
this legendary woman as perniciously dehumanizing, Rich's revision affirms
those characteristics by incorporating them into the gender-transcending
humanity of the female redeemer she imagines.

Although she is a Christlike figure ("more merciless to herself than history"), this heroine's advent is not a second coming but a first appearance. Yet
the messiah of "Snapshots," "Her *mind* full to the wind," draws on imaginative powers invoked by such Romantic and post-Romantic male artists as
Wordsworth ("The winds come to me from the fields of sleep"), Shelley ("O
wild west wind . . . make me thy lyre even as the forest is"), and Lawrence
("Not I, but the wind that blows through me").[80] At the same time, she is both
womanly ("breasted") and masculine ("as beautiful as any *boy*"—though not
an adult *man*) with the Daedalian transcendence and ferocity of a helicopter
("her fine blades making the air wince"). Finally, although herself a redeemer, she has the Madonnalike power to give birth to a new life ("her
cargo . . . delivered / palpable / ours"), fulfilling the "promise" made to
women when they were born human and therefore equal to men.

After *Snapshots*, in both poetry and prose Rich addressed herself with increasing passion to sexual politics. She sought (like Plath, but more openly)
to explore the gender warfare that ensued when the daughters of patriarchal society strove to free themselves from the cultural fiat that had constructed them as daughters-in-*law*. And she attempted (again, like Plath,
but more consciously) to imagine the nature of the new order that might be

"delivered" by feminism. "The tragedy of sex / lies around us, a woodlot / the axes are sharpened for," she wrote in "Waking in the Dark" (1971), describing herself as "a woman dressed in old army fatigues / that have shrunk to fit her" (*F* 153). If "I am death to man / I have to know it," she added in "August" (1972), because "his mind is too simple, I cannot go on / sharing his nightmares" (178). Instead, she struggled to "read . . . the map of the future, the roads radiating from the / initial split" ("Shooting Script" [1970], 145). In doing so, she moved, as Joanne Feit Diehl has put it, "away from painstaking imitation, through encoded representations of women's experience, to a radical poetics that seeks to reimagine the relationship among writing, eros, and sexual identity."[81]

The visions of the new to which Rich's radical poetics gave birth after "Snapshots" included fantasies of the liberation of nature or the natural, imaginings of the transformation of heterosexuality, dreams of the metamorphoses of motherhood and language, and—perhaps most important as a central theme throughout much of her career—visions of a transformed and transformative lesbianism. In the early, surrealistically Romantic "The Trees" (1963), Rich imagined an ecstatic freeing of the forest (and by implication of the flourishing hidden trees into which domesticated women had been turned) that in its way paralleled Plath's fantasy of bees flying toward spring: "The trees inside are moving out into the forest . . . Listen. The glass is breaking. / The trees are stumbling forward / into the night. Winds rush to meet them" (*F* 60–61). More ironically, in "The Demon Lover" (1966) she echoed the conclusion of Woolf's *Between the Acts* to predict the uncertainties that the future might impose on both men and women:

> . . . A new
> era is coming in.
> Gauche as we are, it seems
> we have to play our part.
>
> [82]

But tellingly, Rich had already begun in this poem to relinquish her hopes for a changed heterosexuality. "Posterity trembles like a leaf," she noted wearily, "and we go on making heirs and heirlooms," adding

> how much longer, dear child,
> do you think sex will matter?
> There might have been a wedding
> that never was:
> two creatures sprung free
> from castiron covenants.
> Instead our hands and minds
> erotically waver.
>
> [*F* 84]

Thus, in "The Mirror in Which Two Are Seen as One" (1971) she imagined delivering herself and her sister(s) into a new life, her "nerves the nerves of a midwife / learning her trade" (*F* 161), while in "Diving into the Wreck" (1972) she redefined herself—and her interlocutors—as an unprecedentedly single/plural male/female being, a mermaid/merman, who revisit(s) the primal scene of a wrecked culture "carrying a knife, a camera" and (like H. D.'s goddess bearing "the unwritten book of the new") "a book of myths / in which / our names do not appear" (164). More explicitly, in "Mother-Right" she described the flight of a mother and son, seeking to escape the paternal dominance of a man who "believes in what is his / the grass   the waters underneath   the air" (256).

Yet although Rich's "dream of a common language" of female transfiguration drew on Woolf's earlier, egalitarian notion of a common reader, just as her concept of androgyny echoed the idea outlined in *A Room of One's Own*, that vision was most deeply energized by her emerging belief that "the lesbian in us"—the "woman loving woman"—is most likely to redeem her sisters from "the tragedy of [hetero]sex" and "the phenomenology of anger."[82] "There are words I cannot choose again / *humanism androgyny*," Rich proclaimed in "Natural Resources" (1977), explaining that "such words have no shame in them, no diffidence / before the raging stoic grandmothers" (*F* 262). Instead she sought in greater detail and more desirously than Plath to outline the contours of a world in which women, like the bees of "Wintering," "have got rid of the men // the blunt, clumsy stumblers, the boors" (*PCP* 218–19).

Roped together by a *"cable of blue fire"* in death as in life, the women mountain climbers of "Phantasia for Elvira Shatayev" (1974) appear to have climbed toward such a world. Thus, when they speak in unison from what George Eliot once called "the other side of silence" to tell a male survivor that "we stream / into the unfinished the unbegun / the possible," their quasi-erotic bonding (*"we are moving almost effortlessly in our love"*) adumbrates not only Rich's exploration of lesbian eroticism in *21 Love Poems* but also her definitive association of lesbian desire with aesthetic revelation in "Transcendental Etude" (1977):

> . . . *I am the lover and the loved,*
> *home and wanderer, she who splits*
> *firewood and she who knocks, a stranger*
> *in the storm,* two women, eye to eye
> measuring each other's spirit, each other's
> limitless desire,
>   a whole new poetry beginning here.
>
>   [*F* 168]

As Diehl has observed, Rich's lesbianism is analogous to Walt Whitman's homoeroticism in enabling her to ground "the work of her empathetic imag-

ination in . . . a sensibility alive to sensation and an imaginative endurance
that enables [her, like Whitman] to endow pain with meaning."[83] Rich's
fierce and lucid feminism had in any case empowered her, from "Snapshots"
onward, to adopt a Whitmanesque stance of bardic prophecy as speaker for
and of a female community that she sought to transform into a Herland just
as Whitman strove to metamorphose "these states" into the America of his
dreams.[84] Yet for obvious reasons the "real" (as opposed to fantastic) *specifics*
of the new were often as unclear to Rich as they were to Whitman—or to
Plath, Sexton, Levertov, Wakoski, and their feminist/modernist precursors.

In "From a Survivor" (1972), Rich defined her life after the end of her
marriage and the suicide of her husband "not as a leap / but a succession of
brief, amazing movements // each one making possible the next" (*F* 177). But
in her poetry, as in her prose from this period, she is perhaps deliberately
vague about the nature of these movements, even when (as in the essay "The
Contemporary Emergency and the Quantum Leap" [1978]) she redefines
brief movement as "leap." "The 'quantum leap' of my title," she explains, "is
of course a leap of the imagination [which implies that] we are imagining the
new: a future in which women are powerful, full of our own power, not the
old patriarchal power-over but the power-to-create, power-to-think, power-
to-articulate and concretize our visions and transform our lives and those of
our children" (*L* 271–72).

What would such power actually mean, however? In another essay from
the same year ("Disloyal to Civilization: Feminism, Racism, Gynephobia"),
Rich contemptuously defined what it would *not* mean ("The First Woman to
be Cloned . . . The First Lesbian Secretary of State . . . The First Mother on
the Moon" [*L* 309]) but, understandably, she offered no further particulars.
Indeed, in her carefully argued *Of Woman Born*, published two years earlier,
she had decided that although to "seek visions, to dream dreams, is essential,
and it is also essential to try new ways of living . . . it can seem naive and self-
indulgent to spin forth matriarchal utopias." And again, she had concluded
with a call for an ineffable newness: "We need to imagine a world in which
every woman is the presiding genius of her own body. In such a world
women will truly create new life, bringing forth not only children (if and as
we choose) but the visions, and the thinking, necessary to sustain, console,
and alter human existence—a new relationship to the universe."[85]

Finally, then, for Rich—as for Plath, Sexton, Levertov, Wakoski, and
others of their generation—the new may have been most dramatically defined by her own self-creation as a prophet of transformation, a herald of a
new age who was already striving to live the changes her texts envisioned.
Each of these women struggled to become both a presiding genius of her
own body—as a sexual being, as an intellectual presence, as a public
performer—and a presiding genius of her own body of work. Unlike such
precursors as Moore, Millay, Wylie, and Bishop, all openly grappled with the
problems and possibilities of maternity as well as with the (re)formulations

of the erotic necessitated by a century of sex wars and sexchanges. And in the process of doing so each became, as Robert Lowell wrote of Plath, "something imaginary, newly, wildly and subtly created . . . hardly a woman at all [in the traditional sense], certainly not another 'poetess.'"[86]

That the transformation might be perilous has been suggested to some commentators by the failures of Plath and Sexton to survive their own suicidal impulses. Does Sexton's fantasy of a "death baby" imply a connection between her death and her struggle to be both mother and poet? Does Plath's final vision of a dead woman who has "folded" her children "back into her body" hint that suicide constituted for her the ultimate effort at gender transcendence? Such sex-linked speculations about self-destruction seem both futile and presumptuous, especially in the context of poetic careers which so persistently focused on new modes of *being*.[87]

In this last respect, not only the organization but the title of the manuscript that Plath left behind her when she died on 11 February 1963 seems as relevant to women of her generation as was her struggle to be a triple-threat woman. Before arriving at *Ariel*, she had considered and discarded a number of titles implicitly emphasizing male power and female victimization, most notably "Daddy" and "The Rabbit-Catcher."[88] In settling on *Ariel*, therefore, she was making a profoundly affirmative statement, which referred not just to a turbulent early-morning gallop on the horse Ariel but also, in a larger sense, to an ambitious affiliation with Shakespeare and with the airy spirit who was, along with Prospero, the presiding genius of *The Tempest*.

As such a genius, Shakespeare's Ariel has a history that significantly evokes plots in which Plath had felt herself enmeshed all her life. First, his imprisonment in a cloven pine by the "foul witch Sycorax" echoes the poet's sense that she had early been imprisoned in the body of the witchlike "mum" Medusa, whom she defined as the "bottle in which I live, // Ghastly Vatican" (*PCP* 225). Then, his subsequent thralldom to the patriarchal magician Prospero, from whom he constantly seeks his liberty, parallels Plath's sense of her own enthrallment to a colossal and magical "daddy." (That Prospero is the father of an utterly dependent and devoted daughter is also germane here.) Ariel's two most famous songs, moreover—"Full fathom five" and "Where the bee sucks"—foreshadow key Plathian motifs. In 1958 she actually produced a poem entitled "Full Fathom Five," and of course she wrote a number of other verses which meditate on the sea changes undergone by the lost father who is drowned in the depths of her psyche. At the same time, as a central attempt at self-definition, the bee sequence with which she planned to conclude *Ariel* might be seen as an extended variation on the theme "Where the bee sucks, there suck I."

From the start, of course, Shakespeare's Ariel is a relatively androgynous, or at least sexually indeterminate figure: "he" is never referred to by gender-marked pronouns, and in a number of productions over the centuries "his" part has been played by a woman.[89] In his ultimate liberation from Prospero, moreover ("to the elements / Be free"), "he" becomes a luminous figure for the victorious poet herself as, all air and fire, she enters "the cauldron of morning." That the poem "Ariel," in its play on the Hebrew meaning of the name ("God's lion"), simultaneously changes the gender of the translation (to "God's lion*ess*") and blurs the boundaries between horse and rider ("How one we grow") emphasizes Plath's determination to appropriate for herself as a *woman*-spirit both Ariel's tempest-making powers— including his crucial ability to wreck the king's ship—and his escape from patriarchal bondage. And as, like a "White / Godiva," the speaker of this poem "unpeel[s]— / Dead hands, dead stringencies," she imagines leaving behind her, as Ariel had, not only the torments imposed by the mother/witch and the tasks imposed by the father/magician but also the constrictions of the domesticated (female) body.[90]

An essay entitled "Ariel as Daemon and Fairy" which appears as an appendix to the Arden Shakespeare (edited by Frank Kermode in 1954, so that Plath quite possibly knew the text) describes the characteristics of this supernatural being as traits that would surely have been congenial to a girl who wanted to be God:

> Ariel has nothing of humanity . . . being pure intelligence, 'free from all gross and putrifying mass of a body, immortall, unsensible, assisting all, having Influence over all.' He has the qualities allowed to Intelligences in medieval theology, which include simultaneous knowledge of all that happens; understanding of the cause of things; the power to alter his position in space in no time, and to manipulate the operations of nature, so as, for example, to create tempests; the power to work upon a human being's will and imagination for good or evil ends; and total invulnerability to assault by material instruments.[91]

Obviously these ancient and sacred qualities could not be considered aspects of the *new* in any ordinary sense. Yet in their confounding of the "stringencies" we associate with reality, they are powers Plath fantasized assuming in poem after poem, from "Lady Lazarus" and "Daddy" to "Stings," "Getting There," and "Ariel" itself.

To be sure, Plath could not imagine the self she might achieve *after* her escape from her enslavement to patriarchal tropes and traditions. But then neither does Shakespeare depict Ariel's new life after Prospero bids him "to the elements / Be free." What Shakespeare does tell us, however—and what would have made *The Tempest* still more compelling to the poet who was tired of dwelling in daddy's "black shoe" and weary of the constraining volumes written by the old god of literary tradition—is that Prospero resolves in act 5 of *The Tempest* to break his staff and "bury it certain fadoms in the earth" and "deeper than did ever plummet sound" to drown his book of power. And of course—staffless, bookless—Prospero will no longer command Ariel, a point that would have sealed Plath's identification with that liberated spirit. Freed from the laws and codes that had empowered the father, she may well have felt that, as Ariel, she could at last enter the tradition represented by "Yeats's house" to confront the conundrum that H. D. had called the unwritten volume of the new.

7

The Lives of the Male Male Impersonator, the Loves of the Sextoid: Comedy and the "Sexual Revolution"

Humor is laughing at what you haven't got when you ought to have it. . . .
Humor is when the joke is on you but hits the other fellow first—before it
boomerangs. . . . Humor is your own unconscious therapy.
—Langston Hughes

What You Say to Her   What You Mean
It was only a joke.   I love the sex war because I always win.
—Joanna Russ

Isn't laughter the first form of liberation from a secular oppression? *Isn't
the phallic tantamount to the seriousness of meaning?* Perhaps woman,
and the sexual relation, transcend it "first" in laughter?
—Luce Irigaray

If World War II offered Sylvia Plath a trope of sexual battle which modulated into a search for new ways of (feminine) being, the crisis of total warfare plummeted many literary men into meditations on the artifice, indeed
the bankruptcy, of conventional definitions of the masculine. In Kurt Vonnegut's *Slaughterhouse-Five* (1969), two hospitalized soldiers are traumatized
by life, made "meaningless, partly because of what they had seen in the war":
one "had shot a fourteen-year-old fireman, mistaking him for a German
soldier," while the other had witnessed "the fire-bombing of Dresden. . . . So
they were trying to re-invent themselves and their universe."[1] Like Joseph
Heller's *Catch 22*, Vonnegut's fiction records its protagonists' revulsion
against outworn masculine roles, as well as their absurd efforts to reconstruct their universe and reinvent themselves. Indeed, such hopeless, hapless masculine reinvention repeatedly propels the comic escapades of a host
of antiheroes produced by Vonnegut's and Heller's contemporaries during
the late fifties, the sixties, and the seventies; that is, during the period associated with the sexual revolution.

In its advocacy of sexual license, so-called black humor often exploited farcical incongruities to protest the social malaise and sexual duplicity associated with the postwar era; however, a curious sense of exhaustion lurks behind its defiance. A story entitled "Who Am I This Time?" in Vonnegut's *Welcome to the Monkey House* (1968) makes it clear exactly how self-consciously this author manipulates the humor of male reinvention. The main character—a shy, reclusive man—comes to life only when he takes on various roles in the plays produced by the town theater. As Stanley Kowalski/ Marlon Brando in *A Streetcar Named Desire*, for example, he becomes "a sexy gorilla who was going to beat [Stella's] brains out," but after the show he disappears into "nothing and nobody," much to the disappointment of the amorous woman who plays Stella.[2] To capture her actor-partner, the heroine provides a succession of scripts with suitably passionate identities so that, as she triumphantly explains at the end of the tale, "I've been married to Othello, been loved by Faust and been kidnaped by Paris" (26). Hectically recycling fictive male roles, in this case parts provided by his wife, Vonnegut's man-without-qualities barely keeps his ontological emptiness at bay. Just as important, Vonnegut's wry awareness of the link between potency and violence in, say, Stanley Kowalski, Othello, Faust, and Paris hints at the source of all his heroes' ambivalence about their own ineffectuality, an ambivalence also dramatized by impersonation in the works of Roald Dahl, John Barth, Stanley Elkin, Thomas Pynchon, Vladimir Nabokov, and Ishmael Reed.

From *Lysistrata* to *Tom Jones*, of course, sex has been treated as a laughing matter. However, as a number of critical books from Robert Scholes's *The Fabulators* (1967) on have demonstrated, comedy in the 1960s and 1970s measured the alienation of a generation of authors horrified by a series of atrocities—the Holocaust, Hiroshima and Nagasaki—that made truth stranger and more threatening than even the most bizarre fiction and that made love the only conceivable, but hardly sufficient, antidote to war.[3] The farcical incongruities of experimental humor—its unspeakable practices and unnatural acts—also reflected a rebelliousness that fused the rhetoric of the sexual revolution with that of the Civil Rights and peace movements.

Like Vonnegut, practitioners of black humor or fabulation exploit surreal plots and cartoonlike characters in texts that often feature flagrantly manipulative narrators who demonstrate their authors' consciousness of the inanity of the human (and often the sexual) condition. But the formally more realistic novels of literary women from Mary McCarthy and Muriel Spark to Margaret Atwood, Fay Weldon, Erica Jong, Rita Mae Brown, and Angela Carter also comically incorporate sexually explicit material, turning fiction into a house of mirth.[4] Despite the marked generic asymmetry in the aesthetic productions of men and women during this period, their literature shares a common project: to bring to the surface a critique of male authority in elegiac meditations on the imminent demise of manhood and (heterosexual) eroticism. Paradoxically, throughout the years associated with the liberalization of sexual codes of conduct—the decades bracketed by the widespread dissemination of the Kinsey reports and the research of Masters and Johnson—literary men and women wrote about the problem of sexuality by creating a character whom we will call the "male male impersonator."

If, as social historians have noted, improved birth control, legal abortion, women's growing economic independence, and the beginnings of the gay liberation movement made it possible for women to uncouple sex from reproduction and to insist on their own capacity for (and right to) pleasure,[5] the growing disillusionment of many male artists with what seemed like antiquated myths of virility problematized their ideas about their own capacity for (and right to) pleasure. A male male impersonator like the one in Vonnegut's "Who Am I This Time?" represents men's uncertainty about their own potency, a fear that virility can only be recaptured through a masquerade of masculinity. Alienated from outworn roles for which there seem to be no adequate substitutes, the male manqué makes antic but often doomed efforts to reinvent himself, enabling his author to mourn an endangered eroticism that is either nostalgic in its biological essentialism or perplexing in its textual indecipherability. Even those black humorists purportedly dedicated to eros meditate on the potential demise of phallic sexuality, as if providing evidence for Henry Miller's belief that female laughter creates male impotence, because "the female seldom laughs, but when she does it's volcanic. When the female laughs the male had better scoot to the cyclone cellar."[6]

Miller's dread that laughter will "break down the most 'personal' hard-on in the world" oddly adumbrates Luce Irigaray's notion, expressed in the passage we use as an epigraph here, that laughter may be a form of liberation from the phallic. And Irigaray endorses a view maintained by a number of other French feminists. For Hélène Cixous, "the laugh of the Medusa" has the "volcanic" capacity to "break up the 'truth'" of a "phallogocentric" order. Catherine Clément claims, "All laughter is allied with the monstrous. . . . Laughter breaks up, breaks out, splashes over." And Julia Kristeva points out that "laughter is what lifts inhibitions by breaking through prohibitions."[7] Although most of these thinkers are speculating on the effect of women's laughter, the instability of humor implies that, as Langston Hughes puts it in a passage which we also use as an epigraph, laughter can function as therapy for both sexes.

From Thomas Hobbes to Sigmund Freud and George Santayana, theorists of laughter have examined various aspects of humor, which all appear in the definition supplied by Hughes: these include its release of aggression (it "hits the other fellow first"), its unmasking of vulnerability (it involves "laughing at what you haven't got"), and its self-reflexivity (it "boomerangs"), all of which contribute to its functioning as "unconscious therapy."[8] In the works of male fabulators, jokes about women boomerang against the male male impersonator, ridiculing masculine posturing and undercutting traditional justifications of male primacy. Yet because such radical investigations are frequently embedded in overtly misogynist scripts, some female readers have been distressed by comedy that at least initially seems to be directed against them. For if the male male impersonator demonstrates that a real man is hard to find, he is often partnered with a female figure who is radiant with the eroticism that eludes him, a figure we will call the "sextoid," whose desirousness suggests that a good woman signifies nothing but (heterosexual) desire.

At least in part a reflection of the wholesale commodification and eroticization of the female figure during the sexual revolution, the sextoid is, of course, a sex object. And clearly she alienates many female readers. As Joanna Russ has observed (in a passage that we take as our third epigraph), to those fictions in which literary men can be imagined explaining away such fantasies of dysfunctional men and libidinal playmates with a dismissive "It was only a joke," women often respond by decoding that sentence to mean, "I love the sex war because I always win." The capacity of readers to identify with characters across gender lines, however, meant that some women did laugh with men—and laughing *with* men involved laughing *at* them because of the incongruities that characterize humor: its tendency to attack the other, to reveal the vulnerability of the self, to boomerang. The fiction of the fabulators sometimes attacks that paradigmatic other—the female—first. But when it rebounds to laugh at "what you haven't got when you ought to have it," these same comic fantasies diagnose a masculine identity crisis symptomatic of what can only be construed as a prevalent male penis envy.

Male penis envy: the phrase comes from two of Woody Allen's films, *Annie Hall* (1977) and *Zelig* (1983), in which the comic describes himself as suffering from this strange ailment, and from Joseph Heller's novel *Something Happened* (1974), in which the narrator argues, "*Women* don't suffer from penis envy. *Men* do."[9] Both Allen and Heller are referring, obviously, to Freud's definition of the different effects of the so-called castration complex on boys and girls, a difference that marks their gender identities: "She acknowledges the fact of her castration, the consequent superiority of the male and her own inferiority, but she also rebels against these unpleasant facts."[10] In spite of Allen's assertion that he is one of the few men suffering from penis envy, Heller's protagonist seems more on target when he exclaims in his meditation on "our masculine genitalia" as "our weakest reed": "What a feeble weapon indeed for establishing male supremacy" (368–69). During the years that Jacques Lacan was developing his notion that the phallus is a "transcendental signifier" possessed by no man, a host of comic male characters appeared whose exotic, erotic escapades never quite manage to delude them about what Freud called "organic inferiority" or "the fact of [their] castration." Throughout this chapter, then, we apply Freud's account of the girl's attitude toward her femininity to the male male impersonator's reaction to his masculinity because, for the literary men of Allen's generation, masculinity itself was devolving into a "masculinity complex."

If prevalent male penis envy signals a masculine identity crisis that much black humor uncovers, how do women's comic productions express the muddles and doubts that occurred when neither men nor women knew which was the first, which the second sex? Men's jokes about the male male impersonator opened up a dialogue about the nature of gender into which women entered from a different angle. To the extent that, as Jane Gallop has argued, "postmodernism dephallicizes modernism,"[11] the comedies produced by postwar literary men constitute an interrogation of masculinity that ultimately undercuts traditional justifications of male primacy. Curiously, however, women's markedly different relation to comic traditions shaped works that tend to focus more on the faults of women than on the failures of men, questioning not only the ideology of femininity but also that of feminism, as well as the female literary tradition itself.

In spite of the skepticism men and women shared about themselves and each other, moreover, the male male impersonator threatened literary women with a series of new problems, different from but related to those generated by traditional gender definitions. Considering the dazzling pyrotechnics of fiction in the sixties, Raymond Federman has asked, "In what sense has self-reflexiveness made the writing of fiction . . . even more potent?"[12] Similarly, the women publishing during the second wave of the feminist movement used their comic inventions to examine an odd potency attending the newly anarchic male male impersonator, an examination that may explain the more somber, even gothic, nature of female humor. Lost in the funhouse of sexual comedies, many writers continued to believe that a good man is hard to find, while at least some women of letters took issue with Henry Miller to debate whether a hard man is good or, indeed, possible to find.

———————

In a post–D. H. Lawrence, post–Henry Miller age, many male satirists criticized the hypocrisy and repressiveness of society by presenting explicit celebrations of the body in general and of heterosexuality in particular. In doing so, their fiction accords with the philosophic and psychoanalytic ideas of Herbert Marcuse and Norman O. Brown, whose books promulgated the idea that liberating eros could heal the neurotic citizens of a deathly civilization. What Josephine Hendin calls the "sexualization of social protest,"[13] apparent in Marcuse's *Eros and Civilization* (1955) and Brown's *Love against Death* (1959), issued in comic fantasies dedicated to recovering an endangered eroticism and thereby freeing society of conformity to institutions that were thought to alienate men and women from the joys of sex. But even as male fabulators dramatize aggressively phallic fantasies in stories that hark back to biologically defined sex roles, their fictions inscribe a comedy of male male impersonation within worlds where such stable roles have been delegitimized. Two stories—Kurt Vonnegut's "Welcome to the Monkey House" (1968) and Roald Dahl's "Bitch" (1964)—illuminate how the misogynist plots of much black humor camouflage a subtext which enables their authors to examine the male penis envy of characters who masquerade as sexual liberators.

Vonnegut's "Welcome to the Monkey House," the title story of one of his most popular collections, diagnoses society's sexual ills by seeming to justify the necessity of rape in a culture controlled by repressive and repressed women. In the future world depicted by Vonnegut, a crowded Earth is ruled by "Ma" Kennedy, the president of a World Government that has instituted two programs to curtail overpopulation: the establishment of Suicide Parlors, in which volunteers can ask to be painlessly killed by specially trained "Hostesses," and the enforced consumption of birth control pills that deaden all feeling below the waist. Through "Ma" Kennedy's policies of prudery, carried out by the virgin Hostesses with "advanced degrees in psychology and nursing" (29),[14] Vonnegut's dystopia represents a nightmare vision of a Herland dedicated to "ethical" birth control that does not "interfere with a person's ability to reproduce, which would have been unnatural and immoral," but that instead takes "every bit of pleasure out of sex" (28).

The amazonian Hostesses titillate their customers, potential suicides, into asking for a lethal hypodermic, but they themselves remain virgins, downing pills that make them sexually numb. They are committed to the dream of their society's founder, J. Edgar Nation—obviously based on the FBI director J. Edgar Hoover—who had begun sanitizing American mores by introducing "morality into the monkey house at the Grand Rapids Zoo," thereby making the monkeys "fit things for a Christian family to see": "When he got through with the monkey house, you couldn't tell it from the Michigan Supreme Court" (32, 33, 35). Clearly, Vonnegut is satirizing the puritanical assumption that the pleasures of the body must be evil. But that a rebelliously unconventional hero—Billy the Poet—frees one Hostess from her false consciousness through a therapeutic rape underscores another point; that is, the need for women to be liberated by men into their (heterosexual) eroticism.

Billy the Poet, who "specializes in deflowering Hostesses in Ethical Suicide Parlors" (29), differs from his namesake, Billy the Kid, to the extent that he favors literary over martial arts, sending "dirty poem[s] in the mail" (30). Allied with an underground gang of so-called nothingheads, Billy writes these letters from the front—"*Virgin hostess, death's recruiter, / Life is cute, but you are cuter*" (34)—and impersonates prospective suicides to gain access to the Hostesses. When he forces one Nancy McLuhan out of the Suicide Parlor and into the memorialized Kennedy Compound at gunpoint, he tells her, "A woman's not a woman till the pills wear off" (37). There, injected with truth serum, Nancy undergoes a process of rehabilitation that begins when she answers the question "How does it feel to be a virgin at sixty-three?" with the admission "Pointless" (40).

At the climax of the tale, Vonnegut's philosophically emphatic but mild-mannered hero attempts to retrain the zombie Hostess into her femininity. The bespeckled, pajama'd Billy quietly states that the rape has been planned for the brainwashed Nancy's own "happiness," ignoring her protests that "your idea of happiness is going to turn out to be eight people holding me down on that table, while you bravely hold a cocked pistol to my head—and do what you want" (42). Depressed himself by the "clinical skill" with which he has to deflower her, Billy patiently explains that she will someday become as "*grateful*" as her predecessors (43). Billy's final tactics include attributing Nancy's anger to her disappointment in his "clumsy" lovemaking; promising her that her next, more virile, paramour will restore to sex "a certain amount of innocent pleasure" (45); reading her a sonnet by Elizabeth Barrett Browning that his grandfather recited to his grandmother on their wedding night; and—in order to help her disentangle sexual pleasure from reproduction—leaving her with a bottle of pills labeled "*Welcome to the Monkey House.*"

Presumably liberated into her own "natural sexuality" (44), Vonnegut's Suicide Hostess can now substitute eros for thanatos, freedom for frigidity, the healthy human body for the sick human mind. Vonnegut's tale registers a high degree of what Janice Doane and Devon Hodges call sexual nostalgia, for it contrasts an anaesthetized present with a romantic past (of wedding nights and Barrett Browning's "How do I love thee?" and trips to the zoo).[15] As a rape fantasy, moreover, "Welcome to the Monkey House" expresses precisely the sex antagonism that we traced in *The War of the Words*, even as it typifies the emphasis on female sexualization in much literature from the sixties and seventies. Released by rape into the monkey house of eroticism, Nancy exemplifies the transformation of the prude into the sextoid.

Yet, to the extent that "Welcome to the Monkey House" can be understood as not only an invocation of the sextoid but a critique of the male male impersonator, it illustrates the tendency of comic writing to hit the other fellow first and then boomerang. After all, Vonnegut's deathly future culture has been inaugurated by the puritanical J. Edgar Nation, an advocate of the "Christian family," and by politicians and religious leaders in the United Nations: a sign of Vonnegut's rejection of the ways traditional male authority has degenerated into authoritarianism. Just as important, its dissenting rebel engages in joyless sex so as to raise consciousness, knowing all the while that women like the newly sexualized Nancy will eventually choose more agile lovers. Hardly a virile Billy the Kid, Vonnegut's derivative Billy the Poet is a faintly depressed intellectual whose artillery consists of silly poems and impersonations of suicidal men. Billy may have himself evaded the artificial birth control pills that deaden all feeling, but he can only liberate Nancy by offering her another bottle of pills. Besides implying that sexuality has to be artificially constructed, "Welcome to the Monkey House" presents us with a male character in search of an elusive masculinity. Reduced to a deflowering machine, Vonnegut's hero has become an instrument of an eroticism characterized more by its ideological imperatives than by any pleasure principle. Even as Vonnegut takes female prudery as his target, his joke ridicules the pathetic desires of marginalized men, turning Billy into the schlemiel figure so frequently found in the fiction of the sixties.

Men are just as much in need of fantastic recourses in Roald Dahl's short story "Bitch," which describes the discovery of a bottled scent that even more efficiently returns men and women to the monkey house than would the bottle of "unethical" birth control pills Billy the Poet proffers at the end of Vonnegut's tale. And like Vonnegut's, Dahl's story revises earlier, pejorative evaluations of man's animal sexuality. Here too, however, a comic phallic fantasy ends up ridiculing men's quest for virility. As narrated by the "incorrigible philanderer" Oswald Cornelius, a "Casanova" who finances the venture, Henri Biotte, an olfactory chemist, manages to "produce a perfume which will have the same electrifying effect upon a man as the scent of a bitch in heat has upon a dog! One whiff and that'll be it! The man will lose all control. He'll rip off his pants and ravish the lady on the spot!"[16]

Like Vonnegut's, then, Dahl's fiction analyzes men's desire to recover an endangered sexuality. Because Henri seeks to restore "the eighth pure primary odour" that has been lost since the time "when primitive man . . . still retained the ape-like characteristic of jumping on any right-smelling female" (179, 175), and because such an invention would allow him and Oswald to "control mankind," they decide to go into partnership (181). Once Henri manufactures blend Number 1076, he calls Oswald to his laboratory. Within a scientifically controlled environment that will enable him to measure the effective range of the scent, Henri positions an unsuspecting professional boxer six meters away from a female laboratory assistant. To Oswald, the woman, just before she is sprayed with the perfume—which has no effect whatsoever on the female of the species—resembles a transfixed rat he had seen caged with a python. But after the boxer exhibits his "sheer animal ferocity," she pleads, "Spray me again!" (195–96). The two manufacturers respond by locking her up, naming the stuff *Bitch*, and speculating on marketing ideas that include selling it to "very fat, very rich women" and to men suffering the "loss of virility" (198).[17]

As in "Welcome to the Monkey House," in "Bitch" rape is presented as a therapeutic cure for no-manhood as well as a "natural" desire on the part of women. And in the concluding sequence of events, Dahl delineates—as Vonnegut does—the physiological and political implications of his comic fantasy. After the lab assistant disregards Henri's injunctions and sprays his share of the scent on herself, the scientist, who had a serious heart condition, is "killed in action" at his own lab, the secret of his concoction buried along with him (200). The "infernal" and presumably insatiable desires of women cause the world to lose the benefits of bottled phallic power. But if the story mourns the physical weakness of men whose survival is threatened by their own potentially supra- or subhuman potency, politically it laments the discrepancy between public posturings and private lusts.

Because the English Oswald dislikes a particularly hypocritical President of the United States, he decides to use the last remaining drops to remove this poseur from office. He encapsulates the scent within a corsage equipped with a timing device. Scheming to deliver the flowers to the person designated to introduce the president's next televised speech, he hopes to make the "slippery" president rape this woman "in full sight of twenty million viewers" (202). And the British Don Juan does reach her, a "thoroughly repugnant" giantess, who is "swathed from neck to ankles in the stars and stripes of the American flag" (205–06). An extraordinary image of America as Herland, Dahl's Daughter of the American Revolution punctures the perfume container as she pins on the corsage, leaving Oswald looking down on "my beloved sexual organ" which continues growing "until it had enveloped my entire body and absorbed it within itself. I was now a gigantic perpendicular penis, seven feet tall and as handsome as they come" (209). Filled with a "sense of power" that he has now become an unassailable "Lord of the Universe," he returns to ordinary reality hearing her moan, "You've certainly done me a power of good" (210).

Clearly the fate of Dahl's heroes illustrates the inanities of male phallic fantasies. In "Bitch," women do not need stimulants to trigger what is depicted as their fundamental lustiness, whereas men seek any artificial means to regain a phallicism so overwhelming that it either kills them or subverts their rational intentions. When the frail heart-attack victim Henri is placed beside the "gigantic perpendicular penis" Oswald, and when this odd couple is related to Vonnegut's pathetic rapist Billy the Poet and to his ersatz Stanley Kowalski/Marlon Brando, these figures exemplify a compensatory vision of phallic ascendancy—a clinging to masculinity—that only thinly veils anxiety about deficiency: "The hope of getting a penis sometime is cherished to an incredibly late age and becomes the aim of . . . life" ("FS" 198), as Freud explained in a different discussion of castration. Thus, being a man becomes a fantasy. Sometime around the late 1950s masculinity was being transformed into a masculinity complex just as popular medical theories were emphasizing the physical vulnerability to which male flesh is heir.

As Barbara Ehrenreich has observed, the nineteenth-century association of femininity with illness and masculinity with health was overturned in the middle of the twentieth century. "You, men, are the weaker sex," *Today's Health* explained in 1957, cautioning, "The practice of manliness has become . . . a lethal curse" because "you have a greater chance of dying in each of life's decades than have your women-folk" and by 1976 Herb Goldberg, Ph.D., argued in his evocatively entitled *The Hazards of Being Male* that the "situation is becoming worse": "In 1920, the female life expectancy was only one year higher than that of the male. *Today, the difference is almost eight years and increasing!*" Associating women's professional gains with the liberation of the female body, *The Male Dilemma: How to Survive the Sexual Revolution* (1974) asked, "What is it like to be a man at a time when, with the advent of the Pill, women have the sexual freedom formerly practiced only by men and known to women only in fantasy; a time when every gain for women is paralleled by a corresponding loss of male freedom, job and status?"[18]

From the sixties on, medical research on the multiply orgasmic capacities of women contrasted the male difficulty in having more than one orgasm with the experience of women, who have "no such limitation." On the one hand, sexologists like Hendrik M. Ruitenbeck and Wilhelm Stekel claimed that "men are tortured by the very thought of not being considered virile; their sexuality seems much more in peril than that of contemporary women" and argued that "the percentage of relatively impotent men cannot be placed too high." On the other, feminist thinkers like Mary Jane Sherfey believed that "theoretically, a woman could go on having orgasms indefinitely" if physical exhaustion did not intervene. From Helen Gurley Brown's bestselling *Sex and the Single Girl* (1962) to Anne Koedt's "The Myth of the Vaginal Orgasm" (1970), Betty Dodson's "bodysex" workshops, and Nancy Friday's *My Secret Garden* (1973), a new discourse about female eroticism emphasized the range of possibilities open to women, with or without male partners.[19]

No wonder the hero of Joseph Heller's *Something Happened* glumly states about women, "I'm sorry they ever found out they could have orgasms too" (424). Other commentators offered advice on how men might recapture primitive physicality or recorded compensatory dreams of masculine erotic capabilities. "For the sake of orgasm which is the secret centre of liberation," David Cooper's *Grammar of Living* (1974) argued, "we have to achieve a neat operation—we have to eliminate our poor poisoned brains by effecting a decapitation of ourselves that will at last lead us back to a lost life—and then forward."[20] A description by the popular sexologist David R. Reuben almost seems to gloss the devolution of masculinity into a fantasy—a masculinity complex—even as it locates one way back to the lost life Vonnegut's and

Dahl's heroes seek, at least in part because it functions as a parody of the scene in which Ernest Hemingway took F. Scott Fitzgerald to a mirror so as to assure him about the size of his penis: "In more than one private club," Reuben observes, "the management has thoughtfully installed large magnifying mirrors over the urinals so that each gentleman who avails himself of their facilities can feast his eyes on the reflection of a phallus which would do credit to a bull elephant."[21]

As characters searching not only for sexual potency but also for a reformed society, Vonnegut's Billy the Poet and Dahl's contemporary Casanova also exemplify the efforts of other male male impersonators to assuage a sense of impotence by capturing the lost life of potency. A representative poseur, the hero of David Mercer's "A Suitable Case for Treatment" (1962), which was made into the popular movie *Morgan* (1966), watches Tarzan films, visits the monkeys at the zoo, furnishes his room with a stuffed gorilla, and wishes he had "been planted in the womb of an orangoutang" so he could be "all hairy, and primordial."[22] But his final realization that none of his antics will stop his wealthy wife from divorce proceedings proves that even the most anarchic efforts to recover the lost life of the monkey house cannot heal women of their bourgeois repressions, a point made more angrily through the therapeutic rapes attempted by the entrapped and infantalized heroes of Ken Kesey's *One Flew over the Cuckoo's Nest* (1962) and James Purdy's *Cabot Wright Begins* (1965).[23]

Just as Philip Roth's Portnoy, who is impotent with girls of his own background, recaptures the lost life of potency only through an abusive liaison with an illiterate "Monkey," J. P. Donleavy's hero in *The Ginger Man* (1958) exhibits his recognition of the absurdity of human lives and loves by beating his wife, seducing a succession of working girls, and masquerading in a kangaroo's skin.[24] The sense of disaster and unreality that so often pervades black-humor novels emanates from their authors' focus on the figure Ihab Hassan designates "the victim with a thousand faces," the character Max F. Schulz terms "the common man *manqué*."[25] The multiple identities of this impersonator often call into question masculine myths of virility. For many of the authors of what John Barth tellingly called "the literature of exhaustion," a sense of male biological insufficiency is matched by a recognition of the fictionality, illegitimacy, and anachronism of traditional masculine roles.

Barth and his contemporaries exploited baroque parodies, fantastic burlesques, historical and mythic allusions, and extravagantly textured verbal surfaces—all of which emphasize the artifice of pointedly nonreferential texts—perhaps because, as Barth speculates, "the very idea of the controlling artist has been condemned as politically reactionary, even fascist" or because of a sense of belatedness with regard to Dostoevsky, Tolstoi, Joyce, Kafka, and their successors. As Barth puts it, many critics of his day believed that "the novel, if not narrative literature generally, . . . has by this hour of the world just about shot its bolt."[26] Yet all these factors plummeted him and his contemporaries into the perplexities of envious feelings about the authority of their literary patrilineage: resentment of an authorial control, a literary historical primacy, and an aesthetic potency that inevitably seemed to elude them. At least in part, then, so-called black-humor narratives enact the male artist's unpleasant sense of inferiority by parodying conventional forms of representation, a strategy that simultaneously enables these texts to uncover the factitiousness of outworn, masculine scripts.

Thus, in Barth's *The Sot-Weed Factor* (1960), a novel "which imitate[s] the form of a Novel, by an author who imitates the role of Author," only a magic potion saves the life of the legendary Captain John Smith, enabling him to achieve an eleven-inch erection to deflower the "infrangible" hymen of Pocahontas. Barth's most inventive role-player in this novel—John Smith's descendant Burlingame, who repeatedly tricks all the other characters by disguising himself in a succession of "false identities"—needs recourse to the same "Rites of the Holy Eggplant" to free himself from the "defect" suffered by the men in his family: a member "no greater than a puppy's, nor more useful."[27] Besides motivating male male impersonation, a sense of deficiency pervades formal and thematic efforts to come to terms with elusive or inadequate models of mastery. Thus, many of the tales in Barth's *Lost in the Funhouse* (1969) use intrusive critical comments, typographical eccentricities, fragmented, ungrammatical, or blank passages, and improbable narrators (a sperm, a Siamese twin, a tape recorder) to eschew scripts that seem too trite not only for the author's fictional stories but also for the life stories of his fictive surrogates. Troubled that, like so many artists who "lack lead in their pencils," he cannot find "any new thing to say" or even any "new way to say the old," Barth presents his paradigmatic hero as worrying that "he was merely acting his own role or roles he had no idea who the actor was" (sic).[28]

"We are what we pretend to be," Vonnegut cautioned about the impersonations of one of his male characters, "so we must be careful about what we pretend to be."[29] From Sid Caesar, strutting his stuff as a would-be Nazi who turns out to be a New York City doorman, to Peter Sellers, who plays the roles of German, British, and American Cold Warriors in the movie *Dr. Strangelove* (1963), comics ridiculed male masquerading. Just as sardonic, in this case about impoverished or spurious national mythologies, novelists Thomas Berger (*Little Big Man* [1964]), John Berger (*G.* [1972]), Ishmael Reed (*Mumbo Jumbo* [1972]), and Robert Coover (*The Public Burning* [1977]) undercut stereotypical notions of heroism in love and war, at least in part to emphasize the speciousness not only of hegemonic historical accounts but also of what they have fostered: myths of masculine domination from which the authors remain ironically estranged. Yet like the creators of Billy the Poet and Cornelius, these antiestablishment authors repeatedly call attention to the ways they and their readers remain enmeshed in the Ur-plots being deconstructed and thereby demonstrate the formal link between the parodic self-reflexivity of black humor and its pervasive atmosphere of insufficiency.

That Billy the Poet and Oswald Cornelius use drugs and sex in their social protests and their quest for potency links them to the hipster figure celebrated by the "beatnik" and his grandson, the "hippy." Indeed, the beats' howls against bourgeois puritanism and their sexual experimentations turned them into prototypes of what Herbert Gold called a "new theatrical type—the male impersonator."[30] Transforming their clothes into costumes and their personal adventures into public testimonials to the benefits of dropping out, turning on, and tuning in, figures like Allen Ginsberg, Jack Kerouac, Lawrence Ferlinghetti, and William S. Burroughs used literary performances as advertisements for their flamboyant selves. Their male male impersonations of gurus, drug addicts, criminals, and queers eventually spawned a host of alternative male personae—the Hell's Angels, for example, and the Black Panthers or the Rolling Stones. In three related ways the beats also contributed to the comic traditions established by such writers as Vonnegut, Dahl, Roth, and Barth: their mocking references to the phallus, their analyses of homosexuality, and their espousal of primitivism.

Depicting beat culture as essentially for men, Paul Goodman argued in *Growing up Absurd* (1960) that the "beats are not responsible husbands and fathers of children," for they stalk apart, sharing together the beaten-down beatitude previously reserved for the solitary Byronic hero.[31] Especially in their comic reveries, moreover, the beats amplified Ralph Waldo Emerson's point that "society everywhere is in conspiracy against the manhood of every one of its members"[32] by ridiculing the phallocentrism they associated with the authoritarianism of society and celebrating the phallicism they identified with free-wheeling dissent from such a culture. In "Wichita Vortex Sutra" (1968) Ginsberg asks, "How big is the prick of the President?" His hero in *Howl* (1955–56) is a sainted "cocksman and Adonis," not unlike the hero of Kerouac's *On the Road* (1955). In Ferlinghetti's meditation on the comforts of fantasy, the poet dreams of himself "with penis erectus for spear . . . slay[ing] all old ladies / making them young again / with a touch of my sweet swaying sword." And in much of his work, Burroughs labels love "a fraud perpetuated by the female sex," arguing that "the women of this world were only made to bang."[33]

But the connection between the beatnik and the male male impersonator can also be understood in terms of the analysis of homosexuality undertaken most extensively by Ginsberg, whose belief that "a new kind of man has come to his bliss / to end the cold war he has borne / against his own kind flesh" was less an attack on women than a critique of male heterosexuality.[34] Indeed, Ginsberg's "Archetype Poem" (1950) suggests that both misogyny and heterosexuality need to be understood as the by-products of repression in general and the repression of homosexual desire in particular. "Joe Blow has decided / he will no longer / be a fairy," the poem begins, charting Joe Blow's search for a female sexual partner, his inadequacy in a woman's bed, his contempt for the woman, and finally his relief on regaining his pants and the door. The title and the poem's concluding question—"Why is it that versions / of this lack / of communication are / universal?"—imply that the man who needs a female lover to give him "a man's / position in the world" will suffer a sense of inadequacy.[35] Such a man displays what Eve Kosofsky Sedgwick has called "homosexual panic": if men deny their desire *for* the phallus, according to Ginsberg, they are involved in a denial *of* the phallus and thus doomed to alienation from their own masculinity and to the condition we have been calling male penis envy.[36]

Important as was Ginsberg's interpretation of heterosexuality as a reaction formation against homosexual desire and thus a form of male masquerading, another rhetorical strategy was just as influential in shaping the comic texts of the sixties and seventies: the beats' glorification of a physicality they associated with bestiality. As Norman Mailer explained in *The White Negro* (1957), "Hip is the sophistication of the wise primitive in a giant jungle."[37] While Mailer's essay sings the praises of the irrational, the perverse, and the repressed, his title suggests that, like Mercer's Morgan, he salutes "negritude" in his quest to attain the wise primitivism of the monkey house. As Morris Dickstein has demonstrated, among New Leftists and countercultural dissidents "the black man . . . ironically remain[ed] the mythical phallus, the object of the deepest sexual fantasies and expectations of white people."[38] To the extent that it is impossible to become a "White Negro," then, Mailer's essay displays male penis envy, a symptom of his own masculinity complex.

For two African-American men of letters, precisely this fetishization of the black stud furnishes the locus of comedy. The hero of Cecil Brown's *The Life and Loves of Mr. Jiveass Nigger* (1969) argues that his fictional predecessor, Richard Wright's Bigger Thomas, should have acted on his hatred of whites not simply by murdering a white woman but by raping her: he should have "fucked her so good she would have gotten a glimpse into the immortal soul of the universe and come away . . . feeling he was a man." Yet Brown's con man eventually decides that "Black men fancy themselves potent when they can flatter themselves to be gigolos," a sign of his understanding of the social construction of his role as stud. Similarly, the hero of Charles Wright's *The Wig* (1966) masquerades so as to feel powerful: "Like Cassius Clay. Like Hitler. Like Fats Domino. Like Dick Tracy." For him, "Impersonation is an act of courage, as well as an act of skill, for the impersonator must be cold-hearted, aware of his limitations."[39] But Wright's hero eventually hires himself out in a chicken costume to advertise the King of Southern Fried Chicken and ends up with his penis cauterized, an unmanned Uncle Tom.

Demystifying White Negroes and Jiveass Niggers, Brown and Wright nevertheless focus on the same problem of male penis envy that shaped the impersonations of Vonnegut's Billy the Poet and Dahl's Casanova. Like all the characters whose authors are laughing at what you haven't got when you ought to have it, the hero of Karl Shapiro's *Edsel* (1971) believes himself to be "impotent," although he remains "convinced that man contained a vestigial brain in his genitals, a highly sophisticated brain which thought for itself and lived a life of its own."[40] The only cure for this male penis envy seems to involve a fantasy about acquiring a female—not a woman, but a sextoid— whose essential femaleness confers essential maleness. When even this solution boomerangs, however, the man manqué may respond to his castration by, as Freud would have it, turning his back on sexuality altogether.

———————

The two ways in which the sextoid functions as a proper mate for the male male impersonator reflect, on the one hand, helplessness and, on the other, hopelessness in the face of the masculinity complex. For those writers to whom primitivism offers a consolation devoutly to be wished, the sextoid becomes an animal whose physicality might solve the problem of the masculinity complex; however, for those to whom male male impersonation signifies the artifice of male desire, the female emerges as a collection of body parts that constitute a set of signs which sometimes confirms, but more often confounds, their creator's efforts to achieve mastery or potency.

Stanley Elkin's short story "The Making of Ashenden" (1972) suggests that what Freud called "the phantasy of really being a man" ("FS" 198) depends on a return to a highly improbable, if not impossible, biological essentialism, for here Vonnegut's invitation to enter the monkey house and Dahl's presentation of women as bitches in heat metamorphose into the idea that even the most attractive female may be eclipsed by an animal through whom a man might recover the "vestigial brain in his genitals" or "a phallus which would do credit to a bull elephant." Indeed, "The Making of Ashenden" takes to its logical conclusion a philosophic and literary tradition that opposes the consolations of nature to the absurdities of culture.

The fastidious heir Brewster Ashenden searches for a suitably civilized mate, and he believes he has found her in the elusive Jane Loes Lipton, "a 'prize'" who spends her time dashing around the globe on behalf of a Bangladesh Educational Television series called "Nutritious Meals for a Family of Eighteen from Garbage and without Fire."[41] Given this couple's parodic idealism, their union should consecrate their proud humanism. Yet although they plight their troth, the real making of Ashenden is shown to depend not on a perfected modern female but on a foul-smelling, seven-hundred-pound bear. As the ashen end of a dead civilization, Ashenden manages to enter the monkey house of eroticism only in a game park, where he fearfully encounters a huge Kamchatkan. The bear's erotic gesturing teaches him that having to satisfy her was "the test he'd longed for and was now to have" (49). Given his physical revulsion (her "clit like a baseball"), his efforts to delay the inevitable ("'Foreplay, foreplay,' Brewster hissed"), and his dread that he will not be able to perform (desperately "Aladdinizing" his penis), the scene parodies human copulation: "I'm going to be a man for you, darling," he promises. "Just give me a chance, will you?" This "cheap" talk excites him until he knows, "Yes, I am the wuver of the teddy bear, big bwown bear's wittle white man" (51).

A good woman is hard to find, it seems, but a female bear may be better. Impaling himself on his "pet," a delighted Brewster admits that "he had never felt so male, so much the man, as when he was inside the bear" (53). He therefore determines never to see Jane again, deciding instead to board a train for London, spend a day at the zoo, and book passage to "some place wild, further and wilder than he had ever been" (54). Because of the prudery of human women—Jane remains obsessed with a horror of sexual defilement—the scent of a bear in heat becomes the honey he will hunt in his future days. The crime of Brewster's snobbery has been suitably matched by the punishment of his comic fate. But Elkin's fantasy also implies that male sexual satisfaction remains impossible outside the realm of the fantastic. With the bear deemed preferable to the woman, Elkin's tale raises crucial questions about the possibility of healing the man exiled from his manhood or rescuing him from the grievous diseases of modern life.

Taken together the stories by Vonnegut, Dahl, and Elkin can be understood to constitute rueful elegies on biological essentialism as well as funny meditations on the impossibility of returning to stable sex roles. For women, of course, such mournful meditations may have been more a problem than a solution. Well into the second wave of the women's movement, a participant in *The Hite Report* (1976) explained about the "he-man" figure that "the sexual revolution liberated a vast amount of masculine bestiality and hostility," while Hite herself claimed that "especially since the 1940s the glorification of male sexuality has often been justified as a kind of natural law of the jungle (the product, we are led to believe, of cave-man hormones)." Similarly, a 1969 *Ramparts* essay describing the "heart" of second-wave feminism praised women's knowledge "that they are not inferior—not chicks, nor bunnies, nor quail, nor cows, nor bitches, nor ass, nor meat."[42] What, then, if the magical charms imagined by Vonnegut, Dahl, and Elkin fail to lure men and women into the monkey house of eroticism? Indeed, what if the need for such elixirs itself exhibits a failure of (heterosexual) desire?

Another group of male comic writers, including Thomas Pynchon, Vladimir Nabokov, Donald Barthelme, and Robert Coover, record men's efforts to circumvent anxiety about their potency by constructing a suitable female of their own. While comedies exploiting animal imagery hark back to an endangered essentialism that might save the family of man, contemporary satires exploiting inanimate body parts deconstruct eroticism, unmasking love by viewing the female as a sign system. This second group of writers suggests that the failure of masculine desire can be countered not by sexually mounting the female like an animal but by mounting her on the wall like an objet d'art. But to the extent that male comic characters are ridiculed by their authors for constructing a female sign system, their masculinity is further put into question. In these works, when the sextoid becomes not a monkey, a bitch, or a bear but a compilation of parts, the male male impersonator, at times horrified by his own fetishization of the female, often—to return to our revision of Freud's meditation on castration—"gives up [his] phallic activity and therewith [his] sexuality in general and a considerable part of [his] masculine proclivities in other fields" ("FS" 198).

For Thomas Pynchon in *V.* (1963), the male drained of potency and the reified female symbolize technological, political, and social destructiveness. While Pynchon's Stencil pursues his quest for the sinister, ubiquitous V., she becomes an ever more resonant image of dehumanization—although the indeterminacy of this text opens up the possibility that male (Cold War) paranoia creates the symbolic resonance of the femme fatale. Besides representing a succession of women (Victoria, Veronica, Vera), a corrupt goddess of love (an anti-Venus), and a sign of female genitalia (the vagina as void), V. eventually becomes a compilation of inanimate parts. With feet made of precious metals, a wig, and false teeth, V. embodies the process of petrification that turns human beings into automata. If Stencil's name suggests that men are merely multiply imprinted copies, then Benny Profane voices the only prayer possible for male impersonators in the entropic world of the novel: "Someday, please God, there would be an all-electronic woman. Maybe her name would be Violet. Any problems with her, you could look it up in the maintenance manual. Module concept: fingers' weight, heart's temperature, mouth's size out of tolerance? Remove and replace, was all."[43]

Such an image of the sextoid has, of course, played an important part both in "high" and "low" culture. From the surrealists' broken mannequins in the twenties, their portraits of fractured, often faceless female anatomies, and their furniture composed of female body parts to the pornographic photographers' "beaver" or "pussy" shots in more recent decades, a part of the surveyed female body has frequently stood for the whole, while films like *Mannequin* (1987) pictured the living or dead doll as a dream girl.[44] Two parodies of romance, Vladimir Nabokov's *Lolita* (1955) and Donald Barthelme's *Snow White* (1967), counterpoint male nausea at or indifference to the mediocrity and conventionality of women with masculine attraction to the fetishized sextoid who functions as a muse.

Nabokov's Humbert Humbert compares the "coffin of coarse female flesh" of grown women to the luscious twelve-year-old girls he pursues; but as he records his "parody of incest" with his step-daughter Lolita—or *Dolly*

Haze—he understands that he has "delicately constructed my ignoble, ardent, sinful dream. . . . What I had madly possessed was not she, but my own creation, another, fanciful Lolita—perhaps, more real than Lolita; . . . having no will, no consciousness—indeed, no life of her own."[45] Playing the roles of father and literary genius, Humbert hopes to "be a healthy man" through his "pederosis" with a child who seems "as if she were a photographic image rippling upon a screen" (70, 55, 62). For many readers, therefore, Nabokov jokes at Humbert's expense, suggesting through Humbert's parody of incest just how debilitating might be Freud's view that the "normal feminine attitude" requires young women to take the "father as love-object" ("FS" 199). Read in this way, the humor of *Lolita* boomerangs, for the sextoid's crudity—Lolita's consumerism, her seduction of Humbert, her mind depraved by movie magazines—pales in comparison to the exploitation of the father/genius manqué who has robbed her of her childhood.

While Humbert Humbert sexualizes the family as the only romance left in a culture where love has been so completely debased as to be drained of its excitement, romance has even more definitively disappeared in Barthelme's *Snow White*, which criticizes a male imagination that fetishizes women and women's complicity in their own commodification. In both texts, the sextoid epitomizes a crass American culture: in *Snow White* it is encoded in the Grimm/Disney scripts which lead women to believe that someday their prince will come: "By this Snow White means that she lives her own being as incomplete, pending the arrival of one who will 'complete' her . . . (even though she is in some sense 'with' the seven men, Bill, Kevin, Clem, Humbert, Henry, Edward and Dan)."[46] These men, anesthetized dwarves, withdraw from personal interaction by fetishizing objects as substitutes for her, by voyeuristically spying on her, or by simply leaving. The artist Paul, a candidate for the role of prince, remains "*pure frog*" (169) to Snow White, as insufficient as her dwarflike companions: "The seven of them only add up to the equivalent of about two *real men*, as we know them from the films and from our childhood, when they were giants on the earth. It is possible of course that there are no more *real men* here, on this ball of half-truths, the earth" (41–42).

As in Barthelme's *The Dead Father* (1975), where the patriarch is "dead, but still with us, still with us, but dead" and his sons study "A Manual for Sons," even though they know that "a son can never, in the fullest sense, become a father,"[47] in *Snow White* Barthelme constructs a no man's land where men lack all conviction and women are filled with a passionate but suspect intensity. While the heroine of *The Dead Father* flaunts her own eroticism and degrades that of men—"*I've* got the button" (30), she exclaims à la Gertrude Stein, adding "*No mashing down*. . . . The phallus . . . is next to useless for the purpose" (76–77)—the central character of *Snow White* turns herself into a romance robot who is reduced to body parts by herself, the dwarves, and the narrator. Just as Snow White repeatedly displays her hair, the dwarves view her as a towel, a shower curtain, a "cream-of-wheat belly," or a "delicious assortment" (144) and the teller of the tale begins by drawing the beauty spots on her breast, belly, knee, ankle, buttocks, and the back of her neck.

Nabokov's and Barthelme's antiromances turn on the failures of the male male impersonator (Humbert Humbert as father/genius, Paul as prince) and the sextoid (the nymphet, the fairy-tale heroine) to imply that eroticism has become only one of many contaminated linguistic systems which the comic author decodes as anachronistic, ludicrous, or depersonalizing. Mesmerized by the materiality of female body parts, male characters are often drained of confidence, especially in those texts that diagnose the sextoid as an index of men's anxiety about sexuality.

"A Theological Position" (1972), a closet drama composed by Robert Coover and Gail Godwin, critiques both men's obsession with female body parts and their misogyny as a symptom of penis envy. The priest-protagonist pretends to investigate a pregnant woman to determine whether she is a witch in order to satisfy his own lust, but he discovers that, despite efforts which threaten to give him a heart attack, his subject is somehow constructed so as to stop men from ejaculating: her vagina seems to bite, and it talks, using men's language, "having failed with [her] own."[48] Significantly, the speech of the "cunt" causes the priest to remember a moment of terror in his youth when he walked into a "terrible cave" inhabited by "A wild bear" (157). The mother tongue of the cunt horrifies the priest, as well as the pregnant woman's husband. The cunt's language—she gives "a new history of cunts. . . . She said she'd had enough assaults on the world by the old sausage gods" (164)—frightens both men so much that they relinquish their phallic activity and murder her, only to discover that their own penises then begin talking.

Whether living or dead, the female teaches both men about their alienation from their own sexuality; Coover and Godwin satirize "the fact [of their protagonists'] castration," tallying its costs in terms of female sacrifice. Like the comic productions of Vonnegut, Barth, and Barthelme, "A Theological Position" ridicules notions of male biological primacy and female fetishization, revealing that one is not born a man; one does not become a man; one pretends to be a man. The fabulators, by dislodging the gender hierarchy which feminists then sought to dismantle entirely, laid the groundwork for the second wave of the women's movement and for those women of letters who used humor to confront the perplexities of male desire and male repudiation of desire.

Although, as Godwin's collaborating with Coover indicates and as the capacity of comedy to boomerang suggests, sexual humor about the masculinity complex could provide women with a framework for their own meditations on the phallus as a transcendental signifier of masculine hype, most of the works produced by women during the sixties and seventies eschew the self-reflexiveness of narration so common in the parodic texts of the fabulators in order to meditate on the subjects we have been recording throughout these volumes: the war of the words, sexchanges, and what Jeffrey Weeks has called the "struggle for the future of sexuality."[49] Indeed, many of the women writers who came to prominence during the sixties published gothic, regionalist, domestic, and science fiction, producing texts Molly Hite rightly views as "almost completely outside the dominant experimental movement of postmodernism."[50] Even the works of female satirists and humorists sustain this striking generic asymmetry because they deploy an alternative set of comic strategies.

To the extent that women writers present their heroines as veterans of sexual battles, their comedies illuminate an insight of Margaret Atwood: "'Why do men feel threatened by women?' I asked a male friend of mine. . . . 'They're afraid women will laugh at them,' he said. 'Undercut their world view.' Then I asked some women . . . 'Why do women feel threatened by men?' 'They're afraid of being killed,' they said."[51] If men of letters emphasized the parodic literariness of their texts because they were caught up in the dynamics of male male impersonation, the comic texts of women, both in verse and in prose, are notably less self-reflexive and more hostile, in part because, as Atwood suggests, women may be more anxious about male potency, more suspicious that even its demythologizing might reflect just another move toward mastery.

Like the texts of literary men, sexual comedies by women attribute the death of eros to the transformation of female sexuality into bestiality or textuality and to the anxiety that turns men into impersonators of masculinity. Analyses of the masculinity complex, the male male impersonator, and the sextoid do surface in the comic texts produced by women; but their fiction is shaped by distinctive thematic and formal issues, some of which are related to the societal taboos placed on women's humor in the past and to the history of comedy. Indeed, women's belief that the comic enterprise was itself a form of defiance reinforces Henry Miller's fear and Hélène Cixous's point that when women "break up the 'truth' with laughter," the result is a "volcanic" disruption of the phallogocentric order. For when the "low, slow ha! ha!" of Bertha Mason Rochester, the paradigmatic Victorian madwoman who murmurs the discontents of Charlotte Brontë's *Jane Eyre*, metamorphosed into openly subversive satires during the second half of the twentieth century, it enlisted its authors in the struggle for the future of sexuality.

Because comic texts enabled female characters to begin solving the problem Virginia Woolf had found insoluble even at the end of her successful career—the difficulty of "telling the truth about my own experience as a body" —their authors did not suffer the sense of belatedness experienced by the proponents of the literature of exhaustion. Alluding to the history of humor and the relationship between the sexes in *A Room of One's Own*, Virginia Woolf claimed that future women writers should "learn to laugh, without bitterness, at the vanities—say rather at the peculiarities, for it is a less offensive word—of the other sex" (94).[52] From her point of view, then, women's comic achievements, like their ability to write the truth about the body, were hardly comparable to men's.

To be sure, from Jane Austen's comedies of male pride and female prejudice to Rebecca West's or Edna St. Vincent Millay's humorous depictions of sex war and Zora Neale Hurston's playing the dozens on male pretensions, women of letters have contributed to the literary history of comedy, although with more bitterness than Woolf might have hoped. But as Erica Jong asked in a discussion of her female precursors from Sappho to Emily Dickinson, from Woolf to Sylvia Plath, "Where was the female Chaucer? One lusty lady who had juice and joy and love and talent too?" Self-consciously meditating throughout *Fear of Flying* (1979) on the burdens of the affiliation complex for a comic woman writer, Jong turned to male precursors from Cervantes and Rabelais to Fielding and Nabokov, even though elsewhere she protests against the so-called tough-guy image of the male writer as a hybrid of "Tarzan crossed with King Kong."[53]

At least one anthropological study of "Sexual Inequality in Humor" helps to explain Jong's dilemma by analyzing various social constraints imposed on women. According to Mahader L. Apte, norms of propriety in most cultures have excluded women from verbal duels, institutionalized clowning, trickster legends, and the role of jester, except within the confines of women's own (segregated) communities.[54] Sexual inequality in comedy might also be the result of the roles women have been required to play. Neither the Victorian angel in the house, guarding the standards of morality and serving men, nor the turn-of-the-century New Woman, protesting those standards and bonding with women, was noted for her volcanic laughter. Even after the founding of *Ms.* magazine, women were reminded that their capacity for humor has always been questioned. One *Ms.* cover presented a cartoon in which a man asks, "Do you know the woman's movement has no sense of humor?" to which the female responds, "No . . . but hum a few bars and I'll fake it."[55] Just as important, such satirists as Juvenal, Pope, and Swift often exploited *ad feminam* traditions that suggested not only a link between gender and genre—a link connecting the savage indignation of the satirist with masculine authority—but also a same-sex bond between author and reader. Only a sense of community between humorist and audience facilitates jokes about marginalized groups: outside the religious or racial subculture, such jokes backfire, providing grist for racist, anti-Semitic, or misogynist mills.

The challenge of comedy for twentieth-century women writers was highlighted by the understandable humorlessness of feminist efforts to combat jokes made at women's expense. The members of the editorial boards of the early journals *No More Fun and Games* (1970) and the *Furies* (1971) would very likely have felt about Vonnegut's, Elkin's, and Nabokov's works that they were no laughing matter, as would the central character of Andrea Dworkin's most recent novel, *Ice and Fire* (1986), who defines herself as "a feminist, not the fun kind."[56] "Why We Aren't Laughing . . . Anymore" (1973), the title of a well-known essay by the feminist psychologist Naomi Weisstein, captures the idea, prominent during the second wave of feminism, that because women have been the butt of jokes, they should refuse to identify against the female subject, a position clarified by Alfred Habegger's claim that the "American habit of regarding humor as in some way masculine" has been borne out by literary history.[57]

Besides socially instilled inhibitions, male-dominated literary conventions, and the need for an audience, the distortions of literary historians help explain twentieth-century women's unique relation to the comic. Nancy A. Walker argues that women's contributions to comedy have been overlooked by critics who assumed that "women weren't *supposed* to have a sense of humor." For Walker, as for Zita Dresner, adding the names of, say, Sarah Kemble Knight, Fanny Fern, Frances Whitcher, and Louisa May Alcott enables critics to address the distorted picture we have of the past, thus "redressing the balance."[58] However admirable their efforts, though, these critics fail to account for two related and enduring imbalances. First, few if any of these eighteenth- and nineteenth-century precursors produced a comic oeuvre comparable in scope to those male ancestors whom the fabulists invoke, that is, Cervantes, Rabelais, Fielding, Swift, and Twain. Second, even if they have, their names were marginalized in literary history to such an extent that they could hardly serve as daunting, haunting, or empowering presences for the twentieth-century female artist.

Although contemporary women did look back through their matrilineage, far from feeling that "literary history . . . has pretty well exhausted the possibilities of novelty,"[59] they could view the comic mode itself as providing precisely such a possibility of novelty. If in the nineteenth century George Meredith had explained that "where [women] have no social freedom, comedy is absent; where they are household drudges, the form of comedy is primitive," surely women writing during the second half of the twentieth century would sense that they were among the first generation to attain the "equal footing with men" that, according to Meredith, would allow "pure comedy" to flourish.[60]

The problems and the possibilities comedy posed for women writers led them to examine the sextoid and the male male impersonator in two quite different types of narrative, both of which diverge from standard definitions of black humor or fabulation and both of which enabled their authors to explore the tension between gender defined as biology and gender defined as textuality. In comedies of self-mocking female female impersonation, women of letters fictionalized the strategies deployed by such predecessors as Edna St. Vincent Millay and Marianne Moore to counter feminine subordination. The sextoid, in these works, emerges as just another female masquerade, one that enables its heroine to wrest power over the male male impersonator. In comedies of retaliatory sexchange, women writers imagined themselves as sexual aggressors in fantasies positing a female potency that emerges in the space left by the devolution of the masculine into the masculinity complex.

In both kinds of comedy, literary women's analyses of men's debilitating masculinity complex often lead to an unmasking of femininity and masculinity as supreme but supremely recalcitrant fictions. In both types, also, the relative newness of comedy as a mode of writing, along with the comic boomerang, enables contemporary women writers to ridicule not only their literary patrilineage and matrilineage but also their relationship to contemporary feminism. Most comic narratives by women neither rescue sexuality by excavating an endangered biological essentialism nor eschew it as a contaminated textuality but remain grounded in domestic detail so as to confront the issues raised by female eroticism: standards of feminine attractiveness, pregnancy, childbearing, child rearing, and the repercussions of overturning enduring taboos against female promiscuity. If, according to literary women, biological essentialism seems to mask either a justification for rape or for a return to feminine subordination, then reducing sexuality to textuality appears to figure men's flight not only from women but also from sex itself. The characters of the male male impersonator and the sextoid found in the exuberantly self-reflexive comic fabulations of men slyly present their authors as beleaguered opponents of an obsolete patriarchy, but women of letters exploit these same types to explode myths of masculine and feminine liberation. Whereas their female characters pose as sextoids, their male characters—duped by the feminine images constructed for their benefit—suffer the consequences of no-manhood inflicted by the "low, slow ha! ha!" of the madwoman's progeny.

———————

As Judith Stitzel has observed about the laughter of self-mockery, it can deaden "the pain of acknowledging that we acquiesce in our own destruction"[61] or, even more bleakly, deadpan may deaden the pain of sex antagonism by presenting it as a process devised, controlled, or exploited by women. In *The Golden Notebook*, Doris Lessing's central character muses on "self-parodying humor," which "insulated [men and women] against real hurt."[62] Similarly, in *The Middle Ground* (1980), Margaret Drabble's heroine discovers that "she could avert ridicule by taking the initiative herself," for "one of the ways to avoid being a butt or laughingstock yourself is to make people laugh—not as in the pious old cliché '*with* you rather than *at* you'; no, they had to laugh *at* you, but they had to laugh *because you made them*."[63] Such self-mockery—related to Vonnegut's and Barth's ridicule of their antiheroes —infuses the works of female writers who present their heroines adopting stereotypical roles which they nevertheless manipulate to achieve their own ends and to control or defy their lovers. Margaret Atwood's novel *The Edible Woman* (1969), like her later *Lady Oracle* (1976), focuses on female characters whose victories are qualified by their continued entrapment in debilitating sex roles which they seek to manipulate to their own advantage, a trope quite common in comedies of impersonation.

Marian MacAlpin, the protagonist of *The Edible Woman*, relates how she hopes to escape a dreary job in marketing by accepting a marriage proposal from a respectable, handsome lawyer, Peter; after the engagement, however, her narrative shifts from the first to the third person: a sign—along with the eating disorders she develops—of her self-definition as a marketed good, less consumer than consumable. In particular, Marian suffers from arbitrary yet rigorously enforced and internalized standards of beauty (standards that also obsess the heroines of Cynthia Buchanan's *Maiden* [1971], Alix Kate Shulman's *Memoirs of An Ex-Prom Queen* [1972], and E. N. Broner's *Her Mothers* [1975]). The paraphernalia of sexualization—hairdos and dyes, clothing and diets, seductive makeup and surgical make-overs—exerts a powerful hold over the imaginations of many comic heroines until they construct a model of the sextoid that liberates them from playing that part themselves.

Marian eventually dumps her conventional would-be husband by having a fling with a kinky graduate student. Thus, as Pamela S. Bromberg has pointed out, Atwood "reverses the marriage plot of nineteenth-century fiction" and in particular she revises the two-suitor convention of Jane Austen's novels.[64] At the conclusion of *The Edible Woman*, the anorexic Marian, who had undertaken a virtual masquerade of femininity during her engagement, carves a sponge cake into a replica of herself, shocking her fiancé and ultimately driving him away. Thus, she simultaneously extricates herself from her impending marriage and cures her anorexia by declaring to Peter, "You've been trying to assimilate me. But I've made you a substitute, something you'll like much better."[65] When the "woman made of cake" (280) gazes up at Marian with "its face doll-like and vacant," she understands the significance of its appetizing look: "That's what will happen to you," she tells herself, "that's what you get for being food" (278). She then neatly uses a fork to sever the body from the head, as she recovers from the nausea she experienced throughout her engagement by beginning to devour her feminine self.

Atwood's culinary pièce de résistance in *The Edible Woman* evokes Merit Oppenheim's "Cannibal Feast," a work which she showed at the 1959 surrealist exposition and which protests women viewed as what Barthelme's dwarves called "a delicious assortment." Oppenheim's tableau displays an edible woman laid out on a table, ornamented with fruits and vegetables, as the main course at a dinner party attended by two male mannequins.[66] Similarly, Atwood's Marian—who identifies with the food on her plate— views two dolls on her dressing table as her surrogates until she makes the cake doll. Like Sylvia Plath, whose bride in "The Applicant" is a creature with glass eyes, false teeth, rubber breasts, and an empty head (*PCP* 221), many poets of Atwood's generation satirized the "living doll" to criticize the fetishization of the female form. More pointedly directed against the boring predictability of men's reification of the female, Joanna Russ's play "Window Dressing" (1967) presents a male protagonist's adoration of a female mannequin who seems "better than all" living women. But after he abducts her and confers a kiss which brings her to life, she becomes so horrified by his drab reality that she throws herself out of his apartment window.[67]

Significantly, Atwood's Marian turns to a younger, bohemian lover, Duncan, who seems to understand that the more conventional Peter threatens to trap her in a facade of femininity. Although Duncan's alienation from traditional male scripts appears to hold out the possibility of a less destructive relationship for Marian, this young man acts like a narcissistic wimp whose seeming helplessness forces her to play the role of mother or nurse. Duncan describes himself as a "latent" heterosexual because most sex scenes are "bad imitations" that cause him to "laugh" (195), but his awkwardness proves to be simply a trick to convince her to make love to him. At the close of *The Edible Woman*, the ever-voracious Duncan finishes off Marian's cake: despite his irreverence toward Peter's bourgeois respectability, this male male impersonator will be only too happy to use his rebelliousness against traditional gender arrangements to consume Marian.

In a novel more *about* comedy than comic in its effects, Doris Lessing's *Summer before the Dark* (1973), the middle-aged heroine's youthful lover, Jeffrey, resembles Duncan, for he exhibits "the attractions of non-conformity" that cause her to think he represents an alternative to her husband, an authoritative man whose affairs with younger women make her feel "like a doll whose sawdust was slowly trickling away." Yet Lessing's Kate Brown ends up acting just as maternal toward Jeffrey as Marian does toward Duncan. Before Jeffrey is hospitalized for an illness he contracts during a trip they take together (succumbing to a condition Kate diagnoses as "*opting out*"), this man manqué—"consciously tormented by the multiplicity of his choices of lifestyle"—makes love "like a ten-year-old who has been dared by his gang to climb a high wall, or like a Soviet factory worker overfulfilling a norm."[68]

Thus, even those male male impersonators who appear to be estranged from traditional poses of virility disappoint women whose only recourse remains fighting image with image, role with role.

While Atwood's Marian—fearful about growing larger or smaller, comically adjusting to inane parties, talking to the food she is supposed to eat— finds herself in the perplexing situation of Alice in a contemporary Wonderland, the subplot of *The Edible Woman* revolves around Marian's housemate, Ainsley, who plays the part of a nymphet in order to become pregnant by a man whose sexual proclivities resemble those of Lewis Carroll or Humbert Humbert. But unlike Nabokov, whose narrative perspective conceals Lolita's subjectivity, Atwood focuses on the psychic cost of the "pretty baby" pose: Ainsley as "a little girl" finds it "necessary for her mind to appear as vacant as her face. Her hands were tied. She had constructed her image and now she had to maintain it" (122). Ainsley pays this price in order to turn her Humbert into an unwitting baby-making machine: he is horrified when he discovers that she has duped and seduced him.

Eventually persuaded that her infant-to-be needs a "father image," Ainsley finds a suitable surrogate in an English graduate student (appropriately, a critic of Lewis Carroll) who views poetry as gestation ("the poet was pregnant with his work" [203]) and who calls for the reinstatement of the birth principle ("a new Venus, . . . big-bellied, teeming with life" [205]). Given Ainsley's pregnancy, her future husband's Venus appears to provide her a new and suitable "version of herself" (69) for future female impersonations. Understandably, then, Ainsley, who remains committed to recycling roles, is horrified when Marian begins eating her cake woman: "Marian!" she protests, "You're rejecting your femininity" (280). Ainsley's ongoing determination to use fictive forms of femininity to entrap men whom she manipulates for her own purposes exemplifies what we are calling the comedy of impersonation.

When Dorothy Parker dramatized the discrepancy between her heroine's flirtatious chatter with her dancing partner and her private resentment at having to pander to such a boor in "The Waltz," she established an ironic mode mined by many female descendants who seem to echo Vonnegut's caution that we must be careful about what we pretend to be. Ann Jellicoe's play *The Knack* (1961), for example, displays a female female impersonator entrapping a male impersonator. After being subjected to a series of he-man poses by several housemates, Jellicoe's heroine responds by accusing one nerd of raping her. Ironically, Nancy Jones's decision to fabricate a description of Colin's "Fangs dripping with blood" so flatters her prospective victim that he feels sufficiently masculinized to ask her out for a date.[69] Mary McCarthy aims for a similarly gruesome effect in *The Group* (1963). When one character, Norine, discovers that her husband "just wilts at the approach to intercourse" because she is "a good woman"—"He feels he's fornicating with his mother"—she unsuccessfully attempts to confer potency upon him by buying black chiffon underwear, dark silk stockings, cheap perfume, and a polar-bear rug ("'Venus in Furs'—Sacher-Masoch") so he "would associate [her] with a whore."[70]

Grounded in realistic rather than fantastic details, the humor of female impersonation relies upon heroines exploiting feminine roles that may have originally been thrust upon them but that can be manipulated for their own advantage, a strategy employed in Muriel Spark's *The Public Image* (1968), which narrates sex wars that women wage because of men's insecurity and win through the acting skills they have acquired. Spark's central character, Annabel Christopher, has been constructed through a succession of films into the role of the "English Lady-Tiger," a personage "something between Jane Eyre, a heroine of D. H. Lawrence, and the governess in *The Turn of the Screw*."[71] Initially enamored of the public image he has attained through his relationship to her, Annabel's husband, Frederick, profits from their media exposure. So he consoles himself for her rising fortunes and his own faltering career by privately commenting on her stupidity, by standing firm in his opinion that her acting constitutes "a sort of cheat" (25), and by taking refuge in a succession of affairs with younger women. But a number of episodes indicate that his wife is not the insignificant person he takes her to be. Indeed, in the course of playing the role of the "English Lady-Tiger," she has "become a sort of strong-woman, a sort of tiger at heart" (56).

That Annabel's husband is driven to stage his own suicide in order to tarnish her image and destroy her career indicates the extremity of his masculinity complex and his sexual antagonism. Frederick pays for his own insecurity, as well as his resentment of Annabel's fame, with his death. He makes it appear as if his wife participated in orgies at the moment of his demise, and he sends a succession of sentimental suicide notes taxing Annabel with heartlessness, but she fights these fictional letters from the front with her own carefully studied appearances, orchestrated to ensure her survival as a grieving "widowed Lady-Tiger" (154). At the inquest, the actress even outwits a blackmailer by presenting the damaging letters as evidence of the insanity of her dead husband. Both her husband and her blackmailer have operated on the faith that "she's only a woman. She isn't as tough as you think" (181); however, at the end of the novel the determined Tiger Lady has triumphed over her mortal "enemy" (127).

To the extent that they adopt traditional sex roles, Jellicoe's "rape victim," McCarthy's "whore," and Spark's "grieving widow" practice the dissimulation traditionally ascribed to the female sex. As tricksters, they use to their own advantage the social imperatives against which Olive Schreiner protested when her heroine claimed that while the world tells men to "*Work!*" to women it says, "*Seem!*"[72] Through their masquerades, these heroines protect themselves against men whose entrapment in the masculinity complex poses as grave a threat to women as did traditional patriarchal forms of domination. Yet all three also remain stuck within images of themselves constructed by these same men. A similar comedy of empowerment through impersonation flourished in the skits of comedians like Lucille Ball and Gracie Allen, noted for their harebrained antics as "dumb broads," or in the schticks of Phyllis Diller and Joan Rivers, who present themselves as desperately seeking but never quite attaining the allure of femininity. What Zita Zatkin Dresner has called the "housewife humor" of such popular writers as Betty MacDonald (*The Egg and I* [1945]), Jean Kerr (*Please Don't Eat the Daisies* [1957]), and Erma Bombeck (*The Grass Is Always Greener over the Septic Tank* [1976]) may appear far removed from the sardonic scripts of Jellicoe, McCarthy, and Sparks; however, this comedy also depends on the adoption of a conventional persona: the harried housewife who demonstrates the often absurd obligations attending the feminine mystique of domesticity.[73]

Whereas *The Public Image* implies that wily women can outwit men by manipulating traditional roles, Spark's *The Driver's Seat* (1970) more pessimistically presents women gaining power over men but only by embracing the role of victim with such intensity that even a murderer is reduced to instrumentality. Seeking a man of her own "type," Lise embarks on a holiday bent on self-destruction. She eventually finds a stranger who has had "six years' treatment" and hopes to "start afresh," drives him to a secluded spot, provides him with weapons, and instructs him on the methods he will then use to kill her. The murderer's blundering efforts to evade Lise's suicidal machinations turn the tables in this macabre tale, as Spark dramatizes the power of the madwoman bent on her own homicide. Lise's insane determination to be killed satirizes scripts of female victimization. Recalcitrant and fearful, her antagonist must submit to becoming a character in a plot predicated upon her knowledge of his place as a man, her place as a woman: "She spoke in many languages," Lise's rather pathetic assailant later explains, "but she was telling me to kill her all the time."[74]

The "low, slow ha! ha!" of *The Driver's Seat* depends on Spark's alienation from a masochistic femininity her heroine can control only by adopting. This gallows humor therefore resembles the "humorous grimace" (20) Lessing's Kate Brown uses to ward off her consciousness of the ridiculous role of "love supplier" (54) she has played within her family. Later, Kate remembers "cow sessions" held with a neighbor, in which they found themselves hysterical at certain phrases: "They begin improvising, telling anecdotes or describing situations, in which certain words were bound to come up: wife, husband, man, woman . . . they laughed and laughed" (150). But if women seem entangled in outdated images, if their male partners remain perplexed about their own entrapment in the masculinity complex, why do *wife, husband, man, woman* still exert such a strong hold over the female imagination?

Precisely this question propels the humor of Margaret Atwood's *Lady*

Oracle, which satirizes female female impersonation by linking it to women's inability to disentangle mythologies about male potency from the realities of the masculinity complex. Many readers have noted that the central character of this novel generates a host of identities for herself. As Joan Foster, she copes with her controlling mother, her inaccessible father, and a succession of glumly self-involved male lovers; as Louisa K. Delacourt, she writes the popular "costume gothics" whose heroines function as further fictive surrogates of herself; as the oracular poet of *Lady Oracle*, she imagines herself as a cross between She-Who-Must-Be-Obeyed, the Lady of Shallott, and Sylvia Plath. Although she is frequently "terrified that [she will] be exposed . . . as a fraud, a liar and imposter," Joan multiplies her roles with such dizzying verve that she is driven to stage her own suicide: "I pretended to die so I could live . . . another life."[75]

In many of these guises, moreover, Joan insists on mythologizing her own victim status, as well as the potency of the men in her life, despite these men's patent ineffectuality and insecurity. That *Lady Oracle*'s central character—who wants to "be free not to be myself" (155)—ends up impersonating a suicide signals the ways comedies of impersonation address the issue of female masochism. Unlike the male manqué in the works of Vonnegut, Dahl, and Barth, who uses his masquerades for sexual conquest, female characters in comedies of impersonation adopt the guise of the feminine to wrest control over what they believe to be threatening familial, domestic, social, and professional situations. Even those comic characters who evade the suicidal insanity of Spark's Lise or the virtual renunciation of eroticism that Atwood's and Lessing's heroines eventually espouse tend to suffer from the debilitating roles they adopt in order to manipulate a process of feminization that would otherwise destroy them.

Perhaps Fay Weldon's *The Life and Loves of a She-Devil* (1983) most dramatically meditates on what it means to play such roles. For, after having been dumped by her husband, the hulking central character of this novel takes revenge first by turning herself into a madwoman, then by transforming herself into a host of female personae, and finally by becoming a sextoid. Specifically, Ruth, who believes she is one of the "dogs, as they call us," begins her quest by burning down her home and fobbing her children off on her husband and his seductive mistress, the romance writer Mary Fisher.[76] Then this exceptionally competent housewife takes on a series of identities to avenge herself against her husband and his lover. Under an assumed name, Ruth works in a nursing home where Mary Fisher's mother resides so as to propel the unwanted old lady to her daughter's home; sets up an employment agency in order to steal money from her accountant-husband's clients, pinning the blame on him; takes yet another pseudonym and another costume to become the nanny for a judge who sentences her husband to a long prison term; and masquerades as a charwoman to gain employment from a priest who mounts a campaign against the sort of romances that Mary Fisher has produced. While dainty Mary Fisher ages under the burdens bestowed upon her, Ruth's satanic vow—"I will defy my Maker, and remake myself" (186)—enables her to manipulate all the men who labor under narcissistic delusions of grandeur.

Yet despite her contempt for these dupes, Ruth ultimately uses the money she has stolen to turn herself into "an impossible male fantasy made flesh" (225). The two hundred pound, six-foot-two discarded wife models herself on Mary Fisher, whose "features are so regular and so perfect they are hard to remember. She is all women because she is no woman" (162). The "no woman" Ruth seeks to become wants "to look up to men" (177), but this necessitates a radical transformation which she undergoes through a series of dangerous surgical procedures that prove "there is no such thing as the essential self" (221). Likened to Frankenstein's monster, Ruth controls the doctors who construct her into "an illustration in one of the old *Esquires*" (225). With her teeth capped, her nose "fixed," her fat stripped, her skin "tucked," her hairline moved, her chin reshaped, and her legs sawed off and reassembled, Ruth camouflages the enraged She-Devil behind the facade of the sexy heroine of romance. In spite of the extraordinary pain involved in these operations, Ruth revels in the miseries she inflicts on her insignificant but finally enthralled husband—"As I was, so he is now"—for, like many of the heroines of comedy of impersonation, she believes that "it is not a matter of male or female, after all; it never was: merely of power" (277).

Power, not pleasure, motivates Weldon's heroine. None of the female characters in these comedies of impersonation pursues eroticism for itself and not a few would agree with the sentiments expressed in Fleur Adcock's poem "Against Coupling" (1971). Writing "in praise of the solitary act" and with boredom about the heterosexual act, Adcock explains,

> There is much to be said for abandoning
> This no longer novel exercise—
> for not "participating in
> a total experience"—when
> one feels like the lady in Leeds who
> had seen *The Sound of Music* eighty-six times.

Although the heroines of Jellicoe, McCarthy, Spark, Atwood, and Weldon use sex to conceive children, exact revenge, or gain commitments from men, it is frequently associated with the same "unpleasure" Adcock opposes to the efficiency of "five minutes of solitude" with "no need to set the scene" or "dress up (or undress), make speeches."[77]

Those writers who produced comedies of sexchange, however, present desirous female characters in pursuit of eroticism. Indeed, the heroines in this comic tradition play the traditionally male role of Don Juan and through their sexcapades their authors unmask the male male impersonator while lampooning the female affiliation complex. As Susan Rubin Suleiman has pointed out, Erica Jong's *Fear of Flying* and Rita Mae Brown's *Rubyfruit Jungle* (1973) were "fictional manifestations" of such books as *Our Bodies, Our Selves* (1973), by the Boston Women's Health Book Collective, or Shere Hite's *Sexual Honesty, by Women for Women* (1974).[78] They also represent a group of raunchy, popular, and picaresque bildungsromane dedicated to *Schadenfreude.* Deflating mythologies of male potency, Jong and Brown relate the battle of the sexes to male sexual anxiety and criticize literary traditions that previously omitted explicit erotic activities initiated by female desire.

In *Fear of Flying*, Isadora Wing seeks the free love symbolized by her namesake, Isadora Duncan, through a succession of heterosexual relationships in which she pursues her fantasy of the anonymous, "Zipless Fuck" (11). Yet she continually finds men wanting: her husband advises her to "buy a little dog" (25) to satisfy desires with which he cannot deal; her impotent lover offers her a "sexist put-down" by having a "prick which lies down on the job. The ultimate weapon in the war between the sexes" (90); and her first husband seems lethargic in bed, she decides, because "men reach their sexual peak at sixteen and decline thereafter" (195). All of these episodes provide evidence for Isadora's belief that the "basic inequality" of the sexes can be attributed to the fact that "the female had a wonderful all-weather cunt": "No wonder men hated women. No wonder they invented the myth of female inadequacy" (90). Just as the reality of a "Zipless Fuck" eventually turns out to be insipid, so Isadora speculates about the female quest for Mr. Right that "perhaps there was no man at all, but just a mirage conjured by our longing and emptiness" (101). *Mirage* suggests that historically masculinity has been fictionalized as potency to disguise male passionlessness. Isadora's adventures therefore demonstrate that each of her lovers is "not the stud he thinks he is" (257). Although men believed that "they wanted their women wild," Isadora thinks, "Now women were finally learning to be wanton and wild—and what happened? The men wilted" (272).

Rita Mae Brown's *Rubyfruit Jungle* just as sardonically places its heroine in the male position of philanderer and voyeur in order to unmask masculinity as a pose and just as relentlessly transgresses against the taboo of feminine propriety. This lesbian picaresque begins with the central character urging an uncircumcised childhood friend to exhibit the "wad of pink wrinkles hangin' around" what she advertises as "'the strangest dick in the world.'"[79] As if directly engaging Freud's notion that when little girls notice the "penis of a brother or playmate, strikingly visible and of large proportions," they immediately recognize it "as the superior counterpart of their own small and inconspicuous organ" ("FS" 187), Brown's narrative implies that it is not the girl but the boy who suffers a loss of credit.

A number of Brown's contemporaries retaliated against Freud's imagery
of female envy, male superiority. The speaker of Cynthia Macdonald's poem
"Objets d'Art" (1972), for example, explains that when she was seventeen a
man called her "a real ball cutter," admits "he was right," and goes on to
document how she "began to perfect [her] methods"; advertising to prospective clients, all of whom must be willing volunteers, she has "more subjects than [she] can handle.[80] Just as the sculptor Yayoi Kusama produced
"One Thousand Boat Show" (1962), a construction displaying a boat filled
with male sexual parts, the feminist critic Jane Gallop cracked jokes about
Anna Freud being instructed about the phallus: "Being a man of science,
Freud unbuttoned his pants and showed her. 'Oh,' Anna exclaimed, thus
enlightened. 'It's like a penis, only smaller!'"[81] Not the studs they think they
are, men are depicted as suffering from delusions either of grandeur or
insufficiency when women learn to become "wanton and wild." Thus, Ruth
Stone's "Cocks and Mares" (1978) begins, "Every man wants to be a stud,"
but invokes Elizabeth Bishop's "Roosters" by warning, "He can't tell his cock
from a rooster's."[82]

Not studs in Rita Mae Brown's novel either, men "bore" the adult Molly
Bolt: "If one of them behaves *like* an adult," she explains, "it's cause for
celebration, and even when they do *act* human, they still aren't as good in
bed as women" (174; emphasis ours). Indeed, throughout *Rubyfruit Jungle*
Molly encounters only ineffective or ridiculous men like her "orangutan"
lover—"Right out of the trees he dropped and into my crotch" (180). Ironically, this resident of the monkey house wants her to fantasize during copulation that "we're in the ladies room at the Four Seasons and you're admiring
my voluptuous breasts" (181). The episode, undertaken because of Molly's
curiosity about her female lover's heterosexual relationships, is representative of the source of Brown's comedy of sexchange, which consists of role
reversals embedded in a plot propelled by lesbian desire. As the description
of the "orangutan" who wants his "breasts" admired illustrates, Brown's
humor revolves around the epithet *queer* hurled at her heroine which might
be more aptly applied to the self-defined heterosexuals she meets.

Among them, Ronnie Rapaport, "the grapefruit freak," and Rhea Rha-
din, suffering from "a bad case of the hots," endure "the peculiar twists so
often found in the brains of straight" human beings (127, 160). In addition,
when the properly married Polina Bellantoni succumbs to Molly's seductive
arts, she exhibits the same transsexual yearnings as the "orangutan," for
Polina insists that her lovemaking be accompanied by whispered innuendoes
about her "nice cock, big and juicy" (177). Nor does the gay community in
Rubyfruit Jungle offer more liberated gender assignments. Beyond her attack
on closeted lesbians who condemn younger women for seizing the public
freedom they themselves privately savor, Brown criticizes the reified roles in
supposedly liberated lesbian bars, specifically the "butches and femmes"

described by the "diesel dyke" Mighty Mo (129–30), as well as the seductive, impoverished girls and their wealthy patrons in New York salons, who act like prostitutes and their proprietors. As James Mandrell has pointed out, Molly's alienation from such roles—"Goddammit, I'm not either one" (130)—dramatizes "the healthy a-social, a-gender individual at odds with the rest of society—a sick, smothering morass of guilt and repression."[83]

By adopting the genre of the picaresque, with its traditionally male picaro, Jong and Brown implicitly criticize the limitations of a literary patrilineage that has long associated the adventurous trickster with masculine conquest while defining the female as the object of his quixotic quest. Two comic novels—Jong's *Fanny* (1980) and Joyce Carol Oates's *A Bloodsmoor Romance* (1982)—make this critique of male literary history explicit by constructing historical settings to juxtapose female erotic desire with the distorted literary past erected by men to control women's sexuality. In addition, both *Fanny* and *A Bloodsmoor Romance* present literary men so daunted by female desirousness that they flee the monkey house of eroticism.

"He stole my History": the adventurous heroine in Jong's *Fanny*, a parodic revision of *Tom Jones* and *Fanny Hill*, attacks John Cleland's theft and falsification of her story.[84] "That the Book was written by a credulous Man, not a canny Woman, may easily be seen by the excessive Attention Mr. Cleland pays to the Description of the Masculine Organ," Fanny explains, for "only a Man (and an indiff'rently-endow'd one at that) would dwell so interminably upon the Size and Endurance of sundry Peewees, Pillococks, and Pricks" (176). Also, Cleland's portrait of a strumpet suggests "that the Whore's Life is nought but a Bed of Roses." "Of Clap, Consumption, the Evils of Drink, Death in Childbed (and the other Ravages of the poor Harlot's Life)," Fanny adds, "he hath nought to say" (227). The would-be author of "The Lockiad," a parody of Pope's *Rape of the Lock*—"What dire Distress from Women's Bondage springs! / What Miseries arise from Trivial Things!" (103)—Fanny pursues literary and sexual affairs with alacrity, enabling her author to satirize the sexual politics of the august Augustans who populate her world.

Dean Swift, for example, is shown trying "a fanciful Experiment" not unrelated to his final masterpiece, *Gulliver's Travels*. Urging Fanny to undress, Swift finds a horse, speaks to it in "whinnying Language," and begins to romp "with me stark naked clinging to his Back." When the stallion refuses to copulate with Fanny, a triumphant Swift draws the moral lesson that will inform his utopian vision of the Houyhnhnms, namely that "a Man in Heat will mate . . . with Hens, Sheep, or e'en ripe Melons, a pregnant Woman, or one that flies the Monthly Flag! But a Horse, a Noble Horse, mates only with a Mare to bear a Foal, mates not out of her proper Season, and thus is far more rational than Man!" (221). In comedies of sexchange, men are fearful, disdainful, or horrified by an eroticism that amuses their female creators.

While *Fanny* provides a revisionary view of the literary history of early eighteenth-century England, Oates's *Bloodsmoor Romance* focuses on nineteenth-century America. But here, too, humor at the expense of literary men is generated by a female desire that is at odds with normative notions of feminine chastity. At first, the actress Malvinia seems to epitomize such chastity because both on and off stage, "Malvinia's role was that of the *violated virgin* . . . never moved by any ignoble impulses, let alone carnal passions, of her own."[85] Curiously, however, when the lights go out in her bedroom, "The Beast" appears, causing her to utter "coarse jests" and releasing "unspeakable odors, emanating from the nether regions; as well as an unnatural lubricity of the female organs" (473). Although Malvinia acquires "the discipline of lying immobile, as if paralyzed, or a veritable corpse" with her lovers, she cannot overcome what the narrator calls with pious distaste "unspeakable inclinations" (474, 475).

In spite of all of her female female impersonations, then, Malvinia enters the monkey house of eroticism, and in doing so she allows Oates to mock the nineteenth-century idea of female passionlessness. At the same time, because the Beast emerges when Malvinia makes love to Mark Twain (portrayed here as a lecherous married man), Oates exploits the bestiality of her heroine to poke fun at one of "the highest literary geniuses of all time" (477). When a possessed Malvinia "slap[s], and pinch[es], and jab[s] . . . and *yank[s] at his masculine organ of generation!*" the terrified Twain just manages to gather his wits to crawl "from that bed of bestial extremities, to flee, naked as a newborn babe" (494). The Beast, having turned Malvinia into "a tigress," makes Twain a "prey" (495), who remains haunted by a memory (stirred by Malvinia) of "the antics of a pet monkey" that "jabbered, and twirled about, and foamed at the mouth" (493).

By simply reversing traditional portrayals of masculine license and feminine prudery, comedies of sexchange ridicule sexual stereotypes, enabling humorists shaped by the second wave of feminism to submit definitions of masculinity to the linguistic or physical conditions of femininity. Deriding psychoanalytic discourse, Bette-Jane Raphael's "Myth of the Male Orgasm" (1973) presents the contradictory research findings of Dr. Fern Herpes—"there are two types of male orgasm," the "penile" and the more mature "spherical"—and Dr. Lavinia Shoot, who discovers that men "just think" they have orgasms: "Actually, there is no such thing as the male orgasm." Ridiculing taboos associated with female bleeding, Gloria Steinem speculated on the ways in which "menstruation would become an enviable, boastworthy, masculine event" in her essay "If Men Could Menstruate" (1978): street guys would brag, "I'm a three-pad man," while intellectuals would question whether "without that in-built gift for measuring the cycles of the moon and planets," women could measure "anything at all."[86]

Comedies of sexchange—based, as Raphael's and Steinem's are, on the unacknowledged energy of the female body—inevitably engage in a dialogue not only with the male but also with the female literary past. At least in part, these writers' ambivalence about their female precursors arose because of the modesty and propriety exhibited by the heroines of nineteenth-century women's fictions. Comically critical of her female aesthetic legacy, Margaret Atwood uses the parodic Harlequin novels composed by Joan Foster in *Lady Oracle* to confront the decorum of the romance tradition so popular with women writers and readers. Resisting the happily-ever-after, which "was the way it was supposed to go, . . . the way it had always gone before," Joan eventually relinquishes her proper heroine, a Charlotte whose name recalls the demure facades adopted by the heroines of Charlotte Brontë: "I was getting tired of Charlotte, with her intact virtue and her tidy ways. . . . I wanted her to fall into a mud puddle, have menstrual cramps, sweat, burp, fart" (352).

In *Her Mothers*, Broner's Beatrix—equally ambivalent about her literary matrilineage—composes a book entitled *Unafraid Women*, attempting to fictionalize their power:

> "What does it mean when men say, 'Up against the wall, MF?'"
> "It means, Margaret Fuller."
> "But why?"
> "They're afraid of her."[87]

Yet Beatrix remains convinced that her foremothers "were always short of money," that they were "not beautiful" (105), and that even in the midst of extraordinary efforts they castigated themselves for their "own want of energy, perseverance and application" (132). For a number of the novelists of sexchange, joking about the female affiliation complex enables their heroines to question not only their female literary inheritance but the pieties of a contemporary feminist movement that sought to affirm Woolf's point that "we think back through our [literary] mothers if we are women"(*ROO* 79).

Heralded as "The First Collection of Humor by Women," Deanne Stillman and Anne Beatt's anthology *Titters* (1976) pokes fun at feminist proprieties. Complete with a parodic table of contents for an issue of *Miz* magazine (with articles entitled "Women's Labia, Women's Lobes: The First International Women's Orgasm Roundtable" and "How to Teach Your Son to Wear Dresses and Like It"), Stillman and Beatt's volume also includes spoofs on "Adrienne Poor," "Marge Piercing," and "Ann Sexless." "Sometimes your eyes shimmer like napalm," Adrienne Poor complains in "Trying to Gossip with a Man," adding that the male gaze is "burning . . . through my thin skin / forcing me to look away or at least / reach for my aviator shades."[88] Literary women, increasingly suspicious about prescribed gender roles—whether they came from masculinists or feminists—used the comedy of sexchange to confront a crucial paradox in many people's lives: the vertiginous sense of the fictionality of masculinity and femininity versus the recalcitrance of these definitions.

Precisely this paradox fascinates Molly Hite in *Class Porn* (1987), a novel that considers whether it is possible for women writers to trespass beyond their traditional literary sphere so as to translate the sexist brutalities of pornography into sexy pleasures. Alas, the witty and self-conscious Eleanor Nyland of *Class Porn*, who sets out to become a "lady pornographer" producing "Pussy books for pussies," finds it difficult to perform a sexchange operation on this most masculine of genres.[89] Although she wishes to represent "mutually pleasurable contact," without "this ramming banging . . . violating penetrating invading wounding business," Eleanor eventually relinquishes her efforts to make her heroine overpower her violated, wounded hero. While she suspects that her commitment to erotic pleasure and her refusal to train pornographic tropes of dominance on men will earn the scorn of feminists, Eleanor lands a job with Aureola Books, a publishing house run by the male author of a "feminine" piece of erotica entitled *Till I Faint*.

"'The feminine touch.' In quotation marks" (237): throughout their comic works, contemporaries of Erica Jong and Rita Mae Brown like Hite consider what it means to "take the sexual revolution home with you" (63), and all suggest that despite the fictive nature of femininity and masculinity, men and women continue to recycle farcical but intransigent gender assignments. Lily Tomlin and Whoopi Goldberg—both of whom impersonated male and female characters in their stand-up skits—made a comparable point, for their cute little girls and glitzy rock 'n roll stars demonstrated the comedians' own capacity for sexchange, whereas each of their characters labored under the illusion of a fixed gender assignment. Even the most surrealistic of satires in this period return to the continual dependence of the species on the ineradicable "fact" of sexual difference. A hallucinogenic, fantastic work, Angela Carter's *The Passion of New Eve* (1977), dramatizes the ways biology can be manipulated to destabilize essentialist definitions of gender. This novel, however—which portrays nature as far more malleable than culture—still affirms the role biological difference continues to play.

The Passion of New Eve satirizes the feminist movement through its portrayal of the sexchange operation undergone by its protagonist. The hero, Evelyn, is captured by the Amazonian followers of Beulah, whose emblem is "the broken phallus," and is brought to an underground town built by the holy woman, "Mother." There he is instructed by her acolyte, Sophia, on Mother's "self-constructed theology."[90] A "great, black, self-anointed, self-appointed prophetess," breasted "like a sow—she possessed two tiers of nipples" (58–59)—Mother has perfected her arts as a plastic surgeon and proceeds to castrate Evelyn. Her plan includes impregnating him with his own sperm and reconstructing him into a New Eve as well as a New Mary.

After Mother chides Evelyn for abusing women—"with this delicate instrument that should have been used for nothing but pleasure, you made a weapon" (66)—she launches into self-mythologizing litanies that justify her turning Evelyn into a *"Playboy* centerfold" (75): "I am the Castratrix of the Phallocentric Universe, I am Mama, Mama, Mama!" (67), proclaims the figurative Mother of Herland.

But when Evelyn, now Eve, is captured by Zero the poet and taken to his ranch house in a ghost town, Carter's programmatically feminist Amazons are countered by the novel's subsequent satire of masculinism. Abandoning verbalization for a "bestial locution of grunts and barks" (85), the homophobic, gun-toting Zero has convinced his harem that "women were fashioned of a different soul substance from men, a more primitive, animal stuff" (87). Having had their teeth extracted the better to perform "fellatio on his sacred member" (88), Zero's girls are kept in sexual thrall because they are convinced that his "sacred fluid" is "restorative," although he suffers from sterility, because (he thinks) the screen idol Tristessa had "performed a spiritual vasectomy on him" (92): "Tristessa had magicked away his reproductive capacity via the medium of the cinema screen" (104), thereby plummeting him into the masculinity complex.

Carter's parodic matriarchal and patriarchal societies are dedicated to anatomically determined definitions of gender that are questioned at the climax of the novel. Zero and his menagerie find the decaying "mausoleum" of the movie star Tristessa and discover the celluloid goddess herself, lying like Snow White in a glass coffin. This "most beautiful woman in the world," it turns out, is "an anti-being that existed only by means of a massive effort of will and a huge suppression of fact," for the actress whose figure has become the charismatic icon of femininity bears "the rude, red-purple insignia of maleness" (128): "Tristessa had no function in this world except as an idea of himself; no ontological status, only an iconographic one" (129). Amid the destructive exertions of Zero's girls, whose "clamour and gesticulations were those of the monkey house" (128), Zero stages a mock ceremony between Evelyn-turned-Eve, a biological male surgically reconstructed as a female sextoid but now dressed up as Chopin, and Tristessa, a biologically male female impersonator here wearing a bridal outfit from a film version of *Wuthering Heights*. Their enforced copulation means, Eve thinks, "My bride will become my child's father" (136). After they escape their captors, this odd couple does conceive a child, an indication that anatomical difference—medically transformed and aesthetically fictionalized—will still play a role in the conception of the future.

———

When Carter's Eve-Mary sails away from a war-torn America to nurture the new life within her, a baby whose mother suffers from male penis envy and whose father is a sextoid, what kind of child is she bearing? Eventually, what enfant terrible might slouch toward Bethlehem to be born? The conclusion of *The Passion of New Eve* raises a question posed by Barbara Ehrenreich: "If we cannot have—and do not want—a binding pact between the sexes, we must still have one between the generations, and that means there must be some renewal of loyalty and trust between adult men and women. But what would be the terms of such a reconciliation?"[91] Just as the works in the comic traditions we have traced in this chapter hardly bode well for a binding pact between the generations, the proliferation of satires written by men directed against feminism in the seventies and eighties suggests that a renewal of loyalty and trust between adult men and women may not soon be forthcoming.

Children are rarely seen or heard in the texts summarized here, perhaps because of the incompatibility of the sextoid and the mother, the male male impersonator and the father. This incongruity is clearly marked by Vonnegut's bottle of birth control pills, Nabokov's parody of incest which deprives Lolita of her youth, and Barthelme's sardonic fairy tale of a Snow White who never finds her prince. Many of the other works we have discussed just as effectively dramatize the impossibility of future generations as well as childhood's end. Imagine, for example, the progeny produced by Oswald Cornelius and a bitch in heat or Brewster Ashenden and his seven-hundred-pound bear.

Taken together the works of women ask, Is the family an ongoing romance? In *The Bell Jar*, Esther glimpses a naked man for the first time and discovers that "the only thing [she] could think of was turkey neck and turkey gizzards" (55); later she looks at glass bottles "full of babies that had died before they were born" (75), watches an "enormous spider-fat stomach and two little ugly spindly legs" giving birth on an "awful torture table," and feels nauseated at the sight of the complacently pregnant Dodo Conway, "her head tilted happily back, like a sparrow egg perched on a duck egg" (95). To Atwood's Marian in *The Edible Woman*, a pregnant friend looks "like a boa-constrictor that has swallowed a watermelon" (30). From the fictive "rape victim" in Jellicoe's *The Knack* to the equally fictive "whore" in McCarthy's *The Group*, the murdered Lise of Spark's *Driver's Seat*, and the supposedly dead heroine of *Lady Oracle*, no babies are born. Nor are they produced by Jong's Isadora Wing, unable to find a suitable partner, or Brown's Molly Bolt, dedicated as she is to a life of freewheeling lesbian adventure.

Even when comic heroines do mother, their maternity constitutes a problem for them, for their children, or for their partners. Atwood's Ainsley turns an unwitting man into a sperm bank in order to control every aspect of reproduction only to decide that her infant will need not a father but a "father image"; Weldon's She-Devil repudiates her offspring so as to exploit them as ammunition in the sex war; despite her tenderness, Spark's Tiger

Lady uses her baby as a stage prop. That Carter's pregnant Eve-Mary must sail away from racial and sexual strife in a country where even children organize in militant crusades recalls the anarchic gangs and daemonic or wild children in noncomic literature.[92] The marriage confronted by the heroine of Janet Hobhouse's comedy of manners *Nellie without Hugo* (1982)—who comments about a bedroom she had shared with her husband that "it was, as is proper for scenes of sexual victory and sexual strife, a no-man's-land"—resembles the "emotional no-man's land" inhabited by the heroine of Lessing's pointedly somber *Golden Notebook* and does not bode well for the inheritors of the battlefield.[93]

Most of the works of contemporary comic writers implicitly question whether children can grow into a sexual identity that is more than a sham or a shame. If biological essentialism appears nostalgic to literary men and punitive to literary women, if the unmasking of gender as a sign system leads to a flight from eroticism by literary men which seems just as perverse to literary women as nostalgic essentialism, on what basis can sexual identity be founded? Sex, floating free from marriage in the plots generated during the sexual revolution, no longer sustains either the family or the family romance.

In Caryl Churchill's comedy of sexchange, *Cloud 9* (1979), the children of twentieth-century liberated parents in the second act seem just as badly off as the children found in the first act's depiction of the stifling nineteenth-century family. In act 1, the daughter of a patriarchal marriage is played by a dummy to signify that little girls were supposed to be seen, not heard, in a system that required them to function like objects of exchange; but in act 2, a contemporary lesbian mother has produced a bullying little girl whose aggression is dramatized by having her played by a large man. The Victorian family attempts to suppress the femininity of the son, causing him to disdain his mother and hate his father; but the liberated, contemporary parents of a little boy worry about his bed-wetting, argue over who is supposed to be responsible for him, and fear that he is lost, a fear that seems well founded in light of the fact that he never appears on stage. An admission from a self-defined feminist in Wendy Wasserstein's *The Heidi Chronicles* (1988) epitomizes the narcissism and confusion that thwart the parenting of Churchill's modern characters. Wasserstein's separatist-turned-professional bemoans the nihilism bred of inauthenticity: "By now I've been so many people, I don't know who I am. And I don't care."[94] While Churchill and Wasserstein use comedy to measure the common failings of men and women, some of their contemporaries became less even-handed, more vitriolic, as the impact of the women's movement made itself felt.

The male male impersonators created by George Stade, Ishmael Reed, and Tom Sharpe, self-absorbed and vulnerable, retaliate against ferocious, predatory feminists who appear to have abrogated the pacts between the sexes and the generations. In *Confessions of a Lady-Killer* (1979), Stade's hero manages to murder three feminists associated with the journal *Ms. Chief*. But he ends up still inhabiting a culture whose intellectuals worship at the "First Church of Christ Androgynous" and attending speeches with titles like "Beyond Man: From Society to Sorority." In *Reckless Eyeballing* (1986), Reed's black masculinist finds a baroque way to terrorize a series of female cultural commissars in order to teach them respect for black men. But as a playwright, he can advance his career only by letting members of the journal *Lilith's Gang* dictate a plot that implies black men ought to be lynched if they "recklessly eyeball"—that is, look at—white women.[95]

But perhaps Sharpe's *Wilt* (1976) best illuminates the hostile reaction-formation against the women's movement. The wilted main character has been browbeaten by his wife, a feminist convert who constantly reproves him for not being "a proper man."[96] Women's liberation, according to the nauseated Wilt, stands for "Apes": "If animals do it then humans must. . . . Hitch your wagon to an orang-outang. The egalitarianism of the lowest common denominator" (30). What an earlier generation of male writers found appealing to their male characters this satirist finds appalling. Like Stade's and Reed's antiheroes, Wilt wants his symbolic acts against women to provide "proof that he was a man who could act" (59). But the "intellectual claptrap" of "the revolution of the sexes," the idea that "you're not fully mature unless you're ambisextrous" (74), has turned him into a pathetic lost boy who is painfully attached to a plastic life-sized sexual toy, the sextoid of his wife's lover's husband.

To the extent that Sharpe's childish, childless couples arrive at "checkmate" (219), they reflect the comic war of words literary men and women continue to wage in various genres.[97] For both sexes, the comedies produced before and during the second wave of the women's movement enabled their authors to unravel the family romance in works that evade the terms upon which a reconciliation between the sexes or the generations might be based. The fiascoes encountered by their surrealistic cast of characters—beauties and beasts, living dolls and pure frogs, jabbering genitalia and surgically constructed goddesses—unravel the sense of traditional endings in contemporary letters, lives, and loves. Perhaps satirists from Vonnegut to Sharpe, from Atwood to Carter would advise their readers, as Cynthia Macdonald did in one poem, to return to the traditional Ur-stories about masculinity and femininity, to "consult," for example, "*Snow White* for what would happen"; however, like Macdonald, they would also caution their readers to "remember that the happy ending was because / It was a story for a child."[98]

The Further Adventures of Snow White: Feminism, Modernism, and the Family Plot

8

> We do not want to resemble the women of the past, but where is our future? . . . We live in an unchartered world . . . there are whole new patterns to create.
>
> —Margaret Drabble

> —There was once a poor girl, as beautiful as she was good, who lived with her wicked stepmother in a house in the forest.
> —Forest? *Forest* is passé, I mean, I've had it with all this wilderness stuff. It's not a right image of our society, today. Let's have some *urban* for a change.
>
> —Margaret Atwood

> At the breast there is
> the pounding of the heart
> bearing
>
> story after story.
>
> —Celia Gilbert

Something happened to sex on the way to *Fatal Attraction, Thelma and Louise,* Madonna, Robert Bly's best-selling *Iron John* and Susan Faludi's equally popular *Backlash.* The old fairy tales about relationships between men and women have mutated in increasingly complicated ways, so that many of us— feminist critics, cultural historians—seem to be lost in a forest of stories about the future of sexuality and sex roles. Has any sense of an ending to the gender revolution emerged in recent decades?

Take that age-old favorite, "Snow White." In the seventies, when we were writing *The Madwoman in the Attic,* our first study of the female literary tradition, we dramatized the dilemma of nineteenth-century women, especially women writers, through a discussion of this tale. *There was a good Queen who pricked her finger with a needle, watched blood fall on snow, gave birth to a girl-child, died, and was replaced by another Queen who became stepmother to Snow White,* the nursery classic tells us. When a maternal figure becomes self-assertive, we suggested in our analysis of the story, it is *as if* a good mother had died and been replaced by a wicked stepmother, so that the tale illuminates the contradiction between socially prescribed characteristics of femininity (the silence, immobility, and beauty of the daughter-heroine displayed in a glass coffin) and the rebellious woman artist's desire for power and freedom (the plots of the crafty second Queen to destroy the conventionally feminine Snow White, as well as her ferocious dance of death in fiery shoes).

But as we now conclude *No Man's Land,* we feel we have been reviewing so many new and different plots—all of them explored in various ways by twentieth-century women writers—that it is no longer possible to propose a monolithic "tale" about the female imagination. What had been a single tradition has become many traditions, as women's spheres have widened and the certainties of men's worlds have crumbled. How, after all, would a modern storyteller narrate the dilemmas of Snow White, the Queen, the King, the Prince, and the dwarves? To begin with, she might, like Walt Disney, invoke the Ur-tale:

There was a good Queen who pricked her finger with a needle, watched blood fall on snow, gave birth to a girl-child, died, and was replaced by another Queen who became stepmother to Snow White. "Who is the fairest of them all?" this bad Queen asked her mirror, for she loved herself and hated Snow White. The day came when the mirror told her that Snow White was fairer than she. So she set out to kill the girl. She hired a huntsman to take Snow White into a large dark forest and tear out her heart. But the huntsman pitied the sweet child and let her go, bringing back to the Queen instead the heart of a wild boar, which she ate in triumph, thinking it was her stepdaughter's heart. Still the mirror told her Snow White was the fairest of them all: the beautiful step-daughter had escaped!

Yes, she had gone to live with seven dwarves in a cozy cottage just on the edge of the forest. There she cooked, cleaned, and whistled while she worked. But the Queen, hating the beautiful beloved girl, could not rest, and sought to plot the child's doom. Murderess that she was, she disguised herself cleverly in order to offer three poisonous gifts: first, as a traveling peddler, she sold Snow White a suffocating corset; then, as a gypsy beauty expert, she gave her a deadly comb; finally, as a kindly farm woman, she proffered an evil apple. One bite and Snow White fell into a deathly trance.

The unhappy dwarves lovingly placed her in a splendid glass coffin so that everyone could see how exquisite she was. And sure enough a Prince soon came along, fell in love, and took her back to his palace to ornament his throne room. But miraculously, as soon as she was brought to the royal palace, Snow White threw up the bad apple, lived again, and became a queen herself. And when her wicked stepmother was bidden to the lovely girl's wedding, that bad woman danced herself to death in fiery red shoes. Now Snow White and the Prince could plan to live happily ever after.

But would this version of "Snow White" seem nostalgic, anachronistic, kitschy? Might not our contemporary Scheherazade, like Donald Barthelme in his postmodernist *Snow White,* feel impelled to offer variations on— indeed, radical revisions of—the old theme? If so, surely her variations would reflect the sweeping cultural metamorphoses that attended the entrance of late nineteenth- and early twentieth-century women into the public sphere. First, she would have to take into account the sex wars that were generated by the suffrage movement in particular and by the woman question in general. Next, she would need to dramatize the sexchanges associated with such battles, as well as with transformations of the family romance and altered definitions of the erotic. Finally, she would have to confront a heightened and increasingly widespread consciousness of the artifice of gender itself, its status as a social construct. Indeed, storyteller though she is, she might even be obliged to meditate on current ideas about the artifice of identity. In spite of her best efforts to achieve narrative closure, moreover, she would probably find herself entangled in multiple endings, confused and bemused by a cultural pluralism that makes definitive denouements virtually inconceivable.

Let's imagine the first story she might tell. If she were to address gender issues as they occurred chronologically during the nineteenth and twentieth centuries, her story would probably be a tale of sex antagonism, a tale that asks whether Snow White and the Prince, the Queen and the King, can make love not war. Our first variation on "Snow White" confronts this question, answering it in ways established by authors from Alfred, Lord Tennyson (*The Princess*), to Rider Haggard (*She*) and Charlotte Perkins Gilman (*Herland*), to filmmakers like the creators of *Prizzi's Honor, Fatal Attraction, Sleeping with the Enemy,* and *Thelma and Louise.* All these works explore battles between the sexes. The earlier group in particular focuses on the struggle for women's rights while the second group meditates on what Susan Faludi has defined as a media backlash against the struggle for such rights.

There was a good Queen who pricked her finger with a needle, watched blood fall on snow, gave birth to a girl-child, died, and was replaced by another Queen who became stepmother to Snow White. "Who is the most powerful of them all?" this Queen asked her husband, the King, for she loved herself and hated his smug sense of superiority. But the King quickly told her that he was ten times more powerful than both she and her stepdaughter put together. So she and the lovely girl plotted to kill the King. They lured him into a large dark forest, planning to tear out his heart. But a passing huntsman rescued the majestic man and brought him to a male sanctuary where seven dwarves and a Prince (who was in training for a job at court) disguised him as a statue of god and placed him in a glass coffin.

Still, through her magic arts the enraged Queen knew that her tyrannical husband was alive, and she set out with Snow White to find him. The two women carried a banner demanding their rights and were armed with sticks and stones. But when they arrived at the retreat of the dwarves, their enemies bound them with tight laces, assaulted them with combs, and tried to cram poisoned apples in their mouths. And although the brave Amazons unbound their stays, loosened their locks, and tightened their lips against forced feeding, in the ensuing melee the rocks they flung smashed the glass coffin and woke the King, who rose again, more terrible than ever.

But how would our modern storyteller end this tale? At least three of the following outcomes are implicit in many turn-of-the-century and even contemporary fantasies about sex war. Choose your own adventure.

1. *The King rose again, more terrible than ever. Striking fear into the dark hearts of the rebellious women, the lawful monarch took the Queen and Snow White prisoner and brought them back to his palace, where he locked them in a mirror-lined room. Now at last the foolish pair understood the error of their ways. Snow White spent her time trying on stays, combing her hair, preparing for her marriage to the Prince, and asking the mirrors if she really was the fairest of them all. The Queen happily cooked and cleaned for the King, whistling while she worked.*

Or 2. *The King rose again, more terrible than ever. Yet the Queen and Snow White continued battling until they killed him, captured the Prince, and set the dwarves to cooking and cleaning, even forcing them to whistle while they worked. Triumphant, the two women transformed the sanctuary of the dwarves into a temple staffed by a host of priestesses, all of whom joined them in worshiping the divine spirit of the good Queen Mother who had given birth to Snow White.*

Or 3. *The King rose again, more terrible than ever. But the Queen and Snow White were equal to the occasion. "Come, let us reason together!" they exclaimed, inviting the men to discuss their differences of opinion over a delicious apple pie. Soon the King, the Prince, and the dwarves saw the error of their ways. "The woman's cause is man's," they agreed. Wending their way out of the dark forest and returning to a commodious castle equipped with many labor-saving devices, the King and Queen, the Prince and Snow White, entered into egalitarian and sexually fulfilling marriages. As for the dwarves, they were integrated into a commune run by seven little women, where they raised babies and consciousness, whistling as all worked together for a brave new world.*

While both the first and second waves of feminism clearly generated anxious plots about sexual warfare like those we have just summarized, other cultural phenomena gave rise to a different set of scripts. The free-love movement so important to a writer like Kate Chopin affected and reflected new definitions of female desire, in particular a move away from Victorian notions of women's passionlessness. At the same time, starting with the decadents in England (for instance, Aubrey Beardsley and Aleister Crowley), continuing through the writings of Lawrence, Miller, and Mailer, and still persisting today (in, say, *Playboy* and *Hustler*), these reimaginings of a liberated female libido led to the sexualization and commodification of the female body in both elite erotica and popular pornography. No doubt in response to such reifications, twentieth-century women writers from Willa

Cather and Edith Wharton to Erica Jong and Margaret Atwood either repudiated or critiqued the cultural construction of female heterosexuality. Our second variation on "Snow White" is meant to crystallize controversies about the erotic that have persisted from the turn of the century to the present.

There was a good Queen who pricked her finger with a needle, watched blood fall on snow, gave birth to a girl-child, died, and was replaced by another Queen who became stepmother to Snow White. Every night, the sexually abusive King assaulted the Queen, and every day Snow White tried to comfort her and conceal her bruises. "Who is the fairest of them all?" this battered Queen asked her mirror, and the mirror told her that her stepdaughter was the sexiest girl in the realm. This pleased the Queen because she thought it might please the King: either he could enjoy Snow White himself or he could sell her to a wealthy nearby Prince. So the Queen set out to perfect the child's charms. She hired a huntsman to convey the girl to a finishing school run by dwarves, where she would be taught costuming, hairdressing, and how to stay on a diet. It was her hope that her stepdaughter might become Miss Dark Forest of 1995, maybe even a Playboy *centerfold or a Hollywood starlet.*

But en route to the school, the handsome huntsman seduced Snow White in the middle of the forest. By the time she arrived at the sybaritic mansion of the dwarves, she was quite adept in the arts of love. Indeed, she was ready to teach the dwarves a thing or two. "I give myself when I please, where I please," she told them. And when the Queen arrived on a visit, bringing in tow a charming and fabulously rich Prince, it seemed Snow White was going to live happily ever after.

A range of endings to this tale can be teased out of stories about female desire from *The Awakening* to *Fear of Flying*, stories of the repudiation of female desire from *My Ántonia* to *The Edible Woman*, and male fantasies about female sexuality from *Tropic of Cancer* to *The Story of O*. Feel free to vote for your own favorite.

1. *It seemed Snow White was going to live happily ever after. But alas, the Prince found Snow White's jouissance rather unnerving. He wanted her to marry him and settle down, while she swore that she would never belong to any man. Her plan a failure, the Queen returned gloomily to the King, and beautiful Snow White disappeared into the dark forest, where she is said to be living a bold, free life to this very day.*

Or 2. *It seemed Snow White was going to live happily ever after. But what a shock it was to Snow White when she discovered that the Prince was hardly interested in sex at all and not very good at it. And yet she liked him just as much as he liked her. Besides, when she looked at the battered face of her stepmother she doubted that "a hard man is good to find." "A good man is hard to find," she murmured, renouncing her desire for the exploitative huntsman and her pleasure in the dwarves' school for scandal. True, the King and Queen were still trapped in their old patterns. But Snow White and her new, mild husband relished a relationship surpassing the erotic and settled down to run an apple strudel factory.*

Or 3. *It seemed Snow White was going to live happily ever after. Sadly, though, the Prince wanted Snow White to perform all kinds of unnatural acts, and when the*

Queen saw this she resolved to go along with him, since the King needed money that the millionaire Prince was willing to pay. Before Snow White knew what had happened to her, she was chained and naked in a glass coffin while the Prince took his pleasure and some pictures of her—and the voyeuristic dwarves, along with the excited Queen, watched and whistled as the couple worked. When, quite unexpectedly, the King arrived on the scene, he too joined the happy audience.

Although, as these endings suggest, the issue of heterosexual desire was a central concern for many modernists, a number of their contemporaries were influenced by the new discourse of sexology, which led them to analyze alternate modes of eroticism. During the same period in which, for example, Edward Carpenter and Havelock Ellis defined what they called "the intermediate sex" or "the invert," such writers as Radclyffe Hall, H. D., Gertrude Stein, and Virginia Woolf explored lesbianism, bisexuality, transvestism, and transsexuality in a quest for sex-role metamorphosis that obviously still grips the imagination of novelists and poets in the 1990s. How might these artists tell the story?

There was a good Queen who pricked her finger with a needle, watched blood fall on snow, gave birth to a girl-child, died, and was replaced by another Queen who became stepmother to Snow White. "Who is the fairest of them all?" this new Queen asked the mirror in her closet, and when the mirror told her that Snow White was the most beautiful, the Queen knew that she loved the girl with a love surpassing the love of men. But as the two grew increasingly close, the King became suspicious and plotted to kill Snow White. He hired a huntsman to take the girl into a large dark forest and tear out her heart. The Queen, though, got wind of his plans and arranged for Snow White to take refuge in a commune run by kindly dwarves. Here the girl studied her maternal heritage, as well as the lives of the obscure and the little arts of talk, of dress, of cookery, and whistled while she worked. Sometimes, too, the Queen costumed herself as a huntsman and visited her there. They spent many pleasant nights together.

But the evil King was determined to put a stop to these unnatural activities. So he hired a mercenary Prince to capture the girl. This clever fellow disguised himself as a medical man and offered her three gifts to heal her of what he convinced her was a neurosis: a feminine costume, a new hairdo, and the fruit of his knowledge. When she tasted the latter, though, poor Snow White fell into a deathly trance and the wily Prince immediately locked her up in a glass coffin, so that he could transport her back to her father's kingdom. Before you could say "Abracadabra," however, the wise and loving Queen appeared by the side of the coffin.

Once again, if we translate the meditations of Radclyffe Hall, H. D., Stein, and Woolf on alternative forms of the erotic into the terms of "Snow White," we can propose a number of different solutions to the dilemma presented by this plot. Pick your preference.

1. The wise and loving Queen appeared by the side of the coffin. "Awake, my love, my fair one," cried the Queen. Imagine her sorrow, though, when the entranced girl rose from her coffin murmuring, "I'm sorry, my dear, but my Prince has come." As the

Queen and dwarves sadly conceded that they were no more than a Society of Outsiders, the Prince revealed that he had renounced his mercenary impulses because he had fallen in love with his beautiful patient. And the victorious King emerged from his countinghouse to preside over the wedding feast of the young couple.

Or 2. The wise and loving Queen appeared by the side of the coffin. "Awake, my love, my fair one," whispered the Queen, hoping the Prince and the King would not overhear her. Bewildered, Snow White rose from her glass coffin and whispered back, "What shall I do?" "Marry the Prince but sleep with me too," muttered the Queen, before turning and instructing the dwarves to begin baking apple tarts for the wedding feast. The Prince confessed that he had always worshiped Snow White from afar and promised to impregnate her with a divine child. When last seen, Snow White, the Queen, and the Prince were making movies in the forest, while the beaming King followed them, carrying a jar of myrrh to celebrate the group's sacramental ménage à quatre.

Or 3. The wise and loving Queen appeared by the side of the coffin. "Awake, my love, my fair one," cried the Queen. And imagine her joy when the entranced girl threw up the Prince's bad apple, rose from her coffin, and murmured, "Let us be Queens together and collaborate on translating the works of my lost mother." As an epithalamion chanted by the sisterly dwarves rang out over forest hills, the spirit of Snow White's dead mother appeared on the horizon to bless the new couple and their newfound land. Everyone knew that this magical pair would find a way to reproduce themselves—perhaps mystical, perhaps technological—and that they would bring forth a wonderful daughter of their own. As for the King and the Prince, they soon reconciled themselves to this union they had so long resisted, for when they met again back at the palace, they realized that they had always loved each other, and at last their love dared to speak its name.

Or 4. The wise and loving Queen appeared by the side of the coffin, but then inexplicably vanished. For a long time Snow White lay there. To her it may have seemed as if only a night had passed, but at least ten years went by. (Alas, both the Queen and the King died in that decade.) And when Snow White woke, she was alone in a forest of her own. (The dwarves and the Prince had disappeared.) As she stepped out of the crystal cabinet in which she had been encased, a new day was dawning and a fine wind was blowing the new direction of time. In the distance, she heard the roaring of a sexual conflagration she could not understand: was that what had consumed the King and Queen? Could she ever know? In any case, she need not marry, needn't pass the applesauce across the table. All around her the leaves murmured, and words rose toward her from the woodland floor, wonderful words. But what was their meaning?

If, taken together, all the stories we have thus far told reflect multiple modern responses to sex warfare, heterosexuality, and homosexuality, our new Scheherazade's final version of "Snow White" is meant to represent the radical speculations of many contemporary critical and creative thinkers about the instability of normative categories of gender, race, and identity. Are such terms as *masculinity* and *femininity*, *black* and *white*, *self* and *other* merely supreme fictions? These are issues which not only concerned such major aesthetic innovators as Woolf and Joyce but which still preoccupy theorists from Jacques Lacan and Jacques Derrida to Hélène Cixous, Luce Irigaray and, in a different way, African-American critics from Henry Louis Gates, Jr., to Barbara Christian.

There was a good Queen who pricked her finger with a needle, watched blood fall on snow, gave birth to a girl-child, died, and was replaced by another Queen who became stepmother to Snow White. "Who is the fairest of them all?" this Queen asked her mirror anxiously and incessantly, for she realized that she was no more than a mask, a costume, and so was her King. She loved Snow White and she thought she loved the King, but who were any of them anyway? Merely signifiers, signifying nothing—or so she thought in her bleakest moments. Or were those moments her cleverest moments? Everything seemed terribly indeterminate to the Queen. "Do you even have a 'transcendental signifier?'" she had asked the King one dark night. "I have no 'metaphysics of presence,' I have nothing," he had replied sadly.

The unhappy couple wondered what to do and finally decided to send their brilliant daughter, Snow White, on a quest for an answer to the riddle of gender identity, a subject in which she had always already been interested. Accompanied only by a philosophical huntsman, the girl made her way through circuitous paths into a bewildering forest of no names. Encountering a band of bookish dwarves, she asked, "Am I her was you dreamed before?" incisively quoting Joyce's Ulysses. *But the dwarves were silent: their only speech was gaps, absences, lacunae. "Am I no more than a glass coffin?" she wondered aloud, looking everywhere for a material condition. Suddenly a voice replied—a voice that seemed to come from the wilderness itself but was really the voice of a Prince from a neighboring kingdom.*

Not surprisingly, a storyteller confronted by this plot could only conclude the tale with a dizzying array of indeterminacies, sexchanges, racechanges, and role changes, which ultimately have the effect of undoing the basic premises of the Grimm tale itself. Again, though, choose for yourself your own promised end.

1. She heard the voice of a Prince from a neighboring kingdom. "Yes," boomed the Prince. "You are no more than a glass coffin—that is, a language field. You are merely a construct, an epiphenomenon. As for the King and Queen, they are supreme fictions of your imagination. Liberate yourself, kill them off!" Snow White thought a minute. Then she replied, "Ah, but none of us can be unless we become, none of us can exist unless we at least impersonate our gender assignments." The Prince was bemused. "You sound like an essentialist," he complained. But then she did a radical thing. "How about investigating the pleasure principle by disseminating your symbolic into my semiotic?" the funny girl asked. And before you could say "Abracadabra," the Prince came down out of the trees and fell to with a will. He and Snow White got married and spent many long happy hours in discussion groups with the dwarves. Heartsick, the King and Queen died without discovering any answers to their riddle. Long live the new King and Queen!

Or 2. *She heard the voice of a Prince from a neighboring kingdom. "You are no more than a mask," boomed the Prince. "Take off your face and look at yourself in that forest pool." And when Snow White obeyed him, she discovered he was right: she had never been white at all! She was Coal Black, and so, she realized, were her parents, the King and Queen. "What was all this jive about Snow White, after all?" she wondered. Someone had made her be not herself, but she did have a self. She was Woman and she was Not White. And suddenly she was very angry. Angry at the tellers of this tale, angry at the authors of this book, at the King, the Queen, even the Prince. Who was her real mother anyway, her birth mother? Dimly she remembered a dark face, loving hands.*

Or 3. *She heard the voice of a Prince from a neighboring kingdom. "You are no more than a mask, a costume, a glass coffin," boomed the Prince. Snow White was enthralled. "What a relief!" she exclaimed. "Let's change places!" There was a moment of silence. "What?" asked the Prince, sounding nervous. "Yes," insisted Snow White. "Let's all change our clothes, our masks, let the sexes intermix." She snapped her fingers in a prearranged signal, summoning the King, the Queen, the huntsman, and the dwarves. "No more masks," she cried. "Forget your transcendental signifiers, and off with these lendings!" Suddenly the forest was filled with naked dancers of all colors and many genders. "I'm nobody, who are you? Are you nobody too?" they sang as they pirouetted among the trees. And the forest resounded with their joy, for now the King could at last become the Queen and the Queen the King and the Prince Snow White and the huntsman a dwarf and the dwarves Kings, Princes, Queens, huntsmen, even a pack of cards. "Checkmate," proclaimed Snow White. "The war is over."*

———

Our variations on the theme of "Snow White" are meant to be monitory and ironic, for they reflect just a few of the countless plots proposed not only by the writers whose works we have studied in *No Man's Land* but also by a range of contemporary theorists, critics, and poets. To be sure, all continue to focus on the same question posed by the Ur-story as we interpreted it in *The Madwoman:* how is a woman to achieve personhood in the pleasure palaces of art and the artful palaces of pleasure? What are the dynamics of the family romance in which the figures of father, mother, stepmother, daughter, and son play their various parts? But because the very concepts *woman* and *man* have been rendered increasingly fictive by a century of sex wars and sexchanges, modernist and contemporary writers—female and male—have consistently investigated multiple engenderings of what once seemed to be a single romance.

That we have had to work with such radically unanswerable questions reflects, of course, the sexual ambiguity of the times in which we are living. On the one hand, some of the successes of women's personal and professional lives suggest that we have all "come a long way" out of the glass coffin and the fiery shoes. On the other hand, culturally we often seem to inhabit a misogynistic realm that wants to return women to reification in the coffin or self-destruction in the shoes. So complex is the landscape of stories that those who dwell in it often cannot see the forest (of the historical past and present) for the trees (of fiction).

In 1972, as the second wave of feminism began to crest, Phyllis Chesler ended her influential *Women and Madness* with a series of questions that help map this bewildering terrain. Earlier in her book she meditated on the same sex war that has concerned us, wondering, among other things, "Can women 'win' the sex war, or banish such a war entirely, *without* becoming the dominant sex? . . . *Is* the sex war at the root of other major evils such as race and class slavery, capitalism, puritanism, imperialism, and warfare? And if so, can such evils be exiled from the mass human condition forever by any but a feminist method? (What *is* a feminist method?)." But her concluding questions—besides continuing to explore the issue of sexual battle—touch on many other problems associated with gender transformation, problems still hotly debated. For example, Chesler asks:

> Would intense maternal and paternal mothering in childhood lead to wisdom and strength among women? . . . Can new methods of child-bearing and rearing banish the human tendency to arbitrarily interpret biological differences in oppressive ways? How can we dismiss all "men" as "hopeless"—when some of the by-products of power are knowledge, generosity, and likeableness? . . . Will lesbianism, bisexuality, and homosexuality occur more and more naturally among young people? What will this mean? . . . How shall women learn to go beyond an incestuous and procreative model of sexuality? . . . When can we stop assigning any significance to biological differences?[1]

From the turn of the century to the present, precisely these questions have engaged the attention of literary women, as well as of some of their male contemporaries.

Indeed, whether consciously or not, in response to the persistent problem of gender identity many writers created a complex cast of characters, some of whom inevitably play parts in our various versions of "Snow White": the femme fatale, the New Woman, the mother-woman, the woman warrior, the feminized woman, the no-woman, the female female impersonator, the goddess, the lesbian, the sextoid, the no-man, the New Man, the male male impersonator, the gay man, the transvestite, the transsexual, the androgyne, the he-man. It is as though an increasingly intense consciousness of the artifice of gender, fostered by radical sociocultural disruptions, has impelled many artists to ring what seems to have been every possible change on how the story of the relationship between the sexes can be narrated.

Of course, even these recurring roles in turn-of-the-century and modernist texts should not be understood as monolithic. Olive Schreiner's New

Womanly Lyndall is markedly different from Virginia Woolf's New Womanly Lily Briscoe. Edith Wharton's Lily Bart is not feminized in quite the same way as Willa Cather's agrarian wives. Marianne Moore's sardonic pose as a spinster schoolmarm differs as much from Edna St. Vincent Millay's stance as a hedonistic flapper as it does from H. D.'s impersonation of a chaste Greek nymph. Kate Chopin's Edna Pontellier elaborates a theology of the erotic that should not be conflated with Zora Neale Hurston's excavation of a voodoo goddess. Radclyffe Hall's lesbian Stephen Gordon is not the same as the ironic speaker of *The Autobiography of Alice B. Toklas.* The "invisible" men and "boys" of the black literary tradition cannot be identified with Ernest Hemingway's impotent Jake Barnes or D. H. Lawrence's paralyzed Clifford Chatterley. George Moore's transvestite Albert Nobbs is not to be confused with Virginia Woolf's transsexual Orlando. And yet in some way these characters all represent comparable efforts to solve problems posed by a world of sex wars and sexchange—letters from a (literary) front in which combatants and noncombatants alike report on their experiences in the trenches of transformation.

Although most of these characters have always been seen as crucial figures in modernist literature, few until recently have been defined as important not in spite but *because* of the sexchanges they symbolize. Yet most address or incarnate current feminist answers to questions like those Chesler asks. Thus, if we place second-wave feminist theory in the context of twentieth-century literature's obsession with gender and its discontents, we can see that feminists from Simone de Beauvoir and Kate Millett to Andrea Dworkin, Angela Carter, Mary Daly, and Hélène Cixous have implicitly reconstructed a cast of characters who were of great significance to their aesthetic and intellectual precursors.

More specifically, as they struggled to imagine the engendering of a new age, mid- and late-century theorists aligned themselves in two camps: gradualists (who believed in working within established social structures in order to achieve change) and radicals (who wished to obliterate most extant social institutions). Because of their dissimilar visions of the future of sex roles, these feminists tended to invoke different personae in the cast of characters we have just delineated. In one way or another, such representative gradualists as Simone de Beauvoir, Betty Friedan, Germaine Greer, Carolyn Heilbrun, Dorothy Dinnerstein, Nancy Chodorow, and Carol Gilligan implicitly defined a redeemed future populated by New Women, New Men, mother-women, and androgynes. For their part, representative radicals like Kate Millett, Shulamith Firestone, Andrea Dworkin, Mary Daly, Adrienne Rich, Hélène Cixous, and Susan Griffin imagined a future characterized by escalating sex wars (and therefore ruled by he-men and women warriors), by the triumph of the female principle (and therefore inhabited by goddesses and lesbians), or by a total annihilation of gender categories (and therefore populated by polymorphous bisexuals).

Working from a Sartrean perspective that valorized strength and freedom for the human subject, de Beauvoir was, of course, the first major
contemporary feminist to articulate what now seems to all (except for a
conservative minority) to be woman's basic right to personhood. Complaining that "it is required of woman that in order to realize her femininity she
must make herself object and prey, which is to say that she must renounce
her claims as sovereign subject," the author of *The Second Sex* rejoiced that
the "free woman is just being born" and clearly dreamed of a world jointly
ruled by New Women and New Men. Yet she admitted that "to say in what
degree [woman] will remain different [from man], in what degree these
differences will retain their importance—this would be to hazard bold predictions indeed."[2]

De Beauvoir's American successor, Betty Friedan, was more specific, however, and more willing to prophesy. In her best-selling *Feminine Mystique*
(1963), she called for "a national education program, similar to the GI bill,
for women who seriously want to continue or resume their education—and
who are willing to commit themselves to its use in a profession." And although she too wondered, "Who knows what women can be when they are
finally free to become themselves?" she plainly expected a reorganization of
family structures when and if the New Woman managed to replace the
mother-woman and the sextoid. Moreover, in *The Second Stage* (1981), a
sequel to *The Feminine Mystique,* she heralded the arrival of sensitive New
Men who "can open up to feelings that give them a real sense of inner
strength, especially when they share the daily chores of living and child-
rearing that wives used to shield them from." In addition, rebuking what she
considered the extremism of radicals who constructed a feminist mystique
as dangerous in its way as the earlier feminine mystique, Friedan insisted
that "sexual war against men is an irrelevant, self-defeating acting out of
rage."[3]

Germaine Greer's *Female Eunuch* (1970) clearly supported this last point.
Although Greer, too, refused to prophesy the future of difference, observing that "the sex of the uncastrated female is unknown," she preached love,
not war. Indeed, arguing that "women must humanize the penis, take the
steel out of it and make it flesh again," she rejected lesbianism and re-
proached "'liberated women'" for "taunt[ing] the penis" and "mock[ing]
men for their overestimation of their virility." "The cunt must come into its
own," she proclaimed: her New Woman was not only intellectually but erotically free, in accordance with her belief that the "chief means of liberating
women is the replacing of compulsiveness and compulsion by the pleasure
principle." Declared Greer, "It is possible to use even cooking, clothes, cosmetics and housekeeping for *fun.*"[4]

If Carolyn Heilbrun's concept of androgyny was more utopian than anything de Beauvoir, Friedan, and Greer proposed, it was nevertheless part of

a gradualist program, one in which New Men and New Women would be liberated from "rigidly assigned" sex roles and unite to jointly parent free and joyous families. "I believe that our future salvation lies in a movement away from sexual polarization and the prison of gender toward a world in which individual roles and the modes of personal behavior can be freely chosen," Heilbrun explained in *Toward a Recognition of Androgyny* (1973). And in *Reinventing Womanhood* (1979) she advocated "Dual-Career" or "'symmetrical'" families which would enable women to "appropriate the male model [of professionalism] without giving up the female person" and allow men to experience the "intimacy and nurturance of which they have been long deprived."[5]

Just such a commitment to egalitarian marriage and joint parenting characterized the writings of Nancy Chodorow (upon whose research Heilbrun drew in *Reinventing Womanhood*) and Dorothy Dinnerstein. In her influential *Reproduction of Mothering* (1978), Chodorow complained that the "current organization of parenting separates children and men," with pernicious consequences. She speculated that if instead "children could be dependent from the onset on people of both genders and establish an individuated sense of self in relation to both," then "people's sexual choices might become more flexible, less desperate."[6]

In other words, with new child-rearing practices the frantically "feminine" housewives Friedan had studied and the excessively masculine men responsible for many of their troubles might become New Women and New Men, exploiting the androgynous possibilities of human nature. Similarly, in *The Mermaid and the Minotaur* (1976), Dorothy Dinnerstein blamed a range of social ills—from environmental pollution to warfare and genocide—on family structures in which boy babies early learned to project anxieties about dependency onto a female figure.[7]

But while thinkers from de Beauvoir to Dinnerstein implicitly or explicitly criticized the character whom, following Kate Chopin, we have called the mother-woman, several more recent theorists have sought to overturn the social and intellectual hierarchies that would devalue traditionally feminine modes of knowing and nurturing. The New Woman, argued Carol Gilligan throughout *In a Different Voice* (1982), *should* be in some sense a mother-woman, for women's relational skills, produced by just the child-rearing practices Chodorow studied, allow them to see moral and ethical problems with a "sensitivity" and "care for other's feelings" that men lack because of a culturally constructed male devotion to more abstract notions of "justice." Analyzing a slightly different issue—epistemology—the four authors of *Women's Ways of Knowing* (1986) came to a conclusion which complemented and supplemented Gilligan's. To the extent that "an ethic of responsibility may be more 'natural' to most women than an ethic of rights," they proposed educational schemes that "emphasize connection over separation, understanding and acceptance over assessment, and collaboration over debate."[8] For these writers too, therefore, the New Woman—and a New Womanly education—should be shaped by an acknowledgment of the values represented and promulgated by the mother-woman.

Although many of the thinkers we have defined as radicals obviously shared some of the ideals of the gradualist group, most claimed that the programs these women espoused offered too little, too late. Their exhortations consequently foregrounded a different set of characters. The postscript of Kate Millett's *Sexual Politics* (1969), for instance, attacked such hemen as D. H. Lawrence and Henry Miller, celebrated "Genet's homosexual analyses of sexual politics," and heralded a "cultural revolution" whose "profound changes" might require Amazonian efforts in "the theatrics of armed struggle."[9]

More specific in her prescriptions, Shulamith Firestone in *The Dialectic of Sex* (1970) advocated a "cybernetic socialism" that would foster a "revolt against the biological family" and usher in "what was thought of by the ancients as the Messianic Age." Explaining that "*Pregnancy is barbaric,*" she called for "the full development of artificial reproduction," the abolition of schools for children, the right of children to transfer out of any household, and the lifting of the incest taboo so that "adults might return within a few generations to a more natural 'polymorphously perverse' sexuality." "Relations with children," she explained, "would include as much genital sex as the child was capable of—probably considerably more than we now believe."[10] Clearly her heroine/hero was neither a New Man nor a New Woman (and certainly not a mother-woman) but a polymorphously perverse bisexual, a shape-changing being like Woolf's Orlando, in whom the sexes might happily "intermix."

For Andrea Dworkin, too, "*We are, clearly, a multi-sexed species which has its sexuality spread along a vast fluid continuum where the elements called male and female are not discrete.*" Her *Woman-Hating* (1974) went on to agree with Firestone that the "incest taboo does the worst work of the culture" and to predict that in a brave new world "human and other-animal relationships would become more explicitly erotic, and that eroticism would not degenerate into abuse. Animals would be part of the tribe and, with us, respected, loved, and free." Yet besides celebrating a fluidly multisexed new being, Dworkin also mourned the painful mutilation experienced by the character we have called the feminized woman—the woman whose feet are literally or figuratively bound, whose face is made up, who has become an art object on a marriage market—at the same time that she implicitly defined herself as a woman warrior. For, in a world where the incest taboo still *is* in place, "Every woman raped during a political nation-state war is the victim of a much larger war, planetary in its dimensions—the war . . . that men wage against women."[11]

In her *Intercourse* (1987), moreover, Dworkin advised women to shun sex with men, since most men who make love to women make war on women: "Intercourse remains a means or the means of physiologically making a woman inferior," she argued, "communicating to her cell by cell her own inferior status . . . shoving it into her, over and over, . . . until she gives up and gives in—which is called *surrender* in the male lexicon." Similarly, the speaker of her novel, *Ice and Fire* (1986), declares, "Coitus is punishment," and adds ominously: "I am a feminist, not the fun kind."[12] The villain of her plot is plainly the he-man, her victim the feminized woman, her heroine the fluidly sexual woman warrior.

Like Dworkin, Mary Daly brooded, in *Gyn/Ecology* (1978), on the atrocities of feminization: Indian suttee, Chinese foot binding, African genital mutilation, European witch burnings, American gynecology as gynecide. A more analytic thinker than Dworkin, however, she attributed male sexual aggression to an ontological no-manhood from which all men suffer. Quoting Valeria Solanis's definition of the anatomical distinction between the sexes—"unlike femininity [read femaleness], relaxed masculinity [read maleness] is at bottom empty, a limp nullity. While the female body is full of internal potentiality, the male is internally barren (from the Old French *bar*, meaning man)" (brackets Daly's)—Daly identified the "organized aggression/violence of males" with men's "fear of their own emptiness and weakness." This hollowness causes them to commit "concrete acts of rape, dismemberment, and murder." At the same time, calling the concepts of androgyny and human liberation "mindbinding . . . misbegotten ideas," she resurrected women warriors, "forming and re-forming our Amazon Argosy," and in *Pure Lust* (1984) she praised the idea of the goddess, invoking "metapatriarchal women" who would help her wield "the term *separatism* as our Labrys": the labrys—the Amazon/lesbian weapon of battle—rather than the nurturing consciousness of the mother-woman became her central symbol in the sex war.[13]

Even when radical thinkers did celebrate the mother-woman, they aligned her with the goddess, the lesbian, and the separatism emblematized by Daly's labrys. Adrienne Rich's influential "Compulsory Heterosexuality and Lesbian Existence" (1980), for instance, reasoned from Chodorow's revision of Freud's "Female Sexuality" that since the mother is the first love object for both boys and girls, all girls (and women) are naturally lesbians to some degree while heterosexuality is an arbitrary and artificial behavior imposed by men on women. Thus, "it is the lesbian in us" who is free, desirous, creative—and the mother is a model for the goddess. Yet Rich, who endorsed Daly's *Gyn/Ecology* as a work which burst "the accustomed bounds even of feminist discourse," had also, in *Of Woman Born* (1976), lamented the self-divisions fostered by a mode of "motherhood without autonomy, without choice," and she was brought to her elevation of lesbian separatism by relinquishing a "Phenomenology of Anger" (1972) that turned her into a woman warrior releasing "white acetylene" from her body and training it "on the true enemy" to rake "his body down to the thread / of existence" and leave the he-man "in a new / world; a changed / man": a New Man.[14]

Comparable visions of women warriors, transformed sexuality, and resurrected goddesses marked the writings of Hélène Cixous, Angela Carter, and Susan Griffin. In *The Newly Born Woman*, produced in collaboration with Catherine Clément, Cixous revised what Rich called "the oppressor's language" to confess that "I, revolt, rages, where am I to stand?" and to call for *"the other bisexuality,* the one with which every subject, who is not shut up inside the spurious Phallocentric Performing Theater, sets up his or her own erotic universe." The kind of bisexuality she recommends, she added, involves "the location within oneself of the presence of both sexes . . . the nonexclusion of difference or of a sex . . . the multiplication of the effects of desire's inscription on every part of the body and the other body."[15]

As for Carter, although she complained in *The Sadean Woman* (1979) that "mother goddesses are just as silly a notion as father gods," she defined the Marquis de Sade's polymorphously perverse Juliette as "a New Woman in the mode of irony" and marveled at the sexchanges enacted in his *Hundred and Twenty Days of Sodom,* in which "now the woman, now the man, penetrates and is penetrated in turn; gender itself can become interchangeable, as in the sexual charade that concludes Juliette's career." Like Firestone and Dworkin, as well, she inveighed against the incest taboo: analyzing the moment in Sade's *Philosophy in the Boudoir* when a daughter rapes her mother, she declared, "Were Madame de Mistival [the mother] to have come [instead of fainting], then all the dykes would be breached at once and . . . pleasure would have asserted itself triumphantly over pain and the necessity for the existence of repression as a sexual stimulant would have ceased to exist. There would arise the possibility of a world in which the concept of taboo is meaningless and pornography itself would cease to exist."[16]

Finally, Susan Griffin, arguing from a significantly different perspective about violence and pornography in *Pornography and Silence* (1981), lamented the construction of woman as the sextoid or the female female impersonator —a "'doll,' an actual plastic copy of a woman, made to replace a woman"— and mourned as well the propagation of the he-man, a sadomasochist who, because he is at war with himself, rages against both mother and nature. If Carter's (and Firestone's and Dworkin's) utopia would abolish the incest taboo, Griffin's would more generally eradicate the taboo against matter (and mater) to celebrate the Goddess, the "Great Mother . . . celestial and chthonic at once," in order to redeem the divinity of "the material nature of the world, which pornography degrades."[17]

How, though, would Griffin—or Cixous or Daly—respond to Betty Friedan's call for a national education program for women or to her admonition that sexual war against men is irrelevant and self-defeating? Although such radicals might well approve of the basically utopian impulses that underlie Friedan's first proposition, they would most likely go farther, in an effort to become themselves fictive inhabitants of a utopia Friedan heralds but does not dramatize. As Mary Jo Weaver has argued, for example, Mary Daly's intellectual mode, both on the page and at the podium, constitutes a kind of guerrilla theater, as do the intellectual self-presentations of Cixous and Dworkin, who are both charismatic speakers and compelling icons of a world that has not yet come into being.[18]

Thus, while the figures we have defined as gradualists usually represented themselves as impassioned *commentators* on past and future, the figures we have called radicals generally became desirous *impersonators* of the future even as they sought to anatomize the past. At least in part such differing discursive strategies arose from notably different attitudes toward the very issue of gender, and specifically toward the existence of a category called *man* or *men*. Perhaps for this reason, where the gradualists would opt for those versions of "Snow White" in which the Prince and Snow White, the King and the Queen rearrange social structures to make common cause, the radicals would promote variations on the story in which the Prince and King are either annihilated or relegated to a separate realm so as to liberate Snow White and the Queen into a perfected Herland. Perhaps for this reason too, both the premises and the promises of the two opposing camps have often seemed so alienated from each other that, although each heard the other, neither could respond to the other's sense of an appropriate ending to what now appears to be an interminable war of words.

———

Has this war of words, then, become a war between women? And if so, why? Concentrating primarily on sexual orientation, Betty Friedan wrote in *The Second Stage* that "the hostility that lesbian extremists evince for women who embrace a larger definition of female personhood often seems to exceed their hostility toward men."[19] Considering not only the tendentiousness of Friedan's language ("lesbian extremists," "larger definition of female personhood") but also her threatened attitude, her comment points to an internecine warfare between feminists that is also documented by, among other battle cries, Mary Daly's charge that the women we have defined as gradualists are "fembots"—female robots. Among feminist literary critics, too, such not-so-civil warfare sometimes seems endemic, no doubt because the analysis of literary structures is in some sense inseparable from the revision of social strictures.

In particular, during the seventies and eighties feminist critics on both sides of the Atlantic could be roughly divided into two camps, whose assumptions and priorities paralleled those of the gradualists and radicals. Elsewhere, drawing on M. H. Abrams's influential study of the rise of Romanticism, *The Mirror and the Lamp*, we defined those two groups as "mirrors" and "vamps," figures paradoxically continuous with just the intellectual history they seek to disrupt.[20] Like the political gradualists we have described, the mirror critics advocate an empirical methodology which would foster a reinterpretation of the past in the service of practical, plausible changes for the future. And like the political radicals, the vamp critics reject many conventional modes and categories of analysis in the hope that annihilation of the past will usher in a transformed future.

The mirror: for a number of feminist critics, Abrams's symbol of art as mimetic representation can be said to have become a space in which to capture the shifty historical images of gendered reality. The lamp: for others, his emblem of the heroic poet's self-generated brilliance serves as a paradigm for the critic's expressive autonomy as well as for rebellious impulses associated with "the feminine" that have been repressed but not erased by patriarchal culture. Thus, Abrams's lamp, figuratively speaking, metamorphoses at the hands of these critics into a vamp, both a fatal seductress and a ferociously undead—vampiric—figure who haunts the nightwood of the collective unconscious.

A "realist" as well as a gradualist, the mirror critic works with (and usually within) established structures—the institutional structure of the academy, along with the intellectual structures signified by such words as *author, canon, genre, nationality, class,* and *race*, while the openly ex-centric vamp critic rejects what seems to her the hegemony of such categories. Whether she holds a mirror up to masculinist or feminist texts, the gradualist critic believes that, through careful argumentation and scrupulous documentation, she can persuade readers of both sexes to change the sexual politics represented by the sexual poetics she studies. In their various ways, then, such early works as Elaine Showalter's *A Literature of Their Own*, Barbara Christian's *Black Women Novelists,* Judith Fetterley's *The Resisting Reader*, and Jane Tompkins's *Sensational Designs*, along with Hazel Carby's *Reconstructing Womanhood* and Bonnie Zimmerman's *The Safe Sea of Women* participate in a common project of cultural renovation.[21] For although these books focus on notably different subjects—fiction by British women from the nineteenth century to the present, the literary tradition of African-American women, gender-specific reader responses to American "classics" written by men, and the dynamics of canon formation in the United States—each begins at least implicitly with the assumption that there are knowable, if neglected, aspects of the general past which can be used to re-engender the future.

By contrast, the critics we are calling vamps believe that to renovate literary culture is merely to reinstate (albeit in new configurations) the phallogo-centric hierarchies that have traditionally subordinated the feminine. Therefore, to undo the binary oppositions from which they believe patri-archy has been constituted, such French theorists as Kristeva, Cixous, Clé-ment, and Irigaray seek to excavate and celebrate the semiotic beyond the symbolic, the preoedipal beyond the oedipal, the multiplicity beyond uni-vocality, even the feminine behind or within the masculine.[22] And from Toril Moi to Nelly Furman and Peggy Kamuf, the Anglo-American followers of these thinkers explore the disruptive and contradictory forces of the male or female literary text in order to interrogate the authority of both author and history, with Moi rejoicing in "the free play of the signifier," Furman insisting that "literature is not a representation of experience," and Kamuf arguing that "female writing" is not what some readers "quite banally under-stan[d]" as "works signed by biologically determined females."[23] Finally, then, while the mirror critics are gradualists in their ultimate acquiescence in a sex/gender system which they nevertheless strive to revise, the vamps are radicals in their struggle to transcend a sex/gender system altogether.

In the forest of stories through which we wander, what tales of Snow White would these different critics decide to celebrate, to interpret, to rein-vent? Although each might choose a number of plots and possibilities, much theoretical writing demonstrates that their choices would ultimately set them at odds with each other. The mirrors would no doubt accuse the vamps of being politically irresponsible, of stereotyping the feminine, employing elitist jargon, or living in a philosophical never-never-land. The vamps would probably call the mirrors politically naive and retrograde essentialists and charge that they are collaborating with (or at least complicitous in) a pernicious intellectual status quo. Such vituperative name-calling—like the rancor of gradualists and radicals discussed earlier—can be interpreted in several ways: as a sign of hope (there *is* a future at stake) or a signal of despair (no altered future is possible for such marginalized and therefore divided prophets). Do such quarrels, in other words, signify feminism's healthy cen-trality or its sickening irrelevance in contemporary culture?

At the very least, the intensity with which a range of intellectuals engage in these debates implies the magnitude of the societal disruptions associated with the evolution of feminism in this century. More to the point, women's disagreements over these issues evoke the very multiplicity—indeed, the indeterminacy—of the stories on which we have meditated throughout these three volumes. Perhaps, as what seemed to be the "natural fact" of gender dissolves into fiction, "fictions about gender" inevitably become in-creasingly fantastic and nonreferential, even as, in competition with each other, they are generated with extraordinary rapidity. What single narrative fate, after all, can be imagined by those who no longer believe in monolithic gender destinies dictated by anatomy? For gradualists and radicals, mirrors and vamps, even the concepts *Queen, King, Snow White,* and *Prince,* along with the status of story itself, must constitute grounds for debate.

In spite of the multiple inflections potential in the tale of "Snow White," however, all the thinkers we have been discussing would have to agree that it is premised on one "fact": Snow White is of woman born. Even in an age of *in vitro* fertilization and surrogate motherhood, she would still be of woman born. What are the literary/historical consequences of this single constant? When we juxtapose the plurality of stories which reflect the massive social transformations attendant upon women's entrance into the public sphere with the stability of the biological fact of (female) maternity, we confront two new and interesting literary phenomena: first, the increasing impulse of women writers to historicize and analyze what Rich calls "motherhood as experience and institution," and, second, the emergence of the mother-writer in the mid-twentieth century.[24]

It is as if, for both contemporary novelists (who excavate lost tales of the intersection between the maternal story and patriarchal history) and contemporary poets (who write in the maternal voice in an effort to shape a nonpatriarchal future), the good Queen's entrance into sexuality need not necessitate her transformation into the bad Queen. Instead, the mother as both a bearer of the burden of a newly imagined past and a progenitor of a freshly imagined time-to-come has been redefined as a figure who combines the procreativity of the first Queen with the creativity of the second, the selflessness of the originatory mother with the self-determination of the "step" mother, the magic of biological maternity with the transgressiveness of female craft.

Culturally, as the Ur-story of "Snow White" suggests, maternity has always been the repressed term in the family plot. Just as the matronymic is blanked out by the patronymic, just as the mother's lineage is forfeited to the father's, and just as maternal discourse has been governed by paternal law, so the mother herself has had to die to narrative possibility. Associated with blood, flesh, mater-iality, she has appeared so intransigently imminent that literary, indeed cultural, authority has been predicated on a transcendence or a repudiation of her *being.* From Clytemnestra in the *Oresteia* to Gertrude Morel in *Sons and Lovers,* from Catherine Earnshaw in *Wuthering Heights* to Mary Hyatt, Charity Royall's mother in *Summer,* she has had to be executed or exorcized, most often by her sons but also at times with the connivance of daughters. And even the name Snow White, in its fetishizing of angelic frigidity and spiritual purity, stresses the motherless fairy-tale heroine's freedom from contamination by maternal flesh and blood.

At the same time, the repression of the mother, requiring enormous psychic energy, is often so incomplete, so unsuccessful, that what we might call a ghost of the maternal story haunts artists from Aeschylus to Lawrence, from Emily Brontë to Edith Wharton. In certain cases, this haunting becomes so powerful that the ghostly narrative, despite its cultural ambiguities, becomes the central focus of authorial consciousness. In the nineteenth century perhaps the most striking instance of this phenomenon is *The Scarlet Letter* (1850). Hedged round by tangential documents and masculine moralizings (the Custom House preface, Hawthornean meditations, the sermonizings of Dimmesdale and Chillingsworth), the transgressive Hester Prynne indomitably survives, along with the uncanny signifier and the equally uncanny child she enigmatically presents to her community. And that Hawthorne's romance is set in the Puritan past implies an untold (maternal) story at the center of patriarchal history, a story whose resonance the writer acknowledges even while he denies his heroine the ability to articulate it herself. "In Heaven's own time," Hawthorne allows Hester to muse, "a new truth would be revealed, in order to establish the whole relation between man and woman on a surer ground of mutual happiness." But then he has her admit that she

> had vainly imagined that she herself might be the destined prophetess, but had long since recognized the impossibility that any mission of divine and mysterious truth should be confided to a woman stained with sin, bowed down with shame, or even burdened with a life-long sorrow. The angel and apostle of the coming revelation must be a woman, indeed, but lofty, pure, and beautiful; and wise, moreover, not through dusky grief, but the ethereal medium of joy; and showing how sacred love should make us happy, by the truest test of a life successful to such an end![25]

Hawthorne's excavation of a ghostly maternal narrative in the Puritan past, as well as the prophetic power he at least provisionally offers to an outcast mother, takes on special significance in contemporary writings by women whose historical investigations locate the mother at the heart of the plot of the family and even at the center of the birth of the nation. Unlike Hester Prynne, however, the mother-heroines whom recent women writers discover behind the screen of history are frequently destined prophetesses of a new truth, even though (or perhaps precisely because) most are unquestionably stained with sin, bowed down with shame, or burdened with a lifelong sorrow. Thus, where Hawthorne's fiction ultimately endorses the bifurcation of good (procreative) mother and bad (creative) "step" mother, two novels—Toni Morrison's *Beloved* (1987) and A. S. Byatt's *Possession* (1990)—represent a range of late twentieth-century efforts to construct integrated maternal figures in order to examine the ways the procreative/creative mother can potentially give birth to newfound lands and legends. Veering from a more conventional daughterly perspective to a maternal one, or at least from a focus on the daughter's fate to concentration on the mother's tale and her tale-telling, *Beloved* and *Possession*, in very different ways, can be placed in a tradition that also includes Maxine Hong Kingston's *The Woman Warrior* (1976), Buchi Emecheta's *The Joys of Motherhood* (1979), and Caryl Churchill's *Top Girls* (1982).

Of these three texts, Kingston's is of course the most daughter-centered, for much of the memoir examines the vexed and vexing figure of the Chinese-born mother from the point of view of her American-born offspring. "Don't tell": the repressive maternal injunction is, to be sure, cautionary, meant to ensure the child's safety in an alien culture of "ghosts." Yet the mother herself irrepressibly "talks story," so much so that the daughter, as her scribe, excavates a real "ghost"—the spirit of the dead aunt whom she names No Name Woman. Sexually used and abused, mysteriously impregnated and ritually vilified, this woman without an identity is the paradigmatic lost, elided, dead, forgotten mother who has been sacrificed to the fatality of maternity. Yet her story refuses to die: "My aunt haunts me—her ghost drawn to me because now, after fifty years of neglect, I alone devote pages of paper to her." Moreover, it is arguable that as the muse of the woman warrior, No Name Woman inspires the narrator to reinvent her as the legendary maternal figure with whose tale Kingston concludes the book—the second-century poet Ts'ai Yen, who transcended the trials of exile, rape, and impregnation by transmuting her sorrow into songs. Indeed, like Kingston herself, Ts'ai Yen learns the music of the "barbarians"— of the ghosts—so that she can sing "about China and her family there." And when she does so "her children [do] not laugh but eventually [sing] along when she [leaves] her tent to sit by the winter campfires, ringed by barbarians." Equally important, she "brought her songs back from the savage lands," and three have "been passed down to us."[26]

If the ghost of No Name Woman so haunts Kingston that, figuratively speaking, she is metamorphosed into the illustrious Ts'ai Yen, Nnu Ego, the protagonist of Buchi Emecheta's ironically titled *Joys of Motherhood*, is a pure exemplar of the bitter ways the institution of maternity is so inexorably shaped by changing cultural forces that no liberation can be imagined for the mother-woman. Experiencing herself as stained with sin, bowed down with shame, and burdened with a lifelong sorrow, Nnu Ego is shadowed by the history of her own conception, during which her father, a tribal chieftain, scandalized his household of wives and slaves by giving such noisy pleasure to his favorite mistress that his senior wife sickened and died shortly thereafter. This woman's death, along with the ritual sacrifice of the female slave who had to be buried with her, haunts the daughter born of that mating: a *dibia* (shaman) declares that the murdered servant is Nnu Ego's *chi* (totemic spirit). But besides demonstrating that Nnu Ego has been shaped by this almost legendary event, as well as by her own mother's death following another childbirth, Emecheta shows that her heroine is enmeshed in a far more particular history—the history of the Nigerian shift from a preindustrial tribal culture to an industrialized urban society.

As a bearer of traditional values, Nnu Ego yearns, both at home (in Ibuza) and in the city (Lagos) for "the joys of motherhood." Indeed, her name, with its European allegorical resonance, suggests that sans children Nnu Ego suffers so profound an absence of identity—*No Ego*—that she feels her own personhood can only be gained through the bearing of children: if "I am not a mother," she meditates, "I am not a woman."²⁷ Yet motherhood, as defined both in Ibuza and Lagos, is an institution which just as definitively empties out identity. "The joy of being a mother was the joy of giving all to your children" (224), pronounces the communal wisdom of her society.

And all is what Nnu Ego has given by the end of Emecheta's novel, whose dedication "to all mothers" is therefore as ironic as its title. Repudiated by her first husband because she appears to be barren, sharing her second husband with a succession of other wives, she becomes "a prisoner, imprisoned by her love for her children, imprisoned in her role as the senior wife" (137). But once she has used up all her strength in feeding and educating those children—and especially in nurturing her sons—she is cast aside like a broken vessel. The two boys for whom she has labored vanish into Western culture (one emigrates to America, the other to Canada), and never write her. Although after her death they salve their consciences by giving her "the noisiest and most costly second burial Ibuza had ever seen" and by building a shrine in her name, Nnu Ego nonetheless dies alone, "by the roadside, thinking that she had arrived home. . . . with no child to hold her hand and no friend to talk to her" (224).

Her fate illuminates the insight to which Emecheta has her come too late in her life: "She felt more inadequate than ever. Men—all they were interested in were male babies to keep their names going. But did not a woman have to bear the woman-child who would later bear the sons? 'God, when will you create a woman who will be fulfilled in herself, a full human being, not anybody's appendage?' she prayed desperately" (186). Caught between a tribal system in which women are allowed a certain commercial autonomy but are enslaved or forced to compete with each other in polygamous households, and a posttribal colonized society where black men are subordinated to white men and women while black women are marginalized or nullified even as they bear the burden of sustaining the black family, Nnu Ego has been sacrificed to the joylessness of a fruitless ideology of maternity. Only posthumously does she seem able to protest, by refusing—so the community decides—to grant fertility to the suppliants at her shrine. As a kind of *chi* for her descendants, then, Nnu Ego may be said to have drawn indirectly upon her lifelong sorrow to become the destined prophetess of the mysterious truth that only a new relationship between man and woman can restructure motherhood so as to redeem its "joys."

Caryl Churchill's *Top Girls* begins in a future Nnu Ego will never see but moves rapidly back into the fatalities of the past she so poignantly represents. But both the "top girls" of history and those who populate the modern Top Girls Employment Agency are shown to suffer the consequences of their efforts to combine a life of creative autonomy with one of biological procreativity. The first scene of Churchill's play—featuring a surrealistic dinner party attended by such luminaries as the legendary ninth-century Pope Joan, Chaucer's medieval Patient Griselda, the thirteenth-century Japanese courtesan-nun Lady Nijo, the Victorian traveler Isabella Bird, and the revolutionary Dull Gret of Breughel's fifteenth-century canvas—sets these women's discussions of maternity in a context that crosses historical, cultural, and even generic boundaries. But for most of these figures, regardless of period, culture, or even ontological status, pregnancy and childbirth inexorably recall what Margaret Drabble's heroine in *The Waterfall* defines as "the sexual doom of womanhood, its sad inheritance."[28]

When Pope Joan went into labor during a liturgical procession, she reveals, she was dragged out of town and stoned to death, and her baby died. Nijo's first child died, her second and third were taken away by her lovers, and about her fourth she explains, "Oddly enough I felt nothing for him."[29] Griselda relinquished her daughter and son to the tyrannical husband who was testing her submission to him; even though she feared the children would be killed, she "always knew [she] would do what he said" (23). The childless Isabella Bird was "nearly murdered in China by a howling mob . . . . shouting 'child-eater, child-eater'" (15). Dull Gret saw one son "die on a wheel" and one baby run through by a soldier's sword; she became so enraged that she led her neighbors to hell and gave the devils "a beating" (28). Thus, although these women worthies have been brought together to celebrate how "magnificent" their adventurous lives have been, how "we've all come a long way" (13), their collective stories testify to the universality of the ghostly maternal story that has always and everywhere haunted patriarchal culture.

If Churchill's first scene establishes the ways maternity has tested the lives of even the most successful historical and/or mythical women, the rest of her play focuses on the problems it has posed for the contemporary top girl, Marlene. In addition, Churchill uses the strategy of multiple casting to judge the present against the past so as to investigate exactly how long a way women have come and to demonstrate the ambiguities that mark contemporary efforts to balance professional ambition and maternal destiny. When the actresses who play the parts of the famous and famously eccentric women of the first scene take on the roles of twentieth-century job seekers and employees in the rest of the play, do we experience the history of women as an evolution or a devolution? Tracing the transformation of historical personages into contemporary personalities (Nijo the nun into Win the high-flying, hard-living "tough bird," Pope Joan into Louise the frustrated, alcoholic middle manager, Isabella into both the oppressed adoptive mother Joyce and the worn-down housewife Mrs. Kidd), Churchill implies that *plus ça change, plus c'est la même chose*.

But in metamorphosing Dull Gret into Angie, Marlene's rejected and retarded biological child, the playwright suggests a severer point. Marlene's ferocious independence and ambition, she hints, have spawned a monster child, a pathetic victim of maternal indifference even less likely to "make it" than the rebellious Dull Gret, who at least could invade hell and beat the devil. Using a Marxist analysis to question the ideology of autonomy through which feminism seeks to reform the institution of maternity, Churchill argues that, with the striking exception of the peasant Dull Gret, the top girls of past and present have all too frequently achieved their status at the expense not only of an exploited underclass but also, ultimately, of children. The ghostly narrative that haunts her play, then, in some sense replicates a traditional split between good mother and bad mother, between Joyce, who nurtures and therefore cannot achieve, and Marlene, who achieves and therefore cannot nurture.

Yet in Churchill's script the achieving biological mother cannot evade the fact of her maternity. Although Marlene has kept her identity as Angie's mother a secret and given the girl over to her working-class sister, Joyce, Angie uncannily recognizes Marlene as "mum" and eventually, though more timidly than her precursor Dull Gret, enters the money-worshiping hell that is the Top Girls Employment Agency, a business run entirely on the selfish principles recommended by England's top top girl, Margaret Thatcher. Behind the history of past and present, at the center of a family plot which has heretofore seemed important only insofar as it contributes to the chronicles of the fathers, vibrates the tale of the mother's morally complex struggle for selfhood in the face of a cultural narrative that would deny her centrality and subjectivity. The question that hovers over Churchill's conclusion emerges directly from this untold story: can Marlene remain a top girl while accepting Angie into her life?

"I just come here. I come to you," Angie tells the "aunt" whom she intuitively knows to be "my mother." "I knew you'd be in charge of everything," she adds, and, "It's where I most want to be in the world" (54, 56, 60). Such a haunting of the mother by the inescapable implication of maternity—once the child has been born its fleshly factuality cannot be denied, no matter how its fate has been resolved—is, of course, the crux of *Beloved*. Like the discarded Angie, the murdered Beloved seeks out the place she most wants to be in the world so that she can be with Sethe, the mother who "is the one. She is the one I need. . . . She is the one I have to have," and, as she tells her sister Denver, she plans to "stay here" because "I belong here."[30]

To be sure, unlike Marlene, the tormented Sethe actually hurt her child out of what she experienced as love: when Schoolteacher arrived to return her and her children to slavery, she tried to take "and put my babies where they'd be safe," on "the other side" (164, 203). Moreover, again unlike Marlene, she unequivocally welcomes the lost daughter's eerie invasion of her life. Yet interestingly, these very different texts share a concern with the moral responsibilities enmeshed in the metaphysics of maternity. For if Marlene assumes the right to repudiate her child as utterly other, Sethe assumes the right to sentence *her* baby to death because she so completely identifies with her children that she expects them to share the fate she has chosen for herself. As Paul D observes when he confronts the reality of the infanticide she has committed, her "too-thick love" meant that she acted in a state in which she "didn't know where the world stopped and she began" (165, 164). Thus, while Sethe experiences Beloved's fantastic return as a miraculous opportunity for explanation, expiation, and exultation, the dead girl's entranced insistence that "I am not separate from her   there is no place where I stop   her face is my own" (210) uncannily reflects what Paul D (and others in the community) see as Sethe's own arrogant and narcissistic usurpation of life-and-death power over an other. Read this way, the ghost story at the center of *Beloved* examines the return of the repressed not to celebrate the joys of motherhood—and in particular the mother/daughter "join"—but to analyze the radical ambiguities of maternity.

As a woman yearning to bring her milk to her infants and to keep them "safe" from the evils of the slavery she had herself suffered, Sethe is a prototypical Madonna. But as a murderer of her own offspring she becomes a prototype of Medea. At the same time, although Sethe has to expiate her sin by atoning to her Beloved, feeding her sweets and stories, changing places with the growing girl and physically deteriorating into her daughter's daughter, Morrison's tale historicizes Sethe's psychology in terms of the perverse definitions of ownership generated by the dehumanization and commodification of black families in a slave society. Paul D's condemnation of Sethe's infanticide—"You got two feet, Sethe, not four"—implies that she has acted like an animal not a human being. But Sethe was treated like a breeder by Schoolteacher and the Garners, whipped while lying in a hole dug to protect her unborn baby, and anatomized by Schoolteacher's pupils, who drew her "human characteristics on the left; her animal ones on the right" (193).

Similarly, if Sethe believed the child was her own to do with as she pleased, she herself was purchased as property, and her children were to be sold off by whites whose "property" they constituted. Perhaps the single word *mine* echoes around the house at 124 Bluestone Road because Sethe was dispossessed of herself and her children at the "Sweet Home" farm, which was neither sweet nor home. Thus, every lyrical image of maternity in *Beloved* is qualified and contaminated by images which evoke the horrors of slavery: the waters of the womb breaking and the waters that need to be crossed to get to freedom; the greedy tongue and mouth of the infant and the tongue chewed by the body in pain or mangled inside the iron bit; the umbilical cord and the chain that links the prisoners on the chain gang; the milk meant for Sethe's babies but "taken" by Schoolteacher's nephews while her broken husband crazily slathered himself with butter and clabber "because the milk they took [was] on his mind" (70).

Like the milk that is and is not Sethe's to give, moreover, motherhood in this novel is and is not a function of female self-possession. Sethe's mother-in-law, Baby Suggs, had seen all her children except Halle sold away from her, and she herself had to be bought out of slavery by him. Sethe's own mother had to endure the Middle Passage, where she was impregnated by a series of white men, all of whose babies she "threw away" (62), although she kept Sethe, the fruit of her mating with a black man, whose name she gave the child. Sethe's neighbor Ella "delivered a hairy white thing" fathered by "the lowest yet" (158–59), but she refused to nurse "it," so "it" died after five days. At certain points in the book, indeed, it appears that the power of withholding, of "throwing away," or of annihilating is the only power the slave mother has. Metaphorically, too, it seems at first that the only way Sethe can deal with the trauma of history is by throwing it away, through denial, silence, and repression.

Yet although at the beginning of the novel Sethe believes that "the future was a matter of keeping the past at bay" (42), Paul D's provisional exorcism of the baby ghost from 124, together with his efforts to re-create himself, Denver, and Sethe into a sufficient family, can be said to have forced the grieving mother to abandon the strategy of "throwing away" and to summon up Beloved, who, significantly, rises from the waters of the past at precisely the moment when Sethe needs to receive her. Just as significantly, the process of "rememory" in which Beloved's arrival engages Sethe enables her to speak "unspeakable thoughts, unspoken" (199) to her daughters, sending one of them into a future that includes a revision of the primal scene of infanticide: when Sethe mistakes a white abolitionist for Schoolteacher coming again like one of the four horsemen of the Apocalypse to take Beloved away, she this time attacks not her daughter but the supposed marauder himself, and Denver wrestles her mother to the ground, thereby definitively exorcizing the ghost who embodies the suffering of their common past and ushering in the "tomorrow" with which Paul D wishes to replace their "yesterday" (273).

Throughout *Beloved*, too, Sethe's "rememories" have reconstituted not just for her own daughters but for Morrison's readers a host of lives and griefs that are mostly hidden from history, and they have evoked as well Paul

D's own reconstitutions of an untold male story. In fact, through what Hawthorne's Hester Prynne deprecatingly defined as dusky grief, Morrison's Sethe has become a destined prophetess who is, in Paul D's words, her own "best thing" (273) because she has learned to move from "mine" to "me?"— to reconcile the biological mother-child bond with the historicity of identity.

Where Morrison, like Emecheta, tends to emphasize the historical forces that form and deform the institution of maternity, Byatt, like Kingston and Churchill, stresses the powerful story of motherhood that underlies and, albeit secretly, transforms history. But in Byatt's narrative, as in Morrison's, the "good" (procreative) mother and the "bad" (autonomous) "step" mother are one and the same, selfless and selfish, repressor and representer of a past that gives birth to an unexpectedly promising future. Similarly, in Byatt's novel as in Morrison's, the mother's interiority is embedded in a nineteenth-century cultural context whose consequences, both writers show, continue to affect the present we all inhabit.

Byatt makes this point indirectly, through a plot device that allows her heroine to inherit a surprising legacy, and directly, at the beginning of *Possession*, through an epigraph from Hawthorne's *House of the Seven Gables*, which concludes: "This tale comes under the Romantic definition" in its "attempt to connect a bygone time with the very present that is flitting away from us."[31] Morrison is less explicit, but *Beloved*'s position as the first novel in a projected trilogy which will meditate on African-American history from the time of slavery through the jazz age to the present suggests that she has the same ambition. Tellingly, in a recent book on "whiteness and the literary imagination," she quotes a passage from *Possession* that articulates the ways the present can be transformed through rereadings of the past. In certain reading experiences, "the knowledge that we *shall know* the writing differently or better or satisfactorily runs ahead of any capacity to say what we know, or how. In these readings, a sense that the text has appeared to be wholly new, never before seen, is followed, almost immediately, by the sense that it was *always there*, that we, the readers, knew it was always there, and have *always known* it was as it was, though we have now for the first time recognized, become fully cognizant of, our knowledge."[32] In the reading experience of *Possession: A Romance* the sense of a newness that was "always there" emanates from the excavation of a bygone time shown to contain a fully creative mother and a fully empowering literary matrilineage.

Possession: like the definitions of ownership, of "mine" and "me?" that haunt *Beloved*, Byatt's title evokes a multitude of meanings. Her book touches on how the muse possesses the creative imagination, sexual desire possesses the lover, demons or spirits of the past possess the minds of the present, narrative curiosity possesses the reader of mystery stories, and wives possess husbands, husbands wives. However, two crucial questions in *Possession* address issues of another kind of possession—aesthetic inheritance. First, given Victorian sexual ideologies, could a creative woman be a lover and a mother without losing her self-possession, her autonomy? And given patriarchal historiography, could a literary matrilineage survive, and if so, who would possess it?

The bygone time on which Byatt focuses is a nineteenth-century world of letters populated by such eminent Victorians as Tennyson, Browning, and Carlyle and here dominated by the fictive Randolph Henry Ash, on whose multitudinous texts a covey of modern archivists and biographers has been laboring for decades in what has become known as the Ash Factory. The bastion of traditional scholarship they inhabit is shaken when young Roland Mitchell discovers that the respectably married and sagacious Ash had had an illicit relationship with a relatively obscure woman poet named Christabel La Motte. Maud Bailey, a feminist critic who is a remote relative of La Motte's, enters into a partnership with Mitchell to track down the details of the poets' secret affair. Uncovering the pair's letters to each other and studying the journals, wills, and memoirs of their families and friends, the two modern researchers unearth a story that was "always there" but which lets us know the past "differently."

To the extent that the love letters of Ash and La Motte have been hidden from history because of their transgressive content, they are letters from a Victorian sexual front. Found in a series of resonant locations, they illuminate a striking contrast between patrilineal and matrilineal literary pasts. Roland gets his first glimpse of Ash's correspondence with a mysterious "Madam" when a draft in Ash's hand falls out of the poet's copy of a book by the Renaissance historian Giambattista Vico. An heir and progenitor of male intellectual tradition, Ash occupies a space in the public pages of learning comparable to the site of the "Ash Factory" in the British Museum. Appropriately, therefore, his capacious and philosophical works draw upon monuments of unaging intellect produced by masculine thinkers from Dante and Plotinus to Carlyle and Schleiermacher.

Yet, positioned between the pages of history, his illicit letter to a female counterpart prefigures the discovery of *her* cache of letters in a crumbling Yorkshire country house. Significantly, however, Maud Bailey needs to remember an apparently innocent and childlike poem by La Motte—"Dolly keeps a Secret / Safer than a Friend / Dolly's Silent Symphony / Lasts without end"—in order to find those letters, which are hidden in a doll bed. The remote, isolated, and private setting in which La Motte's letters have been sequestered and the nursery rhyme that gives Maud a clue to their whereabouts typify the reclusive and obscure life of a figure whose compositions include children's tales and mythic allegories comparable to those produced by Christina Rossetti, as well as enigmatic, "slanted" or miniature verses like those written by Emily Dickinson.

Further documentary evidence about the relationship between Ash and

La Motte appears in Yorkshire and Brittany, as well as in the diaries of La Motte's companion, Blanche Glover, and Ash's wife, Ellen. Eventually, after it becomes clear that following a tryst in the summer of 1860 La Motte gave birth to a child who may have been the victim of infanticide, a larger group of scholars—representatives of both the Ash Factory and the growing La Motte industry—literally *unearth* a letter from Christabel to Randolph that had been buried with the Victorian sage by his widow. In a scene that evokes Dante Gabriel Rossetti's exhumation of Lizzie Siddal's coffin in order to retrieve the manuscripts he had buried with her, Byatt suggests how much less control the woman writer has had over the fate of her own words, for the "new truth" of Christabel's life has waited a century to be read. Yet that truth remains powerful and empowering. *"You have a daughter, who is well and married and the mother of a beautiful boy,"* Christabel tells her former lover in this text from the grave. *"I send you her picture. You will see—she is beautiful—and resembles, I like to think, both her parents,* neither of whom *she knows to be her parent"* (542).

Entombed, as it were, in patriarchal history, in the grave of a "Great Man," Christabel's missive tells yet another lost story of the ambiguities of mother-hood. As "in Romance, [where] women's two natures can be reconciled" (404), she reveals herself to have been both creative and procreative, autono-mous and nurturing. At the same time, although she explains that her child is healthy, beautiful, and successful, she admits that the girl, who dislikes poetry, regards her as an aunt who is a kind of witch. Like Marlene in *Top Girls*, Christabel has given her daughter over to her sister to rear, but unlike Angie, the child has never recognized her true mother and has changed the fanciful name the mother bestowed upon her at her birth—Maia—to the more conventional May.

Nonetheless, this very May turns out to be Maud Bailey's great-great-great-grandmother, an ancestress who, as the product of a union between two Victorian artists epitomizing male and female traditions, reveals in this uncanny family romance that the feminist critic has a worthy patrilineage as well as an illustrious matrilineage. The name *Ash*, of course, as well as the aridity of the Ash Factory, implies that the Ash inheritance may be ex-hausted, burnt out, or—like the ashes from which the phoenix rises—ready for some strange and unexpected renewal. But the *word* incarnated in *La Motte* (*mot*), along with the Romance inherent in *Christabel*, may well, Byatt hints, provide such a renewal of a debilitated past.

Christabel La Motte's most famous work, moreover—an epic poem about the mermaid/fairy Melusina, who was said to be both beauty and monster, woman and serpent—analyzes the splits between angel and demon, between "proper" woman and "improper" artist (or indeed between Coleridge's Christabel and his Geraldine) that this poet has, finally, painfully healed in her own life. Together with this text, therefore, her letter to Ash—a letter that was withheld from him by his wife but which she dutifully buried with him—constitutes an epistle to the future which transforms the relationship between Roland and Maud, suggesting that Christabel's lifelong sorrow has made her into the destined prophetess who will help "establish the whole relation between man and woman on a surer ground of mutual happiness." That of all the works discussed here *Possession* is the most optimistic even while it is a *Romance* suggests that the more "realistically" the institution and experience of maternity are analyzed, the more specifically motherhood is located in its cultural contexts, the grimmer is its untold story. Yet although Christabel La Motte may be the *fantasy* mother whom contemporary feminists desirously seek in the nineteenth century, she also functions as a fictive precursor for women who really do exist in the twentieth century, and particularly for women of Byatt's own generation.

In *The Madwoman* we argued that the real story of "Snow White" as it functions paradigmatically for the nineteenth-century female tradition "begins when the Queen, having become a mother, metamorphoses also into a witch—that is, into a wicked 'step' mother."[33] Figuratively speaking, the implication of this transformation for literary women has long been that there is a radical contradiction between biological maternity and aesthetic creativity. For centuries, indeed, it has seemed that the (good) biological mother must die in order for the (bad) infanticidal artist to be born. We would now claim, however, that for contemporary women the tale has an entirely different premise.

Given that women are no longer inexorably silenced and privatized by their culture, there need be no murderous conflict between Snow White and the second Queen and, in addition, given that there are new ways for women to negotiate between procreativity and creativity, there need be no split between Snow White's biological mother and her rebelliously artful stepmother. In the West, access to birth control has long meant that a woman is no longer at the mercy of her biology. Rather, because she is an increasingly active participant in culture, she can choose childbearing as one of many possible projects—a project that need not preclude a commitment to other enterprises. With the breakdown of boundaries between the private (maternal) sphere and the public (paternal) sphere, moreover, maternity itself can enter history.

Although in the Ur-story of "Snow White," and in many of our variations, the death of the good Queen, the self-destructive rage of the bad Queen, and Snow White's inheritance of their conflicted destiny mean that the feminine must always be subordinated or banished from history, the emergence and survival of an artful biological mother implies the possibility of constructing a durable and public female future—a line of literary descent that can speak itself forward. And, in fact, a number of women poets and novelists who came to prominence in the years following World War II were mothers who often focused on maternity as just such an enabling discourse. In fiction, for example, Doris Lessing, Tillie Olsen, Ursula Le Guin, Margaret Drabble, Margaret Atwood, Erica Jong, and Louise Erdrich come to mind, along with Kingston, Emecheta, Churchill, Morrison, and Byatt; in poetry, Denise Levertov, Judith Wright, Ruth Stone, Sylvia Plath, Anne Sexton, Maxine Kumin, Carolyn Kizer, Lucille Clifton, Audre Lorde, Susan Griffin, Louise Gluck, and Sharon Olds.

Considering this newly audible chorus of maternal voices, it seems odd that for the most part feminist criticism has tended either to adopt what Marianne Hirsch has called "*daughterly* perspectives" toward the institution of motherhood or to mystify the maternal as what Julia Kristeva identifies as the unspeakable.[34] Specifically, elaborating upon the literary implications of Nancy Chodorow's *Reproduction of Mothering*, a number of critics have analyzed the fictional representations of daughterly ambivalence toward maternal characters, as well as the conflicts that a range of literary women experience in relation to their own mothers. At the same time, developing a revisionary Bloomian poetics, another group of critics, including ourselves, has examined the dynamics of influence for women writers who, like Elizabeth Barrett Browning, "look everywhere for [literary] grandmothers and see none" or who, with Virginia Woolf, "think back through [their literary] mothers" (*ROO* 79).[35] Thus, to quote Hirsch again, "Feminist writing and scholarship, continuing in large part to adopt *daughterly* perspectives, can be said to collude with patriarchy in placing mothers into the position of object—thereby keeping mothering outside of representation and maternal discourse a theoretical impossibility" (15).

That the discourse of the mother seems such an impossibility is precisely the theory of Kristeva, who argues that because the symbolic linguistic order is necessarily patriarchal, the maternal can never speak itself except through the mediation of the very phallic structures which must repress it. Writes Kristeva: "As long as there is language-symbolism-paternity, there will never be any other way to represent . . . this nature/culture threshold, this instilling the subjectless biological program into the very body of the symbolizing subject, this event called motherhood" (241–42). If the "daughterly" critics for the most part elide or overlook the maternal discourse of recent motherwriters, then, theorists who follow in Kristeva's footsteps deny that there is such a discourse at all. Instead they define mother-writers as ventriloquists' dummies through which a paternal symbolic order issues its commands.

But the notion that the symbolic contract inevitably excludes women—a notion grounded in Lacanian as well as Kristevan theory—is problematic, to say the least, since in most cultures the child acquires language through interactions with the linguistic autonomy of a maternal rather than paternal figure.[36] Perhaps, therefore, injunctions against representations of the nature/culture threshold called motherhood are culturally and historically grounded, not psycholinguistically eternal or essential. If this is the case, the maternal discourse created by the generation of women we are calling mother-writers can be seen as the product of a societal change as dramatic as the one Virginia Woolf located at the moment in the eighteenth century when "the middle-class woman began to write" (*ROO* 68).

Of course, from Anne Bradstreet to Harriet Beecher Stowe to H. D., from Mary Shelley, Elizabeth Gaskell, and Elizabeth Barrett Browning to Rebecca West, women of letters have borne children. But, as Woolf noted in *A Room of One's Own* and Tillie Olsen pointed out in *Silences*, for women literary ambition has long been considered incompatible with the project of parenting. In particular, for modernist women it seems that the archetypal figure of Mrs. Ramsay who always "wanted to have a baby in her arms" had to be exorcized as definitively as Woolf's angel in the house to allow the creativity of, say, the New Womanly Lily Briscoe or indeed of Woolf herself. Among the major female modernists considered in *No Man's Land*, after all, most were childless, including Wharton, Cather, Stein, Barnes, Hall, Richardson, Mansfield, Woolf, Sinclair, Moore, Millay, Sitwell, Larsen, Hurston, McCullers, Bowen, O'Connor, and Bishop. And although each one's childlessness was determined by a complex of quite different personal factors, taken together these writers represent a collective decision to reject the materiality of maternity in order to achieve a transcendence, authority, and independence that most still felt had to be disengaged from the (maternal) feminine. In the versions of "Snow White" these writers might relate, Snow White and the second Queen could perhaps make common cause, but the first Queen still had to die after giving birth because for the most part maternity still appeared incompatible with worldly ambition.

If, then, as we argued in *The Madwoman*, metaphors of creativity elaborated a symbolic equation of pen with penis well into the nineteenth century, even in the early twentieth century—when a range of sophisticated contraceptive methods were available—literal motherhood portended a contradiction between femininity and authorship. What Kristeva even now calls "the abjection of the mother" and what de Beauvoir some time ago saw as woman's figurative immanence means that those writers who felt themselves most exhilaratingly liberated from the traditional constraints of femininity had to reject the threatening constrictions of maternity. Where such male writers as Yeats, Conrad, Joyce, Pound, Hemingway, Fitzgerald, Stevens, Williams, Faulkner, Thomas, Lowell, and Shapiro (all with wives to do most of the child rearing) could easily opt for biological paternity without fearing that such a role would undermine their aesthetic authority, many successful modernist women could not take a biological risk that might incarcerate them in just the sex roles they were striving to critique or repudiate.

How, then, can we account for the achievements of the mother-writers who mostly began to publish in the late fifties and who continue to play a crucial role in contemporary literature by women? Has the first Queen put on the body Judith Shakespeare laid down so long ago? Certainly for contemporary women writers, the materiality of maternity no longer seems to undercut the supposed transcendence of fleshly imperatives necessary for or associated with literary authority. Since the 1950s women of letters have evidently achieved a new kind of solution to the mind/body problem: not a monolithic solution by any means and not one that we are prescribing, but one that seems historically unprecedented. Paradoxically, those who solved this problem in the way we are discussing here were products of just the feminine mystique that gave rise to the second wave of the feminist movement. Yet the paradox is more apparent than real, for if this generation of writers grew up with a cultural ideology admonishing women to fulfill themselves by becoming perfect wives and mothers, they were also citizens of a society that had been radically transformed by the first wave of feminism and that continually urged them to realize their intellectual potential by going to college, getting high grades, and winning prizes and fellowships.

For this generation, then, the parable of the fig tree that Sylvia Plath's Esther Greenwood recounts in *The Bell Jar* is ironic rather than monitory, a joke rather than a sermon. "I saw my life branching out before me like the green fig tree in the story," confides Esther; "from the tip of every branch, like a fat purple fig a wonderful future beckoned and winked. One fig was a husband and a happy home and children and another fig was a famous poet and another fig was a brilliant professor," and so forth. But although Plath's heroine believes that "choosing one [fig] meant losing all the rest," (62–63) the poet-novelist herself, along with many of her contemporaries, actually intended to choose "each and every one of them." Rebelling against the strictures of Buddy Willard's mother, who insists that a man is an arrow into the future and a woman is the place the arrow shoots off from, Esther also rejects what she sees as the sterility of female professionals like Jay Cee and Philomena Guinea. And Plath herself, who planned to be an ambitious arrow into the future, nevertheless proclaimed her determination "to go Virginia Woolf one better" by writing great books and producing wonderful babies.

In this determination, Plath was representative of her generation. To a number of these women, as we have argued elsewhere, it seemed that their immediate female precursors had willfully cut themselves off from the pleasures of procreativity in order to facilitate a painful creativity. About Woolf again, for example, Plath complains in her journal that "what one misses [is] her potatoes and sausage. What is her love, her childless life, like, that she misses it, except in Mrs. Ramsey, Clarissa Dalloway?" (*J* 307). Less explicitly, though comparably, Adrienne Rich, who confesses to having read "the older women poets" with special intensity, reveals her worry that Marianne Moore, "the woman poet most admired . . . (by men)," was "*maidenly*, elegant, intellectual, discreet" ("When We Dead Awaken," *L* 39; emphasis ours). If the choices made possible by contraception, at least for Woolf's generation, were primarily negative—*either* writing *or* motherhood—the choices produced by the feminine mystique of the fifties were parodoxically more fluid, though not less perplexing—*both* writing *and/or* motherhood.

The potential of liberation is inevitably dizzying. For women of the fifties, growing up with Camus and Sartre as well as with de Beauvoir, leaps of faith toward motherhood or not-motherhood were simultaneously vertiginous and exhilarating. For as the poet-activist Robin Morgan has put it, "Since the patriarchy commanded women to be mothers (the thesis), we had to rebel with our own polarity and declare motherhood a reactionary cabal (antithesis). Today a new synthesis has emerged; the concept of mother-right, affirmation of a woman's child-bearing and/or child-rearing when it is a woman's choice. . . . It is refreshing at last to be able to come out of my mother-closet and yell to the world that I love my dear wonderful delicious child" (quoted in Hirsch 163).

Two further journal entries by Plath bring to the surface some of the feelings that may have helped shape Morgan's concept of mother-right. In 1959, when she feared that she might not be able to conceive, Plath explained to herself that "I have always been extremely fond of the definition of Death which says it is: Inaccessability to Experience. . . . And for a woman to be deprived of the Great Experience her body is formed to partake of . . . is a great and wasting Death. After all, a man need physically do no more than have the usual intercourse to become a father. A woman has 9 months of becoming something other than herself, of separating from this otherness, of feeding it and being a source of milk and honey to it" (*J* 309–10). Plath's rhetoric here is in one sense a particularly heated articulation of the feminine mystique; but in another sense it indicates possible aesthetic and metaphysical implications of what might appear merely a physical choice. And four months earlier, when she thought she might have conceived, she had quite specifically formulated a growing consciousness of such implications, remarking that she hoped the experience might yield "*some good pregnant poems*" (300; emphasis ours).

Indeed, although other women had already written "pregnant poems," Plath's verse about her children—like Morgan's yell of delight at coming out of her mother-closet—may be said to have inaugurated a new genre of literature by women, a genre in which a maternal poetic voice addresses or meditates on the mysterious newness and otherness of a child, whose ontological "nakedness / Shadows our safety" ("Morning Song," *PCP* 157). Unlike such nineteenth-century women poets as Maria Lowell and Lydia Sigourney, who tended to produce sentimental effusions about angelic toddlers and dead babies, writers in this new genre frequently provide keen analyses of both the physicality and the metaphysicality of maternity. For these writers, in fact, the crisis of delivery precipitates existential insights at least as grand as those yielded by the confrontations of male artists with the whiteness of the whale or the wilderness of *Deliverance*. And many quite self-consciously ascribe literary historical meanings to such insights.

Sharon Olds's "Language of the Brag," for instance, rivalrously boasts to Walt Whitman and Allen Ginsberg that in bringing forth a baby she has done an all-American, heroic thing:

> I have lain down and sweated and shaken
> and passed blood and feces and water and
> slowly alone in the center of a circle I have
> passed the new person out
> and they have lifted the new person free of the act
> and wiped the new person free of that
> language of blood like praise all over the body.
>
> I have done what you wanted to do, Walt Whitman,
> Allen Ginsberg, I have done this thing,
> I and the other women this exceptional
> act with the exceptional heroic body,
> This giving birth, this glistening verb,
> and I am putting my proud American boast
> right here with the others.[37]

More subtly, in a sardonic apostrophe to Milton, "who made his illegitimate daughters / Read to him in five languages," Bernadette Mayer reveals that she has nicknamed two of her three girl babies after great male literary precursors: Hawthorne and Melville. Caring for these infants absorbs much of her attention—"The Melville one though the smallest wants the most . . . [but] Hawthorne will want to be nursed when she gets up. . . . I can hear Hawthorne, I know she's awake now / But will she stir, disturbing the placid sleep / Of Melville?"—and yet these babies populate the scene of her writing: "They all see the light by which I write."[38]

Just as wittily, Anne Waldman turns to a single and childless female precursor, parodying Emily Dickinson's "I've ceded" and "I'm Wife" to examine not the problematic of female creativity, as Dickinson did, but the literary as well as the literal power of female procreativity:

> I'm wanton—no I've stopped that.
> That old place
> I've changed, I'm Mother
> It's more mysterious.

> How odd the past looks
> When I reread old notebooks.[39]

Perhaps Hélène Cixous best formulates an assumption about the literary implications of maternity that underlies these poems when she asks, in the significantly titled *Newly Born Woman,* "How could the woman, who has experienced the not-me within me, not have a particular relationship to the written?"[40]

From Anne Sexton's hymns to her *"little girl, / my string bean"* (*SCP* 146) and Denise Levertov's meditations on the mystic son "who came forth" to the nursing poems of Elizabeth Socolow and Anne Winters, the verse of women writers has undertaken two projects Cixous calls for: to define the child as "the other, but the other without violence" and to redefine maternity as a "subjectivity that splits apart without regret." As Winters puts it in "Elizabeth Near and Far," a subtly nuanced sonnet sequence to her daughter, no matter how closely bonded the physical mother is with her child, she must always be aware of the metaphysical distance between them: "There is space between me, I know, / And you. I hang above you like a planet— / You're a planet too. One planet loves the other."[41]

Of course, a number of contemporary male poets, from Donald Hall and Galway Kinnell to Philip Levine and Robert Pinsky, have written works to and about their children, with some participating in the projects that Cixous outlines. But the genre in which they work is, curiously enough, far more traditional for father-poets than for mother-artists. Such disparate figures as Ben Jonson, Samuel Taylor Coleridge, and William Butler Yeats, for instance, composed significant verses to and about their offspring. If, as Stephen Dedalus contended in *Ulysses,* paternity is always a fiction, it has also—perhaps for this reason—always been fictionalized. But the factuality and literalness of maternity can be, as we see in the works of the new mother-writers, even more dramatically metaphorized.

Indeed, although almost as many male as female poets have lately indited verses to their children, there are striking, and in some cases almost stereotypically gender-bound, differences between the uses to which the two sexes put the child-poem. For many men, the didactic and homiletic tone of, say, Yeats's "Prayer for My Daughter" becomes virtually paradigmatic: the father-poet instructs, admonishes, and sometimes prophesies to his son or daughter, so that the apparently private occasion of the poem offers an opportunity for public pronouncements on general moral issues. A mini-anthology of works in this mode would include as examples the following representative extracts:

> I give you this bible and more to take.
> Love is the work the hands of man can make,
> so read what this, our fabled history, teaches,

and how the firework, Imagination, reaches
to dignify and sanctify.
                    [Dannie Abse, "Inscription on the Flyleaf of a Bible
                    (For My Elder Daughter)"]

My sons, in whom I am well pleased,
you will learn that a man is not a child,
and there is that which a woman cannot bear.
                    [Marvin Bell, "We Have Known"]

Lie back, daughter, let your head
be tipped back in the cup of my hand. . . .
and let go, remember when fear
cramps your heart, what I told you:
lie gently and wide to the light-year
stars, lie back, and the sea will hold you.
                    [Philip Booth, "First Lesson"]

Daughter, in the place you're going
Many come to less by growing,
Losing what they've had by heart.
                    [Barry Spacks, "Three Songs for My Daughter"]

Remember when you hear them beginning to say "Freedom"
Look carefully—see who it is that they want you to
butcher.
                    [Alex Comfort, "Notes for My Son"]

Jessie, it's as though the whole race is sunk in an
atmosphere of blood
and it's been clotting for so many centuries we can
hardly move now.
                    [C. K. Williams, "The Last Deaths"]

Do not listen to the lies of old men
Who fear your power,
Who preach that you were "born in sin."
A flower is moral by its own flowering.
                    [Etheridge Knight, "Circling the Daughter"]

Someday, when you are twenty-four and walking through
The streets of a foreign city, Stockholm,
Or Trieste,
Let me go with you a little way.
Let me be that stranger you won't notice,
                    [Larry Levis, "Blue Stones"][42]

The powerfully paternal authority that marks all these lines is perhaps most dramatically captured in the juxtaposition of the title of Robert Pinsky's book-length *An Explanation of America* with its subtitle, *A Poem to My Daughter.* The most ambitious of all these works, Pinsky's poem is also the frankest in its admission that the child, as a sort of abstraction of herself, furnishes a pretext for the father's philosophizings:

> As though explaining the idea of dancing
> Or the idea of some other thing
> Which everyone has known a little about
> Since they were children . . . .
> I want to tell you something about our country,
> Or my idea of it: explaining it
> If not to you, to my idea of you.[43]

Such an impulse toward abstraction also infuses a variation on the homiletic child-poem written by men—what we might call the metaphysical child-poem: a verse that is sometimes epitaphic or elegiac but always broods on the vagaries of being and nothingness. Brilliantly typical in this regard is Donald Hall's "My Son, My Executioner," with its elaboration on the old maxim that the birth of the child is the death of the parents. Beginning with the speaker taking his small son into his arms, the poem concludes with a meditation on mortality:

> We, twenty-five and twenty-two,
> Who seemed to live forever,
> Observe enduring life in you
> And start to die together.[44]

"In my child's breath / I face / into my death," writes Philip Dow, in a similar vein, while other poets prophetically imagine a future in which they themselves are already dead but still haunting their offspring. Galway Kinnell, for instance, predicts to his daughter that "you will remember . . . . a specter, descendant / of the ghostly forefathers, singing / to you in the nighttime," and Wendell Berry promises his children: "When you meet the destined ones / now dancing toward you, / we (your parents) will be in line behind you."[45]

By contrast with the relative abstraction of these verses by father-poets, the writings of mother-poets are for the most part intransigently concrete, as if the physicality of the mother-child bond necessarily translates into imagery of dramatic mater-iality. Thus where even the most doting of fathers tends to generalize from flesh to spirit, from the body of the child to a body of knowledge, most women begin with the pulse of uterine beginnings, which, after all, mothers uniquely experience. Pregnancy and abortion, birth and nursing, child watching and childcare: these are topoi on which

mother-poets persistently elaborate, always grounding metaphysical speculations in physical observations. At the same time, like their male counterparts, contemporary women of letters do consider the homiletic and philosophical imperatives that structure parenthood. But perhaps because of
women's immersion in the details of the quotidian, the facticity of the flesh,
their speculations tend to be quirkier, more ironic, even at times more self-
deflating. In the hands of a diaper-changing woman, the homiletic frequently becomes the antihomiletic. In the mind of the mother of teenagers,
the metaphysical often becomes the sardonic.

In Sylvia Plath's pioneering oeuvre, of course, all these modes are represented: the pregnancy poem ("You're"), the nursing poem ("Morning
Song"), the abortion or miscarriage poem ("Parliament Hill Fields"), the
baby/child poem ("Nick and the Candlestick"), even the antihomiletic ("For
a Fatherless Son"), among others. But Plath's contemporaries and descendants also ring all possible changes on these subgenres. Pregnancy poems,
for instance, would include Kathleen Fraser's "Poems for the New" ("I am
round / with his sprouting, / new thing new thing!"); Erica Jong's "The
Buddha in the Womb" ("Bobbing in the waters of the womb, / little godhead"); Anne Winters's "The Stethoscope" ("somewhere you incline your
vast / night-sighted brow—your jointed, swimming hands"); and Carol
Muske's "Sounding" ("the underwater gong / then the regular waves— / an
assault as barbaric as conception, // the soul rung forward into image"). And
nursing poems would include—in addition to those by Socolow and Winters
mentioned earlier—Sandra McPherson's "Pisces Child" ("Your tongue
draws oceans in, not spitting / A word out") and Alicia Ostriker's "Greedy
Baby" from *The Mother/Child Papers* ("your lashes close, your mouth again
clamps on / you are attentive as a business man / your fisted fingers open
relaxing and / all rooms are rooms for suckling in").[46]

More theatrical as singular events than pregnancy and nursing, abortion
and birth offer women similar occasions for lyrical meditation. Like Sharon
Olds's "Language of the Brag," Sharon Libera's "How You Were Born" focuses on the moment of delivery, but unlike Olds's poem, Libera's deploys
self-deprecating humor to recount the modern mother's passive acquiescence in medical technology: "My obstetrician, cool and cynical / checked
me like an oven slow roasting a bird" until "shiny forceps pried you out / as if
I were a can difficult to open." More bleak in its narrative of vulnerability, the
abortion poem explores the mutual victimization of (aborting) mother and
(aborted) child, while attending, still, to the metaphysics implied by the
physical details of maternity. Writes Gwendolyn Brooks in "The Mother,"
one of the best-known contemporary abortion poems, "Abortions will not let
you forget. / You remember the children you got that you did not get." Asks
Lucille Clifton in "the lost baby poem," "the time i dropped your almost body
down / down to meet the waters under the city. . . . what did i know about

drowning / or being drowned?" And Diane di Prima rages that "I want you in a bottle to send to your father / with a long bitter note. I want him to know / I'll not forgive you or him for not being born."[47]

Just as poems about pregnancy, nursing, birth, and abortion inevitably modulate into metaphysical broodings on life and death, scrupulous notations about child rearing and childcare evolve first into analyses of the dynamics of personality and ultimately into homiletic or antihomiletic musings about how (the child's—or even the mother's) life should be lived. Talking to the child, implies Alicia Ostriker in "Bitterness," entails understanding his or her eccentric temperament, always already a source of worry to the mother:

> Somebody said of you when you were young,
> "That child hates being a child"
> —It explained or seemed to explain your resistance
> To love, the creamy family food
> I tried to dish out.

Describing a mother's sense of fatality about a child who sits "glumly on bare linoleum" at least in part because of "the humiliation // Of childhood help-lessness," Ostriker's poem exemplifies not only the kind of detailed, psychological scrutiny so many of these texts embody but also the relinquishing of control that mothers—evidently far more than fathers—understand as a necessity of parenting. "How important it was," observes Colleen McElroy, "When you locked all the doors / Three years old / and instant master of the house."[48]

No doubt as a consequence of the understanding that control must be relinquished, women's homiletic poems tend to become skeptical, parodic, even antihomiletic. A mini-anthology of extracts from women's texts forms a striking contrast to the mini-anthology written by men transcribed earlier:

> How shall I tell anything at all
> To this infant still in a birth-drowse?
>
> [Sylvia Plath, "Candles"]

> Dear children, you must try to say
> Something when you are in need.
> Don't confuse hunger with greed;
> And don't wait until you are dead.
>
> [Ruth Stone, "Advice"]

> A snail is climbing up the window-sill
> Into your room, after a night of rain.
> You call me in to see, and I explain

that it would be unkind to leave it there:
It might crawl to the floor; we must take care
That no one squashes it. . . .
. . . that is how things are: I am your mother
And we are kind to snails.
                    [Fleur Adcock, "For a Five-Year-Old"]

Steal only what you can wear.
Two nickels dont ring like a dime.
Saints come in pints, quarts, gallons.
                    [Alberta T. Turner, "Daughter, Daughter"]

. . . I wrote you good advice—
but the lines have wavered, and fallen short.
                    [Lorrie Goldensohn, "Letter for a Daughter"]

children
when they ask you
why is your mama so funny
say
she is a poet
she don't have no sense.
                    [Lucille Clifton, "Admonitions"]

Granddaughter of my mother,
Listen to my song:
Nothing you do will ever be right,
Nothing you do is wrong.
                    [Ursula K. Le Guin, "An April Fools' Day Present
                    for My Daughter Elisabeth"][49]

By turns doubtful ("How shall I tell anything"), desperate ("don't wait
until you are dead"), modest ("we are kind to snails"), comic ("steal only what
you can wear"), bemused ("the lines have . . . fallen short"), self-deprecatory
("she don't have no sense"), and whimsical ("Nothing you do will ever be
right, / Nothing you do is wrong"), the mother-poet questions the efficacy of
traditional scenes of instruction, interrogating the very possibility of advice
to a being who is at once the same and irremediably other. Culturally, of
course, the superegoistic father has long been constructed as a sagacious and
monitory figure, while the mother has been understood to represent uncon-
ditional love and nurturance. Yet the mother's antihomiletic impulse may
perhaps be reinforced by the physiology of maternity: because she has quite
literally "experienced the not-me within me," the literary mother may understand with special intensity the inexorability with which her child must
and will be born into a world that is beyond her control.

At the same time, in an important subgenre of the child-poem written by women, the mother-writer comes close to at least one of the philosophical impulses that drive the father-poet's work. Like Paul Mariani, who sees in his son an "obsidian mirror image of my / deepest self,"[50] the woman often learns to know herself and her own history by knowing her child. Even the title of Anne Sexton's "The Double Image" summarizes how the poet as mother is forced to confront her own defects through interactions with her daughter ("as if doom had flooded my belly and filled your bassinet"), even while the very fact of childbearing reinstates her in her own genealogy ("You call me *mother* and I remember my mother again"). Similarly, poems by Maxine Kumin, Linda Pastan, and Carolyn Kizer meditate on mother-child mirroring and the self-knowledge that ensues. Defining her children in "Family Reunion" as "the almost-parents of your parents now," Kumin confesses that "having you back to measure us / is harder than having let you go," while Pastan admits in "Letter to a Son at Exam Time" that "You woke up / on the wrong side / of my life." More generally—and most incisively— in "The Blessing" Kizer addresses her "Daughter-my-mother," avowing that "you have observed my worst. / Holding me together at your expense / has made you burn cool."[51]

What accounts for the range and variety of the poems mother-writers produce about and for their children? One answer to this question must surely emphasize the social changes we have been examining throughout these three volumes. No doubt because for the first time women consider themselves able to choose which plots to generate in their personal lives, maternity can be perceived as a narrative of which the woman is an independent author—not, as sometimes in the past, a fiction designed to ensnare a man into a shotgun wedding but a family plot in which she can adopt a role from which she is, by the very gesture of choosing, significantly distanced. In other words, just because she is distanced by the possibility of choosing *against* motherhood, the mother can write about her experience. Her maternal discourse is facilitated, that is, by her sense of herself as constructing and constructed by gender imperatives. At this unusual moment in history, then, she is aware of maternity as a process in which she can represent what Kristeva calls "the subjectless biological program" as an absorbing subjectivity enclosed within her/the "symbolizing subject." Thus, as if paraphrasing Yeats's "Sailing to Byzantium," she might cry, "gather me / Into the artifice of maternity."[52]

But because she experiences the "biological program" as both subjectless and subjective, it may be said that both in body and in mind the self-consciously literary mother encounters a profoundly Emersonian relation between the me and the not-me, and therefore a compelling antidote to that phallocratic structure of domination and colonization which Cixous calls "the Empire of the Self-Same." Simultaneously historian and prophet, the

literal and literary mother has to realize that she has given birth to potentiality, to multiple, possible plots. "At the breast," writes Celia Gilbert in a
poem we took as an epigraph, "there is / the pounding of the heart / bearing // story after story." With Lucille Clifton, the mother knows that her own
history—"my almost me"—is mirrored in the lives and bodies of her children, even while a different destiny—"my more than me"—awaits them.[53]
Addressing her offspring, therefore, the mother-writer looks backward and
forward, always conscious that the child is both a question that the past asks
the future and a question that the future asks the past.

Perhaps for this reason, the emergence of the child-poem in the female
literary tradition signals a major transformation in the situation of the
woman writer in the twentieth century. For despite maternal hesitations and
guilt, the poet who speaks to her child addresses her words to a future she
can now begin to imagine shaping, as she herself has been shaped by a past
she reimagines as empowering rather than debilitating. Although the male
poet has always inserted his voice into the genealogy of literary history,
measuring himself against precursors who *influenced* him as well as those
whom he envisions *influencing*, the contemporary woman poet inhabits new
aesthetic places as she conceptualizes not only a cultural past conceived by
and for women but also a cultural future in which her words may endure in
the minds and lives of those who are either literally or figuratively her
children. Like Audre Lorde, who recalls delivery as a moment of virtually
apocalyptic transfiguration—"my legs were towers between which / A new
world was passing"—the practitioners of this genre employ it to consecrate
their own ongoing creativity "now that [they are] forever with child." Like
Margaret Atwood, who remembers her daughter learning "to spell, / spelling, / how to make spells," the mother as poet begins to heal the fissures of
history, as she realizes that her life need not be torn between creativity and
procreativity but can, rather, encompass both:

> A child is not a poem, a poem is not a child.
> There is no either/or.[54]

How, then, would this newly born mother-writer tell the old story of
"Snow White"? Would she tell it at all or would the disintegration of the
family romance implicit in the self-possession and autonomy of the mother
annihilate the very concept of story? Would the configurations of King,
Queen, Prince, and Snow White be so radically altered as to defamiliarize
and defamilialize these characters altogether? Or would the newly born
Queen pretend that the old stories are still viable and recycle the past in a
series of parodic mimes and masquerades? Would Snow White, in an effort
to differentiate herself from her powerfully integrated mother, be driven to
imagine matricidal plots as lethal as the old infanticidal ones? Would the

King and the Prince so envy the Queen's combination of physical and metaphysical authority that they would completely depart from the story or sternly resolve to reinstate the premises of the primordial tale?

There was a good Queen who pricked her finger with a needle, watched blood fall on snow, gave birth to a girl-child named Snow White, and lived to raise her. And sometimes when this Queen looked into the mirror of her mind, she passed in her thoughts through the looking glass into a forest of stories so new that only she and her daughter could tell them.

Notes

Epigraphs on page vii: H. D., *Trilogy*, in *Collected Poems: 1912–1944*, ed. Louis L. Martz (New York: New Directions, 1983), 570; Rukeyser, "Letter to the Front" (1944), *The Collected Poems* (New York: McGraw-Hill, 1978), 243; Sontag, *Styles of Radical Will* (New York: Farrar, Straus, and Giroux, 1969), 18; Rich, "Phantasia for Elvira Shatayev" (1974), *The Fact of a Doorframe: Poems Selected and New, 1950–1984* (New York: Norton, 1984), 168.

Preface

1 Rich, *The Will to Change* (New York: Norton, 1971); H. D., *Trilogy*, in H. D., *Collected Poems: 1912–1944*, ed. Louis L. Martz (New York: New Directions, 1983), 570.

2 Bloom, *The Closing of the American Mind: How Higher Education Has Failed Democracy and Impoverished the Souls of Today's Students* (New York: Simon and Schuster, 1987), 233, 65, 124, 101.

3 Paglia, *Sexual Personae: Art and Decadence from Nefertiti to Emily Dickinson* (New Haven: Yale University Press, 1990), 12, 11; quoted in *New York*, 4 March 1991, 30.

4 Kamuf, "Replacing Feminist Criticism," in *Feminist Literary Criticism*, ed. Mary Eagleton (London: Longman, 1991), 56.

5 Jacobus, "Is There a 'Woman' In This Text?" in *Feminist Literary Criticism*, 190.

6 Kamuf, "Replacing Feminist Criticism," 59.

7 Brooks, "Bronzeville Woman in a Red Hat," *The World of Gwendolyn Brooks* (New York: Harper and Row, 1971), 351.

8 Spivak, *The Post-Colonial Critic*, ed. Sarah Harasym (New York: Routledge, 1990), 11.

9 Fuss, *Essentially Speaking: Feminism, Nature and Difference* (New York: Routledge, 1989), 21.

10 Faludi, *Backlash: The Undeclared War against American Women* (New York: Crown, 1991), 46.

11 Kristeva, *Revolution in Poetic Language*, trans. Margaret Walker (New York: Columbia University Press, 1984); Cixous and Catherine Clément, *The Newly Born Woman*, trans. Betsy Wing (Minneapolis: University of Minnesota Press, 1986); DuPlessis, *The Pink Guitar: Writing as Feminist Practice* (New York: Routledge, 1990); Jardine, *Gynesis: Configurations of Woman and Modernity* (Ithaca: Cornell University Press, 1985); DeKoven, *Rich and Strange: Gender, History, Modernism* (Princeton: Princeton University Press, 1991).

12 Butler, *Gender Trouble: Feminism and the Subversion of Identity* (New York: Routledge, 1990), 147.

Chapter 1: What Is the Meaning of the Play?

Epigraphs: Woolf, "Journal of Mistress Joan Martyn" (1906), in *The Complete Shorter Fiction of Virginia Woolf*, 2d. ed., ed. Susan Dick (New York: Harcourt, 1989), 48; Woolf, "Ellen Terry," *The Moment and Other Essays* (New York: Harcourt, 1975), 212; Woolf, *Pointz Hall: The Earlier and Later Typescripts of* Between the Acts, ed. Mitchell A. Leaska (New York: University Publications, 1983), 185.

1 Woolf, *Between the Acts* (New York: Harcourt, 1969), 212, 219. Further references will be to this edition, and page numbers will appear in the text after the abbreviation *BA* where necessary. References to other Woolf works will be handled similarly, with pertinent publishing and abbreviation information as follows: *Between the Acts* (New York: Harcourt, 1969), *BA*. *Books and Portraits*, ed. Mary Lyon (New York: Harcourt, 1977), *BP*. *The Captain's Deathbed and Other Essays* (New York: Harcourt, 1978), *CD*. *The Common Reader* (New York: Harcourt, 1953), *CR*. *The Complete Shorter Fiction of Virginia Woolf*, *CSF*. *The Death of the Moth and Other Essays* (New York: Harcourt, 1970), *DM*. *The Diary of Virginia Woolf*, vols. 1–5, ed. Anne Olivier Bell (New York: Harcourt, 1977–84), *D* 1–5. *Jacob's Room* (New York: Harcourt, 1978), *JR*. *The Moment and Other Essays*, *M*. *Moments of Being: Unpublished Autobiographical Writings*, ed. Jeanne Schulkind (New York: Harcourt, 1976), *MB*. *Monday or Tuesday* (New York: Harcourt, 1921), *MT*. *Mrs. Dalloway* (New York: Harcourt, 1985), *MD*. *Night and Day* (New York: Harcourt, 1948), *ND*. *Orlando* (New York: Harcourt, 1956), *O*. *The Pargiters: The Novel-Essay Portion of* The Years, ed. Mitchell A. Leaska (New York: Harcourt, 1977), *P*. *A Room of One's Own* (New York: Harcourt, 1957), *ROO*. *Three Guineas* (New York: Harcourt, 1966), *TG*. *To the Lighthouse* (New York: Harcourt, 1955), *TTL*. *The Voyage Out* (New York: Harcourt, 1948), *VO*. *The Waves* (New York: Harcourt, 1978), *W*. *The Years* (New York: Harcourt, 1965), *TY*.

2 See, for instance, Alex Zwerdling, *Virginia Woolf and the Real World* (Berkeley: University of California Press, 1986), 302–23, and Phyllis Rose, *Woman of Letters: A Life of Virginia Woolf* (New York: Harcourt, 1978), 225–48. In addition, Woolf's responses to the pressures of impending war are revealed in numerous diary entries: e.g., in an entry dated 28 August 1939, she writes "But there's a vast cold gloom. And the strain. Like waiting a doctors verdict. And the young—young men smashed up. But the point is one is too numbed to think" (*D* 5:231).

3 Bell, *Virginia Woolf: A Biography* (New York: Harcourt, 1972), 2: 222. Further references will be to this edition, and volume and page numbers will appear in the text after the abbreviation *QB* where necessary.

4 Woolf, "London in War," Monk's House Papers A20:5, University of Sussex Library, cited in Zwerdling, *Woolf and the Real World*, 307.

5 See Oswald Spengler, *The Decline of the West*, trans. Charles Francis Atkinson. 2 vols. (1923–24; New York: Knopf, 1945). This book, which seemed to many uncannily prophetic, haunted W. B. Yeats, among others.

6 Auden, "Spain 1937," in *The English Auden: Poems, Essays and Dramatic Writings, 1927–39*, ed. Edward Mendelson (New York: Random House, 1977), 212; Eliot, "Little Gidding," *Collected Poems 1909–62* (New York: Harcourt, 1963), 208; Forster, "Post-Munich," *Two Cheers for Democracy* (New York: Harcourt, 1951), 21; Sitwell, "Lullaby," in *Edith Sitwell: Fire of the Mind*, ed. Elizabeth Salter and Allanah Harper (New York: Vanguard, 1976), 219.

7 Zwerdling, *Woolf and the Real World*, 327.

8 See *BA*, 188, 189, where the phrases "orts, scraps and fragments" and "scraps, orts and fragments" appear, as well as *D*, 5:290 (entry dated 31 May).

9 "The other history": see Cixous and Catherine Clément, *The Newly Born Woman*, trans.

Betsy Wing (Minneapolis: University of Minnesota Press, 1986), 83; "breaking the sequence": see *ROO*, 85.

10 Observers as diverse as E. M. Forster, Q. D. Leavis, and Quentin Bell repeatedly made the point that Woolf was a "lady." For Forster's comments on Woolf, see *Recollections of Virginia Woolf by Her Contemporaries*, ed. Joan Russell Noble (London: Cardinal, 1989), 226–42, esp. 240: "She felt herself to be not only a woman but a lady, and this gives a further twist to her social outlook. She was a lady by birth and upbringing [and] her snobbery—for she was a snob—had more courage in it than arrogance." Q. D. Leavis's view of Woolf as "a lady" was much less charitable. See, e.g., this passage from her scathing review of *Three Guineas*, "Caterpillars of the Commonwealth Unite!": "Mrs. Woolf, by her own account, has personally received considerably more in the way of economic ease than she is humanly entitled to and, as this book reveals, has enjoyed the equally relaxing ease of an uncritical (not to say flattering) social circle" (*The Importance of Scrutiny, Selections from* Scrutiny: A Quarterly Review *1932–48*, ed. Eric Bentley [New York: George W. Stewart, 1948], 283). For Bell's account of Woolf's teaching at Morley College, see *QB*, 1:105–07, and for Woolf's own report see his appendix B, 202–04. For Woolf's involvement with the Labour Party, see *QB*, 2:186–88.

11 Patmore's *Angel in the House* (1854) enjoyed immense popularity, going through continually expanded editions and selling over a quarter of a million copies by the time of the poet's death in 1896. The Stephen family library contained an 1866 (fourth) edition signed by the author, who was a favorite of Woolf's grandmother Maria Pattle Jackson. See Diane Gillespie, "The Elusive Julia Stephen," in *Julia Duckworth Stephen*, eds. Diane Gillespie and Elizabeth Steele (Syracuse: Syracuse University Press, 1987), 10–14. For Woolf's vision of her mother as an Angel in the House, see her "Reminiscences," in *MB*, 32–40.

12 See Stephen, *The Mausoleum Book* (Oxford: Clarendon Press, 1977); and Carlyle, *Reminiscences* (London: Longmans, Green, 1881), 2:67–305.

13 For Woolf's reference to Leonard as a "penniless Jew," see her letter to Violet Dickinson, 4 June 1912, in *The Letters of Virginia Woolf*, ed. Nigel Nicolson (London: Hogarth, 1975), 1:500.

14 For the significance of Roger Fry's 1910 exhibition, see Zwerdling, 110–11; for the *Dreadnought* affair, see Rose, 102–03.

15 For a slightly different perspective on the significance of the *Dreadnought* affair, see Jane Marcus, *Virginia Woolf and the Languages of Patriarchy* (Bloomington: Indiana University Press, 1987). In involving herself with the hoax, Marcus asserts, Woolf was "allusively . . . engaged in serious play with the history and ideology of her culture, with biography, autobiography, and with the way in which literature shapes our expectations of life as individuals, couples, families, and generations" (19).

16 On Woolf's involvement with the suffrage movement, see Zwerdling, *Woolf and the Real World*, 212–16, 234, 237–39, 247; In October 1911, Virginia and Adrian Stephen moved from Fitzroy Square to Brunswick Square. According to Leonard Woolf (*Beginning Again: An Autobiography of the Years 1911–18* [New York: Harcourt, 1964]), the Stephens planned to run their establishment on "—for those days—original lines. Adrian occupied the second floor and Virginia the third. Maynard Keynes and Duncan Grant shared the ground floor, and I was offered the fourth floor, or rather a bedroom and sitting room there" (50–51).

17 Nor would Julia have liked her daughter's work on behalf of the suffrage movement; see Gillespie, "The Elusive Julia Stephen," 14–17, for a discussion of George Meredith's criticism of Julia Stephen's conventional views of the woman's role and especially her protestations against women's suffrage.

18 West, "Autumn and Virginia Woolf," *Ending in Earnest: A Literary Log* (Garden City, N.Y.: Doubleday, 1931), 212.

19 Nina Auerbach has recently speculated that Ellen Terry's daughter, Edith Craig, was the original of Miss La Trobe in *Between the Acts;* see Auerbach, *Ellen Terry: Player in Her Time* (New York: Norton, 1987), 247, 427.

20 See Carlyle, *On Heroes, Hero-worship, and the Heroic in History* (London: Fraser, 1841).

21 Susan Squier and Louise De Salvo supplied the title "Journal of Mistress Joan Martyn" when they edited the manuscript for publication in the twenty-fifth anniversary issue of *Twentieth-Century Literature* (1979).

22 Katharine Stephen (1856–1924) was principal of Newnham from 1911 until 1920. After her death, Woolf, waxing nostalgic despite her long-standing aversion to Stephen's rigid brand of fundamentalist Christianity, wrote to Pernel Strachey, Stephen's Newnham replacement: "Never shall I forget her at Newnham, hundreds of years ago, and sitting in that queer grim room with her talking—what a satisfactory and altogether charming human being she was." See *Letters,* 2:126. Ironically, though, despite Stephen's pioneering contributions to higher education for women, little is known of her life and work; she, too, must be counted among the ranks of historically "obscure" women.

23 See Beard, *Woman as a Force in History: A Study in Traditions and Realities* (New York: Macmillan, 1946). For Woolf on "Anon" and women's writing, see *ROO,* 51, *Women and Writing,* passim, and her posthumous essay "Anon" in *Twentieth-Century Literature* 25:3–4 (1979): 380–420.

24 More generally, in contemporary terms the history whose contours Woolf outlined was in some ways comparable to the kind eventually practiced by the "Annales" school in France and in both literary criticism and history by the so-called New Historicists in the United States, although her version of such scholarship was considerably less empirical than are these recent models. (For a concise summary of the "Annales" position, see Traian Stoianovich, *French Historical Method: The Annales Paradigm* [Ithaca: Cornell University Press, 1976]: "The object of *Annales* work is to construct a history of every group and subject whose investigation has been suppressed or neglected. . . . It aims similarly at the 'demasculinization of history' and at the development of a history of women, of youth, of childhood, of oral cultures, of voluntary associations" [158–59].)

25 Schlesinger, "The Role of Women in American History," in *New Viewpoints in American History* (New York: Macmillan, 1921), 126. Half a century earlier, of course, Henry Adams had observed, "The proper study of mankind is woman," adding, "Without understanding the movement of sex, history seem[s] . . . mere pedantry" (*The Education of Henry Adams* [1874], in *Democracy Esther, Mont Saint Michel and Chartres, The Education of Henry Adams* [New York: Library of America, 1983], 1123). Nevertheless, as Nancy Schrom Dye has observed, for "one who insisted on the primacy of sexual force in history, Adams's historical writings are 'curiously empty' of real females"; see Dye, "Clio's American Daughters," in *The Prism of Sex: Essays in the Sociology of Knowledge,* ed. Julia A. Sherman and Evelyn Torton Beck (Madison: University of Wisconsin Press, 1979), 17. See also Elizabeth Waterson, "The Gap in Henry Adams' Education," *Canadian Journal of American Studies* 7 (Fall 1976).

26 Austen, *Northanger Abbey,* ed. Andrew Wright (New York: Holt, Rinehart, 1963), 396–97.

27 Froude's *Carlyle* appeared in 1882–84; Macaulay's *History* in 1849 and 1855; Carlyle's *French Revolution* in 1837; Arnold's *History of Rome* in 1838–42; and Gibbon's *Decline and Fall* in 1776, 1781, and 1788. Catharine Macaulay (1731–91) produced an eight-volume *History of England* (1763–83), which achieved modest success, but there is no evidence that Woolf read it. Bell does note, though, that Woolf also read—among

others—Mandell Creighton's *Queen Elizabeth;* "a work by Lady Barlow"; Charlotte Brontë's *Shirley;* Janet Ross's *Three Generations of English Women* (volumes 2 and 3); George Eliot's *Silas Marner;* and Carlyle's *Reminiscences,* all works written by or dealing with women (*QB* 1:50–51).

28 It is interesting, in this regard, that as Zwerdling observes, Woolf's own father "was very far from believing that women should be decorative objects trained only in the usual feminine 'accomplishments' while preparing themselves for matrimony. His thoughts on the subject were quite uncompromisingly radical for his time and are spelled out in a letter to Julia written before their marriage: 'What I chiefly hold is that women ought to be as well educated as men, indeed a great deal better than men are now. . . . I hate to see so many women's lives wasted simply because they have not been trained well enough to take an independent interest in any studies or to be able to work effectively at any profession'" (*Woolf and the Real World* 184).

29 For discussions of these stories as exemplary analyses of the problem of literary inheritance for women writers, see Gilbert and Gubar, *No Man's Land,* vol. 1: *The War of the Words* (New Haven: Yale University Press, 1988), 189–92 and 173–74.

30 Anne (Anny) Thackeray Ritchie, the sister of Leslie Stephen's first wife, Minnie Thackeray Stephen, wrote impressionistic novels of which Quentin Bell remarks that they "were tenuous, charming productions in which the narrative tended to get lost and in which something of her own vague, erratic engaging personality is preserved" (*QB* 1:10). See also pages 11–12 for further comments; for a biography, see Winifred Gerin, *Anne Thackeray Ritchie* (Oxford: Oxford University Press, 1981); and for Leslie Stephen's comments on his sister-in-law, see his *Mausoleum Book,* 12–15, 23–25.

31 Significantly, too, Katharine's cousin Cassandra—another major character in the romance plot of *Night and Day*—refuses to read Macaulay's *History of England;* see pages 428–29, 433.

32 See Woolf's diary entry of 26 January 1920: "The day after my birthday . . . and happier today than I was yesterday, having this afternoon arrived at some idea of a new form for a new novel . . . . I figure that the approach will be entirely different this time: no scaffolding; scarcely a brick to be seen; all crepuscular, but the heart, the passion, humour, everything as bright as fire in the mist" (*D* 2:13–14).

33 Fever-wracked and dazed by her engagement on her trip down the Amazon, Rachel has lapsed into an altered state of consciousness which she diagnoses as "happiness." For "mother women," see Chopin, *The Awakening* (New York: Bantam, 1981), 10.

34 For every Rachel who is sickened by the prospect of marriage, the plot of *The Voyage Out* suggests, there is a Susan who is delighted at the idea. Similarly, the plot of *Night and Day* suggests that for every Mary who refuses marriage there is a Cassandra who acquiesces in the institution.

35 For a detailed discussion of the relation between World War I and the women's movement, see Gilbert and Gubar, *No Man's Land: The Place of the Woman Writer in the Twentieth Century,* vol. 2: *Sexchanges* (New Haven: Yale University Press, 1989), chap. 7.

36 See Mansfield to John Middleton Murry, November 1919: "My private opinion is that it [*ND*] is a lie in the soul. . . . The novel can't just leave the war out. There *must* have been a change of heart. . . . I feel in the *profoundest* sense that nothing can ever be the same—that, as artists, we are traitors if we feel otherwise: we have to take it into account and find new expressions, new moulds for our thoughts and feelings" (quoted in Jeffrey Meyers, *Katharine Mansfield: A Biography* [London: Hamish Hamilton, 1978], 143–44).

37 For important theoretical discussions of this issue, see Nancy K. Miller, "Emphasis Added: Plots and Plausibilities in Women's Fiction," in Elaine Showalter, ed., *The New Feminist Criticism: Essays on Women, Literature, and Theory* (New York: Pantheon, 1985),

339–60, and Rachel Blau DePlessis, *Writing beyond the Ending: Narrative Strategies of Twentieth-Century Women Writers* (Bloomington: Indiana University Press, 1985).

38 On "Woolf's erotics of chastity," see Marcus, *Woolf and the Languages of Patriarchy*, 115–19. Marcus argues that Clarissa's "honor seems to have derived from her failure to be Richard's sexual partner" (117). See also 204n5, as well as Zwerdling, *Woolf and the Real World*, 120–43, Rose, *Woman of Letters*, 125–52, and Elizabeth Abel, *Virginia Woolf and the Fictions of Psychoanalysis* (Chicago: University of Chicago Press, 1989), 30–44.

39 For a discussion of *MD* from a different perspective, see our *Sexchanges*, 287–89, 314–18, 320–21.

40 For a different perspective on this episode as well as a number of linguistic fantasies in Woolf's novels, see our *War of the Words*, 229–31, 248–51.

41 For another analysis of the song sung by the tube station crone, see Miller, "Virginia Woolf's All Souls' Day."

42 Significantly, the only specific memoir we learn of Clarissa reading is an account of a military *defeat:* in Baron Marbot's *Memoirs*, she "had read late at night of the retreat from Moscow" (*MD* 46).

43 Of course, in Alexander Pope's *The Rape of the Lock*, which features yet another heroic Clarissa, similar themes of male predation and chaste female martyrdom prevail, so that it is possible Woolf had Pope's as well as Richardson's Clarissa in mind when she named her protagonist. In her diary, she notes that she "scrambled through" Pope as a child (*D* 5:86), and she mentions *The Rape of the Lock* in her essay "Lord Chesterfield's Letters to His Son" (*Second Common Reader* [New York: Harcourt, 1986], 86). For further discussions of the name Clarissa, see Marcus, *Woolf and the Languages of Patriarchy*, 117–19, and Beverly Ann Schlack, *Continuing Presences: Virginia Woolf's Use of Literary Allusion* (University Park: Pennsylvania State University Press, 1979).

44 For another view of Elizabeth's role in *MD*, see Bowlby, "Thinking Forward Through Mrs. Dalloway's Daughter," in *Virginia Woolf: Feminist Destinations*, 80–98.

45 On alienation, Chinese eyes, and otherness, see also Julia Kristeva, *About Chinese Women*, trans. Anita Barrows (1974; London: Marion Boyars, 1977). Kristeva writes of her trip to China that she was greeted by "calm eyes . . . piercing, and certain of belonging to a community with which we will never have anything to do" (11).

46 Woolf herself turned forty-four the year she began writing *To the Lighthouse* (1926). Soon after her forty-fourth birthday, she writes of her work on the novel, "Never never have I written so easily, imagined so profusely," and "I am now writing as fast & freely as I have written in the whole of my life; more so—20 times more so—than any novel yet" (*D* 3:58, 59).

47 On Julia Stephen, see, for instance, Marcus, *Woolf and the Languages of Patriarchy*, 96–114; Love, *Woolf: Sources of Madness and Art*, 48–71, 125–26; Diane F. Gillespie and Elizabeth Steele, eds., *Julia Duckworth Stephen: Stories for Children, Essays for Adults;* and Zwerdling, *Woolf and the Real World*, 188–91. For revisionary views of Leslie Stephen, see Love, esp. 14–17, DeSalvo, *Woolf: Impact of Sexual Abuse*, 30–31, and Zwerdling, 184–87. For Woolf's view of the composition of *TL* as an act of exorcism of the ghosts of both parents, see "A Sketch of the Past" (*MB* 80–81, 108), and the 28 November 1928 entry in her *Writer's Diary* (New York: Harper, 1982), 138.

48 For other readings of this sexually charged scene, see Roger Poole, *The Unknown Virginia Woolf* (Cambridge: Cambridge University Press, 1978), 15–18; Maria DiBattista, "*To the Lighthouse:* Virginia Woolf's Winter's Tale," in *Virginia Woolf: Revaluation and Continuity*, ed. Ralph Freedman (Berkeley: University of California Press, 1980), 161–88; Marcus, *Woolf and the Languages of Patriarchy*, 152–56; Gayatri C. Spivak, "Unmaking and Making in *To the Lighthouse*," in Sally McConnell-Ginet, Ruth Borker, and Nelly Furman, eds., *Women and Language in Literature and Society* (New York: Praeger, 1980),

310–27. For a reading of the oedipal and the father/daughter relationships in *TL*, see also Elizabeth Abel, "Cam the Wicked: Woolf's Portrait of the Artist as her Father's Daughter," in Lynda E. Boose and Betty S. Flowers, eds., *Daughters and Fathers* (Baltimore: Johns Hopkins University Press, 1989), 344–60.

49 But on this, see also Jane Lilienfeld, "'The Deceptiveness of Beauty': Mother Love and Mother Hate in *To the Lighthouse*," *Twentieth-Century Literature* 23 (1977): 345–76.

50 Charles Tansley is writing a dissertation about "the influence of something upon somebody" (22) and William Bankes believes that "Carlyle was one of the great teachers of mankind" (71).

51 See "The Charge of the Light Brigade," *Poems of Alfred Lord Tennyson*, ed. Jerome Buckley (Boston: Houghton Mifflin, 1958), 275.

52 For "The Fisherman and His Wife," see *The Complete Grimms' Fairy Tales* (New York: Pantheon, 1972), 103–12. For other discussions of the tale's role in *TL*, see DiBattista, "Virginia Woolf's Winter's Tale," 168–76, and Marcus, *Woolf and the Languages of Patriarchy*, 152–56.

53 See Yeats, "A Prayer for My Daughter," *The Collected Poems of William Butler Yeats* (New York: Macmillan, 1955), 185–87.

54 On Mrs. McNab and Mrs. Bast, see Marcus, *Woolf and the Languages of Patriarchy*, and Abel, "Cam the Wicked," 351.

55 For relevant discussions of these issues, see Zwerdling, *Woolf and the Real World*, 180–209; Spivak, "Unmaking and Making," 310–27; and Paul, *Victorian Heritage*, 168–69. For views about the "mother tongue" in *TL*, see Margaret Homans, *Bearing the Word: Language and Female Experience in Nineteenth-Century Women's Writing* (Chicago: University of Chicago Press, 1986), 277–88.

56 Interestingly, Mrs. Ramsay here becomes a prototype of Dylan Thomas's "long-legged bait," a muselike girl with hooks through her lips who gives the fisherman-poet his poems—as the dead but (in memory) "alive still" mother brings Lily *her* vision. See "Ballad of the Long-Legged Bait," *The Collected Poems of Dylan Thomas* (New York: New Directions, 1946), 166.

57 See "The Castaway," in Cowper, *Verse and Letters*, ed. Brian Spiller (Cambridge: Harvard University Press, 1965), 138–40.

58 Note her echo of Christ, "Es ist vollbracht?"

59 For a range of opinions on these questions, see, e.g., Jane Lilienfeld, "Where the Spear Plants Grew: The Ramsays' Marriage in *To the Lighthouse*," in Jane Marcus, ed. *New Feminist Essays on Virginia Woolf* (Lincoln: University of Nebraska Press, 1981), 148–69; Carolyn Heilbrun, *Toward a Recognition of Androgyny* (New York: Knopf, 1973); Spivak, "Unmaking and Making," 310–27; and Ellen Bayuk Rosenman, *The Invisible Presence: Virginia Woolf and the Mother-Daughter Relationship* (Baton Rouge: Louisiana State University Press, 1986), 112–13.

60 "An escapade": see *D*, 3:131; "theory of biography": see Edel, *Literary Biography* (1959; Bloomington: Indiana University Press, 1973), 139. According to Edel, Strachey himself gave Woolf the first idea for *Orlando*. Commenting on *Mrs. Dalloway*, he remarked to Woolf that "perhaps . . . you should take something wilder and more fantastic, a framework that admits of anything, like *Tristram Shandy*" (*Writer's Diary*, 77; Edel, 138). But what Woolf did "take" as both structure and subject was perhaps more subversive than anything Strachey had in mind.

61 For more on "Nick Greene," see *ROO*, 48–59.

62 For a discussion of the first draft of *Orlando*, see Madeline Moore, "*Orlando:* An Edition of the Manuscript," *Twentieth-Century Literature* 25:3-4 (1979): 303–07.

63 Stevens, "Tea at the Palaz of Hoon," in *The Palm at the End of the Mind: Selected Poems and a Play by Wallace Stevens*, ed. Holly Stevens (New York: Vintage, 1972), 55.

64 Crucial facts of Vita's biography reflected in the text include: her early impassioned affair with Violet Trefusis (here the Russian Sasha because Vita called her "Lushka"), her Spanish grandmother (here as in real life "Rosina Pepita"), her courtship by the foolish aristocrat Lord Lascelles (here the Duke/Duchess of Scandop-Boom), her travels in the East (the Turkish episode), her transvestism (the eighteenth-century escapades), her winning of the Hawthornden Prize for "The Land" (the "Burdett Coutts Prize" for "The Oak Tree"), her legal fight for ancestral property (the "Great Law Suit"), her marriage to the supportive homosexual Harold Nicolson (Marmaduke Bonthrop Shelmerdine), and so forth. In addition, as Nigel Nicolson has pointed out, the symbolic 365 bedrooms and 52 staircases of Orlando's ancestral home are based on the literal architecture of Knole, the Sackville estate, which actually has 365 bedrooms and 52 staircases (Nicolson, unpublished annotations to Orlando; we are grateful to Julia Briggs for sharing these with us and to Nigel Nicolson for allowing her to do so). For more on Vita Sackville-West, both generally and in relation to Woolf and Orlando, see Joanne Trautmann, *The Jessamy Brides: The Friendship of Virginia Woolf and V. Sackville-West* (University Park: Pennsylvania State University Press, 1973); Nigel Nicolson, *Portrait of a Marriage* (London: Weidenfeld and Nicolson, 1973); Victoria Glendinning, *Vita: A Biography of Vita Sackville-West* (New York: Knopf, 1983); Louise De Salvo and Mitchell A. Leaska, eds., *The Letters of Vita Sackville-West to Virginia Woolf* (New York: William Morrow, 1985); and Sandra M. Gilbert, "Introduction: Virginia Woolf's Vita Nuova," in Woolf, *Orlando* (Harmondsworth: Penguin, 1994).

65 For a further discussion of Vita Sackville-West's cross-dressing, see our *Sexchanges*, 324–25, 327, 350.

66 "As centuries go on": see Nicolson, *Portrait of a Marriage*, 200–203, 107.

67 For a more detailed discussion of Woolf's views on higher education, and particularly on the past and future of the "humanities," see Sandra M. Gilbert, "The Battle of the Books/The Battle of the Sexes: Virginia Woolf's *Vita Nuova*," *Michigan Quarterly Review* (Spring 1984): 171–95.

68 For a somewhat different view of "A Society," see Marcus, *Woolf and the Languages of Patriarchy*, 75–95, esp. 88–92. For information about Woolf's decision to omit "A Society" from *A Haunted House*, in which most of the other *Monday or Tuesday* stories are reprinted, see Leonard Woolf's introduction to *A Haunted House and Other Short Stories* (New York: Harcourt, 1972), v–vi.

69 For Woolf's references to "Arthur's song" and "Arthur's education fund," see William Makepeace Thackeray, *The History of Pendennis* (New York: Penguin, 1986), 202–03, where Major Pendennis lays aside all available family funds for the purpose of sending his son to the university, regardless of the boy's inclination or ability.

70 For instance, advising Rachel Vinrace to read Gibbon, St. John Hirst insultingly comments that "it's awfully difficult to tell about women . . . how much . . . is due to lack of training, and how much is native incapacity" (*VO* 154). In *Jacob's Room*, as Jacob crosses the courts of Trinity late at night, the Woolfian narrator hears "the stroke of the clock . . . as if generations of learned men [had] issued it . . . with their blessing, for the use of" the college's living inhabitants (45), and notes the "magisterial authority" of her protagonist's footsteps across the court (46); simultaneously, she has a vision of "the bare hills of Turkey . . . and . . . women standing naked-legged in the stream to beat linen on the stones" (44). Similarly, Rachel's classicist uncle asks "What's the use of reading if you don't read Greek?" (*VO* 171), while in *Jacob's Room* Woolf meditated on a hero who reads Greek, looks like a Greek statue, and actually falls in love in and with Greece. In relation to him, not only the novel's female characters but even its invisible female narrator are inexorably cut off from both language and the culture language represents. From Jacob's semiliterate mother, Betty Flanders, to his practically illiter-

ate mistress Florinda, to his best friend's barely literate sister Clara, these women are exiles from the great procession of male civilization.

71 In her first two novels, indeed, Woolf even depicted upper-class (and, for their time, well-educated) Englishwomen whose only strategy for intellectual expression consisted in repudiations or revisions of male history. Rachel Vinrace in *The Voyage Out* accompanies a dance by impudently playing "hymn tunes . . . very fast, with bits out of Wagner and Beethoven" (165), while Mrs. Hilbery in *Night and Day* perversely decides that "Anne Hathaway had a way, among other things, of writing Shakespeare's sonnets," and her daughter, Katharine, rejects traditional aesthetic forms altogether, substituting instead enigmatic visions of "algebraic symbols, pages all speckled with dots and dashes and twisted bars" (300). For a further discussion of these strategies, see our *War of the Words*, chap. 5.

72 Finch, "The Introduction," in *Selected Poems of Anne Finch, Countess of Winchilsea*, ed. Katharine M. Rogers (New York: Ungar, 1979), 6. For Woolf's further comments on Finch, see *ROO*, 61–64. Tellingly, Woolf's views on Oxbridge were shared by Jane Austen, arguably the woman writer Woolf most admired. See "On the Universities," in *The Works of Jane Austen*, vol. 6: *Minor Works*, ed. R. W. Chapman (New York: Oxford University Press, 1954): "No wonder that Oxford and Cambridge profound / In Learning and Science so greatly abound / since some *carry* thither a little each day / And we meet with so few that *bring any away*" (447).

73 In "A Society" a radical interrogation of traditional pedagogy is implicit even in the seemingly innocuous question asked by Castalia's friends: "Did Oxbridge professors help to produce good people and good books?—the objects of life." Stressing production, generativity, life, this question substitutes a definition of authority as authoring or creating for the baroque academic processional's implied definition of authority as authorization.

74 The rhetoric of Woolf's passage on Fernham's gardens focuses strikingly on *process* through imagery of transformation and, in particular, journeying: "The gardens of Fernham lay before me in the spring twilight, wild and open, and in the long grass, sprinkled and carelessly flung, were daffodils and bluebells, not orderly perhaps at the best of times, and now wind-blown and waving as they tugged at their roots. The windows of the building, curved like ships' windows among generous waves of red brick, changed from lemon to silver under the flight of the quick spring clouds" (*ROO* 17).

75 In "Why?"—a piece Woolf wrote for the Somerville journal *Lysistrata* and a kind of study for the far more elaborate *Three Guineas*—she was even more specific about pedagogical methods. Recalling an occasion when "in a desperate attempt to acquire information about, perhaps, the French Revolution, it seemed necessary to attend a lecture" (*DM* 279), she wrote scornfully about the time-honored but tedious institution of the lecture, asking her readers, "Why encourage your elders to turn themselves into prigs and prophets when they are ordinary men and women? Why force them to stand on a platform for forty minutes while you reflect upon the colour of their hair and the longevity of flies? Why not let them talk to you and listen to you, naturally and happily, on the floor?" (228–29)

76 This vision of the other history strikingly anticipates the central argument of Alice Walker's "In Search of Our Mothers' Gardens." Although this essay begins with a combative discussion of *A Room of One's Own*, Walker proposes, as Woolf did, that the arts of poverty are at least as significant as the arts of wealth—that, for instance, the signature of her black foremothers is paradoxically but powerfully inscribed in the anonymity of bed quilts and flowerbeds. See Walker, *In Search of Our Mothers' Gardens* (New York: Harcourt, 1983), 231–43.

77 Kizer, "Pro Femina," *Mermaids in the Basement* (Port Townsend, Wash.: Copper Canyon Press, 1984), 44.
78 It is relevant, then, that in "A Society" Woolf had sent Castalia to study the modes and mores of Oxbridge in the role of a charwoman.
79 Several black American women of letters have expressed dissatisfaction with Woolf's model of (female) literary history. Comments Alice Walker: If "in order for a woman to write fiction she must have a room of her own . . . and enough money to support herself," what "are we to make of Phyllis Wheatley, a slave who owned not even herself?"; adds Gloria Hull, "Shakespeare had no black sisters." But in England too, from at least the thirties on, Woolf was seen as both snobbish and unrealistic by such thinkers as Wyndham Lewis and Q. D. Leavis. In *Men without Art* (1934), Lewis attacked her "pretty salon pieces," while in "Caterpillars of the Commonwealth, Unite!" Leavis argued that Woolf spoke only for the ruling class, that she had "personally received considerably more in the way of economic ease that she is humanly entitled to," and that "the least damning thing you might say about [her] proposals is that they are irresponsible." Others have offered similar objections to Woolf's theories, although their tone was milder, with Louise Bogan sniping in the *New Republic* that "patently being a lady is difficult," Mary Ellen Chase commenting in the *Yale Review* that Woolf's dream of social transformation is "an unattainable ideal," and even an adulatory reviewer in the *Times Literary Supplement* concluding, "To regain Paradise no number of guineas or societies will avail." See Walker, *In Search of Our Mothers' Gardens*, 235; Hull, "Afro-American Women Poets: A Bio-Critical Survey," in *Shakespeare's Sisters: Feminist Essays on Women Poets*, ed. Sandra M. Gilbert and Susan Gubar (Bloomington: Indiana University Press, 1979), 165; Lewis, *Men without Art*, ed. Seamus Cooney (Santa Rosa: Black Sparrow, 1987), 138–39; Leavis, "Caterpillars," 203, 204, 209 (see also n. 10); Bogan, "The Ladies and Gentlemen," *New Republic*, 14 September 1938, 164–65; Mary Ellen Chase, "A Modern Socratic Dialogue," *Yale Review* 28:2 (1938): 403–05; and "Women in a World of War: A 'Society of Outsiders': Mrs. Virginia Woolf's Searching Pamphlet," *Times Literary Supplement*, 4 June 1938, 379.
80 Zwerdling, *Woolf and the Real World*, 327.
81 For a detailed discussion of this problem, see our *War of the Words*, chap. 5.
82 For a discussion of the "lady of Elvedon" episode from a somewhat different perspective, see our *War of the Words*, chap. 4.
83 For an interesting reading of this aspect of *W*, see Garrett Stewart, *Reading Voices: Literature and the Phonotext* (Berkeley: University of California Press, 1990), 272–77.
84 Living in Oxford, the Pargiters' cousin Kitty Malone studies *The Constitutional History of England by Dr. Andrews* (62) and reads history with a woman tutor (69); Later, Martin Pargiter thinks with revulsion of the Victorian house where he had been brought up: "It was an abominable system . . . family life; Abercorn Terrace. . . . There all those different people had lived, boxed up together, telling lies" (*Y* 223).
85 On this, see Lyndall Gordon, *Virginia Woolf: A Writer's Life* (New York: Norton, 1984).
86 For a discussion of this episode from a slightly different perspective, see our *War of the Words*, chap. 5.
87 "Outline of History": see H. G. Wells, *The Outline of History: Being a Plain History of Life and Mankind*. New illustrated edition, revised and rewritten, with maps and plans by J. F. Horrabin, vol. 1 (New York: Macmillan, 1926). To be sure, Lucy's obsession with "barking monsters" may imply her (and Woolf's) recurrent fear that the war might plunge all supposedly civilized Europeans into a *de*volutionary state of "monstrosity."
88 For Woolf's reference to her own husband as a penniless Jew, see n. 13. See also *QB*, 2:1–4, for further discussions of her views on Judaism, especially her husband's. That the "Woolves" knew themselves to have been endangered by Hitler's *anschluss* during World

War II is demonstrated not only by Leonard's stockpiling of poison (so that they could commit suicide in the event of a German invasion) but also by the fact that their names do actually appear on a Gestapo list of "dangerous" British intellectuals to be exterminated should such an invasion be successfully carried out. (This list is held by the library at Stanford University; see Zwerdling, *Woolf and the Real World*, 289.)

89 The notion of history as a caravan of burdened years had been with Woolf for some time. Interestingly, one of the titles she considered for *The Years* was "The Caravan." See *Writer's Diary*, 229, for her attraction to this title and for her concurrent plan for taking a curtain call (at an upcoming performance of her play *Freshwater, A Comedy*) in "a donkey's head."

90 We are grateful to Chiara Briganti for suggesting this point to us.

91 On the "annunciation" of the starlings, see Harriet Blodgett, "The Nature of *Between the Acts*," *Modern Lanugage Studies* 13 (1983): 27–37.

92 Such a trope for cultural transfiguration was, of course, one that in various ways preoccupied her precursors and contemporaries from Barrett Browning and Swinburne to Yeats, with Yeats's "The Second Coming," "Leda and the Swan," and "Two Songs from a Play" the paradigmatic modernist instances imaging the union of natural and supernatural to beget change. But where Yeats foresaw mostly social chaos as the child of such change—a "rough beast," the "burning roof and tower" of Troy, "Galilean turbulence"—Woolf allows room for more redemptive possibilities, although she cannot name them.

93 See also *TY*, 388, for another reference to the heart of darkness; and it is worth considering the possibility that T. S. Eliot's *The Family Reunion* (1939)—a work roughly contemporary with *The Years*—influenced the structure of Woolf's plot here, especially considering the long friendship between "Great Tom" and the "Woolves."

Chapter 2: Female Female Impersonators

Epigraphs: Bogan, review of Millay, "Huntsman What Quarry?" in *Bogan, A Poet's Alphabet: Reflections on Literary Art and Vocation*, ed. Robert Phelps and Ruth Limmer (New York: McGraw-Hill, 1970), 298; Millay, *Letters of Edna St. Vincent Millay*, ed. Allan Ross Macdougall (New York: Harper, 1952), 76; Costello, *Marianne Moore: Imaginary Possessions* (Cambridge: Harvard University Press, 1981), 246; Moore, "In Fashion, Yesterday, Today and Tomorrow," in *The Complete Prose of Marianne Moore*, ed. Patricia C. Willis (New York: Viking Penguin, 1986), 617.

1 Rivière, "Womanliness as a Masquerade" (1929), in *Formations of Fantasy*, ed. Victor Burgin, James Donald, and Cora Kaplan (London: Methuen, 1986), 35–44; for a fine discussion of the essay, see Stephen Heath, "Joan Rivière and the Masquerade," in ibid., 45–61.

2 See Marjorie Garber, *Vested Interests: Cross-Dressing and Cultural Anxiety* (New York: Harper, 1993), 355, on sexchange and gender bending in early modern literature.

3 "What do women want?": see Freud, quoted in Ernest Jones, *The Life and Work of Sigmund Freud*, vol. 2: *Years of Maturity, 1901–19* (New York: Basic, 1955), 421; among Freud's other meditations on the construction of "femininity," see "Some Psychological Consequences of the Anatomical Distinction between the Sexes" (1925) and "Female Sexuality" (1931), in *Sigmund Freud: Sexuality and the Psychology of Love*, ed. Philip Rieff (New York: Macmillan, 1963), 197–99.

4 De Beauvoir, *The Second Sex*, trans. H. M. Parshley (1949; New York: Bantam, 1961), 502.

5 Goffman, *The Presentation of Self in Everyday Life* (New York: Doubleday, 1959), 77–105; we are grateful to Lisa Jadwin for bringing the relevance of this text to our attention.

6 Griffin, *Pornography and Silence: Culture's Revenge against Nature* (New York: Harper, 1981), 202.

7 Similarly, Griffin adds, "Monroe even referred to this other personality as 'her.' Susan Strasberg . . . tells us that once when she and Monroe walked with a friend through the streets of New York, Monroe turned to Strasberg and her friend and said, 'Do you want me to be *her?*' Suddenly, she took on the 'Marilyn' personality, and just as suddenly, strangers on the street began to recognize her" (*Pornography and Silence*, 204–05).

8 Irigaray, *This Sex Which Is Not One*, trans. Catherine Porter with Carolyn Burke (1977; Ithaca: Cornell University Press, 1985), 132–34. See also on mimicry: "One must assume the feminine role deliberately. Which means already to convert a form of subordination into an affirmation, and thus to begin to thwart it. . . . To play with mimesis is . . . for a woman, to try to recover the place of her exploitation by discourse, without allowing herself to be simply reduced to it" (76).

9 Among the most crucial studies of modern poetry was Richard Ellmann's classic *Yeats: The Man and the Masks* (1948), whose title drew on a major Yeatsian trope to illuminate the significance of feigning—and its corollary, self-distancing—in the career of the Irish poet. And Yeats himself was obviously influenced by such key fin de siècle figures as Oscar Wilde and Max Beerbohm, both of whom half-seriously, half-ironically defended the advantages of cosmetology and costume. (For Beerbohm and others on cosmetology, see Gilbert and Gubar, *No Man's Land: The Place of the Woman Writer in the Twentieth Century*, vol. 2: *Sexchanges* [New Haven: Yale University Press, 1989], 328–31; for Wilde on/and costume, see Richard Ellmann, *Oscar Wilde* [New York: Knopf, 1988], esp. the photographs of the writer in New York, following page 204, and in costume as Salome, facing page 429.)

10 To be sure, as Peter Ackroyd has revealed, Eliot had a penchant for wearing strange costumes and makeup (including lipstick and "green face powder") to certain literary parties; see Ackroyd, *T. S. Eliot: A Life* (New York: Simon and Schuster, 1984), 136. But as Ackroyd notes, "It is significant that the only people who noticed his make-up, and probably the only ones in whose company he wore it, were writers and artists; it is unlikely he powdered his face before going to the bank" (136), and of course as Eliot settled definitively into his ultimate public role of publisher/editor/poet he abandoned this youthful *jeu* in favor of strictly correct business attire.

11 Stevens, "From [Stevens's] Journal," 23 May [1899], in *The Letters of Wallace Stevens*, ed. Holly Stevens (New York: Knopf, 1981), 26.

12 Stevens, "To Harvey Breit," "Journal," 8 August 1942, 415.

13 For discussions of sexual anxiety in "The Love Song of J. Alfred Prufrock," see Gilbert and Gubar, *No Man's Land*, vol. 1: *The War of the Words* (New Haven: Yale University Press, 1988), 31–32, 97–98.

14 Parker, "The Waltz" (1933), *The Portable Dorothy Parker* (New York: Viking, 1944), 77, 81.

15 Parker, "The Satin Dress" (1926), *Portable Parker*, 125; for a comparable poem with the same theme, see also "The Red Dress," ibid., 308.

16 Stevens, "Bowl, Cat and Broomstick," in *The Palm at the End of the Mind: Selected Poems and a Play*, ed. Holly Stevens (New York: Vintage, 1972), 28. All further references will be to this edition, and page numbers will be included in the text.

17 For "lady writers with three names," see Nathanael West, *Miss Lonelyhearts*, in West, *Miss Lonelyhearts and* The Day of the Locust (New York: New Directions, 1962), 13–14; for our earlier discussion of this passage, see *War of the Words*, 146.

18 That Stevens is preaching to himself as well as to his interlocutors is made plain by his assignment of a poem title he himself would later use—"Banal Sojourn"—to Claire's canon. See *Palm*, 30 and 45. For further discussion of this point, see A. Walton Litz, "Introduction to 'Bowl, Cat, and Broomstick,'" *Quarterly Review of Literature* 16 (1969): 230–35.

19 "Yesterday I got a note from Sara Teasdale," Millay wrote her family with naive delight at one point, "inviting me to take tea with her. Whaddayouknowaboutthat! The news of my arrival has *sprud clean* from here to East 29th Street!" (*Letters*, 33–34.) Dell is also quoted in Millay's *Letters*, 84.

20 While she was at Vassar, Millay published poems in *Forum* (9 poems), *Current Opinion* (2 poems), *Smart Set* (1 short story), *Vassar Miscellany Monthly* (4 poems), and *Patient Periodical* (1 poem); her most gratifying part was in a play of John Masefield's about which the Laureate himself wrote her a fan letter. See Karl Yost, *A Bibliography of the Works of Edna St. Vincent Millay* (New York: Burt Franklin, 1937), 160–61.

21 Whether Millay's detractors deplored with Edward Davison the "girlish pretty-pretty-ness" of some of her lines or her admirers decided with Arthur Ficke that in "Renascence" Millay had had "a real vision, such as Coleridge might have seen," and that her poem was, as Floyd Dell said, "comparable in its power and vision to 'The Hound of Heaven,'" they were all defining her as a literary anachronism similar to Stevens's Claire Dupray. Ficke is quoted in Millay's *Letters*, 118; Dell and Davison are both quoted in Norman Brittin, *Edna St. Vincent Millay*. Rev. ed. (Boston: Twayne, 1982), 33.

22 Elizabeth Atkins, *Edna St. Vincent Millay and Her Times* (1936; New York: Russell & Russell, 1964) 70.

23 Edmund Wilson, "The All-Star Literary Vaudeville," *The Shores of Light: A Literary Chronicle of the Twenties and Thirties* (New York: Farrar, Straus, 1952), 242–43; Atkins, *Millay and Her Times*, vii. In answer to the question "What books of 1937 do you nominate for this year's Pulitzer Prize awards?" posed in a 1938 poll in the *Saturday Review of Literature*, "fourteen critics and literary editors—a vote total far ahead of any other title in the poetry field—chose Millay's *Conversation at Midnight*" (William B. Thessing, introduction to *Critical Essays on Edna St. Vincent Millay*, ed. William B. Thessing [New York: G. K. Hall, 1993], 8). Such critical esteem was paralleled by her general popularity. Millay's booming sales, for instance, stood in stark contrast to Wallace Stevens's slow ones (see Peter Brazeau, *Wallace Stevens: Parts of a World* [New York: Random House, 1983], 120). And summarizing the nature and extent of her fame, undergraduate Thomas Lanier Williams (later to rechristen himself Tennessee Williams) wrote: "Sappho, O God, has gone her soundless way, / But spare us a while our glorious Millay!" (quoted in William Jay Smith, "Louise Bogan: A Woman's Words," in *Critical Essays on Louise Bogan*, ed. Martha Collins [Boston: G. K. Hall, 1984], 104).

24 On Lowell, see C. David Heymann, *American Aristocracy: The Life and Times of James Russell, Amy, and Robert Lowell* (New York: Dodd, Mead, 1980), 228; on Wylie, see Judith Farr, *The Life and Art of Elinor Wylie* (Baton Rouge: Louisiana State University Press, 1983), 13.

25 Heymann, *American Aristocracy*, 224; Edith Sitwell, *Taken Care Of: The Autobiography of Edith Sitwell* (New York: Atheneum, 1965), 139–40.

26 Cited by Suzanne Clark in "The Unwarranted Discourse: Sentimental Community, Modernist Women, and the Case of Millay," *Genre* 20 (1987): 139.

27 The cummings address was printed in the *Harvard Advocate*, 24 June 1915, and is discussed in Heymann, *American Aristocracy*, 224; on Millay, see Jean Gould, *The Poet and Her Book: A Biography of Edna St. Vincent Millay* (New York: Dodd, Mead, 1969) 178; on Wylie, see Farr, *Life and Art of Wylie*, 15; for Sitwell, see Sitwell, *Selected Letters 1919–1964*, ed. John Lehmann and Derek Parker (New York: Vanguard, 1970) 247.

28 Leavis, quoted in James D. Brophy, *Edith Sitwell: The Symbolist Order* (Carbondale: Southern Illinois University Press, 1968), xii. Pound, quoted in Heymann, *American Aristocracy*, 198; Eliot's comment on Lowell is quoted in Jean Gould, *Amy: The World of Amy Lowell and the Imagist Movement* (New York: Dodd, Mead, 1975), 3; he speaks of "EDITH Shitwell" in a letter to Ezra Pound of 31 October 1917. See *The Letters of T. S. Eliot*, ed. Valerie Eliot, Vol. 1: *1889–1922* (New York: Harcourt, 1988), 206. See

McAlmon, *Post-adolescence* (Dijon: Darantière, 1923), 50. Wylie is characterized by Wolfe as the object of the "idolatry" of "a precious coterie," who refuses to stay in the same room with a certain novelist because "'I am *not* going to be insulted. . . . He said that Eleanora Duse was the most beautiful woman he had ever seen!' . . . She burst into tears, and turning, fell into the comforting arms of her husband . . . , sobbing convulsively like a child" (Wolfe, *The Web and the Rock* [New York: Harper and Row, 1939], 482–83). Millay was also fictionalized as Rita in Edmund Wilson's *I Thought of Daisy* (New York: Farrar, Straus, 1953).

29 "The monopolisation of literature by women": see letter to Pound, 15 April [1915], in Eliot, *Letters*, 96; "mostly by old maids": see letter to Charlotte Eliot, 13 May 1917, ibid., 179; "I struggle to keep the writing": see letter to his father, 31 October 1917, ibid., 204; "Of course, your superior officer": see letter to Thayer, 30 June 1918, ibid., 236; "there are only half a dozen men": see letter to Pound, 7 November, 1922, ibid., 593; "the feminisation of modern society": see letter to Pound, 23 September 1917, ibid. 198. In an early draft of *The Waste Land*, as if to consolidate all these points, Eliot sketched a composite portrait of a modern "poetess" whose lineaments limned all the faults—critical acclaim, sexual depravity, a derivative style—with which he and his contemporaries associated the Lowells and Wylies, Millays and Sitwells. His whorish Fresca (whose name, it should be noted, rhymes with "Edna") "scribbles verse of such a gloomy tone / That cautious critics say, her style is quite her own": "Not quite an adult, and still less a child," she has "arrived (the Muses Nine declare) / To be a sort of can-can salonniere." (See The Waste Land: *A Facsimile and Transcript . . .* , ed. Valerie Eliot [New York: Harcourt, 1971], 41).

30 See Williams, *Paterson* (1951; New York: New Directions, 1958), 177–200; for a closer analysis of this passage, as well as of the poem's general use of women, see Sandra M. Gilbert, "Purloined Letters: William Carlos Williams and 'Cress,'" *William Carlos Williams Review* 10:2 (1985): 5–15; Williams, *Autobiography* (New York: Random House, 1951), 140; see also Paul Mariani, *William Carlos Williams: A New World Naked* (New York: McGraw-Hill, 1981), 154–55.

31 Ransom, *The World's Body* (New York: Scribners, 1938), 103, 98; "It is with something of a feeling of guilt," this critic added, "that the intellectual male participates in" Millay's early poetry: "His heart wants to be in it but is not. This is because his intellect is not in it. And not entirely in it when Miss Millay is less juvenile, and appears as the adult but unintellectual woman" (99). Although Ransom's are among the best-known comments on Millay, he was clearly influenced by the judgment of his fellow agrarians Allan Tate and Cleanth Brooks, who concluded in a 1935 review of *Wine from These Grapes* that Millay's poetic failures sprang from "an essential immaturity." About her poems on the Sacco and Vanzetti case, Brooks remarked that her "attitude was that of a child whose latest and favorite project has been smashed. Her interest in the trial was like nothing so much as that of . . . a sort of liberal Junior Leaguer," while, more generally, he took her to task because her work lacked "irony" and "toughening" ("Edna Millay's Maturity," *Southwest Review* 20:2 (1935): 1–5.

32 Wheelock, quoted in Brittin, *Millay*, 131. To be sure, as late as 1952 Edmund Wilson was still defending the woman whom he had earlier called "one of the few poets writing in English in our time who have attained to anything like the stature of great literary figures in an age in which prose has predominated" ("Epilogue, 1952: Edna St. Vincent Millay," in *Shores*, 752). But as his memoir demonstrates, his defense was both lonely and ambivalent.

33 Rosenthal, *The Modern Poets* (New York: Oxford, 1960), 254–55.

34 "A poet that matters": see Stevens, "A Poet That Matters," in *Opus Posthumous*, ed. Samuel French Morse (New York: Knopf, 1966), 247–54. Indeed, in letters to friends Stevens confided that Moore's innovative art "is more important than what Williams

does" and that "she is one of the angels: her style is an angelic style" (*The Letters of Wallace Stevens*, ed. Holly Stevens [New York: Knopf, 1981], 278, 290); "Miss Moore . . ." and "the magic name": see *Selected Essays of William Carlos Williams* (New York: Random House, 1954), 121, 292; "a rafter": see Williams, *Autobiography*, 146; "in the verse": see Pound, "Marianne Moore and Mina Loy," in *Marianne Moore: A Collection of Critical Essays*, ed. Charles Tomlinson (Englewood Cliffs, N.J.: Prentice Hall, 1969), 46; "the *refinement*": see Eliot, "Marianne Moore," in ibid., 48. Interestingly, in the last paragraph of his brief piece Pound significantly qualified his praise by remarking patronizingly that "these girls have written a distinctly national product, they have written something which could not have come out of any other country, and (while I have before now seen a deal of rubbish by both of them) they are interesting and readable (by me, that is)" (47). Similarly, Eliot expressed significant reservations about H. D., whose poetry he found "fatiguingly monotonous" (*Letters*, 488) and even—surprisingly, given his later enthusiasm—an early dislike for Moore: "Miss Moore does not seem to have very much to say. . . . She writes . . . a clumsy prose. . . . She has no poetic style," he averred in a *Times Literary Supplement* review of Moore's 1921 *Poems* (*Letters*, 481n3).

35 Although she is not judgmental, Alicia Suskin Ostriker at least in part implies this, associating Lizette Reese, Louise Guiney, Adelaide Crapsey, Sara Teasdale, Elinor Wylie, Genevieve Taggard, Louise Bogan, and others with "an extension and refinement of the traditional lyric style which concentrated on intense personal feeling" and Amy Lowell, Gertrude Stein, Mina Loy, H. D., and Marianne Moore with a poetic mode that "was formally innovative and intellectually assertive but avoided autobiography" (*Stealing the Language: The Emergence of Women's Poetry in America* [Boston: Beacon, 1986], 44; "seem to have little": see Clark, "Unwarranted Discourse," 137; "instructively serve": see Molesworth, *Marianne Moore: A Literary Life* (New York: Atheneum, 1990), 138. Molesworth, Moore's first biographer, reiterates just the stereotypes first defined by Ransom and his colleagues, labeling Millay's poetry "sentimental and rather wan" and emphasizing her public image as "the very essence of the free-living, free-loving poet," in comparison to Moore's privacy, wit, and dedication (138–39).

36 Collins, "Gallantry and Our Women Writers," in Collins, *Taking the Literary Pulse: Psychological Studies of Life and Letters* (New York: Doran, 1924), 118–19. Dell, cited in Allen Churchill, *The Improper Bohemians* (New York: Dutton, 1959), 264. See also Susan Gilmore, "To 'Last the Night': A New Look at the Poetry of Edna St. Vincent Millay" (Honors thesis, Brown University, 1985), 2. We are grateful to Susan Gilmore for sharing this fine thesis with us.

37 Eliot, "Marianne Moore," 51. Significantly, too, Ransom's comment about Moore's lesser "deficiency in masculinity" was made in the context of his essay on the poet as woman, so that his praise of Millay's female "rival" simply meant that Moore was, fortunately for her, a less "womanly woman" than some figures Ransom could think of.

38 Williams liked to remember the "two cords, cables rather, of red hair coiled around [Moore's] rather small cranium" (Tomlinson, "Marianne Moore" [1948], in *Moore: Collection of Essays*, 112). In a similar vein, William Wasserstrom, remembering his first meeting with Moore, confided that "it was . . . no hard task to identify a beautiful woman wearing the tricorn hat and great cape which then served as customary dress" ("Irregular Symmetry: Marianne Moore's *Dial*," in *Festschrift for Marianne Moore's Seventy-Seventh Birthday*, ed. Tambimuttu [New York: Tambimuttu and Mass, 1964], 33), and in another memoir Richard Eberhart focused with similar pleasure on "The tricorne hat, the hale smile, the quick gestures, her grace and charm" ("A Memoir," in *Festschrift*, 73).

39 McAlmon, *Post-adolescence*, 106, 108. Hostile as he occasionally is toward Martha Wullus and her "moralizing" mother, McAlmon does brilliantly capture Moore's conversa-

tional tone (judging from interviews and other descriptions of the poet's personality). Note, for instance, the speech where Martha "chortle[s]" and confesses, "I was quite unable to control myself at the library today, and I fear I spoke curtly to the head librarian for some of her trite insistences. . . . But I find seahorses, lizards and such things, very fascinating. Also a fox's face, the picture of which I saw recently in a magazine, haunts me like a night mare, and contradictory as it seems, I am quite able to appreciate the 'bright beaming expression' that Xenophon talks about, on the face of the hound which was pursueing it'" (110).

40 Jarrell, "Her Shield," in *Moore: Collection of Essays*, 115, 122.

41 Rosenthal, *Modern Poets*, 142; Pearce, "Marianne Moore," in *Moore: Collection of Essays*, 150 (Pearce added that "Her yes! is muted, cautious, and somewhat finicking . . . but it is as authentic as Molly Bloom's" [157–58]); Gifford, "Two Philologists," in ibid., 73. Similarly, as part of a series of widely read attacks on the Eliotian art of allusion out of which modernism's "academic poetry" was constituted, Karl Shapiro rebuked Moore's admirers for the "glove-kissing gallantries" of their blurbs on the dust jacket of *O To Be a Dragon* ("Born of a Lifetime in New York," *New York Times Book Review*, 4 October 1959, 41); later, Shapiro was to speak of Moore's "exquisite timidities"; see *The Poetry Wreck: Selected Essays 1950–1970* (New York: Random House, 1975), 242.

42 See "The Ford Letters," in *A Marianne Moore Reader* (New York: Viking, 1961), 215–24; for the Boston Arts Festival, see Henrietta Holland, "Marianne Moore's New England," *Yankee*, November 1963, 106.

43 See *The Complete Prose of Marianne Moore*, ed. Patricia C. Willis (New York: Viking, 1986): for *Glamour* quotation, 661; *Women's Wear Daily* quotations, 596; *New York Times* quotation, 616.

44 As female female impersonators, therefore, both would have had to agree, albeit with some irony, with a statement made by Louise Bogan in 1963: "Beneath surface like-nesses, women's poetry continues to be unlike men's, all feminist statements to the contrary notwithstanding. Women function differently, in art as in life, and it should be an enlivening rather than a dismal fact that there are some things they either cannot or are unwilling to do, and others that they do very badly" (quoted in Gloria Bowles, *Louise Bogan's Aesthetic of Limitation* [Bloomington: Indiana University Press, 1987], 42).

45 Laura Mulvey, "Visual Pleasure and Narrative Cinema" and "Afterthoughts on 'Visual Pleasure and Narrative Cinema' Inspired by *Duel in the Sun*," in *Feminism and Film Theory*, ed. Constance Penley (New York: Routledge, 1988), 57–68, 69–79; John Berger, *Ways of Seeing* (London: Pelican, 1972), 46.

46 Dinesen, "The Deluge at Norderney," in *Seven Gothic Tales* (1934; New York: Vintage, 1972), 45. See also Joyce Carol Oates's comment that "a woman often feels 'invisible' in a public sense precisely because her physical being . . . figures so prominently in her identity" (*Invisible Woman* [Princeton: Ontario Review Press, 1982], postscript, cited in Ostriker, *Stealing*, 65).

47 Indeed, Dickinson had explained with protomodernist sophistication to Thomas Wentworth Higginson that "when I state myself, as the Representative of the Verse—it does not mean—me—but a supposed person" (Letter to Higginson, July 1862, in *The Letters of Emily Dickinson*, ed. Thomas Johnson. 2 vols. [Cambridge: Harvard University Press, 1955], 2:412). See also our discussion of Dickinson in Gilbert and Gubar, *The Madwoman in the Attic: The Woman Writer and the Nineteenth-Century Literary Imagination* (New Haven: Yale University Press, 1979, 1984), chap. 16.

48 Westkott, *The Feminist Legacy of Karen Horney* (New Haven: Yale University Press, 1986), 190–91.

49 Wilson, *Shores*, 242. In this connection, see also Mary Ellmann's astute remark, "Books by women are treated as though they themselves were women, and criticism embarks . . . upon an intellectual measuring of busts and hips" (*Thinking About Women* [New

York: Harcourt, 1968], 29). Both Wilson and Ellmann are very appositely cited in Gilmore, "To 'Last the Night,'" 13, 31. For Cixous's manifesto, see Cixous and Catherine Clément, *The Newly Born Woman*, trans. Betsy Wing (Minneapolis: University of Minnesota Press, 1986), 63–132.

50 Olson, quoted in Brazeau, *Wallace Stevens*, 211.

51 On Millay, see Dell: "She seemed, as a poet, no mere mortal, but a goddess; and though one could not but love her, one loved her hopelessly as a goddess must be loved" (*Homecoming: An Autobiography* [New York: Farrar and Rinehart, 1933], 301–02). On Moore, see Ostriker: "Her *Paris Review* interview is a self-presentation of the poet as self-deprecating literary virgin pulled reluctantly to the altar of publication"; (*Stealing*, 52). Even the French texts the two chose to translate reinforced these self-defining images: Millay produced a lyric version of Baudelaire's erotically daring *Les Fleurs du Mal*, while Moore decorously translated the moralizing *Fables de La Fontaine*.

52 Millay, *Letters*, 99–100.

53 Moore, quoted in Costello, *Moore: Imaginary Possessions*, 15. (She cites *Quarterly Review of Literature* 16 [1969]: 154.)

54 Williams, "The Great American Novel," in *Imaginations*, ed. Webster Schott (New York: New Directions, 1970), 169; for our earlier discussion of this passage, see *War of the Words*, 155.

55 Plath, *Letters Home*, ed. Aurelia Schober Plath (New York: Harper, 1975), 277; Sexton, "The Uncensored Poet: Letters of Anne Sexton," *Ms.*, November 1977, 53 (see also *A Self-Portrait in Letters*, ed. Linda Gray Sexton and Lois Ames [Boston: Houghton Mifflin, 1977], 79); Rich, "When We Dead Awaken: Writing as Re-Vision," *On Lies, Secrets, and Silence: Selected Prose 1966–78* (New York: Norton, 1979), 39; Bishop, "Efforts of Affection," in Bishop, *The Collected Prose*, ed. Robert Giroux (New York: Farrar, Straus, 1984), 156.

56 Millay, *Collected Poems*, ed. Norma Millay (New York: Harper, 1956), 127, 129. Further references will be to this edition, and page numbers will appear in the text.

57 "The doorstep of the Absolute": see Eliot, "Spleen," *Poems Written in Early Youth* (New York: Farrar, Straus, 1967), 26; "Cousin Nancy," with its quotation of Meredith's "the army of unalterable law" (from "Lucifer in Starlight"): see Eliot, *Collected Poems 1909–1962* (New York: Harcourt, 1963), 22.

58 Norma Millay, introduction to Edna St. Vincent Millay, *Collected Lyrics* (New York: Harper and Row, 1981), xxi–xxii.

59 Nancy Boyd [Edna St. Vincent Millay], *Distressing Dialogues* (New York: Harper, 1924), 84; further references will be to this edition, and page numbers will appear in the text. Millay was known as "Vincent" to her family and friends.

60 Millay, "Diary of an American Art Student in Paris," *Vanity Fair*, March 1919, 44.

61 "Night is my sister, and how deep in love, / How drowned in love and weedily washed ashore, / There to be fretted by the drag and shove / At the tide's edge, I lie—" begins one of many poems devoted to this theme (636). See Jane Stanbrough, "Edna St. Vincent Millay and the Language of Vulnerability," in *Shakespeare's Sisters: Feminist Essays on Women Poets*, ed. Sandra M. Gilbert and Susan Gubar (Bloomington: Indiana University Press, 1979), 183–99.

62 For a more negative appraisal of this poem and its "theatrical" context, see Elizabeth P. Perlmutter, "A Doll's Heart: The Girl in the Poetry of Edna St. Vincent Millay and Louise Bogan," *Twentieth-Century Literature* 23:2 (1977): 162, 164. Perlmutter quotes Horace Gregory and Marya Zaturenska's definition of Millay's "gifts" as "'histrionic'" but sees this judgment as wholly pejorative. Throughout her essay—a comparison between Millay and Bogan which implicitly celebrates Bogan's sincerity as against Millay's theatricality—she faults Millay's writings for being "all so staged, so visible, so temporary" (161, 164).

63 Gilmore points out that, since "I, being born a woman and distressed" is a Petrarchan sonnet, "Millay's choice of the form to . . . convey such an anti-romantic theme is especially ironic. Traditionally, the Petrarchan sonnet expresses a male speaker's feelings of nostalgia or unrequited love; in this sonnet, a female speaker shows her lover that his feelings for her are indeed unrequited" ("To 'Last the Night,'" 71).

64 For a different reading of this poem, see Jan Montefiore, *Feminism and Poetry: Language, Experience, Identity in Women's Writing* (London: Pandora, 1987), 116–18.

65 On the femme fatale, see our *Sexchanges*, chaps. 1, 2, and 4, passim.

66 Millay, "The Key," *Vanity Fair*, December 1922, 45, 94.

67 De Beauvoir, *Second Sex*, 512–13; Goffman also cites this passage (*Presentation of Self,* 112–13).

68 For a different view of this poem, see Perlmutter, "A Doll's Heart," 175.

69 Indeed, in the summer of 1920, when she was probably composing these sonnets, Millay, along with her mother and sisters, lived in a little house lent them by their neighbors George Cram Cook and his wife, Susan Glaspell; see Wilson, *Shores*, 760.

70 Glaspell, *Trifles: And Six Other Short Plays (Two of Them Written in Collaboration with George Cram Cook)* (London: Denn, 1926), 24.

71 Rilke, "Leichen-Wasche," in *New Poems: The Other Part*, trans. Edward Snow (1908; San Francisco: North Point Press, 1987), 82–83; Lawrence, "Odour of Chrysanthemums," in *The Prussian Officer and Other Stories*, ed. John Worthen (Cambridge: Cambridge University Press, 1983), 181–200; Frost, "Home Burial," *The Poetry of Robert Frost* (New York: Holt, Rinehart, 1969), 51–55.

72 For a reading of "An Ungrafted Tree" that treats the same point from an entirely different perspective, see Walter S. Minot, "Millay's 'Ungrafted Tree': The Problem of the Artist as Woman," *New England Quarterly* 48:2 (1975).

73 Wylie, *Collected Poems of Elinor Wylie* (New York: Knopf, 1932), 225–28. Although, like Millay, Wylie was usually seen as a conventionally sentimental love poet, this ambivalently hostile and guilty hymn to a shattered "no man" articulates a theme that frequently recurs in her verse. See, for instance, "The Coast Guard's Cottage" (150), a necrophiliac dramatic monologue spoken by a woman who longs to take the body of a drowned man into her bed, and "Fable" (75), a ballad which implies that the destruction of a (male) knight by a (female) raven leads to the bird's apotheosis.

74 Bogan, letter to Katharine White, 5 February 1936, quoted in Bowles, *Bogan's Aesthetic,* 43.

75 For Millay's view of *Aria da Capo*, see her letter to Cass Canfield, October 1947, *Letters:* "On the stage all its intricacies move into place in a clear and terrible pattern . . . . I am very proud of *Aria da Capo*. I wish I had a dozen more, not like it, but as good" (337).

76 Millay, *Three Plays* (New York: Harper, 1920–26) 42. Further references will be to this edition, and page numbers will appear in the text.

77 For a discussion of Millay's lesbianism at Vassar, see Anne Cheney, *Millay in Greenwich Village* (Tuscaloosa: University of Alabama Press, 1975), 14–28.

78 See Millay, *The Lamp and the Bell*, in *Three Plays*, 146.

79 See Brittin, *Millay*, 82.

80 See Dickinson, J. 1445, *Complete Poems*, 614.

81 See "To Those without Pity," "Hangman's Oak," and "Justice Denied in Massachusetts," *Collected Poems*, 235, 230–31, 232–33.

82 For Millay's political despair in these years, see also "Say That We Saw Spain Die" and "Underground System," *Collected Poems*, 377–380.

83 "Not poems [but] posters": see letter to George Dillon, 29 November 1940, *Letters*, 309. Added Millay, in a letter to another old friend, "How many more books of propaganda poetry containing as much bad verse as this one does, reputation can withstand without

falling under the weight of it and without becoming irretrievably lost, I do not know" (letter to Charlotte Babcock Sills, 2 January 1941, *Letters*, 311–12). She was right: "Edna Makes Supreme Sacrifice," proclaimed a sneering headline in *Vice Versa*, and, more explicitly, a *Time* reviewer of *Make Bright the Arrows* declared that "Millay lashes out at the warring world like a lady octopus caught in a whirlpool (cited in Schweik, *A Gulf So Deeply Cut: American Women Poets and the Second World War* [Madison: University of Wisconsin Press, 1991], 62).

84 Schweik, *Gulf*, 121; letter to Wilson, August 1946, *Letters*, 33.

85 See Eric Partridge, *A Dictionary of Slang and Unconventional English from the Fifteenth Century to the Present Day*. 5th ed. (New York: Macmillan, 1961), 550.

86 As if to anticipate Ransom's remark, however, Millay herself had claimed in an early verse ("To a Poet That Died Young") that "growing old is dying young" (91). Baby talk appears in letters as late as 1949: see, e.g., letters to Norma Millay ("Oh, poor little Wumpty-Woons"—about the deceased Kathleen) and to Margaret Cuthbert and Alice Blinn ("Goody, goody, goody!"—about the prospect of a Christmas present) in *Letters*, 352, 360.

87 Wilson, "Epilogue, 1952: Edna St. Vincent Millay," in *Shores*, 767.

88 Rich, "Twenty-One Love Poems," XI, *The Dream of a Common Language: Poems 1974–1977* (New York: Norton, 1978), 30.

89 Moore, *The Complete Poems of Marianne Moore* (New York: Macmillan/Viking, 1967), 125–26. Unless otherwise noted, further references will be to this edition, and page numbers will appear in the text. "Nevertheless" had its origin in a remark of Moore's mother about "a strawberry that's had quite a struggle." See Marguerite Young, "An Afternoon with Marianne Moore (1946)," in *Festschrift*, 66.

90 For a slightly different reading of "Those Various Scalpels," see Margaret Holley, *The Poetry of Marianne Moore: A Study in Voice and Value* (Cambridge: Cambridge University Press, 1987), 32.

91 On the relationship between the male gaze, female sexual fragmentation, the *blazon*, and Petrarch's *rime sparse*, see Nancy J. Vickers, "Diana Described: Scattered Woman and Scattered Rhyme," in *Writing and Sexual Difference*, ed. Elizabeth Abel (Chicago: University of Chicago Press, 1982), 95–109.

92 Moore, letter to John Warner Moore, 26 November 1915, cited in Taffy Martin, *Marianne Moore: Subversive Modernist* (Austin: University of Texas Press, 1986), 10.

93 Young, "An Afternoon," 64.

94 When Moore was writing the brilliant four-part study of dragonlike saurians that was to become "The Plumet Basilisk," she began to sign her letters to her brother "Yr. affectionate Basilisk" and "Feather B."; see Laurence Stapleton, *Marianne Moore: The Poet's Advance* (Princeton: Princeton University Press, 1978), 82; see also Suzanne Juhasz, *Naked and Fiery Forms: Modern American Poetry by Women, A New Tradition* (New York: Octagon, 1976), 53–54.

95 For the history of Presbyter John—"a legendary medieval character, allegedly the king-priest of the Indies, a mighty Christian potentate in the East, of fabulous wealth and power"—see *Encyclopedia Britannica*, vol. 18 (Chicago: Encyclopedia Britannica, 1971), 480–81, and *Dictionary of the Middle Ages*, vol. 10 (New York: Scribner's, 1987): 118–19.

96 Moers, "Educating Heroinism: Governess to Governor," in *Literary Women* (1972; New York: Oxford University Press, 1985), 211–42.

97 For a somewhat different view of the youthful Moore's censoriousness, see Helen Vendler's comment, "Hers is the aggression of the silent, well-brought-up girl who thinks up mute rejoinders during every parlor conversation." What Vendler fails to note in her analysis of Moore's early "asperity" is the consistency with which the poet's rejoinders (publicly printed so therefore not really "mute") were directed against

powerful male figures or sexually stereotyped female figures. See Vendler, *Part of Nature, Part of Us: Modern American Poets* (Cambridge: Harvard University Press, 1980), 62–63.

98 Moore, "Pouters and Fantails," *Poetry* 6:2 (1915): 70.

99 Moore's *Complete Poems* is, of course, drastically misnamed; as Donald Hall observed, the volume is only "complete in that it includes all the poems Miss Moore has chosen to reprint. As she comments on the flyleaf, 'Omissions are not accidents.'" (Hall, *Marianne Moore: The Cage and the Animal* [New York: Pegasus, 1970], 182.)

100 Bishop, "Efforts of Affection," 144.

101 Ibid.

102 Examining the biographical context of the poem, both Laurence Stapleton and Barbara Guest have pointed to Moore's distress at Bryher's marriage to Robert McAlmon, an event that took place shortly before she began the poem. Guest quotes from a pertinent letter Moore wrote to H. D.: "It may be that there is no such thing as a love affair in the case of people under forty. . . . I think Chesterton is right. . . . (There is no such thing as a prudent marriage) marriage is a Crusade, there is always tragedy in it" (Guest, *Herself Defined: The Poet H. D. and Her World* [New York: Doubleday, 1984], 140–41). See also Stapleton, *Moore*, 41–42. For useful close readings of "Marriage," see, in particular, Pamela White Hadas, *Marianne Moore: Poet of Affection* (Syracuse: Syracuse University Press, 1977), 142–201; David Bergman, "Marianne Moore and the Problem of 'Marriage,'" *American Literature* 60:2 (1988): 241–54; and Joanne Feit Diehl, *Women Poets and the American Sublime* (Bloomington: Indiana University Press, 1990), 61–70.

103 See Adrienne Rich, "Compulsory Heterosexuality and the Lesbian Continuum," *Blood, Bread and Poetry* (New York: Norton, 1986), 23–75.

104 Quoted in Stapleton, *Moore*, 39.

105 On Eliot, see Hugh Kenner, *The Invisible Poet: T. S. Eliot* (New York: McDowell, Obolensky, 1959).

106 Moore, "To Be Liked by You . . . ," *Chimaera* 1:2 (1916): 56. For useful discussions of this piece, see Holley, *Poetry of Marianne Moore*, 41, and Robert Pinsky, "Marianne Moore: Idiom and Idiosyncrasy," in *Marianne Moore: The Art of a Modernist*, ed. Joseph Parisi (Ann Arbor: UMI Research Press, 1990), 13–14.

107 See Stapleton, *Moore*, xii.

108 For a particularly incisive analysis of this poem's literary historical contexts, see John M. Slatin, *The Savage's Romance: The Poetry of Marianne Moore* (University Park: Pennsylvania State University Press, 1986), 208–20.

109 Young, "An Afternoon," 70.

110 Jarrell, *Kipling, Auden & Co.: Essays and Reviews 1935–1964* (New York: Farrar, Straus, and Giroux, 1980) 128.

111 See *Jonah*, 2:2, 10.

112 In Oliver Wendell Holmes's "Chambered Nautilus," the empty shell of the mollusk functions as a "heavenly message" from the departed sea creature, whose architectural toils and ambitions admonish the poet to "Build thee more stately mansions, O my soul" (*Poems of Oliver Wendell Holmes* [Boston: Ticknor and Fields, 1866], 358–59).

One of Moore's early images of women underscores an intention in her work often "missed by the externalist." "Sea Unicorns and Land Unicorns," with its enthralled portrait of the mythic unicorn, notes that, as the old legend suggests, this miraculously elusive beast can be "tamed only by a lady inoffensive like itself— / as curiously wild and gentle" (78). The traditional attraction between virgin and unicorn becomes a poignant paradigm here for the symbiosis between woman, excluded from (or conquered by) the conquests of history, and all the free agents of an alternative, natural history.

113 Schweik, "Writing War Poetry Like a Woman," *Critical Inquiry* 13:3 (1987): 535.

114 Vendler, *Part of Nature*, 61–62.

115 Jarrell, *Kipling, Auden*, 127.

116 Moore, "Interview with Donald Hall," *A Marianne Moore Reader* (New York: Viking, 1961), 261.

117 On the weakness of Moore's late verse, see, for instance, Slatin, *Savage's Romance*, 1–17, passim; for Moore's style, see Borroff, *Language and the Poet: Verbal Artistry in Frost, Stevens, and Moore* (Chicago: University of Chicago Press, 1979), 109, 112.

118 On Moore's revisionary impulses, Borroff comments, "Had I started my investigation on the assumption that Moore really was writing promotional prose, I should have had to conclude that she failed," implying that the poet's incapacity for *real* commercial writing "is the moral of the bathetic tale of her correspondence with the Ford company." (*Language*, 111, 117.)

119 For "the aesthetic of renunciation," see our *Madwoman in the Attic*, chap. 15.

120 Moore, *Prose*, 290–93; Hall, *Moore: Cage and Animal*, 169–70. In meditating on the relationships of both Moore and Millay to female literary precursors, it may be useful for future biographers to consider that both poets were fatherless and each was unusually close to her mother. Moore, of course, lived with her mother all her life and regarded Mary Warner Moore as her major reader. "Vincent" Millay—treated like an adored oldest son—was (like Moore) early encouraged to write by her mother, and her letters to her mother often read like love letters.

121 On Wylie, see Millay, *Letters*, 138, 216–17, and "To Elinor Wylie," *Poems*, 368–75; on Bogan, see Millay, letter to Wilson, *Letters*, 173.

122 Moore, *Prose*, 112–13, 139.

123 See Millay's letter to Cass Canfield, 22 June 1949, in *Letters:* "I have been recently engaged in writing . . . a satire in verse against T. S. Eliot. In this collection of poems, of which I think there will be about twenty . . . [ellipsis Millay's, or her editor's] there is nothing coarse, obscene, as there sometimes is in the work of Auden and of Pound, and nothing so silly as the childish horsing around of Eliot, when he is trying to be funny. He has no sense of humour, and so he is not yet a true Englishman. There is, I think, in these poems of mine against Eliot nothing which could be considered abusive: they are merely murderous" (353). We are grateful to Holly Pepe and Nancy Milford for information about these manuscripts, and grateful to Elizabeth Barnett, Millay's literary executor, for sharing copies of them with us. (They are, in fact, among Millay's most sophisticated, as well as her most venomous, literary productions.)

124 Moore, "A Letter from Kathleen Raine," quoted in *Festschrift*, 111.

125 Stevens, "The Figure of the Youth as Virile Poet," *The Necessary Angel: Essays on Reality and the Imagination* (New York: Vintage, 1965), 52–53.

126 See Ostriker: modernist women poets "tend to write like pagans, as if the death of God (and His civilization and His culture and His myths) were no loss to them. Indeed, it may have been a relief" (*Stealing*, 47).

127 Stevens, "Figure of the Youth," 53.

128 "Scorn . . . the sonnet": See Wordsworth, "Scorn Not the Sonnet," in *Wordsworth: Poetical Works*, ed. Thomas Hutchinson. Rev. ed., ed. Ernest De Selincourt (New York: Oxford University Press, 1967), 206; See Moore, "Humility, Concentration, and Gusto" (1949), in *Prose*, 420–27; on "gusto," see also Costello, *Moore: Imaginary Possessions*, 2–3 and passim; for women and Romanticism, see Sandra M. Gilbert and Susan Gubar, "The Mirror and the Vamp: Reflections on Feminist Criticism," in *The Future of*

Theory, ed. Ralph Cohen (New York: Routledge, 1989), 144–66, as well as Gilbert and Gubar, "'But oh! that deep romantic chasm': The Engendering of Periodization," *Kenyon Review* 13:3 (1991): 74–82.

129 Lowell, "Robert Lowell," in *Festschrift*, 119.

130 Rossetti, prefatory note to "Monna Innominata," *The Complete Poems of Christina Rossetti* (Baton Rouge: Louisiana State University Press, 1986), 86.

131 Tate, "Miss Millay's Sonnets," *New Republic*, 6 May 1931, 336.

132 Fried, "Andromeda Unbound: Gender and Genre in Millay's Sonnets," *Twentieth-Century Literature* 32:1 (1986): 11, 17. Fried also notes that "Millay's final promise—'I will only make him good'—points to her goal in all her sonnets. . . . A pun gives this closure double force. Millay makes the sonnet aesthetically good by tempering the behavior of the unruly subject in its artful cage, making him 'good' in the sense of training him to be well-mannered, obedient, and orderly" (11) and, additionally, that "turning the chastity belt of poetic form into a token of sexual indulgence, Millay invades the sanctuary of male poetic control with her unsettling formalism in the service of freedom" (25). On Millay and the sonnet form, see also Judith Farr, "Elinor Wylie, Edna St. Vincent Millay, and the Elizabethan Sonnet Tradition," in *Poetic Traditions of the English Renaissance*, ed. Maynard Mack and George deForest Lord (New Haven: Yale University Press, 1982), 287–305.

133 Bishop, "One Art," *The Complete Poems of Elizabeth Bishop* (New York: Farrar, Straus, and Giroux, 1983), 178.

134 Bishop, "Pink Dog," *Complete Poems*, 190–91.

135 In conversations, Moore frequently reiterated this point. Donald Hall noted that "she admits influences from prose" but none or few from poetry, adding that "what she means is that she admires certain felicitous phrases which she encounters in prose and which she often includes with full attribution in her poetry" (*Moore: Cage and Animal*, 56).

136 Costello, "The 'Feminine' Language of Marianne Moore," in *Women and Language in Literature and Society*, ed. Sally McConnell-Ginet et al. (New York: Praeger, 1980), 225.

137 It seems relevant here that Bishop's celebrated "The Fish" concludes with a dazzled vision of "rainbow, rainbow, rainbow!" that at least in part persuades the speaker to "let the fish go"; see Bishop, *Complete Poems*, 44.

138 Stevens does often write a "regular" iambic pentameter line, but his experiments with both free verse and stanzaic patterning, ranging from the forms deployed in "Thirteen Ways of Looking at a Blackbird" to those of "The Man with the Blue Guitar" and "Notes Toward a Supreme Fiction," were considerably more various than Millay's even while (in their revisions of "conventional" prosody) they were far more frankly "poetic" than Moore's. Similarly, such notably formal poets as Frost, Archibald MacLeish, and Hart Crane tended to experiment more self-consciously and with a wider range of forms than Millay, Wylie or Bogan.

139 See Chodorow, *The Reproduction of Mothering: Psychoanalysis and the Sociology of Gender* (Berkeley: University of California Press, 1978). On generic dissonance between male and female poets, see Sandra M. Gilbert, "The American Sexual Poetics of Walt Whitman and Emily Dickinson," in *Reconstructing American Literary History*, ed. Sacvan Bercovitch. Harvard English Studies 13 (Cambridge: Harvard University Press, 1986), 123–54.

140 For a specific discussion of structural and imagistic allusions to the pastoral elegy in *The Waste Land*, see our *Sexchanges*, 310–14.

141 Of course, Eliot himself, not altogether disingenuously, defined *The Waste Land* as no more than a "personal grumble" (Waste Land: *Facsimile . . .* , 1).

142 Westkott, *Feminist Legacy*, 193.

143 Bishop, "In the Waiting Room," *Complete Poems*, 159–62. For a particularly illuminating essay which pays special attention to the fictionality of this ostensibly confessional text, see Lee Edelman, "The Geography of Gender: Elizabeth Bishop's 'In the Waiting Room,'" *Contemporary Literature* 26:2 (1985).

144 For a fine analysis of Bishop's memoir of Moore from a different perspective, see Joanne Feit Diehl, *Elizabeth Bishop and Marianne Moore* (Princeton: Princeton University Press, 1993).

Chapter 3: Ain't I a New Woman?

Epigraphs: Godwyn, *The Negro's and Indian's Advocate . . . in Our Plantations* (London: n.p., 1680), 3: for a discussion of this passage, see Henry Louis Gates, Jr., *Figures in Black: Words, Signs, and the "Racial" Self* (New York: Oxford University Press, 1987), 16; Johnson, "Hegira," *Bronze: A Book of Verse* (1923; Freeport, N. Y.: Books for Libraries Press, 1971), 34; Bonner, "On Being Young—a Woman—and Colored" (1925), in *Frye Street and Environs: The Collected Works of Marita Bonner*, ed. Joyce Flynn and Joyce Occomy Stricklin (Boston: Beacon, 1987), 5.

1 Fauset, *There Is Confusion* (1924; Boston: Northeastern University Press, 1989), 232. Further references will be to this edition, and page numbers will appear in the text.

2 Du Bois goes on to state, "America shall rend the Veil" of racism so that "the prisoned shall go free": see *The Souls of Black Folk*, in *Writings: The Suppression of the African Slave-Trade, The Souls of Black Folk, Dusk of Dawn, Essays and Articles*, ed. Nathan Huggins (New York: Library of America, 1986), 364, 545; Dunbar, "We Wear the Mask," *American Negro Poetry: An Anthology*, ed. Arna Bontemps. Rev. ed., American Century Series (New York: Hill and Wang, 1974), 14.

3 Fauset, "The Gift of Laughter," in *The New Negro*, ed. Alain Locke (New York: Atheneum, 1977), 161. See Baker, *Modernism and the Harlem Renaissance* (Chicago: University of Chicago Press, 1987), 17, and Gates, Jr., *The Signifying Monkey: A Theory of Afro-American Literary Criticism* (New York: Oxford University Press, 1988). Of course much contemporary work, including our own, is indebted to Frantz Fanon, *Black Skin, White Masks*, trans. Charles Lam Markmann (1952; New York: Grove Weidenfeld, 1967).

4 Nietzsche, *The Gay Science*, trans. Walter Kaufman (New York: Random House, 1974), 316–17. Nietzsche goes on to argue about Jews that they are a "people who possess the art of adaptability par excellence" and should therefore be viewed "as a world-historical arrangement for the production of actors, a veritable breeding ground for actors."

5 Hurston, "Art and Such" (1938), in *Reading Black, Reading Feminist: A Critical Anthology*, ed. Henry Louis Gates, Jr. (New York: Meridian, 1990), 21. Hurston's remark frames her belief that up through her own time African-American letters "have been little more than the putting into writing the sayings of the Race" (26).

6 Rose, *Jazz Cleopatra: Josephine Baker in Her Time* (New York: Vintage, 1991), 253.

7 Garber, *Vested Interests: Cross-Dressing and Cultural Anxiety* (New York: Routledge, 1992), 281; Rose, *Jazz Cleopatra*, 97. Rose elaborates here on the jungle tree setting, Baker's entrance, "like a monkey," walking on hands and feet, and the use of drums, all of which created the mood of Africa at the Folies-Bergere.

8 Hurston, quoted in Hurst, "A Personality Sketch," in *Zora Neale Hurston: Modern Critical Views*, ed. Harold Bloom (New York: Chelsea House, 1986), 24.

9 Claude McKay, letter to Walter White, 1924, quoted in David Levering Lewis, *When Harlem Was in Vogue* (New York: Alfred A. Knopf, 1981), 124; McKay, *A Long Way from Home* (New York: Lee Furman, 1937), 112.

10 Lewis, *Amsterdam News*, 5 May 1934, quoted in Amritjit Singh, *The Novels of the Harlem Renaissance: Twelve Black Writers, 1923–1933* (University Park: Pennsylvania State University Press, 1976), 62.

11 Bone, *The Negro Novel in America* (1958; New Haven: Yale University Press, 1965), 101. Even contemporary feminist critics assume that Fauset's interest in middle-class characters enmeshed in romance plots invalidates her books, which are condemned either as elitist or as dominated by white values. According to Mary Helen Washington, for instance, "Fauset's novels never shatter the illusions and pretenses of middle-class respectability; they essentially confirm the necessity for black people to struggle harder to attain it" (*Invented Lives: Narratives of Black Women 1860–1960* [New York: Anchor, 1987], 160).

12 Sato, "Under the Harlem Shadow: A Study of Jessie Fauset and Nella Larsen," in *The Harlem Renaissance Remembered*, ed. Arna Bontemps (New York: Dodd, Mead, 1972), 89. Sato also claims that Larsen's "interest lies mainly on the psychological and not on the social side of the matter"(84). Arthur P. Davis has accused the critics Robert Bone, Saunders Redding, and Hugh Gloster of assuming Larsen's and her heroine's problems derive from her status as a "tragic mulatto": see *From the Dark Tower: Afro-American Writers 1900–1960* (Washington, D.C.: Howard University Press, 1974), 96. Even Barbara Christian claims that Larsen's novels typify a "literature of the tragic mulatta," and that their heroines constitute a "stereotype par excellence": see "Images of Black Women in Afro-American Literature" (1973), in Christian, *Black Feminist Criticism: Perspectives on Black Women Writers* (New York: Pergamon, 1985), 8. On the mulatto character in literature, see Judith R. Berzon, *Neither White Nor Black: The Mulatto Character in American Fiction* (New York: New York University Press, 1978); James Kinney, *Amalgamation: Race, Sex, and Rhetoric in the Nineteenth-Century American Novel* (Westport, Conn.: Greenwood, 1985); Joel Williamson, *New People: Miscegenation and Mulattoes in the United States* (New York: Free Press-Macmillan, 1980); and Anna Shannon Elfenbein, *Women on the Color Line: Evolving Stereotypes and the Writings of George Washington Cable, Grace King, Kate Chopin* (Charlottesville: University Press of Virginia, 1988), 1–19.

13 Bone, *Negro Novel in America*, 105–06 (quote, 106).

14 Hurston, *Mules and Men* (1935; Bloomington: Indiana University Press, 1978), 3. Further references will be to this edition, and page numbers will appear in the text after the abbreviation *M* where necessary.

15 Hurst, "Personality Sketch," 23–24.

16 Huggins, *Harlem Renaissance* (New York: Oxford University Press, 1973), 130.

17 Thurman, *Infants of the Spring* (1932; New York: Books for Libraries Press, 1972), 229–30; Hughes, *The Big Sea* (1929; New York: Harvest-Harcourt, 1963), 238–39.

18 For the responses of black women to Woolf's essay, see n.79 of Chapter 1, above. For a consideration of the significance of Sojourner Truth's analysis in slave times, see Deborah Gray White, *Ar'n't I a Woman? Female Slaves in the Plantation South* (New York: Norton, 1985). Elizabeth Fox-Genovese points out that slavery "bequeathed to Afro-American women a double view of gender relations that fully exposed the artificial or problematic aspects of gender identification. Slavery stripped black men of the social attributes of manhood in general and fatherhood in particular. As a result, black women had no satisfactory social definition of themselves as women" ("My Statue, My Self: Autobiographical Writings of Afro-American Women," in *Reading Black, Reading Feminist*, 188).

19 Christian, *Black Women Novelists: The Development of a Tradition, 1892–1976* (Westport, Conn.: Greenwood, 1980), 32. For a critique of the ways in which the black woman has

been set apart from white women, see Abbey Lincoln, "Who Will Revere the Black Woman?" and Frances Beale, "Double Jeopardy: To Be Black and Female," in *The Black Woman: An Anthology*, ed. Toni Cade (New York: New American Library, 1970), 86–87, 90–100. A related point about the "ungendering" effects of slavery is made by Hortense Spillers in "Mama's Baby, Papa's Maybe: An American Grammar Book," *Diacritics* 17:2 (1987): 65–81.

20 Mary Helen Washington notes that when the American Negro Academy—"a kind of think tank" of the intellectual elite—was proposed, it was supposed to be open only to "*men* of African descent"; however, she also claims that African-American culture "was and still is far more egalitarian" than white society (*Invented Lives*, xiii); *All the Women Are White, All the Blacks Are Men, But Some of Us Are Brave*, ed. Gloria Hull, Patricia Bell Scott, and Barbara Smith (Old Westbury, N.Y.: Feminist Press, 1982).

21 Bray, "Taking Sides against Ourselves," *New York Times Magazine*, 17 November 1991, 94.

22 In particular, Wallace points out in this passage that "to blot out the humiliation of working in the white woman's kitchen all day, of being virtually defenseless before the sexual advances of white men, black women enacted a *charade* of teas, cotillions, and all the assorted paraphernalia and pretensions of society life. It was a desperate masquerade" (*Black Macho and the Myth of the Superwoman* [New York: Dial, 1979], 156). We want to extend her point to include middle-class women of color.

23 Hazel V. Carby draws this distinction to explain how and why the fiction of Fauset and Larsen has been dismissed: see *Reconstructing Womanhood: The Emergence of the Afro-American Woman Novelist* (New York: Oxford University Press, 1987), 166.

24 Hurston, *Color Struck* (1926), in *Black Female Playwrights: An Anthology of Plays before 1950*, ed. Kathy A. Perkins (Bloomington: Indiana University Press, 1989), 89–102. Further references will be to this edition, and page numbers will appear in the text.

25 Nella Larsen, *Quicksand and Passing*, ed. Deborah E. McDowell (1928; New Brunswick, N.J.: Rutgers University Press, 1986), 103. Further references will be to this edition, and page numbers will appear in the text.

26 Barrett Browning, "Runaway Slave at Pilgrim's Point," Cambridge edition of *Complete Poetical Works* (Boston: Houghton Mifflin, 1900) 193; Morrison, *Beloved* (New York: Plume, 1988).

27 Graham, "It's Morning," in *Black Female Playwrights*, 217. This murderous mother tells of yet another, who refused to let her sons be sold and sent away: "An' den dat 'oman lift huh big cane knife, / She cry out sompin' in a wild, strange voice, / An' wid one sweep she cut off all dey heads, / Dey roll down at huh feet—All tree ob dem" (217); Johnson, "Black Woman," *Bronze*, 43; all three of Johnson's plays are reprinted in *Black Female Playwrights*, 24–51. According to the editor, Kathy Perkins, these playwrights were protesting against lynchings that took the lives of more than 3,500 people between the years of 1882 and 1927 (9).

28 Grimké, *Rachel* (1916), in *Black Theater, USA*, ed. James V. Hatch (New York: Free Press, 1974), 137–72, and "The Closing Door," *The Birth Control Review*, October 1919, 10. We are indebted to the insights of Patricia Young and Allison Berg and to the discussion of Gloria Hull in *Color, Sex, and Poetry: Three Women Writers of the Harlem Renaissance* (Bloomington: Indiana University Press, 1987), 117–124, 128–29.

29 Owen, quoted in Paula Giddings, *When and Where I Enter* (New York: Bantam, 1985), 184.

30 For a fascinating story that delineates the psychological evolution of boys in a racist culture, see Bonner, "One Boy's Story," in *Frye Street*, 78–91. We are indebted to Laura Dawkins for bringing it to our attention.

31 Hurston, "Isis," *Spunk: The Selected Stories of Zora Neale Hurston* (Berkeley: Turtle Island Foundation, 1985), 11. Further references to this and other stories by Hurston will be to this edition, and page numbers will appear in the text.

32 Hurston, "How It Feels to Be Colored Me," in *I Love Myself When I Am Laughing . . . and Then Again When I Am Looking Mean and Impressive*, ed. Alice Walker (New York: Feminist Press, 1979), 152–53; Hurston, *Dust Tracks on a Road: An Autobiography*, ed. Robert E. Hemenway. 2d ed. (1942; Urbana: University of Illinois Press, 1984), 45–46, 63–64, 262. Further references will be to this edition, and page numbers will appear in the text after the abbreviation *D* where necessary; Hurston, *Their Eyes Were Watching God* (1937; New York: Harper and Row, 1990). Further references to will be to this edition, and page numbers will appear in the text.

33 Barbara G. Walker, *The Women's Encyclopaedia of Myths and Secrets* (San Francisco: Harper and Row, 1983), 454 (on Isis as "Mother in the horizon"); we are grateful to Elyse Demaray for bringing this point to our attention.

34 Du Bois, "The Damnation of Women" (1920), *Writings*, 954.

35 Hurston, *Tell My Horse* (1938; Berkeley: Turtle Island, 1981), 137–38.

36 On Hurston's alienation from a white-dominated publishing world, see Hurston, "What White Publishers Won't Print" (1950), in *I Love Myself*, 169–73.

37 On her conflicted relationship to Mrs. Osgood Mason, see Robert Hemenway, *Zora Neale Hurston: A Literary Biography* (Urbana: University of Illinois Press, 1977), which argues that Mrs. Mason's "ban against publication became a lever for her to govern her young folklorist" (113). Gloria Hull discusses the "personality-patronage" system in terms of male friendships and support groups, likening women's networks to "consolation circles" for the disenfranchised in *Color, Sex, and Poetry*, 9–12. In a party scene in *Passing*, the white patron modeled on Carl Van Vechten is shown to be far less insightful than his black hostess about the racial interactions they are observing; however, when he does begin to understand the central character, she feels threatened and manages to pull the wool over his eyes: see pages 204–06 and 220–22; see Hurston, "The 'Pet' Negro System" (1943), in *I Love Myself*, 156–62. On the "dissembling slave [as] a confidence figure" whose "superficial docility masked independence of mind and resourcefulness," see Valerie Smith, *Self-Discovery and Authority in Afro-American Narrative* (Cambridge: Harvard University Press, 1987), 5.

38 Fauset, *Plum Bun: A Novel without a Moral* (1928; London: Pandora Press, 1985), 88. Further references will be to this edition, and page numbers will appear in the text.

39 At a 1904 suffrage convention, Mary Church Terrell asked "my sisters of the dominant race" to "stand up not only for the oppressed sex but also for the oppressed race": see *History of Woman Suffrage*, ed. Elizabeth Cady Stanton et al. (1922; New York: Arno, 1969), 5:106. A discussion of this speech and of the problematic identification of women with blacks appears in Catharine R. Stimpson, *Where the Meanings Are* (New York: Methuen, 1988), 11–37. For background on Terrell's contribution, see Dorothy Sterling, *Black Foremothers: Three Lives*. 2d ed. (New York: Feminist Press, 1988), 120–57.

40 Ammons, "New Literary History: Edith Wharton and Jessie Redmon Fauset," *College Literature* 14:3 (1987): 212; Sylvander, *Jessie Redmon Fauset, Black American Writer* (Troy, N.Y.: Whitston, 1981) 171. Deborah McDowell's introduction to *Plum Bun* also explores the dynamics of commodification; see pages xiv–xv.

41 For a discussion of *Summer* in the context of a debilitating heterosexuality defined along the lines of father-daughter incest, see Sandra M. Gilbert, "Life's Empty Pack: Notes toward a Literary Daughteronomy," *Critical Inquiry* 11:3 (1985): 355–84, and Chapter 4 of Gilbert and Gubar, *No Man's Land: The Place of the Woman Writer in the Twentieth Century*, vol. 2: *Sexchanges* (New Haven: Yale University Press, 1989), esp. 154–56. In

this connection, Hazel V. Carby's argument that "the most significant absence in the network of social forces" described by turn-of-the-century black women writers is "the black father" takes on added resonance: see "'On the Threshold of Woman's Era': Lynching, Empire, and Sexuality in Black Feminist Theory," *Critical Inquiry* 12:1 (1985): 276. However, powerful paternal figures do play major roles in Fauset's fiction, especially in *There Is Confusion*.

42 Grimké is quoted in *Black Female Playwrights*, 9.

43 McDougald, "The Task of Negro Womanhood," in *The New Negro*, 381.

44 Harper, *Iola Leroy, or Shadows Uplifted* (1892; Boston: Beacon, 1987), 263, 235, 265. For analyses of this novel, see Christian, *Black Women Novelists*, 25–30, and Carole McAlpine Watson, *Prologue: The Novels of Black American Women, 1891–1965*. Contributions in American Studies, no. 79 (Westport, Conn.: Greenwood, 1985), 14–19.

45 Angèle's progressive friend Martha Burden emerges as an exception to her racist friends, and Martha's admiration causes Angèle to believe that white people can be fair to blacks. Similarly, later in the novel several white characters demonstrate their loyalty to Angela after she reveals her racial loyalty.

46 Quoted by Deborah E. McDowell, "New Directions for Black Feminist Criticism," in *The New Feminist Criticism: Essays on Women, Literature, and Theory*, ed. Elaine Showalter (New York: Pantheon, 1985), 193.

47 "New Negro Woman," *Messenger* 5 (1923): 757; see also Paule Marshall's comment that the female artist of color has an obligation to meet the "challenge . . . of being able to give to the Negro man the kind of love and support he so desperately needs in a society that has conspired over the past 400 years to take from him the sense of his manhood" ("The Negro Woman in Literature," *Freedomways* 6:1 [1966]: 24). More recently, in "The Black Lesbian in American Literature: An Overview," Ann Allen Shockley has claimed about the black movement of the sixties that "some black women advocated 'walking ten steps behind the male,' unwittingly encouraging a new master-subserviency at the expense of black womanhood. The shibboleth of the times was to enhance black manhood": see *Conditions: Five, The Black Women's Issue*, ed. Lorraine Bethel and Barbara Smith, 5 (1979): 135.

48 Toomer, *Cane*, ed. Darwin T. Turner (New York: Norton, 1988), 67. According to Turner, Toomer returned to America from the Gurdjieff Institute in Fontainebleau in 1924 because he wished to instruct artists like Wallace Thurman and Nella Larsen: see his introduction to an earlier edition, reprinted in ibid., 137.

49 Carby, *Reconstructing Womanhood*, 163–75; McDowell, introduction, to *Quicksand and Passing*, xvii–xviii.

50 Paula Giddings discusses the problem of the stereotype of black female lust and promiscuity underpinning the repression of female desire: see *When and Where I Enter*, 31, 35, 49–51.

51 McDougald, "Task of Negro Womanhood," 369; Hopkins, *Contending Forces: A Romance Illustrative of Negro Life North and South* (1900; Carbondale: Southern Illinois University Press, 1978). Further references to *Contending Forces* will be to this edition, and page numbers will appear in the text. On the novel, see Hazel V. Carby, "Lynching, Empire, and Sexuality," *Critical Inquiry* 12:1 (1985): 271–76.

52 See Cheryl A. Wall, "Passing for What? Aspects of Identity in Nella Larsen's Novels," *Black American Literature Forum* 20:1–2 (1986): 99.

53 For a discussion of Brontë's influence on Chopin, see our *Sexchanges*, 88 and 100. In *Women on the Color Line*, Anna Shannon Elfenbein observes, "Although it's doubtful that Nella Larsen read Kate Chopin, it is equally clear in a real sense that Helga Crane and Edna Pontellier are linked. For while they are unlike in almost every superficial way, the fact that they are women in a racist, sexist society defines their life chances" (162).

54 Matthew Arnold refers to Brontë's "hunger, rebellion and rage": see *Letters of Matthew Arnold*, ed. George W. E. Russell (New York: Macmillan, 1896), 1:34.
55 Mary Mabel Youman discusses the ironic title in "Nella Larsen's *Passing:* A Study in Irony," *CLA Journal* 18:2 (1974): 235–41; Cheryl A. Wall analyzes doubling in "Passing for What?" ibid., 109; bell hooks examines the paradox that the passer Clare displays love of her race and interprets Clare's death as a sign that "to love blackness is dangerous": see "Loving Blackness as Political Resistance," *Black Looks: Race and Representation* (Boston: South End Press, 1992), 9.
56 Deborah McDowell, who believes that the passing theme camouflages a lesbian subtext, claims that "the novel's opening image is an envelope (a metaphoric vagina) which Irene hesitates to open": see her introduction, xxvi.
57 A different but interesting reading is provided by Beatrice Horn Royster in "The Ironic Vision of Four Black Women Novelists: A Study of the Novels of Jessie Fauset, Nella Larsen, Zora Neale Hurston, and Ann Petry" (Ph.D. diss., Emory University, 1975). She claims that "as third-person storyteller, Irene is the creator of Clare; and in this sense, she becomes the proper middle-class author whose attitude toward the passing mulatto and the literary genre in which she appears shifts so that Clare's death imputes to the title multiple levels of meaning; in addition to the racial act of identity concealment, passing symbolizes the demise of the genteel heroine and the novel form which perpetuates her" (93). But it seems significant that because of Clare's efforts to protect her secret racial identity, only she has the freedom to write or call Irene: "Clare had only to pick up the telephone to communicate with her, or to drop her a card, or to jump into a taxi. But [Irene] couldn't reach Clare in any way" (*Passing* 163).
58 Larsen's story "Sanctuary," which appeared in *Forum* 83 (1930), was accused of being a plagiarism of Sheila Kaye-Smith's "Mrs. Adis," published in *Century Magazine* 103 (1922). Charles R. Larson provides the best overview on Larsen's still mysterious life; in particular, he stresses that she lied about her birth date, her schooling, and her travels, for reasons still obscure. See his introduction to *An Intimation of Things Distant: The Collected Fiction of Nella Larsen* (New York: Anchor, 1992).
59 We are indebted here to the insightful interpretation of Sojourner Truth's speech in Tania Modleski, *Feminism without Women: Culture and Criticism in a 'Postfeminist' Age* (New York: Routledge, 1991), 21.
60 Hurston, "Characteristics of Negro Expression," in *Negro Anthology, 1931–33*, ed. Nancy Cunard (London: Wishart, 1934), 43.
61 See Hemenway's introduction to *Dust Tracks*, x–xv; Barbara Johnson, "Thresholds of Difference: Structures of Address in Zora Neale Hurston," *Critical Inquiry* 12:1 (1985): 278–89; and Henderson, "Speaking in Tongues: Dialogics, Dialectics, and the Black Woman Writer's Literary Tradition," *Reading Black, Reading Feminist*, 116–41.
62 Bennett, "Fantasy" and "To a Dark Girl," in *Shadowed Dreams: Women's Poetry of the Harlem Renaissance*, ed. Maureen Honey (New Brunswick, N.J.: Rutgers University Press, 1989), 159, 108. For other examples of this voyage toward spiritual solutions, compare Anne Spencer's pessimistic "Letter to My Sister" with her "Lady, Lady" in *Shadowed Dreams*, 51, 56.
63 "Race Champions": see Hurston, "Art and Such," in *Reading Black, Reading Feminist*, 22; "On the line," etc.: see Hurston, "How It Feels to Be Colored Me," 153.
64 Garvey, quoted in Mark D. Matthews, "'Our Women and What They Think': Amy Jacques Garvey and *The Negro World*," *Black Scholar* 10:8–9 (1979): 12.
65 Hurston, quoted in Hemenway, *Zora Neale Hurston*, 44, 37.
66 For excellent readings of *Their Eyes Were Watching God* as bildungsroman, see Gates, *The Signifying Monkey*, 170–210; Barbara Johnson, "Metaphor, Metonymy and Voice in *Their Eyes Were Watching God*," *Black Literature and Literary Theory*, ed. Henry Louis Gates,

Jr. (New York: Methuen, 1984), 204–19; and Washington, *Invented Lives*, 237–54. Our analysis of Hurston and the mother tongue appears in Gilbert and Gubar, *No Man's Land: The Place of the Woman Writer in the Twentieth Century*, vol. 1: *The War of the Words* (New Haven: Yale University Press, 1988), 237–39.

67 Du Bois, "Damnation of Women," 967. Du Bois also explains that "not being expected to be merely ornamental, they have girded themselves for work, instead of adorning their bodies only for play" (966).

68 "No-man's land": see Hurston, "The Gilded Six Bits," *Spunk*, 64. Addison Jayle, Jr. explores how the "black man's route to manhood lay in the exploitation of black women" in *The Way of the New World: The Black Novel in America* (New York: Anchor, 1975), 143. See the reading of "Sweat" in our *War of the Words*, 95–97. "Spunk" deals with the competition between men for the ownership of a female who certifies masculinity; similarly, "The Gilded Six Bits" explores the ways in which black men who are obsessed with the trappings of manhood endanger even the most loving of wives.

69 See also the description of the hoodoo doctor Kitty Brown in *Mules and Men*, 209 and 245–51. For an exploration of "Conjure and the Space of Black Women's Creativity," see Houston A. Baker, Jr., *Workings of the Spirit: The Poetics of Afro-American Women's Writing* (Chicago: University of Chicago Press, 1991), 69–101.

70 Davies, "Zora Neale Hurston's *Their Eyes Were Watching God*: Speaking Out of the Lips of Flowers," in "The Goddess in the Landscape: A Tradition of Twentieth-Century American Women's Pastoral" (Ph.D. diss., Indiana University, 1991), 146.

71 John Dryden, "Song for Saint Cecilia's Day" (1687), in *Poems of John Dryden*, ed. James Kinsley. 4 vols. (Oxford: Clarendon, 1958), 2:539.

72 In its meditation on the possibilities of resurrection and its use of the dog, Hurston's conclusion may be "signifying" on T. S. Eliot's *Waste Land* and in particular on the conclusion of "The Burial of the Dead" section: "That corpse you planted last year in your garden, / Has it begun to sprout? Will it bloom this year? / Or has the sudden frost disturbed its bed? / O keep the Dog far hence, that's friend to men, / Or with his nails he'll dig it up again!" (*The Complete Poems and Plays, 1909–50* [New York: Harcourt, Brace, and World, 1962], 39).

73 Naylor, *Mama Day* (New York: Vintage, 1989), 310.

74 Lorde, "Who Said It Was Simple," *Chosen Poems Old and New* (New York: Norton, 1982), 50.

75 H. D., "The Master," in *H. D.: Collected Poems, 1912–1944*, ed. Louis L. Martz (New York: New Directions, 1983), 461.

Chapter 4: H. D.'s Self-Fulfilling Prophecies

Epigraphs: Nin, "The New Woman" (1974), *In Favor of the Sensitive Man and Other Essays* (New York: Harcourt Brace Jovanovich, 1976), 13; Benedict, journal entry of October 1912, in *An Anthropologist at Work: Writings of Ruth Benedict*, ed. Margaret Mead (Boston: Houghton Mifflin, 1959), 119; Freud, "Femininity," lecture 33 of *New Introductory Lectures on Psychoanalysis*, ed. and trans. James Strachey (New York: Norton, 1965), 135; H. D., *Tribute to Freud* (New York: McGraw-Hill, 1974), 17. Further references to "The Writing on the Wall" and "Advent" will be to this edition, and page numbers will appear in the text after the abbreviation *TF* where necessary.

1 Lacan's "The Line and Light," in *Of the Gaze*, is discussed by Homi Bhabha, "Of Mimicry and Man: The Ambivalence of Colonial Discourse," in *Politics and Ideology*, ed. James Donald and Stuart Hall (Philadelphia: Open University Press, 1986), 198–205.

2 Russo, "Female Grotesques: Carnival and Theory," in *Feminist Studies/Critical Studies*, ed. Teresa de Lauretis (Bloomington: Indiana University Press, 1986), 224. For the Nietzsche quotation, see chap. 3, n.4.

3 See Gilbert and Gubar, *No Man's Land: The Place of the Woman Writer in the Twentieth Century,* vol. 1: *The War of the Words* (New Haven: Yale University Press, 1988), 242–43, for a meditation on H. D.'s name. On Pound's name for H. D., "Dryad," see H. D., *End to Torment: A Memoir of Ezra Pound* (New York: New Directions, 1979), with the poems from "Hilda's Book" by Ezra Pound, ed. Norman Holmes Pearson and Michael King (New York: New Directions, 1979), 17 and 84. Further references to *End of Torment* will be to this edition, and page numbers will appear in the text after the abbreviation *ET* where necessary; for "Astraea," and "Atalanta," and "American Aphrodite," see Barbara Guest, *Herself Defined: The Poet H. D. and Her World* (New York: Doubleday, 1984), 99, 272, 221; for "Artemis," see Bryher, *The Heart to Artemis: A Writer's Memoirs* (New York: Harcourt, Brace and World, 1962); Lawrence, *Aaron's Rod* (1922; New York: Viking, 1961), 23, 28. H. D.'s fictional surrogate, Julia, is called "person, *Personne,* Nobody" in *Bid Me to Live* (1960; New York: Dial, 1983), 172, 196. Further references will be to this edition, and page numbers will appear in the text after the abbreviation *BML* where necessary. Compare her *Palimpsest,* in which the Roman Verrus calls the Greek Hipparchia "Person" (1926; Carbondale: Southern Illinois University Press, 1968), 48. Further references will be to this edition, and page numbers will appear in the text after the abbreviation *P* where necessary; "Greek publicity girl": see Pearson, "Interview," *Contemporary Literature* 10 (1969): 441.

4 Martz, introduction to *H. D.: Collected Poems, 1912–1944,* ed. Louis L. Martz (New York: New Directions, 1983), xix–xxiii. Further references to H. D.'s poems will be to this edition, and page numbers will appear in the text after the abbreviation *CP* where necessary.

5 Dickinson, J. 1335, in *The Complete Poems of Emily Dickinson,* ed. Thomas Johnson (Boston: Little, Brown, l960).

6 Collecott, "Images at the Crossroads: The 'H. D. Scrapbook,'" in *H. D.: Woman and Poet,* ed. Michael King (Orono: University of Maine: National Poetry Foundation, 1986), 319–67; for Dinesen, see Chapter 2, n. 46, above. "Oread" is, of course, H. D.'s most famous imagist poem.

7 Guest, *Herself Defined,* 84. See also Susan Stanford Friedman, *Penelope's Web: Gender, Modernity, H. D.'s Fiction* (Cambridge: Cambridge University Press, 1990), 13–17; on the "neurotic" character played by H. D. in the movie, see Adalaide Morris, "The Concept of Projection: H. D.'s Visionary Powers," *Contemporary Literature* 25:4 (1984): 424–25.

8 For a discussion of the image he calls "The Nymph with the Broken Back" in painting, see Bram Dijkstra, *Idols of Perversity: Fantasies of Feminine Evil in Fin-de-Siècle Culture* (New York: Oxford University Press, 1986), 96–108.

9 Modleski uses the idea of compensation implicit in Joan Rivière's analysis to distinguish masquerade from performance: see *Feminism without Women: Culture and Criticism in a 'Postfeminist' Age* (New York: Routledge, 1991), 54.

10 Susan Stanford Friedman, *Psyche Reborn: The Emergence of H. D.* (Bloomington: Indiana University Press, 1981), 17–154. For a Lacanian reading of how "H. D.'s writing language is fractured by the family romance," see Claire Buck, *H. D. and Freud: Bisexuality and a Feminine Discourse* (New York: St. Martin's, 1991), 8. Havelock Ellis, Hans Sachs, Walter Schmideberg, and Eric Heydt were H. D.'s therapists before and after Freud, a sign of her lifelong fascination with psychoanalysis.

11 See Gilbert and Gubar, *War of the Words,* 165–224. The pertinent passage in Freud appears in "Female Sexuality" (1931), in *Sigmund Freud: Sexuality and the Psychology of Love,* ed. Philip Rieff (New York: Macmillan, 1963), 197–99. Further references will be to this edition, and page numbers will appear in the text after the abbreviation "FS" where necessary.

12 H. D., "The Gift," typescript. Collection of American Literature, Beinecke Rare Book and Manuscript Library, Yale University, 10.

13 Friedman, *Penelope's Web*, 22, 27–28.

14 Gary Burnett's excellent study, *H. D. between Image and Epic: The Mysteries of Her Poetics* (Ann Arbor: UMI Research Press, 1990) discusses and fills in this gap. See especially page 92. Clearly, we disagree with Cheryl Walker's view that Greek culture functioned "as an escape from the terrifying, violent, and destructive aspects of patriarchal history" and that Greece represented for H. D. a place where "gender divisions could be dissolved": see *Masks Outrageous and Austere: Culture, Psyche, and Persona in Modern Women Poets* (Bloomington: Indiana University Press, 1991), 110–11.

15 DuPlessis, "Family, Sexes, Psyche: An Essay on H. D. and the Muse of the Woman Writer," *Montemora* 6 (1977): 145.

16 *HERmione* (composed 1927; New York: New Directions, 1981), 212. Further references will be to this edition, and page numbers will appear in the text after the abbreviation *HER* where necessary. Also see *ET*, 12.

17 For background information, see Peter E. Firchow, "Rico and Julia: The Hilda Doolittle-D. H. Lawrence Affair Reconsidered," *Journal of Modern Literature* 8:1 (1980): 51–76.

18 On the identity of the male figure, Guest mentions Pound (*Herself Defined* 169), while Burnett interprets him as a response to Richard Aldington (*H. D. between Image and Epic* 80). Given H. D.'s propensity to read multiple layers of palimpsestic meaning onto an image, the figure is probably both the ex-fiancé and the ex-husband.

19 DuPlessis, *Writing beyond the Ending: Narrative Strategies of Twentieth-Century Women Writers* (Bloomington: Indiana University Press, 1985), 66–83.

20 Pound, "Revolt" (1909), in *Collected Early Poems of Ezra Pound*, ed. Michael John King (New York: New Directions, 1976), 96–97.

21 See, for example, Pound's "To E. B. B." and "The Summons," in *Collected Early Poems*, 262–63; our discussion of Stevens's "Bowl, Cat and Broomstick" appears in Chapter 2.

22 Pound's comment appears in an essay appended to the poem "Shalott" (notebook compiled 1908) and reprinted in *Collected Early Poems*, 322.

23 See Guy Davenport, "Persephone's Ezra," *New Approaches to Ezra Pound* (London: Faber, 1969), 145–73, and in particular, "Woman for Pound is the stillness at the heart of a culture" (168).

24 Pound, "Ortus," *Collected Shorter Poems* (London: Faber, 1968), 93; Pondrom, "H. D. and the Origins of Imagism," in *Signets: Reading H. D.*, ed. Susan Stanford Friedman and Rachel Blau DuPlessis (Madison: University of Wisconsin Press, 1990), 104–05. Pondrom points out that "H. D. wrote powerful poems which support Pound's definitions of the image and the vortex—*before* he formulated these ideas and before his own poetry showed any consistent effort to achieve these goals." For a theoretical discussion of how the identification of woman with nature excludes women from a poetic voice, see the introduction of Margaret Homans, *Women Writers and Poetic Identity* (Princeton: Princeton University Press, 1980), 12–29.

25 Pound, "The Tea Shop," *Collected Shorter Poems*, 127. Janice S. Robinson points out the significance of this and other poems by Pound in *H. D.: The Life and Work of an American Poet* (Boston: Houghton Mifflin, 1982), 44–45.

26 Pound, "Tempora," *Collected Shorter Poems*, 121.

27 "Tampered with [H. D. as] an oracle": see H. D., *Paint It To-Day*, composed 1921 and printed in part in *Contemporary Literature* 27 (1986): 440–74 (quotation, 447).

28 Pound, "Canto 29," *The Cantos of Ezra Pound* (New York: New Directions, 1970), 144.

(See also H. D., *ET,* 27 and 31); on Pound and Gaudier-Brzeska, see Charles Norman, *Ezra Pound* (New York: Macmillan, 1960), 136.

29 Pound, postscript to Rémy de Gourmont, *Natural Philosophy of Love,* trans. Ezra Pound (New York: Rarity Press, 1931), 169. Pound's postscript is discussed and quoted by Lawrence S. Dembo in *Conceptions of Reality in Modern American Poetry* (Berkeley: University of California Press, 1966), 158, and in the preface to Gilbert and Gubar, *No Man's Land: The Place of the Woman Writer in the Twentieth Century,* vol. 2: *Sexchanges* (New Haven: Yale University Press, 1989).

30 Pound, "Canto 47" (1937), *Cantos,* 237. See Robert Casillo, *The Genealogy of Demons: Anti-Semitism, Fascism, and the Myths of Ezra Pound* (Evanston: Northwestern University Press, 1988): "In Pound's mythology the paternal *logos* and the light of the sun are associated interchangeably with the phallus and its seed, the plough and the father's sowing" (26).

31 Pound, quoted in David Perkins, *A History of Modern Poetry: From the 1890s to the High Modernist Mode* (Cambridge: Harvard University Press, 1976), 484 (also see the discussion of the ideogram as "the one form of writing free from the risk of ambiguity" in Michael André Bernstein, "Image, Word, and Sign: The Visual Arts as Evidence in Ezra Pound's *Cantos,*" *Critical Inquiry* 12:2 [1986]: 358); Pound, "Canto 99" (1958), *Cantos,* 697, 702; "gynocracy": see Robert Casillo, "Pound and Mauberley: the Eroding Difference," *Papers on Language and Literature* 21:1 (1985): 51; "the phallus 'inspire[s] primitive religions'": see unpublished letter of Pound's quoted in Paul Smith, *Pound Revised* (London: Croom Helm, 1983), 55.

32 Lawrence, letter to Cecil Gray, 7 November 1917, in *The Collected Letters of D. H. Lawrence,* ed. Harry T. Moore, vol. 1 (New York: Viking, 1962), 532. See the account in Robinson, *H. D.,* of the deletion of H. D.'s name in Huxley's 1932 edition of the letters (108).

33 Lawrence, "Medlars and Sorb-apples" and "Bavarian Gentians" (1923), in *The Complete Poems,* ed. Vivian De Sola Pinto and F. Warren Roberts (New York: Penguin, 1984), 280–81, 697. Further references to Lawrence's poems will be to this edition and will appear in the text after the abbreviation *LCP.*

34 See Helen Sword's discussion of "the *gloire*" as maleness and femaleness in "Orpheus and Eurydice in the Twentieth Century: Lawrence, H. D., and the Poetics of the Turn," *Twentieth-Century Literature* 35:4 (1989): 422.

35 "Only gods": see Lawrence to Gordon Campbell, 2 September 1914, in *The Letters of D. H. Lawrence,* ed. George J. Zytaruk and James T. Boulton (New York: Cambridge University Press, 1981) 3:218, and Lawrence, "Hopi Snake Dance" (1924), *The Later D. H. Lawrence* (New York: Knopf, 1952), 279 (for an extended discussion of how Lawrence solved the problem of female primacy, see Sandra M. Gilbert, "Potent Griselda: 'The Ladybird' and the Great Mother," in *D. H. Lawrence: A Centenary Consideration,* ed. Peter Balbert and Phillip L. Marcus [Ithaca: Cornell University Press, 1985], 130–61; "woman as the goddess": see Lawrence, *Phoenix: The Posthumous Papers of D. H. Lawrence,* ed. Edward D. McDonald (New York: Viking, 1936), 630–31 (Lawrence's misogyny is discussed in Cornelia Nixon, *Lawrence's Leadership Politics and the Turn against Women* [Berkeley: University of California Press, 1986], 199–200. See also Nixon's analysis of "Phallic knowledge," ibid., 44); "a race falls" and "all the germs": see Lawrence, *The Symbolic Meaning: The Uncollected Versions of Studies in Classic American Literature,* ed. Armin Arnold (Fontwell, Arundel, England: Centaur, 1962), 109, and "Education of the People," *Phoenix,* 621.

36 Anne Bradstreet's line "Let *Greeks* be *Greeks,* and Women what they are, / Men have precedency, and still excell" contextualizes H. D.'s determination to be both Greek and woman, as well as the dread she shared with Bradstreet that "it is but vain unjustly to wage war; / Men can do best, and women know it well" ("The Prologue" (1650), in *The*

Complete Works of Anne Bradstreet, ed. Joseph R. McElrath, Jr., and Allan P. Robb [Boston: Twayne, 1981], 7). On the mask and the woman poet, see Dolores Rosenblum, "Christina Rossetti: The Inward Pose," and Terence Diggory, "Armored Women, Naked Men: Dickinson, Whitman, and Their Successors," *Shakespeare's Sisters: Feminist Essays on Women Poets*, ed. Sandra M. Gilbert and Susan Gubar (Bloomington: Indiana University Press, 1979), 82–98 and 135–50.

37 Bryher defends H. D.'s poems—"they are not cold, they are not passionless"—in a review essay (*Poetry* [March 1922]) discussed by Burnett, *H. D. between Image and Epic*, 31.

38 Chernin, *Reinventing Eve: Modern Woman in Search of Herself* (New York: Harper & Row, 1988), 61. H. D.'s *Hippolytus Temporizes* (1927; Redding Ridge, Conn.: Black Swan, 1985), can also be read as a meditation on frigidity.

39 In her "Pygmalion" (1917), H. D. identifies herself as poet with the sculptor, although it is also possible to view this poem as expressing her identification with the sculpted (*CP* 49–50). See Collecott's discussion of the poem in terms of H. D.'s "need to step down from the marble base on which artist-poets like Pound had placed her" ("Images At the Crossroads," 347, 357). Robert Duncan suggests that H. D.'s knowledge of Shaw's play meant that she may have identified with his Miss Doolittle: see "H. D.'s Challenge," *Poesis* 6 (1965): 23.

40 H. D., *Hedylus* (1928; Redding Ridge, Conn.: Black Swan Books, 1980), 140.

41 See the discussion of bisexuality and H. D.'s *HERmione* in Susan Friedman and Rachel Blau DuPlessis, "'I Had Two Loves Separate': The Sexualities of H. D.'s *Her*," *Signets* 8 (1981): 205–32. On *Hermione*, also see Rachel Blau DuPlessis, *H. D.: The Career of That Struggle* (Bloomington: Indiana University Press, 1986), 61–68; and Friedman, *Penelope's Web*, 123–25.

42 See Marilyn Arthur's discussion of "Red Roses for Bronze" in "Psychomythology: The Case of H. D.," *Bucknell Review* 28:2 (1983), 65–79, as well as Susan Stanford Friedman's in "Modernism of the 'Scattered Remnant': Race and Politics in the Development of H. D.'s Modernist Vision," in *H. D.: Woman and Poet*, 113–14.

43 On "Priest," Louis L. Martz argues that the poem is based on H. D.'s "fifteen-year fixation upon Peter Rodeck (Peter Van Eck of 'Advent'" (*CP* xxvi), who had recently lost his wife. See also David Roessel's answer to Gary Burnett, who views "Priest" as an allusion to Lawrence, in "H. D. and Lawrence: Two More Allusions," *H. D. Newsletter* 1:2 (1987): 46–50.

44 Poe, "The Philosophy of Composition," in *The Complete Poems and Stories of Edgar Allan Poe, with Selections from his Critical Writings*, ed. A. H. Quinn (New York: Knopf, 1951), 2:982; see our discussion in Gilbert and Gubar, *The Madwoman in the Attic: The Woman Writer and the Nineteenth-Century Literary Imagination* (New Haven: Yale University Press, 1979), chap. 1.

45 H. D., *Kora and Ka* (Dijon: Imprimerie Darantière, 1934), 7, 40; See Robert Duncan's analysis in "The H. D. Book: Part 2, Chapter 6," in *H. D.: Modern Critical Views*, ed. Harold Bloom (New York: Chelsea House, 1989), 145.

46 H. D., *Nights* (1935; New York: New Directions, 1986), 51, 52.

47 Claire Buck counters the emphasis by DuPlessis and Friedman on vulval metaphors by pointing to the dancer's transformation into the phallus: see *H. D. and Freud*, 79–80.

48 Burnett, *H. D. between Image and Epic*, 128, 138.

49 Poems from *Trilogy*, which appear in *Collected Poems*, will be identified in the text by poem number followed by page number after the abbreviations *WDNF* (for *The Walls Do Not Fall*), *TA* (for *Tribute to the Angels*), and *FR* (for *The Flowering of the Rod*) where necessary.

50 See Barbara Kiefer Lewalski, *Protestant Poetics and the Seventeenth-Century Religious Lyric*

(Princeton: Princeton University Press, 1979): "The Pauline terms—election, calling, justification, adoption, sanctification, glorification—mark the important stages (some of them concomitant rather than sequential) in the spiritual life of any Protestant Christian" (16).

51 See H. D., *The Gift* (New York: New Directions, 1982), 73–100. There, H. D. identifies herself as the recipient of ancient wisdom inherited through her maternal grandmother who "spoke with tongues—hymns of the spirits in the air—of spirits at sunrise and sunsetting" (87); "vessel of divine inspiration": see Katharine M. Wilson, *Medieval Women Writers* (Athens: University of Georgia Press, 1984), xvii. Lewalski, in *Protestant Poetics*, explains that "prophecy, though often directed to the mind and heart, is a public mode, concerned to mediate through testimony, archetypal symbol, and story the prophet's inspired visions of transcendent reality or of apocalyptic transformations, present or future" (4); see the excellent discussion of chastity, redirecting erotic desire, and spiritual visions in Elizabeth Alvilda Petroff's introduction to *Medieval Women's Visionary Literature* (New York: Oxford University Press, 1986), 3–59.

52 A full discussion appears in Susan Gubar, "The Echoing Spell of H. D.'s *Trilogy*," in *Shakespeare's Sisters*, 200–218.

53 Unpublished letter to Bryher (1934) quoted by Friedman and DuPlessis, "'I have two loves separate,'" *Signets*, 226.

54 Paul Fussell, *Poetic Meter and Poetic Form* (1965; New York: Random House, 1979) 131. On *Trilogy's* use of rhyme, rhythm, and couplets, see Alicia Ostriker, "No Rule of Procedure: The Open Poetics of H. D.," *Agenda* 25:3–4 (1987–88): 145–54.

55 Again, we are elaborating upon a pattern of protestant spiritual evolution discussed by Lewalski, *Protestant Poetics*, 18.

56 See Gilbert and Gubar, *War of the Words*, 242–43 and 247.

57 H. D., *Notes on Thought and Vision and the Wise Sappho* (San Francisco: City Lights Books, 1982), 20, 21.

58 Ibid., 18–20.

59 Kloepfer, "Mother as Muse and Desire: The Sexual Politics of H. D.'s *Trilogy*," in *H. D.: Woman and Poet*, 200.

60 See Donna Krolik Hollenberg, *H. D.: The Poetics of Childbirth and Creativity* (Boston: Northeastern University Press, 1991), for a full discussion of H. D.'s analysis of her experiences of pregnancy.

61 Lawrence, *Aaron's Rod*, 250.

62 "Book means *penis*": Hollenberg quotes an unpublished letter from H. D. to Bryher (1933) in *H. D.: The Poetics of Childbirth*, 110.

63 Holland, *Poems in Persons: An Introduction to the Psychoanalysis of Literature* (New York: Norton, 1973), 23. Also see Joseph Riddel, "H. D.'s Scene of Writing—Poetry As (And) Analysis," *Studies in the Literary Imagination* 12:1 (1979): 41–59, and Rachel Blau DuPlessis and Susan Stanford Friedman, "'Woman is Perfect': H. D.'s Debate with Freud," *Feminist Studies* 7:3 (1981): 417–30.

64 Duncan, "The H. D. Book: Part 2: Nights and Day, Chapter 5," *Caterpillar* 2:2 (1969): 60. On the association of jars with "the old, old jars of Egypt" that Freud in "The Master" bequeaths to the speaker of that poem, see Dianne Chisholm, *H. D.'s Freudian Poetics: Psychoanalysis in Translation* (Ithaca: Cornell University Press, 1992), 61.

65 See Marcel Detienne, *The Gardens of Adonis: Spices in Greek Mythology*, trans. Janet Lloyd (Sussex: Harvester Press, 1977), 48–49, 59–71.

66 Rosemary Radford Ruether, *Mary—The Feminine Face of the Church* (Philadelphia: Westminster, 1977), 41.

67 In *The Man Who Died*, the wounded Jesus rejects Mary Magdalene and journeys to the goddess Isis whose efforts to bring him back to life issue in the jubilant cry, "He is risen."

Clearly, Lawrence is identifying resurrection and erection. See Burnett's reading of
A Dead Priestess as H. D.'s response to *The Man Who Died* and especially his discussion of
the priestess's vision of a Christ who "would see worlds in a crystal . . . or a shell," a
clear adumbration of Kaspar in *Trilogy* (*H. D. between Image and Epic*, 171).

68 We are indebted to Alice Falk's research on Sophia as well as to Susan Cady, Marian
   Ronan, and Hal Taussig, *Sophia: The Future of Feminist Spirituality* (San Francisco: Har-
   per and Row, 1986). Elisabeth Schussler Fiorenza discusses Matthew's use of Sophia in
   In Memory of Her: A Feminist Theological Reconstruction of Christian Origins (New York:
   Crossroads, 1985), 133–34.

69 Schweik, *A Gulf So Deeply Cut: American Women Poets and the Second World War* (Madison:
   University of Wisconsin Press, 1991), 255.

70 Kloepfer, "Mother as Muse and Desire," *H. D.: Woman and Poet*, 202.

71 Ibid., 201.

72 Freud's footnote to his essay "If Moses Was an Egyptian . . ." argues, "There is hardly a
   doubt that in those obscure times mother deities were replaced by male gods (perhaps
   originally their sons). Especially impressive is the fate of Pallas Athene, who was no
   doubt the local form of the mother deity; through the religious revolution she was
   reduced to a daughter, robbed of her mother, and eternally debarred from motherhood by the taboo of virginity" (*Moses and Monotheism*, trans. Katherine Jones [1937;
   New York: Vintage, 1967], 16–65; quote, 55–56).

73 Schweik, *Gulf So Deeply Cut*, 286. Schweik also associates myrrh with Myrrhine in Aris-
   tophanes' *Lysistrata* and with "Myrine," an amazon or woman warrior who founds the
   city of Mitylene in Lesbos. Significantly, in "Let Zeus Record," H. D. praises Bryher
   using the image of myrrh: "Yet when Love fell / struck down with plague and war, / you
   lay white myrrh-buds / on the darkened lintel" (*CP* 284).

74 See, for example, Smith, *Pound Revised*, 128.

75 Mary Beaton, Mary Seaton, Mary Carmichael, and Mary Hamilton—from the Childe
   ballad—are, of course, used throughout *A Room of One's Own;* see our discussion in *War
   of the Words*, 93. In *The Gift*, H. D. remembers her uncle singing, "*Last night there were four
   Marys,*" and wonders, "Who were the four Marys, and why were there four?" (19 and
   84).

76 Freud, *Civilization and Its Discontents* (1930; London: Hogarth, 1982), 6.

77 Chernin, *Reinventing Eve*, 94.

78 This line appears in H. D., *Borderline—A Pool Film with Paul Robeson* (1930; *Sagetrieb* 6:2
   [1987], 34), and is discussed in the context of H. D.'s evolving relationship to film by
   Gary Burnett in *H. D. between Image and Epic*, 103.

Chapter 5: Charred Skirts and Deathmask

Epigraphs: Stein, *Everybody's Autobiography* (1937; New York: Vintage, 1973), 133; H. D.,
Helen in Egypt (New York: New Directions, 1974), 99. Further references will to be this
edition, and page numbers will appear in the text; Plath, "Getting There" (1962), in *The
Collected Poems*, ed. Ted Hughes (New York: Harper and Row, 1981), 249. Further references to Plath's poems will be to this edition, and page numbers will appear in the text after
the abbreviation *PCP* where necessary.

1 H. D., *The Gift* (New York: New Directions, 1982), 135–37.

2 See our discussion of this passage from the unpublished "The Thorn Thicket" (Collection of American Literature, Beinecke Rare Book and Manuscript Library, Yale University) in Gilbert and Gubar, *No Man's Land: The Place of the Woman Writer in the Twentieth
  Century*, vol. 2: *Sexchanges* (New Haven: Yale University Press, 1989), 308.

3 Bryher, *The Days of Mars: A Memoir, 1940–1946* (New York: Harcourt Brace Jovanovich,
  1972), 120.

4 Stein, *Wars I Have Seen* (London: Batsford, 1945), 122; see the chapter "Soldier's Heart" in our *Sexchanges*, 258–323.
5 Lessing, *Martha Quest* (1952; New York: New American Library, 1970), 26.
6 Bowen, "The Demon Lover," *The Collected Stories of Elizabeth Bowen* (New York: Random House, 1982), 661–66. Further references to Bowen's stories will be to this edition, and page numbers will appear in the text.
7 Buck, *Of Men and Women* (New York: John Day, 1941), 155.
8 Stein, *Wars I Have Seen*, 49–50.
9 Vernon Scannell makes this point in *Not without Glory: Poets of the Second World War* (London: Woburn Press, 1976), 17–18. See also Chester E. Eisinger, *Fiction of the Forties* (Chicago: University of Chicago Press, 1963), 23–24. Larkin, "MCMXIV," *The Whitsun Weddings* (London: Faber, 1964), 28; Read, "To a Conscript of 1940," *Collected Poems* (New York: Horizon, 1966), 152 (see also Vance Bourjaily, *Confessions of a Spent Youth* [New York: Dial, 1960], whose hero enters World War II haunted by the poetry of the earlier war); Douglas, "Desert Flowers," in *The Terrible Rain: The War Poets 1939–1945*, ed. Brian Gardner (London: Methuen, 1983), 109; Lewis, "Where Are the War Poets?" (1943) *Poems of C. Day Lewis 1925–1972*, ed. Ian Parsons (London: Cape-Hogarth, 1977), 138; Spender's remarks are quoted in the *Norton Anthology of English Literature*, vol. 2, ed. M. H. Abrams et al. (New York: Norton, 1986), 2320.
10 Matthews, quoted in Margaret Goldsmith, *Women at War* (London: Lindasay Brummond, n.d.), 98. For statistics on female employment, see William Chafe, *The American Woman: Her Changing Social, Economic, and Political Roles, 1920–1970* (New York: Oxford University Press, 1972). A number of historians have questioned Chafe's view that an upsurge of paid employment of married women during World War II led to the later women's liberation movement. The most recent to do so is D'Ann Campbell in *Women at War with America* (Cambridge: Harvard University Press, 1984). Vera Brittain describes her generation's skepticism in *Lady into Woman: A History of Women from Victoria to Elizabeth II* (New York: Macmillan, 1953), 188 and 198.
11 Maureen Honey discusses the Adel ad in *Creating Rosie the Riveter* (Amherst: University of Massachusetts Press, 1984), 84. John Costello focuses on the advertisements of cosmetic companies, which argued that lipstick symbolizes what soldiers are fighting for, "the precious right of women to be feminine and lovely" (*Love, Sex and War: Changing Values 1939–45* [London: Pan, 1986], pl. 63 and 64).
12 Women's uniforms and status are discussed in Jack Cassin-Scott and Angus McBride, *Women at War: 1939–45* (London: Osprey, 1980), 15–18; "expression of free-flowing penis-envy": see Ferdinand Lundberg and Marynia F. Farnham, *Modern Woman, The Lost Sex* (New York: Harper, 1947), 214–215, 353–54.
13 Matthews, quoted in Goldsmith, *Women at War*, 98; War Department brochure, quoted by Eleanor F. Straub, "Women in the Civilian Labor Force," in *Clio Was A Woman: Studies in the History of American Women*, ed. Mabel E. Deutsch and Virginia C. Purdy (Washington, D.C.: Howard University Press, 1980), 218; "majority of girls": see Peggy Scott, *They Made Invasion Possible* (London: Hutchinson, 1944), 8; Mead, "The Women in the War," in *While You Were Gone: A Report on Wartime Life in the United States*, ed. Jack Goodman (New York: Simon and Schuster, 1946), 278; Costello, *Love, Sex and War*, 361.
14 Fussell, *Wartime: Understanding and Behavior in the Second World War* (New York: Oxford University Press, 1989), 132.
15 For background on the general cultural effects of war conditions, see Alan Sinfield, *Literature, Politics, and Culture in Postwar Britain* (Berkeley: University of California Press, 1989), 6–22; Thomas, "A Refusal to Mourn the Death, by Fire, of a Child in London," in *The War Poets: An Anthology of the War Poetry of the 20th Century*, ed. Oscar Williams (New York: John Day, 1945), 32; Sitwell, "Still Falls the Rain" (1942), *The Collected Poems* (New York: Macmillan, 1957), 272.

16 Dickey, "The Firebombing" (1946), *Buckdancer's Choice* (Middletown, Conn.: Wesleyan University Press, 1964), 17; Ciardi, "Take-Off Over Kansas," *Other Skies* (Boston: Little, Brown, 1947), 21–22.

17 Graves, quoted in Ian Hamilton's introduction to *The Poetry of War, 1939–45*, ed. Ian Hamilton (London: Alan Ross, 1965), 3; Press, "Poets of World War II," in *British Writers*, ed. Ian Scott-Kilvert, vol. 7 (New York: Scribner's, 1978), 421–50. Fussell quotes William Manchester's assessment that "all who wore uniforms are called veterans, but more than 90 per cent of them are as uninformed about the killing zones as those on the home front" as well as statistics that the United States Army, which grew in 1943 by two million men, contained only about 365,000 in combat units and an even smaller number in rifle companies (*Wartime* 283).

18 Yeats, "Lapis Lazuli" (1938), *The Collected Poems of W. B. Yeats* (New York: Macmillan, 1956), 292.

19 Jarrell, "The Death of the Ball Turret Gunner" (1945), *The Complete Poems* (New York: Farrar, Straus, and Giroux, 1969), 144.

20 Fussell, *Wartime*, 153.

21 Woolf, *Leave the Letters Till We're Dead: The Letters of Virginia Woolf*, vol. 6: *1936–41*, ed. Nigel Nicolson, with Joanne Trautmann (London: Hogarth, 1980), 379.

22 Bishop, "Roosters" (1946), *The Complete Poems 1927–1979* (New York: New Directions, 1971), 35. Further references will be to this edition, and page numbers will appear in the text.

23 "Mov[e] from a country morning": see William Spiegelman, "Natural Heroism," in *Modern Critical Views: Elizabeth Bishop*, ed. Harold Bloom (New York: Chelsea House, 1985), 99–100; see also Anne R. Newman, "Elizabeth Bishop's 'Roosters,'" in ibid., 117.

24 Beard, *On Understanding Women* (1931), excerpted in *Mary Ritter Beard: A Sourcebook*, ed. Ann J. Lane (New York: Schocken, 1977), 144.

25 Holtby, *Women and a Changing Civilization* (1935; Chicago: Academy Chicago, 1978), 159–60.

26 Burdekin, *Swastika Night* (Old Westbury, N.Y.: Feminist Press, 1985). In her introduction, Patai distinguishes the consciousness of "gender ideology" in Burdekin's text with its absence in *1984* (xiii–xiv). Further references will be to this edition, and page numbers will appear in the text.

27 Carson McCullers more elliptically hints at the relation between masculinism and fascism when a heroine is baffled by two words—*Pussy* and *Mussolini* scrawled on a neighborhood wall: see *The Heart Is a Lonely Hunter* (1940; New York: Bantam, 1953), 31.

28 Rukeyser, "Letter to the Front" (1944), *The Collected Poems* (New York: McGraw-Hill, 1982), 235. Further references to Rukeyser's works will be to this edition, and page numbers will appear in the text.

29 Smith and Snelling, "Man Born of Woman," *North Georgia Review* 6:1–4 (1941): 10, 17.

30 Brittain, *Lady into Woman*, 198.

31 Holtby, *Women and a Changing Civilization*, 166.

32 Stein, *The Mother of Us All* (1946), in *Gertrude Stein: Last Operas and Plays*, ed. Carl Van Vechten (New York: Vintage, 1975), 80–81.

33 Bernikow, *Among Women* (New York: Harmony, 1980), 190–92.

34 Bowen, *The Heat of the Day* (1948; New York: Knopf, 1949), 24–25. Further references will be to this edition, and page numbers will appear in the text.

35 Smith, *Over the Frontier* (1938; London: Virago, 1980), 271.

36 Sitwell, "Lullaby," *Collected Poems*, 274–75.

37 Sitwell, "Serenade: Any Man to Any Woman," *Collected Poems*, 276.

38 Uris, *Battle Cry* (1953; New York: Bantam, 1982), 48; Earle, "Cannoneer's Lady," in *Reveille: War Poems by Members of Our Armed Forces*, ed. Daniel Henderson, John Kieran, and Grantland Rice (New York: Barnes, 1943), 31.

39 Costello, *Love, Sex and War*, 120.
40 Ciardi, "The Health of Captains" (1955), *As If: Poems New and Selected* (New Brunswick, N.J.: Rutgers University Press, 1955), 13; Kirstein, "Snatch," *Rhymes of a PFC* (1964; Boston: David R. Godine, 1981), 128. For the slippage between *puellis* (girls) and *duellis* (battles), see Henry Reed's "Lessons of the War: Naming of Parts," *A Map of Verona and Other Poems* (New York: Reynal and Hitchcock, 1947), 27–29.
41 Quoted in Costello, *Love, Sex and War*, 123.
42 Roberts-Jones, "Battalion H.Q. Burma," in *Poems from India by the Members of the Forces*, ed. R. N. Currey and R. V. Gibson (London: Oxford University Press, 1946), 125.
43 *"Fuck"*: see Karen Lee Schneider, "Altered Stories, Altered States: British Women Writing the Second World War" (Ph.D. diss., Indiana University, 1991), 7–8; "I won't describe": see Fussell, *Wartime*, 109.
44 May, *Homeward Bound: American Families in the Cold War Era* (New York: Basic, 1988), 110–11.
45 Connolly, "Comment," *Horizon* 3 (1941): 5.
46 Kirstein, "Load" (1964), *Rhymes of a PFC*, 152; Hersey, *The War Lover* (New York: Knopf, 1959), 387.
47 Don Jaffe, "Poets in the Inferno: Civilians, C.O.'s and Combatants," in *The Forties: Fiction, Poetry, Drama*, ed. Warren French (Deland, Fla.: Everett/Edwards, 1969), 36.
48 Auden, "September 1, 1939" (1939), in *The English Auden*, ed. Edward Mendelson (London: Faber, 1977), 245. Mendelson argues in *Early Auden* (London: Faber, 1981) that "social revolution" is a "male preserve" for Auden and Isherwood, who present an avid warmonger in *The Dog Beneath the Skin* as a mother who has lost her sons in battle (276).
49 Wilbur, "Place Pigalle," *The Beautiful Changes* (New York: Harcourt Brace, 1947), 12; Major Fred B. Shaw, Jr., "Lydia of Libya," in *Reveille*, 217; Douglas, "Cairo Jag" (1943), in *Complete Poems*, ed. Desmond Graham (Oxford: Oxford University Press, 1978), 97. Also see Bernard Gutteridge, "Sunday Promenade: Antisirane," originally published in *Traveller's Eve* (1947) and reprinted in *Old Damson-Face: Poems 1934–1974* (London: London Magazine Editions, 1975), 43.
50 Manifold, "The Sirens," in *War Poets*, 191; Patric Dickinson, "War," in *Reveille*, 241; Bourjaily, *Confessions of a Spent Youth*, 345 (also see the cartoons of Sgt. George Baker that show servicemen afraid to shake hands with women after army sex education courses, reprinted in James Jones, *World War II* [New York: Grosset and Dunlap, 1975], 55. Fussell describes American movies with names like *Good Girls Have VD Too*, as well as British slogans like the one used in Egypt: "Remember, flies spread disease. Keep yours shut!" [*Wartime*, 108]); Tolson, "The Furlough," *Rendezvous with America* (New York: Dodd, Mead, 1944), 23–24. (Because Tolson is black, his femicidal text is especially interesting in the context of Gwendolyn Brooks's poetry about black male femicidal rage. See the discussion later in this chapter.)
51 Corporal John Readey, "A Woman's a Two-Face," in *Reveille*, 215. In this regard, the proliferation of popular songs on infidelity is pertinent: "Don't Sit under the Apple Tree with Anyone Else but Me," "Paper Doll," and "Somebody Else Is Taking My Place," for example.
52 Barker, "To Any Member of My Generation," in *War Poets*, 321; Kunitz, "Careless Love," in ibid., 166; Shapiro, "Conscription Camp" (1941) *Collected Poems, 1940–1978*, (New York: Random House, 1978), 47–48; Causley, "A Ballad for Katharine of Aragon" (1951), *Collected Poems, 1951–1975* (London: Macmillan, 1975), 14.
53 May, *Homeward Bound*, 70.
54 Pynchon, *V.* (New York: Lippincott, 1963), 318.

55 Mary Cadogan and Patricia Craig, *Women and Children First: The Fiction of Two World Wars* (London: Gollancz, 1978), 173.

56 Fussell, *Wartime*, 116.

57 Mailer, *The Naked and the Dead* (1948; New York: Holt, Rinehart and Winston, 1981), 721; Pynchon, *Gravity's Rainbow* (New York: Bantam, 1974), 21.

58 Cynthia Enloe, *Does Khaki Become You? The Militarisation of Women's Lives* (London: Pluto, 1983), 2. In *Love, Sex and War*, Costello mentions that members of the WAAF were also referred to as "Pilots' Cockpits" in British slang and he quotes one WAAF member who recalled that "soldiers often tried to rape us" (79–80); Robert Hewison, *Under Siege: Literary Life in London, 1939–45* (London: Weidenfeld and Nicolson, 1977), 25.

59 Sally Van Wagenen Keil, *Those Wonderful Women in Their Flying Machines: The Unknown Heroines of World War II* (New York: Rawson, Wade, 1979), 197, 202, 212. D'Ann Campbell quotes Virginia Gildersleeve explaining, "If the Navy could possibly have used dogs or ducks or monkeys" instead of women, certain admirals would have preferred them (*Women at War with America*), 37.

60 For Millay, see discussion in Chapter 2; on Rukeyser, see "Grandeur and Misery of a Poster Girl," *Partisan Review* 10:5 (1943): 472–73; on Moore, see Randall Jarrell, "Poetry in War and Peace," *Kipling, Auden & Co.* (New York: Farrar, Straus, and Giroux, 1980), 129–30; on H. D., see Jarrell, "*Tribute to the Angels* by H. D.," ibid., 135.

61 Deutsch, "For a Young Soldier" and "To My Son," *Take Them, Stranger* (New York: Henry Holt, 1944), 58–59.

62 Schweik, *A Gulf So Deeply Cut: American Women Poets and the Second World War* (Madison: University of Wisconsin Press, 1991), 85–109. See the discussion of this picture in Fussell, *Thank God for the Atom Bomb and Other Essays* (New York: Summit, 1988), 49. Although he believes the *Life* photo and caption are "without a trace of irony or outrage," Fussell does not examine what its effect might be on the female viewer.

63 David Geraint Jones, "The Light of Day," in *Terrible Rain*, 154 (see also Gervase Stewart's "Poem" in ibid., 149); inscription on the memorial at Kohima, quoted in ibid., 161.

64 Shapiro, "V-Letter" (1944), *Collected Poems*, 87–88.

65 Douglas, "*Vergissmeinnicht*" (1943), *Complete Poems*, 111.

66 "There's the girl I 'left behind,'" the speaker of "Nebraska Gunner at Bataan" (1943) exclaims, "I wonder, would she love me yet / If she could watch me grimly kill," and so he wants to "keep her safe back there": see Corporal Richard F. Ferguson in *Reveille*, 71.

67 Uris, *Battle Cry*, 2.

68 Eberhart, "Brotherhood of Men," *Collected Poems, 1930–1976* (New York: Oxford University Press, 1976), 101; Jones, *From Here to Eternity* (New York: Scribner's, 1951), 16. Consider, also, A. A. Milne's war verse: "I march along and march along and ask myself each day: / If I should go and lose the war, then what will Mother say? / The Sergeant will be cross and red, the Captain cross and pink / But all I ever ask myself is, What will Mother think?" ("Song for a Soldier," *Behind the Lines* [New York: Dutton, 1940], 31).

69 Orwell, *1984* (1949; New York: New American Library, 1981), 81, 206, 222. Daphne Patai also argues that "Orwell assails Big Brother's domination but never notices that he is the perfect embodiment of hypertrophied masculinity" (*The Orwell Mystique: A Study of Male Ideology* [Amherst: University of Massachusetts Press, 1984], 251).

70 Ciardi, "Health of Captains," 13; Jarrell, "Death of the Ball Turret Gunner," 144. See the similar imagery in Ciardi, "Two Songs for a Gunner" (1951), *As If*, 24; Oscar Williams, "The Man in that Airplane," in *War Poets*, 443.

71 Jarrell, "Gunner" (1945), *Complete Poems*, 204.

72 Lewis, "On Embarkation" (1945) and "Christmas Holiday" (1942), *Selected Poetry and Prose* (London: Allen and Unwin, 1966), 84, 99.

73 Boyle, "Army of Occupation" (1947), "Men" (1941), and "Defeat" (1941), *50 Stories* (New York: Penguin, 1980), 439–53, 275–87, and 294–304.
74 Boyle, *American Citizen Naturalized in Leadville, Colorado* (New York: Simon and Schuster, 1944), 6, 11, 12, 6, 7.
75 Mead, "Women in the War," 125.
76 See Ursula Vaughan Williams, "Penelope" (1948), Juliette de Bairacli-Levy, "Threnode for Young Soldiers Killed in Action" (1947), and Rachael Bates, "The Infinite Debt" (1947), in *Chaos of the Night: Women's Poetry and Verse of the Second World War*, ed. Catherine Reilly (London: Virago, 1984), 125, 8, and 27, as well as the war fiction composed by Elizabeth Taylor, Betty Miller, and Elizabeth Jane Howard; "as long as there be war": see Fussell, *Wartime*, 168.
77 Quoted in Ranes Minns, *Bombers and Mash: The Domestic Front 1939–1945* (London: Virago, 1980), 37.
78 Coats, "The 'Monstrous Regiment'" (1950), in *Chaos of the Night*, 29–30.
79 Schneider, "Altered Stories, Altered States," 117; Smith, "Who Shot Eugenie?" *Harold's Leap* (1950), *The Collected Poems of Stevie Smith* (London: Allen Lane, 1975), 292–93. See also Sylvia Lynd, "The Searchlights" (1945), Catherine Brewster Toosey, "Colour Symphony" (1941), and Margery Lawrence, "Garden in the Sky" (1950), in *Chaos of the Night*, 81, 121, and 74.
80 Quoted in Minns, *Bombers and Mash*, 33.
81 Warner, "Noah's Ark," *A Garland of Straw: Twenty-Eight Stories by Sylvia Townsend Warner* (New York: Viking, 1943), 97, 100, 104. In this volume, also see "The Trumpet Shall Sound" and "From Above," both about the impact of the blitz on women (68–79 and 189–96).
82 Brooks, "Gay Chaps at the Bar" (1945), *The World of Gwendolyn Brooks* (New York: Harper and Row, 1971), 51, 53. Further references to Brooks's poems will be to this edition, and page numbers will appear in the text.
83 Melhem, *Gwendolyn Brooks: Poetry and the Heroic Voice* (Lexington: University Press of Kentucky, 1987), 42.
84 Shaw, *Gwendolyn Brooks* (Boston: Twayne, 1980), 62.
85 Stevens, "Sunday Morning" (1915), "How red the rose that is the soldier's wound" (sect. 6 of *Esthetique du Mal* [1942]), "Examination of the Hero in a Time of War" (1942), and "[Prose statement on the poetry of war]" (1942), in *The Palm at the End of the Mind: Selected Poems and a Play by Wallace Stevens*, ed. Holly Stevens (New York: Archon, 1984) 7, 256–57, 201, 205, and 206. Also see "Dutch Graves in Bucks County," in ibid., 236–39.
86 McCullers, *The Member of the Wedding* (New York: Bantam, 1981), 39, 127. Further references will be to this edition, and page numbers will appear in the text.
87 In respect to its elaboration of a father-daughter model of heterosexuality, *Member of the Wedding* resembles Edith Wharton's *Summer*. See our *Sexchanges*, 155–56.
88 Petry, *The Street* (New York: Pyramid, 1961), 162. Jean Bethke Elshtain quotes a black domestic who took a high-paying factory job: "Hitler was the one that got us out of the white folks' kitchen" (*Women and War* [New York: Basic, 1987]), 190). Fussell points out that until well into the war, Red Cross workers segregated the blood plasma of blacks from that of whites (*Thank God for the Atom Bomb*), 141. One of the most insightful journalists during the forties, Rebecca Stiles Taylor, wrote columns about women, mobilization, and the war effort that emphasize the special vulnerability and resiliency of black women: see *The Chicago Defender*, 1939–44.
89 Nemerov, "IFF," *War Stories: Poems about Long Ago and Now* (Chicago: University of Chicago Press, 1987), 29.
90 Mailer, *Naked and the Dead*, 568, 580, 322.

91 Ibid., 672; Aichinger, *The American Soldier in Fiction, 1880–1963: A History of Attitudes Toward Warfare and the Military Establishment* (Ames: Iowa State University Press, 1976), 41. In the film version of *From Here to Eternity*, Deborah Kerr sadly tells Bert Lancaster that he has married the military.

92 Orwell, "Looking Back on the Spanish War" (1943), *A Collection of Essays by George Orwell* (New York: Doubleday, 1954), 214.

93 Eberhart, "Brotherhood of Men," 103, 105.

94 Ford, quoted in our *Sexchanges*, 301. The homoerotic overtones of works by Wilfred Owen, Herbert Read, and Ford contrast with the aggressively heterosexual context established in the literature of World War II.

95 Bérubé, *Coming Out under Fire: The History of Gay Men and Women in World War Two* (New York: Penguin, 1991), 97, 188–89.

96 The best discussion of the violently destructive, suicidal homosexual in the literature of World War II is in Peter G. Jones, *War and the Novelist* (Columbia: University of Missouri Press, 1976), 113–61; Eve Kosofsky Sedgwick, *Between Men: English Literature and Male Homosocial Desire* (New York: Columbia University Press, 1985).

97 Corsellis, "What I Never Saw" (1940), in *Terrible Rain*, 71.

98 Plagemann, *The Steel Cocoon* (New York: Viking, 1958), 63–64, 20.

99 Jones, *From Here to Eternity*, 643.

100 Parker, "The Lovely Leave," *The Portable Dorothy Parker* (New York: Penguin, 1944, 1977), 17. Hannah Lees's *Till the Boys Come Home* (New York: Harper, 1944) is reviewed by Diana Trilling and praised for depicting the boredom of wives left by men eager for an adventure together during the war: see *Reviewing the Forties* (New York: Harcourt Brace Jovanovich, 1978), 101.

101 Lessing, *A Proper Marriage* (1952; New York: New American Library, 1970), 238. See also Olivia Manning, *The Levant Trilogy* (London: Penguin, 1983), 154–56 and 197, and Robert K. Morris, "Olivia Manning's *Fortunes of War*: Breakdown in the Balkans, Love and Death in the Levant," in *British Novelists Since 1900*, ed. Jack I. Biles (New York: AMS Press, 1987), 247.

102 Lessing, *Proper Marriage*, 238; Lessing, *The Golden Notebook* (New York: Bantam, 1979), 63.

103 Weil, "The *Iliad*, Poem of Might" (1940–41), in *The Simone Weil Reader*, ed. George A. Panichas (New York: David McKay, 1977), 171.

104 Smith, "I had a dream . . . ," *Collected Poems*, 421–23.

105 H. D., *Gift*, 133–37.

106 Brittain, *Account Rendered* (London: Virago, 1982), 214. Further references will be to this edition, and page numbers will appear in the text.

107 We are here presenting an alternative to the more optimistic readings of *Helen in Egypt* offered by Susan Stanford Friedman in "Creating a Women's Mythology," in *Signets: Reading H. D.*, ed. Susan Stanford Friedman and Rachel Blau DuPlessis (Madison: University of Wisconsin Press, 1990), 373–405, and Cheryl Walker, *Masks Outrageous and Austere* (Bloomington: Indiana University Press, 1991), 128–30.

108 H. D., *Vale Ave* (1957), in *New Directions in Prose and Poetry 44*, ed. J. Laughlin (New York: New Directions, 1982), 18–68. Further references will be to this edition, and page numbers will appear in the text.

109 Weil, "*Iliad*, Poem of Might," 158, 159.

110 Porter, *Ship of Fools* (Boston: Atlantic-Little, Brown, 1962), 144.

111 Lessing, *Golden Notebook*, 98, 153.

112 See Elizabeth Bowen, "The Happy Autumn Fields," *Collected Stories*, 671–85, for a tale that presents the daydreams of a woman in a bombed house, visions that link her to a Victorian (female) world of love and ritual that is as beyond renovation as the house.

113 Arnow, *The Dollmaker* (New York: Avon, 1972), 151. Further references will be to this edition, and page numbers will appear in the text.

114 Barnes, *The Antiphon* (London: Faber, 1958), 94–95.

115 Rich, "The Eye of the Outsider: The Poetry of Elizabeth Bishop," *Boston Review* 8:2 (1983): 16.

116 Marshall, *Brown Girl, Brownstone* (Old Westbury, N.Y.: Feminist Press, 1981), 100. Further references will be to this edition, and page numbers will appear in the text.

117 Spark, *The Girls of Slender Means* (New York: Knopf, 1963), 27–28. In *The Prime of Miss Jean Brodie* (New York: Laurel, 1980), Spark's heroine is described as "a born Fascist" (150 and 153).

118 Rhys, "The Insect World" (1976), *The Collected Short Stories* (New York: Norton, 1987), 356. Further references will be to this edition, and page numbers will appear in the text.

119 Cooper, "Nothing Has Been Used in the Manufacture of This Poetry that Could Have Been Used in the Manufacture of Bread" (1974), *Scaffolding: New and Selected Poems* (London: Anvil, 1984), 35.

120 Coleman, "No Woman's Land," *Mad Dog Black Lady* (Santa Barbara, Calif.: Black Sparrow, 1979), 26.

121 Piercy, *Gone to Soldiers* (New York: Fawcett Crest, 1988), 318. Further references will be to this edition, and page numbers will appear in the text.

122 See May, *Homeward Bound*, 58–91.

123 For a similar point, see Porter, *Ship of Fools:* When La Condesa states her belief that to be a German is "an incurable malady . . . as hopeless as being a Jew," her lover replies, "Or a woman" (236).

124 See Margaret Fuller, *Woman in the Nineteenth Century* (1845; Columbia: University of South Carolina Press, 1980), 30. On Schreiner, see *An Olive Schreiner Reader*, ed. Carol Barash (London: Pandora, 1987), 202–03 and 248.

125 Weininger, *Sex and Character* (London: William Heinemann, [1906]), 306; Hitler, quoted and discussed in Susan Griffin, *Pornography and Silence* (New York: Harper, 1981), 172.

126 Jackson, *Behold the Jew* (New York: Macmillan, 1944), 21, 22. See also Schweik, *Gulf So Deeply Cut*, 17–22.

127 De Beauvoir, *The Second Sex*, trans. and ed. H. M. Parshley (New York: Bantam, 1961), xxiii; Friedan, *The Feminine Mystique* (New York: Dell, 1983), 308. Further references will be to this edition, and page numbers will appear in the text.

128 "His simple nobility": see Spiegelman, "Natural Heroism," 98; Bishop, "Visits to St. Elizabeths" (1950), *Complete Poems*, 133–35.

129 Smith, *Over the Frontier*, 158.

130 Boyle, "Winter Night" (1946), *50 Stories*, 606.

131 O'Connor, "The Displaced Person" (1955) *The Complete Stories of Flannery O'Connor* (New York: Farrar, Straus, and Giroux, 1971), 196.

132 Lessing, *The Four-Gated City* (New York: Knopf, 1969), 516. See also Denise Levertov, "During the Eichmann Trial" (1961), *Poems: 1960–1967* (New York: New Directions, 1983), 65, as well as the final poem in *The Sorrow Dance*.

133 Yamada, "To the Lady," *Camp Notes and Other Poems* (San Lorenzo, Calif.: shameless hussy press, 1976), n.p. See Susan Schweik's more extended discussion of Nisei women poets, *Gulf So Deeply Cut*, 173–212, and Hisaye Yamamoto, *Seventeen Syllables and Other Stories* (Albany, N.Y.: Kitchen Table, Women of Labor Press, 1988). On government policies to fingerprint and intern Italian-American "enemy aliens," see Concetta Doucette, "Fingerprinting Children Is Not New," *Italian Americana* 10:1 (1991): 79–82,

and Stephen Fox, *The Unknown Internment: An Oral History of the Relocation of Italian Americans during World War II* (Boston: Twayne, 1990).

134 Spark, "The First Year of My Life" (1975), *The Stories of Muriel Spark* (New York: Dutton, 1985), 268.

Chapter 6: In Yeats's House

Epigraphs: Plath, *The Journals of Sylvia Plath*, ed. Frances McCullough and Ted Hughes (New York: Dial, 1982), 237–39. Further references will be to this edition, and page numbers will appear in the text after the abbreviation *J* where necessary; Hughes, "The Virgin Knight," *Moortown* (New York: Harper, 1979), 162; Yeats, "To Dorothy Wellesley" (1936–39) *The Poems of W. B. Yeats: A New Edition*, ed. Richard J. Finneran (New York: Macmillan, 1989), 304; Plath, letter to Aurelia Plath, 14 December 1962, in *Letters Home*, ed. Aurelia Plath (New York: Harper, 1975), 488. Further references to Plath's letters will be to this edition, and will appear in the text after the abbreviation *LH* where necessary.

1 Plath, "Superman and Paula Brown's New Snowsuit," *Johnny Panic and the Bible of Dreams: Short Stories, Prose, and Diary Excerpts* (New York: Harper, 1980), 271. Further references to pieces in this volume will be to this edition, and page numbers will appear in the text after the abbreviation *JP* where necessary.

2 George Steiner, for instance, claims that Plath's "association of her own pain with that of the Jews in Europe" is "a subtle larceny" (cited by Elizabeth Hardwick, "On Sylvia Plath," in *Ariel Ascending: Writings about Sylvia Plath*, ed. Paul Alexander [New York: Harper, 1985] 109).

3 For a discussion of this episode, see Sandra M. Gilbert and Susan Gubar, *No Man's Land: The Place of the Woman Writer in the Twentieth Century*, vol. 1: *The War of the Words* (New Haven: Yale University Press, 1988), 61–62.

4 "Sadie" was a frequent name with which "Sivvy" rechristened herself in romans à clef. For a more extensive discussion of "The Fifty-ninth Bear," see Sandra M. Gilbert, "A Fine, White, Flying Myth: The Life/Work of Sylvia Plath, in *Shakespeare's Sisters*, ed. Sandra M. Gilbert and Susan Gubar (Bloomington: Indiana University Press, 1979), 245–60.

5 Plath, "Lyonesse" (1962) in *The Collected Poems*, ed. Ted Hughes (New York: Harper, 1981), 234. All further references to Plath's poetry will be to this edition, and page numbers will be included in the text after the abbreviation *PCP* where necessary.

6 For an interesting discussion of the gradual depersonalization of these terms—"Herr God, Herr Lucifer," etc., in the drafts of this poem, see Susan Van Dyne, *Revising Life: Sylvia Plath's Ariel Poems* (Chapel Hill: University of North Carolina Press, 1993), 58–63.

7 Lowell, foreword to Sylvia Plath, *Ariel* (New York: Harper, 1966), vii.

8 Rich, "Power," *The Dream of a Common Language* (New York: Norton, 1978), 3.

9 Yeats "He and She" (1935), *Collected Poems*, 285.

10 John Keats, letter to George and Georgiana Keats, Sunday 14 February–Monday 3 May 1819: "A Man's life of any worth is a continual allegory—and very few eyes can see the Mystery of his life—a life like the scriptures, figurative. . . . Lord Byron cuts a figure—but he is not figurative—Shakespeare led a life of Allegory: his works are the comments on it" (*The Selected Letters of John Keats*, selected Lionel Trilling [New York: Doubleday Anchor, 1951], 229); rather extravagantly, one set of critics praises or blames Plath's suicidal intensity, tracing an allegorical, psychodramatic, even melodramatic relation between life and art. More conservatively, the second set explains or analyzes her stylistic influences, tracing a somewhat less problematic though still allegorical relation between art and art. For the first group, see, e.g., Denis Donoghue, in

New York Times Book Review, 22 November 1981, 1, 30; David Holbrook, *Sylvia Plath: Poetry and Existence* (London: Athlone, 1976), 131; Hugh Kenner, "Sincerity Kills," in *Sylvia Plath: New Views on the Poetry,* ed. Gary Lane (Baltimore: Johns Hopkins University Press, 1979), 42–44; Marjorie Perloff, "Sylvia Plath's 'Sivvy' Poems: A Portrait of the Poet as Daughter," in ibid., 173. For the second, see Judith Kroll, *Chapters in a Mythology: The Poetry of Sylvia Plath* (New York: Harper, 1976); Gary Lane, "Influence and Originality in Plath's Poems," in *Plath: New Views;* Margaret Dickie Uroff, *Sylvia Plath and Ted Hughes* (Urbana: University of Illinois Press, 1979); John Frederick Nims, "The Poetry of Sylvia Plath," in *Ariel Ascending,* 46–60.

11 See Pope, Gay, and Arbuthnot, *Three Hours after Marriage* (Ann Arbor, Mich.: UMI, 1978).

12 "Mob of scribbling women": see Nathaniel Hawthorne, quoted in Caroline Ticknor, *Hawthorne and His Publishers* (Boston: Houghton Mifflin, 1913), 142. For a more detailed discussion of these literary battles, see our *War of the Words,* chaps. 2 and 3.

13 Plath, quoted in Lois Ames, "Notes toward a Biography," in *The Art of Sylvia Plath,* ed. Charles Newman (Bloomington: Indiana University Press, 1971), 166.

14 Arnold, "The Forsaken Merman," in *The Portable Matthew Arnold,* ed. Lionel Trilling (New York: Viking, 1959), 62.

15 See Yeats, *Collected Poems:* "No Second Troy" (89); "To Dorothy Wellesley" (301–02); "Nineteen Hundred and Nineteen" (204–08).

16 Yeats, "On a Political Prisoner," "In Memory of Eva Gore-Booth and Con Markiewicz," "On Woman," and "A Prayer for My Daughter," *Collected Poems,* 181, 229, 144, 186.

17 Langdon-Davies, quoted in Aurelia Plath's introduction to *LH,* 32–33.

18 Katherine Stern, unpublished paper; Judith Kroll, *Chapters,* passim.

19 Hughes, "Sylvia Plath and Her Journals," in *Ariel Ascending,* 155; Yeats said in *A Vision* (New York: Collier, 1956) that his "ghostly instructors" came to bring him "metaphors for poetry" (8).

20 Interestingly, Nancy Hunter Steiner locates the origins of *The Bell Jar*'s bloody and wounding devirgination episode in a real event that took place when she and Plath were attending Harvard Summer School in 1955, and Plath began to hemorrhage after a sexual experience, implying that sex itself was ontologically wounding. See Nancy Hunter Steiner, *A Closer Look at Ariel: A Memory of Sylvia Plath* (New York: Harper's Magazine Press, 1972), 64–67.

21 For the significance of these references, see Hughes's early poems "The Thought Fox" and "Pike," in Ted Hughes, *New Selected Poems* (New York: Harper, 1982), 1, 47–48.

22 See Suzanne Juhasz, "The Double Bind of the Woman Poet," *Naked and Fiery Forms: Modern American Poetry by Women, A New Tradition* (New York: Octagon, 1978), 1–6; see also E. M. Forster, *Howards End* (New York: Vintage, 1954).

23 Lawrence, "The Woman Who Rode Away," *The Complete Short Stories* (New York: Viking, 1961), 2:581, 569.

24 Plath, *The Bell Jar* (New York: Bantam Books, 1972), 68. All further references will be to this edition, and page numbers will appear in the text after the abbreviation *BJ* where necessary.

25 For a more detailed discussion of this passage from a slightly different perspective, see our *War of the Words,* chap. 5.

26 For Woolf's comments on *The Waves* as a "play-poem," see *WD,* 139. In this chapter, references to *The Waves* will be to *Jacob's Room and The Waves* (New York: Harvest, 1959) and page numbers will appear in the text after the abbreviation *W* where necessary.

27 Hardwick, "On Sylvia Plath," 115.

28 Yeats, *Collected Poems,* 254, 251, 254, 335.

29 Yeats, "Two Songs from a Play," *Collected Poems*, 210–11.

30 Yeats, "A Prayer for My Son" and "A Prayer for My Daughter," *Collected Poems*, 212, 188–90.

31 Interestingly, some of Plath's key female precursors had comparable feelings about Yeats. Dorothy Richardson, for instance, wrote in *The Trap* about Yeats's symbolic significance: associating the poet's image with the thunder and lightning Plath connected with her own lover/rival Hughes, Richardson remarked of Dorothy/Miriam's experience with Yeats, that "as the thunder rolled bumping and snarling away across the / sky, they saw the figure of a man appear from the darkness / . . . . A brilliant flash lit up the white face and its / frame of heavy hair. . . . / Yeats: and he lived here. . . . all the time his presence / would cast its light upon their frontage" (in Richardson, *Pilgrimage*, vol. 2 [New York: Knopf, 1938]); on *The Oresteia*, see Sandra M. Gilbert, "Life's Empty Pack: Notes toward a Literary Daughteronomy," *Critical Inquiry* 11:3 (1985): 365, 369, 375–76.

32 Not only had Plath earlier boasted, as we have seen, that she was "younger than Yeats in [her] saying," she had also claimed that she would find "images of life: like Woolf found. But . . . I will be stronger" (*J* 165). In fact, some of her most rivalrous comments about Woolf were made in the context of a reading of *The Waves:* "I underlined & underlined: re-read that," she confessed to her journal, but then added "I shall go better than she" (164).

33 Kenner, "Sincerity Kills," 42.

34 Nims, "The Poetry of Sylvia Plath," in *Ariel Ascending*, 46–60. In rimas dissolutas, each line rhymes with the corresponding lines of all other stanzas.

35 Nims, "Poetry of Plath"; McPherson, "The Working Line," in *A Field Guide to Contemporary Poetry and Poetics*, ed. Stuart Friebert and David Young (New York: Longman, 1980), 59.

36 Hall, "The Line," in *Field Guide to Contemporary Poetry*, 75.

37 Coleridge, "Kubla Khan" (1816), in *The Portable Coleridge*, ed. I. A. Richards (New York: Viking, 1950), 156–57.

38 In a different connection, Nims insightfully discusses Plath's use of what he calls "ghost rhyme"; see "Poetry of Plath," 52.

39 Yeats, "Adam's Curse," *Collected Poems*, 78.

40 Hughes, "Plath and Her Journals," 162.

41 Ibid., 161–62.

42 Plath had undertaken to produce a series of poems on paintings, including Giorgio De Chirico's "The Disquieting Muses," for *Art News*. Other poems in the same series include "On the Decline of Oracles" (based on the painting "The Enigma of Oracle," by De Chirico), "Snakecharmer" (after a painting by Douanier Rousseau), "Yadwigha, on a Red Couch, among Lilies: A Sestina for the Douanier" (based on the painting "The Dream," also by Rousseau), "Virgin in a Tree" (after an etching by Paul Klee), "Perseus: The Triumph of Wit over Suffering" (also inspired by an etching by Klee, "Perseus, of the Triumph of Wit over Suffering"), "Battle Scene: From the Comic Operatic Fantasy 'The Seafarer'" (after Klee's painting, "The Seafarer"), and "The Ghost's Leavetaking" (from "The Departure of the Ghost," a painting by Klee).

43 The drafts of "Daddy," along with most of the other *Ariel* drafts, are held by the Smith College Library. "Daddy" is a particularly interesting work to study, since its composition was unusually swift in comparison to the composition of, say, "Elm"; the final stanza of "Daddy," however, was added after the body of the poem had evidently emerged in a rush of inspiration.

44 Lynda K. Bundtzen, *Plath's Incarnations: Woman and the Creative Process* (Ann Arbor: University of Michigan Press, 1983), 91. See also Sister Bernetta Quinn, "Medusan

imagery in Sylvia Plath," in *Plath: New Views*, 98: "Several scholars have called attention to another name for the common medusa, *Aurelia aulita*—moon jellyfish—the first element suggesting Sylvia's mother, Aurelia Schober Plath, and the second lunar symbolism." Although our final interpretation of the poem is somewhat different from hers, Quinn's attentive and patient analysis of "Medusa" is still the most brilliant reading of all the details of this difficult text.

45 For an incisive discussion of this point, see Joanne Feit Diehl, *Women Poets and the American Sublime* (Bloomington: Indiana University Press, 1990), 130.

46 To such definitional bravura the narrator of "By Candlelight" adds a brilliant double entendre, as she defines the season, the darkness, and her situation: "*This is* winter, this is night, small love" (*PCP* 236). (Does the phrase "small love" refer to the child she is addressing or to her own dilemma—i.e., "This is winter, this is night, [this is] small love"?)

47 Plath, radio interview on BBC, 31 October 1962, cited in Linda Wagner-Martin, *Sylvia Plath: A Biography* (New York: Simon and Schuster, 1987), 224.

48 For an analysis of this point from a slightly different perspective, see Gilbert, "Fine, White, Flying Myth."

49 See Diehl, *Women Poets*, 138, and Van Dyne, *Revising Life*.

50 See John, 11:1–45; in her poem, Plath follows the contours of the biblical story very closely in a number of ways.

51 Cixous, "Sorties," in Cixous and Catherine Clément, *The Newly Born Woman*, trans. Betsy Wing (Minneapolis: University of Minnesota Press, 1986), 95.

52 See Otto Plath as "scapegoat" and consider biology of bees as well as "dead man" in first draft.

53 See Susan Van Dyne's useful analysis of the drafts of the bee sequence in *Revising Life*, 98–115. The brackets are Van Dyne's, indicating Plath's deletions. We are grateful to Van Dyne for sharing much of this material with us when it was still in manuscript.

54 For a now classic and influential discussion of the circumstances of Plath's suicide, see A. Alvarez, "Sylvia Plath," in *The Art of Sylvia Plath: A Symposium*, ed. Charles Newman (Bloomington: Indiana University Press, 1978), 56–68.

55 Hughes, "Plath and Her Journals," 164.

56 Berryman, *The Dream Songs* (New York: Farrar, Straus, 1974), 206; Lowell, "Sylvia Plath," *History* (New York: Farrar, Straus, 1973), 135. For a more detailed discussion of these comments, see our *War of the Words*, chap. 3.

57 Hughes, *Cadenza, Wodwo* (London: Faber, 1967), 20.

58 Faas, *Ted Hughes: The Unaccommodated Universe* (Santa Barbara: Black Sparrow, 1980), 11 and passim.

59 Hughes, *Gaudete* (New York: Harper, 1977), 186. A. Alvarez comments on what appears to be this scene in "Sylvia Plath" (212). Because of the eventual suicide of Hughes's second wife, Assia Gutman (and also, of course, because of the highly mythologized nature of his own determinedly nonconfessional poetry), it is not possible to identify autobiographical references in his work with any real certainty. But Faas, on the evidence and chronology and allusion, makes a convincing case for the symbolic significance of Plath in Hughes's imagination, as does Stuart Hirschberg in *Myth in the Poetry of Ted Hughes* (Totowa, N.J.: Barnes and Noble, 1981).

60 Hughes, *Gaudete*, 189, 191. Hughes's "Bite. Again, bite" is strikingly reminiscent of Joyce's "agenbite of inwit," his phrase for the remorse that Stephen Dedalus suffers over his treatment of his dying mother. For what is perhaps Hughes's most poignant and personal elegy for Plath, see "You Hated Spain" (1979), *New Selected Poems*, 131–32.

61 Hughes, "Lovesong," *New Selected Poems*, 123–24. See esp. "His kisses sucked out her

whole past and future or tried to / He had no other appetite / She bit him she gnawed him she sucked . . . . Her smiles were spider bites." For a more detailed discussion of "Lovesong," see our *War of the Words*, chap. 1.

62 Rich, "When We Dead Awaken: Writing as Re-Vision" (1971), in Rich, *On Lies, Secrets, and Silence: Selected Prose, 1966–1978* (New York: Norton, 1979), 36. Further references will be to this edition, and page numbers will appear in the text after the abbreviation *L* where necessary.

63 Sexton, "Sylvia's Death," in Sexton, *The Complete Poems* (Boston: Houghton Mifflin, 1981), 126–27. Further references to Sexton's work will be to this edition, and page numbers will appear in the text after the abbreviation *SCP* where necessary.

64 Jong, "Alcestis on the Poetry Circuit," *Half-Lives* (New York: Holt, Rinehart, and Winston, 1971), 25–26.

65 Oates, "The Death Throes of Romanticism: The Poetry of Sylvia Plath," *New Heaven, New Earth: The Visionary Experience in Literature* (New York: Fawcett, 1974), 114. See also Oates's comment, later in the same essay, that "the experience of reading [Plath's] poems deeply is a frightening one: it is like waking to discover one's adult self, grown to full height, crouched in some long-forgotten childhood hiding place, one's heart pounding senselessly, all the old rejected transparent beasts and monsters crawling out of the wallpaper" (120).

66 Rich, "Snapshots of a Daughter-in-Law" (1958–60), *The Fact of a Doorframe: Poems Selected and New, 1950–1984* (New York: Norton, 1984), 38. Unless otherwise noted, further references to Rich's poetry will be to this edition, and page numbers will appear in the text after the abbreviation *F* where necessary; Kizer, "Pro Femina, Three" (1963, 1965), *Mermaids in the Basement: Poems for Women* (Port Townsend, Wash.: Copper Canyon Press, 1984), 43; Salter, "A Poem of One's Own," *New Republic*, 4 March 1991, 31.

67 Kizer, "Pro Femina, Two," *Mermaid*, 42 (for a more extended discussion of literary women's overt battles against, or contempt for, male rivals, see our *War of the Words*, chap. 4); Salter, "Poem of One's Own," 32.

68 There is no space here to review the reciprocal stylistic influences between the two poets, but they were of course manifold.

69 To be sure, in the context of Sexton's oeuvre (and her life), as indeed in Plath's, such a swallowing—especially of pills—can imply a delivery/rebirth into death.

70 For a discussion of Sexton's reading in the absence of "a traditional education in Donne, Milton, Yeats, Eliot, and Pound," see Maxine Kumin, "How It Was," foreword to *SCP*, xxvii–xxviii.

71 While the two men watch—dying and thinking "'This is the last of a man like me'"— "over the mists / of Venus, two fish creatures stop / on spangled legs and crawl / from the belly of the sea. / And from the planet park / they heard the new fruit drop" (*SCP* 15).

72 For a more extensive discussion of witchcraft and the female imagination, see our *War of the Words*, chap. 5.

73 Levertov, "Song for Ishtar," in Levertov, *Poems: 1960–1967* (New York: New Directions, 1983), 75. Unless otherwise noted, further references to Levertov's poems will be to this edition, and page numbers will appear in the text after the abbreviation *LP* where necessary.

74 But consider the rage implicit in Levertov's depiction of a "white sweating bull of a poet" who "told us // our cunts are ugly" ("Hypocrite Women," *LP* 142).

75 Wakoski, "Poem to the Man on My Fire Escape," *Trilogy: Coins and Coffins, Discrepancies and Apparitions, The George Washington Poems* (Garden City, N.Y.: Doubleday, 1974), 26. Unless otherwise noted, further references to Wakoski's poems will be to this edition, and page numbers will appear in the text.

76 Wakoski, "Looking for a Sign on the Fulham Road (The Star)," *Inside the Blood Factory* (Garden City, N.Y.: Doubleday, 1968), 78.

77 Auden, introduction to Adrienne Rich, *A Change of World* (New Haven: Yale University Press, 1951), 11.

78 For further discussion of Rich's "move away from painstaking imitation," see Diehl, *Women Poets*, 142.

79 De Beauvoir, *The Second Sex*, trans. H. M. Parshley (1949; New York: 1953), 729.

80 For the wind as a Romantic metaphor for inspiration, see M. H. Abrams's classic "The Correspondent Breeze: A Romantic Metaphor," in *English Romantic Poets: Modern Essays in Criticism*, ed. M. H. Abrams (New York: Oxford University Press, 1960), 37–54; Rich comments on her feelings about (and sometime indebtedness to) Shelley and Lawrence in "Three Conversations," in *Adrienne Rich's Poetry*, ed. Barbara Charlesworth Gelpi and Albert Gelpi (New York: Norton, 1975), 112–17.

81 Diehl, *Women Poets*, 142.

82 Rich, "The Phenomenology of Anger," *Diving into the Wreck: Poems 1971–72* (New York: Norton, 1973), 27–31.

83 Diehl, *Women Poets*, 160. Diehl begins by observing: "Like Whitman, Rich grounds the work of her empathic imagination in a homoeroticism that confirms the power of bodily sensation" (160).

84 Among Rich's most Whitmanesque poems are the relatively early "From an Old House in America" (Rich, *Poetry*,) and—especially—"An Atlas of the Difficult World," *An Atlas of the Difficult World* (New York: Norton, 1991), 3–26.

85 Rich, *Of Woman Born: Motherhood as Experience and Institution* (New York: Norton, 1976), 282, 285–86.

86 Lowell, foreword to *Ariel*, vii.

87 It is significant that such speculations are seldom offered in the comparable cases of such male artists as Hart Crane, Ernest Hemingway, Randall Jarrell, and John Berryman.

88 Plath also considered as possible titles "The Rival" and "A Birthday Present," both of which focus on competitive violence and (given the nature of the poem "A Birthday Present") suicidal desire.

89 We are grateful to Bob Griffin for drawing this point to our attention, and for a number of helpful discussions of *The Tempest*.

90 See Van Dyne's discussion of Godiva/God's lioness in *Revising Life*.

91 Shakespeare, *The Tempest*, ed. Frank Kermode. Arden Shakespeare (New York: Routledge, 1954), 143.

Chapter 7: Lives of the Male Male Impersonator

Epigraphs: Hughes, "A Note on Humor," in *The Book of Negro Humor*, ed. Langston Hughes (New York: Dodd, Mead, 1966), vii; Russ, "Dear Colleague: I Am Not an Honorary Male," in *Pulling Our Own Strings*, ed. Gloria Kaufman and Mary Kay Blakely (Bloomington: Indiana University Press, 1980), 180; Irigaray, "Questions," *This Sex Which Is Not One*, trans. by Catherine Porter with Carolyn Burke (Ithaca: Cornell University Press, 1985), 163.

1 Vonnegut, *Slaughterhouse-Five* (New York: Laurel, 1988), 101.

2 Vonnegut, "Who Am I This Time," *Welcome to the Monkey House: A Collection of Short Works by Kurt Vonnegut, Jr.* (New York: Delacorte Press, 1968), 17, 24. Further references to stories in this collection will be to this edition, and page numbers will appear in the text.

3 See Robert Scholes, *The Fabulators* (New York: Oxford University Press, 1967); as well as Charles B. Harris, *Contemporary American Novelists of the Absurd* (New Haven: College and University Press, 1971); Morris Dickstein, *Gates of Eden: American Culture in the Sixties* (New York: Basic, 1977); and Raymond Federman, "Self-Reflexive Fiction,"

Columbia Literary History of the United States, ed. Emory Elliot (New York: Columbia University Press, 1988), 1142–57.

4 Three publications that reflect the critical attention women's comedy has received from feminist critics: *Last Laughs: Perspectives on Women and Comedy*, ed. Regina Barreca (New York: Gordon and Breach, 1988); Nancy A. Walker, *A Very Serious Thing: Women's Humor and American Culture* (Minneapolis: University of Minnesota Press, 1988); *Redressing the Balance: American Women's Literary Humor from Colonial Times to the 1980s*, ed. Nancy Walker and Zita Dresner (Jackson: University Press of Mississippi, 1988). On the disparity between women's use of realism as opposed to men's "dazzling pyrotechnics," see Gayle Greene, *Changing the Story: Feminist Fiction and the Tradition* (Bloomington: Indiana University Press, 1991), 3 and 19.

5 See, for example, Barbara Ehrenreich, Elizabeth Hess, and Gloria Jacobs, *Re-Making Love: The Feminization of Sex* (Garden City, N. Y.: Anchor, 1987), esp. 67–73.

6 Miller, *Tropic of Capricorn* (London: John Calder, 1964), 171. We are indebted to Rolande Diot's discussion of Miller in "Sexus, Nexus and Taboos versus Female Humor: The Case of Erica Jong," *Revue Française d'Etudes Américaines* 30 (1986): 491–99.

7 Miller, ibid.; Cixous and Clément, *The Newly Born Woman*, trans. Betsy Wing (Minneapolis: University of Minnesota Press, 1986), 33, 68–69; Kristeva, *Revolution in Poetic Language* (New York: Columbia University Press, 1984), 224.

8 For background on laughter and aggression, see Regenia Gagnier, "Between Women: A Cross-Class Analysis of Status and Anarchic Humor," in *Last Laughs*, 135–46.

9 Heller, *Something Happened* (New York: Knopf, 1974), 369. Further references will be to this edition, and page numbers will appear in the text.

10 Throughout this chapter, we will refer to and revise the brief discussion of "female castration" that appears in Freud's "Female Sexuality" ("FS" 194–211, esp. the passage on 198). An extended discussion of the literary implications of Freud's essay appears in Gilbert and Gubar, *No Man's Land: The Place of the Woman Writer in the Twentieth Century*, vol. 1: *The War of the Words* (New Haven: Yale University Press, 1988), chap. 4.

11 Gallop's remark pertains to her discussion of male theorists who dephallicize modernism so as to appear "current" by "trying to be not male" (*Thinking through the Body* [New York: Columbia University Press, 1988], 100).

12 Federman, "Self-Reflexive Fiction," p. 1142.

13 Hendin, *Vulnerable People: A View of American Fiction Since 1945* (New York: Oxford University Press, 1978), 14–15. On the impact of existentialism on the sexualization of culture, see Ihab Hassan, *Radical Innocence: Studies in the Contemporary American Novel* (Princeton: Princeton University Press, 1961), 68–69. On the influence of sexologists like Weilhelm Reich and Lawrence Lipton, see Charles I. Glicksberg, *The Sexual Revolution in Modern American Literature* (The Hague: Martinus Nijhoff, 1971), 230–32.

14 Vonnegut's satire on women presidents and Ph.D.s takes on a more sinister light in terms of his comment, "Educating a woman is like pouring honey over a fine Swiss watch. It stops working," quoted in *Words on Women: Quotes by Famous Americans*, ed. Evelyn L. Belenson and Sharon Melnick (White Plains, N.Y.: Peter Pauper, 1987), 25.

15 Doane and Hodges, *Nostalgia and Sexual Difference: The Resistance to Contemporary Feminism* (New York: Methuen, 1987), 10–11. Throughout the self-reflexive comedies of the fabulators, women's art is associated with kitsch, nostalgia, sentimentality, or degraded commercialism.

16 Dahl, "Bitch," *Switch Bitch* (New York: Knopf, 1974), 9, 174. Further references will be to this edition, and page numbers will appear in the text.

17 In this regard, it is interesting to note that Dahl's children's books, *James and the Giant Peach* and *Charlie and the Chocolate Factory*, as well as his horror stories, focus on issues of endangered masculinity. For background on Dahl's contribution to horror fiction, see Alan Warren, "Roald Dahl: Nasty, Nasty," in *Discovering Modern Horror Fiction*, ed.

Darrell Schweitzer (San Bernardino, Calif.: Borgo, 1986), 120–28. A number of stories discussed in this essay—including "Lamb to the Slaughter" and "William and Mary"—directly address the issue of the battle between the sexes.

18 Ehrenreich, *The Hearts of Men: American Dreams and the Flight from Commitment* (Garden City, N. Y.: Anchor, 1983), 67–84; Lemuel C. McGee, "The Suicidal Cult of 'Manliness,'" *Today's Health* 35:1 (1957): 28; Goldberg, *The Hazards of Being Male: Surviving the Myth of Masculine Privilege* (New York: New American Library, 1976), 172; Anne Steinmann and David J. Fox, *The Male Dilemma: How to Survive the Sexual Revolution* (New York: Jason Aronson, 1974), 3. We are indebted to Lori Landay for bringing this text to our attention.

19 "No such limitation": see David R. Reuben, *Everything You Always Wanted to Know about Sex, But Were Afraid to Ask* (New York: David McKay, 1970), 38; Ruitenbeek, *The New Sexuality* (1974), and Stekel, *Impotence in the Male* (1971), quoted in Paul Hoch, *White Hero Black Beast: Racism, Sexism and the Mask of Masculinity* (London: Pluto, 1979), 19, 65; Sherfey, "A Theory of Female Sexuality," in *Sisterhood Is Powerful*, ed. Robin Morgan (New York: Vintage, 1970), 220–21; Brown, *Sex and the Single Girl* (New York: Random House, 1962); Koedt, "The Myth of the Vaginal Orgasm," in *Notes from the Second Year: Women, Liberation, Major Writings of the Radical Feminists*, ed. Anne Koedt and Shulamith Firestone (New York: Radical Feminism, 1970); Friday, *My Secret Garden* (New York: Pocket, 1974). See also Ehrenreich, Hess, Jacobs, *Re-Making Love*, 74–99.

20 Cooper, *Grammar of Living* (New York: Pantheon, 1974), 52–53. See the useful discussion of sexology in Stephen Heath, *The Sexual Fix* (New York: Schocken, 1984), esp. chap. 6: "The Erotic Path to the 'Big O.'"

21 Reuben, *Everything*, 5–6.

22 Mercer, "A Suitable Case for Treatment," *Collected T.V. Plays*, vol. 2 (London: John Calder, 1982), 43. Further references will be to this edition, and page numbers will appear in the text.

23 On the significance of rape in the novels of Kesey and Purdy, see Mary Allen, *The Necessary Blankness: Women in Major American Fiction of the Sixties* (Urbana: University of Illinois Press, 1976), 58–69. In his interpretation of Purdy's novel, Tony Tanner argues that the motive for Cabot's repeated rapes is desire for "an emancipation—a stepping out of the stuffy library room full of word-patterns into the refreshing liberation of the empty room and speechless physical contact" (*City of Words: American Fiction 1950–1970* [New York: Harper and Row, 1971], 100).

24 Roth, *Portnoy's Complaint* (New York: Random House, 1969); Donleavy, *The Ginger Man* (New York: Delacorte, 1965).

25 Hassan, *Radical Innocence*, 61, 69; Schulz, *Black Humor Fiction of the Sixties: A Pluralistic Definition of Man and His World* (Athens: Ohio University Press, 1973), 10.

26 Barth, "The Literature of Exhaustion," *Atlantic*, August 1967, 30, 32, 33.

27 Barth, *The Sot-Weed Factor* (Garden City, N. Y.: Anchor, 1987), 569–73.

28 Barth, *Lost in the Funhouse* (New York: Doubleday, 1988), 112, 120.

29 Vonnegut, introduction to *Mother Night* (New York: Dell, 1966), v.

30 Gold, "The Beat Mystique" (1958), in *The Beats*, ed. Seymour Krim (Greenwich, Conn.: Gold Medal, 1960), 161. A different perspective is provided in the same collection by David McReynolds, who defends the "greater freedom" in sexual relations of the "hipster," noting that it reflects the "sudden equality of the sexes" ("Hipsters Unleashed"), 207, 204. More critically, Norman Podhoretz argues that the beats believed "performance and 'good orgasms'. . . [were] the first duty of man and the only duty of woman" ("The Know-Nothing Bohemians" (1958), ibid., 117), a point illuminated by Gold's condemnation of Kerouac and his followers for keeping "score of [their] heroes' erotic blitzes, forgetting that—if you are the trooper who uses sex as a weapon—every notch in a weapon weakens the weapon" ("Beat Mystique," 163).

31 Goodman, *Growing up Absurd* (New York: Vintage, 1960), 185.

32 Emerson, "Self-Reliance" (1841), in *Essays and Lectures,* ed. Joel Porte (New York: Library of America, 1983), 261.

33 Ginsberg, "Wichita Vortex Sutra" (1968), *Collected Poems 1947–1980* (New York: Harper and Row, 1984), 395; Neal Cassady is described as "a sainted cocksman" in Ginsberg, *Howl, Collected Poems,* 128; Ferlinghetti, "[Frightened]," *A Coney Island of the Mind* (New York: New Directions, 1958), 33; Burroughs, quoted in John Tytell, *Naked Angels: The Lives and Literature of the Beat Generation* (New York: McGraw-Hill, 1976), 203, 205.

34 Ginsberg, "Who Be Kind To," *Collected Poems,* 362.

35 Ginsberg, "The Archetype Poem," *Collected Poems,* 61–62.

36 Sedgwick, *Between Men: English Literature and Male Homosocial Desire* (New York: Columbia University Press, 1985), 89. See also Sedgwick's *Epistemology of the Closet* (Berkeley: University of California Press, 1990), 15 and 19.

37 Mailer, *The White Negro* (San Francisco: City Lights Books, 1957), 6. See also Mailer's claim that "the hipster had absorbed the existentialist synapses of the Negro, and for practical purposes could be considered a white Negro" (4).

38 Dickstein, *Gates of Eden,* 169.

39 Brown, *The Life and Loves of Mr. Jiveass Nigger* (New York: Farrar, Straus, and Giroux, 1969), 22–23, 203; Wright, *The Wig* (New York: Manor, 1966), 90, 89. Also see the discussion of this novel in Schulz, *Black Humor Fiction of the Sixties,* 108–09.

40 Shapiro, *Edsel* (New York: Bernard Geis Associates, 1971), 4.

41 Elkin, *The Making of Ashenden* (London: Covent Garden Press, 1972), 4. Further references will be to this edition, and page numbers will appear in the text. A different meditation on why and how human beings should turn to the beasts for an education occurs in Saul Bellow, *Henderson the Rain King* (1958): see Helen Weinberg, *The New Novel in America: The Kafkan Mode in Contemporary Fiction* (Ithaca: Cornell University Press, 1970), 88–98. For a fantasy of a woman mating with a bear, see Marian Engel's more lyrical, less comic *Bear* (New York: Atheneum, 1976).

42 Hite, *The Hite Report: A Nationwide Study of Female Sexuality* (New York: Dell, 1977), 459, 465. See also Christopher Lasch, *The Culture of Narcissism* (New York: Warner, 1979), 196; "they are not inferior": see Marlene Dixon, "Women's Liberation" (1969), in *America in the Sixties,* ed. Ronald Lora (New York: Wiley, 1974), 308.

43 Pynchon, *V.* (New York: Lippincott, 1963), 385. V. is linked by Bernard Bergonzi to the eponymous heroine of Marshall McLuhan's *The Mechanical Bride* (1951) and by R. W. B. Lewis to D. H. Lawrence's Gudrun Brangwen, "a new Daphne, turning not into a tree but a machine": see Bergonzi, *The Situation of the Novel* (London: Macmillan, 1970), 99; Lewis, "Days of Wrath and Laughter," *Trials of the Word: Essays in American Literature and the Humanistic Tradition* (New Haven: Yale University Press, 1965), 231. On Cold War paranoia in *V.,* see Schultz, *Black Humor Fiction of the Sixties,* 78–79.

44 An early piece of science fiction represents the robot Helen—composed of alloyed metals, chemical endocrines, and rubber—as her creator's ideal mate; "No woman ever made a lovelier bride or a sweeter wife" (Lester del Rey, "Helen of O'Loy" [1938], in *The Science Fiction Hall of Fame,* vol. 1, ed. Robert Silverberg [New York: Avon, 1970], 72). In contrast to del Rey's science-fiction version of the Pygmalion story, C. L. Moore's "No Woman Born" (1944) describes the constructed female not in terms of male delight but in relation to women's fantasies, for her metallic, constructed heroine defies her creators: *The Best of C. L. Moore,* ed. Lester del Rey (New York: Ballantine, 1975), 243. On surrealism and pornography, see Susan Gubar, "Representing Pornography: Feminism, Criticism, and Depictions of Female Violation," in *For Adult Users Only: The Dilemma of Violent Pornography,* ed. Susan Gubar and Joan Hoff (Bloomington: Indiana University Press, 1989), 47–67. On photographic and filmed dismemberment of the

female figure, see Annette Kuhn, *The Power of the Image: Essays on Representation and Sexuality* (London: Routledge, 1985), 35–40.

45 Nabokov, *Lolita* (New York: Putnam's, 1955), 46, 289, 64. Further references will be to this edition, and page numbers will appear in the text. Significantly, early in their relationship Lolita shows Humbert a photograph of "a surrealist painter relaxing, supine, on a beach, and near him, likewise supine, a plaster replica of the Venus di Milo, half-buried in sand" (64). It is possible, then, to read this novel as Nabokov's critique of the uses to which the male imagination puts the female/muse.

46 Barthelme, *Snow White* (New York: Atheneum, 1967), 70. Further references will be to this edition, and page numbers will appear in the text. Useful background information on this novel is provided by Lois Gordon, *Donald Barthelme* (Boston: Twayne Publishers, 1981), 62–83; Dickstein, *Gates of Eden*, 243; Lasch, *Culture of Narcissism*, 263; and Maurice Couturier and Regis Durand, *Donald Barthelme* (London: Methuen, 1982), 68.

47 Barthelme, *The Dead Father* (New York: Farrar, Straus, and Giroux, 1975), 1. A refrain that appears throughout first paragraph and page 33. Further references will be to this edition, and page numbers will appear in the text. We are indebted to Joan Hope for bringing this book to our attention.

48 Coover, "A Theological Position" (with Gail Godwin), in Coover, *A Theological Position* (New York: Dutton, 1972), 155, 161. Further references will be to this edition, and page numbers will appear in the text.

49 Weeks, *Sexuality and Its Discontents* (London: Routledge, 1985), 5. We are suggesting that Gershon Legman's belief that women's hostility toward the penis cannot be found in jokes "since jokes are primarily invented by men" no longer holds true during the sexual revolution: see *Rationale of the Dirty Joke* (New York: Grove, 1968), 1:331. During the second wave of the women's movement, both sexes devised jokes to handle the fallout from heightened sex antagonism. See Allan Dundes, *Cracking Jokes: Studies of Sick Humor Cycles and Stereotypes* (Berkeley: Ten Speed, 1987), 82–95.

50 M. Hite, *The Other Side of the Story* (Ithaca: Cornell University Press, 1989), 14.

51 Atwood, "Writing the Male Character" (1982), *Second Words: Selected Critical Prose* (Toronto: Anansi, 1982), 413.

52 See the discussion of Woolf's contribution to comedy in Judy Little, *Comedy and the Woman Writer: Woolf, Spark, and Feminism* (Lincoln: University of Nebraska Press, 1983), 7.

53 We discuss Austen's comedy in chapters 4 and 5 of Gilbert and Gubar, *The Madwoman in the Attic: The Woman Writer and the Nineteenth-Century Literary Imagination* (New Haven: Yale University Press, 1979); West's comic story "Indissoluble Matrimony" is analyzed in our *War of the Words*, 96–100; for Millay's and Hurston's humor, see Chapters 2 and 3 of this volume; Jong, *Fear of Flying* (New York: New American Library, 1973), 101. Further references will be to this edition, and page numbers will appear in the text; Jong, "The Artist as Housewife/The Housewife as Artist" (1972), *Here Comes & Other Poems* (New York: New American Library, 1975), 262. See also Emily Toth, "Dorothy Parker, Erica Jong, and New Feminist Humor," *Regionalism and the Female Imagination* 2 and 3 (1977–78): 70–85. This special double issue on female humor provides useful background information on gender and comedy.

54 Apte, *Humor and Laughter: An Anthropological Approach* (Ithaca: Cornell University Press, 1985), 67–81.

55 Marie Severin, cover, *Ms.*, November 1983. Nancy A. Walker discusses gender bias in relation to humor as a masculine trait: see *Very Serious Thing*, 74 and 83. Also see *Last Laughs*, 4. Significantly, the word *satire* has often mistakenly been thought to derive from *satyr*, the lusty god dedicated to Bacchus.

56 Dworkin, *Ice and Fire* (New York: Weidenfeld and Nicolson, 1986), 110. For background on the journals mentioned, see Todd Gitlin, *The Sixties: Years of Hope, Days of Rage* (New

York: Bantam, 1987), 371–72, and Silvia Federici, "Putting Feminism Back on its Feet," in *The 60s without Apology*, ed. Sohnya Sayres, Anders Stephanson, Stanley Aronowitz, and Fredric Jameson (Minneapolis: University of Minnesota Press, 1985), 344–45.
57 Weisstein, "Why We Aren't Laughing . . . Anymore," *Ms.*, November 1973, 49–51; Habegger, *Gender, Fantasy, Realism* (New York: Columbia University Press, 1982), 117.
58 Walker, *Very Serious Thing*, ix; Walker and Dresner, *Redressing the Balance: American Women's Literary Humor from Colonial Times to the 1980s* (Jackson: University Press of Mississippi (1988). See esp. their useful introduction.
59 Barth, "Literature of Exhaustion," 30.
60 Meredith, "The Idea of Comedy" (1877), in *Comedy: An Essay on Comedy, by George Meredith, and Laughter, by Henri Bergson*, ed. Wylie Sypher (Baltimore: Johns Hopkins University Press, 1980), 32.
61 Stitzel, "Humor and Survival in the Works of Doris Lessing," *Regionalism and the Female Imagination* 4:2 (1978): 61–68. Commentators on Jewish humor have made a comparable point; Joseph Boskin, "Beyond *Kvetching* and *Jiving:* The Thrust of Jewish and Black Folkhumor," in *Jewish Wry: Essays on Jewish Humor*, ed. Sarah Blacher Cohen (Bloomington: Indiana University Press, 1987), 60–62.
62 Lessing, *The Golden Notebook* (New York: Bantam, 1979), 488.
63 Drabble, *The Middle Ground* (New York: Ivy, 1980), 18.
64 Bromberg, "The Two Faces of the Mirror in *The Edible Woman* and *Lady Oracle*," in *Margaret Atwood: Vision and Forms*, ed. Kathryn VanSpanckeren and Jan Garden Castro (Carbondale: Southern Illinois University Press, 1988), 14.
65 Atwood, *The Edible Woman* (New York: Popular Library, 1976), 279. Further references will be to this edition, and page numbers will appear in the text.
66 Oppenheim's work is discussed in Sarane Alexandrian, *Surrealist Art* (London: Thames and Hudson, 1970), 90, 145, and 150. A contemporary of Atwood's, Patricia Goedicke, presents the female persona of her poem "Sprinkle Me, Just" as "adjusting a chocolate and straw- / berry ice-cream tit" and "sitting here on your juicy plate / like a stack of puffy pancakes," but she warns, "I'm not pressure cooked for nothing": EAT ME but watch out, / nothing I do is true" (*Psyche: The Feminine Poetic Consciousness*, ed. Barbara Segnitz and Carol Rainey [New York: Dell, 1973], 163). In her written work, Judy Chicago has also ridiculed the fetishization of body parts: see her "Cock and Cunt," *Through the Flower: My Struggle as a Woman Artist* (New York: Doubleday, 1975), 208–13. In "Woman's House Kitchen," Chicago and her collaborators positioned sliced-off women's breasts as wall hangings to symbolize (the cost of) female nurturance and the sexual division of labor.
67 Russ, "Window Dressing," in *The New Women's Theatre: Ten Plays by Contemporary American Women*, ed. Honor Moore (New York: Vintage, 1977), 61–74. On the commodification of women, see also Cynthia Buchanan, *Maiden* (New York: William Morrow, 1972), and Beth Henley, *The Miss Firecracker Contest* (New York: Dramatists Play Service, 1985).
68 Lessing, *The Summer before the Dark* (New York: Bantam Books, 1973), 60, 65, 112, 67, 102. Further references will be to this edition, and page numbers will appear in the text.
69 Jellicoe, *The Knack* (London: Faber, 1961), 94.
70 McCarthy, *The Group* (New York: Harcourt, Brace, and World, 1963), 130–31.
71 Spark, *The Public Image* (London: Macmillan, 1968), 13, 31. Further references will be to this edition, and page numbers will appear in the text.
72 Schreiner, *The Story of an African Farm* (New York: Schocken, 1976), 175.
73 Dresner, "The Housewife as Humorist," *Regionalism and the Female Imagination* 2 and 3 (1977–78): 29–38. Also see Emily Toth, "A Laughter of Their Own: Women's Humor in the United States," in *Critical Essays on American Humor*, ed. William Bedford Clark and W. Craig Turner (Boston: G. K. Hall, 1984), 207–09. For a discussion of Rivers's "*ad*

hominem insults," see Sarah Blacher Cohen, "The Unkosher Comediennes: From Sophie Tucker to Joan Rivers," in *Jewish Wry*, 119–22.

74 Spark, *The Driver's Seat* (London: Macmillan, 1970), 120, 159.

75 Atwood, *Lady Oracle* (New York: Fawcett Crest, 1976), 347. Further references will be to this edition, and page numbers will appear in the text.

76 Weldon, *The Life and Loves of a She-Devil* (New York: Pantheon, 1983), 6. Further references will be to this edition, and page numbers will appear in the text.

77 Adcock, "Against Coupling," *High Tide in the Garden* (London: Oxford University Press, 1971), 26.

78 Suleiman, "(Re)writing the Body: The Politics and Poetics of Female Eroticism," in *The Female Body in Western Culture: Contemporary Perspectives*, ed. Susan Rubin Suleiman (Cambridge: Harvard University Press, 1986), 8.

79 Brown, *Rubyfruit Jungle* (Plainfield, Vt.: Daughters, 1973), 4–5. Further references will be to this edition, and page numbers will appear in the text. Similar jokes about the penis appear in Sharon Olds, "The Connoisseuse of Slugs" (1983), in *Deep Down: The New Sensual Writing by Women*, ed. Laura Chester (Boston: Faber, 1988), 60, as well as in Alix Shulman, *Memoirs of an Ex-Prom Queen* (New York: Bantam, 1972), 49 and 68, and in Lisa Alther, *Kinflicks* (New York: Knopf, 1975), 59 and 126.

80 Macdonald, "Objets d'Art," *Amputations* (New York: Braziller, 1972), 6.

81 A photograph of Kusama's "One Thousand Boat Show" appears in Lucy Lippard, *From the Center: Feminist Essays on Women's Art* (New York: Dutton, 1976), 78; Gallop, *Thinking through the Body* (New York: Columbia University Press, 1988), 124.

82 Stone, "Cocks and Mares," *Cheap* (New York: Harcourt, Brace, Jovanovich, 1975),54. A number of contemporary women deflate male poseurs by meditating on their devolution into animals. See, for instance, Judith Rechter, "FayWray to the King," in *No More Masks!* ed. Florence Howe and Ellen Bass (Garden City, N. Y.: Anchor, 1973), 257; Mona Van Duyn, "Leda," in ibid., 129; Kathleen Fraser, "Bestiality . . . (from The Leda Notebooks)" (1987), in *Deep Down*, 194; Margaret Atwood, *You Are Happy* (New York: Harper and Row, 1974), 47–48; and Jeanette Winterson, *Oranges Are Not the Only Fruit* (London: Pandora, 1985), 72–73.

83 Mandrell, "Questions of Genre and Gender: Contemporary American Versions of the Feminine Picaresque," *Novel* 20:2 (1987): 156.

84 Jong, *Fanny: Being that True History of the Adventures of Fanny Hackabout-Jones* (New York: New American Library, 1980), 175. Further references will be to this edition, and page numbers will appear in the text.

85 Oates, *A Bloodsmoor Romance* (New York: Warner, 1982), 472. Further references will be to this edition, and page numbers will appear in the text.

86 Raphael, "The Myth of the Male Orgasm" (1973), in *Issues in Feminism*, ed. Sheila Ruth (Boston: Houghton Mifflin, 1980), 19, 21; Steinem, "If Men Could Menstruate," *Ms*, October 1978.

87 Broner, *Her Mothers* (Bloomington: Indiana University Press, 1985), 83.

88 *Titters: The First Collection of Humor by Women*, ed. Deanne Stillman and Anne Beatts (New York: Macmillan, 1976), 43. Two novels that poke fun at feminist pieties are Beverly Lowry's *Daddy's Girl* (New York: Viking, 1979) and Noretta Koertge's *Valley of the Amazons* (New York: St. Martin's, 1984).

89 M. Hite, *Class Porn* (Freedom, Calif.: Crossing Press, 1987), 49. Further references will be to this edition, and page numbers will appear in the text.

90 Carter, *The Passion of New Eve* (New York: Harcourt, Brace, Jovanovich, 1977), 54, 58. Further references will be to this edition, and page numbers will appear in the text.

91 Ehrenreich, *Hearts of Men*, 181–82.

92 From William March's *The Bad Seed* (1954) to Sol Yurick's *Warriors* (1965) and Doris

Lessing's *The Fifth Child* (1988), contemporary fiction has focused on the sick, demonic, wild, or savage child.

93 Hobhouse, *Nellie without Hugo* (New York: Penguin, 1982), 11. We are grateful to Cornelia Nixon for bringing this text to our attention; Lessing, *The Golden Notebook* (New York: Bantam, 1979), 457.

94 Wasserstein, The Heidi Chronicles *and Other Plays* (New York: Vintage, 1991), 224.

95 Stade, *Confessions of a Lady-Killer* (New York: Norton, 1979); Reed, *Reckless Eyeballing* (New York: St. Martin's, 1986), 139.

96 Sharpe, *Wilt* (New York: Vintage, 1984), 12. Further references will be to this edition, and page numbers will appear in the text. A number of other texts deal directly with men's anxiety about feminism, among them Donald Barthelme's *Paradise* (1986), David Lodge's *Small World* (1985), and John Updike's *The Witches of Eastwick* (1984).

97 See, for example, Margot Sims, *On the Necessity of Bestializing the Human Female* (Boston: South End Press, 1982), which parodically presents the scientific revelation that "Men and Women Belong to Different Species!" with mock charts, graphs, and statistics. On performance artists like Annie Sprinkle, Linda Montano, Karen Finley, Carolee Schneemann, and Sapphire, see *Angry Women*, ed. Andrea Juno and V. Vale (San Francisco: Re/Search Publications, 1991).

98 Macdonald, "A Story for a Child," *Transplants* (New York: Braziller, 1976), 35.

Chapter 8: The Further Adventures of Snow White

Epigraphs: Drabble, "A Woman Writing," in *On Gender and Writing*, ed. Michelene Wandor (Boston: Pandora, 1983), 157; Atwood, "There Was Once," *Good Bones* (Toronto: Coach House Press, 1992), 19 (we are grateful to Margaret Atwood for supplying us with this book); Gilbert, "Unfinished Business," *Bonfire* (Cambridge, Mass: Alice James Books, 1983), 37.

1 Chesler, *Women and Madness* (New York: Avon, 1973), 241–42, 303–04.

2 De Beauvoir, *The Second Sex*, trans. H. M. Parshley (New York: Bantam, 1961), 642, 673.

3 Friedan, *The Feminine Mystique* (New York: Dell, 1963), 356, 364; Friedan, *The Second Stage* (New York: Summit, 1981), 153, 257.

4 Greer, *The Female Eunuch* (London: Paladin, 1971), 20, 318, 326.

5 Heilbrun, *Toward a Recognition of Androgyny* (New York: Knopf, 1973), ix–xi; *Reinventing Womanhood* (New York: Norton, 1979), 193, 196, 212, 195.

6 Chodorow, *The Reproduction of Mothering: Psychoanalysis and the Sociology of Gender* (Berkeley: University of California Press, 1978), 217, 218.

7 Dinnerstein, *The Mermaid and the Minotaur: Sexual Arrangements and the Human Malaise* (New York: Harper and Row, 1976), passim.

8 Gilligan, *In a Different Voice: Psychological Theory and Women's Development* (Cambridge: Harvard University Press, 1982), 10; Mary Field Belenky, Blythe McVicker Clinchy, Nancy Rule Goldberger, Jill Mattuck Tarule, *Women's Ways of Knowing: The Development of Self, Voice, and Mind* (New York: Basic, 1986), 229.

9 Millet, *Sexual Politics* (New York: Avon, 1969), 473.

10 Firestone, *The Dialectic of Sex: The Case for Feminist Revolution* (New York: Morrow, 1970), 274, 226, 230, 248, 265, 272.

11 Dworkin, *Woman Hating* (New York: Dutton, 1974), 183, 189, 188, 94.

12 Dworkin, *Intercourse* (New York: Free Press, 1987), 137; *Ice and Fire* (New York: Weidenfeld & Nicolson, 1986), 100.

13 Daly, *Gyn/Ecology: The Metaethics of Radical Feminism* (Boston: Beacon, 1978), 360, 361, 386; *Pure Lust: Elemental Feminist Philosophy* (Boston: Beacon, 1984), 350, 364.

14 Rich, "Compulsory Heterosexuality and Lesbian Existence" (1980), *Blood, Bread, and Poetry: Selected Prose 1979–1985* (New York: Norton, 1986), 32–35; Rich, "It is the

Lesbian in Us . . ." in *L*, 199–202; Rich, *Of Woman Born: Motherhood as Experience and Institution* (New York: Norton, 1976); Rich, "The Phenomenology of Anger," *Diving into the Wreck: Poems 1971–1972* (New York: Norton, 1973), 29.

15 Cixous, in Cixous and Clément, *The Newly Born Woman*, trans. Betsy Wing (Minneapolis: University of Minnesota Press, 1986), 85; "the oppressor's language": see Rich, "The Burning of Paper instead of Children" (1968), in *Adrienne Rich's Poetry*, ed. Barbara Charlesworth Gelpi and Albert Gelpi (New York: Norton, 1975), 48.

16 Carter, *The Sadeian Woman: An Exercise in Cultural History* (New York: Virago, 1979), 5, 79, 111–12, 131–32.

17 Griffin, *Pornography and Silence: Culture's Revenge against Nature* (New York: Harper and Row, 1985), 40, 72.

18 Weaver, *New Catholic Women: A Contemporary Challenge to Traditional Religious Authority* (San Francisco: Harper and Row, 1985), 170–77.

19 Friedan, *Second Stage*, 318.

20 See Abrams, *The Mirror and the Lamp: Romantic Theory and the Critical Tradition* (1953; New York: Norton, 1958); and Gilbert and Gubar, "The Mirror and the Vamp: Reflections on Feminist Criticism," in *The Future of Literary Theory*, ed. Ralph Cohen (New York: Routledge, 1989) 144–66.

21 Showalter, *A Literature of Their Own: British Women Novelists from Brontë to Lessing* (Princeton: Princeton University Press, 1977); Christian, *Black Women Novelists: The Development of a Tradition, 1892–1976* (Westport, Conn.: Greenwood, 1980); Fetterley, *The Resisting Reader: A Feminist Approach to American Fiction* (Bloomington: Indiana University Press, 1978); Tompkins, *Sensational Designs: The Cultural Work of American Fiction, 1790–1860* (New York: Oxford University Press, 1985); Carby, *Reconstructing Womanhood: The Emergence of the Afro-American Woman Novelist* (New York: Oxford University Press, 1987); Zimmerman, *The Safe Sea of Women: Lesbian Fiction, 1969–1989* (Boston: Beacon, 1990).

22 Kristeva, *Revolution in Poetic Language*, trans. Margaret Waller (New York: Columbia University Press, 1984); Cixous and Clément, *Newly Born Woman;* Irigaray, *This Sex Which Is Not One*, trans. Catherine Porter with Carolyn Burke (Ithaca: Cornell University Press, 1985).

23 Moi, *Sexual/Textual Politics: Feminist Literary Theory* (New York: Methuen, 1985), 106–07; Furman, "The Politics of Language: Beyond the Gender Principle?" in *Making a Difference: Feminist Literary Criticism*, ed. Gayle Greene and Coppélia Kahn (New York: Methuen, 1985), 69; Kamuf, "Writing Like Woman," in *Women and Language in Literature and Society*, ed. Sally McConnell-Ginet, Ruth Borker, and Nelly Furman (New York: Praeger, 1980), 285.

24 See Rich, *Of Woman Born*.

25 Hawthorne, *The Scarlet Letter* (New York: Penguin, 1983), 275.

26 Kingston, *The Woman Warrior* (New York: Vintage, 1977), 19, 243.

27 Emecheta, *The Joys of Motherhood* (New York: Methuen, 1985), 62. Further references will be to this edition, and page numbers will appear in the text.

28 Drabble, *The Waterfall* (Harmondsworth: Penguin, 1971), 154.

29 Churchill, *Top Girls* (New York: Samuel French, 1982), 29.

30 Morrison, *Beloved* (New York: Knopf, 1987), 76. Further references will be to this edition, and page numbers will appear in the text.

31 Hawthorne, *House of the Seven Gables*, quoted as epigraph to Byatt, *Possession: A Romance* (New York: Vintage, 1991).

32 Morrison, *Playing in the Dark: Whiteness and the Literary Imagination* (Cambridge: Harvard University Press, 1992), xi–xiii.

33 Gilbert and Gubar, *The Madwoman in the Attic: The Woman Writer and the Nineteenth-Century Literary Imagination* (New Haven: Yale University Press, 1979), 37.

34 Hirsch, *The Mother/Daughter Plot: Narrative, Psychoanalysis, Feminism* (Bloomington: Indiana University Press, 1989), 163; Kristeva, "Motherhood according to Giovanni Bellini," in *Desire in Language: A Semiotic Approach to Literature and Art,* ed. Léon S. Roudiez (New York: Columbia University Press, 1980). Further references will be to these editions, and page numbers will appear in the text.

35 Barrett Browning, *The Letters of Elizabeth Barrett Browning,* ed. Frederic G. Kenyon (New York: Macmillan, 1899), 1:230–32.

36 See Gilbert and Gubar, "Sexual Linguistics," *No Man's Land: The Place of the Woman Writer in the Twentieth Century,* vol. 1: *The War of the Words* (New Haven: Yale University Press, 1988), chap. 5.

37 Olds, "The Language of the Brag," *The Sign of Saturn: Poems 1980–1987* (London: Secker and Warburg, 1991), 8–9.

38 For a discussion of the Miltonic legacy in women's writings, see our *Madwoman in the Attic,* chap. 6, "Milton's Bogey."

39 Waldman, "Complaynt (after Emily Dickinson)," *Helping the Dreamer: New and Selected Poems, 1966–1988* (Minneapolis: Coffee House Press, 1989), 108.

40 Cixous in Cixous and Clément, *Newly Born Woman,* 90.

41 Levertov, "He-Who-Came-Forth," *Relearning the Alphabet* (New York: New Directions, 1970); Cixous in Cixous and Clément, *Newly Born Woman,* 88, 90; Winters, "Night Light," *The Key to the City* (Chicago: University of Chicago Press, 1986), 25.

42 Abse, "Inscription on the Flyleaf of a Bible (For My Elder Daughter)," *Poems, Golders Green* (London: Hutchinson, 1962), 34; Bell, "We Have Known," *Marvin Bell: New and Selected Poems* (New York: Atheneum, 1987), 39; Booth, "First Lesson," *Relations: Selected Poems 1950–1985* (New York: Viking, 1986), 4; Spacks, "Three Songs for My Daughter," *Spacks Street: New and Selected Poems* (Baltimore: Johns Hopkins University Press, 1982), 12; Comfort, "Notes for My Son" (Sect. 4 of "The Song of Lazarus") *The Song of Lazarus* (New York: Viking, 1945), 93; Williams, "The Last Deaths," *With Ignorance* (Boston: Houghton Mifflin, 1977), 9; Knight, "Circling the Daughter," *The Essential Etheridge Knight* (Pittsburgh: University of Pittsburgh Press, 1986), 109; Levis, "Blue Stones," *The Dollmaker's Ghost* (New York: Dutton, 1981), 68.

43 Pinsky, *An Explanation of America: A Poem to My Daughter* (Princeton: Princeton University Press, 1979), 5.

44 Hall, "Epigenethlion: First Child," *Exiles and Marriages* (New York: Viking, 1956), 106.

45 Dow, "Sunday Afternoon Nap with My Three Year Son, Colin," *Paying Back the Sea* (Pittsburgh: Carnegie-Mellon University Press, 1979), 66; Kinnell, "Under the Maud Moon," *Selected Poems* (Boston: Houghton Mifflin, 1982), 101; Berry, "Our Children, Coming of Age," *The Wheel* (San Francisco: North Point, 1982), 52.

46 Fraser, "Poems for the New," *In Defiance of the Rains* (San Francisco: Kayak Books, 1969), 19; Jong, "The Buddha in the Womb," *At the Edge of the Body* (New York: Holt, Rinehart, and Winston, 1979), 23; Winters, "The Stethoscope," *Key to the City,* 25; Muske, "Sounding," *Wyndmere* (Pittsburgh: University of Pittsburgh Press, 1985), 59; McPherson, "Pisces Child," *Elegies for the Hot Season* (New York: Ecco, 1982), 60; Ostriker, "Greedy Baby," *The Mother/Child Papers* (Santa Monica, Calif.: Momentum, 1980), 18.

47 Libera, "How You Were Born," in *The Ploughshares Poetry Reader,* ed. Joyce Perseroff (Watertown, Mass.: Ploughshares, 1986), 177; Brooks, "The Mother," *The World of Gwendolyn Brooks* (New York: Harper and Row, 1971), 5; Clifton, "the lost baby poem," *Good Woman: Poems and a Memoir 1969–1980* (Brockport, N.Y.: BOA Editions, 1987),

60; di Prima, "Brass Furnace Going Out: Song after an Abortion," *Selected Poems: 1956–1976* (Plainfield, Vt.: North Atlantic, 1977), 92–99.

48 Ostriker, "Bitterness, *Green Age* (Pittsburgh: University of Pittsburgh Press, 1989), 16; McElroy, "Where the Iguanas Still Live," *Queen of Ebony Isles* (Middletown, Conn.: Wesleyan University Press, 1984), 26.

49 Plath, "Candles," *PCP,* 149; Stone, "Advice," *Second-Hand Coat: Poems New and Selected* (Boston: Godine, 1987), 112; Adcock, "For a Five-Year-Old," *Selected Poems* (Oxford: Oxford University Press, 1983), 8; Turner, "Daughter, Daughter," *Lid and Spoon* (Pittsburgh: University of Pittsburgh Press, 1977), 26; Goldensohn, "Letter for a Daughter," *The Ploughshares Poetry Reader,* 87; Clifton, "Admonitions," *Good Woman,* 51.

50 Mariani, "What the Wind Said: For Paul," in *Crossing Cocytus,* ed. Robert Pack (New York: Grove, 1982), 48.

51 Sexton, "The Double Image," *To Bedlam and Part Way Back* (Boston: Houghton Mifflin, 1960), 53, 61; Kumin, "Family Reunion," *Our Ground Time Here Will Be Brief* (New York: Viking, 1982), 18; Pastan, "Letter to a Son at Exam Time," *Waiting For My Life* (New York: Norton, 1981), 15; Kizer, "The Blessing," *Mermaids in the Basement: Poems for Women* (Port Townsend, Wash.: Copper Canyon Press, 1984), 16.

52 Yeats, "Sailing to Byzantium" (1927), *The Collected Poems of W. B. Yeats: A New Edition,* ed. Richard J. Finneran (New York; Macmillan, 1989), 193–94.

53 Clifton, "last note to my girls (for sid, rica, gilly and neen)," *Good Woman,* 124.

54 Lorde, "Now That I Am Forever with Child," *Chosen Poems Old and New* (New York: Norton, 1982), 13; Atwood, "Spelling," *True Stories* (New York: Simon and Schuster, 1981), 63.

Index

Numbers in italics indicate illustrations.

Acknowledgments

The authors gratefully acknowledge permission to reprint material from the following sources: from *Trilogy*, by H. D., from *Collected Poems: 1912–1944*, © 1982 estate of Hilda Doolittle, reprinted by permission of New Directions Publishing Corporation; from "Letter to the Front," by Muriel Rukeyser, from *Out of Silence*, by Muriel Rukeyser (Evanston, Ill.: TriQuarterly Books, 1992), © William L. Rukeyser, reprinted by permission of William L. Rukeyser; from "Phantasia for Elvira Shatayev," by Adrienne Rich, from *The Fact of a Doorframe: Poems Selected and New, 1950–1984*, © 1984 Adrienne Rich, copyright © 1975, 1978 W. W. Norton and Company, copyright © 1981 Adrienne Rich, reprinted by permission of the author and W. W. Norton and Company; "And if I loved you Wednesday," "Was it for this I uttered prayers," and "I will put Chaos into fourteen lines," by Edna St. Vincent Millay, from *Collected Poems*, © 1922, 1950, 1954, 1982 Edna St. Vincent Millay and Norma Millay Ellis, reprinted by permission of Elizabeth Barnett, literary executor; from "O to Be a Dragon," by Marianne Moore, from *The Complete Poems of Marianne Moore*, © 1957 Marianne Moore, renewed 1985 Lawrence E. Brinn and Louise Crane, executors of the estate of Marianne Moore, reprinted by permission of Viking Penguin, a division of Penguin Books USA; from "An Egyptian Pulled Glass Bottle in the Shape of a Fish," by Marianne Moore, from *Collected Poems of Marianne Moore*, © 1935 Marianne Moore, renewed 1963 Marianne Moore and T. S. Eliot, reprinted by permission of Macmillan Publishing Company; from "Hegira," by Georgia Douglas Johnson, from *Bronze: A Book of Verse*, © 1923, reprinted by permission of Ayers Company Publishers; from *Trilogy*, by H. D., from *Collected Poems: 1912–1944*, © 1982 estate of Hilda Doolittle, reprinted by permission of New Directions Publishing Corporation; from *Helen in Egypt*, by H. D., © 1961 Norman Holmes Pearson, renewed 1989 by Perdita Schoffner, reprinted by permission of New Directions Publishing Corporation; from "Getting There," by Sylvia Plath, from *Ariel* from *The Collected Poems*, © 1963 Ted Hughes, reprinted by permission of HarperCollins Publishers; from "The Virgin Knight," from "Stained Glass" by Ted Hughes, from *Moortown*, © 1979 Ted Hughes, reprinted by permission of Faber and Faber; from "To Dorothy Wellesley," by W. B. Yeats, from *The Poems of W. B. Yeats: A New Edition*, ed. Richard J. Finneran, © 1934 Macmillan Publishing Company, renewed 1962 Bertha Georgie Yeats, reprinted by permission of Macmillan Publishing Company; "He and She," by W. B. Yeats, from *The Poems of W. B. Yeats: A New Edition*, ed. Richard J. Finneran, © 1934 Macmillan Publishing Company, renewed 1962 Bertha Georgie Yeats, reprinted by permission of Macmillan Publishing Company; from "Unfinished Business," by Celia Gilbert, from *Bonfire* © 1983, reprinted by permission of Alice James Books.